Sports Media, Marketing, and Management:

Breakthroughs in Research and Practice

Information Resources Management Association
USA

IGI Global
DISSEMINATOR OF KNOWLEDGE

Published in the United States of America by
IGI Global
Business Science Reference (an imprint of IGI Global)
701 E. Chocolate Avenue
Hershey PA, USA 17033
Tel: 717-533-8845
Fax: 717-533-8661
E-mail: cust@igi-global.com
Web site: http://www.igi-global.com

Library of Congress Cataloging-in-Publication Data

Names: Information Resources Management Association, editor.
Title: Sports media, marketing, and management : breakthroughs in research and practice / Information Resources Management Association, editor.
Description: Hershey, PA : Business Science Reference, 2018. | Includes bibliographical references.
Identifiers: LCCN 2017045862| ISBN 9781522554752 (hardcover) | ISBN 9781522554769 (ebook)
Subjects: LCSH: Communication in sports. | Sports--Marketing. | Sports administration. | Mass media and sports. | Social media.
Classification: LCC GV567.5 .S77 2018 | DDC 796.06/9--dc23 LC record available at https://lccn.loc.gov/2017045862

British Cataloguing in Publication Data
A Cataloguing in Publication record for this book is available from the British Library.

For electronic access to this publication, please contact: eresources@igi-global.com.

List of Contributors

Table of Contents

Preface

In the sports, fitness, and recreation industry, the constant advancement of new business strategies can make it very difficult to stay on the forefront of innovative trends. That is why IGI Global is pleased to offer this one-volume comprehensive reference that will empower students, researchers, practitioners, academicians, professionals, and consultants with a stronger understanding of the challenges and strategic opportunities associated with sports media, marketing, and management.

This compilation is designed to act as a single reference source on emerging topics in the sports industry, including but not limited to spectator engagement, organizational leadership, sponsorships, event management, sports fan loyalty, mass media, and brand anthropomorphism. The chapters within this publication are sure to provide readers the tools necessary to develop effective leadership, consumer engagement, and brand positioning strategies for professional and non-professional sports organizations.

Sports Media, Marketing, and Management: Breakthroughs in Research and Practice is organized into three sections that provide comprehensive coverage of important topics. The sections are:

1. Branding and Marketing;
2. Management, Sponsorship, and Strategic Planning; and
3. Spectatorship and Consumerism.

The following paragraphs provide a summary of what to expect from this invaluable reference source:

Section 1, "Branding and Marketing," opens this extensive reference source by highlighting the latest trends in sports branding and brand management, and how new marketing tools are expanding the reach of sports organizations. Focusing on the use of sports mascots, emotional branding, and social media, this section demonstrates the importance of digital marketing strategies to create brand commitment and attachment.

Section 2, "Management, Sponsorship, and Strategic Planning," includes discussions on leadership, brand image, competitive advantage, and the importance of both financial and in-kind sponsorships. Readers will benefit from research that will help them to develop comprehensive strategic plans, maintain sound corporate social responsibility, and execute sponsorship-linked marketing initiatives.

Section 3, "Spectatorship and Consumerism," presents coverage on sporting event culture and sports fan motivation. Through innovative discussions on shared rivalry, fantasy sports leagues, and community engagement, this section highlights the changing landscape of modern sports media environments. These inclusive perspectives contribute to the available knowledge on sports ecosystems and the sense of community during sporting events.

Although the primary organization of the contents in this work is based on its three sections, offering a progression of coverage of the important concepts, methodologies, technologies, applications, social issues, and emerging trends, the reader can also identify specific contents by utilizing the extensive indexing system listed at the end.

Section 1
Branding and Marketing

Chapter 1
Getting Brand Commitment Through Internet and Mobile Sports Marketing:
An Insight on Real Madrid Football Team

Verónica Baena
European University of Madrid, Spain

ABSTRACT

This chapter provides a better understanding of the impact that the Internet and mobile sports marketing are having on a business's ability to achieve customer engagement. To achieve this goal, the case of Real Madrid football team is analyzed, as it is calculated to have over 200 million supporters worldwide. Information about Real Madrid was gathered from September 2012 to March 2013 by repeatedly browsing the team's Website, Facebook, Twitter, Instagram, and apps. Data from interviews of Real Madrid's marketing department published in business press and posts was also compiled. Additionally, a focus group was conducted to discuss the customer engagement of Real Madrid's fans. The findings offer new opportunities to get customer engagement. They also highlight the important role of social media to gain insight about the fans.

INTRODUCTION

"Consumers love events, corporations love consumers – this is a match made in heaven" (D'Alessandro, 1993, p. 507). Although this statement originates from 1993 it is still true, maybe more than ever.

Marketers know that brands are a strategic choice for companies that operate in markets where technological innovation is a basic premise (Jensen and Beckmann, 2009). This is especially relevant in the 21st century, as due to the globalization of the economy, companies have nowadays the possibility to consider the entire market instead of focusing only on their local region (Ratten and Ratten, 2011). To do so, every organization needs to have a strong brand.

DOI: 10.4018/978-1-5225-5475-2.ch001

According to the above discussion, brands can be considered as a strategic choice for companies that operate in markets where technological innovation is a basic premise (Jensen and Beckmann, 2009). The goal is getting customer engagement, which drives brand loyalty. In this sense, literature highlights the role of a company's brand community as it has the power to influence the strength of the relationships between community participants and the firm's brand (Hur, Ahn and Kim, 2011). Moreover, when customers are affectively committed to a company, they identify themselves with the firm's vision and values, and in turn, they are interested in the growth of the company. In addition, interaction among members may influence the choice of brands and enhance the company's brand loyalty, making this issue very relevant for both academics and practitioners (Sicilia and Palazón, 2008). For instance, committed customers show proactive behaviors such as positive word-of-mouth (Patwardhan and Balasubramanian, 2011).

The above discussion is especially relevant in the sports sector, as it has become increasingly commercialized and internationalized over the past decades. Specifically, sports marketers have to consider what benefits the team could provide to their fans to get customers' support. In particular, strategies such as finely tuned communications through a variety of media (e.g., e-mail, and special limited access events) are able to boost and reinforce the degree to which committed fans feel they are receiving special treatment and are truly part of a team (Kaynak, Gultekin and Tatoglu, 2008). Furthermore, the advance of the Internet, including also social media and mobile phone, offers marketers and immense variety of new possibility to communicate with the customers, but also fans and fans. That's why professional sports is one of the sectors of activity that most uses interactive marketing mediums to contact their followers in real time. In short, cell phones, iPads and iPhones have enabled marketing to be more interactive (Cooke and Buckley, 2008), which helps professional sports to attract new followers and collect fan feedback through Facebook, Twitter or Instagram, among others (Ratten and Ratten, 2011).

Besides, PricewaterhouseCoopers (2011) predicted the sports market to grow from almost $120 billion in 2011 to over $145 billion in 2015. Specifically, over a third ($50 billion) of the 2015 sports market revenue will be generated in Europe, Africa and the Middle East. The growing importance of this market gave the impulse to focus on the sports business in this research. That is, to get customer commitment sports marketers need to make consumers feel as a part of the team, and discover ways to keep them by highlighting the importance of the team in their lives.

Moreover, the internationalization of the global economy has meant that many sports marketers now look to the global market instead of one region in their marketing efforts. Specifically, as noted by Ratten and Ratten (2011), entrepreneurial sport ventures that adopt an international focus are likely to achieve success in the competitive marketplace. This implies, however, that successful sports brands have to transcend their cultural origins to develop strong relationships with consumers across different countries and cultures (Hollis, 2008). In alignment with the to the above arguments, adopting marketing strategies that allow the sports team to contact their followers without physical restrictions is crucial to achieving customer engagement and loyalty. For instance, of six billion people living on earth; about 5 billion have a mobile device and interact between 40 and 80 minutes with the device every day. Therefore, sports managers have to be up-to-date with the latest trends and developments of digital and mobile marketing. In other words, implementing branding strategies through Internet and mobile phone applications is not an option for sport marketers; it's a must.

Even though prior studies proved emotional relationships of customers towards brands in the consumer goods market (Keller, 2001), the feeling of brand commitment in sports is still little explored. That is, despite the growing importance of this topic, there is a dearth of research on this issue (Kaynak, Salman and Tatoglu, 2008). In an attempt to contribute to literature, the present chapter analyzes the brand management and customer engagement strategy implemented by Real Madrid through digital marketing and mobile phone applications. We have focused on this football team as it is one of the most successful sports teams in terms of worldwide supporters. More specifically, the annually published Football Money League report of Deloitte highlights the special significance of this soccer team. In this sense, in the season 2003/04 the biggest football club was Manchester United, generating a yearly turnover of almost $260 million (Deloitte, 2005). By the time of 8 years, this amount almost doubled. Nevertheless, as highlighted by Deloitte (2013), Real Madrid is nowadays at the lead, showing total revenue of $513 million. It is also worth mentioning that when Deloitte started their Football Money League in the season 1996/97, Real Madrid generated total revenue of €85 million, resulting in a compound annual growth rate (CAGR) of 12.7% between 1996 and 2012 (Deloitte, 2013). A fact that is especially notable in a period of crisis in Europe. Figure 1 shows the composition of the total revenue of Real Madrid. Deloitte Football Money League's Report splits the revenue of a club into three categories, depending on the origin of the revenue: i) revenue generated on match-day (e.g. tickets); ii) revenue related to broadcasting; and iii) commercial revenue. As this study focuses on the latest one (sports marketing strategies) we need to have a detailed look on this issue.

From the season 2003/04 to 2008/09 the match-day revenue was showing a CAGR of 10.3% with similar CAGR values in broadcasting (12.8%), and commercial (10.1%) revenues. Now considering only the last three seasons from 2009/10 to 2011/12 a significant development can be determined. In those three years the match-day revenue shows a CAGR of -1.1%, whereas the revenues of broadcasting and commercial items continue with a constant CAGR of 12.0%, respectively 11.4%, as depicted in Figure 2. This increased difference between the growth rate of the revenue generated on matchday compared to the growth rates of the revenue raised by broadcasting and commercial components leads to a shift in the composition of the total revenue of Real Madrid.

Besides, regarding the number of worldwide supporters, it is worth mentioning that Real Madrid is one of the most successful sports teams with more than 200 million people. In terms of virtual followers, Real Madrid has more than 17 million Facebook fans and nearly 40 million views of videos on YouTube. It is also the football team with the largest number of Twitter followers in Europe.

Figure 1. Real Madrid revenue composition in million Euros in 2012. Source: Own elaboration based on Deloitte (2013).

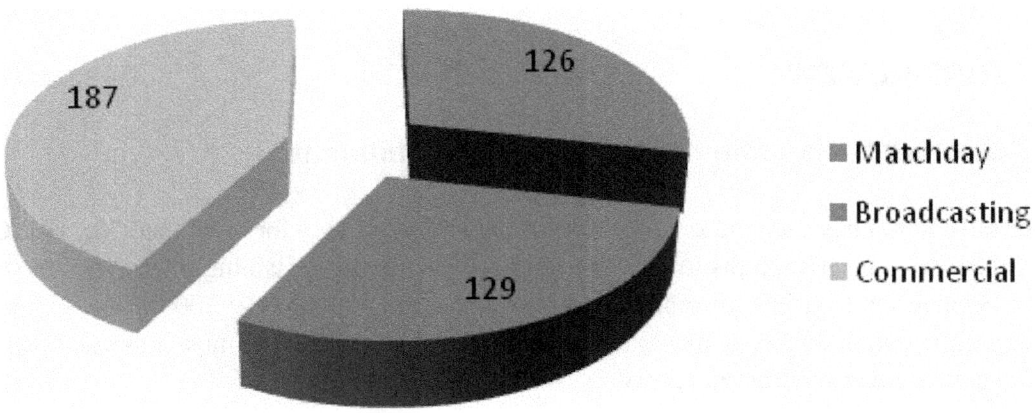

Figure 2. Real Madrid C.F. Revenue from 2003/2004 to 2011/2012. Source: Own elaboration based on Deloitte (2005-2013).

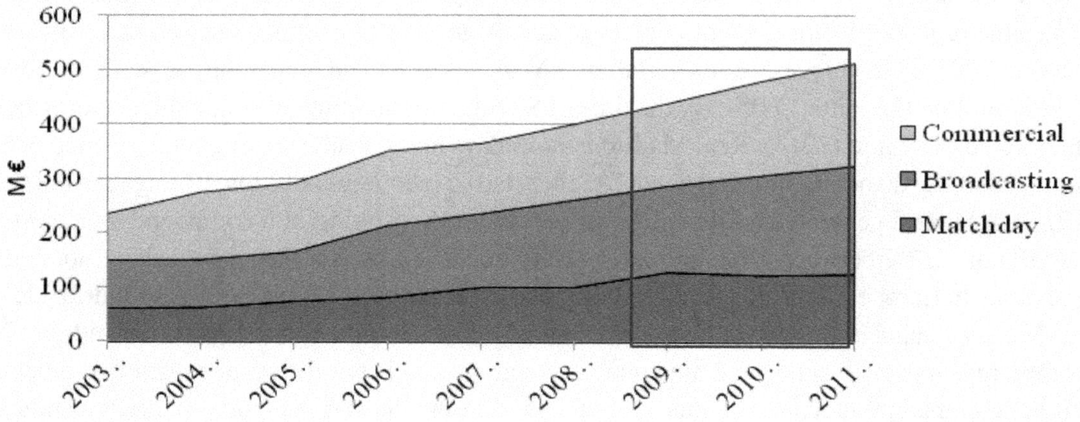

Prior sports literature has conducted single case studies to analyze Manchester United as an example of network orchestration (Shaw, 2007), David Beckham as a brand (Vincent, Hill and Lee, 2009), or the brand elements and local inspiration of FIFA World Cup (Weszka, 2011). However, to the author's knowledge, no one has addressed the analysis of the Real Madrid as an example of branding strategy to achieve customer commitment and loyalty. Specifically, through the combination of the customer engagement approach provided by Carroll and Ahuvia (2006) and the adaption of Keller's (2001) concept of active engagement to the latest marketing communication media, this study will contribute to the identification of the effects of cutting-edge digital and mobile marketing towards the emotional relationship to a sports brand. This will be our contribution.

With this objective in mind, we have structured the present work into various sections. Firstly, we discuss the role of Internet as a tool to transform the traditional company's communication strategy. Then, Real Madrid football team is introduced as well as the present work's methodology. Subsequently, the marketing strategy implemented by Real Madrid through digital marketing and mobile phone applications is discussed, as well as its effectiveness in terms of customer commitment. The study ends with the conclusions of the research and some thought on its limitations, as well as suggestions for future lines of research.

LITERATURE REVIEW

From Customer Satisfaction to Customer Commitment

Customer satisfaction has been the key objective of marketing strategy for more than 50 years. Of late, however, there have been attempts to move beyond satisfaction in explaining differences in strategic consumer behavior and getting customer commitment (Carroll and Ahuvia, 2006). That is, managers need to concentrate their efforts on managing their brands, as it is one of the most important company's assets (Kaynak, Salman and Tatoglu, 2008).

To achieve this goal, many companies have embarked on some customer-facing processes and solutions (CFPS), which might include customer relationships management (CRM), customer engagement management (CEM), customer satisfactions cells, call centers, and so on. However, just stand-alone CFPSs are not enough to keep the customer with the organization. Unless such CFPSs are strategically integrated to the entire customer life cycle, it would have limited usefulness, and the organization would not be able to exploit the potential of such mechanisms. In short, companies and their customers must define what the customer experience should be. In doing so, a thorough knowledge of the market and customers becomes essential to know what customers want and also differentiate between customers (Triparthi, 2009).

The most successful companies build deeply emotional relationships with their customers, who stay faithful to their brands that earn both their rational trust as well as their affection. This is especially relevant as customers who are emotionally engaged behave quite differentially than those who just prefer certain brand because of rational arguments. Particularly, emotionally engaged consumers spend more, are less price sensitive and are more likely to get through a problem than other consumers who are not so engaged (Triparthi, 2009). In other words, companies interested in winning, retaining, and deepening customer relationships can no longer do so by launching winning products, or holding down costs or even improving customer service. They need to engage their customers (Triparthi, 2009).

Besides, managing a firm's brand in a proper and continuous way can contribute positively to the value of the company. According to Feldwick (2002), a brand is simply a collection of perceptions in the mind of the consumer. Hollis (2008) expands this perspective, explaining that these perceptions and associations that people have with the brand must them also make them wanting to buy the product. This statement led Faris (2007), former chief innovation officer at MDC Partners[1] to define a brand as a collective perception in the minds of consumers. This implies the fact that the perceptions and emotions towards a brand need to be shared, to create this collective image. That is, the stronger, more coherent and motivating those perceptions are, the more likely they will be to influence purchase decisions and add value to a business.

In line with the above discussion, Pedersen (2004) highlights the idea that branding could even be the most important mechanism for a sports organization to grow. Customer engagement is built through a strong brand, as the customers will trust the brand and interpret the brand as a sign of quality. In extreme cases, this can lead to the "religion" phenomenon, meaning that the customer will stick to the brand in every case. Consequently the customers will be willing to accept higher prices, not only paying for the product, but also for competence, quality, image and prestige. As shown in Figure 3, today's market conditions do not allow a proper differentiation utilizing only objective product features, making it essential for marketers to add an emotional value to the brand, trying to build brand love. This is especially important in sports, where fans dedicate their time and efforts to support their teams and they contribute an unconditional love to the team (Kaynak, Salman and Tatoglu, 2008).

The Role of Internet in the Marketing Evolution

Nowadays, companies are faced with two incommensurable challenges. On the one hand, they need to be constantly innovative and ready for change. On the other hand, they are expected to create an enduring and recognizable identity that attracts attention in a world saturated with communication (Jensen and Beckmann, 2009).

Figure 3. The "Religion" phenomenon in branding. Source: Own elaboration based on Pedersen (2004).

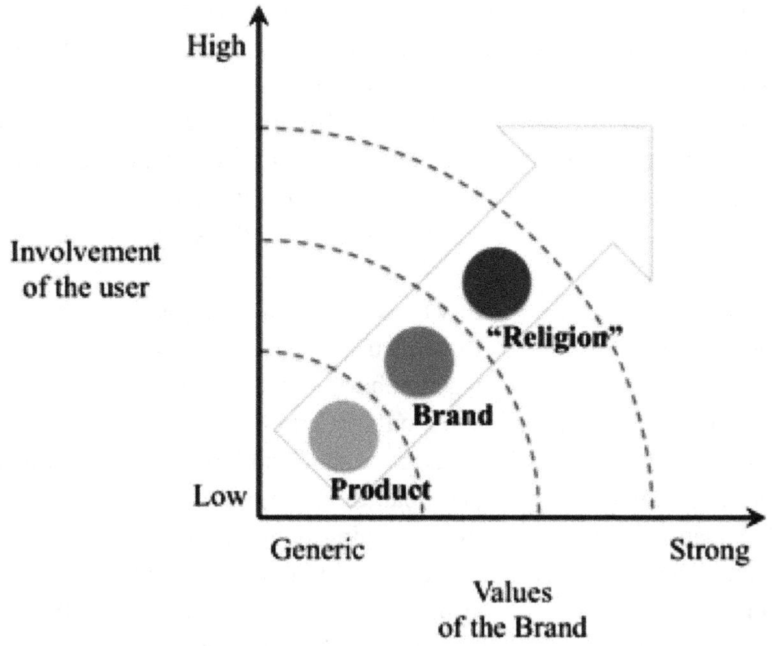

An important channel for brands to interact with their customers is the Internet. The advance of this tool, including also social media and mobile applications, offers marketers an immense variety of new possibility to communicate with the customers. Beyond that, with Web 2.0, the interactive communication left being a one-way siege and became an intercourse between fans and organizations, but also among fans. In this sense, from Fischel (2004) some advantages for digital marketing are derived. Firstly, one advantage valid for all channels is the 24-hour availability. This development means that consumers request those information they consider important at the, for them, most convenient moment. Secondly, every consumer is able to individually select only the information she/he is interested in. These data are spread throughout various online channels, giving the consumer easy access to the content. Thirdly, the Internet presents new sales channels, for example in form of online shops or mobile applications and at the same time offers easy and precise ways for success monitoring. The last and one of the most important benefits of the Internet is the possibility for consumers to be always up-to-date. Fischel (2004) suggests adopting the online-marketing-mix accordingly to Kolibius's (2001) eco-online-marketing-mix. This model transforms the "4Ps" (Product, Price, Place and Promotion) into "4Cs," namely Content, Commerce/Convenience, Co-location and Communication/Community. Even though the "4Cs" do not replace the "4Ps" their importance, with the increased importance of new media is growing immensely.

Considering to the above discussion, Internet has transformed the marketing paradigm from physical offerings to the virtual marketplace. It allows shifting attention from one-way communication to interactive and real-time relationships with a company's customers. As a result, without Internet, brand communities couldn't be as vigorous and relevant as they currently are. In fact, cconsidering the possibility for sport marketers to reach a global market, the appearance of Internet becomes even more important. Therefore, many sports organizations have implemented relationship marketing programs designed to appeal to their most avid fans (Fullerton and Mertz, 2008). Also, a team's website provides a brilliant tool for boosting the frequency with which fans can follow the team. For example, video clips from past games and on-going or current press conferences allow the fans to be involved with the team more frequently (Kaynak, Gultekin and Tatoglu, 2008). This issue is very important as sports offer massive potential for revenue generation of a global scale because of its cross-cultural ability to appeal to different generations of people from multiple geographic locations.

In line with the above arguments, customer engagement has been finding increasing use largely in the digital context where website providers finding it increasingly challenging to hold on to visitors to their sites, in an effort to sell or communicate with them (Triparthi, 2009). Moreover, Internet plays an important role in achieving customer commitment and brand loyalty, as it allows brand communities not to be restricted to geographic co-presence of members. That is, interaction takes place through a technological interface, making a physical context unnecessary. As a result, a corporate Web site can allow the birth of a virtual space around the brand. The site also becomes a meeting point where members develop their relationships inside an environment where the brand is always present (Sicilia and Palazón, 2008). However, managing a Web page is not enough to get succeed in customer engagement (Hur, Ahn and Kim, 2011).

Brand Communities as a Tool to Get Customer Engagement

Most companies use brand communities for the strategic purpose of getting closer to particular target market segment. In fact, members of a brand community drive an organization's brand-building agenda by virtue of the communication among the community members who support the same brand (Muniz and Schau, 2005). This issue is very important as sports offer massive potential for revenue generation of a global scale because of its cross-cultural ability to appeal to different generations of people from multiple geographic locations.

In particular, digital marketing and mobile phone applications may help sports organizations such as the Real Madrid to implement further marketing strategies oriented to increasing customer commitment. This is because brand community members may establish a brand related discussion but they may also share opinions about any other topic of interest (Hur, Ahn and Kim, 2011). This helps to achieve brand engagement, as members can join the group without the limitations of geographical barriers. This aspect is very relevant for every organization, especially if we consider the high cost of acquiring new customers as compared to maintaining the current customer portfolio (Kaynak, Gultekin and Tatoglu, 2008). Then, both digital and mobile marketing play an important role in achieving customer commitment, as they allow brand communities not to be restricted to geographic co-presence of members.

To sum up, as it will be discussed in the next sections, digital and mobile marketing actions may help sports organizations, such as the Real Madrid, to implement further marketing strategies oriented to increasing customer commitment and fans retention.

METHODOLOGY

As stated, the present study focuses on the Real Madrid soccer team. Information about this club was gathered from September 2012 to March 2013 by repeatedly browsing the team's Web site, Facebook, Twitter, Instagram and apps. More specifically, actions implemented by the club to get customer engagement were analyzed.

Moreover, information from interviews of the Real Madrid's marketing department published in business press and posts was compiled. A similar procedure was followed in previous research to analyze Nutella's and Coca-Cola's brand communities (see, e.g., Cova and Pace, 2006 and Sicilia and Palazón; 2008, among others).

Finally, two exploratory focus groups were conducted to discuss the customer engagement of Real Madrid's fans. A non-probability sample of 28 undergraduate students was selected on the basis that they are potential followers of sport teams. Most participants were men (68%) and aged between 18 and 25 years (78%) resulting in a mean age of 22 years. In this sense, it's worth mentioning that, as noted by Jackson and Shaw (2009), the use of non-probability samples is particularly relevant to management research. Literature has also highlighted the benefits of using young people as a sample to explore customer engagement (Hayes et al, 2006), as they represent future earners and spenders (Ross and Harradine, 2011).

REAL MADRID AS AN EXAMPLE OF BRAND MANAGEMENT

Founded in 1902 as the Madrid Football Club, the team has traditionally worn a white home uniform ever since. The word Real (royal in Spanish) was conferred to the club by King Alfonso XIII of Spain in 1920 together with the royal crown in the emblem. The team has played its home matches in the 85,454 people capacity *Santiago Bernabéu Stadium* in downtown Madrid since 1947. As of 30 July 2013, Real Madrid won a record 32 National League championships (*La Liga*) and a record 9 European Cup/UEFA Champions' League trophies. The club was awarded with the recognition of FIFA Club of the 20th century on 23 December, 2000. It also received the FIFA Order of Merit in 2004. Furthermore, Real Madrid is allowed to wear a multiple–winner badge on their jersey during UEFA Champions League matches as they have won more than five European Cups.

As regards brand value, the most successful sports teams in Europe has traditionally been Manchester United (US$259 million brand value), Real Madrid (US$155 million brand value), and Bayern Munich (US$150 million brand value) (Bauer, Sauer and Schmitt, 2005). In 2010, Forbes estimated Real Madrid's worth to be approximately US$1,323 million, ranking them second after Manchester United. Nevertheless, according to Deloitte (2010), Real Madrid had revenues of US$535 million in the same period, ranking it first. In 2012, Forbes's Most Valuable Football Brand ranking established that Manchester United remains the world's most valuable football club brand valued at US$853 million despite a season without any trophies. Real Madrid dropped down to 3rd place at US$600 million, just ahead of FC Barcelona with a brand value of US$580 million.

As discussed in this study, Real Madrid has realized the importance of the brand and grasped the ability to market in a way not seen anywhere else in the world of soccer. In particular, this football team is one of the most recognizable brands in sports. With some of the world's greatest players on the field, Real Madrid understood the need to make businesses decisions to embrace new technologies and communication tools in order to increase their profitability. In addition, the team exemplifies that brand equity is mainly based on brand awareness and image. For example, in terms of brand awareness, the fusion of the potent Real Madrid brand with equally powerful global football superstars such as David Beckham and Cristiano Ronaldo was a profitable decision. Specifically, once the two famous footballers started to wear the Real Madrid jersey, the club was able to dramatically increase the price paid by their major corporate sponsors such as Siemens, Audi, and Adidas (Vincent, Hill and Lee, 2009).

Real Madrid's Internet and Mobile Marketing Strategy

Sport's fans dedicate their time and efforts to support their teams. Thus, the fans become customers who consume their team's services and products, since they unconditionally love their club.

Generally, only a small part of a team's turnover is derived from the traditional revenue stream of tickets sales. That is, an important percentage of a club's gross revenue comes from sponsorship deals, television rights, and other media royalties. Specifically, sports leagues and other sports-related companies have five of the top 20 positions among global merchandise licensors (Ratten and Ratten, 2011). However, the costs associated with purchasing and employing top quality players have also hugely increased over the last decade. This means that sports teams have had no choice but to find new revenue sources, which has made it ever more important to remain gain and develop popularity with the general public. Figure 4 shows the list of sponsors of Real Madrid in 2013.

In view of the above arguments, many professional sports teams are turning to long-term strategic brand management as the dominant viewpoint for their marketing efforts. While short-term tactics centering on winning matches such as firing a head coach, or hiring or renting a star player in the middle of the season are commonly used by sports managers, these tactics do not guarantee long-term and steady revenue flows (Kaynak, Gultekin and Tatoglu, 2008). Consequently, it is necessary to increase the target market and get fans interested in the team by keeping them up to date with developments via television and Internet (Ratten and Ratten, 2011). To achieve this goal is vital that clubs build a virtual community for their fans and dispose of mobile integration.

Then, we can argue that interaction with the fans is one of the most relevant aspects in terms of digital marketing strategy to be considered. Thanks to Real Madrid's virtual community the club has an estimated 280 million fans this communications with their followers. Furthermore, Real Madrid has its own encrypted Digital TV channel, Real Madrid TV, which is available both in Spanish and English. A

Figure 4. Official sponsors of Real Madrid football team. Source: www.realmadrid.com. Retrieved on July 2nd, 2013.

YouTube channel was also created in addition to the club's Web page, RealMadrid.com. Nevertheless, none of these strategies helped the team to know how people react with the club's messages inside the official website. Therefore, some years ago Real Madrid started its Facebook page and Twitter account in which the team could gain insight into their fans in terms of number of visits, topics they like, etc.

Currently, social media allowed the club to reach 19 million Madridistas (Real Madrid followers) overseas, thus making it the most popular sports club in social networks in 2012 according to FameCount.com. In particular, since its launch, the club's Facebook page has been a success and has built up a huge following with millions fans and with an average of approximately 3,000 new fans joining every day. Hence, although the social network started as a way for Real Madrid to test fan interaction, the team's official social network pages have also become a source of information for Madridistas worldwide, since it is published in five different languages (Spanish, English, French, Arabic, and Japanese).

Real Madrid also uses social media to encourage fans to join club membership programmes. For example, the club encourages its fans to join the eMadristas club, which gives access even more content. Social media also opens up additional opportunities for sponsors and Real Madrid partners. That is, sponsors not only have the chance to be in the stadium, on the shirts, and on RealMadrid.com but they can also publish their messages via the club's social media channels and provide engaging content for the Real Madrid's fans. For instance, every week Bwin (Real Madrid's current jersey sponsor) hosts an interview with the team talking about the next game. In addition, the Real Madrid Fantasy Manager game on Facebook and iPhone (which has 140,000 users on average per month) allows fans to coach the team. Besides, the YouTube channel makes a difference by offering exclusive free content in Spanish, English and Arabic.

In conjunction with the above mentioned marketing strategies (website and social network), Real Madrid has been working with mobile technologies to implement them in the club's marketing strategy. As a result, "Real Madrid Mobile" was created. It generates extra revenue for the team through the distribution of their mobile content portfolio and the creation of new mobile services. Moreover, "Real Madrid Mobile" allows the club to build a new mobile community for Real Madrid fans which is significant because mobile phones generate in some cases a much better response than other forms of communication, such as email or traditional letters. For instance, when the team wins a trophy, it sends out video calls to all of its mobile subscribers and once the fans respond to such a call, they see a video of one of the players saying "*Madridista we have won La Copa! Thanks very much for your support!*" This type of communication is much more personal, reaches out to fans, and enhances customer engagement. It is also worth mentioning the partnership with CISCO systems announced on March 2012 to make the stadium Santiago Bernabéu one of the most technologically advanced stadiums in the world. Using CISCO's Connected Sports Solutions, Real Madrid's arena was fully optimized to improve Web connectivity and facilitate social media access to their supporters.

Finally, the club's decision to join *The Mobile Marketing Association* (MMA) as a Regional Member gave the team the opportunity to launch several successful mobile marketing strategies such as MyMadrid's mobile community. This is a multi-platform and multi-language community for fans used by Real Madrid to communicate exclusive special offers and ticket availability, regardless of their phone model. The mobile platform also offers supporters real time news, access to the club's official Youtube channel, minute by minute game updates, real time 3D goals from matches and chat, MSN services, as well as a mini games service. In other words, MyMadrid goes beyond a conventional mobile community as it allows creating and sparking interaction amongst the fans.

DISCUSSION AND CONCLUSION

The goal of any organization is not only their customers to be satisfied with the product but also they were willing to promote, defend and do battle with others, of behalf of the brand. This is because a person emotionally attached to a brand usually accepts to pay premium prices for this specific brand (Thomson, MacInnis and Park, 2005) in order to avoid separation distress (Sarkar, 2011). Therefore, strategic brand management has become a key issue in the last decade, especially in sports (Blumrodt, Bryson, and Flanagan, 2012).

The present study confirms that sport is becoming increasingly commercialized and sport entities have become more professional over the years. Real Madrid shows a highlighted position, being one of the most important brand names in sports with players that are well-known and highly supported. Specifically, over 200 million people worldwide follow Real Madrid. In addition, the club has more than 1,800 *peñas* (official club-affiliated supporters' groups) in Spain and around the world. In terms of virtual followers, Real Madrid has more than 17 million Facebook fans and nearly 40 million views of videos on YouTube. It is also the team with the largest number of Twitter followers in Europe. Real Madrid players are also very popular in social networks. Particularly, Cristiano Ronaldo is the most popular sportsman in the world, having more than 31 million Facebook fans, over three million Twitter followers, and more than 4 million views on YouTube. We can then argue that Real Madrid has also the best online presence and largest communication activity in social networks.

Based on the above arguments, the marketing strategy adopted by Real Madrid football team has been analyzed to study the importance of both digital marketing and mobile phone applications to open up many new opportunities, gain customer commitment, and understand the customer perspective. More specifically, this paper argues that customer engagement enables companies to extend beyond their core product. This is especially true in professional sports where customer commitment is demonstrated by consumers who purchase season tickets and/or watch all of a team's games on television. Additionally, new services such as team-related merchandise stores and restaurants in close proximity to the stadium enable the team to create additional revenue streams through licensing agreements (Gladden, and Funk, 2001).

To achieve this goal (getting customer commitment), sports marketers have to implement new tools that allow the team to interact with their followers without physical restrictions. This is very relevant as most sports teams focus on international branding to build a global fan base (Ratten and Ratten, 2011). In this sense, Internet usage and its derived applications (i.e., social networks and mobile phones) allow the appearance of virtual brand communities. This helps the team to get feedback from their followers (Patwardhan and Balasubramanian, 2011), and open new opportunities for the club's partners as well as sponsors. In this way, Real Madrid has reached agreements with the main media partners in Spain, in which the football team launches monthly SMS challenges on TV and in newspapers giving theirs fans the opportunity to win exclusive prizes. As an example, in 2009 Real Madrid launched a special contest that gave their fans the opportunity to win the official AUDI cars of the players, those that had been used by the team's stars.

In addition, the present work confirms that social media has provided new opportunities to gain insight about the brand's fans. Specifically, when Real Madrid posts content, many people immediately answer by saying they like it or they don't. Supporters' feedback is very important. For instance, when Real Madrid started to include links to the club's online shop on their Facebook page, it took fans a while to realize that this was Real Madrid's official online store. This made the club think of this fact and consider that maybe it needs to include on their posts that this was the official online store, as the previous information was not as clear for fans as the team thought.

Mobile Marketing has also offered new opportunities for Real Madrid, such as the promotion of sponsors through mobile services. The mobile services not only give the customers a sense of proximity and confidence about the Real Madrid brand itself but also about the sponsors of the brands. This type of marketing strategy increases the brand's popularity while also adding value to the brand. As Pedro Duarte, former Mobile Marketing Manager at Real Madrid CF, said, "Real Madrid is one of the leaders in terms of mobile technology and sports here in Europe. One of the main things that separates us from other sports organizations in terms of mobile success is that we have a department dedicated to our mobile platforms and mobile marketing – that is the main difference between Real Madrid and many other companies, some of them have digital teams, but we specialize in mobile marketing and building a mobile community for Real Madrid" (Read, 2010).

Moreover, one of the participants of the focus group we conducted in this study noted that "While showing these pictures in my phone, so you can realize that Real Madrid is always trying to get involved with their fans, because the team knows that it is very important for the fans to see everything that is happening. Followers not only buy the shirt and wear it when they go to the stadium. They like to feel they join the team and belong to their Football Team Community as one special member". In this sense it is worth mentioning that contrary to expectations, recent literature discusses negative reactions, like irritation, that mobile marketing may provoke among customers. This is because mobile marketing is often perceived disturbing, which negatively affect the customer engagement with the brand (Li, Edwards and Lee, 2002). Therefore, one of the main challenges and opportunities for mobile marketing is to understand and respect the personal nature of the usage of mobile phones (Barwise and Strong, 2002), as done by Real Madrid.

Academic and Practical Contributions

The findings of this study have certain academic and practical implications for management literature that worth to be addressed. Firstly, brand virtual community marketing enhances customer commitment. Specifically, since customer participation often leads to brand loyalty, Internet and mobile marketing have to be considered as tools to improve marketing effectiveness. This finding is consistent with recent research (Patwardhan and Balasubramanian, 2011; Ratten and Ratten, 2011). Brand communities also offer new insight for customer relationship management and related marketing activities as suggested in prior literature (i.e., Sicilia and Palazón, 2008; Hur, Ahn and Kim, 2011).

Besides, this study highlights the importance of mobile marketing strategies. Developing an interactive Web site is not enough to get brand loyalty, understood as an actual and profound behavior that consistently supports and repurchases referred products or services, despite competitors' marketing efforts to change their behavior (Oliver, 1997). Specifically, traditional Web sites are no longer motivating customers to return to the site (Sicilia and Palazón, 2008). As a result, sports managers need to use interactive marketing mediums to connect with consumer in real time. That is, technological innovative media made possible by Web 2.0. has enable marketing to be more interactive and socially complex (Cooke and Buckley, 2008).

In addition, by integrating different elements of social media such as blogs, YouTube, Facebook, and Twitter, companies elevate presence (Larson, 2011) and create virtual communities (Ratten and Ratten, 2011), which influence the choice of brands and impact brand loyalty. Furthermore, interaction among members may influence the choice of brands and enhance the company's brand loyalty (Sicilia and Palazón, 2008).

Finally, football's industry is nowadays characterized by difficulty to obtain new incomes derived from traditional business. Faced to this situation football clubs have designed new strategies that have turned them into modern sports&media companies. Real Madrid is a perfect example of this new strategic view in a Spanish sport organization. The main contribution of the new management model applied to the club has been value brand progressive enhancement and new forms of brand exploitation from a new marketing strategy. As a result of this new strategy, incomes from brand exploitation have increased importantly and Real Madrid is quite near to obtain a leadership position between football clubs around the world (Blanco and Forcadell, 2006). Then we think both academia and managers may find useful the findings of the present study.

Limitations and Direction for Future Research

The present study provides some insights that may help teams and their managers to realize the relevance of their brand in business success. Specifically, it's is confirmed that sports managers should focus increasing loyalty of their brands as well as on developing strong, favorable and unique associations in the heads of the team's followers. However, some limitations should be considered.

A first limitation of this work is its sports business environment, more exactly the European football market. Real Madrid represents a leading football entity in this market, offering the possibility to consider it as example model. It should however be noted that the digital and mobile environment is constantly changing and new marketing trends can surge and might be considered in further studies.

Secondly, the analysis developed in this study is qualitative. It could be improved with a quantitative study in which supporters were asked about the degree to which their functional, social, and emotional needs are satisfied through the digital and mobile marketing strategy implemented by the club. Therefore, we propose it as a further research line.

Finally, with a focus on the Real Madrid football club, our findings are limited to this institution. Then, we encourage replicating this study by considering any other successful organization that operates in an area different from sports, and see whether findings obtained in this research could be generalized independently of the sector of activity.

REFERENCES

Barwise, P., & Strong, P. (2002). Permission-based mobile advertising. *Journal of Interactive Marketing*, *16*(1), 14–24. doi:10.1002/dir.10000

Bauer, H. H., Sauer, N. E., & Schmitt, P. (2005). Customer-based brand equity in the team sport industry: Operationalization & impact on the economic success of sport teams. *European Journal of Marketing*, *39*(5/6), 496–513. doi:10.1108/03090560510590683

Blanco, M., & Forcadell, F. J. (2006). El Real Madrid club de fútbol: La aplicación de un modelo empresarial a una entidad deportiva en España. *Universia Business Review*, *11*, 1698–5117.

Blumrodt, J., Bryson, D., & Flanagan, J. (2012). European football teams CSR' engagement impacts on customer-based brand equity. *Journal of Consumer Marketing*, *29*(7), 482–493. doi:10.1108/07363761211274992

Cooke, M., & Buckley, N. (2008). Web 2.0: Social networks & the future of market research. *International Journal of Market Research*, *50*(2), 267–292.

Cova, B., & Pace, S. (2006). Brand community of convenience products: New forms of customer empowerment: The case of my nutella community. *European Journal of Marketing*, *40*(9/10), 1087–1105. doi:10.1108/03090560610681023

Deloitte - Football Finance. (2011). *Football money league 2011*. Retrieved June 30, 2013, from http://www.deloitte.com/view/en_GB/uk/industries/sportsbusinessgroup/sports/football/deloitte-football-money-league-2011/5596840c99e9d210VgnVCM2000001b 56f00aRCRD.htm

Deloitte - Football Finance. (2012). *Football money league 2012*. Retrieved June 30, 2013, from http://www.deloitte.com/view/en_GB/uk/industries/sportsbusinessgroup/sports/football/deloitte-football-money-league-2012/index.htm

Deloitte - Football Finance. (2013). *Deloitte football money league 2013*. Retrieved June 30, 2013, from http://www.deloitte.com/view/en_GB/uk/industries/sportsbusinessgroup/sports/football/deloitte-football-

Deloitte - Sports Business Group. (2005). *Football money league 2005*. Retrieved June 30, 2013, from http://www.deloitte.com/view/en_gb/uk/b55e85ed081fb110V gnVCM100000ba42f00aRCRD.htm

Deloitte - Sports Business Group. (2006). *Football money league 2006*. Retrieved June 30, 2013, from http://www.deloitte.com/view/en_GB/uk/industries/sportsbusiness group/b54ae8e99defd110VgnVCM100000ba42f00aRCRD.htm

Deloitte - Sports Business Group. (2007). *Football money league 2007*. Retrieved June 30, 2013, from http://www.deloitte.com/view/en_GB/uk/industries/sportsbusiness group/4fe98445881fb110VgnVCM 100000ba42f00aRCRD

Deloitte - Sports Business Group. (2008). *Football money league 2008*. Retrieved June 30, 2013, from http://www.deloitte.com/view/en_GB/uk/industries/sportsbusiness group/sports/football/703f4159f0c4 1310VgnVCM3000001c56f00aRCRD.htm

Deloitte - Sports Business Group. (2009). *Football money league 2009*. Retrieved June 30, 2013, from http://www.deloitte.com/view/en_GB/uk/industries/sportsbusiness group/a02ee3dad5181210VgnVCM100000ba42f00aRCRD.htm

Deloitte - Sports Business Group. (2010). *Football money league 2010*. Retrieved June 30, 2013, from http://www.deloitte.com/view/en_GB/uk/industries/sportsbusiness group/6a5fb29b3f907210VgnVCM 100000ba42f00aRCRD.html

Faris, Y. (2007). *Brands: Socially constructed reality: Talent imitates, genius steals*. Retrieved March 10, 2013, from http://farisyakob.typepad.com/blog/2007/01/brands_socially.html

Feldwick, P. (2002). *What is brand equity, anyway? Selected papers on brands and advertising*. Oxfordshire, UK: World Advertising Research Center.

Forbes. (2009). *Soccer team valuations*. Retrieved May 10, 2013, from http://www.forbes.com/lists/2009/34/soccer-values-09_Soccer-Team-Valuations_Rank.html

Forbes. (2010). *The business of soccer*. Retrieved May 10, 2013, from http://www.forbes.com/2010/04/21/soccer-value-teams-business-sports-soccer-10-intro.html

Forbes. (2012). *The Forbes fab 40: The world's most valuable sports brands*. Retrieved May 10, 2013, from http://www.forbes.com/sites/mikeozanian/2012/10/17/the-forbes-fab-40-the-worlds-most-valuable-sports-brands-4/

Fullerton, S., & Metz, R. (2008). The four domains of sports marketing: A conceptual framework. *Sport Marketing Quarterly*, *17*(2), 90–108.

Hayes, J., Alford, B., Silver, L., & York, R. (2006). Looks matter in developing consumer-brand relationships. *Journal of Product and Brand Management*, *15*(5), 306–315. doi:10.1108/10610420610685875

Hollis, N. (2008). *The global brand: How to create & develop lasting brand value in the world market*. New York: Milward Brown.

Hur, W.-M., Ahn, K.-H., & Kim, M. (2011). Building brand loyalty through managing brand community commitment. *Management Decision*, *49*, 1194–1213. doi:10.1108/00251741111151217

Jackson, T., & Shaw, D. (2009). *Fashion marketing*. Baskingstroke, UK: Palgrave-McMillan.

Jensen, M. B., & Beckmann, S. C. (2009). Determinants of innovation & creativity in corporate branding: Findings from Denmark. *Journal of Brand Management*, *16*(7), 568–479. doi:10.1057/palgrave.bm.2550138

Kaynak, E., Gultekin, G., & Tatoglu, E. (2008). An integrative framework linking brand associations & brand loyalty in professional sports. *Journal of Brand Management*, *15*(5), 336–357. doi:10.1057/palgrave.bm.2550117

Keller, K. L. (2001). *Building customer-based brand equity: A blueprint for creating strong brands* (Working Paper). Marketing Science Institute.

Larson, D. (2011). Global brand management – Nike's global brand. *The ISM Journal of International Business*, *1*(3), 1–14.

Li, H., Edwards, S. M., & Lee, J.-H. (2002). Measuring the intrusiveness of advertisements: Scale development and validation. *Journal of Advertising*, *31*(2), 37–47. doi:10.1080/00913367.2002.10673665

Muniz, A., & Schau, H. (2005). Religiosity in the abandoned Apple Newton brand community. *The Journal of Consumer Research*, *31*(4), 737–747. doi:10.1086/426607

Oliver, R. (1997). *Satisfaction: A behavioral perspective on the consumer*. New York: McGraw-Hill.

Patwardhan, H., & Balasubramanian, S. K. (2011). Brand romance: A complementary approach to explain emotional attachment towards brands. *Journal of Product and Brand Management*, *20*(4), 297–308. doi:10.1108/10610421111148315

Pedersen, L. (2004). *Why is branding so important?* Retrieved March, 12, 2013, from http://www.fiba.com/pages/mod/v3/util/downMana.asp?fileID=406

Ratten, V., & Ratten, H. (2011). International sport marketing: Practical & future research implications. *Journal of Business and Industrial Marketing*, *26*(8), 614–620. doi:10.1108/08858621111179886

Read, A. (2010). *Real Madrid & mobile marketing*. Post on UKSN – The Social Media & Sport.

Ross, J., & Harradine, R. (2011). Fashion value brands: The relationship between identity & image. *Journal of Fashion Marketing & Management*, *15*(3), 323–325.

Sarkar, A. (2011). Romancing with a brand: A conceptual analysis of romantic consumer-brand relationship. *Management & Marketing Challenges for the Knowledge Society*, *6*(1), 79–94.

Shaw, D. (2007). Manchester United football club: Developing a network orchestration model. *European Journal of Information Systems*, *16*, 628–642. doi:10.1057/palgrave.ejis.3000702

Sicilia, M., & Palazón, M. (2008). Brand communities on the internet. *Corporate Communications: An International Journal*, *13*(3), 255–270. doi:10.1108/13563280810893643

Site Ross, J., & Harradine, R. (2011). Fashion value brands: The relationship between identity & image. *Journal of Fashion Marketing & Management*, *15*(3), 323–325.

Stavros, C., & Westberg, K. (2009). Using triangulation & multiple case studies to advance relationship marketing theory. *Qualitative Market Research: An International Journal*, *12*(3), 307–320. doi:10.1108/13522750910963827

Thomson, M., MacInnis, D., & Park, W. (2005). The ties that bind: Measuring the strength of consumers' emotional attachments to brands. *Journal of Consumer Psychology*, *15*(1), 77–91. doi:10.1207/s15327663jcp1501_10

Triparthi, M. N. (2009, March). Customer engagement: Key to successful brand building. *Journal of Management*, 131–140.

Vincent, J., Hill, J. S., & Lee, J. W. (2009). The multiple brand personality of David Beckham: A case study of the Beckham brand. *Sport Marketing Quarterly*, *18*(3), 173–180.

Weszka, P. (2011). FIFA world cup brand elements & local inspirations. *Sport Marketing Quarterly*, *20*(3), 174–186.

ENDNOTE

[1] MDC is a Business Transformation Organization that utilizes technology, marketing communications, data analytics, and strategic consulting solutions to drive meaningful returns on Marketing and Communications Investments for multinational clients in the United States, Canada, Europe, and the Caribbean.

This research was previously published in Strategies in Sports Marketing edited by Manuel Alonso Dos Santos, pages 203-218, copyright year 2014 by Business Science Reference (an imprint of IGI Global).

Chapter 2
Digital Marketing:
Relationship Between Real Madrid's Actions and Brand Promotion and Customer Loyalty

Cesar Pereira da Mota
Universidade Aberta, Portugal

Pedro Isaías
The University of Queensland, Australia

ABSTRACT

Despite the fact that the branding of football is not a new phenomenon, the emergence of new media has provided the means and the opportunity for the widespread promotion of football club's brands. At the same time, the growing popularity of social media among football fan has empowered them to express their opinions and has granted them unlimited resources for information search and exchange. This chapter aims to examine the relationship that exists between Real Madrid's digital marketing actions and its promotion as a brand and the loyalty of its supporters. An online questionnaire was distributed among sports and football fans in order to identify their profile, their preferred communication channels, their use of social media and their knowledge about Real Madrid.

INTRODUCTION

Football is the most loved sport worldwide, with millions of fans of various ages, ethnicities and social classes. It is experiencing a phase of new management, in which it is presented as a large company, with a sizeable investment in marketing, especially digital marketing, to allow the inclusion and satisfaction of both fans and customers. Real Madrid Football Club's management model stands out for its business strategy, which has transformed the club into a sports-media organisation and has caused interest from other teams and sectors of the economy. It has over 100 years of history and it has been considered by the International Federation of Association Football (FIFA), the best club of the 20th century.

DOI: 10.4018/978-1-5225-5475-2.ch002

Supporters have become more involved and active in their use of the new media, which has empowered them to voice their opinions namely on forums (Cleland, 2011). Platforms like Twitter allow fans to comment on live events as they happen. While these new forms of media represent an opportunity for fans, their potential is also being maximised by football clubs to engage in direct dialogue with their fans and for commercial reasons (Dixon, 2016).

This study intends to address the following question: "What is the relationship between Real Madrid's digital marketing actions and brand promotion and customer loyalty?" The relevance of this question pertains to the importance of building a close relationship between the team and its supporters, in order to maintain their loyalty. Real Madrid's team invests in digital marketing because it knows that the team does not exist without its supporters just as it does not exist without its players. This chapter begins by providing a brief overview of relevant literature about digital marketing, football branding, fan engagement and Real Madrid. It then describes the empirical research and presents and discusses the results in the final sections.

MARKETING FOOTBALL

Marketing has always been affected by technological changes, from the printing press to the emergence of the internet. Technology has been providing marketing with innovative means to engage consumers. As consumers become more active in the digital world and require more engagement and interaction, traditional marketing is being overtaken by digital marketing (Ryan, 2016).

Brand Promotion and the Fans

Digital marketing entails the "management and execution of marketing using electronic media such as the web, e-mail, interactive TV and wireless media in conjunction with digital data about customers' characteristics and behaviour" (Chaffey, Ellis-Chadwick, Mayer & Johnston, 2009, p. 10). A fundamental aspect of marketing is knowing the customer. Organisations need to know their customers, their profiles and their preferred digital channels so they can reach them (Chaffey & Smith, 2008). Society is becoming increasingly digital. The percentage of EU28 individuals that use the internet on a daily basis has risen from 53% in 2010 to 71% in 2016 (Eurostat, 2017). Also, there is a growing tendency for people to engage with social media for a variety of reasons, namely to assert their role as consumers (Stephen, 2016). In 2016 Facebook had 1.609 billion monthly active users, while YouTube had over 1 billion, Google+ had 440 million, Instagram had 430 million, Twitter had 325 million and Pinterest had 110 million (Calcutt, 2016).

Kaufman and Horton (2015) postulate that there are five core steps to incorporate digital marketing in an organisation: mindset, the need to incorporate a digital culture with the existing culture; model, which concerns the integration of the principles of digital marketing within the organisation's marketing actions; strategy, the formulation of digital marketing techniques; implementation, which refers to the execution of the digital marketing tactics that were formulated; and sustainability, a alignment between the organisation's digital marketing values and actions. With regards to sports marketing itself, it isn't merely limited to attracting more fans to events. It entails both the use of marketing to promote sports products and the use of sports to promote other products and services (Fullerton & Merz, 2008). The evolution of consumers' profile and the growing competition for fans and financial support has placed a greater emphasis on the importance of marketing within the sport sector (Mullin, Hardy & Sutton, 2007).

According to Kennedy and Kennedy (2012), the "massive expansion in football finances is driven, directly and indirectly, by the commercial exploitation of a 'brand loyalty' that generates money from fan allegiance to football clubs nurtured over generations" (p.330). The commitment of the supporters can no longer be assured by the traditional once a week sports event. To ensure the loyalty of their mass of fans, sports organisations have to foster a continuous relationship with them and guarantee their constant engagement (García, 2011). With the internet, sports organisations began to develop internal channels for communicating directly with the fans, such as the creation of official websites. This type of communication with the supporters is independent of external media (local/national media) (Cleland, 2011). Sports organisations have, thus, been empowered to distribute their content, without having to depend on traditional media coverage (Sherwood, Nicholson & Marjoribanks, 2016). Moreover, numerous sports organisations have become aware of the importance of social media for brand development and have asserted their presence in several platforms (Parganas, Anagnostopoulos & Chadwick, 2015).

With the pervasiveness of Web 2.0 technology, consumers have become more active and informed. They have a greater control over the content they see, they are getting increasingly involved in the creation of products, they can create and share content and they use online platforms to post their opinions (Ryan, 2016). Additionally, the existence of different media sources has driven fans to be more interested in obtaining information about several aspects of the game and not just about the results and the players (Cleland, 2011). Sports fans are resorting to online platforms for entertainment and to search for information about their teams. Also, they have the expectation that their teams will have a social media presence to communicate with them (Parganas, Anagnostopoulos & Chadwick, 2015). Football fans are increasingly buying tickets online and have become accustomed to using the internet for price comparison platforms (Delloitte, 2016).

Fans Engagement

Besides social media, football fans also use the clubs' websites and other traditional media. Cleland (2011) study about four English football clubs (Aston Villa, Birmingham City, Coventry City and Northampton Town), revealed that the media sources that the supporters used for news and information were the clubs' official websites and local and national newspapers. Although the author also argues that the official websites are sometimes criticised for failing to provide the fans with interaction features, which are more easily found on non-official platforms that offer, for example, chat options (Cleland, 2011).

According to Miranda, Chamorro, Valero and Maestre (2010) football clubs websites can be assessed according to three types of factors, informational, transactional and communicational. Content is a fundamental element in any website, so it is important to provide current and accurate information. Also, football clubs' websites have to include features that allow the sale of tickets and merchandise. Finally, in terms of communication, it is important that they include contact information and feedback options for visitors. Silva and Isaías (2014) conducted a study about Sporting Clube de Portugal and the interaction between the club and its website users. The authors showed that information quality was the aspect that the users considered to be most important on the website. Other factors that were considered as important were information that is easily understandable, the website security, the efficiency of the system and the visual aspect. The study also concluded that only 18.5% of the participants used the official website to purchase products.

An important aspect of the relationship of fans with football clubs is the purchase of merchandise. There seems to be a football consumption, with the promotion of merchandise that targets the fans' communal identity (Kennedy & Kennedy, 2012). Sports marketing requires the development of strategies to match the consumers to sports' products (Mullin, Hardy & Sutton, 2007). Football paraphernalia helps fans to express both their private and their collective identities. Football fans purchase their club's merchandise mainly for its symbolism. Football merchandise translates the fans' devotion to a team, which then fosters a sense of belonging to a community (Derbaix & Decrop, 2011). There is a growing tendency for people to purchase sports products online, which has led sports organisations to invest in their internet channels for the distribution of their merchandise (Yoo & Ross, 2014).

Sponsors are also part of the relationship that fans have with their teams. The engagement of fans constitutes an incentive for sponsors (Kennedy & Kennedy, 2012). Sponsorship enables the sponsor to capitalise on their relationship with a team or a player (Fullerton & Merz, 2008). Although the use of advertising on football clubs' websites can be a nuisance, it can also serve as a form of local contextualisation and a connection to the community. Since websites are depleted of location, in some cases the links to the sponsors are the only content that provides any geographical identification (Crolley, 2008). Furthermore, sponsor awareness can be used as a measurement to determine the success of a sponsorship. This awareness is positively influenced by the fans behavioural loyalty, i.e. their financial investment in merchandise, their match attendance and their media use for following the team (Biscaia, Correia, Rosado, Ross & Maroco, 2013).

Real Madrid Football Club

Real Madrid's president Florentino Pérez started his mandate in mid-2000 and began to transform Real Madrid into a professional organisation whose business model has been described as an example of success (García, 2011). The idea behind the transformation of Real Madrid into a contemporary sports-media organisation derives from the notion that sports clubs, like brands, can be commercially exploited. The football industry has become one of the most lucrative businesses from the entertainment and leisure sector (Callejo & Forcadell, 2006).

Some of the strategies that Real Madrid employed to widen and enrich its relationship with its supporters included event planning, its own Real Madrid TV, the official website and social media presence. With concern to event planning, Real Madrid has turned traditional events, such as players' presentations into massively covered events that fans all over the worlds could witness. By granting its fans with access to events that were previously private or exclusive of the media, Real Madrid not only strengthen its relationship with the fans, but it also projected its image throughout the world, resulting in added revenue from merchandise and media. Real Madrid's TV channel is an important information instruments for fans and the media as well as a valuable tool for the promotion of Real Madrid's services and products. Its reach is, nonetheless, limited by the fact that it is a paid channel and not available in open access. The official website, realmadrid.com, provides an access point for fans that cannot be easily reached and a platform for community building. It grants access to the club's news, interviews with players and special promotions and products (García, 2011). In a study by Miranda et al. (2010) Real Madrid's website received a good evaluation in terms of navigability and of providing its content in multiple languages. Real Madrid's website is also considered to be strongly branded, with a commercial orientation that includes a notorious presence of its sponsors and advertising to its products (Crolley, 2008).

The use of social media constitutes another instrument of Real Madrid's promotion. Its presence in several social media websites, such as Facebook and Twitter enables them to interact with the supporters and provide them with access to content. (García, 2011). Baena (2016) examined the effect that the online and mobile marketing strategies that Real Madrid uses, have on the development of brand love. Their mains findings demonstrate that Real Madrid's mobile application did not have a relevant impact on brand love and that Real Madrid's social media presence should be asserted, as these media are predominant with relation to the traditional official websites.

METHODOLOGY

This study is exploratory, descriptive and correlational. Initially, a literature review was conducted using scientific papers obtained from b-on, a Portuguese online library (http://www.b-on.pt), Scielo (Scientific Electronic Library Online - http://www.scielo.br/); and from information that was collected from different websites, in order to capture a more realistic picture of the current football context and of digital marketing. Real Madrid Football Club's official website (http://www.realmadrid.com) was also consulted, its social media pages (Facebook, Twitter, Instagram, YouTube) and its fans' pages.

In order to address the main research question more specific objectives were outlined:

- Identify the marketing strategies that Real Madrid uses;
- Recognize the impact of Real Madrid's marketing in terms of sponsor dissemination;
- Identify the profile of Real Madrid's supporters, through its social channels;
- Examine the use of digital channels by the supporters;

In an attempt to establish a relationship between the supporters and the team, some hypotheses were delineated:

H1: Despite the multiplicity of Real Madrid's marketing actions for brand promotion, there is still some superficiality in the loyalty of its customers;
H2: Regardless of the team's popularity, the supporters do not usually access Real Madrid's official website;
H3: In spite of being a worldly famous team, people have no knowledge of their sponsors;
H4: Many of the supporters purchase the team's merchandise through Real Madrid's official website.

The empirical research consisted of an online questionnaire, using Google Forms, which was distributed among sports and football fans, people who use the team's social media and also on the Portuguese Open University platform. The questionnaire was available from the 11th of January until the 11th of February, 2016. Given the complexity of identifying and reaching the target population, snowball sampling, a non-probability sampling technique was used. In a study by Isaías, Pífano and Miranda (2012), the authors argued the validity of this sampling technique within dispersed populations and concluded that it allows the collection of valuable data deriving from the chain of contacts that is created. Hence, the respondents were asked to disseminate the questionnaire to people from their network of contacts, who were also interested in this subject. Initially the questionnaires were to be distributed among different communities of Real Madrid supporters, but as their closed nature became evident, different websites and online communities were contacted to complete the questionnaire. There was an attempt to reach different regions of the world by using some platforms from Brazil and by using the Portuguese Open University's platform, which has students from all over the world.

The questionnaire was composed of five sections: the first section concerned general data from the respondents; in the second part the respondent was asked to answer questions about the internet and social networks; the third section related to digital marketing itself; the fourth section was about sports and football; and the fifth part concerned Real Madrid.

The quantitative data that was collected with the questionnaire was analysed via IBM SPSS Statistics 23, where a correlation between the variables was performed with pertinent statistical analysis.

RESULTS

In total there were 192 responses, with an equal distribution among the genders, 96 from male respondents and 96 from female respondents. The average age of the respondents was 37.6 (SD: 12.8 years) and the majority of the respondents were 36-45 years old (48 respondents) and 26-35 years old (46 respondents). Despite the fact that the questionnaire was in Portuguese, the results were collected from several countries. Portugal was the country with the higher number of participants (53.1%) followed by Brazil (32.3%). France, Belgium, Angola and Spain were some of the other countries where responses were collected.

As the questionnaire was distributed solely on the internet, all the participants reported using it. In Table 1 it is possible to see that the great majority of the respondents use the internet on a daily basis (55.7%) or several times a day (42.7%). Only a very small percentage of the participants (1.6%) uses the internet only once to three times a week. Hence the sample is characterised by a frequent use of the internet, which is in line with the reality of the internet use in Europe, where in 2016, 71% of the individuals in EU28 reported using the internet on a daily basis (Eurostat, 2017).

In terms of the purpose of their internet use (Table 2), 88.5% of the respondents chose online banking, 79.2% said they use the internet to search for information and access to the university, school and courses and 77.6% uses the internet for online shopping. It is also important to highlight the fact that the use of social networks and channels was selected by 73.4% of the participants, which is important for this research.

An overwhelming majority of the respondents (185) stated that they were registered in at least one social network. Facebook was the most popular social network among the respondents (93.8%), reiterating its global dominance in terms of social media (Calcutt, 2016).

Table 1. Internet Use

Do You Use the Internet?		Frequency	Percentage	Valid Percentage	Cumulative Percentage
Valid	Yes, I use it once a week	1	0.5	0.5	0.5
	1 to 3 times a week	2	1.0	1.0	1.6
	Daily	107	55.7	55.7	57.3
	Several times a day	82	42.7	42.7	100.0
	Total	192	100.0	100.0	

Table 2. Purpose of internet use

What is the Purpose of Your Internet Use?		Responses		Percentage of Cases
		N	Percentage	
Valid [a]	Access news	133	10.8%	69.3%
	Search for information	152	12.4%	79.2%
	Access to information about sports	73	5.9%	38.0%
	Access to the university, school and courses	152	12.4%	79.2%
	For work	115	9.3%	59.9%
	Online banking	170	13.8%	88.5%
	Email access	100	8.1%	52.1%
	Social networks and channels	141	11.5%	73.4%
	Online shopping	149	12.1%	77.6%
	Other	45	3.7%	23.4%
	Total	1230	100.0%	640.6%

a. Dichotomous group tabulated at 1

Table 3. Social networks

Are You Registered in Any Social Network? Which One?		Responses		Percentage of Cases
		N	Percentage	
Valid [a]	No	7	1.6%	3.6%
	Yes, Facebook	180	40.4%	93.8%
	Yes, Twitter	52	11.7%	27.1%
	Yes, Instagram	65	14.6%	33.9%
	Yes, Google +	74	16.6%	38.5%
	Yes, YouTube channel	42	9.4%	21.9%
	Yes, Blogs	18	4.0%	9.4%
	Other	7	1.6%	3.6%
	Total	445	100.0%	231.8%

a. Dichotomous group tabulated at 1

With regards to the frequency of use, the majority of participants uses social networks daily (53.6%), 32.8% use them several times a day and 6.8% use them once or three times a week. Solely a very small percentage (3.1%) claimed they use them only once a week and 3.6% of the respondents don't use them at all.

In terms of content sharing (Table 4), 48.7% of the participants stated that they do not share any sports content through social networks. Those who do share sports content, prefer to do so via Facebook (32.8%), Twitter (7.3%) and Google+ (5.2%). It was also possible to conclude that men share more sports content through social networks ($p = 0.001$).

Figure 1. Age vs. social network use

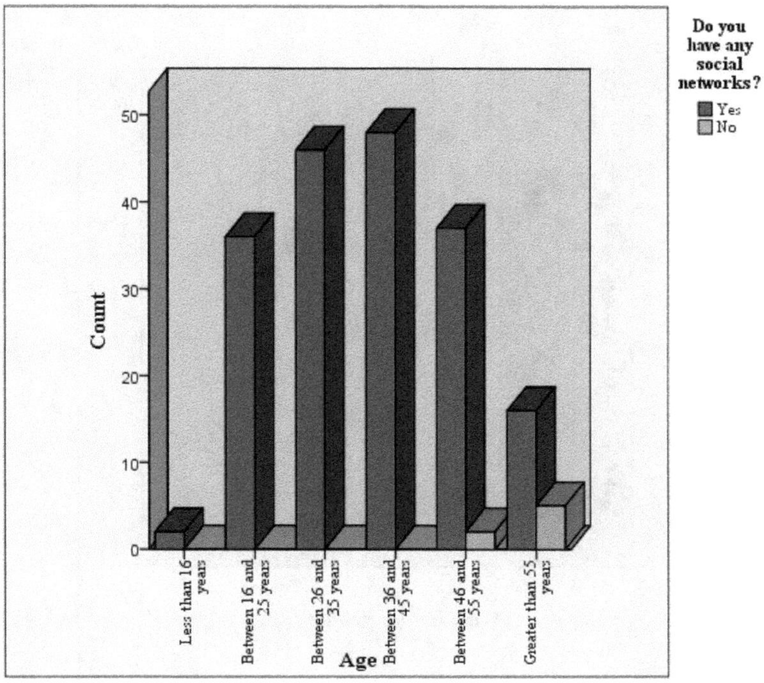

Table 4. Content sharing via social networks

Do You Share Any Sports Content? Where?		Responses		Percentage of Cases
		N	Percentage	
Valid [a]	I do not share	113	48.7%	58.9%
	Facebook	76	32.8%	39.6%
	Twitter	17	7.3%	8.9%
	Instagram	8	3.4%	4.2%
	Google +	12	5.2%	6.3%
	YouTube channel	1	0.4%	0.5%
	Blog	1	0.4%	0.5%
	Other	4	1.7%	2.1%
	Total	232	100.0%	120.8%

a. Dichotomous group tabulated at 1

With concern to sports, 153 participants claimed they liked sports. This question revealed some differences in terms of gender (Figure 2), since 83 respondents are male and 70 are female. The same difference occurs within the number of participants who do not like sports, 13 are male and 26 are female ($p = 0.02$). This portrays men's preference for sports.

There was also a significant statistical difference with regards to the love for sports and age, $p = 0.03$, as can be seen in Figure 3.

Figure 2. Love for sports and gender

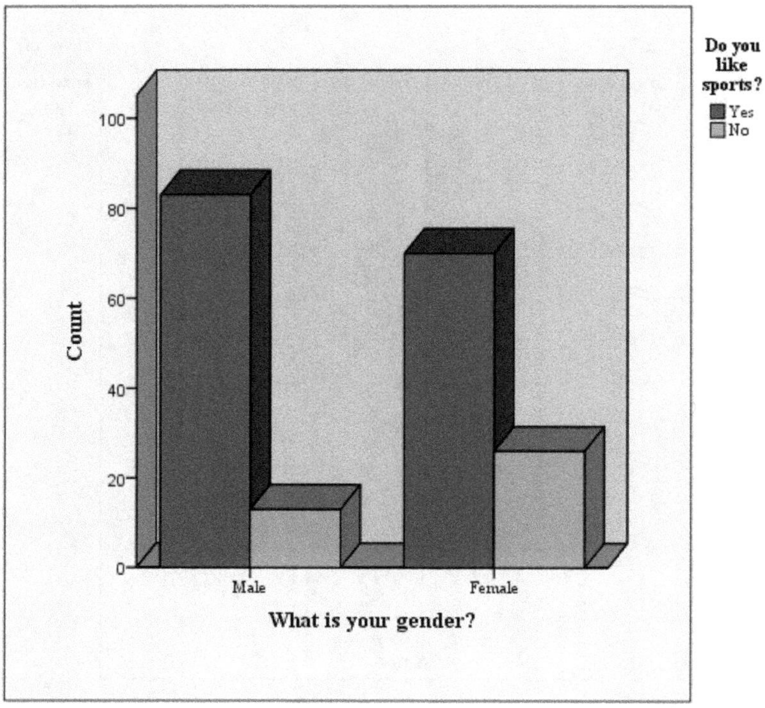

Figure 3. Love for sports and age

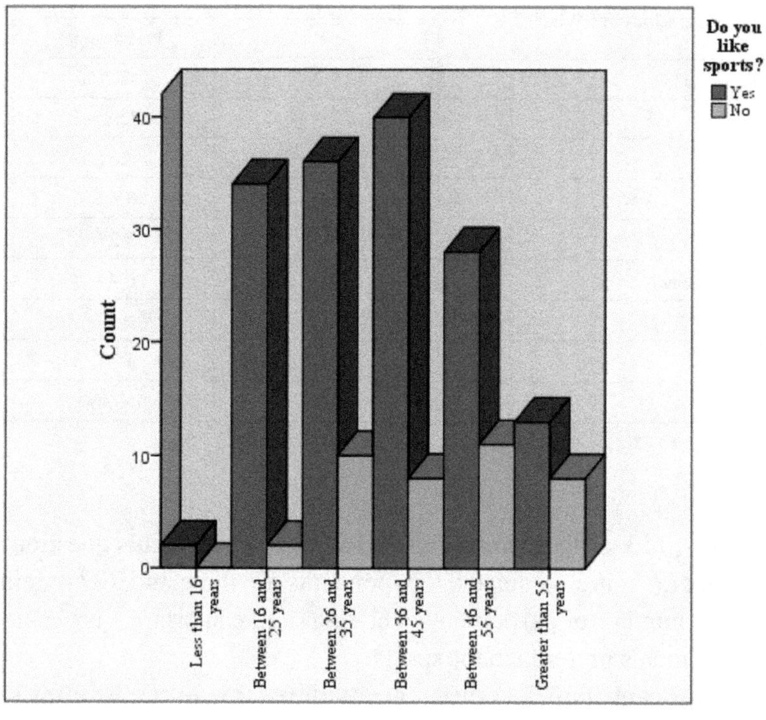

Although 153 respondents stated that they liked sports, only 138 follow some type of sports activity. The main means for following sports activities are public television channels, (50.5%), websites (43.2%), social networks (41.1%) and private television channels (35.4%), as is illustrated by Table 5. There seems to be a growing use of digital means to follow sporting activities, which is a tendency that is also reported by previous studies (Cleland, 2011; Parganas, Anagnostopoulos & Chadwick, 2015).

In term of sports products, 134 participants (78.2%) stated that they have some type of sports item. In this question, there were no age or gender differences. For these respondents the acquisition of the sports items was done mainly in non specific sports stores (32.3%), Table 6. This question also reveals that only a small percentage of the purchases are done online (17.7%), contrary to the growing use of online shopping for sports products that the literature reports (Yoo & Ross, 2014).

The great majority of the participants stated that they liked football (70.8%) and 58.9% of them follow a team. There were significant statistical differences with regards to the love for football and gender, with the predominance of male respondents (p = 0.000).

In terms of following football championship, 147 participants claimed that they follow at least one. The Portuguese league was the most popular (18.7%), followed by the Spanish (17.5%), the English (14.5%) and the Brazilian (13.8), as can be observed in Table 7.

Currently, it is possible to follow teams and championships through several communication means with various technological possibilities. When enquired about their use of these sports applications, only 31.8% of the respondents use them. This group of participants is mainly young (Figure 4) and male (p = 0,000).

With concern to the section about Real Madrid, in particular, the majority of the respondents 64.1% stated that they like the team, while 35.9% stated that they don't like the team. Although the number of male participants was higher among those who liked the team, there was no significant statistical difference (p = 0.051). There were also no significant statistical differences in terms of age (p = 0.300).

Table 5. Following sporting activities

Do You Follow Any Sports? Through Which Means?		Responses		Percentage of Cases
		N	Percentage	
Valid [a]	No	54	8.5%	28.1%
	Yes, on the radio	39	6.1%	20.3%
	Yes, on newspapers	52	8.2%	27.1%
	Yes, on sporting newspapers	47	7.4%	24.5%
	Yes, on public television channels	97	15.3%	50.5%
	Yes, on private television channels	68	10.7%	35.4%
	Yes, on websites	83	13.1%	43.2%
	Yes, on official sporting websites	49	7.7%	25.5%
	Yes, on social networks	79	12.4%	41.1%
	Yes, on YouTube	31	4,9%	16,1%
	Yes, through mobile applications	36	5,7%	18,8%
	Total	635	100,0%	330,7%

a. Dichotomous group tabulated at 1

Table 6. Sports products

Do You Have Any Sports Item? Where Did You Buy It?		Responses		Percentage of Cases
		N	Percentage	
Valid [a]	I don't have	58	21.8%	30.2%
	Yes, I do. I bought it in an official store	45	16.9%	23.4%
	Yes, I do. I bought it on an official website	22	8.3%	11.5%
	Yes, I do. I bought it on other websites	25	9.4%	13.0%
	Yes, I do. I bought in sporting stores	86	32.3%	44.8%
	Yes, I do. I bought it in other physical stores	28	10.5%	14.6%
	Other	2	0.8%	1.0%
	Total	266	100.0%	138.5%

a. Dichotomous group tabulated at 1

Table 7. Football championships that the participants follow

Do You Follow Any International Football Championship?		Responses		Percentage of Cases
		N	Percentage	
Valid [a]	I do not follow any championship	45	11.1%	23.4%
	Portuguese championship	76	18.7%	39.6%
	Spanish championship	71	17.5%	37.0%
	English championship	59	14.5%	30.7%
	Brazilian championship	56	13.8%	29.2%
	French championship	28	6.9%	14.6%
	Italian championship	25	6.2%	13.0%
	German championship	25	6.2%	13.0%
	Belgian championship	6	1.5%	3.1%
	Turkish championship	5	1.2%	2.6%
	USA championship	6	1.5%	3.1%
	Argentinean championship	1	0.2%	0.5%
	Swiss championship	3	0.7%	1.6%
	Total	406	100.0%	211.5%

a. Dichotomous group tabulated at 1

The analysis of the results also shows that from the 153 people who like sports, 109 also like Real Madrid. Moreover, the 14 participants who claimed that they don't like sports, stated that they like Real Madrid (p = 0,000). Hence, it is possible to conclude that the majority of people who like sports, also likes Real Madrid (Figure 5). Similar data was collected, when comparing the people who like Real Madrid and those who like football (Table 8).

Figure 4. Sports apps use and age

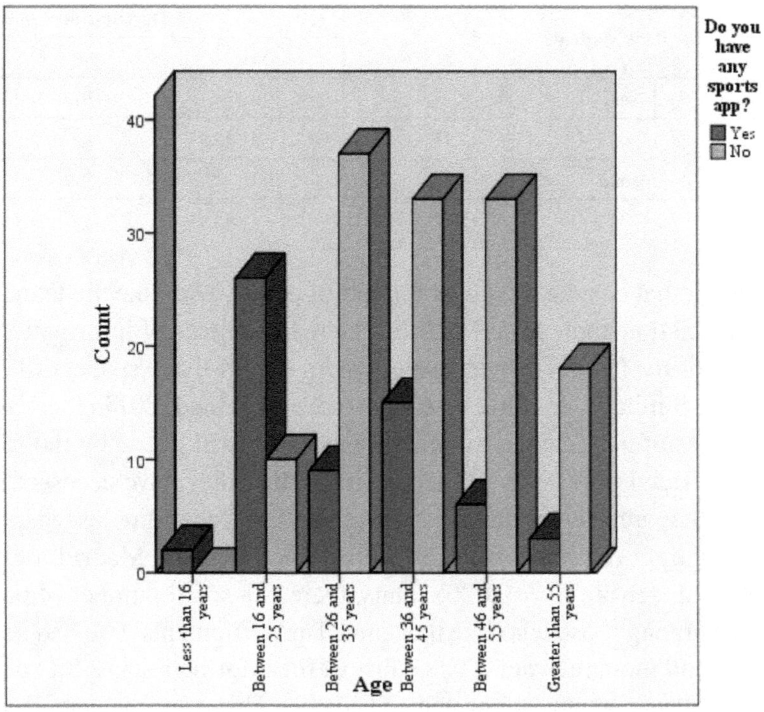

Figure 5. Liking real madrid vs. liking sports

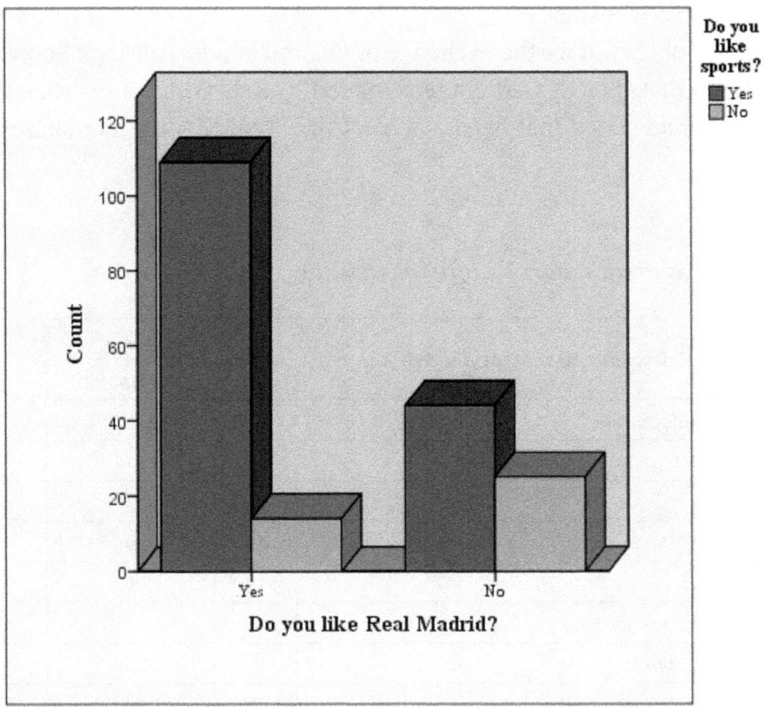

Table 8. Liking real madrid vs. liking football

Do You Like Real Madrid?		Do You Like Football?		
		Yes	No	Total
Valid	Yes	107	16	123
	No	29	40	69
	Total	136	56	192

It also became evident that despite the large number of people who like the team, only 43.8% of the participants access information about Real Madrid. The main sources of information are the television (17.1%) non-official websites (13.2%), sports newspapers (12.9%), newspapers (8%), official website (7.7%) and radio (3.1%). Similarly, to other research studies (Cleland, 2011) these results demonstrate that in spite of the success of new media, traditional media are still in use by the fans. In terms of accessing Real Madrid's official page, only 49 people stated that they have accessed it, which is in line with previous literature that argues that the official websites are becoming less visited (Baena, 2016).

It is important to highlight that from the 123 people who like Real Madrid, only 45 of them have already visited the official website (p = 0,000). Thus, there is a small number of people who have accessed the website even among those who like the team. The participants who had accessed the website were asked what they found more relevant. The quality of the information (12.8%) and the visual aspect (11.7%) were considered the most important items (Table 9). This data was very similar to the one that was obtained from the responses of the participants with relation to websites in general. Also, these results reiterate Silva and Isaías (2014) findings in terms of the importance of the quality of information, the website's security and its visual aspect and Miranda et al. (2010) argument for the importance of content on football clubs' websites.

Similarly, to what was observed for the exchange of general content on social networks, not too many people, only 32, claimed that they shared content related to Real Madrid on social networks. Among those participants only 1 had stated that he/she doesn't like Real Madrid, but shares content related to

Table 9. Relevant aspects on real madrid's official website

What Do You Find More Relevant on Real Madrid's Website?		Responses		Percentage of Cases
		N	Percentage	
Valid [a]	Quality of information	34	27.4%	68.0%
	Visual aspect	31	25.0%	62.0%
	Ease of use	21	16.9%	42.0%
	Security and Privacy	11	8.9%	22.0%
	Website's speed	10	8.1%	20.0%
	Relationship with the user	12	9.7%	24.0%
	None of the above	5	4.0%	10.0%
	Total	124	100.0%	248.0%

a. Dichotomous group tabulated at 1

the club on his/her social networks. As it happened with the exchange of general content, Facebook is the mostly used social network (96.8%), Table 10.

In terms of Real Madrid's products, only 35 participants purchased some type of sports product from Real Madrid and 34.3% of them used physical stores. Only 28.6% of the respondents had used the official website to make a purchase, while 22.9 has used official stores (Table 11). There were no significant statistical differences with regards to gender and age.

With regards to Real Madrid's evaluation in the media there was no negative response that would characterise it as a "bad brand". The majority of the respondents, 33.5%, evaluated it as a good brand, while 25% stated their indifference (Table 12).

The questionnaire also intended to examine the respondents' knowledge of the team's players and sponsors. Only 52 respondents stated that they don't know any Real Madrid player, while 140 claimed to know at least one player and 11 respondents stated that they know all the players in the team. The results also show that from the 123 respondents that like Real Madrid, 103 claimed to know at least one player. On the other hand, from the 69 respondents that do not like the team, 37 claim to know at least one player (p = 0,000). Hence, it is possible to conclude that the respondents that like Real Madrid, have a wider knowledge of their players. In terms of gender and the knowledge of the players there were

Table 10. Exchange of content related to real madrid on social networks

Content Exchange on Social Networks		Responses		Percentage of Cases
		N	Percentage	
Valid [a]	Facebook	31	60.8%	96.9%
	Twitter	5	9.8%	15.6%
	Instagram	5	9.8%	15.6%
	Google +	7	13.7%	21.9%
	YouTube	1	2.0%	3.1%
	Blog	1	2.0%	3.1%
	Other	1	2.0%	3.1%
	Total	51	100.0%	159.4%

a. Dichotomous group tabulated at 1

Table 11. Purchase of real madrid team's products

Real Madrid Official Products		Responses		Percentage of Cases
		N	Percentage	
Valid [a]	Official store	8	22.9%	25.8%
	Official website	10	28.6%	32.3%
	Other websites	5	14.3%	16.1%
	Other stores	12	34.3%	38.7%
	Total	35	100.0%	112.9%

a. Dichotomous group tabulated at 1

Table 12. Real madrid's evaluation in the media

Media Evaluation		Responses		Percentage of Cases
		N	Percentage	
Valid[a]	Indifferent	56	25.0%	29.2%
	A good brand	75	33.5%	39.1%
	Only another club	4	1.8%	2.1%
	The best club	28	12.5%	14.6%
	A reasonable brand	2	0.9%	1.0%
	A symbol of the ideology	32	14.3%	16.7%
	No evaluation	27	12.1%	14.1%
	Total	224	100.0%	116.7%

a. Dichotomous group tabulated at 1

significant statistical differences (p = 0,000), with male respondents being predominant in terms of their knowledge of the players.

The participants who claimed to know at least one player from the team were given the option of identifying the players. The most cited players were Cristiano Ronaldo (54 participants) followed by Bale, Benzema and Pepe (8 participants each).

With respect to the sponsors, only 43 participants (22.4%) referred that they don't know any. From those who claimed to know at least one sponsor, the most popular was Emirates (37.1%) and Adidas (26.8%) as can be seen in Table 13. These are international companies, whose logos are highlighted on the team's jerseys. Similarly, to what occurred in the question related to the respondents' knowledge of the players, from the 123 respondents who like Real Madrid, 112 know at least one sponsor (91%). From the 43 people that stated that they don't know any sponsor, 32 (74.4%) claimed not to like Real Madrid. Again, those who like Real Madrid have a wider knowledge of their sponsors (p = 0,000), reiterating the belief that sponsor awareness improves with behavioural loyalty (Biscaia et al., 2013). Another similarity with the previous question is the fact that the male participants were predominant with regards to their knowledge of the team's sponsors (p = 0,009).

DISCUSSION

Through the data collection it was possible to attain the proposed objectives as well as to reflect on the hypotheses that were outlined.

Hence, H1, which considered the existence of superficiality in the loyalty of Real Madrid's team customers, even with the various marketing actions, was confirmed. Many of the participants that like the team don't search for information related to it (63.4%), don't share sports content about the club on their social networks (74.8%) and they don't have official products (76.4%).

H2 that suggested that the supporters do not access the official website was also confirmed. Despite being a worldly famous and appreciated team (64.1% stated that they like Real Madrid), the results demonstrated that there is a high number of supporters, but they don't access the official website (63.4%) to obtain news and information (39%), nor to make any purchase online (28.6%).

Table 13. Real Madrid Sponsors

Do you know any of Real Madrid's sponsors? Which one?		Responses		Percentage of cases
		N	Percentage	
Valid [a]	Emirates FLY	119	37,1%	79,9%
	Adidas	86	26,8%	57,7%
	Coca-Cola	32	10,0%	21,5%
	Audi	36	11,2%	24,2%
	Microsoft	17	5,3%	11,4%
	BBVA	29	9,0%	19,5%
	Other	2	0,6%	1,3%
	Total	321	100,0%	215,4%

a. Dichotomous group tabulated at 1

With regards to H3, which assumed that there was a lack of knowledge in terms of the team's sponsors, it was partly rejected. There is a high percentage of respondents (77.6%) that claimed to know at least one sponsor and even those who don't like Real Madrid know some of its sponsors, especially those that have a greater importance in the history of the club (Emirates 79.9% and Adidas 57.7%).

Finally, H4, which referred to the purchase of the brand's products through Real Madrid's official website, was also rejected. Real Madrid's official website is not the main venue (28.6%) that the supporters chose to buy their sports products. Even with the options available on the team's channel and the marketing strategies that are developed by the club. Table 14 portrays the summary of this discussion.

CONCLUSION

Football is one of the most popular and loved sports in the world and in a world that is technologically so advanced and where information reaches anyone at anytime, being at the forefront of technology al-

Table 14. Discussion Summary

Hypothesis	Status	Results
H1	Confirmed	The supporters: • Do not search for information about the team. • Do not share sports content on the social networks they use. • Do not have official sports products from the brand.
H2	Confirmed	• The supporters do not access the team's official website. • It is not the main source of information. • It is not the main venue for the purchase of official products.
H3	Rejected	• People in general know Real Madrid team's sponsors. • The supporters have a great knowledge of the sponsors. • Emirates and Adidas are the most popular sponsors.
H4	Rejected	• The official website is not the most used venue for the purchase of official products. • Supporters prefer to purchase products in the physical stores.

lows a team to win inside and outside the field. There is an increasing number of clubs, sponsors and institutions like FIFA and UEFA (e Union of European Football Associations that harness the market of digital publicity. This tendency was the motivation of this study.

In the context of the digital world, Real Madrid's team is present on several social channels and networks, mainly on Facebook, Twitter, Google+, Instagram, YouTube, Smartphone app and its official website. Since the results showed that Facebook is the social network that has more impact and a higher number of users, the majority of Real Madrid's campaigns should be directed at it.

It was equally possible to identify the profile of the sample of supporters that answered the questionnaire. The sample was composed of mainly young and male people. Additionally, since they are part of the digital world they are the main users of the team's social channels and networks. They know the players and the sponsors, they search for information and they use the team's website. These are the kind of supporters that Real Madrid should concentrate on, since they are there main followers. With regards to Real Madrid's marketing strategies, it has assured its presence in various social channels and networks such as Facebook, Twitter, Google+, Instagram, YouTube, Smartphone app, official website, online shop and Real Madrid TV. Its marketing strategies has an impact on the promotion of sponsors: there are global and regional main sponsors; only 22.4% of the participants had no knowledge of the team's sponsors; those with a wider knowledge, were part of the group that liked Real Madrid; and the male respondents had a wider knowledge of the sponsors than the female respondents. With regards to the use of digital channels by the supporters, all of the team's channels are used, with a predominance from Facebook. Despite the pervasiveness of digital channels, people also look for physical channels.

With respect to this study's limitations, there were some difficulties in gaining access to certain websites for the publication of the questionnaire and in obtaining responses from the users. Also, since the literature is scarce in this area, much of the information that was used about Real Madrid derived from its own official channels, specially its website. The fact that the questionnaire was in Portuguese limited the scope of platforms where it could be distributed and also the number of participants.

Future research should focus on a wider distribution of the questionnaire in terms of both platforms and respondents, to allow a comparison between different countries. Other options include concentrating solely on the supporters as the target population and examine other teams' digital marketing strategies to establish a comparison. Additionally, it would be important to explore more closely the profile and behaviour of the followers, the loyalty of current supporters and the acquisition of prospective ones.

REFERENCES

Baena, V. (2016). Online and mobile marketing strategies as drivers of brand love in sports teams: Findings from Real Madrid. *International Journal of Sports Marketing & Sponsorship*, *17*(3), 202–218. doi:10.1108/IJSMS-08-2016-015

Biscaia, R., Correia, A., Rosado, A. F., Ross, S. D., & Maroco, J. (2013). Sport sponsorship: The relationship between team loyalty, sponsorship awareness, attitude toward the sponsor, and purchase intentions. *Journal of Sport Management*, *27*(4), 288–302. doi:10.1123/jsm.27.4.288

Calcutt, V. (2016, February 9). Social Media User Statistics 2016. Socialnomics. Retrieved from http://socialnomics.net/2016/02/09/social-media-user-statistics-2016/

Callejo, M. B., & Forcadell, F. J. (2006). Real Madrid football club: A new model of business organization for sports clubs in Spain. In *Global Business and Organizational Excellence* (pp. 51-64).

Chaffey, D., Ellis-Chadwick, F., Mayer, R., & Johnston, K. (2009). *Internet marketing: strategy, implementation and practice* (4th ed.). Pearson Education.

Chaffey, D., & Smith, P. R. (2008). eMarketing eXcellence: Planning and optimizing your digital marketing (3rd ed.). Routledge.

Cleland, J. (2011). The media and football supporters: A changing relationship. *Media Culture & Society, 33*(2), 299–315. doi:10.1177/0163443710393866

Crolley, L. (2008). Using the Internet to strengthen its identity: The case of Spanish football. *Sport in Society, 11*(6), 722–738. doi:10.1080/17430430802284003

Delloitte. (2016). Annual Review of Football Finance 2016.

Derbaix, C., & Decrop, A. (2011). Colours and scarves: An ethnographic account of football fans and their paraphernalia. *Leisure Studies, 30*(3), 271–291. doi:10.1080/02614367.2010.527356

Dixon, K. (2016). Fandom. In E. Cashmore & K. Dixon (Eds.), *Studying Football*. Oxon, New York: Routledge.

Eurostat. (2017). Individuals - Frequency of internet use. Retrieved from http://appsso.eurostat.ec.europa.eu/nui/show.do?dataset=isoc_ci_ifp_fu&lang=en

Fullerton, S., & Merz, G. R. (2008). The four domains of sports marketing: A conceptual framework. *Sport Marketing Quarterly, 17*(2), 90.

García, C. (2011). Real Madrid Football Club: Applying a relationship-management model to a sport organization in Spain. *International Journal of Sport Communication, 4*(3), 284–299. doi:10.1123/ijsc.4.3.284

Isaías, P., Pífano, S., & Miranda, P. (2012). Subject Recommended Samples: Snowball Sampling. In P. Isaías & M. B. Nunes (Eds.), *Information Systems Research and Exploring Social Artifacts: Approaches and Methodologies*. IGI Global.

Kaufman, I., & Horton, C. (2015). *Digital Marketing: Integrating Strategy and Tactics with Values, A Guidebook for Executives, Managers, and Students*. Oxon, New York: Routledge.

Kennedy, P., & Kennedy, D. (2012). Football supporters and the commercialisation of football: Comparative responses across Europe. *Soccer & Society, 13*(3), 327–340. doi:10.1080/14660970.2012.655503

Miranda, F. J., Chamorro, A., Valero, V., & Maestre, J. (2010). Quantitative assessment of football web sites: An empirical study of the best European football club. *Journal of Service Science and Management, 3*(01), 110–116. doi:10.4236/jssm.2010.31014

Mullin, B. J., Hardy, S., & Sutton, W. A. (2007). *Sport Marketing* (3rd ed.). Human Kinetics.

Parganas, P., Anagnostopoulos, C., & Chadwick, S. (2015). Youll never tweet alone: Managing sports brands through social media. *Journal of Brand Management, 22*(7), 551–568. doi:10.1057/bm.2015.32

Ryan, D. (2016). *Understanding digital marketing: marketing strategies for engaging the digital generation*. London, Philadelphia: Kogan Page Publishers.

Sherwood, M., Nicholson, M., & Marjoribanks, T. (2016). Controlling the Message and the Medium? *Digital Journalism*, *5*, 513-531.

Silva, J., & Isaías, P. (2014). Website Interaction between a Football Club and its Supporters: The Case of Sporting Clube de Portugal. In Human-Computer Interfaces and Interactivity: Emergent Research and Applications (pp. 72-100). Hershey, PA: IGI Global.

Stephen, A. T. (2016). The role of digital and social media marketing in consumer behavior. *Current Opinion in Psychology*, *10*, 17–21. doi:10.1016/j.copsyc.2015.10.016

Yoo, J., & Ross, S. D. (2014). Understanding Online Purchase Intentions of Licensed Sports Merchandise through Integration of Technology Acceptance Model and Trust. *The Journal of SPORT*, *3*(1), 3.

ADDITIONAL READING

Bohnsack, D., Jostol, G., Maher, R., Sundar, A., Pokrywczynski, J., & Berg, K. (2016, January). Tracking Sports & Event Marketing Analytics for Marketing Effects: Relevant Research Questions the Industry Knows and Needs. *Proceedings of the American Academy of Advertising Conference* (p. 154). American Academy of Advertising.

Bruns, A., Weller, K., & Harrington, S. (2014). *Twitter and sports: Football fandom in emerging and established markets. In Twitter and society* (Vol. 89, pp. 263–280). Peter Lang.

DeSarbo, W., & Madrigal, R. (2012). Exploring the demand aspects of sports consumption and fan avidity. *Interfaces*, *42*(2), 199–212. doi:10.1287/inte.1110.0575

DeSarbo, W. S., & Madrigal, R. (2011). Examining the behavioral manifestations of fan avidity in sports marketing. *Journal of Modelling in Management*, *6*(1), 79–99. doi:10.1108/17465661111112511

Filo, K., Lock, D., & Karg, A. (2015). Sport and social media research: A review. *Sport Management Review*, *18*(2), 166–181. doi:10.1016/j.smr.2014.11.001

García, B., & Welford, J. (2015). Supporters and football governance, from customers to stakeholders: A literature review and agenda for research. *Sport Management Review*, *18*(4), 517–528. doi:10.1016/j.smr.2015.08.006

Giulianotti, R. (2002). Supporters, followers, fans, and flaneurs: A taxonomy of spectator identities in football. *Journal of Sport and Social Issues*, *26*(1), 25–46. doi:10.1177/0193723502261003

Hur, Y., Ko, Y. J., & Claussen, C. L. (2011). Acceptance of sports websites: A conceptual model. *International Journal of Sports Marketing & Sponsorship*, *12*(3), 13–27. doi:10.1108/IJSMS-12-03-2011-B003

Koronios, K., Psiloutsikou, M., Kriemadis, A., Zervoulakos, P., & Leivaditi, E. (2016). Sport Sponsorship: The Impact of Sponsor Image on Purchase Intention of Fans. *Journal of Promotion Management*, *22*(2), 238–250. doi:10.1080/10496491.2016.1121739

Kriemadis, T., Kotsovos, A., & Kartakoullis, N. (2009). A strategy for managing customer relations on the internet: Evidence from the football sector. *Direct Marketing: An International Journal*, *3*(4), 229–243. doi:10.1108/17505930911000847

Lu, H. (2016). Inspiration of Successful Experience of US and European Enterprises Leveraging Sports Marketing on "Going Global" of Chinese Enterprises. *Journal of Sports Sciences*, *4*, 250–255.

McCarthy, B. (2013). Consuming sports media, producing sports media: An analysis of two fan sports blogospheres. *International Review for the Sociology of Sport*, *48*(4), 421–434. doi:10.1177/1012690212448240

Mudrick, M., Miller, M., & Atkin, D. (2016). The influence of social media on fan reactionary behaviors. *Telematics and Informatics*, *33*(4), 896–903. doi:10.1016/j.tele.2016.01.005

Richelieu, A., & Desbordes, M. (2009). Football teams going international–the strategic leverage of branding. *Journal of Sponsorship*, *3*(1), 10–22.

Ruddock, A., Hutchins, B., & Rowe, D. (2010). Contradictions in media sport culture: The reinscription of football supporter traditions through online media. *European Journal of Cultural Studies*, *13*(3), 323–339. doi:10.1177/1367549410363200

Schmid, B., Kexel, C., & Djafarova, E. (2016). Multidimensional Sports Spectators Segmentation and Social Media Marketing. *World Academy of Science, Engineering and Technology, International Journal of Social, Behavioral, Educational, Economic. Business and Industrial Engineering*, *10*(8), 2558–2561.

Stander, F. W., Van Zyl, L. E., & Motaung, K. (2016). Promoting fan engagement: An exploration of the fundamental motives for sport consumption amongst premier league football spectators. *Journal of Psychology in Africa*, *26*(4), 309–315.

Szymoszowskyj, A., Szymoszowskyj, A., Winand, M., Winand, M., Kolyperas, D., Kolyperas, D., & Sparks, L. et al. (2016). Professional football clubs retail branding strategies. *Sport, Business and Management. International Journal (Toronto, Ont.)*, *6*(5), 579–598.

Thoo, A. C., Radzi, N. F. M., Merlinda, F., & Ho, P. H. (2016). Factors Affecting Football Fans' Purchase Intention Toward Sponsoring Product—A Conceptual Model. *Advanced Science Letters*, *22*(12), 4241–4244.

Witkemper, C., Lim, C. H., & Waldburger, A. (2012). Social media and sports marketing: Examining the motivations and constraints of Twitter users. *Sport Marketing Quarterly*, *21*(3), 170.

Woisetschläger, D., Haselhoff, V., & Backhaus, C. (2014). Fans resistance to naming right sponsorships: Why stadium names remain the same for fans. *European Journal of Marketing*, *48*(7/8), 1487–1510. doi:10.1108/EJM-03-2012-0140

Zhang, Z., & Won, D. (2010). Buyer or browser? An analysis of sports fan behaviour online. *International Journal of Sports Marketing & Sponsorship*, *11*(2), 21–36. doi:10.1108/IJSMS-11-02-2010-B003

KEY TERMS AND DEFINITIONS

Brand Promotion: Concerns the strategies and techniques that are employed to create a positive image of a brand and stimulating its demand. It aims to create an awareness of services and products, increase sales and enhance customer loyalty.

Customer Loyalty: Refers to consumers' commitment to a specific brand. When customers are loyal to a particular brand they consistently chose products and services from that brand, despite the actions of competitors or even price.

Digital Marketing: It is a facet of marketing that uses digital technologies to promote products, services and brands. It uses the internet and digital media to reach its target population and it can occur in real time.

Social Media: Represent the collective of internet applications that enable individuals to create and share content. Unlike the traditional media, the information can be edited and controlled by the users. Wikipedia, Facebook, Twitter and LinkedIn are just some examples of social media websites.

Social Networks: Derive from Web 2.0 technologies and allow people to use an internet platform to build an online profile and a social network of contacts. They can have a general nature like Facebook or have a particular vocation such as LinkedIn, which is professional.

Sponsor: Refers to an entity or an individual that provides financial support or other type of contribution to an organisation, person or event, usually in exchange of advertising and promotion.

Sports Marketing: Refers to a specialisation of marketing that focuses on the promotion of sports teams, events, services and products. It involves a variety of sectors, namely broadcasting, customer relations, social media and advertising.

This research was previously published in User Innovation and the Entrepreneurship Phenomenon in the Digital Economy edited by Pedro Isaias and Luísa Cagica Carvalho, pages 28-49, copyright year 2018 by Business Science Reference (an imprint of IGI Global).

Chapter 3
Brand Anthropomorphism:
Collegiate Mascots and Social Media

Tamara L. Wandel
University of Evansville, USA

ABSTRACT

This chapter addresses brand anthropomorphism, in particular how sports mascots can be utilized on social media to increase emotional connectivity with fans and their affiliated teams. The history and role of mascots and present day usage encourages understanding of how narratives are a positive and promising tool for marketing communication professionals and those in the sports and entertainment industry. Interviews were conducted with personnel associated with mascots to gain insights into the concept of brand anthropomorphism. Also, an online survey was conducted on mascot brand attributes and results were presented. The ability to personify a brand has significant managerial implications, and this chapter demonstrates how social media platforms may drive brand loyalty.

INTRODUCTION

Goals. Assists. Touchdowns. Homeruns. Shutouts. Championship Records.

Statistics dominate the sports world, determining who sees field or floor time, when and where games are played, and in salary caps and arbitration. Statistics help determine successful seasons, assess coaching talent, measure athletic prowess, and provide clear evidence of whether a stadium's seats are packed or empty. These are the tangibles that make or break a sports bank, and the financial fallout to not only sports teams but also to the surrounding communities is significant.

In 2015, the global sports market had a value of approximately 145 billion U.S. dollars, and the National Collegiate Athletic Association (NCAA) revenue is now approaching the billion dollar mark in college sports (Statista, 2016). Whether you are a sports fantastic, casual fan or a student of marketing and communication, sports is big business. The managerial implications of anthropomorphism and sports are noteworthy, offering a mechanism to create strong feelings in fans by attributing human characteristics to the mascots and encouraging a sense of connectivity.

DOI: 10.4018/978-1-5225-5475-2.ch003

Loyalty is heated and intense among fans, and sports organizations count on this. Social media has heightened this fervency, and it has become an important and relied upon platform for marketing the brand of a team. Social media allows organizations unparalleled levels of audience engagement (Littlewood, Bick, & Treen, 2017), so that online exchanges with customers may take place to encourage an emotional attachment extending far beyond any given game's win or loss.

Research into the determinants of sports emotional branding and loyalty has grown in recent years, but it did not include the variable of social media (Munnukka, Karjaluoto, & Hokkanen, 2017). This chapter provides history, context, and original information to further understanding of the topic. In particular, the chapter has three main objectives:

- To offer managers ideas and methods of personifying brands via mascots
- To demonstrate specific examples of social media being used successfully by collegiate teams to create innovative anthropomorphic marketing campaigns
- To increase awareness of trends in emotional branding

These objectives extend beyond the sports world and into business and nonprofit sectors. In all fields, brands are identities and offer meaning and value to an organization (Kozinets, 2017). The chapter begins, in Section 1, with a literature review on emotional branding. This section describes a model identifying stages of consumer choice and also addresses various types of emotions, which may ultimately impact purchasing decisions. Section 2 offers a historical context to anthropomorphism and how mascots may serve as critical links to the brand of a company. Section 3 details information on social networking as a valuable mechanism to connect consumers and fans. In Section 4, information gleaned from original interviews is given, providing inside understanding by individuals working closely with four well-known mascots. Section 5 moves from the previous qualitative research to original quantitative research undertaken. Data from an online survey addresses how respondents felt toward various attributes of mascot Twitter accounts. Section 6 identifies trends managers should be aware of for anthropomorphizing sports mascots. In particular, managers should consider the diversification of social media, offer more stadium-specific experiences for fans, provide more breadth and depth in mascot storytelling, and find more effective means to measure the value in emotional branding efforts. Section 7 constitutes the conclusion of the chapter, with a summary of the relevance and implications of using mascots for emotional branding purposes.

EMOTIONAL BRANDING

In the last decade, literature regarding branding has focused on the important role of emotions as a mechanism to connect consumers and brands (Yoo & MacInnis, 2005). The premise of emotional branding was discussed even before that, however, when it was realized that benefit-driven only approaches to brands may not have the longevity and enduring competitive advantage that a personal and meaningful bond between a consumer and a brand may possess (Luther, 2006). People tend to think of the world in terms of the human experience, and humans are emotional creatures at heart. Emotional branding is the feeling of attachment toward a specific brand, one which is relational in nature and often story-driven. Traits associated with emotional branding may be trust, resonance, companionship, and love (Rossiter & Bellman, 2012).

The premise of emotional branding for a company or organization is to develop a trusting and intimate emotional connection that transcends any material satisfaction (Gobe, 2011). For marketing and communication professionals, this means that emotional branding can make the difference between otherwise equal choices a consumer possesses. A five-stage model developed by O'Shaughnessy and O'Shaughnessy (2003) helps illustrate the process of consumer choice:

1. The value system or key concerns of consumers
2. Emotive stimuli (the object, service or event)
3. Appraisal of the emotive stimuli
4. Beliefs and desires
5. Emotional response

The fifth stage is most pertinent to emotional branding, as it is when arousal of feelings toward the product, object or service takes place. This in turn brings about consumer action as choices are made of which product or brand to align with and support. Likability, comfort, and bonding with a brand can be a significant determinant for a consumer, even overriding logic. Ten major kinds of emotion were categorized by Balaji, Londhe and Shukla (2016): aspiration, admiration, affection, anticipation, assurance, empathy, enjoyment, interest, fulfillment and optimism. By understanding and managing the customer emotional experience, a company or organization can establish competitive differentiation. When emotional branding succeeds, the consumer is not only approving of the brand but actually begins to identify as part of it because the brand is positioned into the core of his or her life (Akgün, Koçoğlu, & İmamoğlu, 2013).

When this alignment occurs in the sports industry, the team becomes an extension of the fan. This notion of devoted fans, referred to as fandom, includes feelings of camaraderie and belongingness with others who share a love for the same team. In addition to feelings of pride, benefits of fandom include social prestige, crossing boundaries of age, sex and race, and the fact that skill is not necessary for audience participation (Zillman, Bryant & Sapolsky, 1989). A sports crowd is unique from other types of crowds in the way the group possesses certain commonalties before even coming together as a collective unit.

Melnick (1993) noted that being a fan in a crowd of like-minded fans offer a sense of a quasi-intimate relationship and a feeling they truly belong to that group. It is why we hear the term "We bleed purple!" for the University of Evansville Purple Aces metaphorically bleeding their hearts out in loyalty. The fans are coming together in allegiance for a greater good, a greater enjoyment, which ultimately makes them feel part of something greater.

This sentimental attachment is emotional branding. The strategy has seen success in companies such as Coca Cola and Harley Davidson (Thompson et al., 2006). When studying the most successful campaigns, there is an understanding consumers are getting much more than a product. They are participating in an experience. When the branding takes place via social media, it is even more emotionally charged, as they are getting warm feelings and intangibles from other brand users (Muniz & Schau, 2005). Other consumers become part of the marketing mix, creating dialogue and personal anecdotes associated with the product.

Existing research on the subject centers primarily on social identity theory in understanding how individuals use social groups to support their own personal and collective identities (Wann & Dolan, 1994; Madrigal, 1995). People often see themselves based on characteristics and behaviors of a group in which they are members. Being a devoted fan can help individuals find their small place in a larger societal space. Sport sociologists have even suggested that sport is a microcosm of society (Eitzen, 2005). Through sports, people can learn values such as honor, glory, resilience, courage, wit, acceptance of authority, and self-discipline (Synder & Spreizter, 1989).

The social identification-brand equity model proposed by Underwood, Bond and Baer (2001) describes social identification as the means to tap the emotional connection between a service brand and a consumer. The more devoted a fan is to a team, and therefore identifies with that team, the more value the brand equity of the team. Brand equity is the commercial value comprising a set of assets and liabilities closely linked with a brand name, separate from the actual product or service.

Branding for customers can be divided into three major categories: attributes, benefits and attitudes (Keller, 1993). In a marketplace more competitive than ever before, according to Zhang (2015), brand emotion is the key to expanding the market.

ANTHROPOMORPHISM AND THE MAKING OF A MASCOT

A company's intent to reach a client or customer via emotion is similar to an author striving to elicit emotion in a reader. In literature, anthropomorphism is used as an emotive device to encourage a strong connection with the reader. It is a type of personification that gives human traits to nonhumans. Anthropomorphism distinguishes itself from personification, though, in that personification describes abstract objects using human characteristics. An example of personification would be pollution, and this is why so many environmentalists frame the topic to be humanized by referencing "Mother Earth" (Epley, Waytz, & Cacioppo, 2007).

With anthropomorphism, the animal or object actually behaves as if it were a human. The trait or behavior can come in many forms, for example, possessing human intelligence or having the ability to talk. Anthropomorphic figures have been found in Palaeolithic art, and many authors have used it as creative expression. George Orwell's *Animal Farm* uses anthropomorphic examples to help readers examine society. In the story by Beatrix Potter, *The Tale of Peter Rabbit*, the rabbits in the story wear clothes and live in a rabbit hole with furniture. In the 1883 novel by Carlo Collodi, *Pinnocchio*, we learn of the lovable, wooden marionette which Geppetto has carved in his Italian village. Pinocchio, dreaming of being a real boy and attaining many of those human characteristics, embodies the spirit of the anthropomorphic object.

Anthropomorphism helps lessen gaps between ages, making objects seem friendly or relatable. The worrywart Cogsworth, the Clock, and the sweet but rebellious Lumière, the Candlestick, in *Beauty and the Beast* are each likeable, understandable and relatable to kids and adults alike. This same desire authors – or even movie directors given the 2017 remake of the beloved tale – possess to entertain audiences of all ages can be considered useful in the sports industry. Mascots help appeal to young audiences, and young audiences eventually become ticket holders.

The word mascot originates from the French word mascotte, meaning lucky charm, and mascoto, meaning witchcraft and charm. The word became more known after its introduction in the 1880 opera "La Mascotte", first performed in Paris. The basic plot revolves around a maid who is thought to bring good luck to everyone around her, albeit with the caveat she remains a virgin.

Later, the term mascot started to be linked to animals thought to bring good luck. Sports provided the impetus in the 1800s for using animals as mascots in order to entertain fans. Lions and tigers were the main choices, as these predators embody bravery, strength and could offer the spectators spine-tingling roars. Many live mascots are still used today in college sports, including tigers. A plethora of other live animal mascots are used, too, including gamecocks, greyhounds, buffalo, horses, steer, eagles, falcons, goats, owls, bears, mules and different breeds of dogs.

In 1955, a shift away from live mascots was seen and lifelike puppets, each cuddly and endearing, were created. These puppets were visibly soft, friendly and quite quirky with their unique personalities. They were called Muppets. The creation of the Muppets by Jim Hanson, who was a University of Maryland student at the time, resonated with audiences. Kermit, Gonzo and Beaker are still beloved by many. The Muppets helped propagate a new type of mascot as corporate ambassadors of goodwill and good luck, according to the International University Sports Federation (2016).

Today, mascots—live or costumed—are integrated into every college and college athletic team. Most schools having a live mascot also have one of the costumed variety. At the University of Georgia, the live mascot who ranked number one out of the Best Mascots in College Football in 2014 (Siegel, 2014), is a pure white English bulldog. It was in the 1950s when attorney Sonny Seiler first brought a bulldog to a game. Coach Wally Butts asked Seiler for permission to use the dog as Georgia's mascot. From that day forward, Uga, an abbreviation for the University of Georgia, has been the University's greatest ambassador, said Media Operations Coordinator Karen Huff (Figure 1).

The costumed version of the University is referred to as *Hairy Dawg*. Huff said, "In a relatively short time, Hairy has created his own fan base nationally and is able to represent the school in ways a live mascot physically could not.

Being physically present in multiple places is key, and the University of Georgia recognizes the value of the Internet as an important piece in emotional branding. This way, fans have 24-7 access to information about the mascot.

According to Internet World Stats Usage and Population Statistics (2016), 3.6 billion people regularly use the Internet. That means those people are using words and phrases to search the Internet, it is often a trademark first keyed in when looking for information about a product, service or a sports-related organization. Type in the word swoosh and sites featuring the multinational giant seem endless. Nike has

Figure 1. University of Georgia's Uga
© 2016, UGA Sports Communications. Used with permission.

found great success with emotional branding through it use of struggle, determination and heroism in campaigns. Trademarks, whether in the form of designs or text, are valuable to brand strategy.

As of September 2016, the University of Georgia had almost 20 trademarks, several relating to athletics: Georgia Bulldogs, Bulldogs, Dawgs, UGA, University of Georgia Athletic Association, Between the Hedges, How Bout Them Dogs, Go You Silver Britches, Hairy Dawg, and the Football Helmet mark.

Trademarks surrounding Uga are essential in the case of University of Georgia, because the University is not the only sports team using a bulldog as its mascot. In fact, 43 other colleges and universities use the bulldog and its symbol of tenacity. The bulldog was the first mascot in the U.S., chosen by Yale University. Besides Yale and the University of Georgia, 13 other Division I institutions have a bulldog mascot: Alabama A&M, Bryant University, Butler University, Fresno State University, The Citadel, Drake University, Gardner-Webb University, Gonzaga University, Louisiana Tech University, Mississippi State University, University of North Carolina at Asheville, Samford University and South Carolina State University.

Given bulldogs are the most popular animals of all college sports mascots, it is important for sports communication and marketing professionals to differentiate their mascots. While there have been numerous live Ugas, each residing in Savannah, Georgia, they all have their own unique personality and achievements, which get touted to fans. For instance, Uga IV stands out for having been the only Georgia mascot to attend a bowl game every year of his service, and he was also the first mascot invited to the Heisman Banquet. He is reported to have looked dashing for the event, sporting his game jersey plus a collar and black tie. Unfortunately, at times his zest for the team took a toll. The night before a big game against Vanderbilt, Uga injured himself while jumping off a hotel bed. Uga IV reigned from 1981 through 1989 and received a Varsity letter posthumously, another example of anthropomorphism.

Uga can also add the title of actor to his resume. According to Huff, Uga has appeared in two movies – "Midnight in the Garden of Good and Evil" and "Gator" – and has been featured on the Animal Planet channel. Uga serves as the rallying point for the University of Georgia fans, and he has been involved in many charitable functions through the years, including events benefiting the March of Dimes, Easter Seals and the Humane Society.

Besides Uga and his buddy Dan the bulldog at Yale, there are seven other live bulldog mascots used by Division I schools, those being Butler University, Fresno State University, The Citadel, Drake University, Louisiana Tech University, Mississippi State University and University of North Carolina at Asheville.

While the University of Georgia and Uga have shied away from him having his own social media account or page, citing the fact that Uga is a family pet and lives four hours from Athens, Georgia, where the campus is located, the owners have recently been working with the University to include various photographs and snippets of the everyday life of Uga to be posted on wht is referred to as the "Bulldog Trending Wall".

SOCIAL MEDIA AND SPORTS MASCOTS

College athletic departments possess an arsenal of tools in order to build a distinctive emotional brand strategy for engaging fans and encouraging connectivity. But in an industry full of statistics, concrete facts and hard data comes a surprising social media star: the mascot. This chapter explores the benefits of brand anthropomorphism to an organization, how mascots can serve as a valuable tool in increasing brand equity of a college sports team, and analyzes several sports mascots finding success in engaging fans via the social media.

Many industries such as the food industry or automotive industry have studied how branding, including emotional branding, has played a role in encouraging dialogue and loyalty (Mumby, 2016). However, the sports industry with its die-hard fans, constant need to fill seats at regular games, and clients of all ages, may well provide the most ideal business context in which to view how mascots, and social media in particular, can be used to engage fans for a loyal, long-term relationship (Achen, R.M., 2016).

Rothschild (2011) analyzed how sports and entertainment managers utilized social media, and it was found that 57 percent have a definitive strategy when it comes to using these platforms. Moreover, those who have a social media strategy experience higher revenues than those who do not.

Social media has provided a vehicle for marketing communication professionals to create emotional branding strategies with anthropomorphic mascots. These collective, online community channels allow storytelling and expended belief in a way that makes mascots, and therefore teams, understandable, and relatable. When the mascots begin to converse via social media, people play along in a purposeful distortion of reality while still gaining real facts and information about the team.

Social media is defined as the various platforms and applications that allow consumers to connect, communicate, and collaborate with each other (Williams & Chinn, 2010). From an organizational standpoint, Twitter, Facebook, Instagram, Snapchat, Vine, YouTube, and other social media offer an opportunity to facilitate conversations around a brand in a way that feels more personal. Twitter, the micro-blogging service that allows users to communicate with one another in 140 characters or less, reported 319 million monthly active users in the first quarter of 2017. The average number of tweets per day was calculated at 58 million. Thousands of brand pages exist on Twitter, and every professional sports team in North America uses Twitter. Even more pertinent to this chapter is that sports are the most talked about topic on Twitter, with 41 percent of all tweets being about sports (Stoll, 2014).

College sports receives its due attention on Twitter. In the 2015-16 season, through the second quarter of 2016, the College Football Playoff National Championship of 2015 was the fourth most tweeted about sporting event with 2.04 million tweets (Statista, 2016). The only events more popular in tweets were from the professional realm: Super Bowl 50, the NBA Jazz versus Lakers game, and the NFL Patriots versus Broncos game.

Facebook, another popular social networking site, had 1.9 billion active users as of April 2017. It was the first social network to surpass 1 billion registered accounts, and it remains one of the most popular social networking sites. This fact already made Facebook important to marketing communication professionals, but it comes even more apparent why when it is critical for brand strategy consideration when this fact is considered: When a person hears about a product or service through a Facebook friend, it has been found that he or she becomes a customer at a 15 percent higher rate than if information about the good or service had been received through another route (comScore, 2011). It is an old-fashioned word-of-mouth concept, only online and possessing more far-reaching outcomes. It was Facebook that acquired Instagram in 2012, and it appears it was a smart business move. Instagram has 700 million monthly active users as of early 2017. Snapchat was launched in 2011, and it has 301 million monthly daily active users. Each of these social networking sites – Twitter, Facebook, Instagram and Snapchat – is mentioned in the interviews taking place for this chapter.

With the proliferation of social media, marketers and communicators are able to encourage emotional ties for brand value. Sports fans seek more entertainment and access to information on their favorite teams, and they often do so through social media platforms (Ballouli, 2010). Many of these fans are loyal and passionate, and they expect regular dialogue delivered in an interesting, entertaining way. Mascots can make the task easier for marketing communication professionals.

In April 2016, the top Twitter accounts of college mascots were identified by Athlon Sports & Life (Watkins, 2016). Ranking in the top 10 were Oregon Ducks, Brutus the Buckeye, Sparty, HokieBird, Cocky, Goldy the Gopher, Butler Blue III, Aubie and Tiger, Bevo, and Mike the Tiger.

QUALITATIVE RESEARCH

Attempts to interview professionals associated with the top 10 Twitter mascots took place in August and September 2016, resulting in a minimum of three semi-structured phone interviews with those aligned with Sparty, Brutus, Bevo and Mike. These interviews provide context and insight to the chapter.

Sparty

In 1995, Sparty won the Leadership Award from his peers at the U.S.'s largest mascot camp, and his foray into the social media world began 15 years later (Figure 2). As of April 2017, Sparty boasted 23,000 Twitter followers @TheRealSparty, and in 2016 he created a SnapChat account.

One of the things that makes Sparty special is that his social media accounts are run entirely by students, and they are always ones that wear the costumed mascot outfit. "Sparty isn't run by our athletic or marketing teams," said Clint Stevens, coordinator of the Sparty mascot program. "Sparty only tweets about stuff he would actually say and do."

So when Sparty visits the latest Nike store grand opening, the mascot uses Twitter, Facebook, Instagram and Snapchat to let his fans know. When he waves an American flag during an Independence Day parade, fans get to see him in action.

Figure 2. Michigan State University's Sparty
© 2016, MSU Athletics. Used with permission.

Sparty is used to appeal to kids and people at the age of 100 and everyone in between, Stevens said, "We're always trying to innovate, and we give the students a chance to participate and help run those sites." Sparty is one of the most active college mascots, and he makes approximately 600 event appearances a year. "I've been in my job 6 months, and I've already traveled to Los Angeles twice with Sparty," said Stevens. "We do as many meet and greets with fans as possible. We kiss babies and show people we love them as much as they love us."

Much like a political party candidate, Sparty needs to play to all ages and travel to make his presence known. But when it comes to social media, Sparty stays away from any subject that can have controversy, including politics. "Sparty is always looking for a silver lining," said Stevens. "We don't touch politics. We're more a cheerleader keeping people informed and excited about what we're doing."

The mascot does exchange in playful jibes on social media with other mascots and regularly has Twitter battles, usually with mascots in the same conference. "Sparty goes back and forth with Bucky and other mascots. We try to have fun with it since mascots are friends with other mascots. Conferences have really changed the way mascots interact with each other, so even though we're rivals, the mascots remain friendly."

"We're always building and expanding the brand as much as possible through social media, and we'll work with whatever sites the mascot squad says college students are using," said Stevens.

Sparty has a humorous side, but fans take him seriously. Stevens said there was a lot of passion recently when Sparty's trademark image was altered. Some loved the new trademark and others did not. "Everyone has an opinion about brands, and sometimes the loudest are those who don't agree. It's like armchair quarterbacks thinking a head coach did something wrong and going online to be a keyboard hero and tell everyone."

Other than those types of passionate displays of discontent, Stevens said Sparty only sees positivity. "He's more a rallying cry to get people excited." On his Facebook page, Sparty says his personal interests are cheering on all MSU sports, Wolverine hunting, lifting weights and being awesome.

Sparty is one of only a few mascots to have his own signature licensed, a task undertaken in 2016, which helps keep authenticity with autographs and other visual representations. Many things like passion and loyalty make a good Sparty, but height also matters. To fit right in the 7-foot costume, those wearing it have to be between 5'10" and 6'2" in height.

Bevo

Imagine a stadium filled with over 100,000 people singing "The Eyes of Texas". That's University of Texas football. At its heart is its mascot, Bevo XV, a Texas longhorn and the largest live mascot in college athletics (Figure 3). On September 4, 2016, Bevo XV made his first appearance at Royal-Memorial Stadium, a big year, considering it was the 100th anniversary of the original Bevo making his game debut.

Despite the excitement of Bevo XV's first game, a game ending in double overtime with Texas beating the Notre Dame, the steer seemed to take it all in stride. At one point, he decided to give his 1,100-pound body a rest and lay down to watch his team's victory. He is a young male, after all, having been born the prior year. He's already well-known, though, with over 11,000 likes on his Facebook page, 14,000 Twitter followers and almost 10,000 Instagram followers.

The University of Texas has long recognized the importance that the mascot has on its fans. Around 2010, the University began utilizing social media to engage a wider fan base and make them feel a closer connection to the Bevo tradition and behind-the-scenes game day activities. Social media allows

Figure 3. University of Texas's Bevo

these fans "… to see and participate in aspects of the University that were previously only available to a select few," said Ricky Brennes, Executive Director at BEVO for Neighborhood Longhorns Program.

Brennes acknowledged the challenges associated with anthropomorphic mascots. "It can be difficult to speak on behalf of a beloved symbol that can't actually talk," he said. But the best way to do this, to communicate and engage a fan base, is through first-person posts coming from the mascot, believes Brennes. Fans must agree, as they respond to the posts as if they are actually having a dialogue with Bevo.

"I think it's because the mascot is a symbol of something that they probably have incredible passion for in both the University and its athletic teams," said Brennes. "A live mascot is almost viewed as a family pet. Fans have great affinity for the mascot and want to participate with the tradition."

This allegiance to Bevo is used for more than athletics. Bevo is the face of the Neighborhood Longhorns, a program which offers scholarships and encourages grade-school children to stay in school. Through social media, Bevo is able to promote these campaigns and scholarships.

The University of Texas has its own network, and of the top 10 social media posts last year, four were related to Bevo, according to Brennes. The video unveiling the new Bevo (Bevo XV) had over 1 million views in the first 24 hours.

Brutus Buckeye

In both professional and collegiate sports, Brutus Buckeye is "America's Most Followed Mascot" (Figure 4). The Ohio State's costumed mascot shined, as of April 2017, with 131,000 Instagram followers and 154,000 Twitter followers. Brutus likes to stay close to his fans, and he makes about 40 posts on any given week.

Figure 4. Ohio State University's Brutus

The inspiration behind Brutus originated from a paper mâché and chicken wire-inspired project that made an appearance during a homecoming game against Minnesota. At that time, there was no mascot for Ohio State. "The marching band was doing a routine and out walks this guy wearing this creation," said Ray Bourhis, who witnessed the excitement. "A lot of fans – 85,000 fans – went nuts."

Soon after, the Ohio Staters helped provide the funding for a new and much more durable mascot creation, and Brutus was born. He celebrated his 50th birthday in 2015. Photos from the event were seen on various social media, and photos from every state were submitted by fans vying for the best Brutus birthday cake. The people behind Brutus, managed by the athletics department digital team, are always looking for posts that play on human emotions.

"Celebrating and reacting to team success obviously does well," said Aaron Green, Emerging Media Specialist at Ohio State. "People love to laugh and we try to take advantage of that by playfully poking fun at other mascots or photoshopping Brutus into celebrity selfies and famous movie scenes. Sharing photos of Buckeye babies and puppies are a close second, though."

Game days are a busy time for Brutus and the fans. "Buckeye fans flood our social media channels responding to messages initiated by Brutus to submit their game day photos or 'Shoe Selfies' as we call them," said Green. "We collect those photos and display about 45-50 during the game on the video board and another 60-75 in a video slideshow the following week, with dozens more left on the cutting room floor."

One of the ways in which Brutus stays in touch with his fans is the linking into larger conversations already existing on social media and participating in playful posts with rivals. In 2015, when the cover art for music artist Drake's "Views" album was a popular meme, " … that team up north published a photo shopped image of football coach Jim Harbaugh perched atop Michigan Stadium's scoreboard in similar fashion to Drake sitting on the CN Tower in Toronto." This is when the digital team decided to have a little fun. They posted their own photo shopped version, with Brutus sitting atop Michigan

State's scoreboard (Figure 5). They used a photo from 2015 when the two teams played each other in Ann Arbor, with the score prominently displayed.

Brutus plans to stay cutting-edge, and the digital team behind him is currently exploring virtual reality-like interfaces to bring the mascot directly to fans.

Mike

Perhaps in no better way can the importance of emotional branding be explained than when research for this chapter was being undertaken on Mike the Tiger (Figure 6). As this chapter was being written, Mike IV, the beloved mascot of Louisiana State University, was a live Bengal tiger with the distinction of being the only tiger to live on a college campus.

At half the weight of Bevo, Mike was equally busy on social media. Each day all year long since first stepping foot in social media with a Facebook page in January 2010, fans have been able to interact with Mike online.

In May 2016, Mike was diagnosed with cancer. That summer, he received radiotherapy for spindle cell sarcoma. With his cancer diagnosis, a photo of Mike was shown every day on various social media platforms so fans were able to see how he was doing, said Ginger Guttner, director of PR for LSU's School of Veterinary Medicine.

In October 2016, Bevo sent Mike flowers after learning of his move to hospice care. With all the rivalry, with all the banter, there is a special bond between fans, their live mascots, and their caretakers. The outpouring of love of a creature who symbolizes so much exemplifies emotional branding's very real impact, and fans of other colleges also posted well wishes to Mike's social media accounts.

Figure 5. Ohio State University's Brutus on Michigan's scoreboard

Figure 6. Louisiana State University's costumed Mike
© 2016, Credit LSU Athletics. Used with permission.

Mike VI died on October 11. Guttner said Mike did not belong only to the University but to everyone (Figure 7). The voice behind Mike's social media account, Guttner found herself in unchartered territory when she took over the task of talking like a tiger six years ago. It all began when someone unaffiliated with LSU created a Facebook page acting on behalf of Mike. The University had the page taken down, but personnel quickly realized there was a fan demand for a legitimate site.

At 19,000 Twitter followers and 18,000 Instagram followers as of October 2016, and 214,800 likes to his Facebook page, social media gave fans a look into Mike's persona, said James Lowder, Team Mike coach. Mike's Snapchat account is new and the University is just now experimenting with that tool.

"We believe that it's very important to view Mike as a brand ambassador to not only the Athletic Department but also the University," said Lowder. "By using his playful, fun-loving character and his large presence on social media, we're able to use Mike to connect to all audiences, whether young or old."

Whether it is an athletic event to encourage fan turnout or a promotional event, Lowder said, "Mike helps us bring joy to the world around us." Guttner struggled with talking on behalf of a tiger at first, unsure of what to say or how to say it. But after a person posted a photo to Mike's page asking for thoughts on behalf of his sick child, Guttner realized people were allowing their beliefs to be temporarily suspended and wanted to hear from Mike, and not a spokesperson of Mike.

Guttner soon realized, "If a child writes to Santa Claus, he doesn't want to hear back from Santa's secretary."

Figure 7. Louisiana State University's Mike VI
© 2016, Credit LSU. Used with permission.

As the only tiger living on a college campus, Mike was used to help educate the public on the plight of tigers worldwide, said Guttner. "I'd love to interact more on social media with other live mascots. We already do that to some extent, but I think it would be great if we could pool our collective resources to do something fun and educational for all of our respective fans."

A balance of education and fun always seemed to be at the heart of Mike's personality. One post in particular of the beautiful beast captured the spirit: "Do these stripes make me look fat?" Mike asked. "Just because we work in academia doesn't mean we can't be a little silly," said Guttner. I don't think a mascot page is a place to get involved in deep philosophical or political discussions. It's all about engaging with fans and giving them a place to share their stories and memories and ask questions. If you can have fun while making fans feel closer to their university and possible educating them a little, too, you're golden."

LSU has done an outstanding job continuing social media efforts, despite losing their beloved Mike. The costumed "furry" Mike has 54,000 Twitter followers. The real life tiger habit is currently undergoing renovations, and the University hopes to have Mike VII (a young male tiger) picked out and ready to be part of the team before the start of the Fall 2017 academic calendar.

QUALITATIVE RESEARCH

Building on an extensive literature review, numerous antecedents of mascot brand attributes were identified focusing on brand personality traits, consumer interaction, and marketing behaviors (Hudson, Huang, Roth & Madden, 2016). For data collection, an online survey was conducted in August 2016, and 2,000 participants were asked for their feedback on 19 attributes of the mascot Twitter accounts of Bevo, Brutus, Mike, and Sparty (Table 1). The attributes were commonly linked to feelings of connectivity in consumers and chosen brands (Parganas, Anagnostopoulos, & Chadwick, 2015). An 18.8

Table 1. Attributes of Twitter accounts

Account Attributes	Mean Rating
Helps me feel connected to the team	3.22
Would recommend this team to friends/family	3.17
Offers an inside scoop on the team	3.13
Increases excitement leading to game days	3.07
Like learning about the mascot's personality	3.05
Willing to spend more for items with my team brand	3.05
Makes me feel more connected to the university	3.04
Helps me feel connected to other fans	3.03
My team brand makes me feel good	3.02
This page is popular with my friends	3.01
Provides up-to-date information	3.00
Gives me information I wouldn't otherwise know	2.95
Affords me access to special giveaways	2.90
Allows me to express myself in comments or posts	2.89
Is part of my weekly routine	2.89
Feel like they care about fans	2.86
Entertains me	2.85
Would like more behind-the-scenes photos/video	2.74
Provides information about community events	2.64

percent response rate was achieved (375 surveys were completed) using a four-point Likert scale – with four being very high and one being very low. Likert (1932) developed the scale to measure attitudes by asking individuals a series of questions in relation to how much or how little they disagree. Likert scales use a fixed choice format with ordinal scales measurement (Bowling, 1997).

The T-test of the two groups (General Fans Vs Students/Alumni) produced significant differences for eight of the 19 criteria, meaning the results are not explainable by natural skewing. General fans rate the mascot accounts as higher than students/alumni on the following: "Makes me feel more connected to other fans", "Makes me feel more connected to the University"; "Willing to spend more items with my team brand", "Allowed me to express myself in comments or posts", "Would like more behind-the-scenes photos/videos", "Affords me access to special giveaways", "Gives me information I wouldn't otherwise know", and "Makes me feel more connected to my team".

This T-test offers a way to compare means between the two groups. Based on the findings for this study, managers may wish to take into account creating separate marketing strategies for the two main groups of fans. Of course, this can be extended beyond the sports field into other industry factions. In order to reach consumers who are already heavily linked to an organization or company as opposed to those not physically located near the company, the use of mascots and emotional branding requires psychographic segmentation in the marketing campaign. Table 2 demonstrates numerous areas impacted in this particular study based on segmentation of lifestyles, interests and geographic location.

Table 2. Significant differences of students/alumni and general fans

Account Attributes	Students/Alumni		All Other Team Fans (Non-Students / Non-Alumni)		T-Value	Probability
	Mean	SD	Mean	SD		
Makes me feel more connected to other fans	2.93	.67	3.11	.58	-258	.010
Makes me feel more connected to the university	2.95	.76	3.11	.70	-2.08	.039
Willing to spend more for items with my team brand	2.94	.69	3.14	.66	-2.56	.011
Allowed me to express myself in comments or posts	2.77	.73	2.99	.65	-2.78	.006
Would like more behind-the-scenes photos/video	2.63	.87	2.82	.69	-2.12	.034
Affords me access to special giveaways	2.79	.73	2.99	.72	-2.55	.011
Gives me information I wouldn't otherwise know	2.81	.73	3.06	.63	-3.33	.001
Makes me feel more connected to my team	3.09	.72	3.33	.65	-3.08	.002

TRENDS IN ANTHROPOMORPHISING SPORTS MASCOTS

Based on interviews and industry observations, four trends can be expected in the area of brand anthropomorphism and college sports mascots that have implications for marketing communication professionals: 1) diversification of social media channels; 2) the introduction and expansion of stadium-specific experiences via smart phones; 3) greater online storytelling of anthropomorphic mascots; and 4) independent, third-party validation measurements to assess brand equity through social media.

Diversification of Social Media Channels

To encourage fans to have an emotional attachment to a team means a need exists to create and maintain communication modes in ways which circumvent traditional linear models of communication. Frequent updates by the mascot in terms of posts and tweets, plus a sense of dialogue to encourage ongoing interaction, are key to fan engagement. Achieving increased visibility of the brand means marketing communication professionals have the unique task of needing to closely manage information while encouraging more dialogue and transparency than ever before.

Interviews conducted for this chapter show that sports communication personnel and those involved with college mascots feel strongly that the biggest impact on a user's decision to interact with content centers on the quantity of existing views, likes and retweets. Ensuring opportunities for social media interaction among mascots can be a timely task for sports communication professionals. Fans interested in the brand story expect regular communication provided in a creative way to help them enjoy the social media experience. This kind of psychological engagement is crucial as fans are participants as opposed to passively receiving information (Schmitt, 2012). Depending on demographics and psychographics, fans may utilize any number of preferred social media sites. Having a social media presence on one site will no longer be enough. Multiple platforms will be expected, and these may change year to year based on consumer desire.

Not only is there a need for constant communication in multiple platforms, but transparency will reach new heights as fans have the opportunity to read what other fans have to say via posts and tweets. This constant communication from a plethora of sources located anywhere in the world and often containing an element of anonymity means marketing communication professionals must find a way to monitor the mascot sites. Marketers are going to need more diligence in limiting inappropriate or disparaging comments and tracking down imposter sites which can spread misinformation or damage a brand.

Loran Smith, Executive Secretary of the Georgia Bulldog Club, said it recently came to light that someone unrelated to the family was running a Facebook page supposedly from Uga. After reviewing the page, he said they realized "... it was loaded with fabricated information and bogus activities that Uga was doing unrelated to his mascot duties. We found out who was behind it and politely asked them to stop. They did. As a family, we were afraid this misinformation was not good for the image of the mascot we have been blessed to handle since 1956."

Trust is the foundation of relationships, and relationships and emotional attachment are what fuel long-term fan loyalty. Transparency on multiple social media sites will be crucial to sustaining fan interest, but monitoring to ensure accurate representations of the brand will present new challenges for marketing professionals.

Stadium-Specific Experiences

Smartphone apps account for more than half of all Americans' time spent online, according to comScore (2016). A second trend for college sports will be stadium-specific strategies for emotional branding purposes. Many professional sports teams are now offering apps for mobile ordering of food and beverages with in-seat delivery, high-definition video replays, and way finding on their phones to navigate through the stadium. The stadium the NFL Jacksonville Jaguars use, Jacksonville EverBank Stadium, has two 363-foot video boards that display posts created by fans. Fans of the NHL New Jersey Devils who appear on the jumbotron or videoboards can have personalized video clips instantly sent to their mobile device so they can share the clips on the social media of their choice.

These extra ways of encouraging fandom are becoming more common in professional sports, and college sports will need to follow in order to ensure fan engagement. John Brams, director of sports and entertainment for Extreme Networks, said, "Kids leave at halftime at college games because they don't have connectivity, and they don't want to be in a connectivity black hole."

Storytelling via Mascots

The third trend anticipated is a heavier online usage of mascots for brand storytelling. One implication of this, beyond the usage of multiple platforms as already discussed, is the mascot replacing other more traditional spokespersons. This may include celebrity spokespersons or high-profile athletes who have served as the face and voice of the brand. Both anthropomorphic mascots and celebrities can create appeal, a memorabilia factor to messaging, attachment with customers and keep a brand top of mind, but the anthropomorphic mascot costs less and is easier to control. With people, external factors can at times negatively impact a brand. An example of this can be seen in the numerous sponsors, including Speedo and Ralph Lauren, disassociating their brands from Ryan Lochte after his 2016 Rio Olympics debacle.

Certainly, mascot mayhem does occur, but it is less frequent. The Chicago Bulls made headlines when the man who portrayed the mascot was charged with marijuana delivery from his car ("Da Bulls arrested", 2004). The most talked about and published controversy of mascots surrounds Native American mascots, such as the Chicago Blackhaws, Washington Redskins and Kansas City Chiefs. Some feel these mascots are positive acknowledgements toward the indigenous people from which the team name or mascots derived their name. Others view these mascots as perpetuating stereotypes and creating long-term misunderstanding and damage.

Mascot scandals are rare, however, and rarer still on social media. While Lochte made headlines around the world for his actions, the 2016 Olympic mascot Vinicius was busy spreading good cheer to fans. Vincius, a mixture of various Brazilian animals, is said to have the agility of a cat, the balance and sway of a monkey, and the grace of a bird. He was named after a famous Brazilian poet, essayist and musician. Most Americans might know him from the song lyrics he created for "The Girl from Ipanema". The creators of the Vincius mascot say he's a happy, communicative and hyper-connected animal who helps celebrate sports, forge friendships and share news on social networks (Rio Olympics, 2016).

Both celebrities and mascots can be legitimate ways to communicate messages and gain and sustain interest in a brand. But as negative Ryan Lochte memes were popping up all across social media, it can be appreciated how simple and easily controlled Vincius is in comparison. It is expected that more anthropomorphized mascots will appear on social media, and elaborate back-stories and behind-the-scenes information will be given to satisfy social-media savvy fans. Mascots traditionally do not use words, but they are animated in gestures. Social media storytelling provides a way for mascots to have a voice.

Measurement

The fourth trend is the need for independent, third-party validation measurements to assess effectiveness of emotional branding on mascot profiles and sites. As transformative changes occur in how fans utilize technology and consume media, marketing professionals in college sports will need to devote more time to creating and managing mascot visibility and dialogue in social media. Measuring the return on investment in time will be important.

Social media management dashboards and other software tools will move to the forefront to allow understanding of how content—posts, videos, photographs and more—on social media sites is being shared and by whom. It will also be important to gauge the quality of that content. It will no longer be enough to track the number of likes, posts and views and to consider anecdotal evidence. As emotions influence purchase behavior, marketing communications professionals will be asked to quantify efforts expended on emotional branding.

CONCLUSION

The anthropomorphic mascot is experiencing a renewed life in social media, providing a unique and personal way to establish a marketable feature to a brand. These mascots can be one of the ways in which college sports teams get uniquely identified and forge emotional attachment to improve brand equity.

For years, team performance and top players and even coaches have been thrust in the spotlight. The addition of the mascot as a social media darling with a unique following is expected to increase dramatically. However, the ability of marketers to use emotional branding to capitalize non-product attributes, such as the image, history, tradition and even intangibles such as the team's stadium or brand mark (Parganas, Anagnostopoulos, & Chadwick, 2015), can be encouraged through storytelling and relationship building on mascot social media pages and sites.

To allow fans to play along with what has been created, and add to it through their own comments, strengthens the relationships and allegiance to both the mascot and the team. The mascots offer a sense of adventure through storytelling – blurring nonfiction data with fictional thoughts via posts or photographs. Then the fan has the option to move from passive observer to active participant by engaging in dialogue. By making comments, fans add more depth and texture, which perpetuates even more texture from other actively engaged consumers (Patterson & Hodgson, 2013). In doing so, the fans become part of the story, making the hero of the story – the anthropomorphic mascot – seem all the more human.

This often playful approach is actually building loyalty by engaging fans on a personal level and deepening emotions, values and aspirations of customers (Poon, 2016). In many cases, marketers can use stories to help create common ground, meaning and purpose. Storytelling across multiple media platforms offers endless ways to connect with fans. Anthropomorphizing a mascot in multiple mediums is one of the most creative techniques marketers can use for the emotional branding purposes of building relationships, sustaining loyalty and offering a sense of community and belonging.

When fans participate in the mascot narrative, they are part of the team's culture. Social media, and mascots in particular, provide fans a means to use their imagination and share their passion of a team. It's a relationship – a team over me philosophy – paramount to emotional branding. Just as mascots serve as cheerleaders for the team, brand anthropomorphism via social media unites consumers – fans, in this case – to become cheerleaders for the brand.

Researchers have shown that consumer demand for authentic brands is on the rise (Fritz, Schoenmueller & Bruhn, 2017), and this chapter offers a means for managers to influence and increase the perceived authenticity of a brand. In order to directly appeal to the emotional state of a fan or consumer, mascots help create an atmosphere of long-lasting connection. The mascot may trigger feelings of loyalty, happiness, success and belonging, all of which ultimately impact the economic livelihood of a team or company.

REFERENCES

Achen, R. M. (2016). Examining the influence of Facebook Fans, Content, and Engagement on Business Outcomes in the National Basketball Association. *Journal Social Media for Organizations, 3*(1), 1.

Adler, P. A., & Adler, P. (1988). Intense loyalty in organizations: A case study of college athletics. *Administrative Science Quarterly, 33*(3), 401–417. doi:10.2307/2392716

Akgün, A. E., Koçoğlu, İ., & İmamoğlu, S. Z. (2013). An emerging consumer experience: Emotional branding. *Procedia: Social and Behavioral Sciences, 99*, 503–508. doi:10.1016/j.sbspro.2013.10.519

Ashley, C., & Tuten, T. (2015). Creative strategies in social media marketing: An exploratory study of branded social content and consumer engagement. *Psychology and Marketing, 32*(1), 15–27. doi:10.1002/mar.20761

Balaji, D., Londhe, B. R., & Shukla, R. P. (2016). Successful Emotional Branding Campaigns on Television in India: An Exploration. *Indian Journal of Science and Technology, 9*(15). doi:10.17485/ijst/2016/v9i15/92152

Bowling, A. (1997). *Research Methods in Health*. Buckingham, UK: Open University Press.

Boyle, B. A., & Magnusson, P. (2007). Social identity and brand equity formation: A comparative study of collegiate sports fans. *Journal of Sport Management, 21*(4), 497–520. doi:10.1123/jsm.21.4.497

Button, P., Green, K., & Galvin, D. (2013). *The Principles of Pride: The Science behind the Mascots*. Arlington, VA: Rare.

comScore (2016). *Consumers are mobile. Where are they going?* Retrieved September 22, 2016, from http://www.comscore.com/Products/Audience-Analytics/Mobile-Metrix

Da Bull arrested on drug charge (2004, January 21). *Chicago Tribune*. Retrieved September 15, 2016, from http://www.chicagotribune.com/

Drori, G. S., Delmestri, G., & Oberg, A. (2013). Branding the university: Relational strategy of identity construction in a competitive field. *Trust in Higher Education Institutions*, 134-147.

Eitzen, D. S. (2005). *Sport in contemporary society: An anthology* (7th ed.). London: Paradigm Publishers.

Epley, N., Waytz, A., & Cacioppo, J. T. (2007). On seeing human: A three-factor theory of anthropomorphism. *Psychological Review, 114*(4), 864–886. doi:10.1037/0033-295X.114.4.864 PMID:17907867

Fagerberg, J. (2009). *Beyond Deflategate: Ranking the Patriots Top 10 Scandals*. Bdcwire.com

Fritz, K., Schoenmueller, V., & Bruhn, M. (2017). Authenticity in branding–exploring antecedents and consequences of brand authenticity. *European Journal of Marketing, 51*(2), 324–348. doi:10.1108/EJM-10-2014-0633

Gobe, M. (2001). *Emotional Branding*. New York, NY: Allworth Press.

Hudson, S., Huang, L., Roth, M. S., & Madden, T. J. (2016). The influence of social media interactions on consumer-brand relationships: A three-country study of brand perceptions and marketing behaviors. *International Journal of Research in Marketing*, *33*(1), 27–41. doi:10.1016/j.ijresmar.2015.06.004

Hudson, S., Roth, M. S., Madden, T. J., & Hudson, R. (2015). The effects of social media on emotions, brand relationship quality, and word of mouth: An empirical study of music festival attendees. *Tourism Management*, *47*, 68–76. doi:10.1016/j.tourman.2014.09.001

International University Sports Federation. (n.d.). Retrieved September 1, 2016, from http://www.fisu.net/en/International-university-sports-federation-3137.html

Internet World Stats Usage and Population Statistics. (n.d.). Retrieved on September 15, 2016 from http://www.internetworldstats.com/stats.htm

Keller, K. L. (1993). Conceptualizing, measuring, and managing customer-based brand equity. *Journal of Marketing*, *57*(1), 1–22. doi:10.2307/1252054

Khogeer, Y., Patterson, A., & Hodgson, J. (n.d.). *Influential Marketing: The Literary Life of Anthropomorphic Mascots*. University of Liverpool.

Kozinets, R. (2017). Brand Networks as the Interplay of Identities, Selves, and Turtles: Commentary on Interplay between intended brand identity and identities in a Nike related brand community: Co-existing synergies and tensions in a nested system. *Journal of Business Research*, *70*, 441–442. doi:10.1016/j.jbusres.2016.06.020

Likert, R. (1932). A Technique for the Measurement of Attitudes. *Archives de Psychologie*, *140*, 1–55.

Littlewood, K., Bick, G., & Treen, E. (2017). A Measurement Construct for Social Media: The SM Value Chain—An Abstract. In *Creating Marketing Magic and Innovative Future Marketing Trends* (pp. 605–605). Cham: Springer. doi:10.1007/978-3-319-45596-9_114

Luther, T. S. (2006). Emotional Branding: Where Heart and Wallet Collide. *Luther Media*. Retrieved September 20, 2016, from http://www.luthermedia.com/emotional-branding/

Madrigal, R. (1995). Cognitive and Affective Determinants of Fan Satisfaction with Sporting Event Attendance. *Journal of Leisure Research*, *27*, 205–227.

Melnick, M. J. (1993). Searching for socialbility in the stands: A theory of sports spectating. *Journal of Sport Management*, *7*(1), 44–60. doi:10.1123/jsm.7.1.44

Morrison, S., & Crane, F. G. (2007). Building the service brand by creating and managing an emotional brand experience. *Journal of Brand Management*, *14*(5), 410–421. doi:10.1057/palgrave.bm.2550080

Mumby, D. K. (2016). Organizing beyond organization: Branding, discourse, and communicative capitalism. *Organization*, *23*(6), 884–907. doi:10.1177/1350508416631164

Muniz, A. M. Jr, & OGuinn, T. C. (2001). Brand Com-munity. *The Journal of Consumer Research*, *27*(4), 412–432. doi:10.1086/319618

Munnukka, J., Karjaluoto, H., Mahlamäki, T., & Hokkanen, V. (2017). Effects of Social Media on Consumers' Sports Brand Experiences and Loyalty. In *Creating Marketing Magic and Innovative Future Marketing Trends* (pp. 1051–1064). Cham: Springer. doi:10.1007/978-3-319-45596-9_194

O'Shaughnessy, J., & O'Shaughnessy, N. J. (2003). *The Marketing Power of Emotion*. New York: Oxford University Press.

Parganas, P., Anagnostopoulos, C., & Chadwick, S. (2015). Youll never tweet alone: Managing sports brands through social media. *Journal of Brand Management*, *22*(7), 551–568. doi:10.1057/bm.2015.32

Patterson, A., Khogeer, Y., & Hodgson, J. (2013). How to create an influential anthropomorphic mascot: Literary musings on marketing, make-believe, and meerkats. *Journal of Marketing Management*, *29*(1-2), 69–85. doi:10.1080/0267257X.2012.759992

Poon, S. (2016). Identifying and comparing mystery and honesty as emotional branding values in brand personality design. *International Journal of Recent Scientific Research*, *7*(3), 9241–9248.

Rio Olympics. (2016). Retrieved September 16, 2016, from https://www.rio2016.com/mascots/#!olympic-mascot

Rossiter, J., & Bellman, S. (2012). Emotional branding pays off. *Journal of Advertising Research*, *52*(3), 291–296. doi:10.2501/JAR-52-3-291-296

Rothschild, P. C. (2011). Social media use in sports and entertainment venues. *Sports International Journal of Event and Festival Management*, *2*(2), 139–150. doi:10.1108/17582951111136568

Rutter, R., Lettice, F., & Nadeau, J. (2016). Brand personality in higher education: Anthropomorphized university marketing communications. *Journal of Marketing for Higher Education*, 1–21.

Schmitt, B. (2012). The consumer psychology of brands. *Journal of Consumer Psychology*, *22*(1), 7–17. doi:10.1016/j.jcps.2011.09.005

Siegel, A. (2014). The 10 best mascots in college football of 2014. *College Football Fan Index*. Retrieved September 25, 2016, from http://fanindex.usatoday.com/2014/10/06/the-10-best-mascots-in-college-football/

Snyder, E. E., & Spreizter, E. A. (1989). *Social aspects of sport* (3rd ed.). Englewood Cliffs, NJ: Prentice Hall.

Statista. (2016a). *Global sports market – total revenue from 20016 to 2015*. Retrieved September 23, 2106, from https://www.statista.com/statistics/194122/sporting-event-gate-revenue-worldwide-by-region-since-2004/

Statista. (2016b). *Most popular sports events during the 2015/16 season*. Retrieved September 2, 2106, from http://www.statista.com/statistics/290997/popular-sports-events-tweets-united-states/

Stoll, B. (2014). *The current status of digital transformation within football at IFA Berlin*. Retrieved August 20, 2016, from www.theuksportsnetwork.com

Tsosie, R. (2016). Indigenous Identity and Sports Mascots: The Battlefield of Cultural Production. *Fed. Law.*, *63*, 9.

Underwood, R., Bond, E., & Baer, R. (2001). Building service brands via social identity: Lessons from the sports marketplace. *Journal of Marketing Theory and Practice*, *9*(1), 1–13. doi:10.1080/10696679.2001.11501881

Van Riper, T. (2008). *Psychological viewpoints* (2nd ed.). Hillsdale, NJ: Lawrence Erlbaum.

Yoo, C., & MacInnis, D. (2005). The broad attitude formation process of emotional and informational ads. *Journal of Business Research*, *58*(10), 1397–1406. doi:10.1016/j.jbusres.2005.03.011

Zavattaro, S. M., Daspit, J. J., & Adams, F. G. (2015). Assessing managerial methods for evaluating place brand equity: A qualitative investigation. *Tourism Management*, *47*, 11–21. doi:10.1016/j.tourman.2014.08.018

Zhang, Y. (2015). The impact of brand image on consumer behavior: A literature review. *Open Journal of Business and Management*, *3*(01), 58–62. doi:10.4236/ojbm.2015.31006

KEY TERMS AND DEFINITIONS

Brand Awareness: The extent, often expressed in percentages, to which consumers are familiar with distinctive attributes or images of a particular brand.

Brand Equity: The commercial value comprising a set of assets and liabilities closely linked with a brand name, separate from the actual product or service.

Competitive Differentiation: A positioning tactic for an organization to be strategic in setting products or services apart from competitors.

Division I (D-I) Collegiate Athletics: The highest level of intercollegiate athletics sanctioned by the National Collegiate Athletic Association (NCAA) in the U.S.

Emotional Branding: The practice of creating brands, and ultimately intrinsic relationships, which appeal to the emotional needs and desires of consumers.

Fandom: A group of fans characterized by feelings of empathy and camaraderie with others who share a common interest.

Social Media: Computer-mediated technologies allowing users to create and share content and participate in social networking.

Storytelling: Both a cultural and social activity to share stories; includes a narrative point of view.

This research was previously published in Driving Customer Appeal Through the Use of Emotional Branding edited by Ruchi Garg, Ritu Chhikara, Tapan Kumar Panda, and Aarti Kataria, pages 171-193, copyright year 2018 by Business Science Reference (an imprint of IGI Global).

Chapter 4
Play It Like Beckham!
The Influence of Social Networks on E-Reputation – The Case of Sportspeople and Their Online Fan Base

Sylvaine Castellano
Paris School of Business, France

Insaf Khelladi
ICN Business School, France

ABSTRACT

New opportunities and challenges are emerging thanks to the growing Internet importance and social media usage. Although practitioners have already recognized the strategic dimension of e-reputation and the power of social media, academic research is still in its infancy when it comes to e-reputation determinants in a social networks context. A study was conducted in the sports setting to explore the impact of social networks on the sportspeople's e-reputation. Whereas the study emphasized (1) the influence of social networks' perception on the sportspeople's e-reputation, and the neutral roles of (2) the motives for following sportspeople online, and (3) the negative content on the Internet, additional insights are formulated on maintaining, restoring and managing e-reputation on social networks. Finally, future research directions are suggested on the role of image to control e-reputation.

INTRODUCTION

It takes 20 years to build a reputation and five minutes to ruin it. If you think about that, you'll do things differently. - Warren Buffet

Today, there are more than 3.2 billion Internet users globally (International Telecommunication Union, 2015), making them able to see whatever happens online. One of the major abilities of the Internet, beyond its mass communication technology dimension, is its bi-directionality (Dellarocas, 2003). The

DOI: 10.4018/978-1-5225-5475-2.ch004

Internet allows firms to reach a very large audience at low cost and individuals to diffuse their personal thoughts, opinions and reactions, making them available to any Internet user (Dellarocas, 2003).

Social media are global, open, transparent, non-hierarchical, interactive and real-time, and are completely shifting individuals' behaviors and expectations (Dutta, 2010). Online social platforms are used by billions of people around the world, making them a genuine phenomenon. The leading social networks worldwide ranked by number of active users are:

- Facebook (1.5 billion users),
- WhatsApp (900 million users), and
- QQ (860 million users) (Statista, 2016a).

Almost two-thirds of American adults use social networking sites. 35% of 65-year-olds and older is doing the same. Such behavior has entirely rebuilt the way people get and share information about everything related to their every day's life (Perrin, 2015).

The top ten Twitter accounts having the highest number of followers worldwide belong mainly to celebrities from the music industry, except Obama's account which is ranking third with more than 70 million followers. The most viewed YouTube channels worldwide per month are those of:

- Music stars (David Guetta and Justin Bieber), and
- Labels (T-Series),
- YouTubers (Ryan ToysReview and Family Fun Pack), and
- Nursery videos (LittleBabyBum) (Statista, 2016b).

Sportspersons have well grasped the social media phenomenon. Indeed, almost all websites of sports clubs have links to their Twitter, Facebook, YouTube official pages and accounts. Moreover, soccer players are a typical example of this social medial mania. As of April 2016, Cristiano Ronaldo has more than 41.5 million followers on Twitter, followed by Kaka (24.5 million) and Neymar (21.6 million). Other sports are not left out. Players such as Rafael Nadal (9.2 million followers) and Serena Williams (6.1 million followers) are topping the ranking of most followed Twitter accounts in tennis. Sprinters such Usain Bolt is nearing 4 million followers and F1 pilots such as Lewis Hamilton is having more than 3.2 million followers. Soccer players (Cristiano Ronaldo and Lionel Messi) and clubs (FC Barcelona and Real Madrid) are listed in the top ten most popular Facebook pages based on number of fans (Statista, 2016c).

Sports events are having their share of fame. The retirement of Sir Alex Ferguson in 2013 was the third most tweeted event after the reelection of Barack Obama and the resignation of Pope Benedict. The 2014 World Cup was of the top of conversations on Twitter, generating more than 670 million tweets worldwide (TwitterData, 2014). However, sports events are also having their share of shame. During the 2012 London Olympic Games, several athletes were banned from the competition because of their misbehavior on the Internet. The FIFA corruption crisis in 2015 and the tennis player Maria Sharapova's doping scandal in 2016 were also large online bad buzzes. Finally, it's worth mentioning that an anti-doping database Twitter account (@Dopinglist) was created in September 2008, displaying the most complete database of athletes sanctioned for doping.

The sports industry grows faster than global GDP on average (Kearney, 2011). It is expected to achieve global revenues of US$ 145.3 billion (PricewaterhouseCoopers, 2011). When it comes to social media, it is increasingly used by the sports world, with Facebook, YouTube and Twitter being the most privileged platforms to exchange with fans and online communities (Rothschild, 2011).

Even though social media help to increase the lead generation, to monitor conversation about their brand while mimicking the competition (Rothschild, 2011), social media is still a conundrum for sports firms because of their double-edge facet (Sanderson, 2011). On one hand, athletes can break news, share public and private information, and interact with their fan base via online social platforms. This gives to athletes a feeling of control over the content released. On the other hand, when debatable content is posted by athletes, sports firms become clueless in front of the bad buzz generated by unlimited online users (Sanderson, 2011).

Sports events do not only occur on stadiums but also on the virtual sphere. While athletes represent real business opportunities – sponsorship accounts for more than 30% of the total sports market (PricewaterhouseCoopers, 2011) – a video on YouTube, a picture on Facebook or a tweet can ruin the reputation of sportspeople. Hence, what athletes say online appears to be of great deal for their e-reputation.

So far, few studies have analyzed the concept of e-reputation (Chun & Davies, 2001), and fewer articles have investigated the extent to which social media influences the reputation online (Castellano & Dutot, 2013). Indeed, while 87% of firms' executives rate reputation risk as a top strategic risk (Deloitte, 2014), 56% of global consumers use research engines (e.g., Google, Yahoo!) as the first step of their purchasing journey (PricewaterhouseCoopers, 2014). Moreover, almost 80% of global consumers are influenced by social media in their decisions to buy products (PricewaterhouseCoopers, 2016), and more than 50% of web-consumers frequently use Facebook in their purchasing journey (PricewaterhouseCoopers, 2015). Nevertheless, knowing that more than one-quarter of crises spread internationally within an hour; and over two-thirds within 24 hours, it takes about 21 hours for firms to respond to bad buzzes; and more than half of bad news remains in the spotlights, a month after their first release. Also, only one firm out of ten was well-prepared to manage a crisis, 40% of firms have no contingency plan, and the situation is worse when it comes to manage a behavioral crisis (Freshfields, Bruckhaus, & Deringer, 2013). In short, e-reputation is no longer the affair of some marketing and communication professionals. It became a wider concern which pushed insurance companies, training centers and standardization institutions to develop offers and solutions to address individuals' as well as firms' concerns (Alloing, 2013).

Hence, it is paramount to understand the perception of fans regarding the online reputation of their favorite athletes and to explore how sportspeople manage their relationship with their community through social media in general and social networks more specifically. The aim of this chapter is fourfold:

1. Investigate the perception of online communities of sportspersons' e-reputation,
2. Understand the factors that might affect athletes' e-reputation,
3. Formulate further insights on how to maintain, restore and manage e-reputation, and
4. Propose future directions on the role of image to control e-reputation.

In the next paragraphs, a background exploring e-reputation in a social networks context is presented, followed by the investigation of the growing importance of social networks in the sports industry in general and the specific case of the French context. The chapter concludes with key recommendations and future research areas on e-reputation and image management.

BACKGROUND: E-REPUTATION IN A SOCIAL NETWORKS CONTEXT

Understanding e-reputation and its perception issues on social networks requires defining the concepts that have been widely used in the professional world but still need clarification on the academic level.

The Social Networks' Era

From Social Media to Social Networks

Social media represent the production, consumption and sharing of information through social interaction mostly on the Internet (Castellano & Dutot, 2013). Therefore, the growing importance of the Internet and of social media has many consequences. For instance, from marketing perspective, social media have a great impact on consumer-to-consumer communications (Mangold & Faulds, 2009). In management, Kaplan & Haelein (2010) emphasize the opportunities and benefits for decision makers deriving from the social media usage. For example, the use of blogs or virtual teams positively influences the collaborative projects and ultimately the performance of the firm.

Social media are various (Kaplan & Haelein, 2010). Among them, social network sites (also called social networking sites or social networks) which are "web-based services that allow individuals to:

1. Build a public or semi-public profile within a bounded system,
2. Articulate a list of other users with whom they share a connection, and
3. View and traverse their list of connections and those made by others within the system." (Boyd & Ellison, 2007, p. 211).

In short, social networking sites are the applications which connect strangers in the virtual sphere (Kaplan & Haelein, 2010), while allowing them to make visible their social links (Boyd & Ellison, 2007).

Social networks are the most popular online places worldwide. Indeed, more than 90% of online adults have an account on at least one social network site (GlobalWebIndex, 2016). In addition, individuals spend almost one hour and a half per day on their social networks, making their social networking accounts for almost 30% of their daily Internet activities (GlobalWebIndex, 2016). Also, the high user engagement on social networks highlights its universal appeal and emphasizes this global cultural phenomenon (comScore, 2011). Nevertheless, the fact that all users, through their social networks, share messages, links, videos, pictures, or even games with other members from the same network, they are creating a community with a multi-directional content. Additionally, the average digital consumer has about 7 social accounts (GlobalWebIndex, 2016). This makes social networks perfect places to observe and analyze individuals' opinions regarding a subject whether it is a person, a brand, a firm or an official institution (Cuvelier & Aufaure, 2011).

People use social networks to communicate and maintain relationships, to update others and get updates on activities and situations, to store events, or to post testimonials (Dwyer et al., 2007). People also use social networks for the enjoyment they feel, for the number of peers they collect as well as for the usefulness they perceive (Lin & Lu, 2011).

Social Networks Diversity and Challenges

Social networks are tremendously diverse. One way to usually categorize social networks is to consider the manner people use them. Some social networks are used to nurture the social connections (e.g., Facebook, Twitter, Google+, Myspace). Others are used to share multimedia contents (e.g. YouTube, Flickr, Pinterest). Some social networks are used for professional purposes such as finding job or business opportunities (e.g. LinkedIn, Viadeo) or to connect with counterparts of the same area of expertise (e.g., Classroom 2.0, Nurse Connect). Individuals also use social networks to connect with informational communities and get information related to their daily issues (e.g., Super Green Me, Do-It-Yourself Community). Other individuals target educational social networks to interact with students and professors (e.g., The Student Room, ePALS School Blog) or academic-specific social networking to share research and look for peer-reviews (e.g., Academia.edu). Finally, people also use social networks for their hobbies such as gardening (Oh My Bloom), or scrapbooking (My Place at Scrapbook.com) (White, 2012).

Social networks can be utilized in several ways which makes them so popular and at the same time raises several challenges for individuals as well as for the firms. For individuals, social networks question the privacy and trust principles which guide their willingness to share content and develop new social connections (Dwyer et al., 2007). More specifically, young individuals (i.e. children and adolescents) are highly concerned by cyberbullying and online harassment, sexting, as well as dealing with self-esteem and being addicted to the online life (O'Keeffe et al., 2010). Additional challenges related to individuals' online presence on social networks are setting the right boundaries between their personal and professional spheres and audiences, selecting the right content to disclose (Dutta, 2010), as well as managing the digital footprint.

Social networks also represent challenges that firms need to take into account. First, because many forms of user-generated contents emerged on the Internet, the credibility of the information shared on social networks is questioned (Castillo et al., 2011). Second, an overload of information flourished on social networks, which make it more difficult for followers to find the right information in the right social network (Bian et al., 2008). Third, the fact that individuals in online communities can very easily register, disappear and re-register under completely different identities with almost no costs, is problematic to handle (Dellarocas, 2003). Fourth, managers and decisions makers are not aware to the full extent of the influence of social networks on the firm's survival and on their sales because Internet users can use social networks as media to create, share or modify content on the Internet (Kietzmann et al., 2011). Fifth, because of the myriad social networks, firms cannot be active in all of them, to avoid making their efforts be meaningless and diluted. Hence, firms will need to select the most efficient and relevant social networking platforms to their target groups and to their messages (Kaplan & Haelein, 2010).

Nevertheless, one of the major challenges in using social networks is the reputational risk. The reputation might be at risk because of information leakage, piracy, data loss, etc. (Shullich, 2011). Moreover, losing reputation affects competitiveness, market positioning, stakeholders' trust and loyalty, and the legitimacy of operations (Aula, 2011). Consequently, firms lose the control of the information they and other Internet users create and diffuse. Overall, ignoring the relevance of the Internet on reputation management is no longer possible.

From Reputation to E-Reputation

Reputation and the Internet

Reputation is a "lasting perception held of an organization by an individual, group or network that forms a collective system of beliefs and opinions that influences people's actions with regards to an organization." (Balmer, 2001). Reputation is defined as "a summary of one's past actions within the context of a specific community, presented in a manner that can help other community members make decisions with respect to whether and how to relate to that individual" (Dellarocas, 2010, p. 34). It reflects the extent to which users can identify their standing and the standing of others (Kietzmann et al., 2011).

Frombrun (1996) highlighted key attributes of reputation that might be affected by the Internet and social media, more specifically social networks. First, reputation is based on perceptions. Because perception is subjective, reputation is to some extent out of the hands of the corporation (Brown et al., 2006). Therefore, when taking into account the Internet, the perception of virtual sphere individuals hold influences reputation. For example, if individuals are not technology savvy, their perception of IT-based products or services will be biased in comparison to individuals who appreciate such products and services. Consequently, the perception people have of social media and social networks influences the perception they have of a firm's reputation online. Second, reputation represents the aggregate perception of all its audiences (Fombrun, 1996). Both internal and external stakeholders' perception forms the overall reputation. However, previous studies pointed out that reputation is often issue specific; and that an organization can have a different reputation per stakeholder group constituents (Brown et al., 2006). Internet users can represent a new category of stakeholders. Consequently, their motivation to create and follow user-generated content can influence the perceived reputation they form towards the evaluated entity. Information is spread faster on the Internet by online communities. Such communities are empowered as they can create and diffuse information of the Internet. Third, reputation can be positive or negative (Wartick, 2002). Similarly, the retention of online information, based on user-generated content, can also be positive and negative. Because of limited cognitive capacity and because of an overload of information, the retention of information is limited. One can assume that people tend to better remember events with negative content. Therefore, one can deduce that especially on the Internet, the retention of negative content is higher than the retention of positive content. Fourth, reputation is stable and enduring (Wartick, 2002), but it does not prevent from change. Several authors implicitly or explicitly refer to the notion of time in their definition of reputation. Building a reputation takes time (Mahon, 2002; Rhee & Haunschild, 2006; Roberts & Dowling, 2002) and one can question whether the time issue is relevant on the Internet. Fifth, reputation summarizes relevant past actions (Dellarocas, 2010). Reputation links the past to the future as it results of a firm's past actions and future prospects (Fombrun, 1996). However, the Internet changed the rules of the game. While traditional reputation takes time to be built, e-reputation is immediate. One can deduce that the past and the immediate dimensions of reputation are both needed to be taken into consideration. Sixth, reputation is a matter of trust, a very difficult attribute to guarantee in an Internet setting. Hence, social media rely on automatic tools that aggregate user-generated information to ensure trustworthiness (Kietzmann et al., 2011). Finally, with the Internet, people are connected, and they want to know everything, from everywhere and at any time. Therefore, firms such as Twitter fit these new trends. People are motivated to follow other people on the Internet based on exclusivity of information, develop some kind of virtual proximity, etc. One can deduce that Internet users' motivations influence their perceptions of e-reputation.

Perspectives on E-Reputation

E-reputation, online reputation, cyber reputation, web reputation, and digital reputation are some of the several terms used to designated different practices, technologies or professional services (Alloing, 2013). E-reputation is viewed by the practitioners as "the image Internet users have about a company or a person based on information published on the web, on what is said by the others, on the messages diffused by various users (customers, competitors, employees, etc.), or by the footprints left involuntarily." (Frochot & Molinaro, 2008, p. 13). In the academic world, e-reputation refers to the elements of reputation which are derived specifically from electronic contacts (Chun & Davies, 2001). The e-reputation of an object is defined as "the reputation built on a set of perceptions that stakeholders have on that object, based on any information circulating on the Net." (Paquerot et al., 2011, p. 281).

E-reputation shares many common features with reputation (i.e. image, opinion, identity) but differs in the formation process using Internet in general or social media in particular (Alloing, 2013). E-reputation is often related to electronic Word-of-Mouth. The latter refers to positive or negative statement individuals express about products, brands or firms, and diffuse them on Internet (Hennig-Thurau et al., 2004). E-reputation is also often related to image. E-reputation refers to an overall image formed by an Internet user about an object. E-reputation is also the result of the several images formed by Internet users about an object and that are restituted by them to the Internet (Alloing, 2013). Finally, e-reputation is often related to digital identity. The latter helps to manage the e-reputation through highlighting the attributes that influence online users' perceptions about a firm (Alloing, 2013).

Putting reputation and e-reputation into perspective allows inferring the following features. E-reputation is first based on the perception of the evaluating audience. Second, e-reputation is strongly linked to social networks, considered as the most popular platforms for the expression and diffusion of opinions (Alloing, 2013). Third, online communities represent stakeholders that evaluate online reputation. Fourth, the retention of negative online content is higher than the retention of positive one. Fifth, the motivation of the multiple constituencies varies, which influences their perception of e-reputation. In addition, positive and negative elements need to be considered when analyzing perceived reputation. Finally, because reputation is built over time and e-reputation is immediate, two dimensions of reputation need to be considered: the present dimension ('awareness' as the creating stage of reputation); and the past dimension ('image' as the management stage of reputation). Awareness is the short-term initial stage of reputation whereas image is the long-term development stage of reputation.

THE GROWING IMPRORTANCE OF SOCIAL NETWORKS IN THE SPORTS INDUSTRY

Studies on Sports and Social Networks in the French Context

The image of an athlete is important since it can help to receive the support of the general public. In addition, sportspersons are ambassadors of their own sports. They also represent brands as a mean of celebrity endorsement. They carry specific values and can become heroes for a whole generation.

The impact of social networks on athletes' e-reputation in the French context has previously been investigated. Interviews with three sports experts were conducted. These experts explained that different elements play a significant role for sportspersons on social networks, such as:

1. The frequency of social networks usage,
2. The opinion towards social networks,
3. The reasons to follow (or not) athletes on social networks,
4. The number of athletes and sports followed on social networks,
5. The need for athletes to be present on social networks,
6. The role of social networks for athletes,
7. The 'memory' of the internet by giving a positive example (and respectively a negative example)
8. Involving a social network and an athlete and/or a sports event (open-ended question to assess the top of mind), and
9. The reasons to stop following an athlete on social networks.

While it takes many years to build traditional reputation (offline), e-reputation is more instantaneous as social media spread information rapidly. Therefore, when analyzing e-reputation, it seems pertinent to differentiate short-term and long-term e-reputation (see table 1).

In addition, when it comes to factors that influence e-reputation in the sports context, table 2 further displays the elements mentioned by the three experts. Overall, it is important to differentiate factors that are related to the use of social networks in general, to the sports discipline itself, or to the athlete him/

Table 1. Dimensions of e-reputation

Variable	Dimensions	
e-reputation	Short-term: awareness	Long term: Image

Source: *(Castellano et al., 2014)*

Table 2. Elements that influence athletes' e-reputation

Variable	Dimensions	
Perception of Social Network	Positive perception: • An opportunity. • A new media. • An entertainment.	Negative perception: • A danger. • Not useful.
Motivation for following sportsmen on social networks	• Sport (the specific discipline). • Sportsman's personal information. • "Proximity" developed with the athlete. • Type of information shared online, which is rather 'exclusive'.	
Motivation for not following sportsmen on social networks	• Social networks-related reasons. • Sport-related reasons. • Sportsman-related reasons.	
Retention of Information	Positive negative elements of information retention.	• No retention • Partial retention (participants remember the name of the sportsman or the event mentioned on social networks). • Full retention (name both the name of a sportsman and a particular event or comment he/she made on social networks).

Source: (Castellano et al., 2014)

herself and his/her behavior on the Internet, and within or outside of sports fields. Each factor, and/or the combination of these factors can potentially influence the sportspeople's e-reputation (see table 2).

The above-mentioned elements were used to create an online survey and test corresponding hypotheses in order to investigate the relationship between social networks and e-reputation in the sports context. Among the 155 respondents who participated to the online questionnaire 44% were male and 56% female; most of them (53%) were below 25 years old, 19% between 26 and 30, 16% between 31 and 45, and 12% above 45.

Concerning the attitude towards social networks, the results showed that 84% of the respondents connected on social networks several times a day. First, social networks represent an unprecedented way to create some proximity between an athlete and his/her community. The respondents felt closer to the sportspersons (37%) and they had a sense of interactivity. It is also interesting to notice that respondents mostly looked for sports news (88%), but also for some more personal information about the athlete, and to gain some kind of exclusivity (72%). Second, according to the respondents, social networks represent a new relationship between athletes, sports, and fans. Although, most respondents did not follow sportspersons on social networks (60%), among the remaining 40%, half of them followed between 1 and 4 athletes, 12% between 5 and 10. Surprisingly, half of them followed 10 or more athletes. They mainly followed soccer, tennis, swimming and rugby. Third, most respondents said that athletes must be present on social networks (66%). The main reason evoked was to manage their image and e-reputation. Results showed that when the interactivity increased, so did the level of e-reputation.

However, the results also showed the dark side of social networks. Only 4% did not find them useful. But, 40% of them considered social networks as dangerous, even for a professional use. The privacy issue for instance has been already mentioned in previous studies (Boyd & Ellison, 2007). Finally, when it comes to top of mind illustrations related to athletes and social networks, respondents unexpectedly rather remembered positive examples in comparison to negative examples. Positive examples are for instance, posting the picture of a new born kid (Gerald Piqué from FC Barcelona and his famous wife Shakira). It can also be sharing a victory online. This showed that social networks cannot mainly be associated with short-term memory. Whatever an athlete can write or share, people will tend to remember it.

The results of the study showed that the way people perceive social networks influences e-reputation, both present-based (awareness) and past-based (image) e-reputation. In addition, the study also found that both short and long-term e-reputation derives from the combination between the perception of social networks and the motivation to use them. However, the underlying motivations to use social networks do not influence short and long-term e-reputation. Finally, the study found that respondents recall equally positive and negative information on the Internet. Women tend to remember positive events (mean = 0.37) over negative events (0.19). For men, a difference was noticed (retention means: positive = 0.5 and negative = 0.48). However, the mean difference for men is not significant. Overall, some results supported previous research (the double-edge of social networks), while others were counter-intuitive (Internet has a memory).

Initial Perspectives on Social Networks and E-Reputation

The main objective of this study was to explore the relationship between social networks and online reputation. More specifically, the study aimed at investigating the perception of online communities of sportspersons' e-reputation, and understanding the factors that affect such perception in line with previous research (Chun & Davis, 2001; Castellano & Dutot, 2013).

First, regarding the perception of online communities of sportspersons' e-reputation, results showed that fans and communities pay attention to the information that exists and that circulates online. Internet users do not only remember negative information (e.g., bad buzz), and the retention of positive events is higher. Internet has a memory for good news! Bad buzz can quickly be replaced by other types of information. However, the retention of information (both positive and negative) is limited as Internet users tend not to remember many things.

Second, the perception of social networks influences the e-reputation of sportspersons. When social networks are positively perceived, audiences tend to have a better awareness and image of the athlete. However, when social networks are negatively perceived, audiences tend to have negative perception of athletes' reputation. More specifically, technical problems of social networks (e.g., access issues, saturated networks), or the limited use of such networks have a negative impact on athletes' e-reputation. In addition, the literature also identified limits of social networks. Privacy and vulnerability (Baker, Gentry & Rittenburg, 2005; Aguirre et al., 2012) represents two main dangers of social networks and the Internet in general. Such dangers affect people's perception of e-reputation.

Third, athletes cannot only perform on the field, but also in the virtual scene in order to increase their potential revenues and sponsorship contracts. No matter the type of motivation to follow sportspersons on the Internet, such motivations have no influence on the sportspeople's e-reputation. Therefore, several questions arise regarding the type of information that athletes can share, and the new ways of communication with their online communities to consider. Another option is to reconsider the relationship with online audiences in order to increase e-reputation (Boyd et al., 2010).

Fourth, the interaction effect between perception and motivation has an impact on e-reputation. The combination of positive perception of social networks and the right motivation to use them was found to be the winning combination. It is not the number of tweets or provocative contents that matter but rather the right tweet for the right audience at the right time that matters to build and keep a high e-reputation.

Overall, e-reputation in the sports industry results from factors related to social networks, to the sports and to the sportspeople. Throughout the empirical investigation in the sports industry, online communities and fans were found to perceive differently the signals sent (videos, posts, tweets, etc.) by sportspersons. These aggregate perceptions form the overall e-reputation of an athlete. These athletes are the ambassadors of their sports and they often represent brands. It is therefore crucial for them to control their image in order to build and manage their e-reputation.

SOLUTIONS AND RECOMMENDATIONS

Maintain E-Reputation

First, the manner how sportspersons maintain good e-reputation on social networks is illustrated through the example of David Beckham. David Beckham created the Footwork Productions Limited in 1996 in order to manage his image. Such a strategy proved to be successful as he earned 31.5 million euros in 2012. Early 2013, David Beckham signed with the French football team Paris Saint-Germain, where he ended his career on May, 23rd, 2013. Even though his professional sport activities are over, David Beckham is still very active and he possesses many followers on social media and social networks. His presence on social networks kept on growing after he retired from football. For instance, his Facebook page has 54 million fans, and his latest post has been viewed more than one million times, with more than 11,000 likes in less than 24 hours. These numbers signal high level of interests from his audience all over the world. Similarly, his Twitter account has more than 610,000 followers, and his Instagram account is followed by 22 million users with only 350 publications.

How to explain this constant growth on social media from a retired professional sportsman? Managing efficiently one's presence online would ultimately have an impact on e-reputation.

The type of information shared and social networks used are further examined. For instance, the example of a picture posted on both Facebook and Instagram for David Beckham to celebrate the birthday of his famous wife Victoria Beckham is very instructive. Posted on Facebook on April 20th, 2016, the picture has almost 800,000 likes, 6,830 comments and 6,860 shares. On Instagram, there were 5923 comments and 805,000 likes. Such use of cross-social networks dynamics creates a spillover effect, and ultimately represents exponential visibility on social networks.

Besides cross social networks presence, another mean to keep a high level of visibility in the case of David Beckham is connected to the diffusion of information not directly related to sports activities. For instance, out of the 20 latest posts on Facebook, 6 were directly related to sports (i.e., meeting former Real Madrid team players, sponsorship activities with Adidas, celebrating Kobe Bryant career, tribute to Johan Cruyff, etc.). This means that more than 75% of the content posted was not related to sports. Among them, 4 posts were related to promotional activities (i.e., celebrity endorsement with the fashion brand H&M). Also, 8 additional posts were related to his family. Beckham's sons appeared on 6 of these 8 family posts. This strategy is not surprising as recent articles online explained that David has full control of his son Brooklyn's social media accounts (Shenton, 2015). Even though it is quite difficult to control what is said about oneself online, it is of strategic importance to at least have a certain control on one's official social network accounts.

Overall, the reputation and e-reputation of sportspersons are not only built on the sports arenas but also on a virtual field, either through cross social networks dynamics or through activities not directly related to sports. However, even though the case of David Beckham illustrates how to maintain high levels of e-reputation, the virtual sphere rather emphasizes the negative impact of the Internet on online reputation.

Restore E-Reputation

Online reputation management is about controlling the information shown on the Internet (specifically search engines) in order to manage what is visible to the general public (The Armchair Athletes, 2016). When typing the keywords 'athletes + reputation' on the most popular Internet search engine, the first five results emphasize the negative influence of the Internet on sportspersons' online reputation. These results specifically mention terms such as:

- 'Risks',
- 'Terrible reputation',
- 'E-Reputation in question',
- 'Bad reputation', and
- 'Coach killer reputation'.

As the David Beckham example exhibited, sportspersons should not only pay attention to their behavior on the real sports fields, but also to the virtual arena. Hence the question of maintaining high reputation and e-reputation, but also repair e-reputation in times of crisis should be further investigated.

There is a double-edge of being present on social networks. On the one hand, social networks can help to increase e-reputation. Teddy Riner, the first and only judoka to have won 8 World Championships gold medals, is very present on social media. He considers that there is no barrier between him and his 'friends' on the virtual sphere. For instance, Facebook is a good mean to keep in touch with his fans. That's the way he manages his image and closeness with his online communities, while preserving his private life simultaneously (Dixte, 2012). Other sportsmen consider that Twitter decreases physical distances and increases the opportunity to share information with fans. On the other hand, social networks give sportspersons little room for error because of the endless scrutiny. Online reputation problems can arise in different ways. They can be related to misleading news, outdated information, and other poisonous materials that populate the Web (The Armchair Athletes, 2016). Below are some examples of such problems:

- Sportspersons may wish to provide exclusive news but ultimately disclose private or secret information. For example, football player Eden Hazard gave the name of his new club while the news was not yet official. Eden gained 250,000 followers on Twitter, but was very much criticized by his new club at the same time.
- Sportspersons are not in full control of what is said about them online. Fox Sports posted in 2012 a message on their Latin American Twitter site and declared that Lionel Messi died. A 'hashtag' stating '#RIP Messi' was also included with the post (RecoverReputation, 2016).
- When sportspersons do not themselves post and monitor the news on their own official accounts, mistakes out of their control can damage their reputation. When famous Dutch football player Johan Cruyff (among the top 10 players of all time) passed away, Morgan Schneiderlin a French football player posted his tribute on Instagram - but sadly not only put up a picture of the wrong person but also spelled Cruyff's name wrong. The e-reputation of the French football player was damaged even though the tribute was posted by the community manager, not directly by the player, and the PR never publicly apologized (Bourdet, 2016).
- Finally, while sportpersons tend to better control established Internet-based media, they need to pay particular attention to new types of social networks. For instance, the football player Serge Aurier wanted to interact with fans through Periscope. At some point, he insulted his coach and the video was spread through the live video streaming app. New networks, apps, features, etc. increase interactivity and speed of information for the best but also for the worst. The video was posted by many YouTubers and got more than 1.5 million views. However, the video of Serge Aurier apologies on the official YouTube channel of his football club reached only 75,000 views. This examples shows some asymmetry between the damage done and attempts efforts to restore e-reputation.

Overall, it will always be better to avoid controversies and bad buzz as they can drag on for long periods of time (Miller, 2011). This consequently provides sportspersons new and challenging means to act and react efficiently and successfully on the Internet. The correct interaction with general audiences (fans, online communities, experts, business analysts, etc.) is crucial when it comes to e-reputation. In addition, sportspersons must ensure that all communication channels are covered accordingly so as to easily convey the information they wish to address. Those "new technologies enable audiences to move from a passive stage to an active one, playing, therefore, a dynamic role and allowing public controversies and crises." (Hearit, 1999, p. 303).

FUTURE RESEARCH DIRECTIONS: THE ROLE OF IMAGE TO CONTROL E-REPUTATION

When it comes to better understanding e-reputation dynamics, the previous illustrations show that maintaining high levels of e-reputation and restoring damaged e-reputation seem to be the main challenges and provide complementary perspective to examine issues related to e-reputation.

Internet users can influence each other and affect other users' perception of the sportsperson (Siano et al., 2011). As reputation is based on perceptions, it is to some extent outside the control of the sportsperson (Brown et al., 2006), especially with the development of the Internet because it is more difficult to distinguish or differentiate between official information posted by the athlete, and subjective interpretations deriving from information on blogs and social networks, for which sources of information are difficult to identify. For instance, positive or negative Word-of-Mouth would spread faster on the Internet because sportspersons cannot control such messages. Immediate and sudden online reactions and comments can boost or destroy the e-reputation of sportspersons faster than ever (Ory, 2009).

Because it becomes more challenging for the sportspeople to control what is said about them, they need to rely on stronger anchor points in order to protect their e-reputation. One of these points is their image, which can be defined as the general impression that audiences hold and which is directly linked to reputation.

For some scholars, image and reputation are interchangeable (Dowling, 1994). Other scholars differentiate image and reputation (Chun & Davies, 2001). Image is based on the perception of external audiences only whereas reputation is based on the perception of all audiences, both external and internal (Chun & Davies, 2001). Many authors implicitly or explicitly refer to the notion of time in their definition of reputation (Fombrun, 1996; Gotsi & Wilson, 2001), as evaluations are formed over time by repeated impressions of image, whether positive or negative (Gray & Balmer, 1998). In short, better managing one's image can better help to manage e-reputation.

Crisis Communication to Restore E-Reputation

A crisis is defined as "any emotionally charged situation that, once it becomes public, invites negative stakeholder reaction and thereby has the potential to threaten the financial wellbeing, reputation, or survival." (James & Wooten, 2005, p. 142). A crisis can be described as a chain of events that can have negative consequences on reputation (online and offline) (Bloch, 2012). Crisis can escalate and spread even more rapidly than before.

The Internet can act as "an agent that accelerates the crisis news cycle and breaks geographical boundaries." (Gonzalez-Herrero & Smith, 2008, p. 144). This "gives the crisis a new viral dimension although the same crisis would most probably occur at a slower pace without the existence of the Internet." (Gonzalez-Herrero & Smith, 2008, p. 145). "It is often the handling of a crisis that leads to more damage than the crisis event itself." (James & Wooten, 2011, p. 61).

Sometimes, the sports-related activity is not the core of the online discussions anymore, but rather the numerous social media reactions. Once the e-reputation is hurt on social media, the sportspersons' eagerness to defend themselves just makes the whole thing worst, or even funnier. Specifically, sportspersons try to "change or delete information available on the Internet, [which] will lead to a greater diffusion of information that would be kept confidential in case of no manipulation. That is called the Streisand effect." (Liarte, 2013, p. 103). Consequently, the more control sportspersons try to have on the Internet, whether it is on their brand image in general or a specific situation, the greater the negative consequences. "By monitoring the blogosphere and quickly correcting rumours that could be perceived as facts, companies were able to prevent the crisis from escalating to mainstream media." (Crush, 2006, as cited in Gonzalez-Herrero & Smith, 2008, p. 147).

E-Reputation Management

Online reputation management is an ongoing process (Jones et al., 2009). Sportspersons must monitor and participate to online activities, and they also measure their impact on their e-reputation.

In the age of social media, almost every public figure has dealt with a mocking tweet at one time or another. Today, it is not only the sports performances that are discussed online, but also the private life of these sportspersons, their links to celebrities in other industries (music, movies, etc.), or even make personal judgements of their look, their behavior outside of the sports fields, etc. (Depta, 2016).

A online monologue is no longer efficient. With the development of Web 2.0, sportspersons need to engage in virtual discussions with their online communities. A good e-reputation mainly depends on the right balance between "blogs, social networks, wikis, podcasts, mail groups, newsgroups, forums and chat rooms." (Jones et al., 2009, p. 930). In addition, image and e-reputation are now co-created with all types of audiences (fans, experts, etc.), leading to online communities. These online conversations need to be managed and coordinated efficiently. Overall, "when used effectively the Internet is the best tool for improving reputation that has yet been created." (Valor, 2009, quoted in Jones et al. 2009, p. 9).

Finally, some firms specialized in creating; managing and monitoring e-reputation in the sports industry are also being more and more established. Communication and PR firms, such as SportMarket© and Digidium©, aim to monitor information online. They screen the tone of the discussions online, whether positive or negative. They even provide follow-ups and recommendations based on the specific objectives of their clients who are professional sportspersons but also sports clubs and even agents.

New Perspectives on Managing E-Reputation on Social Networks

The digital era changed the traffic and the speed of information diffusion, as new technologies are creating an acceleration phenomenon. New challenges occur nowadays, companies are much more fragile with the faster diffusion of information on Internet, and crises arise more often. Social media and blogs have further fragmented the audience, which makes it more difficult for sportspersons to manage their communication on social networks. Different audiences can voice their opinion in a much easier and effortless way on social networks. Such dynamics can have an influence on the sportspeople's image and e-reputation.

For example, one particularity of e-reputation is that information spreads much faster among many more people than ever before. How is this happening within the sports sphere? The Facebook might appear to be privileged for regular daily conversation. During sports events such as the Olympic Games and football competitions, blogs represent interesting means to spread and analyze some information. Still, Twitter tops all social networks to comment sports events, whether the audience discusses sports brands or sportspersons. Interestingly, depending on the type of sports events, audiences will rather tend to be ethnocentric (i.e., discuss teams and/or sportspersons from their own country), such as during football competitions, while audiences tend to mention sportspersons from different countries during events such as the Olympic Games, which shows the truly global dimension of such sports events, with overall rather positive comments (Martins, 2012). Twitter is a pertinent way to develop a brand – in the case of professional athletes, they are the brand – and to interact with online communities by forming a connection with their fans. Sportspersons can use their Twitter accounts to give themselves more exposure for endorsements. But negative reactions from social networks can cost sportspersons / brands dearly. If the athlete as a brand is thought of to be controversial, then audiences are less likely to become associated with that athlete / brand.

CONCLUSION

In this chapter, the authors aimed at analyzing the factors that influence the perception of athletes' e-reputation, which is mainly observed on social networks. Many types of social networks exist and people tend to spend more and more time to discuss their favorite topics and sports is among them. Athletes are considered celebrities and online communities share their opinions on what athletes say, what is said by other Internet users, and any information published on the Web that overall form the e-reputation of athletes. Fans and online communities perceive the online reputation of athletes based on characteristics related to the specificities of the social networks, of the sports or sports event under scrutiny, and of the athletes themselves.

The Internet provides many opportunities from communication perspectives, such as greater interactivity, greater diffusion of information, wider reach, etc. Very few athletes such as David Beckham rather have a positive image and high reputation online. In fact, there are some risks in communicating through social networks, mainly because of the lack of control on the virtual sphere. These dangers are related to the diversity and sometimes conflicting types of audiences, and to the new types of apps and virtual tools recently created. When the e-reputation is damaged, negative consequences can appear on many levels – sponsorship contracts cancelled, lower sports-related performance, etc. – which requires a communication strategy to be defined. Sometimes, the management of the crisis is worse than the origin of the crisis itself. Communication crisis is a key to restore e-reputation on social networks and bring back good relationships between the athlete and the fans.

REFERENCES

Aguirre, M. E., Mahr, D., de Ruyter, K., Wetzels, M., & Grewal, D. (2012). The Impact Of Vulnerability During Covert Personalization – A Regulatory Mode Approach. *41st EMAC Conference.*

Alloing, C. (2013). *Processus de veille par infomédiation sociale pour construire l'e-réputation d'une organisation. Approche par agents-facilitateurs appliquée à la DSIC de La Poste* (Doctoral dissertation). Université of Poitiers.

Aula, P. (2010). Social media, reputation risk and ambient publicity management. *Strategy and Leadership, 38*(6), 43–49. doi:10.1108/10878571011088069

Baker, S. M., Gentry, J. W., & Rittenburg, T. L. (2005). Building Understanding of the Domain of Customer Vulnerability. *Journal of Macromarketing, 25*(2), 128–139. doi:10.1177/0276146705280622

Bloch, E. (2012). *Communication de crise et media sociaux. In Collection: Fonction de l'Entreprise.* Paris: Dunod.

Bourdet, A.-S. (2016). *Bourdes des sportifs sur les réseaux sociaux: c'est pas moi, c'est mon CM!* Retrieved April 24, 2016, from http://www.lequipe.fr/Football/Article/Bourdes-des-sportifs-sur-les-reseaux-sociaux-c-est-pas-moi-c-est-mon-cm/646602

Boyd, B. K., Bergh, D. D., & Ketchen, D. J. (2010). Reconsidering the Reputation-Performance Relationship: A Resource-Based View. *Journal of Management, 36*(3), 588–609. doi:10.1177/0149206308328507

Boyd, D. M., & Ellison, N. B. (2007). Social network sites: Definition, history, and scholarship. *Journal of Computer-Mediated Communication, 13*(1), 210–230. doi:10.1111/j.1083-6101.2007.00393.x

Brown, T. J., Dacin, P. A., Pratt, M. G., & Whetten, D. A. (2006). Identity, intended image, construed image, and reputation: An interdisciplinary framework and suggested terminology. *Journal of the Academy of Marketing Science, 34*(2), 99–106. doi:10.1177/0092070305284969

Castellano, S., & Dutot, V. (2013). Une analyse de l'e-réputation par analogie ou contraste avec la réputation: Une approche par les médias sociaux. *Revue Française du Marketing, 243*, 35–51.

Castellano, S., Khelladi, I., Chipaux, A., & Kupferminc, C. (2014). The Influence of Social Networks on E-Reputation: How Sportspersons Manage the Relationship with Their Online Community. *International Journal of Technology and Human Interaction, 10*(4), 65–79. doi:10.4018/ijthi.2014100105

Chun, R., & Davies, G. (2001). E-reputation: The role of mission and vision statements in positioning strategy. *The Journal of Brand Management, 8*(4), 315–333. doi:10.1057/palgrave.bm.2540031

comScore. (2011). *It's a Social World. Social Networking Leads as Top Online Activity Globally, Accounting for 1 in Every 5 Online Minutes.* Retrieved April 20, 2016, from http://www.comscore.com/Insights/Press-Releases/2011/12/Social-Networking-Leads-as-Top-Online-Activity-Globally

Cuvelier, E., & Aufaure, M. A. (2011). A buzz and e-reputation monitoring tool for twitter based on Galois Lattices. In *Conceptual Structures for Discovering Knowledge* (pp. 91–103). Springer Berlin Heidelberg. doi:10.1007/978-3-642-22688-5_7

Dellarocas, C. (2003). The digitization of word of mouth: Promise and challenges of online feedback mechanisms. *Management Science*, *49*(10), 1407–1424. doi:10.1287/mnsc.49.10.1407.17308

Dellarocas, C. (2010). Online reputation systems: How to design one that does what you need. *MIT Sloan Management Review*, *51*(3), 33.

Deloitte. (2014). *Global survey on reputation risk*. Reputation@Risk.

Depta, L. (2016). *25 People Sports Social Media Hilariously Called Out, Part 1*. Retrieved April 24, 2016, from http://bleacherreport.com/articles/2630187-25-people-sports-social-media-hilariously-called-out-part-1

Dixte, M. (2012). *La e-réputation sportive se joue sur tous les terrains*. Retrieved April 20, 2016, from http://blog.youseemii.fr/la-e-reputation-sportive-se-joue-sur-tous-les-terrains

Dowling, G. (1994). *Corporate Reputations*. London: Kogan Page.

Dutta, S. (2010). What's your personal social media strategy? *Harvard Business Review*, *88*(11), 127–130. PMID:21049685

Dwyer, C., Hiltz, S., & Passerini, K. (2007). Trust and privacy concern within social networking sites: A comparison of Facebook and MySpace. *AMCIS 2007 Proceedings*, 339.

Fombrun, C. J. (1996). *Reputation: realizing value from the corporate image*. Boston, MA: Harvard Business School Press.

Freshfields Bruckhaus Deringer. (2013). *Containing a crisis. Dealing with corporate disasters in the digital age*. Author.

Frochot, D., & Molinaro, F. (2008). *Livre blanc sur l'e-réputation*. Paris: Les Infostratèges.

GlobalWebIndex (2016). *Social summary. Quarterly report on the latest trends in social networking*. Author.

Gonzalez-Herrero, A., & Smith, S. (2008). Crisis communications management on the Web: How Internet-based technologies are changing the way public relations professionals handle business crises. *Journal of Contingencies and Crisis Management*, *16*(3), 143–153. doi:10.1111/j.1468-5973.2008.00543.x

Gotsi, M., & Wilson, A. M. (2001). Corporate reputation: Seeking a definition. *Corporate Communications: An International Journal*, *6*(1), 24–30. doi:10.1108/13563280110381189

Gray, E. R., & Balmer, J. M. T. (1998). Managing Corporate Image and Corporate Reputation. *Long Range Planning*, *31*(5), 695–702. doi:10.1016/S0024-6301(98)00074-0

Hearit, K. M. (1999). Newsgroups, activist publics, and corporate apologia: The case of Intel and its Pentium chip. *Public Relations Review*, *25*(3), 291–308. doi:10.1016/S0363-8111(99)00020-X

Hennig-Thurau, T., Gwinner, K. P., Walsh, G., & Gremler, D. D. (2004). Electronic word-of-mouth via consumer-opinion platforms: What motivates consumers to articulate themselves on the Internet? *Journal of Interactive Marketing*, *18*(1), 38–52. doi:10.1002/dir.10073

International Telecommunication Union. (2015). *ICT facts and figures*. Geneva: ITU.

James, E. H., & Wooten, L. P. (2005). Leadership as (Un)usual: How to display competence in times of crisis. *Organizational Dynamics*, *34*(2), 141–152. doi:10.1016/j.orgdyn.2005.03.005

James, E.H. & Wooten, L.P. (2011). Crisis Leadership and Why It Matters. *European Financial Review*, 60-64.

Jones, B., Temperley, J., & Lima, A. (2009). Corporate reputation in the era of Web 2.0: The case of Primark. *Journal of Marketing Management*, *25*(9-10), 927–939. doi:10.1362/026725709X479309

Kearney, A. T. (2011). *The Sports Market; Major trends and challenges in an industry full of passion*. Retrieved April 20, 2016, from https://www.atkearney.com/documents/10192/6f46b880-f8d1-4909-9960-cc605bb1ff34

Liarte, S. (2013). Image de marque et Internet: Comprendre, éviter et gérer leffet Streisand. *Décisions Marketing*, *69*(69), 103–110. doi:10.7193/dm.069.103.110

Lin, K. Y., & Lu, H. P. (2011). Why people use social networking sites: An empirical study integrating network externalities and motivation theory. *Computers in Human Behavior*, *27*(3), 1152–1161. doi:10.1016/j.chb.2010.12.009

Martins, D. (2012). *E-réputation marques et sportifs: les JO plus « sociaux » que l'Euro*. Retrieved April 24, 2016, from http://www.synthesio.com/fr/blog/francais-e-reputation-marques-et-sportifs/

Miller, S. (2011). *Lessons in social media brand reputation: observing athletes on Twitter*. Retrieved April 24, 2016, from http://www.cision.com/us/2011/06/brand-reputation-social-media/

OKeeffe, G. S., & Clarke-Pearson, K. (2011). The impact of social media on children, adolescents, and families. *Pediatrics*, *127*(4), 800–804. doi:10.1542/peds.2011-0054 PMID:21444588

Ory, W. (2009). *La réputation de l'entreprise ne se limite pas à Internet*. Retrieved April 24, 2016, from http://www.marketing-professionnel.fr/outil-marketing/reputation-entreprise-depasse-internet-perception-globale-marque.html

Paquerot, M., Queffelec, A., Sueur, I., & Biot-Paquerot, G. (2011). L'e-réputation ou le renforcement de la gouvernance par le marché de l'hôtellerie? *Management & Avenir*, (5), 280-296.

Perrin, A. (2015). *Social networking usage: 2005-2015*. Pew Research Center. Retrieved April 24, 2016 from http://www.pewinternet.org/2015/10/08/2015/Social-Networking-Usage-2005-2015/

PricewaterhouseCoopers. (2011). *Changing the game. Outlook for the global sports market to 2015*. Author.

PricewaterhouseCoopers. (2014). *Consommateurs connectés. La distribution à l'ère digitale. 4ème étude mondiale sur les web-acheteurs*. Author.

PricewaterhouseCoopers. (2016). *Global total retail survey. They say they want a revolution*. Author.

RecoverReputation. (2016). *Who Should Manage Your Online Reputation For Athletes, Tennis Players.* Retrieved April 24, 2016, from http://www.recoverreputation.com/who-should-manage-your-online-reputation-for-athletes-tennis-players/

Rothschild, P. C. (2011). Social media use in sports and entertainment venues. *International Journal of Event and Festival Management, 2*(2), 139–150. doi:10.1108/17582951111136568

Sanderson, J. (2011). To tweet or not to tweet: Exploring Division I athletic departments social-media policies. *International Journal of Sport Communication, 4*(4), 492–513. doi:10.1123/ijsc.4.4.492

Shenton, Z. (2015). *David Beckham reveals he has full control over son Brooklyn's social media accounts.* Retrieved April 24, 2016, from http://www.mirror.co.uk/3am/celebrity-news/david-beckham-reveals-full-control-6472971

Siano, A., Vollero, A., & Palazzo, M. (2011). Exploring the role of online consumer empowerment in reputation building: Research questions and hypotheses. *Journal of Brand Management, 19*(1), 57–71. doi:10.1057/bm.2011.23

Socialbakers. (2016). *David Beckham Facebook statistics.* Retrieved April 20, 2016, from http://www.socialbakers.com/statistics/facebook/pages/detail/84218631570-david-beckham

Statista. (2016a). *Leading social networks worldwide as of April 2016, ranked by number of active users (in millions).* Retrieved April 20, 2016, from http://www.statista.com/statistics/272014/global-social-networks-ranked-by-number-of-users/

Statista. (2016b). *Most viewed YouTube channels worldwide as of March 2016, by monthly views (in millions).* Retrieved April 20, 2016, from http://www.statista.com/statistics/373729/most-viewed-youtube-channels/

Statista. (2016c). *Most popular Facebook fan pages as of April 2016, based on number of fans (in millions).* Retrieved April 20, 2016, from http://www.statista.com/statistics/269304/international-brands-on-facebook-by-number-of-fans/

The Armchair Athletes. (2016). *Online Reputation Management.* Retrieved April 24, 2016, from http://www.thearmchairathletes.com/services/online-reputation-management/

TwitterData. (2014). *Insights into the #WorldCup conversation on Twitter.* Retrieved April 20, 2016, from https://blog.twitter.com/2014/insights-into-the-worldcup-conversation-on-twitter

Wartick, S. L. (2002). Measuring corporate reputation: Definition and data. *Business & Society, 41*(4), 371–393. doi:10.1177/0007650302238774

White, M. G. (2012). *What Types of Social Networks Exist?* Retrieved April 20, 2016, from http://socialnetworking.lovetoknow.com/What_Types_of_Social_Networks_Exist

KEY TERMS AND DEFINITIONS

E-Reputation: The reputation that derives from electronic contacts on the Internet.

Image: Overall public perceptions and beliefs over organizations, institutions, individuals, etc. based on their experience and observation.

Reputation: Past and present signals that influence the overall evaluation – either positive or negative – that different audiences hold towards organizations, institutions, individuals, etc.

Social Media: Social media represent the production, consumption and sharing of information through social interaction mostly on the Internet.

Social Network: Social networks represent one type of social media that connect different audiences on the virtual sphere in order to reach different purposes.

This research was previously published in Research Paradigms and Contemporary Perspectives on Human-Technology Interaction edited by Anabela Mesquita, pages 43-61, copyright year 2017 by Information Science Reference (an imprint of IGI Global).

Chapter 5
Fantasy Sports and Gambling in Sport:
Marketing Implications for Branding and Fan Engagement

Amber A. Ditizio
Texas Woman's University, USA

ABSTRACT

Modern sports/media complex may be the result of complex inactions of communication technologies, social developments, and the increased sophistication of businesses in understanding the intrinsic and extrinsic aspects of consumer behavior. From the promotion options of print media, television and radio, to the self-engaging aspects of Internet sport coverage and gaming, the spectator is rapidly becoming an integral part of the branding process. Media, especially fantasy sports, has transcended the traditional roles of television's function as agents of exposure to engagement and personal involvement in athletic contest and its merchandising. Although the media aspect may been neglected in sports research, media research traditionally has considered sports too popular for traditional research. This paper explores some of the major topics for research that combines sports and newer forms of media exploitation for marketing purposes.

INTRODUCTION

Fantasy Sports and Office Betting Implications

Although the sport literature is fairly sparse on the roles of fantasy sports and/or gambling in sport in relation to academic research and its impacts on fan engagement in sport organizations, there has been considerable interest on the topic. Aspects that the current paper will deal with include revenue generation of fantasy sports and/or gambling, branding implications for leagues, and other relevant issues related to gambling and sport enterprise operations. In general, the roles of fantasy and gambling in sport

DOI: 10.4018/978-1-5225-5475-2.ch005

are many and can be more difficult to separate from more traditional sporting venues. Schirato (2012) suggested that in gaming and fantasy sport engagement allow the fan or user to be located in the field of vision, permitting the fan to do more than simply watch, but to some extent contributing to or even making the sport. It is a type of visual enhancement that is promoted by technology that both disposes and facilitates continuous mobile vision. Fantasy sport foregrounds watching as an active and productive process. Hence, at least from the fan perspective, it is game that he/she watched and is produced out of their work efforts, choices, and literacies. Sports-related organizations have promoted a brand image and loyalty that transcends all levels of social-economic levels, especially at the collegiate, professional and international sport teams' competition (Bouchet, Ballouli, & Bennett, 2011; Coates & Humphreys, 1999; Pedersen, 2013; Seguin, Richelieu, & O'Reilly, 2008).

Social media and its related technological developments has especially accelerated branding experiences, such as Facebook™, MySpace™, YouTube™, and Wikipedia™, that ultimately allow the consuming public the opportunity to express their opinions and shape their future viewing experience (Zimmerman, Clavio, & Lim, 2011). Fantasy sports, in particular, allow the participant to strategic trade, manage, and alter the contest in ways never available before. The degree of involvement is dictated by the levels of active and productive processes, based on individual degree of effort, choices, and literacies (Schirato, 2012). Coupled with the engaging activities associated with fantasy sports participation, sport-relating office pooling and gambling provide additional avenues for fans to become engaged in the sport industry. One of the fastest growing forms of sports gambling is online betting, which typically consists of poker, betting on the outcomes of certain popular sporting events, bingo, and online casinos. However, the consuming public is not the only stakeholder involved in the media experience. Corporate sponsors, sports writers, broadcasters, sports executives, and players must all be considered in setting an agenda that meets their needs as well.

Revenue Generation in Sport Enterprises

As with most modern businesses, sport organizations need to shift the sport promotion mix to ensure continuous positive cash flows from its products and services. Changing from sport as a product to entertainment as a personalized consumer product essentially needs a shift in sport promotion mix paradigm. If the current focus is on the entertainment aspect of the sport, it would need a very different marketing campaign. In such a case, while there is no direct transaction is derived and/or expected, there is an expectation from the consumer for marketing the entertainment aspect to be done in a certain way. With entertainment as the focus, the promotion mix needs to become focused on fans and friends enjoying the event together in the imagery rather than the sport being the focus in the imagery. As the debate of the entertainment versus the consumerism aspects of sport, is there any way that the promotion could stay the same and still effectively attract consumers to the entertainment aspect?

It is essentially true that tangible products differ from intangible services, but even most manufacturers offer services for their products. In fact, the single fasting growing cost section for manufacturers is warranty costs (Helo, Anussornnitisarn, & Phusavat, 2008; Ifinedo & Nahar, 2009; Johansson & Sudzina, 2008). Tailgate parties certainly illustrate the growth of entertainment as the focus, as the promotion mix becomes focused socially enjoying the event and engaging the fans outside the sport event. As a diehard

Cleveland Browns fan for the last 12 years, there is very little left to enjoy in a Browns game except for the social engagement -- there is no fun in having a series of losing seasons. Yet, the NFL franchise still flourishes through good promotional mixes and proper market segmentation. There are other sources of revenue that can be directly tied to being successful, as in professional sports' championships typically have some of the highest ratings in terms of viewing, so can the case be made at the collegiate level. Die-hard fans to causal spectators are drawn to media coverage that, in turn, creates significant sources of revue for these athletic contests.

For example, there is a Big 10™-television network that requires a separate subscription in order to be viewed. Several cable networks will offer pay-on-demand to watch re-runs of these championship and bowl game appearances. Then there are advertising fees paid by commercial entities that add to the coffers of these teams for broadcasting and marketing rights. The officially licensed merchandise available before and after successful athletic contest tends dominates the retail and online stores. The list is almost endless. Burden and Li (2009), Burden, Li, Masiu, and Savini (2006), Pantuosco and Stone (2007), and Park and Nahm (2011) all have cited that the commercial hype, commercialization, and advertising campaigns resemble the same coverage received by professional sport teams in term of their championships. Hence, there are numerous opportunities for sport organizations to make profit through both entertainment and engagement outside the actual game attendance by having a proper marketing strategy.

Sports-related online and face-to-face betting activities in a professional work environment are relatively common place, although there are very few studies that academically study it potential impacts productivity in the office (Bradley, 2008). Sound fiscal management practices, such as curbing spending and matching revenues with expenses, coupled with innovative management approaches, should be requirements for all business enterprise to survival and thrive in today's challenging global environment. Office pooling and gambling, especially on sporting events, in the workplace is considered unethical and a distraction by many. The Safe and Secure Internet Gambling Initiative estimates that Americans bet over US$100 billion a year using offshore gaming websites. It has been reported, for example, that companies lose up to US$3.8 billion in wages during the month of March each year due to the men's NCAA national collegiate basketball tournament (Bradley, 2008; Simers, 2008). However, studies (Simers, 2008) illustrated that about 69% of working U.S. citizens do not wager in office pools and that half of these people have no interest in the March Madness tournament at all. It may be successfully argued that employees who favor March Madness pools in the workplace do not think it is unethical, especially because it fosters camaraderie among those involved in the office pools by providing them a common topic of discussion and networking and they receive the blessing from management.

Nesbit and King (2010) cited that the fantasy sports industry, driven mainly by the love for fantasy football, has grown to over 18 million players, resulting in over US$2 billion dollars. Nesbit and King, via survey methods, tested whether actual engagement in fantasy football league play, both passively and actively, significantly increased NFL game attendance rates. They found that engagement in fantasy football league play was positively correlated with actual NFL games that participants attended. In general, fantasy participants are likely to attend at least one game per year and that they attend between 0.22 and 0.57 more games per season as compared to their counterparts that are not involved in fantasy football league play. However, Nesbit and King did not statistically differentiate among the classifications participants, such as season ticket holders or casual fans.

LOYAL TO FANTASY GAMING THROUGH MARKETING AND BRANDING

Theoretical Approaches

Undoubtedly, as a doctoral student interested in future trends associated with fantasy sports, there must be current research designs that adequately address and measure the impacts of the other stakeholders in promoting appropriate messages in mass media, especially in fantasy sports and related gambling activities. Some designs may be technology-specific, while other designs are more strategic than tactical in that they are ensuring that the proper goals of the organization are properly communicated in the selected media channel. Websites of organizations should be organized to maximize positive corporate image control and minimizing the impact of competing stimuli, not just maximizing merchandising opportunities. Although research studies can be designed to look at the individual behavior level, there needs to be a renewed focus on understanding the strategic goal of a sport organization, both in its formulation and implementation, and how best to utilize the various media channels available to convey the messages that sport organizations want to project. To strategically frame sport and media-related research, academics should understand the needs of the intended audience. Fans are demanding more direct interaction or engagement with their sport entertainment, developing a sense of belonging, not just spectatorship (Dees, 2011; Evans & Smith, 2004; Hutchins, 2011). Sport businesses need to create an agenda that adequately addresses their clients' needs and simultaneously satisfied the corporate desires for marketing penetration and revenue generation.

Virtual Gaming Applications and Options

For example, Quidditch, a virtual game inspired by Harter Potter's movies, is currently played at 100s of locations, both domestically and globally. As suggested by Cohen, Brown, and Welty Peachey (2012), the successful start of this game was totally based on a lack of marketing research on nontraditional, coed sports and the innovative nature of the game. This situation defies most traditional thought on successful marketing of video games and related merchandise. The authors found that this viable niche market within the sports industry was based on a collection of intrinsic and extrinsic motivational factors [i.e. identification with a noted figure (Harry Potter), camaraderie and friendship, desire to have fun, desire to try something new, and desire to get in shape. The shear participation in Quidditch allowed users to deeper commitment to the HP franchise. This lifestyle change, coincided with passion towards the HP franchise, was important. Lifestyle in niche sports is associated with a wiliness to consume and participate in sports (Miloch & Lambrecht, 2006). This cyclical relationship is unique due to the pop culture aspect of Quidditch and builds on the suggestion that social identity can be drawn from extracurricular activities such as sport participation and interweaved into an organization's e-commerce activities.

Quidditch allowed participants to fulfill social outlets which they may not have had otherwise. This could suggest that the sport has the potential, because of its ability to foster new relationships, to reach young people who normally would not partake in a more traditional sport. Of course, the negative side of virtual sport participation is that it may add to the global obesity and lack of physical exercise. Such research adds to the notion that sport has value as entertainment, merely a social outlet. The growth of

Quidditch and fantasy sports emphasizes psychosocial involvement or engagement. Such engagement seems to be integrated into one's lifestyle. Cohen, et al. (2012) postulated that sport is capable of reaching people who may not have motivation or interest in participating in traditional sports.

Gaming and Branding Opportunities

Businesses are rapidly finding that fantasy sports and related gaming activities offers management a significant opportunity for branding within this marketing segment. Green (2001) discussed the importance of utilizing subcultures in sports, of which fantasy sports may be classified as an example. These subcultures are generally defined as, "segments of society that embrace certain distinctive cultural elements" (p. 4). Green further explained that these subcultures can include direct and indirect participation. Green specifically noted that a form of direct participation can be through fantasy league sports. Steinberg (2013) pointed to a situation where a fantasy football team "owner" sought corporate sponsorship to pay for the league's entrance fee. This particular situation was successful for both the owner and the sponsor, although there may still be some legal issues associated with selling naming rights and corporate sponsorship within fantasy leagues (i.e. fantasy sports usually bases their information on NFL or other professional leagues' statistics that are readily available from websites, such as ESPN). As the original question that was given to me suggests that although subculture and sponsorship relationships are less common among types of sponsorship, they can still be strategically leveraged by both owners and corporate sponsors of fantasy leagues. Such efforts many prove mutually beneficial for fans as well as corporate sponsors, as suggested by research by Doherty and Murray (2007).

From research literature on the popularity of fantasy sports, there may be a very a number of potentially profitable opportunities for both website owner and the corporate sponsor. The real question may be if such practices are sustainable in the long-term. Is that the true future of sport and its competition is merely for entertainment, regardless of its form? Can we expect that in some near future that elitism and big business will drive sport activities out of the reach of ordinary citizens? Do fans rather want to be engaged in cyber space then as spectators or active participants in formal and informal sports?

Sport-related organizations and their corporate sponsors equally benefit from strategic efforts of leveraging social networking via developing and direct fan involvement and coordinated direct marketing activities. Individually, athletes can simultaneously develop and promote their branding opportunities with fans as well as satisfying the marketing goals of their teams and corporate sponsors (Filo, Funk, & Alexandris, (2008). Strategically leveraging social media (e.g. Facebook™, MySpace™, YouTube™, Twitter™) for dual goals of self-promotion and representation ultimately mediates and disturbs influence of mass media and sports officials (Hutchins, 2011). The unpredictability and lack of rationality that sometimes accompany rapid acceptance of newer modes of communications in redefining relationships among the various stakeholders (i.e. athletes, fans, managers, corporate sponsors) are obvious consequences associated with the volume, speed, ubiquity, and active experimentation of mobile and wireless devices. Perhaps this has led to an overload of information, adding to social complexity in trying to frame scholarly endeavors in sport-related research, but it also makes the problems more challenging and interesting to investigate. It is an exciting time to do sport-related research. It is no longer a stepchild to business and the social sciences, but a legitimate discipline, worthy of its own methodologies and research agendas.

CORPORATE SPONSORSHIP IMLICATIONS

Effects of Direct Competition

As noted by Doherty and Murray (2007), due directly to increased competition for more discriminating corporate sponsorships showcase the needs for nonprofit sport organizations to develop sponsorship packages that are sophisticated, with the needs of the sponsor well established. Of course, this trend may be equally true for for-profit enterprises, such as professional sport leagues. All sport organizations need to differentiate themselves in such a way that they add value over and beyond other sponsorship proposals that the corporations will undoubtedly be receiving for their considerations. The basic premise is that such sponsorship must provide added value to the firm. We live in an age where accountability, responsibility, and value added are common vocabulary to successful management employees. Why should fantasy sports be let out of that equation? Studies have shown that participation in fantasy sports by professional NFL fans actually increases attendance at games (Nesbit & King, 2010). Nesbit and King cited that the fantasy sports industry, driven mainly by the love for fantasy football, has grown to over 18 million players, resulting in over US$2 billion dollars. Based on similar research, whether actual engagement in fantasy football league play, both passively and actively, significantly increased NFL game attendance rates. They found that engagement in fantasy football league play was positively correlated with actual NFL games that participants attended. The point is that there are many fans that a corporate sponsor can reach by using the social media and, in particular, fantasy sport venues. Is it sustainable? It would be a similar question in asking if social media and networking are sustainable.

Fantasy League Sponsorship

Although there are several examples of companies sponsoring either a fantasy league and/or a fantasy team owner' it is still one company supporting another through sponsorship, publicity, promotion, and general marketing activities. It is relatively obvious that fantasy football and the NFL seem like they are becoming bigger and better each day in terms of recruiting and retaining a stable fan base. Many people are actively involved in fantasy football leagues, which have boosted NFL ratings, and it has historically been a win-win situation for both parties. But what about the other types of fantasy sports, such as soccer, basketball, golf, not just football. What about the risks/procedures of companies or people sponsoring not athletes or teams or other companies, but individuals that are controlling a team. Are there more risks for this type of sponsorship than by sponsoring an athlete? Or are there more benefits? What are some of the risks and benefits associated with sponsoring a fantasy team? There are many factors that are for and against each other when dealing with fantasy sports. Corporate sponsors follow the money trail, which means they typically go after fantasy leagues that are tied to professional sports, like football and basketball. They fed on each other and develop the win-win situation. As with trading in fantasy sports, higher preforming athletes get more attention and become more attractive to corporations to sponsor. However, golf, soccer, tennis, and other sports are not attractive enough to get the attraction needed for big business sponsorship. An alternative to fantasy sports would be allowing star athletes in these other fields develop stronger ties with their fan base via social media. Such interaction promotes fan loyalty, provides a platform where fans and directly engage in the sports and athletes they admire. Over time, such popularity and corporate branding may lead to the type of sponsorship in lesser known fantasy sports.

Scholarly Applications and Future Research

In terms of scholarly pursue in studying the strategic impact of agenda-setting goals and tactics that influence media on sports coverage and its implications, a variety of techniques and research designs are available. In terms of theoretical frameworks to research the effects of adequate branding techniques on the stakeholder (i.e. fan, consumer, corporate sponsor, management, owners, tax collector) is exchanging their scare resources (i.e. money, time, effort) for a value-added activity (i.e. personalized experience) or product (i.e., merchandise, service). It is extremely important to understand the inherent needs of the various stakeholders (Harrison, Bosse, & Phillips, 2010; Husted & Allen, 2011). By using applications of Stakeholder Theory, for example, the expectations of an organization's stakeholders can be directly involved in developing and satisfying the mission of the organization through agenda-setting activities that are found throughout the sport literature (Sotiriadou, Shilbury, & Quick, 2008; Zimmerman, Clavio, & Lim, 2011). Scholarly studies have evolved from merely reporting or describing how fans of sport-related reacted to content of media materials (i.e. websites, media coverage of scandals, fantasy sports, social media, blogs) to how such stakeholders interact, engage, and partner with their counterparts in the development and creation of new media options in sports.

BRANDING AND MARKETING OPPORTUNITIES FOR FANTASY SPORTS

Examining Interplay With Professional and Fantasy Sports

Collegiate and professional sports, such as the NBA and the NFL, have provided entertainment to its customers for over 90 years. While the marketing plan employed by professional sports has been relatively successful and there are several definitive factors that attract fans to fill stadiums and purchase leagued-sponsored merchandise, they have received competition in recent years through the development and promotion of fantasy sports, especially fantasy football. Basically, participation in fantasy sports allows fans the virtual ability to trade, cut, and sign players at will and simulate the outcomes of such decisions in real time. For example, fans using NFL.com Fantasy League can create interactive competition where "general managers" create virtual teams by selecting real players through drafting and trading. The NFL will soon select the top NFL fantasy coach who be used as an aid in the drafting of 2014 Pro Bowl in Hawaii. Hence, participants, by behaving similar to a real sports owner, can build a team that competes against other fantasy owners. The simulations as based on the individual performance statistics of real individual players involved in professional sports. Complexities can even generate statistics and game points based on third-party sources and actual inputs from face-to-face collegiate and professional sports competition. Interestingly, Shandler (2009) noted that the U.S. Congress is currently promoting consumer protection legislation in terms of gambling activities. With the passage of the Unlawful Internet Gambling Enforcement Act of 2006, it established a legal definition for fantasy sports and states that fantasy sports in general cannot be considered gambling based on that definition. So, there is less of an ethical issue at stake and more of a financial one.

Fantasy sports are extremely popular, so corporate sponsors want to be where the action is and where their fans are participating. Evidence from the sport management literature suggests that the same basic model used for sponsorship for the best athletes can carry over into the realm of sponsorship for the best fantasy team "owner." There are current sponsorships that fit this model and the best fantasy sport owner does have a legitimate change of being directly sponsored.

Many of the basic intrinsic motivations, such as escapism, entertainment, and social interactions, for attracting a loyal professional sport fan are similar to the many reasons participants are attracted by fantasy sports (Brock, 2006; Davis & Duncan, 2006; Moorman, 2008). Lee, Seo, and Green (2013) recently completed a detailed study on the particular motivations of fantasy player. In their research, via factor analysis, they reduced the motivations to 12 dimensions of fantasy sport motivation. The motivations were quite diverse and ranges from game interest, becoming a general manager/head coach, love of sport, prize, competition, entertainment value, bonding with friends/family, social interaction with other participants, knowledge application, hedonic experience, escapism, and substitute for a losing team. Interestingly, most of the factors were outside the traditional motivation of competition and skill, especially in terms of social interactions.

It is estimated by 2014 that 19.4 million people age 12 and above in the U.S. and Canada will play fantasy sports and 34.5 million people have ever played fantasy sports (Moorman, 2008). In a comprehensive study (Allen, Kustov, & Recck, 2007) it was found that 22% of U.S. adult males with Internet access, aged 18 to 49 years old, played fantasy sports. In general, the fantasy sports-related activities are estimated to have at least a US$3 to 4 billion annual economic impact across the sports industry (Grady, 2007). This apparent appeal in fantasy sports may lead to increased office pooling that has the potential to become a global workplace disruption as reported in studies that focused on similar office betting on major sporting events, such as the annual NCAA sponsored March Madness basketball tournaments (Smith & Smith, 2008).

Fantasy sports are extremely popular throughout the world with leagues for soccer cricket and other nondomestic based sports. More complex variants use computer modeling of actual games based on statistical input generated by professional sports. Erlbaum (2006) noted that in fantasy sports there is the ability to trade, cut, and sign players, like a real sports owner. Although there are several different types of fantasy sports, fantasy football is by far the most popular (Nesbit & King, 2010). If fact, Davis (2012) estimated that 32 million people presently engage in fantasy football and it is especially popular with college students. Davis (2012) suggested that empirical evidences points to active engagement in fantasy football is a classic vehicle that enhances knowledge of basic sport marketing concepts to undergraduate students.

Management's Role in Promoting Branding and Communication

Management has since developed many online public relations campaigns, taking advantage of the extreme popularity of fantasy sports to rebuild a strong and personalized relationship with its fan base, as evident by the extreme popularity of the fantasy sports among active ticket holders to NFL games (Nesbit & King, 2010). In general, fantasy sports and its many gaming activities has caught the attention of a significant following of professional team sports fans because of its ease-of use, accessibility, and entertainment qualities. The popularity of the four major message boards of fantasy sports websites, namely ESPN.com Fantasy Games, Yahoo! Fantasy Sports, FOX Fantasy Sports, and NFL: Fantasy Events. Hence, the popularity of fantasy sports are testimony to the successful interrelationship between fantasy and professional sports (Dwyer & Drayer, 2010).

POTENTIAL GENDER INFLUENCES

Technology Sophistication and Fantasy Sport Participation

A number of researchers have suggested that significant gender differences exist in the acceptance of technology in personal use (Dautzenberg, 2012; Ong & Lai, 2006; Venkatesh & Morris, 2000; Yeh, Hsiao, & Yang, 2012). The results may have significant bearing on the acceptance of fantasy sport applications and its overall acceptance among males and females. In all the studies, there are specific ease-of-use inhibitors, especially for women. Unfortunately, there is a significant void in the literature concerning gender difference via these technology-based factors in the fantasy sports area from an academic perspective. There is some empirically-based research that suggests the traditional motivational factors of technology sophistication and convenience are primary enhancers of fantasy sports-gaming participation. Suh (2012) explored in a recent dissertation dealing with the psychological factors associated with fantasy sports participation, found that certain motivation factors had a statistically positive affect on attitude, but certain constraints had a statistically negative affect on attitude. Using a service-quality model, Suh found that there were statistically significant positive relationships among perceived service quality and satisfaction, attitude, and between attitude and actual amount of time and usage.

Specifically, in terms of overall technology sophistication, Ong and Lai (2006) found that men's rating of technology-rated variables of computer self-efficacy, perceived usefulness, perceived ease-of-use, and behavioral intention to use e-learning and computer software applications were higher than women's rating. Interestingly, Ong and Lai found that women were strongly influenced by perceptions of computer self-efficacy and ease of use, and that men's usage decisions were significantly influenced by their perception of usefulness of e-learning. The authors suggested that to increase effectiveness of e-learning, men must generally perceive that the system is useful to enhance their job productivity thereby attracting them to more useful content.

Behavioral Considerations

The perceived usefulness had the most significant effect on behavioral intention to use for men only, suggesting that females perceived usefulness is important, but more so for males. In fantasy sports, regardless of gender, active and successful participation generally requires a working knowledge of the technology and player centric strategies in order to become successful in fantasy player trades and other tactics. Perhaps this emphasis details and technological sophistication may explain the apparent dominance of males in fantasy sports engagement. It was found that perceived ease-of-use has even stronger effects than perceived usefulness both for women and men. Since it is assumed that technological sophistication is important to increasing active participation in fantasy sports, especially in football, women may significantly be hampered by perceived ease-of-use inhibitors.

Lin and Chang (2011), in similar research efforts, found that that technology readiness influenced the same set of technological variables of perceived usefulness, perceived ease-of-use, attitudes, and behavioral intentions in self-service applications. They suggested that in order to achieve better self-service technologies effective outcomes for both genders, management should pay increased attention to customers' readiness to accept such technologies. Management may positively influence the use of technology-related services by promoting opportunities that enhances optimistic and innovative outcomes for technological services. It is also important to reduce technological readiness inhibitors, especially discomfort, insecurity, and identity threat factors in order to simultaneously reduce 'reluctance to use' service technology. These concepts were at least partially validated by Deng, Liu, and Qi (2011), who examined research based on the Unified Theory of Acceptance and use of technology models. The authors found that ease of use factors were extremely important and by reducing technology readiness inhibitors can significantly increase acceptance of new technologies.

Maldonado, Khan, Moon, and Rho (2011) validated a modified unified theory of acceptance and use of technology model by adding an e-learning motivation construct in order to specify the role of e-learning motivation in the use and adoption of related technology systems. The authors found that the constructs of e-learning motivation and social influence had a positive influence on behavioral acceptance and intention for both males and females.

Lee, Kwak, Lim, Pedersen, and Miloch (2011), found that the that the perceived roles of gender, sensation seeking, locus of control, and need for cognition in predicting attitudes and intentions relative to participating in fantasy football league had similar results in most technology or knowledge-based research. Specifically, they used technological knowledge of the fantasy sport [domain-specific construct (i.e. fantasy football knowledge)] to serve as a moderator to control the potential attenuating effects of personality and other related behavior effects. The authors found that males exhibited significant sensation seeking, locus of control, and domain-specific behaviors that were related to both attitudes and intentions toward participating. For males, knowledge of the game acted as a moderator between locus of control and intentions. Interestingly, none of the personality traits were associated with attitudes or intentions for females. It was hypothesized that males should exhibit statistically significant traits in their attitudes and behaviors towards fantasy sport applications as compared with their working professional female counterparts.

GENERAL CONCLUSION

Continued Transformational Aspects of the Internet

There is little doubt that the Internet has become a prominent tool in sport management, as evident from its vast array of communication reach and range in terms of becoming a preferred provider of sport content, e-commerce, and video clips and spectator engagement. It is now evolving into more than that. Based on the seven key internet strategy themes presented in Evans & Smith (2004): leadership, managers' perceptions of online commerce, IT assimilation theory, Internet vision statements, project trams, partnership/alliances, and online communities, fantasy sporting and branding opportunities are rivaling both collegiate and professional sports. Despite having the best of intentions, occasionally sports marketing promotional efforts can cause unintended harm. When attitude and behavior change occurs in the direction opposite to that which was intended (i.e., boomerang effect). Many ways messages cause confusion by becoming lost in the translation, sport marketers need to ensure that the message is properly articulated as intended? There are many examples that can be found on YouTube of advertisements where the message was not properly articulated or failed to send the message that was intended.

Hence, commercialization is a double-edged sword; in that it provides for corporations' need for increased visibility and a place that may win the attention of fans, as many companies believe that the emotional meaning of the game or the team will be transferred to the sponsoring company. On-the-other-hand, the reverse may also be true; emotional meaning is just as easily transferred from the company to the club that it sponsors. Therefore, sports managers must be careful to find a good match before signing up with a sponsor. For example, in the past, the Coors Company, a family-run and controlled firm, is infamous for its past unethical business practices, and has been the target of consumer boycotts since the 1960s, as a result of its anti-labor policies and attitudes towards racial groups. In addition, the company openly supported the apartheid regime in South Africa. Therefore, a sports management team would likely be criticized for choosing Coors as a sponsor, as association with this company could cause the team to lose fans. As commercialization in sports grows, management teams will increasingly have to make ethical choices about where money flows into the game and what and whose values they choose to be associated with. The video that especially emphasized the boomerang effect was the YouTube video entitled "When Sport Stars Get ANGRY!" (2014). As the coaches and star athletes acted very poorly (e.g., throwing chairs and calling people foul names), the logos of corporate sponsors are prominently displayed in the background.

Branding and Corporate Sponsorships

It would be very difficult to create a one-size-fits-all sponsorship policy manual in order to meet the specific needs of a sponsor, as all such events and promotional campaigns must be highly customized. However, there is little doubt that such a manual should include a description and history of the organization; especially if the sponsorship is specific to an event, then a description and history of the event should be included. Reviewing a number of sponsorship agreements and letters, the Web contains a number of examples of previous sponsors with quotes from them about why they supported the sport organization and/or event and what benefits they directly received from such sponsorship. Other items typically include a brief overview of why to sponsor the organization and/or event as well as a list of sponsorship levels and benefits associated with each level as well as the value of each level. Of course, there should be detailed instructions for how the potential sponsor can contact the program director to purchase sponsorship. The objectives of position enhancement, status enhancement, and trade networking can probably be best served by ensuring visibility is properly matched with the level a sponsor contributes. Essentially if someone who contributes more gets more visibility than someone that contributes less, so it is important to build sponsorship levels and benefits appropriately. As suggested by Wang, Cheng, Purwanto, and Erimurti (2011), sports team sponsor's brand equity was could to be empirically congruent between the sponsor and the sponsored team directly affects the sponsor's credibility, which has an impact on the sponsor's brand equity. Therefore, it is important to get it right by matching the sponsor's image with the organization's or event's image.

However, there is little doubt that effective communication is important in successful marketing practices (Weeks, Cornwell, & Drennan, 2008). The use of pretest communication concepts and intervention has become standard practices in social marketing. Pretesting communication is the use of assessing consumer's response to messages and other intervention components. Communication messages can become lost in translation when you target the wrong audience; this mistake almost always results in disaster because the message does not relate to a particular audience. Marketers can ensure that they use pretesting communication because it reduces the risk of delivering the wrong message and also help to assure that there is strong match between the consumers and the program interventions and gauge the consumer's response to a concept to determine early if the strategy will be effective. It is an interesting question whether the boomerang effect is fair to judge an athlete's character right after a football game either in wins or loss's during an interview. Brown, Linderberger, & Bryant (2008) gave convincing evidence that athletes' performance and emotional/physical presence are all part of a sound sport marketing strategy. As evident through this paper, fantasy and more traditional sport marketing branding and corporate sponsorships are not immune.

ACKNOWLEDGMENT

The author wishes to thank the valuable contributions by the reviewers for their input into the final paper.

REFERENCES

Allen, E. G., Kustov, K., & Recck, G. (2007). Building a better fantasy baseball team. *Quality Progress*, *40*(4), 24–29.

Bouchet, A., Ballouli, K., & Bennett, G. (2011). Implementing a ticket sales force in college athletics: A decade of challenges. *Sports Marketing Quarterly*, *20*(2), 84–92.

Brock, D. (2006). Leagues of their own. *Nine (Edmonton)*, *15*(1), 110–114. doi:10.1353/nin.2006.0036

Brown, K., Linderberger, J., & Bryant, C. (2008). Using pretesting to ensure your messages and materials are on strategy. *Social Marketing and Health Communication*, *9*(2), 116–122. PMID:18340086

Burden, W., & Li, M. (2009). Minor league baseball: Exploring the growing interest in outsourced sport marketing. *Sport Marketing Quarterly*, *18*(3), 81–91.

Burden, W., Li, M., Masiu, A., & Savini, C. (2006). Outsourcing intercollegiate sport marketing operation: An essay on media rights holders' strategic partnership decisions. International. *Journal of Sport Management*, *7*(1), 474–490.

Coates, D., & Humphreys, B. R. (1999). The growth effects of sports franchises, stadia and arenas. *Journal of Policy Analysis and Management*, *14*(4), 601–624. doi:10.1002/(SICI)1520-6688(199923)18:4<601::AID-PAM4>3.0.CO;2-A

Cohen, A., Brown, B., & Welty Peachey, J. (2012). The intersection of pop culture and non-traditional sports: An examination of the niche market of Quidditch. *International Journal of Sport Management and Marketing*, *12*(3/4), 180–197. doi:10.1504/IJSMM.2012.052666

Dautzenberg, K. (2012). Gender differences of business owners in technology-based firms. *International Journal of Gender and Entrepreneurship*, *4*(1), 79–98. doi:10.1108/17566261211202990

Davis, D. J. (2012). Project NFFL: The Niagara Fantasy Football League and sport marketing education. *College Student Journal, 46*(2), 235–242.

Davis, N. W., & Duncan, M. C. (2006). Sports knowledge is power: Reinforcing masculine privilege through fantasy sport league participation. *Journal of Sport and Social Issues, 30*(3), 244–253. doi:10.1177/0193723506290324

Dees, W. (2011). New media and technology use in corporate sport sponsorship: Performing activational leverage from an exchange perspective. *International Journal of Sport Management and Marketing, 10*(3/4), 272–285. doi:10.1504/IJSMM.2011.044795

Deng, S., Liu, Y., & Qi, Y. (2011). An empirical study on determinants of web based question-answer services adoption. *Online Information Review, 35*(5), 789–798. doi:10.1108/14684521111176507

Doherty, A., & Murray, M. (2007). The strategic sponsorship process in a non-profit sport organization. *Sport Marketing Quarterly, 16*(1), 49–59.

Dwyer, B., & Drayer, J. (2010). Fantasy sport consumer segmentation: An investigation into the differing consumption modes of fantasy football participants. *Sports Marketing Quarterly, 19*(4), 207–216.

Erlbaum, L. (2006). Handbook of Sports and Media. Retrieved from www.nytimes.com/2005/01/22/sports/football/22sportsbiz.html

Evans, D. M., & Smith, A. C. T. (2004). The Internet and competitive advantage: A study of Australia's four premier professional sporting leagues. *Sport Management Review, 7*(1), 27–56. doi:10.1016/S1441-3523(04)70044-3

Filo, K., Funk, D. C., & Alexandris, K. (2008). Exploring the role of brand trust in the relationship between brand associations and brand loyalty in sport and fitness. *International Journal of Sport Management and Marketing, 3*(1/2), 39–57. doi:10.1504/IJSMM.2008.015960

Grady, J. (2007). Fantasy stats case tests limits of intellectual property protection in the digital age. *Sport Marketing Quarterly, 16*(4), 230–232.

Green, B. C. (2001). Leveraging subculture and identity to promote sport events. *Sport Management Review, 4*(1), 1–19. doi:10.1016/S1441-3523(01)70067-8

Harrison, J. S., Bosse, D. A., & Phillips, R. A. (2010). Managing for stakeholders, stakeholder utility functions, and competitive advantage. *Strategic Management Journal, 31*(10), 58–74. doi:10.1002/smj.801

Helo, P., Anussornnitisarn, P., & Phusavat, K. (2008). Expectation and reality in ERP implementation: Consultant and solution provider perspective. *Industrial Management & Data Systems, 108*(8), 1045–1158. doi:10.1108/02635570810904604

Husted, B. W., & Allen, D. B. (2011). *Corporate Social Strategy: Stakeholder Engagement and Competitive Advantage*. Cambridge, UK: Cambridge University Press.

Hutchins, B. (2011). The acceleration of media sport culture. *Information Communication and Society, 14*(2), 237–257. doi:10.1080/1369118X.2010.508534

Ifinedo, P., & Nahar, N. (2009). Interactions between contingency, organizational IT factors, and ERP success. *Industrial Management & Data Systems*, *109*(1), 118–126. doi:10.1108/02635570910926627

Johansson, B., & Sudzina, F. (2008). ERP systems and open source: An initial review and some implications for SMEs. *Journal of Enterprise Information Management*, *21*(6), 649–659. doi:10.1108/17410390810911230

Lee, S., Seo, W. J., & Green, B. C. (2013). Understanding why people play fantasy sport: Development of the Fantasy Sport Motivation Inventory (FanSMI). *European Sport Management Quarterly*, *13*(2), 166–199. doi:10.1080/16184742.2012.752855

Lee, W.-Y., Kwak, D. H., Lim, C., Pedersen, P. M., & Miloch, K. S. (2011). Effects of personality and gender on fantasy sports game participation: The moderating role of perceived knowledge. *Journal of Gambling Studies*, *27*(3), 427–441. doi:10.1007/s10899-010-9218-9 PMID:20865303

Maldonado, U. P. T., Khan, G. F., Moon, J., & Rho, J. J. (2011). E-learning motivation and educational portal acceptance in developing countries. *Online Information Review*, *35*(1), 66–85. doi:10.1108/14684521111113597

Miloch, K., & Lambrecht, K. W. (2006). Consumer awareness of sponsorship at grassroots sport events. *Sport Marketing Quarterly*, *15*(3), 147–154.

Moorman, A. M. (2008). Fantasy sports leagues challenged as illegal gambling. *Sport Marketing Quarterly*, *17*(4), 232–234.

Nesbit, T. M., & King, K. (2010). Impact of fantasy football participation on NFL attendance. *Atlantic Economic Journal*, *38*(1), 95–108. doi:10.1007/s11293-009-9202-x

Ong, C.-S., & Lai, J.-Y. (2006). Gender differences in perceptions and relationships among dominants of e-learning acceptance. *Computers in Human Behavior*, *22*(5), 816–829. doi:10.1016/j.chb.2004.03.006

Pantuosco, L., & Stone, G. (2007). Capitalism for the cooperative: The NCAA and NFL model of parity and profit. *Journal of Economics & Economic Education Research*, *8*(2), 65–92.

Park, Y., & Nahm, A. Y. (2011). Classification of mass customisation: A Socio-Technical System perspective. *International Journal of Services and Operations Management*, *8*(3), 322–334. doi:10.1504/IJSOM.2011.038975

Pedersen, P. M. (2013). Reflections on communication and sport: On strategic communication and management. *Communication and Sport*, *1*(1/2), 55–67. doi:10.1177/2167479512466655

Schirato, T. (2012). Fantasy sport and media interactivity. *Sport in Society: Cultures, Commerce, Media. Politics*, *15*(1), 78–87.

Seguin, B., Richelieu, A., & O'Reilly, N. (2008). Leveraging the Olympic brand through the reconciliation of corporate and consumers' brand perceptions. *International Journal of Sport Management and Marketing*, *3*(1/2), 3–22. doi:10.1504/IJSMM.2008.015958

Smith, A. D., & Smith, A. A. (2008). Exploring the service location strategies behind super bowl venue selection. *Services Marketing Quarterly*, *29*(4), 66–84. doi:10.1080/15332960802218778

Sotiriadou, K., Shilbury, D., & Quick, S. (2008). The attraction, retention/transition, and nurturing process of sport development: Some Australian evidence. *Journal of Sport Management*, *22*(1), 247–272.

Suh, Y. I. (2012). Examining the psychological factors associated with fantasy sports participants, Dissertation. Retrieved from http://udini.proquest.com/view/examining-the-psychological-factors-goid:594581088/

Venkatesh, V., & Morris, M. G. (2000). Why don't men ever stop to ask for directions? Gender, social influence, and their role in technology acceptance and usage behavior. *Management Information Systems Quarterly*, *24*(1), 115–139. doi:10.2307/3250981

Wang, M., Cheng, J. M.-S., Purwanto, B. M., & Erimurti, K. (2011). The determinants of the sports team sponsor's brand equity. *International Journal of Market Research*, *53*(6), 811–829. doi:10.2501/IJMR-53-6-811-829

Weeks, C. S., Cornwell, T. B., & Drennan, J. C. (2008). Leveraging sponsorships on the Internet: Activation, congruence, and articulation. *Psychology and Marketing*, *25*(7), 637–654. doi:10.1002/mar.20229

When sport stars get ANGRY! (2014). *TalkSPORT Magazine*. Retrieved from http://www.youtube.com/watch?v=uQTATWUtvHQ

Yeh, J.-C., Hsiao, K.-L., & Yang, W.-N. (2012). A study of purchasing behavior in Taiwan's online auction websites: Effects of uncertainty and gender differences. *Internet Research*, *22*(1), 98–115. doi:10.1108/10662241211199988

Zimmerman, M. H., Clavio, G. E., & Lim, C. H. (2011). Set the agenda like Beckham: A professional sports league's use of YouTube to disseminate messages to its users. *International Journal of Sport Management and Marketing*, *10*(3/4), 180–195. doi:10.1504/IJSMM.2011.044789

This research was previously published in the Journal of Electronic Commerce in Organizations (JECO), 14(4); edited by Pedro Isaías, pages 52-65, copyright year 2016 by IGI Publishing (an imprint of IGI Global).

Chapter 6
Strategic Use of Facebook to Build Brand Awareness:
A Case Study of Two National Sport Organizations

Ann Pegoraro
Laurentian University, Canada

Olan Scott
University of Canberra, Australia

Lauren M. Burch
Indiana University-Purdue University Columbus, USA

ABSTRACT

Social media provides a strategic means for non-profit organizations to build and maintain strong relationships with consumers. The purpose of this study was to apply branding theory and frameworks to the use of Facebook by National Olympic Committees in two countries, Australia and Canada over specific time periods related to three Olympics Games. These Facebook pages were examined to determine the types of brand-related post content and communication style utilized as well as the consumer response to these posts. The two organizations generally used Facebook to broadcast product related brand attributes such as information about athletes and teams. There was also a significant difference in Facebook post use and focus by two organizations indicating some international differences in using Facebook for branding a sport organization. The results also provide practical implications for non-profit sport organizations using Facebook to build positive brand images, promote fan engagement and ultimately create brand ambassadors.

DOI: 10.4018/978-1-5225-5475-2.ch006

INTRODUCTION

The rise in use and popularity of the Internet has dramatically changed the way sport organizations communicate with their stakeholders (Pedersen, Miloch, & Laucella, 2007). Social media (SM) platforms such as Twitter and Facebook provide a central location for social engagement and a means for sport organizations to disseminate their messages directly to mass audiences (Pegoraro, 2010). A SM usage survey of sport fans found that 40% report that SM has made them bigger fans of their respective teams (Broughton, 2011) confirming findings from an earlier study that 61% of Major League Baseball (MLB) fans and 55% of National Football League (NFL) fans considered themselves bigger fans of the leagues since they started following their favourite teams on SM platforms (Broughton, 2010). Additionally, 51% of MLB fans and 43% of NFL fans reported spending more time watching the league as a result of following their favourite team on SM (Broughton, 2011). Therefore interacting with sport organizations or other fans on SM can increase a fan's level of identification and loyalty.

As SM use has grown marketers have come to see it as a viable medium grow brand awareness (Dittmore & McCarthy, 2014), which is a key component of building brand equity for a sport organization, as without awareness the consumer cannot form a brand association. Research has established the link between brand awareness, association and brand identity to enhanced loyalty among consumers and sports fans (Aaker, 2007; Bauer, Stokburger-Sauer, & Exler 2008; Gladden & Funk, 2001; Keller, 1998; Ross, 2006). Brand loyalty involves building a two-way collaborative relationship through communication and interaction between organizations and their consumers or fans in the case of sport (Wallace, Wilson, & Miloch, 2011).

SM use by sport organizations is largely driven by two key factors: the relatively inexpensive cost of SM when compared to traditional marketing tools and the ability to connect with millions of fans with ease (Dittmore & McCarthy, 2014). SM allows for interaction, providing a unique channel of communication that shifts communication from one-way (e.g., television advertisements) to a more interactive method. SM is a cost-effective tool for building brand relationships through interactive dialogue between sport organizations and fans (Williams & Chinn, 2010).

National Olympic Committees (NOCs) are one segment of the sport industry that could greatly benefit from SM, as these organizations are not-for-profit and operate on rather limited budgets when compared to those of professional sports. NOCs are responsible for development of sport and athletes in their respective countries and are largely funded through government and sponsorship revenue. While all sport organizations stand poised to benefit from SM, most NOCs and the sports they represent do not have budgets allowing for full utilization of traditional marketing outlets such as paid television, radio, print, internet, and outdoor advertising (Eagleman, 2013). Many Olympic sports can largely be considered niche sports, or those that do not receive mainstream media coverage on a daily basis (Greenhalgh, Simmons, Hambrick & Greenwell, 2011). Niche sports are relatively on their own and therefore they must create their own publicity, their own market share and fan base in order to survive (Greenhalgh et al., 2011). Eagleman, Pedersen, and Wharton (2009) found that while mainstream sports like men's football and basketball in the United States, enjoy a mutually beneficial relationship with the mass media, it is much more difficult for other sports to generate awareness and build fan bases, and therefore they must seek channels other than mass media to achieve these goals.

SM is a unique marketing communications tool that niche sport organizations like NOCs can use to attempt to overcome the challenge of lower budgets, less media coverage, and low fan interest levels. It could also be used to increase brand awareness, reach more fans and stakeholders, and maintain public interest in non-Olympic years when traditional media coverage of these organizations is typically at its lowest (Fernandez Pena, Ramajo, & Arauz, 2014). Therefore, the purpose of this study was to examine the use of SM as a brand management tool in the context of Olympic Sport Organizations in different parts of the world. Specifically, this study investigated the use of the SM platform Facebook by two NOCs, the Canadian Olympic Committee (COC) and the Australian Olympic Committee (AOC). This cross-country comparative case study analysis examined the Facebook pages of these two NOCs to determine how this SM communication tool was utilized to build relationships with fans thereby increasing brand loyalty. Ultimately such a case study provides a unique exploration into the various stages of the use of SM as a branding tool over time, and in two parts of the world.

LITERATURE REVIEW

Social Media and Sport Organizations

There is a growing body of literature surrounding the use of SM in sports, much of the focus to date has been on the use of various forms of SM by athletes, teams and leagues in professional sport (e.g., Ballouli & Hutchinson, 2010; Pegoraro, 2010). Many scholars argue that the issue of SM is so prominent for sport organizations that researchers and practitioners can no longer ignore this under researched topic (Ballouli & Hutchinson, 2010).

Stavros, Meng, Westberg, and Farrelly (2014) examined fan's motivations for using NBA teams' Facebook pages finding four key motivations: passion (i.e. team-directed displays of strong affection); hope (i.e. team-directed pronouncements centered on desirable outcomes); esteem (i.e. comments directed toward the team and/or fellow fans that share personal fandom); and camaraderie (i.e. community directed comments that reflect a desire for identification and interaction within the community). Researchers have also found that SM enables consumers to interact with one another as SM defies geographic barriers creating a truly global community (Scott, Bradshaw, and Larkin, 2013). Pronschinske, Groza, and Walker (2012) examined how Facebook page attributes influenced fan participation and found that the number of fans on a Facebook page is determined by authenticity (i.e. perception the site is official) and engagement (i.e. fan-centric strategies designed to facilitate two-way dialog). Therefore it is important for sport organizations to engage with fans on Facebook, as this engagement can positively impact interaction with a sport brand's content in terms of interaction or likes and followers (Pronschinske et al., 2012).

Research on sport organizations and SM has found that these platforms present a unique opportunity for sport organizations to communicate and foster interaction with the public (Williams & Chinn, 2010). Further, Hopkins (2013) found that each SM platform enables sport organizations to engage with their publics in different ways and the author suggests that Twitter is best for interaction and real-time updates whereas Facebook can be used to enhance customer experiences. Waters, Burke, Jackson, and Buning (2011) utilized stewardships strategies as a basis to explore the use of both Facebook and websites of NFL teams for the purpose building relationships with fans. The authors found that teams placed greater emphasis on relationship management strategies on their website than on Facebook, suggesting that perhaps this was due to a lack of flexibility in the prescribed formats of SM, lack of control or lack of a measurable return on investment (Waters et al., 2011).

Wallace et al. (2011) studied the Facebook pages of NCAA sports and athletic departments to understand how these organisations utilized the platform for brand management. The authors concluded that both types of organizations used Facebook as a tool for creating long-term relationships with fans and that the content posted on their Facebook pages focused on ''experiencing the brand through real-time online interaction'' (p. 439). Eagleman (2013) examined the existing role of SM within National Sport Organizations (NSO) in the United States and found that 100% of the organizations studied had a Facebook page. NSO participants in the study indicated that there were two key goals for SM use: enhancing the organization's relationship with fans and promoting the organization's brand and sport. The study also noted the benefits of SM as identified by NSOs as the ability to developing a greater connection between the organisation and its fans in a cost-effective manner as SM provides the ability to reach a large number of fans at a very low cost (Eagleman, 2013). Thompson, Martin, Gee, and Eagleman (2014) studied SM use of one specific NSO, Tennis New Zealand, and concluded that NSOs need to have a sustained SM presence to build social interaction and engagement with their publics. Further, the authors found that it is important for organizations to cater SM content to their users and not adopt a one-size-fits-all approach (Thompson et al., 2014).

Branding, Sport, and Social Media

The introduction and widespread uptake of SM has enabled consumers to connect with friends, brands, and high profile personalities such as athletes and movie stars (boyd & Ellison, 2007). SM has enabled sport organizations to directly connect with their fans and build relationships through a more one-to-one interactive approach (Abeza, O'Reilly, & Reid, 2013), linking the fan to the sport brand, while simultaneously broadcasting these interactions to fans' and brand networks alike (Wallace et al., 2011; Pegoraro 2010). While SM is still a relatively young medium, the growth in platform numbers and usage rates requires that sport organizations pay attention and develop specific strategies to use SM to enhance fan loyalty and build brand equity (Aaker, 2007; Ioakimidis, 2010).

Marketers have come to see SM as a viable medium to grow brand awareness (Dittmore & McCarthy, 2014). Strong brand elements that are identifiable, enduring, and meaningful to consumers provide a unique competitive advantage, building equity for the brand (Keller, 1999). In Keller's model (1993) brand equity consists of two components: brand awareness and brand image. Brand awareness is based upon a consumer's ability to recognize and recall a brand (Bauer et al., 2008). Brand awareness is the vital first step in building brand associations stored in a consumer's memory, as without brand associations desired consumer behaviour (i.e. purchasing) cannot occur (Bauer et al., 2008). Brand associations have been investigated in several sport domains (Ross, Bang, & Lee, 2007; Ross, James, & Vargas, 2006) with Gladden and Funk (2002) concluding that brand-association factors contribute to the creation of brand equity for sport organizations.

Brand image is the cumulative product of brand associations in the consumer's mind and are comprised of three different elements: brand attributes, brand benefits and brand attitudes (Bauer et al., 2008). Brand equity is created if a consumer has favourable, strong, and unique associations in their memory for that brand. When considering how a brand projects itself on SM, brand attributes are the most evident of the three elements and are comprised of product- and non-product-related attributes. The tangible attributes of a sport brand are usually easy to identify, (i.e. logos, colours), but intangible features of a sport brand are less visible can involve elements such as nostalgia for a team, performance of a star player, team success, and peer-group acceptance (Funk & James, 2006). The latter builds on fan group identity, which involves a group of people collectively connected to a sport entity through participation and consumption and this is unique to the sport industry (Foster & Hyatt, 2008). In terms of brand attributes in sport, Bauer et al. (2008) demonstrated that non-product-related attributes, or attributes that do not affect the outcome of a sporting event (i.e. logo and tradition) yielded stronger brand-attitude and behavioural loyalty outcomes than product-related attributes (i.e., success, players) which are directly related to the actual sporting event.

According to Ross (2007) brand awareness and associations create loyal sport consumers with identifiable preferences in behaviours and attitudes. Brand loyalty manifests itself in two ways: attitude towards the brand and behaviour, or consumption of that brand (Kaynak, Salmon & Tatoglu, 2008). Behaviour is easiest to identify and quite often involves repeat purchasing or consumption behaviour. Attitude is more difficult as it is subjective and indirect (Pritchard & Funk, 2010). Although the attitude toward a particular team may not generate direct revenue, Kaynak et al., (2008) note that consumers' enduring attitude toward a team or organization contributes to social aspects of interpersonal communication and identification with that team and these can be used as indicators of brand loyalty.

Effective SM use by brands must not appear as an advertisement to the customer but rather appear as an attempt to build a relationship and establish trust (Wright, Khanfar, Harrington, and Kizer, 2010). Usulu (2010) examined users' engagement with brands and advertising via Facebook and found that users are interested in brand announcements and that they feel part of the brand communities they choose to follow. This engagement, and feeling as if one is 'part of' a brand is important to build brand loyalty as satisfied members of online brand communities are more likely to be loyal and spread positive word of mouth (Yang, 2012). Chow and Shi (2015) utilized customer value theory as a framework to investigate consumer satisfaction with brand pages on Facebook and found information quality, economic benefit, social presence, entertainment, and arousal significantly influence customers' satisfaction with brand pages. Customer satisfaction significantly influences the intention to spread positive word of mouth building brand awareness (Chow & Shi, 2015). Aaker (2015) states if a brand focuses their SM strategy on what a person is passionate about, what motivates that person to reach out, to share experience, or to express an opinion, the end result will be increased brand awareness and loyalty. Perhaps nowhere is passion more evident than in the world of sport and related fandom and therefore communication and marketing strategies must connect these fans to brand building initiatives (Casteleyn, Mottart, & Rutten, 2009).

RESEARCH QUESTIONS

The purpose of this study is to examine the use of SM, specifically Facebook, as a brand management tool by the NOCs of Canada and Australia to determine how these major national non-profit sport organizations utilize Facebook to build relationships with fans. To investigate this, a series of research questions were developed.

Previous research on Olympic Sports and SM have suggested that communication on SM platforms should also promote interaction with the organization's website as well as provide information in a close-up way, through the one to one mode of communication that SM facilitate (Fernandez Pena et al., 2014). Therefore, RQ1 was developed to ascertain what communication strategy each organization was using:

RQ1: What type of post style type (e.g., status update, video, link) are most frequently used on Facebook by NOCs

RQ1a: What type of communication style (i.e. broadcast or engagement) is most frequently used on Facebook by NOCs

Involvement with a sports team provides a different set of experiences for fans, which create unique brand associations that strengthens the brand equity for the team (Watkins, 2014). Bauer et al. (2008) suggests that brands have high customer-based brand equity when the consumer has developed strong, favourable, and unique brand associations with a sport brand. Therefore the use of SM by any sport organization should focus on building positive brand associations in the minds of fans. The second research question, RQ2, focuses analyzing the content of the Facebook posts by each of the NOC for the inclusion of content focused on creating brand awareness.

RQ2: How are Brand Awareness Categories (i.e. brand attributes, brand associations and marketing strategies) utilized by NOCs on their Facebook pages?

When fans engage with a sport brand on SM, this helps to create brand awareness, favorable brand associations and ultimately brand loyalty. Engagement on SM refers to how the public becomes involved with and participates in content provided by on that platform (Fernandez Pena et al., 2014). On Facebook, there are three participation levels for fans, with the most passive level being press the 'Like' button on a post, the next level is commenting on a post and the third level is sharing the post with your network of friends. While the option of sharing content shows both engagement and spreadability of content, (Fernandez Pena et al., 2104), this measure could not be included in the study as the Facebook API does not provide for collecting this data. Therefore, RQ3 focused on the highest level of participation available through the time periods of the study (i.e. comments).

RQ3: What content are fans engaging (i.e. commenting) with on the Facebook pages of NOCs?

The period between Games, known as the Olympiad, is the time that NOCs receive the least media attention, making it much more difficult to generate brand awareness and build a fan base (Fernandez Pena et al., 2014; Eagleman, 2013). Therefore, NOCs must seek other means by which to achieve these goals and RQ4 focused on investigating how NOCs utilized SM during the different time periods in the study.

RQ4: Is there any difference in the use of Facebook by NOCs during Pre-Games, Game and Post Game time periods?

METHODS

For this research, content analysis was employed as the methodological approach. Content analysis enables researchers to make replicable and valid inferences from texts and other meaningful matter (Krippendorf, 2004). Furthermore, this methodology allows for systematic and objective analysis of pre-existing content (Wimmer & Dominick, 2006). Recently, sport-specific content analyses have been applied to SM content, (e.g., Frederick, Burch & Blaszka, 2015). In this particular content analysis study, posts from the AOC and the COC Facebook pages served as the unit of the analysis.

The decision to incorporate two different countries into the data set was based on several factors. In terms of the Olympics Games, the inclusion of two different countries assured that the analysis was not biased by only including a country that is predominately successful in the Summer Olympic Games (i.e. Australia) or a country that is predominately successful in the Winter Olympic Games (i.e. Canada). In terms of Olympic medals won in both Summer and Winter Olympic Games, Australia ranks 12th overall, and Canada is 15th and each have participated in a total of 25 games (International Olympics Games Results 2015). In addition, both of these NOCs were the top English-speaking NOCs on the overall medal list outside of the perennial powerhouses of the United States (ranked 1st) and Great Britain (ranked 3rd).

In terms of SM use, Australia ranked 6th in the world with 57% of their population active on SM and Canada was 8th with 56% of the population active, indicating that there was a large user base in each country (We Are Social, 2015). Facebook was the top used SM platform in each country with 40% of Australians and 47% of Canadians active on Facebook. Therefore, the decision was made to include two different countries in the data set, to focus on the dominant SM platform (i.e. Facebook) in these countries and to provide cross-country comparisons of the data.

Collecting online data, and in particular SM data, often presents a methodological issue related to coding, as online information is constantly updated and removed (Riffe, Lacy, & Fico, 2008). NVivo10 is text analytic software that allows researchers to capture web content directly from SM sites through its add on NCapture and import it as a static data set (NVivo, 2012). NCapture was utilized in to collect data from the Facebook pages of the AOC and the COC to ensure that all coders were analyzing the same data set.

DATA COLLECTION AND CODING

This study involved a qualitative and quantitative analysis of the development and maintenance of a SM strategy on Facebook by the COC and the AOC. Triangulation of data involves gathering slices of data at different times and situations, as well as on multiple subjects (Denzin, 1978). Data triangulation was utilized in this study to crosscheck data from two sources (i.e. the AOC and COC), to search for regularities in the research data and to enhance confidence in the findings (O'Donoghue & Punch, 2003). Data were collected from the Facebook pages of the AOC and COC yielding a data set of posts and comments ranging from September 2009 to March 2014, covering 3 Olympic Games time periods, two Winter Olympics Games (Vancouver 2010 and Sochi 2014) and one Summer Olympic Games (London 2012). To facilitate analysis of such a large data set and to ensure data triangulation, a purposeful sample was selected for the following time periods: Pre-Games and Games (lead up to and during an Olympic Games), post Games (one month) and one year out from an Olympic Games both pre and post. For example, related to the 2012 Summer Olympics, the following time periods were selected for each NOC: July and August 2011 (out year out) May, June (pre-Games), July and August (Games) and July and August 2013 (One year post period). This purposeful sample was in keeping with previous research (Fernandez Pena et al, 2014) and the results are detailed in Table 1.

Multiple variables were adopted and modified from previous content analytic research specific to the Olympic Games (e.g., Frederick et al., 2015); from previous branding studies related to sport (e.g. Bauer et al., 2008) and from previous research related to use of Facebook by sport teams (Wallace et al., 2011). Major themes included communication tools, brand attributes, brand associations and marketing strategy, (see Table 2 for definitions). For the analysis related to communication type, each post for coded for presence of each variable (i.e. status, photo, video, link) and posts could be coded in one or more of the variables. For instance, a post that contained a *photo* and a *link* would be coded for the presence of both communication type variables. For the brand awareness categories (i.e. brand attributes, brand associations and marketing strategies), the variables within each category were mutually exclusive so posts

Table 1. Purposeful sample of data for inclusion in the study

Time Period	Date	AOC Posts	Percentage	COC Posts	Percentage
2010 Winter Olympics Pre Games	Nov-09	11	2.23	30	2.39
	Dec-09	7	1.42	30	2.39
	Jan-10	10	2.02	83	6.62
2010 Games	Feb-10	13	2.63	79	6.30
Post Games	Mar-10	1	0.20	31	2.47
2010 - 1 Yr. Post	Feb-11	13	2.63	71	5.67
2012 - 1 Yr. Pre	Jul-11	18	3.64	30	2.39
	Aug-11	30	6.07	21	1.68
2012 Summer Olympics Pre Games	May-12	30	6.07	76	6.07
	Jun-12	26	5.26	64	5.11
2012 Games	Jul-12	17	3.44	85	6.78
	Aug-12	62	12.55	63	5.03
Post Games	Sep-12	12	2.43	47	3.75
2014 - 1 Yr. Pre	Feb-13	13	2.63	91	7.26
	Jul-13	16	3.24	32	2.55
2012- 1 Yr. Post	Aug-13	26	5.26	25	2.00
2014 Winter Olympics Pre Games	Nov-13	15	3.04	47	3.75
	Dec-13	21	4.25	59	4.71
	Jan-14	13	2.63	50	3.99
2014 Games	Feb-14	122	24.70	221	17.64
Post Games	Mar-14	18	3.64	18	1.44
Total		494	100	1253	100

Table 2. Categories and variables

Category	Variable
Type of Communication (based on Frederick, et al. 2015; Wallace et al., 2011)	Status, photo, video, link, other
	Broadcast (one-directional message; posting score updates; general information dissemination)
	Engagement (socially interacting with a user or user group; calling followers or fans to action; trying to elicit feedback and opinions)
Brand attributes (based on Frederick, et al. 2015; Wallace et al., 2011; Bauer et al., 2008)	Product: *athlete* (individual athlete), *sport* (rules and requirements, teams; not specific athletes), *team/game* (focus on results from team sports); *team/non-game* (about the national teams but not results); *sport*
	Nonproduct*: other people* (coaches, fans, Olympic officials; no athletes), *sport issue* (steroids, tickets, injuries, etc.; not specific athletes),
Brand Associations (based on Frederick, et al. 2015; Wallace et al., 2011)	*IOC* (anything related to the International Olympic Committee), *host city/country* (e.g. London, England; could include opening or closing ceremonies; focus is on the city/country itself), *other city/country* (city/country other than the host city/ country; focus is on the city/country itself),
Marketing Strategies (based on Frederick, et al. 2015; Wallace et al., 2011)	*Media* (mentions of media, media relations), and *promotion* (posts promote team related products, selling).

could be coded only in one of the focus categories. In order to ensure consistency in coding between the data sets each category was precisely defined and coders were instructed to only code for the primary content of the post to ensure that posts did not fall into more than one category.

Intercoder reliability was established prior to coding the entire data set. According to Riffe, Lacy, and Fico (2008), an overlap of 10%–20% is acceptable for the purposes of intercoder reliability. A 10% subsample for each NOC data set was randomly selected and coded by each coder to establish intercoder reliability. Cohen's kappa coefficients were at or above .75 for all variables (.75–.91), which is considered sufficient based in previous research standards (e.g., Wimmer & Dominick, 2006). The coders then completed the coding process and frequency distributions and chi-square tests were conducted in SPASS 20 to help answer the research questions. These statistical tests were deemed appropriate due to the exploratory nature of the current study and the use of categorical data.

RESULTS

When the coding was complete, the categories of *Sport* and *Sport Issue* were removed due to low numbers of posts (i.e. 8 posts total for *Sport* and 1 for *Sport Issue).* This left 9 categories of coded posts and examples of each of the types of posts by category are provided in Table 3.

Before providing analysis specific to the RQs, the researchers analyzed the posting levels by each NOC to determine if there were any significant differences in Facebook usage over the time periods included in the study the results are provided in Figure 1. The COC had a higher utilization of Facebook throughout all the time periods except for one, August 2011, one-year pre the 2012 Summer Games. The chi-square test revealed a significant difference for Facebook post numbers between the AOC and the COC, ($\chi2$ (2) = 50.31, p = .001).

To investigate RQ1, an analysis of the type of post characteristics was conducted and the results are presented in Table 4. The COC utilized *photos* the most in their posts (49.64%), followed by links (36.31%) while these were reversed for the AOC with *links* (62.55%) the most used then *photos* (44.74%). *Status update* and *videos* were used the least by both organizations and when looking at the post style, both NOCs utilized the *broadcast* style the most with the AOC using it in 78.96% of posts and the COC in 66.59%.

To investigate RQ2, data triangulation method were employed to find similarities in the data and to ensure confidence in the findings related to the overall data for both NOCs. Chi-square results indicated a significant difference in the use of the categories of variables related to brand awareness (i.e. brand attributes, brand associations and marketing strategies ($\chi2$ (8) = 111.99, p = .001) by the NOCs. The coding results for both AOC and COC are presented in Tables 5 and 6 respectively. ($\chi2$ (8) = 111.99, p = .001). The frequency of category type and variable are presented in Table 6.

Although a significant difference existed overall between the AOC and COC use of brand awareness categories, both committees devoted the largest amount of posts to the product related variable of *athletes*, with the AOC referencing *athletes* in 55.55% of posts and the COC in 36.9% of posts. Following the focus on *athletes*, the COC next employed the marketing strategy related variable of *media* related posts (15.7%), while the AOC utilized continued to utilize product related brand attributes by providing content that focused on *teams/non-game* setting (16.3%). The COC did, however, employ this same category as their third most frequently utilized category (14.4%). For the AOC, they utilized the non-product variable of *people/not athletes* for their third most utilized category of content.

Table 3. Examples of posts by category for AOC and COC

Category	Variable	AOC	COC
Brand Attributes *Product*	Athlete	*Super Sally Pearson just won gold for Australia in the 100m hurdles. What a great Day 11 for Australia! Who was up at the crack of dawn watching? [link]*	*Erik Guay won World Cup gold in alpine's super-G on the weekend – he is the 2nd Canadian man ever to win a World Cup downhill and super-G race over a career*
	Team/Game	*The Australian men's indoor volleyball team have qualified for the London Olympic Games after a dominant win over China! Congratulations to the team on an amazing effort. Watch out London!*	*It's Canada vs. Greece in FIFA's first International matchup of 2011! Watch the battle live here [link]*
	Team/non-game	*Video action from the selection announcement today. If only mixed trio synchro was an olympic event!*	*Canucks fans: 2010 athletes set to drop the puck on Saturday night!*
Brand Attributes *Non-Product*	People/not Athletes	*Volleyroos coach Jon Uriarte will go up against his son Nicolas who plays for Argentina at the London Olympics. Check out what he thinks about the match up*	*Canadian MP's were spotted wearing red mittens as they Painted the Town Red in the House of Commons on Parliament Hill.*
Brand Associations	IOC focus	*A cool 500 Days to Go to the next Winter Olympics-Sochi 2014 Winter Games! Give this post a like to show your support for our Winter athletes!*	*The luge team relay is a new event at #Sochi2014.*
	Host City/ Country	*It's a long journey to the #Olympic stage... We're warming up for #Rio2016 for the next 857 days. Here's a snapshot of what we got up to this weekend*	*It's coming fast! London 2012 full schedule of events is unveiled: link] Here's a video from the last time London hosted, the Olympic Cauldron being lit in 1948 (how time has changed)! [Link]*
	Other Country	*Our AUStrian friends raise the bar in Sochi! #GoAUS*	*Fingers crossed: Friday, in Guadalajara, Mexico, we will find out if Toronto wins the 2015 Pan/Parapan Am Games. Watch the final decision live between 5:30 and 6:30 p.m. EST. [Link]*
Marketing Strategies	Media focus	*Some of the best Getty Images photos from a huge day at the #Olympics: [link] #GoAUS*	*This is our playground. Watch #WeAreWinter: [Link] & subscribe to our YouTube channel for more great videos.*
	Promotion	*Who is going to be Australia's #1 performer at #Sochi2014? You could win an awesome pair of gloves from XTM Ski Team! #ASPIREtoSochi*	*Attention last minute #Christmas gift givers: [Link]- check out our holiday gift guide. #TeamCanada #Sochi2014 #Rio2016*

Figure 1. Number of posts by both NOCs

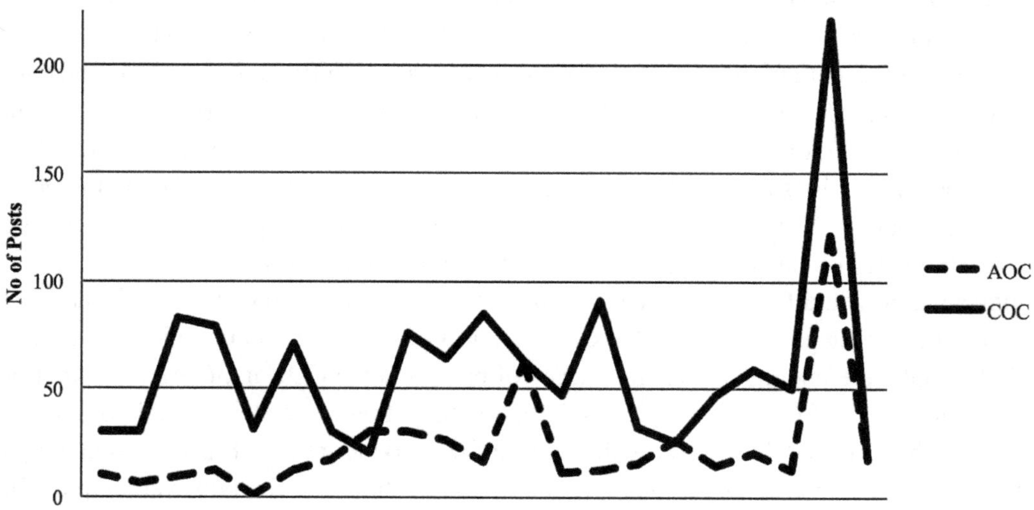

Table 4. AOC and COC post characteristics

	AOC		COC	
	No. of Posts	**Percentage**	**No. of Posts**	**Percentage**
Status	25	5.06	106	8.46
Link	309	62.55	455	36.31
Photo	221	44.74	622	49.64
Video	43	8.70	69	5.07
Post Style				
Broadcast	409	78.96	899	66.59
Engagement	109	21.04	451	33.41

Table 5. AOC coding results by category of Facebook posts

	Date	Brand Attributes Product			Non-Product	Brand Associations			Marketing Strategy	
		Athlete	**Team/ Game**	**Team/ Non-Game**	**People/ Not Athletes**	**IOC/ Olympic Focus**	**Host City/ Country**	**Other Country**	**Media Focus**	**Promotion**
2010 Winter Olympics Pre Games	Nov. 2009	5	0	4	1	0	0	0	0	1
	Dec. 2009	5	0	0	2	0	0	0	0	0
	Jan. 2010	5	0	4	0	0	0	0	1	0
2010 Games	Feb. 2010	5	2	2	1	1	1	0	0	1
Post Games	Mar. 2010	0	1	0	0	0	0	0	0	0
2010 - 1 Yr. Post	Feb. 2011	9	1	2	0	0	1	0	0	0
2012 - 1 Yr. Pre	Jul. 2011	4	0	4	1	5	0	2	1	0
	Aug. 2011	26	0	2	0	0	0	0	0	2
2012 Summer Olympics Pre Games	May 2012	13	0	11	0	4	0	0	1	1
	Jun. 2012	9	2	6	5	1	2	0	0	1
2012 Games	Jul. 2012	5	0	10	0	0	1	0	1	0
	Aug. 2012	37	16	5	3	1	0	0	0	0
Post Games	Sept. 2012	5	0	3	1	3	0	0	0	0
2014 - 1 Yr. Pre	Feb. 2013	3	1	0	2	4	1	0	1	1
	Jul. 2013	7	2	5	1	0	0	1	0	0
2012- 1 Yr. Post	Aug. 2013	16	2	3	2	1	1	0	1	0
2014 Winter Olympics Pre Games	Nov. 2013	10	0	0	3	2	0	0	0	0
	Dec. 2013	11	0	2	2	2	0	1	3	0
	Jan. 2014	6	0	4	0	1	0	0	0	1
2014 Games	Feb. 2014	79	2	12	12	1	5	1	3	3
Post Games	Mar. 2014	11	1	1	3	0	1	0	0	1
Totals		271	30	80	39	26	13	5	12	12

Table 6. COC coding results by category of Facebook posts

			Brand Attributes Product		Non-Product		Brand Associations		Marketing Strategy	
	Date	Athlete	Team/Game	Team/Non-Game	People/Not Athletes	IOC/ Olympic Focus	Host City/ Country	Other Country	Media Focus	Promotion
2010 Winter Olympics Pre Games	Nov-09	6	0	4	1	8	3	2	5	1
	Dec-09	14	2	5	2	2	3	0	1	1
	Jan-10	48	8	7	5	1	0	0	4	10
2010 Games	Feb-10	37	8	2	2	0	5	0	20	5
Post Games	Mar-10	24	1	2	0	1	0	0	2	1
2010 - 1 Yr. Post	Feb-11	20	3	2	6	2	1	0	35	2
2012 - 1 Yr. Pre	Jul-11	1	0	1	4	8	2	0	11	3
	Aug-11	4	0	0	2	1	2	0	12	0
2012 Summer Olympics Pre Games	May-12	32	1	13	4	4	0	0	12	9
	Jun-12	31	1	6	1	0	0	0	2	23
2012 Games	Jul-12	31	5	14	5	4	0	1	12	13
	Aug-12	28	6	12	5	2	0	0	2	8
Post Games	Sep-12	23	0	12	4	2	0	0	1	5
2014 - 1 Yr. Pre	Feb-13	33	1	39	2	2	0	0	6	8
	Jul-13	10	0	7	3	1	4	1	5	1
2012- 1 Yr. Post	Aug-13	16	0	3	2	1	3	0	0	0
2014 Winter Olympics Pre Games	Nov-13	20	1	5	1	4	2	1	4	8
	Dec-13	16	9	14	2	0	0	0	10	8
	Jan-14	12	2	19	2	1	0	0	6	8
2014 Games	Feb-14	76	75	10	4	7	1	0	45	2
Post Games	Mar-14	13	0	3	0	0	0	0	1	1
Total		495	123	180	57	51	26	5	196	117

As differences in regard to the type of post were observed in the dataset, the next step was to investigate the causes, if any behind these differences to ensure confidence in the overall findings and to determine regularities within the data. Therefore, standardized residuals were calculated to determine where the significant differences occurred within the Chi-square results. An adjusted residual value of +/- 1.96 is significant at the 0.05 level, while +/- 2.58 is significant at the .01 level (Agresti, 2012). Standardized residuals for each type of post by the AOC and COC are provided in Table 8.

Based on this analysis, the types of post that contributed to the statistically significant difference in post type between the AOC and COC were *athletes, team/game*, *people/not athletes*, *media focus*, and *promotion*. Positive standardized values listed in Table 8 as significant contributors indicate values that were over-represented in regard to their expected values, while negative standardized values indicated under-represented values (Agresti, 2012). These results indicate that the AOC and COC were similar in their use of brand association variables (i.e. *host city/country, IOC focus*) but differed in their use of brand attributes (i.e. *athletes*) and marketing strategies (i.e. *media focus*). For example, the AOC under utilized variables related to marketing strategies (i.e. *media focus, promotion*), while these categories

Table 7. Number of comments and avg. comments/post by category

Category	Variable	AOC					COC				
		Posts	%	Comments	%	Avg. Com/ Post	Posts	%	Comments	%	Avg. Com/ Post
Brand Attributes	Athlete	271	55.53	4,573	58.71	16.87	495	39.6	5,848	43.58	11.81
Brand Attributes: Product	Team/Game	30	6.15	1,115	14.32	37.17	123	9.84	3,027	22.56	24.61
	Team/non-game	80	16.39	785	10.08	9.81	180	14.4	1,640	12.22	9.11
Brand Attributes: Non-Product	People/not Athletes	39	7.99	518	6.65	13.28	57	4.56	196	1.46	3.44
Brand Associations	IOC focus	26	5.33	339	4.35	13.04	51	4.08	453	3.38	8.88
	Host City/Country	13	2.66	170	2.18	13.08	26	2.08	117	0.87	4.50
	Other Country	5	1.02	14	0.18	2.80	5	0.4	12	0.09	2.40
Marketing Strategy	Media focus	12	2.46	167	2.14	13.92	196	15.68	1,568	11.68	8.00
	Promotion	12	2.46	108	1.39	9.00	117	9.36	558	4.16	4.77

Table 8. Type of post standardized residuals

Category	Post Type	AOC	COC
Brand Attribute - Product	Athlete	3.8**	-2.4*
	Team/Game	-2.0*	1.20
	Team/non-game	0.80	-0.50
Brand Attribute – Non-Product	People/not Athletes	2.30*	-1.40
Brand Association	IOC focus	0.90	-0.60
	Host City/Country	0.60	-0.40
	Other Country	1.30	-0.80
Marketing Strategy	Media focus	-6.10**	3.80**
	Promotion	-4.0**	2.5*

Note: *Significant at the $p < 0.05$ level; ** Significant at the $p < 0.01$ level.

were over represented in the COC data set. In addition, in the AOC dataset, content related to the non-product variable of *people/not athletes* was over represented. While the most utilized category for the COC was *athletes,* it was actually under represented in the dataset overall.

To answer RQ 3 investigating fan engagement with the posted content, the first step was to identify a measure of engagement. While NCapture did provide the number of likes for each post, the number of comments provides a more robust measure of participation or engagement by fans (Fernandez Pena et al., 2014). An individual who follows either the AOC or COC on Facebook can easily click a like button for any post, but if they take the time to compose a comment, this would be an indication of higher engagement (Miranda, Chamorro, Rubio, and Rodriquez, 2014). Table 7 provides data on number of post for each organization by category, the total number of comments for each category as well as the average number of comments per post. Chi square test for RQ3 revealed that the difference in engagement by post category was significant ($\chi2$ (8) = 2115.48, p = .001).

As noted early the product related variable of *athletes* was utilized the most by both organizations, therefore it is not surprising that this variable also received the highest number of comments. But when the comment numbers are normalized by the number of posts to provide an average number of comments per post, the results are different. The highest average number of comments per post for both the AOC and the COC was for the product related variable of *team/game* (n=37.71 and 24.61 respectively), which is the fourth (6.15%) most utilized category for AOC and second (22.56%) for the COC.

After the analysis was complete for the first three research questions, the differences between the NOCs and their respective use of Facebook that emerged through the data triangulation were noted. To investigate RQ4, the COC was chosen as the case study example given the higher utilization of Facebook by this organization as well as chi-square residual results which indicated the COC's focus on marketing strategies. To further analyze the use of Facebook by the COC, post characteristics and content were analyzed over the time periods selected in the original sampling: Pre-Games, Games and Post Games and. The results are presented in Tables 9 and 10.

In terms of type of communication utilized, *links* are the predominate type used in both the Pre-Games and Games periods, followed by *photos* in both time periods. The order switches in Post Games period, where *photos* are predominately used followed by *links*. There is also an increase in the use of videos during Games time periods. It should be noted that the majority of the use of *status* communication type happened in the time periods around the 2010 Games and then *status* alone disappears from use. When looking at the use of *broadcast* versus *engagement* style of communication posts, the COC uses broadcast predominately in the Pre-Games (65.79%) and Games (70.81%) time periods. But in the Post Games period, the use of engagement increases to 40.43% of all posts.

Table 9. COC communication types over time periods (% of posts)

	Pre Games	Games	Post Games
Status	7.18	7.99	6.00
Link	72.86	63.91	60.00
Photo	33.39	48.32	69.79
Video	3.29	8.09	3.40
Broadcast	65.79	70.81	59.57
Engagement	34.21	29.19	40.43

Table 10. COC brand category variables over time periods (% of posts)

	Pre Games	Games	Post Games
Brand Attributes - Product	61.31	68.01	62.05
Brand Attributes - Non-Product	4.49	3.58	6.70
Brand Associations	7.94	4.47	7.14
Marketing Strategies	26.25	23.94	24.11

Lastly, when investigating the use of brand awareness strategies of the COC over the time periods, the use of *product-related brand attributes* dominates each time period (61.31%, 68.01% and 62.05% respectively). The COC tends to use more *non-product related* content in the Post Games period, while content related to *marketing strategies* remain fairly constant throughout. The use of *brand associations* does see some fluctuation

DISCUSSION

The purpose of this study was to analyze the use of Facebook as a brand management tool in the context of two National Olympic Committees, the AOC and the COC. The analysis revealed statistically significant findings in coverage of brand attributes, communication tools, and marketing coverage by these two organizations. These results present both theoretical and practical implications.

Overall, the COC utilized Facebook more than the AOC except in during one non-games year. It could have been expected that the AOC would utilize Facebook more often during the 2012 Games, because Australia is typically a summer sport nation and has had high medal winnings during Summer Games. Whereas, Canada could have been expected to post more often around and during the Vancouver and Sochi Games, as Canada could be described as more successful during the Winter Games. Even though the countries are very similar in profile for Olympic success and SM use, there were significant differences in how each NOC utilized Facebook. In terms of practical issues, each NOC may want to revisit their strategy for Facebook to enhance its use for brand management.

The style of post used can influence the way the Facebook users interact (Wallace et al., 2011). As more fans are consuming sports online, relationship management is an important aspect of the sport industry (Foster & Hyatt, 2008). Both NOCs used links in their post that brought users to Web sites outside of Facebook. This perhaps reveals the strategy to bring the user deeper into the NOC's richer content on their corporate websites as SM platforms are only a part of any organization's overall online presences and cross-pollination between SM and an organization's website should be a part of any marketing strategy. As Fernandez Pena and Arauz (2011) indicate, traditional websites represent more static content and SM platforms are a way of making that static content become more dynamic. Visual images could potentially generate fan involvement and interaction in a way that is uniquely different than other communication tools (Mehdizadeh, 2010) and the NOCs did capitalize on this by utilizing photos in their posts. In fact the COC utilized photos the most in the Post Games time period, when the organization would expect to receive less media and fan attention. This is perhaps a good strategy given that photos are one of the main drivers of engagement on Facebook (Malhotra, Malhotra & See, 2013). Videos were less used, perhaps an indication of the evolving nature of Facebook over the time of the study or the lower budgets available to NOCs. It is important for sport organizations to pay attention to video as an opportunity on Facebook, given the use of videos increases shared content and provides spreadability of a branding message (Malhotra, et al., 2013).

The NOCs tended to focus their content on a broadcast feature rather than engagement such as asking a question of fans. While fans responded well to these broadcast messages, recent research by Malhotra et al. (2103) has indicated that asking fans to get involved increases engagement in the form of comments, but can also decrease message spreadability due to a decrease in sharing. Therefore, sport organizations need a clear strategy for both the use of broadcast and engagement focused content on Facebook.

In terms of content that would create brand awareness for the NOCs, the organizations tended to utilize product related brand attributes the most. Both NOCs discussed athletes the most, which is not a surprise as athletes are the face of the Olympics for each nation. The frequent use of product-related attributes demonstrated that the NOCS are using Facebook to further the brand image of the product and emphasize the experience of sport and their athletes. Product related brand attributes have been associated with higher purchase intentions and are a factor influencing consumption behavior (Gladden & Funk, 2002; Kaynak et al., 2008). These results also support the notion that the type of brand coverage may influence fan interactions and communication on Facebook pages (Pedersen, Laucella, Miloch, & Fielding, 2007).

The NOCs did post content over 9 different categories in this study, illustrating a willingness to provide many ways for fans to interact with content. A variety of communication tools and content coverage has previously demonstrated a positive association with consumer behavior (Wilson, Fornasier, & White, 2010). These findings indicate that a variety of communication tools in combination with different types of content are strategies employed by NOCs to engage in building brand awareness through engaging content.

The use of marketing strategy related content was primarily focused on garnering media attention for the NOCs. These results are in line with previous studies that found that sport organizations are more focused on providing information and building their image, than on short-term marketing activations (Schultz & Sheffer, 2010; Wallace et al., 2011). In fact Fernandez Pena et al., (2014) advocate that SM not only be used by Olympic organizations as a marketing tool, that it has the power to do more, to create relationships and further the Olympic ideals.

There is a heightened level of nationalism during world events, such as the Olympic Games and previous research has suggested that ''the athletic component of the Olympics is often secondary to the nationalistic pride people feel toward the competition'' (Billings & Eastman, 2002, p. 351). This was definitely evident in the study at fans were most interested in content related to team and/or games results. NOCs and their related organizations are able to capitalize on feelings of nationalism during world events through the posting of team and individual successes, as interest in home nation athletes may be higher than at any other period in the year. Kassing and Sanderson (2010) indicated that event-specific information increases interactivity with fans using SM. While the response to team/game content was high, there was a disconnect in strategy as the team/game category was not the most utilized type of post and the NOCs should take note of what their fans want as they adjust their SM strategy. If they do so, they will help fans form the brand associations that are necessary to build brand loyalty, which is what is required to maintain interest and profile for these organizations.

LIMITATIONS AND FUTURE RESEARCH

Facebook pages represent only one SM platform for examination and therefore future research should incorporate other platforms. While the data were collected over an extended period of time, it did not include equal an equal number of Games (i.e. 2 Winter Games 1 Summer Games). Also, the inclusion of the 2010 Winter Games data could introduce a bias into the data as Canada was the host nation for these Games. The addition of Facebook user-interaction values (e.g. comments/user) would be important for determining whether fan interaction is has increased or decreased over time. In addition, a qualitative analysis of actual Facebook user comments may provide more specific information about consumer behavior and depth of relationship with the organization. Therefore, future research could include a qualitative analysis of user comments together with a content analysis of post data on Facebook pages. And lastly, future research should include qualitative interviews with key stakeholders at sport organizations to determine their brand management goals and objectives for SM platforms.

CONCLUSION

The findings from this study revealed one approach to evaluating communication, branding, and marketing techniques utilized by a sport organization on the SM platform Facebook. As a fan's experience with content on Facebook may influence their perceptions of that sport brand, sport marketers can utilize Facebook to create brand awareness, manage brand image and communicate with fans in real time. The results of this study show that while the use of Facebook over time has changed for the sport organizations studied; there is still a great opportunity for improvement in its use as a brand management tool for non-profit sport organizations. Facebook pages examined in this study were generally used to cultivate long-term relationships with Facebook users, and content was focused on experiencing the brand through the broadcast of athlete related information. The findings suggest that the management of communication techniques and the content posted to Facebook can potentially increase brand exposure and, as a result, create positive brand associations for a sport organization. In addition, use of product-related brand attributes on Facebook helps to facilitate two-way interaction with fans, engaging them as part of the brand community. In the future, NOCs can focus content in areas that promote the best interaction opportunities in order to build a stronger relationships, positive brand images and ultimately turn fans into brand ambassadors.

REFERENCES

Aaker, D. (2007). Innovation: Brand it or lose it. *California Management Review*, *50*(1), 8–24. doi:10.2307/41166414

Aaker, D. (2015). Four ways digital works to build brands and relationships. *Journal of Brand Strategy, 4*(1), 37–48.

Abeza, G., O'Reilly, N., & Reid, I. (2013). Relationship marketing and social media in sport. *International Journal of Sport Communication, 6*(2), 120–142.

Agresti, A. (2002). *Categorical data analysis* (2nd ed.). New York, NY: Wiley. doi:10.1002/0471249688

Ballouli, K., & Hutchinson, M. (2010). Digital-branding and social-media strategies for professional athletes, sports teams, and leagues: An interview with Digital Royalty's Amy Martin. *International Journal of Sport Communication, 3*(4), 395–401.

Bauer, H. H., Stokburger-Sauer, N. E., & Exler, S. (2008). Brand image and fan loyalty in professional team sport: A refined model and empirical assessment. *Journal of Sport Management, 22*, 205–226.

Billings, A. C., & Eastman, S. T. (2002). Selective representation of gender, ethnicity, and nationality in American television coverage of the 2000 Summer Olympics. *International Review for the Sociology of Sport, 27*(3-4), 351–370. doi:10.1177/101269020203700302

boyd, D., & Ellison, N.B. (2007). Social network sites: Definition, history, and scholarship. *Journal of Computer-Mediated Communication, 13*(1), 210-230.

Broughton, D. (2010, July 26). Survey: Social-media use builds fan avidity. *SportsBusiness Journal.* Retrieved from: http://www.sportsbusinessdaily.com/Journal/Issues/2010/07/20100726/This-Weeks-News/Survey-Social-Media-Use-Builds-Fan-Avidity.aspx

Broughton, D. (2011, June 27). Survey spots social media trends among fans. *SportsBusiness Journal*, 9.

Casteleyn, J., Mottart, A., & Rutten, K. (2009). How to use Facebook in your market research. *International Journal of Market Research, 51*(4), 439–447. doi:10.2501/S1470785309200669

Chow, W. S., & Shi, S. (2015). Investigating Customers' Satisfaction With Brand Pages In Social Networking Sites. *Journal of Computer Information Systems, 55*(2), 48–58. doi:10.1080/08874417.2015.11645756

Denzin, N. K. (1978). *Sociological Methods*. New York: McGraw-Hill.

Dittmore, S. W., & McCarthey, S. T. (2014). Sports Marketing and New Media. In A. C. Billings & M. Hardin (Eds.), *Routledge Handbook of Sport and New Media* (pp. 165–176). Oxford, UK: Routledge.

Eagleman, A. N. (2013). Acceptance, motivations, and usage of social media as a marketing communications tool amongst employees of sport national governing bodies. *Sport Management Review, 16*(4), 488–497. doi:10.1016/j.smr.2013.03.004

Eagleman, A. N., Pedersen, P. M., & Wharton, B. (2009). Coverage by gender in ESPN The Magazine: An examination of articles and photographs. *International Journal of Sport Management, 10*(2), 226–242.

Fernández Peña, E., & Arauz, M. (2011). *Social networking and the Olympic movement: social media analysis, opportunities and trends*. Centre d'Estudis Olimpics. Universitat Autònoma de Barcelona. Report commissioned by the International Olympic Committee. Retrieved 8th August, 2015 from http://doc.rero.ch/lm.php?url=1000,10,38,20110929154239-FE/2011_-_Social_Networking_and_the_Olympic_Movement_-_UAB_OSC.pdf

Fernández Peña, E., Ramajo, N., & Arauz, M. (2014). Social media in the Olympic Games. In A. C. Billings & M. Hardin (Eds.), *Routledge Handbook of Sport and New Media* (pp. 153–164). Oxford, UK: Routledge.

Foster, W., & Hyatt, C. (2008). Inventing team tradition: A conceptual model for the strategic development of fan nations. *European Sport Management Quarterly*, *8*(3), 265–287. doi:10.1080/16184740802224183

Frederick, E., Burch, L., & Blaszka, M. (2015). A Shift in Set: Examining the Presence of Agenda Setting on Twitter during the 2012 London Olympics. *Communication and Sport*, *3*(3), 312–333. doi:10.1177/2167479513508393

Funk, D., & James, J. (2006). Consumer loyalty: The meaning of attachment in the development of sport team allegiance. *Journal of Sport Management*, *20*, 189–217.

Gladden, J., & Funk, D. (2001). Understanding brand loyalty in professional sport: Examining the link between brand associations and brand loyalty. *International Journal of Sports Marketing & Sponsorship*, *3*(1), 67–86. doi:10.1108/IJSMS-03-01-2001-B006

Gladden, J., & Funk, D. (2002). Developing an understanding of brand associations in team sport: Empirical evidence from consumers of professional sport. *Journal of Sport Management*, *16*, 54–81.

Greenhalgh, G. P., Simmons, J. M., Hambrick, M. E., & Greenwell, T. C. (2011). Spectator support: Examining the attributes that differentiate niche from mainstream sport. *Sport Marketing Quarterly*, *20*(1), 41–52.

Hopkins, J. L. (2013). Engaging Australian Rules Football fans with social media: A case study. *International Journal of Sport Management and Marketing*, *13*(1/2), 104–121. doi:10.1504/IJSMM.2013.055197

International Olympics Games Results. (2015). *Results by Games*. Accessed 8 August 2015 from http://www.olympic.org/olympic-results

Ioakimidis, M. (2010). Online marketing of professional sports clubs: Engaging fans on a new playing field. *International Journal of Sports Marketing & Sponsorship*, *11*(4), 271–282. doi:10.1108/IJSMS-11-04-2010-B002

Kassing, J., & Sanderson, J. (2010). Fan-athlete interaction and Twitter: Tweeting through the Giro: A case study. *International Journal of Sport Communication*, *3*(1), 113–128.

Kaynak, E., Salmon, G., & Tatoglu, E. (2008). An integrative framework lining brand associations and brand loyalty in professional sports. *Brand Management*, *15*(5), 336–357. doi:10.1057/palgrave.bm.2550117

Keller, K. (1999). Brand mantras: Rationale, criteria and examples. *Journal of Marketing Management, 15*(1-3), 43–51. doi:10.1362/026725799784870513

Keller, K. L. (1993). Conceptualizing, measuring and managing customer-based brand equity. *Journal of Marketing, 57*(1), 1–22. doi:10.2307/1252054

Krippendorf, K. (2004). *Content analysis: An introduction to its methodology* (2nd ed.). Thousand Oaks, CA: Sage.

Malhotra, A., Malhotra, C. K., & See, A. (2013). How to Create Brand Engagement on Facebook. *MIT Sloan Management Review, 54*(2), 18–20.

Mehdizadeh, S. (2010). Self-presentation 2.0: Narcissism and self-esteem on Facebook. *Cyberpsychology, Behavior, and Social Networking, 13*(4), 357–364. doi:10.1089/cyber.2009.0257 PMID:20712493

Miranda, F.J., Chamorro, A., Rubio, S., & Rodriquez, O. (2014). Professional Sports Teams on Social Networks: A Comparative Study Employing the Facebook Assessment Index. *International Journal of Sport Communication, 7*, 74-89.

NVivo. (2012). Retrieved April 26, 2015 from http://www.qsrinternational.com/products_nvivo.aspx

O'Donoghue, T., & Punch, K. (2003). *Qualitative Educational Research in Action: Doing and Reflecting*. London: Routledge.

Pedersen, P., Laucella, P., Miloch, K., & Fielding, L. (2007). The juxtaposition of sport and communication: Defining the field of sport communication. *International Journal of Sport Management and Marketing, 2*(3), 193–207. doi:10.1504/IJSMM.2007.012400

Pedersen, P. M., Miloch, K. S., & Laucella, P. C. (2007). *Strategic sport communication*. Champaign, IL: Human Kinetics.

Pegoraro, A. (2010). Look who's talking: Athletes on Twitter: A case study. *International Journal of Sport Communication, 3*(4), 501–514.

Pritchard, M., & Funk, D. (2010). The formation and effect of attitude importance in professional sport. *European Journal of Marketing, 4*(7/8), 1017–1036. doi:10.1108/03090561011047508

Pronschinske, M., Groza, M. D., & Walker, M. (2012). Attracting facebook tans': The importance of authenticity and engagement as a social networking strategy for professional sport teams. *Sport Marketing Quarterly, 21*(4), 221–231.

Raacke, J., & Bonds-Raacke, J. (2008). Myspace and facebook: Applying the uses and gratifications theory to exploring friend-networking sites. *Cyberpsychology & Behavior, 11*(2), 169–174. doi:10.1089/cpb.2007.0056 PMID:18422409

Riffe, D., Lacy, S., & Fico, F. G. (2008). *Analyzing media messages: Using quantitative content analysis in research* (2nd ed.). New York, NY: Taylor and Francis Group.

Ross, S. (2006). A conceptual framework for understanding spectator-based brand equity. *Journal of Sport Management, 20*, 22–38.

Ross, S. (2007). Segmenting sport fans using brand associations: A cluster analysis. *Sport Marketing Quarterly, 16*, 15–24.

Ross, S., Bang, H., & Lee, S. (2007). Assessing brand associations for intercollegiate ice hockey. *Sport Marketing Quarterly, 16*, 106–114.

Ross, S., James, J., & Vargas, P. (2006). Development of a scale to measure team brand associations in professional sport. *Journal of Sport Management, 20*, 260–279.

Sanderson, J. (2010). Framing Tiger's troubles: Comparing traditional and social media. *International Journal of Sport Communication, 3*(4), 438–453.

Schultz, B., & Sheffer, M. (2010). An exploratory study of how Twitter is affecting sports journalism. *International Journal of Sport Communication, 3*, 226–239.

Scott, O. K. M., Bradshaw, R., & Larkin, P. (2013). Exploring ways in which social networkers contribute to online groups: A case study of one Facebook group's discussion of Australian broadcaster channel 9 during the 2010 Winter Olympic Games. *First Monday, 18*(4). Retrieved from http://firstmonday.org/ojs/index.php/fm/article/view/4316/3426

Stavros, C., Meng, M. D., Westberg, K., & Farrelly, F. (2014). Understanding fan motivation for interacting on social media. *Sport Management Review, 17*(4), 455–469. doi:10.1016/j.smr.2013.11.004

Thompson, A-J., & Martin, A. J., Gee, S., & Eagleman, A., N. (2014). Examining the development of a social media strategy for a national sport organisation: A cast study of Tennis New Zealand. *Journal of Applied Sport Management, 6*(2), 42–69.

Usulu, Y. (2010). Determinant factors of time spent on Facebook: Brand community engagement and usage types. *Journal of Yasar University, 18*(5), 2949–2957.

Wallace, L., Wilson, J., & Miloch, K. S. (2011). Sporting Facebook: A content analysis of NCAA organizational sport pages and big 12 conference athletic department pages. *International Journal of Sport Communication, 4*(4), 422–444.

Waters, R. D., Burke, K. A., Jackson, Z. J., & Buning, J. D. (2011). Using stewardship to cultivate fandom online: Comparing how national football league teams use their web sites and facebook to engage their fans. *International Journal of Sport Communication, 4*(2), 163–177.

Watkins, B. (2014). Social Identification and Social Media in Sports. In A. C. Billings & M. Hardin (Eds.), *Routledge Handbook of Sport and New Media* (pp. 200–210). Oxford, UK: Routledge.

We are Social. (2015). *Digital, Social and Mobile Worldwide Report*. Accessed 8 August 2015 from http://wearesocial.net/blog/2015/01/digital-social-mobile-worldwide-2015/

Williams, J., & Chinn, S. J. (2010). Meeting relationship-marketing goals through social media: A conceptual model for sport marketers. *International Journal of Sport Communication*, *3*(4), 422–437.

Wilson, K., Fornasier, S., & White, K. (2010). Psychological predictors of young adults' use of social networking sites. *Cyberpsychology, Behavior, and Social Networking*, *13*(2), 173–177. doi:10.1089/cyber.2009.0094 PMID:20528274

Wimmer, R. D., & Dominick, J. R. (2006). *Mass media research: An introduction* (8th ed.). Belmont, CA: Thomson Higher Education.

Wright, E., Khanfar, N., Harrington, C., & Kizer, L. (2010). The lasting effects of social media trends on advertising. *Journal of Business & Economics Research*, *8*, 73–80.

Yang, T. (2012). The decision behavior of Facebook users. *Journal of Computer Information Systems*, *52*(3), 50–59.

This research was previously published in the International Journal of Public Administration in the Digital Age (IJPADA), 4(1); edited by Christopher G. Reddick and Manuel Pedro Rodríguez Bolívar, pages 69-87, copyright year 2017 by IGI Publishing (an imprint of IGI Global).

Chapter 7
Sports Marketing and Social Media

Reza Mohammadkazemi
University of Tehran, Iran

ABSTRACT

In this chapter, we are going to focus on the impact of Social media to change the marketing world in every industry. Social media marketing (SMM) has had a particular impact in the field of sports marketing. Social media in sports has effectively rendered a new style of communication with important implications for the field. The fans' connection to sports is changing and social media is creating a whole new channel for the fans to interact and be a part of the action beyond that which they may hope to achieve by physically being present at the stadium or the ballpark. Sports organizations today are reliant upon social media for their continued success and growth. This chapter describes how social media is being used amongst sports organizations and how it has changed the sports industry.

INTRODUCTION

Sport is not just a game. Ever since the first bookkeeper took the first bet from the first punter on a game's result, sport has been a business. Sports constitute big business. For instance, the combined, the four big leagues in America, National Basketball Association (NBA), Major League Baseball (MLB), the National Football League (NFL) and the National Hockey League (NHL) generate approximately $23 billion in revenue over a typical year; and, that's just the tip of the iceberg. U.S. sporting equipment sales at retail sporting goods stores are $42.6 billion yearly, according to U.S. government figures. The myriad avenues for profit in the sports industry contribute its complexity; these include ticket sales, sports video games, licensed products, and copyrights, sporting goods, sports-related advertising, Sport Media, stadium naming fees and facilities income. Social media can be an effective solution to increasing revenues by targeting the various avenues for profit effectively (Plunkett, 2012)

DOI: 10.4018/978-1-5225-5475-2.ch007

What Is Social Media?

According to Wikipedia, social media is defined as internet-based tools for sharing and discussing information among human beings. The term 'social media' is the combination of two words: 'social' and 'media.' Media commonly refers to advertisement and the communication of ideas or information through publications or channels. Social represents the interaction of individuals within a group or community. Taken together, social media refers to communication and collaboration platforms which are sustained generated by the interpersonal interaction of individuals through the privileged tool or medium (Szu, 2014).

Social media is the social interplay among people, through which they share, or create information and opinions in virtual communities and social networks. Media for social interaction is using highly accessible and scalable communication techniques (Wysocki, 2012). Social media is the use of web-based and mobile technologies to turn communication into interactive dialogue. Kietsmann, Hermkens, McCarthy, and Silvestre (2011) stated "social media is comprised of mobile and web based technologies that provide interactive platforms for the public to share, create, discuss, and modify content".

Generally Social media enables us to watch and share videos and photos, engage in online conversations, read and write blogs, and post on social network sites or comment on others' postings. Thus, it can be gathered from the diversity of these activities that social media is a vast term for multifarious platforms, tools and content that enable people to exchange, create and use information (Mohammadkazemi, 2013).

Classification of Social Media

Social media has many different forms including magazines, Internet forums, weblogs, social blogs, micro blogging, wikis, social networks, podcasts, photographs or pictures, video, rating and social bookmarking. By applying a set of theories in the field of media research (social presence, media richness) and social processes (self-presentation, self-disclosure Table 1), Kaplan and Haenlein created a classification scheme (Table 1), with seven different types of social media (Haenlein, 2010).

1. Collaborative projects (for example, Wikipedia).

Projects research focuses on technology that affects societies groups, organizations and communities, for example, text chat and voice mail and text chat. It has improved from collaborative work study of supporting people's work activities and working relationships (Klieber, 2009).

2. Blogs and microblogs (for example, Twitter).

A blog is a Web page that serves as a publicly available personal journal for an individual. Commonly updated daily, blogs often reflect the personality of the author. A microblog varies from a traditional blog in that its content is generally smaller in both actual and aggregated file size (Humphreys, 2010).

3. Social news networking sites (for example, Digg and Leaker net).

A social news website reflects user-posted stories that are ranked based on amicably. Users can comment on these posts, and these comments may also be ranked. Since their emergence with the birth of web 2.0, these sites are used to link many types of information including support, news, humor, and discussion. Social news sites allegedly facilitate democratic participation on the web (By Jesse Holcomb, 2013).

4. Content communities (for example, YouTube and Daily Motion).

Content communities permit users to share online multimedia materials. Famed content communities include Flickr, YouTube and SlideShare. After registering for an account, users upload their materials, describe them, and make them publicly available. Visitors search the content communities by subscribe, keyword, to individual users, and send feedback on the content (Carlisle George, 2007).

5. Social networking sites (for example, Facebook).

A social networking service is a platform to build social networks or social relations among people who, for example, share activities, interest, backgrounds, or real-life connections (Cecconi, 2007).

6. Virtual game-worlds (e.g., World of Warcraft).

Virtual gaming is where a person can experience being in a three-dimensional environment and interact with that environment during a game. This is a vital part of the game (Whitton, 2008).

7. Virtual social worlds (e.g. Second Life).

A virtual world is a computer-based online community environment that is designed by and shared among individuals so that they can interact in a tailored, simulated world. Users interact with each other in this simulated world using text-based, two-dimensional or three-dimensional graphical models called avatars (haenlein, 2009). These segmentations between the different types of social media have become increasingly blurred. For example, Shi, Rui and Whinston (Whinston, 2013)allege that Twitter, as composition of broadcasting service and social network, classes as a social broadcasting technology.

Who Are Social Network Sites Users?

There is a great deal of demographic variation (e.g., age, sex, race, income, and educational attainment) among those who use different social networks.

Table 1. Classification of Social Media by social presence/media richness and self-presentation/self-disclosure

		Social Presence/Media Richness		
		Low	**Medium**	**High**
Self-presentation / Self-disclosure	High	Blogs	Social networking sites (e.g., Facebook)	Virtual social worlds (e.g., Second Life)
	Low	Collaborative projects (e.g., Wikipedia)	Content communities (e.g., YouTube)	Virtual game worlds (e.g., World of Warcraft)

According to a 2011 report from the Pew Research Center's Internet &American Life Project (Humpton, Goulel, Rainie, &Purcell, 2011) that you can see in Figure 1, about half of American adults (47 percent), or 59 percent of Internet users in America, state that they use at least one social networking site (common reasons cited for use of social networking are illustrated in Figure 2). This is close to double the 26% of adults (34% of internet users) who used a social network site in 2008. Internet users of all ages are more likely to use a social network site today than they were in 2008 the growth of social network site use has been most pronounced among those who are over the age of 35. In 2008 only 18% of internet users 36 and older used a social network site, by 2010 48% of internet users over the age of 35 were using a social network site. This is about twice the growth experienced by internet users 18-35; 63% of whom used a social network site in 2008 compared with 80% in 2010. Among other things, this means the average age of adult-social network site users has shifted from 33 in 2008 to 38 in 2010.

Why Do People Use Social Network Sites?

In 2011, IBM developed a survey of almost 1,000 consumers for its annual CRM Study. One of the questions asked was why consumers were active on social networks. At the top of the list with 70%, not surprisingly, was the aim of connecting with family and friends. In second with 49%, consumers revealed that they were looking to stay connected to relevant news and information. Just behind with

Figure 1. Age distribution of social networking site users in 2008 and 2012. % of social networking site users in each age group for instance in 2008, 28% of social networking sites users were 18-22, but in 2010 that age group made up 16% of social networking site users.

Source: Pew Research Center's Internet &American Life social Network site survey conducted on landline and cell phone between October 20-November 28, 2010. N for full sample is 2,225 and margin of error is +/- 2.3 percentage points. N for social network site and Twitter users is 975 and margin of error is +/- 3.5 percentage points.

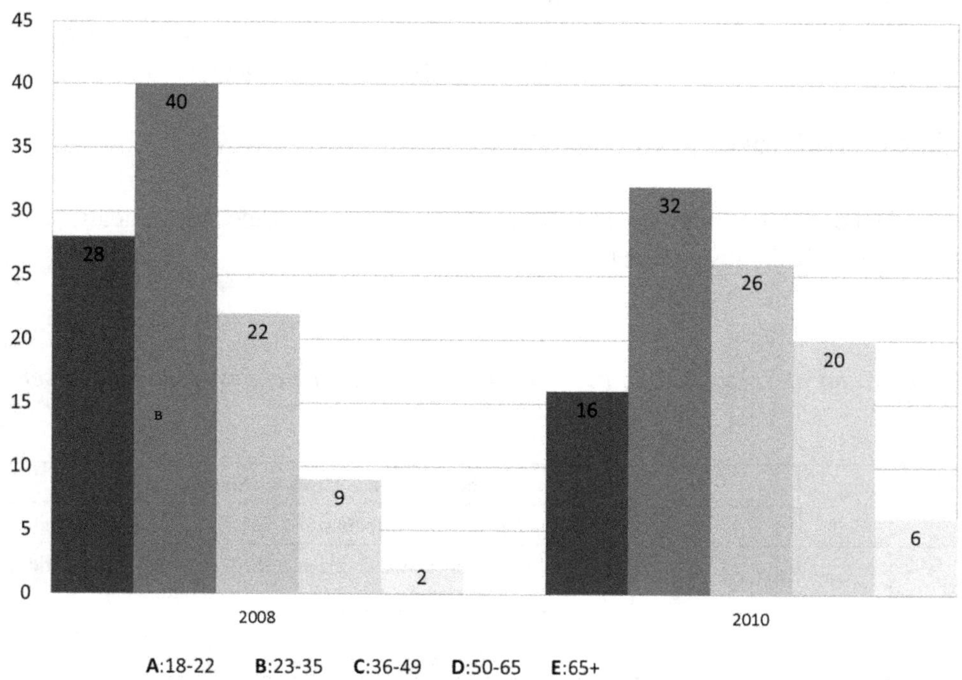

46%, consumers expressed the desire for entertainment. And, last but certainly not least, 42% wished to share reviews of company or product experiences (Parasnis, 2011). Figure 2 shows some reasons why people use social network sites.

And Why Do Sport Fans Use Social Networks?

Through the social network sites fans can:

- **Get a Pre-Game Buzz Going:** While their players and coaches are warming up, they can go over the game plan, and get in the zone, some social media company will be hard at work, connecting with fans online who can't wait for the game to begin.
- **Live Tweet Their Games:** When a fan can't make a game, how can he be part of the action? Through social media! Regular updates can make fans feel like they're really there (Lee, 2014).
- **Participate in Discussions After Games:** There's nothing like a good debate after a close match. Social media enables fans to continue discourse about matches and their favorite teams beyond the actual game times and thus foster a continued dialogue.
- **Promote Each Player:** The most loyal fans feel as if they have a connection with their favorite players. Social media can provide exclusive interviews, and contests for autographed jerseys and caps. Thus, social media can enable fans to more easily and closely interact with teams and engender a sense of greater closeness with individual players.

Figure 2. Reasons consumers go to social media or social networking sites. Note: Sample size N = 1056.
Source: IBM institute for Business Value analysis. CRM study 2011.

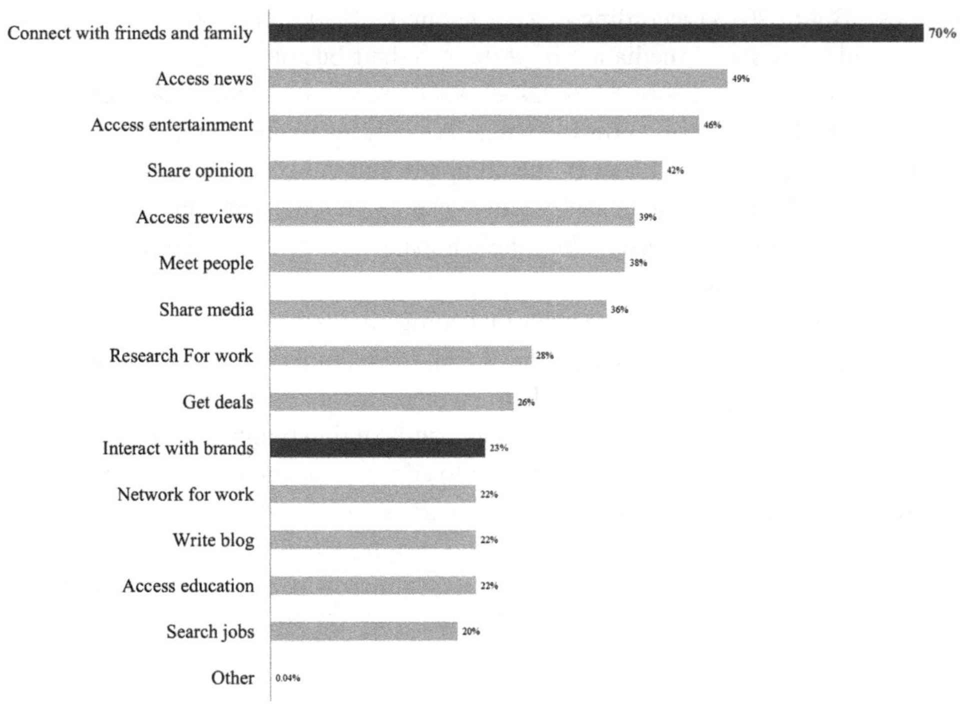

- **Stay Active During the Off-Season:** A consistent social media schedule will keep the engagement going until the next season comes around.
- **Handle a Scandal:** Unfortunately, scandals are often a part of sports. An online presence gives fans the platform they need to address these little hiccups, but will they know what to say? A good social media company will have just the right words.

Social Media and Companies

Social Media and social networking sites today are the best route available to a brand for connecting with potential customers because they allow companies to reach out to potential customers without spending exorbitant amounts of money on advertising. Through interactive exchanges that can often be financially of little or no cost for companies, social media enables continued brand presence and brand engagement which can contribute to fostering brand awareness and loyalty. These new media inspire public trust of audiences by connecting with them at a more significant level. Social media marketing is the new motto for many brands; Social networking Traders are taking note of many social media opportunities and beginning to achieve new social improvisation at a higher rate than ever before. Social media marketing and the businesses that take advantage of it have become more experienced (Almotairi, 2014).

Not surprisingly, firms of all types and sizes are using social media for marketing and public relation fuss. The increase of the social media and sequential advances in technology obviously create incomparable and excellent opportunities for those able to invest on them.

In fact Social media is now essential demands. Social media has altered the way we communicate with others and how we exchange information. And for companies it provides a marketing opportunity that overcomes the traditional medium and connects them directly with customers. This is why many businesses—from giants like Starbucks and IBM to the local ice cream shops—are exploring social media marketing initiatives (Neti, 2011). Not so long ago, marketers were unsure about using social media for business .But in 2013 (according to a survey in the USA, over 3000 marketers) a significant 86% of marketers said that social media are important to their businesses (Stelzner, 2013)In the early days, emails and websites first supported businesses, social media is the next marketing wave. With the appearance of social media, marketing now has a wholly different reach and return (Story, 2007). Social media makes a two-way connection between the company and the customer, where both can communicate with one another. It can be one of the practical examples for a win-win condition, the customer can state his opinion and get a response, while the company gets to dive deep into customer care and distinguish their overall performance.

Mangold and Faulds (2009)noticed nine ways that companies use social media successfully; (1) provide networking platforms, (2) use blogs and other social media tools to engage customers, (3) use both traditional and Internet-based promotional tools to engage customers, (4) provide information, (5) be outrageous, (6) provide exclusivity, (7) design products with talking points and consumers' desired self-images in mind, (8) support causes that are important to consumers, and (9) utilize the power of stories.

The advent of mobile technology, particularly in regard to increased availability of social media and mobile marketing has become vital to business efforts. Wright, Khanfar, Harrington, and Kizer (2010) hypothesize that using mobile technology to contact a customer is becoming more efficient than traditional methods of marketing, communication, and advertising. Traditional methods of marketing like radio, television, and magazine are capable of connecting to a large population but these mediums are too general (Hana S. Noor Al-Deen, 2013). Social media efforts, specifically through mobile technology, are becoming more valuable in reaching particular audiences and tailoring the message based on each individual consumer. The increase in mobile marketing and interactive marketing is expected to continue its growth (Wright et al., 2010).

Sport Marketing

The term 'marketing' is being used in a variety of ways. Some think of marketing as the use of advertising, publicity and personal selling strategy to make others know about a product, or to attract more consumers to purchase it. However, marketing is much more comprehensive than this narrow conception. Simply stated, marketing means to be focused on satisfying the needs and wants of customers or consumers. In turn, this means that sport marketing is focused on meeting the needs of sport customers or consumers, including people who take part in playing sport, watching or listening to sport news and programmers, collecting memorabilia, purchasing merchandise, buying sporting goods like shirts and shoes, or even surfing a sport website to find out the latest about their favorite team, player or event. A sport consumer is someone who generally uses sport products or services. A sport customer is someone who pays for the use of a specific product or service (BLlythe, 2005). It is acceptable to use the terms inter-changeably to refer to those people who use and pay for sport products and services.

Sport Is a Unique Product

Sports marketing are the combination of marketing concepts to sport services and products, and the marketing of nonrelated sport products through sport events (Merz, 2008). Sports marketing therefore have two principal aspects. First, it is the usage of general marketing practices to sport products and services. Second, it is the marketing of other industrial products or services through sport. Like any other marketing, sport marketing tracks to meet the needs and wants of consumers. It attains this by providing sport-related products and services to consumers. However, sport marketing is dissimilar to formal marketing in that it also has the ability to encourage the consumption of non-sport products and services by association. It is rational to understand that sport marketing means the marketing of sport plus the use of sport as a tool to market other products and services.

For example, the marketing of sport products and services directly to sport consumers could include sporting equipment, professional competitions, sport events and local clubs. Other examples include selling season tickets, team advertising, designing a publicity stunt to promote an athlete, and developing licensed apparel for sale. Marketing through sport happens when a non-sport product is marketed through an association to sport. Some examples could include a well-known athlete endorsing a biscuit, a firm sponsoring a sport event, or even beverages companies arranging to have exclusive rights to provide drink at a sport venue or event (Coca Cola n.d.).

The two aspects of sport marketing are central to understanding the full range of ways in which sport is used. But the weakness is that they tend to emphasize the selling part of sport marketing (Smith A., 2008). Before any dealing occurs, a long term strategic analysis must be planned in order to find out what sport customers want and what the best methods of delivering it are. As a result, sport marketing should also be considered as a set of planning and accomplishment activities related to the delivery of a sport product or service.

Before any sales, a sport product or service must take a place in the mind of a consumer. Actually, this demands that a costumer is cognizant of the sport product or service and has responded to it in some way. The process of developing such a response is known as branding, and when a sport brand has found a firm place in consumers' minds, then can be said that it is positioned (Smith A Z., 2008a)The result of successful branding and having strong market position are not only a single transaction but also sport marketing has mirrored the establishment of a steady relationship between a sport brand and its users.

Sport Marketing Mix Elements

A strategy sports organization utilized commonly is the "Marketing Mix". This tool consists of four variables known as the "Four P's" of marketing. The marketing mix blends these variables together to produce the results it wants to gain in its specific target market. The following describes the four P's of marketing:

- **Product:** Products are the goods and services that business provides to sale to target market (Gates, 2013). When developing a product quality, design, features, packaging, customer service and any subsequent after-sales service must be considered. Usually it is manufacturers who decide what products to produce and people have to choose among them. However, through social network interactions, customers can post about their needs and product desires and companies can react. For example Adidas blogs and sites receive customers' demands and produce exclusive products for customers (Anderson, 2014).
- **Place:** Place refers to distribution, location and methods of delivering the product to the customer. This includes the location of the business, shop front, distributors and logistics. E-commerce and social networking has given a new future to this element (Rank, n.d.). Customers are able to purchase directly from manufactures independent from any brokers.
- **Price:** Price is the amount of money that customers have to pay in order to buy products. The price charged for a product will depend on a number of factors: the cost to make it, the amount of profit required, competitor prices and the price consumers are willing to pay (Owomoyela, 2013). Customers can utilize the internet and social media to discuss and compare prices.
- **Promotion:** Promotion concerns the act of communicating with consumers to aware of value of the product. It then involves persuading general consumers to become customers of the business using methods such as advertising, direct marketing, personal selling and sales promotion (Moor Hall, 2009). Social media have the key role in this element. This can be better conceptualized via the social media marketing mix strategy of Manchester United.

What are the key elements of the marketing mix of Manchester United? All *products* consist of presenting an excellent football team that plays and wins in an incredible way. Moreover, there are other components of the product including trading such as the sale of shirts, and a variety of memorabilia (for more information visit www.manutd.com. The product also allocated to television rights, and Manchester United's own television channel. In one respect the *place* is Old Trafford where home games are played, but Manchester United also plays at a range of other venues. And, of course its products are sold through club's website and a range of other social media.

Manchester United markets as a worldwide brand. The club also engages in a variety of *promotional* activities, for example with the mobile phone company Vodafone. Manchester United books, shirts, key rings, programs and many other items are sold and promoted through its website. Positioning or repositioning a product - refers to locating that product within a market for example presenting it is a down-market or up-market product. It is a product for younger consumers or older consumers (Matthey, 2012).

A Move From the 4 P's to the 4c's

Today's companies, marketers and brands face an ever changing environment and with the continuing developments in computers and communication technology, the increase in consumers' knowledge about what they want and needs, the way we communicate to consumers should change as well. A different perspective to marketing is necessary to provide for the consumer effectively and efficiently in order to build long lasting relationships. Marketing in this day and age needs to be a two-way communication process.

Bob Lauterborn, professor of advertising at the University of North Carolina has tracked the success of new products introduced into the U.S (Lemly, 2013). According to Bob, 80 percent of new products fail each year. With such a high failure rate, Bob notes that something isn't working with our "mindset". He wants to replace the Four P's with his Four C's.1-Product is replaced by Consumer, 2- Price is replaced by Cost, 3- Place is replaced by Convenience, 4-Promotion is replace by Communication.

- **From Product to Consumer**

The rule of four C's of marketing mentions that customers should be the priority. Inversely, the traditional marketing mix focus is on Products, in the 4 C's model, the primary focus is on the customer. So the companies which follow this strategy believe in producing products which satisfy their consumers. While the extreme interpretation of focusing on the customer would be to provide customizable products informed by individual customer desires and preferences, this is typically only an option for smaller marketing and not for mass markets. For mass markets, the traditional marketing mix can be used (curvecommunications, 2013). The Consumer model could be known as a conversation between the customer and the business, they come together to create a custom-tailored product to satisfy a customer's demands. One of the most important innovations that the social media has contributed to products is enhanced personalization and customization. Two complete processes that allow customers to design their own product that will satisfy their needs and wants (Thirumalai, 2011). By providing "the right content in the right format to the right person at the right time (Ho, 2005)", companies are trying to provide solutions to their customers, rather than selling them a single product. The Consumer model could be known as a conversation between the customer and the business, they come together to create a custom- tailored product to satisfy a customer's demands.

- **From Price to Cost**

Cost replaces to pricing in the traditional marketing mix. Cost is a very important consideration during consumer decision making and hence in the 4 C's rule, the cost variable is given special attention. Online customers don not only look at the price that is quoted on the websites, but also compare competitor prices (Pradeep Kr, 2011).

- **From Place to Convenience**

Convenience replaces placement or distribution of the traditional marketing mix. Companies must think of convenience to buy for costumers instead of place.

Thus convenience, like place, plays a critical role. The customers the will not buy the product if it is not convenient to them. Convenience is one of the most important reasons that users come online to do transactions or to make sales enquiries. The core meaning of "convenience" in marketing mix is "accessibility to the service" which became easy via the Internet (McClean, 2012). In sport industry place could be a stadium, gym, tennis court, etc. They can't be easily moved to accommodate customers. The matter is how can it be convenience for customers to buy and use sports product? And how can sport product be available to customers at their home? Official sites for many types of sports like NFL, NHL, and MLB are the solution to the place versus convenience concept. For example listener can pay to have all MLB broadcasts in their home, car or on their mobiles (Chelladturai, 2013).

- **From Promotion to Communication**

Promotion concept in traditional marketing is a one-way message but communication is a two-way interaction. Instead of virtuous pronouncement about how good the product or service is, consumer today seek to be engaged and have meaningful interactions with companies. Even traditional media like television channels and radio are starting to have their own websites and use social media like Twitter and Facebook. Recently, many kinds of sports organizations have found out that Lauterborn's fourth C is more effective (Chelladturai, 2013).

Why Should Sport Companies Use Social Networks?

There are many reasons why companies should use social networks. Ten key reasons are summarized below:

Cost-Effective

Social networking in a business promotional plan allows stretching advertising dollars further than usual. The budget that companies set for promotions can be used for other forms of advertising or to prepare prizes for social networking contests or promotions. some sports organization allocated budget which remained from advertising for their active online fans redeem tangible prizes of their choice (Evans, 2010). For example Baylor football team offers prizes including season tickets to a sport of the winner's choice, lunch with the coach or team gear (visit www.baylorbears.com).

Reach

Social networking allows the sport companies to reach a wide audience and fans. Consumers are increasingly reliant on technology and social media. The 2012 London Olympics could have about 1 billion fans but how is it possible? Sports fans worldwide viewed events, received updates, and monitored results by using digital device and social network sites (Media[BM], 2012).

Connection

Traditional marketing campaigns miss out on the two -way communication between their business and customers. Social networking gives companies a more personal connection with their customers. For instant Mufaddal Choonia, Chief Executive Officer, Mahindra Racing, believes that one of the reasons for their success comes back to digital and social media. He says "social network site is extremely important for us since it's the only two-way conversation we can have with the fan. We get members to interact with the team and (Chopra, 2014).

Flexibility

Online marketing through sports social sites gives companies more flexibility in the type of promotion they do. Companies can send out information on special deals, general information or tips about their industry, company information and contests. The informal nature of the sites allows sharing things that companies wouldn't with traditional print advertising. Brazil is selling World cup ticket online and through social network sites fans can sell and buy thicket for this event (Smith A., 2014)

Timely

Social networking allows companies to instantly disseminate information to their followers. Traditional marketing requires printing time and may only run a few times (Kerley, 2011). Companies had to plan out their marketing and promotions well in advance. With social media, they can post information immediately as they deem appropriate.

Easier Referrals

Customers need to trust before purchasing. They trust their friends. Technology makes it easier for customers to share company's information with their online friends. When the customers follow a company's profile online, they can refer it to their friends (Frost, 2014). Many sports club use this theory and provide a social site for their members and obtain many new members because their present consumers invite their friends to join the same club and gym.

Promotions

Special promotions persuade customers to purchase more from the business. This kind of promotion gives new customers an opportunity to try new products or services (Healey, 2014). For these promotional ideas to work effectively, companies need to get the word out. Social networking allows sharing information about the promotions to a large audience.

Increased Web Traffic

Social networking profiles provide a tool for driving traffic to the company's main website. This is particularly beneficial for web-based companies who do most of their business virtually. Including, the website address in social networking profiles and mentioning it in the regular posts leads more people to visit it.

Branding

Social media aids in branding the company. The messages, photos and videos they post on their profile pages build an image of the company. Carefully planned posts that consistently promulgate the company's brand by maintaining a consistent tone and message help to build and maintain a company's success.

Hiring

When a company builds an online presence, it likely will reach potential employees who are savvy in social networking. The larger candidate pool of individuals with technology experience allows the company to find the best candidates when you have openings. These individuals can then use their social networking skills to further promote the company online (Frost, 2014).

Integration of Sports Communication, Marketing and Social Media

Sports touches people live in unique ways, so it should come as no surprise that communication about and marketing sports through social media also require unique approaches. Sport as an agent for bringing people together and as a unique product means that it is an industry where social media can have a dramatic impact on communication and marketing (Chelladturai, 2013). But why is sport a unique product?

1. Aspects of the sport product are intangible.
2. Sport is subjective and heterogeneous.
3. Sports are inconsistent and unpredictable.
4. Sport is perishable.
5. Sport evolves emotions.

Sport Communication

Sports communication is the heart of the sports industry. Pedersen, Miloch and Laucella (2011) define sports communication as the "process by which people in sport, in a sport setting, or through a sport endeavor share symbols as they create meaning through interaction (Neti, 2014a)". Sports communication underline the relationship development between organizations, players, fans, and third parties. Basically, these relationships have pivotal role in the success of each individual team. Sports organizations use mixed media to improve these relationships via internet, television, radio, and papers.

Sports communication is a multi-dimensional phenomenon which includes branding, reputation management, and customer service to sales, marketing, and sponsorship. Further, Rein, Kotler, and Shields impart five principal goals in effective sports communication (1) to increase the tendency for stockholders, (2) to set the sports brand's identity for a long time, (3) to humanize the sports brand, (4) to persuade the stakeholder to identify with the sports brand and feel a personal connection with the participants, and (5) to place the outcomes of competition in more than just a winning context (Wysocki, 2012).

These strategies are vital in relating with stakeholders, sparking interest, and continually building and retaining the fan base.

Sport Communication and Social Media

The number of professional sports teams which use the social networks is increasing swiftly. Social media have changed sports media and its consumption. Fans, athletes and teams now are able to connect with one another easily. Sanderson and Kassing state that social media provide an opportunity to professional teams and athletes together and publish sports news in addition to increasing their self-preservation management (Blair Browning, 2012)

In the past magazines, newspaper then radio and television were the only way of accessing athletes, games, events and news about sports. The feedback of audiences was limited. Sports organization couldn't get direct feedback from audiences. In the 1970s people could watch games live by satellite program (F.Wayne Blann, 2011).Later the technologies like computer, Internet and networks influenced on sport communication. At this time Fans could chose whatever they want from many available options and they were not obliged to consume what media had made for them. Through the social media every person is able to create and transfer information about world of sport at any time. In other words fans have commenced to challenge the media by creating and sharing content independent from them (Mohammmadkazemi, 2011).

Sport World and Social Media

The use of social media by sport industry is increasing steadily. *Teams*, *athletes* and *fans* derive benefit of social media phenomena.

1. **Teams:** Nowadays professional teams and amateur ones use social media because they desire to provide timely updates, to communicate with fans, to receive publicity, etc. Here are a few examples of teams that used social media to grow their brand (Chelladturai, 2013).
    a. **Milwaukee Bucks:** The Milwaukee Bucks are a professional basketball team based in Milwaukee, Wisconsin. They are part of the Central Division of the Eastern Conference in the National Basketball Association (NBA). In 2009 this team built the "Fear the deer" campaign around Twitter, bloggers and YouTube .the team filmed special "fear the deer" videos and showed them at the games and posted them to You tube. Fans and broadcasters have energetic discussion about team via social media.
    b. **Cleveland Indians:** The Cleveland Indians are a professional baseball team based in Cleveland, Ohio, United States Team launched the "Indian Social Media Deck" in 2009.The Indians took a big step into social media. In 2011, The Deck dedicated raised seats in the left field grandstand with WIFI which allows hosting fans to blog or tweet live from the game. More recently, the Indians has moved the Social Deck from left to a luxurious enclosed seating area. It is a great effort to satisfy the social media-savvy fans.
    c. **AFL Alumni Association:** The Arena Football League (AFL) is the highest level of professional indoorAmerican football in the United States(visit w*ww.arenafootball.com)*. The AFL creates a network for members and provides benefits including greater opportunities for community involvement, discounts and promotions, charity communications, job postings, event

advertisements and invitations, Hall of Fame nominations, and opportunities for voting on League issues.

d. **NHL Connect:** NHL Connect is the official fan community of the National Hockey League and includes groups, videos and photos.

2. **The Athletes:** Social media burst into the society and it has been reflected in sports with athletes keeping in touch with their fans to promote themselves and products through Facebook, Twitter and Instagram among other outlets. The athletics, formerly had to rely on traditional media to tell their story but nowadays they just write a blog post or tweet or can make a video to You tube to reach fans. Popular athletes can make substantial sums of money when they are enlisted by third parties to post promotional tweets or pictures to their social media pages.
3. **Fans:** Fans are the largest part of the sports social media. They talk about their favorite team and discuss about the match and referee. Some sports fans preferring to go online for game updates and sports news. It's clear how crucial it is for sports teams to be on social media. Now people can stay up-to-date with the score via Facebook, Twitter, and sports apps. No matter where a fan is for what he or she is doing, it is possible to be interacting with a given team and being apprised of any updates.

Mobile Sport Marketing

Mobile Phone: Mobile phone usage has also become beneficial for social media marketing. Today, many cell phones have social networking capabilities. Individuals are notified of any happenings on social networking sites through their cell phones, in real-time (Kietzmann, 2013). This constant connection to social networking sites means products and companies can constantly remind and update followers about their capabilities, uses, importance, etc. Because cell phones are connected to social networking sites, advertisements are always in sight. Also many companies are now putting QR codes along with products for individuals to access the company website or online services with their smart-phones.

Mobile marketing is a very formidable tool for sports organizations and teams. It permits them to interact and engage, on a personal level, with their fans (consumers), both at the stadium and throughout the season. Additionally, it is a communication medium that is ideal for the sports fans that tend to be younger, more educated, tech savvy, and more in-touch with trends. Sports marketers can take advantages of mobile tactics and campaigns to reach fans in many ways (Nick, 2013)

Text Message: As early as 2011, professional basketball teams like the Chicago Bulls and Phoenix Suns began using sports text marketing to raise the numbers of their fans bases and retain current fans engaged (Nick 2013b). With SMS marketing, fans can be updated on the latest stats, scores and other information via text messages. At that year, famous league soccer team Chicago Fire also began using text message to connect with fans directly (Neman, 2014). The soccer team now makes use of a variety of text marketing tools, including polls in the arena, games, advertising, special offers, and text-to-win promotions. They study the results and use them to understand what fans are looking for and what levels of engagement is convenient for them.

The feedback these teams have received so far has been numerous. It seems the fans enjoy the personalized engagement with their favorite sports organizations. This intimate Communication has proven to make fans feel more closed to their teams and also to get a new, more tech-savvy crowd to become interested in games. Here are just a few ways organizations are using text message marketing for Sports.

1. **Ticket Promotions:** Teams continually run ticket promotions in order to increase ticket sales as well as to attract new fans into the stadium. For example, the team might run an opted-in text message in their stadium programs or on their TV commercials: "Text us to 212121 for an opportunity to win tickets to the playoffs!" When customers text in, organization can repeat market these fans. This increases ticket sales, helps team management to understand what kinds of promotions work and what levels of engagement consumer are willing to commit to.
2. **Scores and Stats:** Teams often use sports text marketing to send out up-to-the-minute scores and statistics to their growing lists of opted-in fans. By giving fans such a simple way to keep up with their favorite teams, sports organizations have an easier time of both maintaining their fans for current or future promotions (Szu, 2014). Stats and Scores are two of the outstanding points of interest for fans, and it's vital for teams to transfer the information that their audience want. So they consumers can trust the organization and brand.
3. **Schedules and Information:** Text message marketing makes it easier for teams to keep fans informed with the very latest schedules and team announcements, which effects being in attendance at games and interest in the teams. Because of text messaging Marketing is one of the most effective communications with consumers, sports organizations can be rather certain that fans are always up to date with the latest changes and team announcements, and so able to plan to watch or attend games (Nick, 2013a). This has a noticeable effect on maintaining consumer and revenue base for sports teams.

Mobile Advertising: Mobile advertising is a form of advertising via mobile (wireless) phones or other mobile devices. It is a subdivision of mobile marketing (Story, 2007)Some commonly types of mobile advertising are mobile web banner or banner advertising that is a kind of advertising on the World Wide Web provided by an advertising server. By click on it, it will be connected to a related-company.

Mobile Application: Mobile applications, also referred to as mobile apps, are software programs that run on smart phones and other mobile device that enable users to connect to websites on their mobile devices in more streamlined and user friendly ways. A mobile app can be a mobile Web site bookmarking utility, a mobile-based instant messaging client, Gmail for mobile, and many other applications (webopedia, 2014). Many sports teams and leagues have their own mobile applications. For example NHL Ice Time is the official app from the National Hockey League; NBA Game Time is the official app from the National Basketball Association.

Mobile Website: A Mobile Site is a website which is especially designed for optimized performance on a mobile. Today, sport fans preferred to access sports scores, feeds, news stories and fantasy leagues through their mobile browsers. One example of a sport mobile website is Sky Sports .It provides the latest sports news, views and video and range of mobile services and applications. Have a general look (Figure 3): Social networking and sports apps dominate in popularity among advertising source (Szu, 2014a).

Competitive Factor: Represents the average number of bids auction.

Today's the evaluation of social media are finding unique ways of generating revenue from the very beginning. Here are a few of the revenue models that some sport organizations use them (Lehtinen, 2013).

1. **Freemium Model:** The word "freemium" is a combining the two aspects of the business model: "free" and "premium" (Hayes, 2008). This business model offers a basic service for free, while users are charging for advanced futures. The freemium business model is popular for companies just starting out as they try to lure users to their software or service. An example of a freemium

Figure 3. 2014. MoPub Mobile Advertising Insights Report

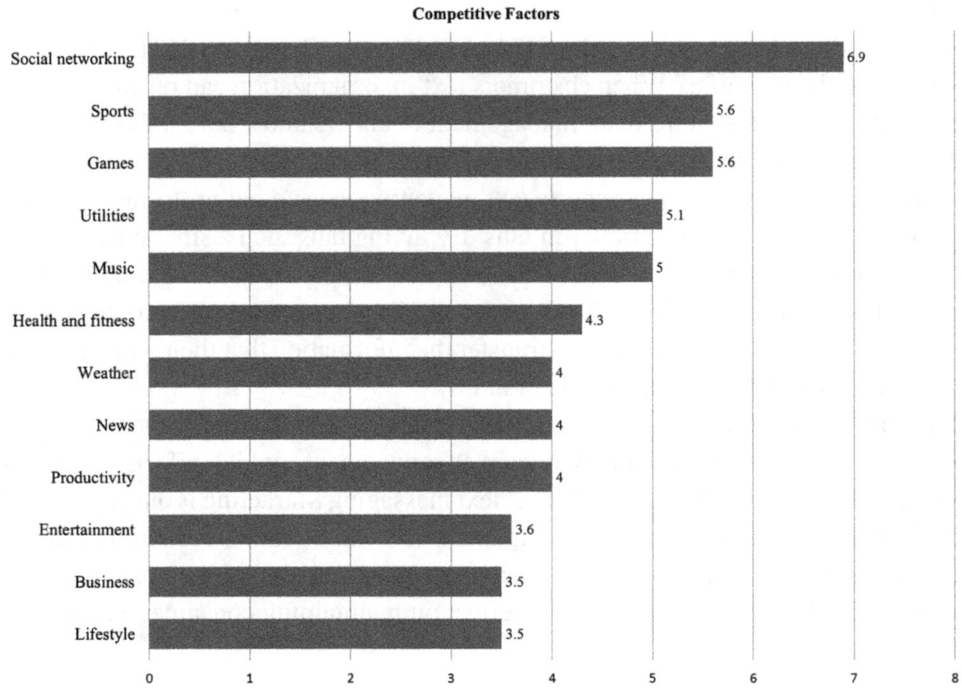

business model is Skype, a company that allows you to make calls over the Internet. Their basic service is free, but for more advanced services you have to pay a premium.

2. **Affiliate Model:** The service generates revenue streams by increasing traffic, leads, or sales to another, affiliated company's website (Helmut Krcmar, 2011). Businesses that sell products depend on affiliated sites service, to send them the traffic or leads that are needed in order to sell. Although high traffic sites use this model more since even low traffic rates can create high revenue streams, there are examples of individual blogs that have been able to yield income using this model (e.g. Shoe Money site).
3. **Subscription Model:** This model asks users to pay monthly or yearly to access to a product or service (Noren, 2013). It gives a chance to companies to have long-term relationships with their customers, which can be better in the long run. Getting the price-points right and preserving personal touch with subscribers are the major challenges in this model (e.g. Netflix, Spotify).
4. **Virtual Goods Model:** Users are paying for virtual goods, such as upgrades, points, or gifts, on a website or in a game. The margins of virtual goods are high, since goods essentially do not cost anything for the service provider (Wauters, 2007). There is little or no marginal or production cost once the economy of the service has been set (e.g. Facebook Gifts, Playdom).
5. **Advertising Model:** This model emphasizes on selling advertising against their traffic. According this model as much as traffic site has the more can be charged for advertising in this site (e.g. Myspace, Yahoo!).

CONCLUSION

Social media in sport marketing explores sports marketing goals in relation to social media tools and concept being used today. The most important change to the sports world dues to the advent of social media. With platforms such as Facebook and Twitter, there are millions of users for sports brands to promote themselves to. The social media industry has incredible effect all businesses including sports businesses. Social media in sport world created a quick and efficient way to communicate with fans and customers by specializing and detailing information in addition, conventional advertising and promotion is enhanced through these communications. Generally it can be said that Social media is speedily becoming a new force in any organizations around the world.

REFERENCES

Almotairi, M. (2014). Social media marketing (SMM) and business organizations. *Journal of Service Science and Management*, 368-376.

Anderson, D. (2014, Jun 27). *Supply Chain Case Study: the Definitive Guide*. Retrieved September 13, 2014, from Supply hainOpz: http://www.supplychainopz.com/2013/07/principles-of-supply-chain-management.html

Armstrong, K. L. (2007). *Sport Marketing*. Ithaca, NY: California State University at Long Beach.

Blair Browning, S. (2012). The positives and negatives of Twitter: Exploring how student-athletes Use Twitter and respond to critical Tweets. *International Journal of Sport Communication*, (5), 503-521.

Bliythe, J. (2005). *Essentials of Marketing*. London: Pearson Education Limited.

Carlisle George, J. (2007). *User-Generated Content Online*. London: Academic Press.

Cecconi, A. (2007). *Management and Evaluation of Instructional Technology and Distance Education Program*. Nova Southeastern University.

Chelladturai, T. N. (2013). *Social media in sport marketing*. Scottsdale, AZ: Holocomb Hathaway.

Chopra, R. (2014, Jun 11). *Campaign India Agency Report Card*. Retrieved Jun 17, 2014, from Campaign of India: http://www.campaignindia.in/Author/242587,raahil-chopra.aspx

Coca-Cola Company. (n.d.). *A Short History of Coca Cola*. Retrieved 7 27, 2014, from The Coca-Cola Company: www.thecoca-colacompany.com

Curvecommunications. (2013, May 10). *4C's of marketing*. Retrieved 5 8, 2014, from curve communication: http://www.curvecommunications.com/2013/05/the-four-cs-of-marketing/

Evans, D. (2010). *Social media marketing*. New York, NY: Wiely Publishing.

Frost, S. (2014, March). *Top 10 reasons a business should use social networking in its promotional plan.* Retrieved December 11, 2014, from Chron: http://smallbusiness.chron.com/top-10-reasons-business-should-use-social-networking-its-promotional-plan-20337.html

Gates, W. (2013, January 9). *The 4p's of marketing*. Retrieved May 22, 2014, from Small Biz Connect. Retrieved from http://toolkit.smallbiz.nsw.gov.au/part/3/12/56

Haenlein, A. M. (2010). Users of the world, unite! The challenges and opportunities of social media. Elsevier.

Haenlein, A. M. (2009). *The fairyland of second life: virtual social worlds and how to use them.* Elsevier.

Hana S. Noor Al-Deen, J. (2013). *Social Media: Usage and Impact.* Lanham, MD: Lexington Books.

Hayes, T. (2008). How Network Culture is Revolutionizing Business. *Jump Point*, 195.

Healey, M. (2014, February 16). *The business of going digital.* Retrieved September 25, 2014, from Jumping The Digital Shark: http://reports.informationweek.com/abstract/83/12521/IT-Business-Strategy/The-Business-of-Going-Digital.html

Helmut Krcmar, M. B. (2011). Innovation, Society and business:Internet-based business models. *Berlin Symposium.*

Ho, T. (2005). Web Personalization as a Persuation Strategy. *Information Systems Research*, 271–291.

Humphreys, L. (2010). Technological Determinism. Encyclopedia of Science and Technology Communication, 2, 869.

Jan, H., & Kietzmann, K. (2011). Social media? Get serious! Understanding the functional building blocks of social media. Elsevier.

Jesse Holcomb, J. G. (2013). *News use across social media platforms.* Retrieved 5 7, 2014, from Pew Research Center: http://www.journalism.org/2013/11/14/news-use-across-social-media-platforms

Kerley, P. (2011, March 28). *How businesses can survive a product recall using social media.* Retrieved September 28, 2014, from Mashable: http://mashable.com/2011/03/28/social-media-product-recalls/

Kerley. (2011). Retrieved from http://mashable.com/2011/03/28/social-media-product-recalls/

Kietzmann, J. C. (2013). Bittersweet! Understanding and Managing Electronic Word of Mouth. *Journal of Public Affairs*, 146-159.

Klieber, P. (2009). (n.d.). Document Classification Through data Mining Social media Networks. *Steson University.*

Kotler, P. (2012). *Marketing Managment.* Pearson Education.

Lee, A. (2014). *Socila Media Examiner.* Retrieved from http://www.socialmediaexaminer.com/

Lemly, A. (2013, January). *The 4 Cs of marketing*. Retrieved May 12, 2014, from Prezi: http://prezi.com/sqhc9apzsstu/the-4-cs-of-marketing

Matthey, J. (2012, March 15). *International marketing*. Retrieved August 5, 2014, from Businesscasestudies: http://businesscasestudies.co.uk

McClean, R. (2012, October 19). *The 4 C's versus the 4 P's of Marketing*. Retrieved 4 19, 2014, from Custom Fit: http://www.customfitonline.com/news/2012/10/19/4-cs-versus-the-4-ps-of-marketing/

Media, B. (2012, September 21). *Sports Fans and Digital Media*. Retrieved May 4, 2014, from Online Insights: http://www.onlineinsight.com

Merz, S. F. (2008). The four domains of sports marketing: A conceptual framework. *Sport Marketing Quarterly*, 90-108.

Mohammmadkazemi, R. T. (2011). Comparative Study of Promotion element among Pro league of Iran, South Korea & Japan. *Journal of Business Management Perspective*, *10*(7). (In Persian).

Moor Hall, C. (2009). *How to achieve an effective promotional mix*. Berkshire, UK: The Chartered Institute of Marketing.

Neman, S. (2014). *SMS campaigns are boosting mobile engagement for sports teams*. Retrieved April 26, 2014, from ez texting: https://www.eztexting.com/mobile-marketing-center/resources/boosting-mobile-engagement-for-sports-teams

Neti, S. (2011). Social media and its role marketing social media. *International Journal of Enterprise Computing and Business Systems*, 2.

Nic. (2013). *How Sports Organizations are Using Text Messaging*. Retrieved from https://www.callfire.com/blog/2013/11/19/how-sports-organizations-are-using-text-messaging

Nick. (2013, November 19). *How sports organizations areusing text messaging*. Retrieved February 25, 2014, from Callfire: https://www.callfire.com/blog/2013/11/19/how-sports-organizations-are-using-text-messaging

Noren, E. (2013). *The subscription business model*. Retrieved from digitalbusinessmodel: http://www.digitalbusinessmodelguru.com

Owomoyela. (2013). Investigating the impact of market mix elements on consumer loyalty: an emprical study on nigerian breweries plc. *Interdisciplinary of Contemporary Research in Business*, 59-62.

Parasnis, C. H. (2011). *IBM Institute for Business Value*. IBM Institute.

Plunkett, J. (2012). *Market Research*. Retrieved 3 5, 2014, from Plunkettresearch: http://www.plunkettresearch.com

Pradeep Kr, J. (2011). Break Down Of Marketing P's: "A New Evolution". *International journal of Business and Management Research*, 59-63.

Rank, J. (n.d.). *Distribution channels*. Retrieved August 5, 2014, from In Encyclopædia Reference for Business: http://www.referenceforbusiness.com/small/Di-Eq/Distribution-Channels.html

Smith, A. (2008). *Introduction to sport marketing*. New York, NY: Butterworth Heinemann. doi:10.1016/B978-0-7506-8685-3.50004-2

Smith, A. (2014, July 7). *Footballticketexchange*. Retrieved August 13, 2014, from Worldfootballticketexchange: www.worldfootballticketexchange.com

Stelzner, M. (2013). *Social media marketing industry report*. San Diego, CA: Social Media Examiner.

Story, L. (2007). *media and advertising*. Retrieved from nytimes: http://www.nytimes.com/2007/06/28/business/media/28adco.html?_r=1&

Story, L. (2007). *Media and Advertising*. Retrieved from The New Yourk times: http://www.nytimes.com

Szu, E. (2014, September 13). *Mobile advertising market report*. Retrieved November 19, 2014, from slideshare: http://www.slideshare.net/lainians/mo-pub-mobile-advertising-marketplace-report-2012-q3

Thirumalai, S. (2011). An Empirical Exploration of the Sources and Financial Consequences. Carlson School of Management, 376 - 392.

Wauters, R. (2007). *Virtual Goods: the next big business model*. Retrieved from http://techcrunch.com/2007/06/20/virtual-goods-the-next-big-business-model/

Wayne Blann, F. K. L. (2011). Sport Marketing. Ithaca, NY: California State University at Long Beach.

webopedia. (2014). Retrieved from www.webopedia.com/TERM/M/mobile_application.html

Whinston, L. Q. (2013). Two Formulas for Success in Social Media: Social Learning and Network Effects. Department of Economics, The University of Texas at Austin, School of Information Systems, Singapore Management University.

Whitton, N. (2008). Collaborative virtual gaming worlds in higher education. Routledge.

www.manutd.com/en.aspx. (2014). Retrieved from www.manutd.com/en.aspx

Wysocki, M. (2012). *The Role of Social Media in Sports Communication: An Analysis of NBA Teams*. A capstone project. Washington, DC: School Communication American University.

Yonev, M. C. (2014). *Sports business introduction: How marketing and social media help sports business?* Retrieved from Salford Business School blog: http://blogs.salford.ac.uk/business-school/

KEY TERMS AND DEFINITIONS

Social Media: In this paper, any kinds of mobile application or websites in which fans/consumers can make their networks.

Social Media Marketing (SMM): Marketing through social media which is creating a new channel for the fans/costumers to interact with their Producers.

Social Networking: Is a platform to build social relations among people.

Sport Communication: A process in which people develop their relationship through organizations, players, fans inside a sport community.

Sport Industry: Is a market in which people, activities, business, and organizations involved in producing focused on sports.

Sport Marketing: Marketing for any kinds of goods & services through different kinds of sport.

This research was previously published in the Handbook of Research on Integrating Social Media into Strategic Marketing edited by Nick Hajli, pages 340-358, copyright year 2015 by Business Science Reference (an imprint of IGI Global).

Chapter 8
The Ball Is in Your Court:
Using Socially Responsible Actions as an Effective Marketing Tool

Marina Mattera
European University of Madrid, Spain

Verónica Baena
European University of Madrid, Spain

ABSTRACT

This chapter conducts an in-depth study regarding a European football club's marketing strategy and brand management approach in order to evaluate customers' perceived ethicality and how consumers value corporate social responsibility activities. Specifically, the cases of Real Madrid and Barcelona FC (also named Barça) are analyzed. These two football teams are considered as they are two of the most successful sports teams in terms of worldwide supporters and revenues. The findings highlight how European football clubs should incorporate corporate social responsibility into their marketing strategy through the evaluation of consumer's perceived corporate social responsibility values and ethicality.

INTRODUCTION

Global society has become increasingly more aware of firm's actions in terms of social accountability, including not only environmental matters but also social problems. Among these, we find social inequalities, analphabetism, poverty, lack of access to clean water, waste disposals, pollution endangering human life, and a large etc. Previous literature has identified a positive association between investing in business efficiency and investing in corporate social responsibility (CSR) to create and enhance a sustainable competitive advantage (McGuire et al, 1988; Shepard et al, 1997; Buchholtz et al, 1999; Quazi and O' Brien, 2000; Jones et al, 2007; among others). However, in many cases it has been identified that a lack of appropriate diffusion of this information can mislead consumers or undermine the efforts conducted in terms of their real corporate social responsibility efforts. Consequently, it is deemed essential to

DOI: 10.4018/978-1-5225-5475-2.ch008

conduct marketing actions specifically oriented towards notifying all the firm's stakeholders regarding their CSR policies and activities (Mattera, Baena y Cerviño, 2014).

It is important to denote that the firm shall first hold strong ethical values related to CSR activities upon which their strategies are based. In the event this does not happen, consumers will view the corporate marketing activities as a way of masking the image and reputation, without any true substance, commonly referred to as "greenwashing" (Lyndenberg, 2002). In the sports sector, and especially in football, this is especially true as, one of the most important assets of a company is the brand. Therefore, managers need to concentrate their efforts on managing this strategic business asset. The company's goal is getting brand loyalty, which signifies a measure of attachment that a customer has to a brand. Customer loyalty mostly creates brand value to a firm, which then can aid to create and enhance brand equity (Kaynak, Salman and Tatoglu, 2008).

However, despite the above arguments, strategic brand management has only become a key issue in the last decade (Blumrodt, Bryson, and Flanagan, 2012). This is especially relevant in sports, as it has become increasingly commercialized internationally over the past decade. It implies that sport companies in today's global market need to be progressive service sellers in order to compete with other leisure activities, and entrepreneurial sport ventures that do this succeed in the competitive marketplace (Ratten and Ratten, 2011).

Metrics of brand performance should include contemporary issues, such as CSR, in measuring consumer's expectations and how each brand fulfills them. Along these lines, Blumrodt et al. (2012) conducted an analysis of European Football teams and how their engagement in terms of CSR activities impacted on customer-based brand equity. Findings concluded that football club's involvement in community activities and other CSR actions has an impact on brand image and customer behavior. Additionally, the authors highlighted the need to implement a brand management strategy to assess customer's perceived ethicality and integrate it as a part of the marketing strategy.

In an attempt to contribute Literature, and based on Blumrodt et al. (2012), the present chapter conducts an in-depth study about two of the most relevant European Football clubs to analyze their brand management approach and evaluate their fans' perceived ethicality and how supporters value CSR activities. Specifically, the case of Real Madrid and Barcelona FC (also named Barça) are analyzed. We have focused on these football teams as they are two of the most successful sports teams in terms of worldwide supporters. With this objective in mind, we have structured the paper into various sections. The first one provides a Literature Review. Subsequently, the marketing strategy implemented by Real Madrid and FC Barcelona through CSR actions is addressed, as well as its effectiveness in terms of customer commitment and loyalty. The final section sets out the conclusions.

BACKGROUND

The basement for a successful commercialization is a strong brand. In sports, branding could be defined as a long-term relationship between the sponsor and the sponsee, in which both are equivalent and have a brand status (Adjouri and Stastny, 2006). This partnership is based in trust where both partners have a high common identification and pursue common strategic goals.

Sport is becoming increasingly commercialized and sport entities have become more professional over the years. While North American sport organizations have traditionally led this development, the European ones are catching up (Bauer, Sauer and Schmitt, 2005). Nowadays, sports brands all over the world have as a major objective becoming globally recognized, especially in the case of professional football clubs (Chanavat and Bodet, 2009). Furthermore, the internationalization of sports results as a consequence from the maturation of traditional markets in Western Europe and North America. That is, many brands particularly spots brands have transcended geographically by focusing on the global appeal of the sport.

Under these conditions, sports marketing is necessary to the businesses growth and survival (Ratten and Ratten, 2011). More specifically, many sports teams have been focusing on international branding efforts by building a global fan base and implemented relationship marketing programs designed to appeal to their most avid fans. This is especially true in soccer teams, which have turned into corporations where they share their wealth with their stockholders. Although ticket revenue used to be the number one source of income, now it has been declining due to the emergence of other source of income such as merchandising, broadcasting rights and season combined tickets (Kaynak, Salman and Tatoglu, 2008). In other words, among the evolution of diverse highly competitive sports, football clubs have started to think global and tackle an audience beyond where they compete. In this sense, literature coincides in emphasizing Manchester United as the pioneer in the football sports industry in terms of expanding their marketing and brand to other markets and regions (Hill and Vincent, 2006).

More specifically, in order to expand the image and commercialization of a specific sports entity, it is important to have strong brand equity, which engages sports fans and to which diverse individuals can relate. The reason behind this rationale is that brand consists of four dimensions: i) brand awareness; ii) brand image; iii) perceived quality, and iv) brand loyalty (Keller, 1993). In each of those dimensions the consumer, in this case sports fan, feels identified with the brand in one way or another. Furthermore, having a strong brand implies that customers maintain a favorable brand through age, have high brand-names awareness, and perceive that a brand is of high quality. Therefore, they all are loyal to it (Chavanat and Bodet, 2009). This holds especially true in the case of sports, as fans tend to maintain their choice of teams for a specific sport through life.

Achieving Supporters' Commitment Through Social Causes

Literature has emphasized the importance of showing strong brand for sport organizations as this may help them to enhance their competitive positioning in the marketplace. In essence, it is the development of this effective "brand" that allows sport entities to maximize their financial efficiency when interacting with consumers and stakeholders. Moreover, knowing what affects brand awareness and brand positioning constitutes a potential management tool for developing both marketing strategies and their operational components (Chavanat and Bodet, 2009). In short, brand has become a primary area of emphasis in the sport marketing literature (Cooper, 2010), as well as understanding the specific factors driving the four dimensions of brand equity in the case of sports brands.

According to the above arguments, it is also worth mentioning that sports fans are becoming more conscious and demanding of their team's commitment with society. This is consistent with Blumrodt, Bryson and Flanagan's (2012) results, which confirmed a positive impact of clubs' engagement in humanitarian programs, and show that the club's supporters expect a serious involvement in society from their sport brand.

As a result, we can argue that the club's commitment to social causes becomes a factor to take into account when building a sports brand. In particular, during recent years, professional sports clubs and associations have become more involved with social causes, creating their corporate social responsibility actions and strategies. For instance, in the United States, the Green Sports Alliance was created by professional teams from the Pacific Northwest, in collaboration with the Environmental Protection Agency (James, 2011). According to the International Olympics Committee (2013), sports have a significant role in society and organizations that are in this industry should embrace and promote their social responsibility. Also, in the case of sports teams, considering they are individual companies and represent various stakeholders' interest, they have a need for Corporate Social Responsibility (CSR) measures and strategies. In this case, CSR translates into some of the following actions:

1. Ensuring corporate values are shared, respected and promoted by all the members of the organization and its supporters.
2. Employing the best people for the job (players, coaches, etc.) based on skills and qualifications (not basing judgment on age, race, social class or other).
3. Always respecting and encouraging fair play.
4. Having clear equipment guidelines (protecting players from injuries, setting an example for followers or fans).
5. Being transparent in decision making, accounting procedures and especially in disciplinary actions.
6. Show that through health and fitness a better quality of life can be accomplished.
7. Using sustainability as a standpoint for the development of the sport's engagement.
8. Focusing on community benefit (could be a potential source of new players).
9. Promoting heroes and heroines (players with exemplary behavior) as role models for supporters and society in general.

Moreover, individuals playing sports at a competitive level can play a significant part in shaping youngsters' future as they constitute a role model, an example of what some children wish to accomplish in the near future. Then, there is a high responsibility that relies in the way these individuals act, whether they play an individual or a team sport.

Sports Marketing Based on Social Commitment

By engaging in CSR actions, these sports icons can set a path to be followed by children of all ages. Additionally, regarding how CSR translates in the sports industry, firms that incorporate the abovementioned elements may gain more supporters and get a better image in the eyes of society in general. In particular, the former President of the International Olympics Committee, Jacques Rogge, mentioned that sports do not have a power on its own, they depend on people who play and follow it, creating a movement that has the power to improve the values of the society we live in *(2003)*.

Having said that, it's worth mentioning that Babiak and Wolfe (2013) have evidenced that CSR is becoming institutionalized in professional sport agents (clubs, sponsors, etc.). Findings also identified the internal resources and external pressures that served as the drivers of these changes. Complementary to this contribution, it was previously explored socially responsible activities around mega-sport events, specifically analyzing the Super Bowl event (Babiak and Wolfe, 2006). It was also shown that sport executives delivered their community outreach efforts during the event through an altruistic and strategic perspective.

Moreover, other authors have assessed CSR from a marketing perspective in sports. For instance, Landreth Grau and Garretson Folse (2007) evaluated cause-related marketing in the sports industries, which involved contributing to non-profit organizations, informing their consumers about it and translating those contributions into higher sales. Additionally, it was explained that cause-related marketing can only be sustainable over time if CSR activities contribute to the social causes and sport executives include CSR in the overall corporate strategy (see, e.g., Irwin et al., 2003; Lachowetz and Gladden, 2002; Lachowetz and Irwin, 2002; Roy and Graeff, 2003).

Incorporating Social Causes to Sports Companies' Culture

Contributing to social causes voluntarily it is not only relevant for sports organizations. It is equally important for them to ensure that the firm and anyone who represents it (i.e. players) comply with legal requirements (Carroll, 1979). That is, if a player engages in illegal activities, even if he is individually responsible, his bad reputation reflects on the sports brand, thus damaging the sports' reputation and image (Smart and Rechner, 2007).

Considering professional sports organizations hold a high profile in the communities where they are based, each team is dependent on those social contexts for their own commercial success (Extejt, 2004). This holds especially true in the case of European Football clubs, as football is the most widespread watched, played and followed sport in the world, being European Championships and Teams regarded as the best clubs in where players from all over the world wish to play (FIFA, 2013). For instance, when Barcelona footballer Lionel Messi, four times FIFA World Player of the Year, was accused with his father Jorge Messi of defrauding the Spanish authorities of more than 4m euros ($5.4m; £3.4m), many journalists published this information and Barcelona FC's brand name was seriously damaged as its main player was said of setting up shell companies in South America to avoid various million in payments. To avoid this negative effect on Messi's reputation, he and his father denied these charges, and argued they had always fulfilled their tax obligations following the advice of their tax consultants who would take care of clarifying this situation. As shown in Figure 1, the player also received support from Barcelona president Sandro Rosell and predecessor Joan Laporta who was in charge during the years of the allegations.

Due to the arguments abovementioned, almost all professional teams participate in philanthropic activities (Babiak and Wolfe, 2006). Particularly, Sheth and Babiak (2010) conducted a study through using a mixed-methods approach (i.e. survey and a qualitative content analysis of responses to open-ended questions) to assess how professional sport executives define CSR, and the priorities teams have regarding their CSR activities. It was concluded that the professional sports industry focuses on many approaches, including philanthropic activities and ethical behaviors. Additionally, the authors argued that executives consider CSR to be a basic component of their business strategy and that there are a number of elements to take into consideration, mainly: philanthropy (altruistic giving), an emphasis on the local community, partnerships, and ethical concerns.

More recently, Sheth and Babiak (2010) identified there is a need for a greater understanding of a definition of CSR in the sports industry, together with the relationship between CSR practices and sports team's success (matches won, championships won, etc.). The present chapter directly addresses these matters through an in-depth study of two of the most renowned sports teams in the European Football industry.

Figure 1. Messi receives backing from the FC Barcelona's President. Source: Official Twitter of FC Barcelona, on June 13, 2013

DO AS YOU WOULD BE DONE BY

As stated in the Introduction of this work, for the purpose of this study, Real Madrid and Barcelona FC were selected, as they are firstly the top teams in Spanish football and among the top three most valuable brands in the European sports industry. Both soccer teams are very successful. Specifically, founded in 1902, Real Madrid was the world's richest football club in 2012 in terms of revenue, with an annual turnover of €513million and the most valuable, worth €3.3billion (Deloitte, 2013). As shown in Table 1, the team was also the most valuable football club in 2013. Internationally the club has won a record of nine European Cup/UEFA Champions League titles and a joint of three Intercontinental Cups, as well as two UEFA Cups, and one UEFA Super Cup. Additionally, Real Madrid was awarded with the recognition of "FIFA Club of the 20th Century" on December 23rd, 2000. It also received the FIFA Order of Merit in 2004. Added to this, Real Madrid is allowed to wear a multiple–winner badge on their shirt during UEFA Champions League matches as they have won more than five European Cups.

Related to Barcelona FC, the team was founded in 1899 and is currently placed at the top of the UEFA club rankings. In particular, a recent study by Goal.com found Barcelona to be the most successful club in the UEFA Champions League (since the current format was adopted in 1992). Moreover, in international football, Barcelona has won four UEFA Champions League, four UEFA Super Cup, a record of three Inter-Cities Fairs Cup, and a record of two FIFA Club World Cup trophies. In 2010, the club created history when three players who came through its youth academy (Messi, Iniesta and Xavi Hernández) were chosen as the three best players in the world, having bagged the top spots at the FIFA Ballon d'Or, an unprecedented feat for players from the same football school.

These two soccer teams are highly the most supported worldwide, having the largest fanbase among all sports teams on all major social networks (with over 46 million fans on Facebook, around 10 million followers on Twitter). Based on the above profile, they were studied in this research.

Additionally, as part of the look at the world's 50 most valuable sports teams, Forbes (2013) also broke down the social media universe of those teams. Table 2 ranks the teams considering the combined number of Facebook fans and Twitter followers. As shown, Barcelona occupies the firs position in this ranking courtesy of 60 million followers, with Real Madrid in second place and Man United third.

Table 1. The most valuable football clubs in 2013

Rank	Team	Country	Value ($M)	% change on year	Revenue ($M)
1	Real Madrid	Spain	3,300	76	650
2	Manchester United	England	3,165	42	502
3	Barcelona	Spain	2,600	99	613
4	Arsenal	England	1,326	3	368
5	Bayern Munich	Germany	1,309	6	468
6	Milan	Italy	945	-4	326
7	Chelsea	England	901	18	409
8	Juventus	Italy	694	17	248
9	Manchester City	England	689	35	362
10	Liverpool	England	651	5	296
11	Tottenham Hotspur	England	520	-8	226
12	Schalke 04	Germany	498	-15	221
13	Borussia Dortmund	Germany	436	16	240
14	Internazionale	Italy	401	-18	236
15	Lyon	France	368	-4	167
16	Corinthians	Brazil	358	-	119
17	Napoli	Italy	330	16	188
18	Hamburg	Germany	300	-16	154
19	Marseille	France	285	-18	167
20	Newcastle United	England	263	9	146

Source: Own elaboration based on Forbes' list of the most valuable football clubs. Retrieved October 13, 2013 from http://www.forbes.com/sites/mikeozanian/2013/04/17/soccers-most-valuable-teams-real-madrid-dethrones-manchester-united-from-top-spot-at-3-3-billion/

Data Gathering Process

Information about both Real Madrid and Barcelona FC was gathered from December 2012 to March 2013 by repeatedly browsing the teams' Web site. Results are portrayed on Table 1, as follows. Comments posted on social media and articles published in specialized newspapers were also considered. Additionally, one exploratory focus group was conducted to discuss the customer engagement of Real Madrid and Barcelona's fans.

As noted by Jackson and Shaw (2009), the use of non-probability samples is particularly relevant to marketing research. Literature has also highlighted the benefits of using young people as a sample to explore customer engagement (Hayes et al, 2006), as they represent future earners and spenders (Ross and Harradine, 2011). During the focus group[1], participants were immersed in a discussion regarding

Table 2. Social media top 10 ranking 2013

Rank	Team	Number of Followers
1	Barcelona	60.6 M
2	Real Madrid	49.8 M
3	Manchester United	34.5 M
4	Chelsea	20.2 M
5	Los Angeles Lakers	19.6 M
6	AC Milan	17.2 M
7	Arsenal	16.8 M
8	Chicago Bulls	9.7 M
9	Bayern Munich	8 M
10	New York Yankees	7.3 M

Source: Own elaboration based on Top Forbes' Social Media Rankings. Retrieved October 13, 2013 at http://www.whoateallthepies.tv/barcelona/170189/real-madrid-top-forbes-social-media-rankings-courtesy-of-50-million-followers.html

Barcelona and Real Madrid's social responsibility actions. All students except two actively practiced sports and followed European football competitions yet every one of the students in the focus group knew of at least two social initiatives conducted by each of those clubs, FC Barcelona and Real Madrid.

Also, the students acknowledge that it is very important for firms to commit to social causes, and in doing so, to promote their actions so that others can follow their example. In the case of FC Barcelona and Real Madrid, they mentioned that both of the Spanish leading clubs had set an example for other football teams to engage in social activities. Additionally, it was outlined the importance of marketing for sports companies, especially in this case, as it serves as a tool to promote firms' commitment to the community, whether locally, nationally or internationally; which according to the students surveyed, shows a more trustworthy company, enhancing the image and the brand.

In general, they were aware of most of the initiatives that both clubs have set up in practice, based on TV advertisements, social media, comments from the players, and comments from the journalists in newspaper articles or during games. Table 3 shows the social actions that students knew either FC Barcelona or Real Madrid carried out and they described them accurately. This shows that both firms not only have a strong commitment that is embedded in their corporate culture and values, but they have conducted effective marketing strategies to inform and publicize their brands.

Based on the above discussion, it was herein determined that there was a need for a greater understanding of the relationship between CSR practices and sports team's success (Sheth and Babiak, 2010). In this context, both Real Madrid and FC Barcelona have achieved a greater success thanks to their CSR initiatives (e.g. FC Barcelona helped Messi when he was a child and had a hormone deficiency but great potential as a football player; later on, Messi became an excellent football player, one of the most valued in the world). More specifically, based on the evidence gathered from these two Football Clubs, it is understood that there is a cause-effect relationship between the sports brand identity, shared values and community with their consumers (sports fans). By combining the club's internal culture and values with those shared with the community (and a noble purpose or corporate philanthropy), the sports brand can create a solid structure, which has the power to translate CSR actions into success. For instance, supporting players that later on become the greatest figures in the club's history (i.e., Messi),

Table 3. CSR actions conducted by FC Barcelona and Real Madrid

Actions	FC Barcelona	Real Madrid
CSR-Sponsor	Unicef	N/A
Foundation	Fundació Barcelona	Fundación Real Madrid
Schools for children	Barçakids, "Leer te hace grande"	Escuelas de la Fundación
Fight against diseases	More than a Goal: End Polio	N/A
Social inclusion	Inclusive sport sessions	Escuelas Deportivas de Integración Social
Health	"We are what we eat," FutbolNet	Baloncesto en hospitales
Donating Materials	Dignity for children	Not specified
Senior citizen programs	N/A	Actividad física para mayores
Collaborations with international organizations	Unicef, IDB	N/A
Collaborations with NGO	Bill and Melinda Gates Foundation, Fundación Pies Descalzos, Fundación Leo Messi	N/A
Collaborations with firms	Qatar Airways, Nike, Shell (as examples)	Emirates, Adidas, Bwin (as examples)

Source: Own elaboration

or contributing to schooling of children in impoverished areas (namely Africa, Latin America, etc.) leads to strong linkages between fans and the team.

Figure 1 shows the interactions between the different elements that determine sports industry's agents brand identity, based on Kapferer (2008)'s Brand Identity Prism. The author identified a company's brand identity was based on seven main elements: capabilities, internal culture & values, noble purpose, personality, shared values & communities, aspirational self-image and rallying cry. The first element makes reference to what the company owner of the brand does, the quality or performance standards it uses or represents, and how well it performs. The internal culture & values represents the firm's core beliefs, mainly those elements that the brand will never compromise on; while noble purpose represents the larger goal or cause that the brand aspires to serve. The brand's personality shows the way in which the firm delivers its capabilities; the shared values & community portrays the ideas that customer and the company owner of the brand see as important (passions and affinities); and the aspirational self-image represents what people think of consumers of a brand when they wear that specific brand. Finally, the rallying cry summarizes the vision, heart and soul of the brand.

In the case of sports marketing and building sports brands based on social commitment, it has been evidenced that the noble purpose, shared values & community and internal culture & values represent the basis for the Brand Identity model. This is complemented by the capabilities and the personality. As a result, by having a strong commitment with social causes, the sports brand can create a solid basis for their brand identity model. This has a constant feedback with the rallying cry and aspirational self-image, representing both what the society needs and what the consumer wants to show to society as they embrace and wear the brand.

Moreover, as the brand is established linked to these strong social values, and the eagerness to contribute to the community, there is a need for a specific marketing plan to transfer this information to consumers and the general public. An effective marketing strategy, combined with effective communication, achieves strong sports consumer (fan)'s support of the brand, thus building the brand reputation.

Additionally, by engaging in social causes, through effective communication the brand can learn the social interests of the fan, thus designing their social commitment and corporate strategy accordingly, and tackling the specific elements that interest him. Figure 2 summarizes this discussion.

DISCUSSION AND CONCLUSION

Being global and well-known is the major objective of sport brands in general and professional football clubs in particular (Chanavat and Bodet, 2009). In fact, the transfer of soccer star David Beckham to Real Madrid, which was mainly explained by brand considerations, serves as an example for the growing importance of marketing aspects in the management of professional sports teams. We can then say that sport organizations have to be progressive service sellers in order to successfully compete with other leisure offers (Bauer, Sauer and Schmitt, 2005). However, only recently has case research been used to extend the understanding of relationship marketing in sports (Stavros and Westberg, 2009).

To cover this gap, the present study qualitatively explores how European football clubs should incorporate CSR into their marketing strategy through the evaluation of consumer's perceived CSR values and ethicality. Our findings highlight that professional sport teams and leagues have unique resources at their disposal in order to put into practice specific CSR programs and raise awareness in the general public with greater impact than organizations operating in other industries. Among these resources, those which stand out are: donating tickets, usage of their facilities for events (stadiums, arenas, etc.), access to media and social media, vendors, sponsors and support of professional staff (lawyers, accountants, trainers, experts in kinesiology, etc.).

Figure 2. Sports brand management and marketing model. Source: Own elaboration based on Kapferer (2008).

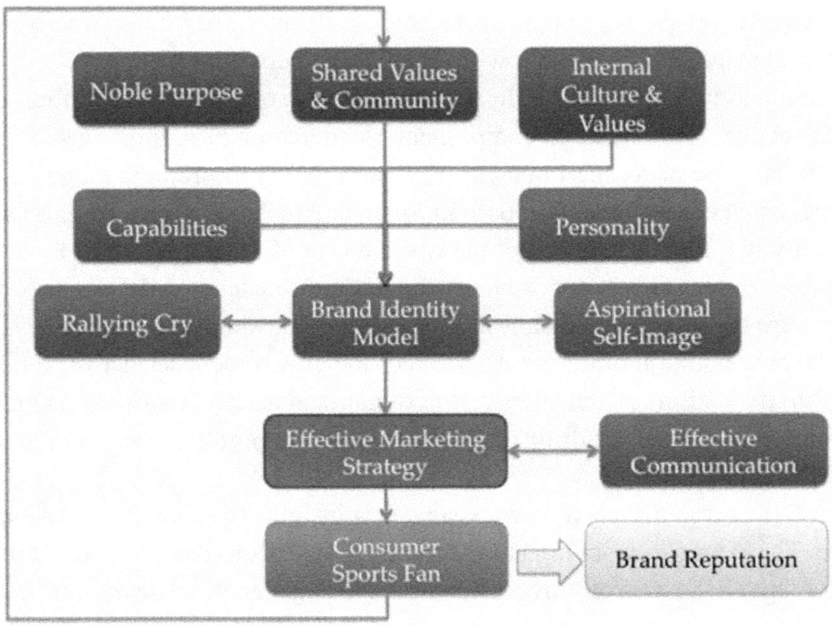

In particular, concerning Barcelona FC, their actions with Lionel Messi, the agreements they have with UNICEF, and many other initiatives show how the firm's CSR actions result in a variable for brand enhancement, as well as alleviating social problems. The case of Lionel Messi shows not only an act of good faith but also how this event constituted a significant marketing element for the firm. Specifically, FC Barcelona first heard about Messi when this young Argentinian was barely 12 years old. He was a significantly better football player than any other child yet he had just been diagnosed with a growth hormone deficiency (GHD). Though the disease had a cure, it was too expensive for Messi's family, and without it his future as a professional football player was doubtful.

When FC Barcelona's coach at the time saw Messi playing, he saw he had a lot of potential, so the club offered to pay for the treatment if Lionel moved to Barcelona from his hometown in Rosario (Argentina). Not only Messi was cured from his GHD but also he was the third youngest player ever to play for Barça's top-team and the youngest in Spain's Prime national league (*La Liga*). Additionally, the FC Barcelona Foundation signed an agreement with UNESCO in 2007 to combat racism and violence in sport. In the framework of this alliance various awareness campaigns have been developed, with the participation of FC Barcelona players, like the one launched in 2011 called 'Put Racism Offside', starring Messi, Piqué and Keita. Thanks to this arrangement it has also been achieved that football clubs belong to ECA (European Clubs Association) include anti-racist clauses in their players' contracts.

Related to Real Madrid, participants in the focus group highlighted that one of the many initiatives the team has through the "Real Madrid Foundation" is the creation of schools in Latin-America and India, which support the development of young athletes. This Foundation recently received the Corporate Social Responsibility award from the Football is More Foundation, which was created by S.D. Prince Constantin von und zu Liechtenstein to promote development and peace through football. In addition, Real Madrid uses sport to reach out to demographic groups in risk of social exclusion through its Foundation. In doing so, an ever-growing network of academies in youth, penitentiary centers were created throughout Spain to achieve the insertion of these groups into society, and make society aware of the situation these groups are in. Particularly, in penitentiary centers the Foundation aims to facilitate the reinsertion of inmates into society through the practice of football or basketball, and promoting the development of positive values and competences, such as team work, the acceptance and respect for established rules, and respect for one's fellow man, among others.

Real Madrid Foundation also facilitates the social integration of immigrant children and their families through the joint practice of football and complimentary education programs. In short, as published in Real Madrid's official Web page, the Foundation's main goal is to promote values inherent in sport, and to use the latter as an educational tool, both in Spain and the rest of the world. It uses the universal nature of Real Madrid CF to make the rest of the world aware of the importance of teaching values and promoting charitable causes. Therefore, events such as benefit matches, the Foundation's annual Gala, or benefit concerts are organized in which it instills values to be emulated by society. This Foundation exists thanks to the collaboration of different offices of the government services and the generous support it receives from the patronage and sponsorship of national and international companies, as well as the donations from thousands of Madridistas (Real Madrid supporters) who wish to strengthen their bond with Real Madrid.

Moving forward, the present analysis has revealed new insights from how CSR and sports brands are related in practice. The examples from Real Madrid and FC Barcelona can serve as a standpoint for other sports teams, especially in the case of European football, to engage in social commitments and use these as a basis for their marketing strategy. In doing so, they will not only create significant benefits for the communities that they collaborate with, but also position the sports brand as a socially-committed one, which holds stronger value for fans compared to other brands. Moreover, as shown in this work, having a noble purpose and internalizing social commitment into the sports firm's culture and values adds greater meaning to the brand identity model. It also creates a strong link between fans and other stakeholders and the sports brand, which ensures a long lasting relationship consumer/fan-sports club. Therefore, through this study, managers working in the sports industry can use Real Madrid and FC Barcelona as examples-to-be-followed; considering social commitment as a valuable input in their corporate strategy, as well as in their marketing strategy.

In sum, we hope this research serves as a basis for further investigations, observing the gradual development of the most important sports clubs start to adopt social responsibility strategies.

Limitations and Direction for Future Research

This study has been concluded within the framework of some limitations. Firstly, results of the research have been obtained by a qualitative approach. Besides, another limitation is the use of a convenience sample. Due to the difficulty to reach all population subject to the research, convenience-sampling method has been chosen. But, it is not possible for the sample to represent all population. Thus, generalization may not be made.

Based on the above limitations, further research in this area can be conducted in different directions. A first research in this area could be the same study protocol and apply it to other European clubs. Findings can then be compared to those from Real Madrid and FC Barcelona clubs analyzed in this research. Also, the understanding obtained from such investigations would be useful for the development of CSR dimensions in sport marketing, as well as for the formulation of sport industry practices.

REFERENCES

Adjouri, N., & Stastny, P. (2006). *Sport-branding: Mit sport-sponsoring zum markenerfolg*. Wiesbaden: Gabler.

Babiak, K., & Wolfe, R. (2013). Perspectives on social responsibility in sport. In *Routledge handbook of sport and corporate social responsibility*. New York: Routledge.

Babiak, K. R., & Wolfe. (2006). More than just a game? Corporate social responsibility and Super Bowl XL. *Sport Marketing Quarterly*, *15*(4), 214–224.

Bauer, H. H., Sauer, N. E., & Schmitt, P. (2005). Customer-based brand equity in the team sport industry: Operationalization and impact on the economic success of sport teams. *European Journal of Marketing*, *39*(5/6), 496–513. doi:10.1108/03090560510590683

Blumrodt, J., Bryson, D., & Flanagan, J. (2012). European football teams' CSR engagement impacts on customer-based brand equity. *Journal of Consumer Marketing*, *29*(7), 482–493. doi:10.1108/07363761211274992

Brand Finance. (2011). *European football brands 2011*. Retrieved September 18, 2013 from http://brandfinance.com/images/upload/top_30_european_football_brands_2011_final_website.pdf

Braunstein, J. R., & Ross, S. D. (2010). Brand personality in sports: Dimension analysis and general scale development. *Sport Marketing Quarterly*, *19*(1), 8–16.

Buchholtz, A. K., Amason, A. C., & Rutherford, M. A. (1999). Beyond resources: The mediating effect of top management discretion and values on corporate philanthropy. *Business & Society*, *38*(2), 167–187. doi:10.1177/000765039903800203

Chanavat, N., & Bodet, G. (2009). Internationalisation and sport branding strategy: A French perception of the big four brands. *Qualitative Market Research: An International Journal*, *12*(4), 460–481. doi:10.1108/13522750910993356

Copper, C. G. (2010). New media marketing: the innovative use of technology in NCAA athletic department e-branding initiatives. *Journal of Marketing Development and Competitiveness*, *5*(1), 23–32.

Deloitte. (2013). *Deloitte football money league 2013*. Retrieved October 28, 2013 from http://www.deloitte.com/view/en_GB/uk/industries/sportsbusinessgroup/sports/football/deloitte-football-money-league/c0d0cc64dac5c310VgnVCM3000003456f70aRCRD.htm

Dix, S., Phau, I., & Pougnet, S. (2010). Bend it like Beckham: The influence of sports celebrities on young adult consumers. *Young Consumers*, *11*(1), 36–46. doi:10.1108/17473611011025993

Fédération Internationale de Football Association (FIFA). (2013). *Corporate website*. Retrieved October 3, 2013 from http://www.fifa.com/tournaments/index.html

Forbes. (2013). *World's most valuable soccer teams 2013*. Retrieved September 20, 2013 from http://www.forbes.com/pictures/mlm45eigjk/3-barcelona-2/

Hayes, J., Alford, B., Silver, L., & York, R. (2006). Looks matter in developing consumer-brand relationships. *Journal of Product and Brand Management*, *15*(5), 306–315. doi:10.1108/10610420610685875

Hill, J. S., & Vincent, J. (2006, May). Globalization and sports branding: The case of Manchester United. *International Journal of Sports Marketing & Sponsorship*, 213–230.

International Olympic Committee. (2013). Retrieved June 30, 2013 from www.olympic.org/uk/news/olympic_news/review_uk

Irwin, R. L., Lachowetz, Cornwell, & Clark. (2003). Cause-related sport sponsorship: An assessment of spectator beliefs, attitudes, and behavioral intentions. *Sport Marketing Quarterly*, *12*(3), 131–139.

James, S. (2011, March 24). The green league: CSR hits pro sports. *Forbes*. Retrieved October 2, 2013, from http://www.forbes.com/sites/csr/2011/03/24/the-green-league-csr-hits-pro-sports/

Jones, T. M., Felps, W., & Bigley, G. A. (2007). Ethical theory and stakeholder-related decisions: The role of stakeholder culture. *Academy of Management Review*, *32*(1), 137–155. doi:10.5465/AMR.2007.23463924

Kapferer, J. N. (2008). *The new strategic brand management: Creating and sustaining brand equity long term*. Philadelphia: Kogan Page.

Kaynak, E., Gultekin, G., & Tatoglu, E. (2008). An integrative framework linking brand associations and brand loyalty in professional sports. *Journal of Brand Management*, *15*(5), 336–357. doi:10.1057/palgrave.bm.2550117

Lachowetz, T., & Gladden. (2002). A framework for understanding cause-related sport marketing programs. *International Journal of Sports Marketing & Sponsorship*, *4*(4), 205–225.

Lachowetz, T., & Irwin. (2002). FedEx and the St. Jude Classic: An application of a cause-related marketing program (CRMP). *Sport Marketing Quarterly*, *11*(2), 114–116.

Landreth Grau, S., & Garretson Folse. (2007). Cause-related marketing (CRM). *Journal of Advertising*, *36*(4), 19–33. doi:10.2753/JOA0091-3367360402

Lydenberg, S. D. (2002). Envisioning socially responsible investing. *Domini Social Investments*. Retrieved September 12, 2013, from http://live.domini.com/common/pdf/SL_SRI_Vision.pdf

Mattera, M., Baena, V., & Cerviño, J. (2014). Investing time wisely: Enhancing firm's brand awareness through stakeholder engagement in the service sector. *International Journal of Management Practice*.

McGuire, J. B., Sundgren, A., & Schneeweis, T. (1988). Corporate social responsibility and firm financial performance. *Academy of Management Journal*, *31*(4), 854–872. doi:10.2307/256342

Quazi, A. M., & O'Brien, D. (2000). An empirical test of a cross-national model of corporate social responsibility. *Journal of Business Ethics*, *25*(1), 33–51. doi:10.1023/A:1006305111122

Ratten, V., & Ratten, H. (2011). International sport marketing: Practical and future research implications. *Journal of Business and Industrial Marketing*, *26*(8), 614–620. doi:10.1108/08858621111179886

Ross, J., & Harradine, R. (2011). Fashion value brands: The relationship between identity and image. *Journal of Fashion Marketing and Management*, *15*(3), 323–325.

Roy, D. P., & Graeff. (2003). Consumer attitudes toward cause-related marketing activities in professional sports. *Sports Marketing Quarterly*, *12*(3), 163–172.

Shaw, D. (2007). Manchester United football club: Developing a network orchestration model. *European Journal of Information Systems*, *16*, 628–642. doi:10.1057/palgrave.ejis.3000702

Shepard, J. M., Betz, M., & O'Connell, L. (1997). The proactive corporation: Its nature and causes. *Journal of Business Ethics*, *16*(10), 1001–1010. doi:10.1023/A:1017957618855

Sheth, H., & Babiak, K. M. (2010). Beyond the game: Perceptions and practices of corporate social responsibility in the professiona sport industry. *Journal of Business Ethics*, *91*(3), 433–446. doi:10.1007/s10551-009-0094-0

Stavros, C., & Westberg, K. (2009). Using triangulation and multiple case studies to advance relationship marketing theory. *Qualitative Market Research: An International Journal*, *12*(3), 307–320. doi:10.1108/13522750910963827

Suddaby, R. (2006). What grounded theory is not. *Academy of Management Journal*, *49*(4), 633–642. doi:10.5465/AMJ.2006.22083020

ENDNOTE

1 A non-probability sample of 13 undergraduate students was selected on the basis that they are potential followers of sport teams. As noted by Jackson and Shaw (2007), the use of non-probability samples is particularly relevant to marketing research. Literature has also highlighted the benefits of using young people as a sample to explore customer engagement (Hayes et al, 2006), as they represent future earners and spenders (Ross and Harradine, 2011).

This research was previously published in Strategies in Sports Marketing edited by Manuel Alonso Dos Santos, pages 74-87, copyright year 2014 by Business Science Reference (an imprint of IGI Global).

Chapter 9
The Marketing Implications of International Sports Rating Systems

Raymond T Stefani
California State University – Long Beach, USA

ABSTRACT

Recognized world sports federations appear to have chosen their official rating systems with marketing in mind. 87% of the 105 official rating systems involve the simple accumulation of points, which encourages top competitors to enter as many tournaments as possible. Most of those systems recognize a seasonal champion. A marketer can exploit the importance of the end-of-season events and the appearance of top athletes. To be successful in a combat sport like wrestling, boxing, and judo, physically overcoming the opponent is intensely personal. Top competitors can be advertised in personal terms to encourage the awaiting audience to buy into the upcoming contest on an equally personal level. In other sports such as running, swimming, and rowing, each competitor performs unimpeded by the opponent. Often the best performance for a season is used to crown a yearly champion. A rating in seconds and meters is more tangible than one in points. A marketer can illustrate the small gap between top competitors making every stride important to potential ticket buyers. Some of the object-control sports like basketball, cricket, ice hockey, rugby, soccer, and tennis are rated by point accumulators and some are rated by more sophisticated systems that self adjust, based on the relative strengths of the opponents. Mind sports such as chess and bridge are included because these competitions are recognized by the International Olympic Committee and by SportAccord. The specifics of those rating systems are provided in this chapter as are suggested marketing opportunities.

INTRODUCTION

In spite of the amount of money at risk, organizations may approach a sports competition with no marketing plan in mind, Stotlar (1993). On the other hand, effective marketing evolves when a brand actively aligns itself with a favorite team, Mitre and Ordonez de Pablos (2009), when an affinity can be

DOI: 10.4018/978-1-5225-5475-2.ch009

established between a company and a sport, Bloom et al. (2006), and when fanship can be exploited as motivation to attend a sports event, Kahle and Close (2011). This chapter suggests strategies for the effective marketing of sports, based on the special attributes of each type of sport, made clear by the types of rating systems chosen by the stakeholders of recognized international sports federations.

It would be a marketing dream to handle a match between the two top-ranked players in the world. It is not nearly as obvious that the rating system itself could discourage or encourage that matchup. Suppose a world governing federation creates ratings by averaging points earned per tournament, based on the most recent 52-week period. Player A has earned 1000 points on 10 matches for a rating of 100 while player B has acquired 900 points on 9 matches for the same rating. The two are tied as the best in that sport. A marketer wants to promote a small tournament in the home nation of Player B. The marketer invites Players A and B. Unfortunately for the marketer, Player A declines, realizing that his worst score of 10 points happened 52 weeks before. By doing nothing for one week, the 10 points will "age out" and his rating will become 990/9 or 110. His rating rises 10% by doing nothing. Player B wants to help promote the match in his own country. Unfortunately for the marketer, the end of the season is fast approaching and Player B wants to win the top honors in his sport. He realizes that if he wins, he would only earn 30 points for the minor tournament. His rating would become 930/10 or 93, a drop of 7% while winning. Both players are discouraged from entering because of the averaging system.

Suppose the federation recognizes the above flaws in the averaging system. The federation votes to rate players based on the sum of all points accumulated in the last 52 weeks. Had that been true prior to the tournament, by not entering, Player A's rating would drop from 1000 to 990, punishing him for inactivity. Player A might as well enter the tournament. Player B could have a rating increase from 900 to 930 should he win in his native country, a bonus for his loyalty. Point accumulation systems encourage entries by top players in as many competitions as possible, aiding in the marketing of those competitions. Such was the marketing-based motivation of the men's Association of Tennis Professional, the ATP, when they changed from an averaging system to the current point accumulation system. The women's tour, the WTA, followed suit. After the change, both organization expressed satisfaction that more top players were entering tournaments under the new point accumulation system than under the old averaging system.

There is another feature of a point accumulation rating system with huge marketing implication. Many sports crown an end-of-season champion by using a 52-week moving total. A marketer can chronicle the battle among top players in the tournaments leading up to the finale. If the scoring system is understood, then it's possible to build up interest in a tournament, advertising what is needed for a player to overtake another or for a player to gain enough points to be guaranteed becoming the seasonal winner. The media will publicize that competition, providing free advertising of the sport and creating excitement for the following season.

A marketer's career may begin with one sport, but that person may later become involved in other sports. If marketing is done for a sports venue, that job will require an understanding of all sports that may be played there and the rating systems that need to be understood and exploited to keep the seats filled. This chapter will serve as a resource into world sports and into the official rating systems for those sports, as published by the federations that organize competition. I will compare and contrast the various rating systems, giving marketing implications and advice.

TYPES OF SPORTS AND SOURCES OF RECOGNITION

To assist the marketing of sports so as to make an intelligent use of rating systems, a comprehensive and organized list of sports and their rating systems is needed. Space limitations make it necessary to decide which sports to include. The Official World Encyclopedia of Sports and Games (1979) and Random House Encyclopedia (1983) include many sports with various categories. There are racquet sports, stick-and-ball sports, and water sports, for example. A sport can be classified as being a team sport vs. being an individual sport. There is some ambiguity to that demarcation, though. Tennis is an individual sport in singles but there is a team element in doubles. Swimmers compete individually, but placement points can be added to create team competition. Basketball is clearly a team competition. A more organized taxonomy of sports and rating systems is given in Stefani (1999) leading to a survey of recognized federations and their ratings systems in Stefani (2011). For this chapter, the latter two studies of sports and sports rating systems are updated through November 2013 and carefully analyzed to identify marketing implications.

To avoid ambiguities, I suggest separating sports into the three mutually exclusive ways that competitors can interact. First, a *combat sport* involves direct contact between competitors (as for boxing, wrestling and judo) in which each competitor tries to control the other. Second, an *independent sport* does not allow contact at all, that is, each competitor performs unimpeded by opponents (as for swimming, athletics, and golf). We might say that each competitor tries to control the competitor's own self for success. Third, in what I call an *object sport*, contact is indirect in a quest to control an object (as in basketball, football, and tennis). Those three categories are unambiguous and mutually exclusive.

As to selecting sports, and not to do so arbitrarily, I will chose sports recognized by well-known international organizations. The International Olympic Committee (IOC) selects sports for inclusion in the Summer and Winter Olympic Games. As unambiguous as inclusion by the IOC might seem, there is a problem in terminology. When the IOC uses the term "sport," the IOC refers to a sports federation that organizes competition. The IOC defines aquatics as a sport because the federation, abbreviated FINA, organizes competition in four water-related "disciplines": synchronized swimming, swimming, diving and water polo. Since it is common outside of the IOC to define those four disciplines as sports, I will count all IOC disciplines as sports. I have examined all IOC-recognized federations as of November, 2013 and counted 39 recognized Summer Olympic disciplines/sports, 15 more in the Winter Olympics and another 57 sports that are recognized but are not currently on the Olympic program, for a total of 111 sports. See the linkable list of international federation on the webpage http://www.olympic.org/ioc.

There is an anomaly with two of those 111 sports. The IOC lists bridge and chess as recognized sports, while bridge and chess would not normally be classed as sports al all, certainly not in the same way as swimming and golf. The term "game" is often used regarding chess and bridge, yet "game" is ambiguous in that we also have a game of football and basketball. Rather than become arbitrarily exclusive, disqualifying chess and bridge as sports, I will be inclusive and adopt a term that has recently been used: a *mind sport*. The first two World Mind Sports Games were held just after the 2008 and 2012 Olympic Games. The Third World Mind Sports Games is planned in Brazil in 2016. Normally, a sport is defined as a competition with a set of rules for determining the winner *requiring physical prowess*. I will let that definition hold for a "physical sport" of which we have noted three types, while a sport in which the italicized term does not hold will be called a "mind sport". Of course, thinking is required of all sports; therefore, I will define a mind sport as one in which a surrogate can make a valid play on behalf of the competitor. For example, it would be perfectly legal for a surrogate to move the chess piece or hold the cards for a mind sport player in chess and bridge; but, the athlete must swim 100 m or hit a golf ball in a physical sport such as swimming and golf.

At this point we have defined four types of sports: mind sports and three types of physical sports (combat, independent and object). These four categories are mutually exclusive and yet inclusive of all possible modes of competition.

Like the IOC, SportAccord is a Swiss-based international organization that recognizes sports federations which, in turn, organize sports competition. As of November, 2013, SportAccord recognizes the same 111 sports also recognized by the IOC plus another 21. Among the additional 21 sports are two more mind sports, draughts (checkers) and Go. The first two World Mind Sports Games following the Olympic Games included the four mind sports recognized by the IOC and SportAccord, bridge, chess, draughts and Go, as well as Xiang Qi or Chinese Checkers, which does not appear on any source of recognition; hence, it is not included among the mind sports in this chapter. For a list of all recognized federations with a link to each see http://www.sportaccord.com/en/members/.

Finally, I examined http://en.wikipedia.org/wiki/List_of_International_Sport; which contains all of the IOC-recognized federations and all of the SportAccord-recognized federations. In addition, Wikipedia identifies additional international federations organizing competition in another 27 sports as of November, 2013. That website is a useful resource, providing links to the all of the federations organizing competition in the 159 sports.

In the tables that will follow, the 159 sports are coded in terms of recognition.

- **IOC Summer:** The 39 sports to be contested at the 2016 Summer Olympics
- **IOC Winter:** The 15 sports to be contested at the 2014 Winter Olympics
- **IOC:** The 57 sports recognized by the IOC but not currently in the Olympics.
- **SportAccord:** An additional 21 sports recognized by SportAccord.
- **Wikipedia:** An additional 27 significant international sports listed by Wikipedia.

TYPES OF RATING SYSTEMS

I prefer to divide rating systems into three mutually exclusive categories. First, a small number of combat sports have a *subjective system*. There are then two types of objective rating systems: one type in which a rating is non-decreasing and one type in which a rating may increase, decrease or remain the same.

A point accumulation system (*accumulative system* for short) is one in which points are accumulated over some period in a non-decreasing running sum as shown in (1). The worst that happens is that no points are gained in which case the running sum does not change. Competitors are then ranked in order based on rating values.

Accumulative Rating = Sum over a period (result points, importance, ageing) (1)

For example, a third place result might gain 100 result points. That competition may have a relative importance of 2 (earning 100x2 = 200 points). The period may include the last four years of results; where values from the most recent 52 weeks are multiplied by 100%, the next oldest year by 75%, the third year by 50% and the fourth year by 25%, counting backwards. If the 200 points were earned in the fourth of the four years, counting backwards, that result would be age-weighted as 200x0.25 or 50 points. The accumulative system encourages players to compete, enhancing ticket sales.

The remaining system is the most sophisticated. A self-adjustive system (*adjustive system* for short) causes each rating to seek its own level. Each rating self adjusts after every competition up, down or making no change at all using the following equation.

New Adjustive Rating = Old Adjustive Rating + factor (actual result - target) (2)

A rating increases (decreases, remains the same) when the actual result exceeds (is less than, is equal to) the target. The target can compensate for the relative strength of the competitors. A weak team playing a strong team will have a small value for the target. A strong team playing a weak team will have a large value for the target. Teams of equal strength will have a medium target. Over many competitions, the rating seeks a level determined by the individual's or team's performance relative to that of the typical opponent.

As one example of an adjustive system, a team might secure a win so that the actual result may have value 1 (compared to 0.5 for a tie and 0 for a loss), while the target may be the estimated probability of winning which was 0.4 before the match. Suppose the Old Adjustive Rating was 150 and the factor is 50. Then the New Adjustive Rating would be 150 + 50 (1 - 0.4) or 180. In most of the adjustive systems, the opposing team would lose 50 points to create what is knows as a point exchange system. The sophistication comes in selecting a compatible actual result and target and in selecting the multiplying factor which provides sensitivity but must not be so large as to create instability for the rating values. Competitors are then ranked in order based on rating values.

Table 1 shows the breakdown of the three types of rating systems for the four types of sports. Of the 159 sports, four are mind sports, 18 are combat sports, 74 are independent sports and 63 are object sports. The world marketplace seems to be partial to independent sports and object sports. Of the 159 sports, 54 have no rating system, leaving 105 with a rating system. Three of the four mind sports have the sophisticated adjustive rating system; which is in keeping with that type of sport. All four of the subjective systems are applied to combat sports, where the winner is also determined subjectively, which is intuitive. The most common rating system is the accumulative system, comprising 91 (87%) of the 105 rating systems. Of those 91 accumulative systems, 58 use a one year period (64% of the accumulative systems and 55% of all rating systems). The influence of marketing on world rating systems is obvious: a one-year window results in the crowning of a yearly champion; which in turn, provides excellent marketing leverage.

The remainder of this chapter will examine the special interaction of sports marketing and rating systems for each of the four types of sport which have rating systems. In order, we will consider object sports, independent sports, combat sports and mind sports. The marketing of the sports lacking a rating system is then discussed. The last section summarizes the conclusions from this chapter.

MARKETING IMPLICATIONS FOR OBJECT SPORTS

Table 2 contains the 36 object sports with a rating system, where the sources of recognition are defined above. Of the 36 rated object sports (13 of which are Olympic sports), 30 are rated via accumulative

Table 1. Sports rating systems and types of sports

		Type of Sports Rating System				
Sport	Number of Sports	No rating System	Number of Systems	Subjective	Accumulative	Adjustive
Mind Sports	4	0	4	0	1	3
Combat Sports	18	9	9	4	5	0
Independent Sports	74	18	56	0	55	1
Object Sports	63	27	36	0	30	6
Total	159	54	105	4	91	10

systems and six are rated by more sophisticated adjustive systems. As mentioned above, the accumulative systems encourage entrants in as many competitions as possible which enhances ticket sales. Further, 14 of the 30 accumulative systems cover a one year period allowing a seasonal champion to be crowned. The six adjustive rating systems are intended to cause ratings to seek a level based on past performance compared to current performance.

Some of the most viewed sports with accumulative systems are basketball, ice hockey, rugby league, rugby sevens (to be an Olympic sport for the first time in 2016), tennis, volleyball and beach volleyball. Effective marketing is enhanced by becoming familiar with the point table and with current rankings.

- As a competition is approaching, include specifics as to who are top ranked, who are challenging for the top position and how far apart top competitors/teams are in points. People tend to give special importance when numerical values are assigned.
- Play up the number of points available for the winners and runners-up.
- Indicate specifically how well-known competitors/teams can to move up in the rankings and what the top ranked need to earn to remain top ranked.
- Look for those making recent ranking gains to create curiosity among fans on how the upward-movers perform in the competition being marketed.
- A sports federation will usually show the ranking positional changes which can be used flag the ones to specially tout.
- Badminton, beach volleyball and tennis are among the 14 sports that crown an end-of-season champion. Exploit that throughout the season, touting the race among top competitors for the championship.
- There is a sense of permanence to being a seasonal champion. The media will give free advertising if they report on the chase to the trophy.
- For the multi-year accumulative systems, mention the number of years involved, which gives added credibility to the player or team.

Cricket, croquet, football, netball, rugby union and squash are rated by their federations using sophisticated adjustive systems, as summarized in Table 3. FIFA uses a different adjustive system for women's football than for men's football. The more that a marketer understands the rating system for a sport; the more effectively can that system can be used for promotional purposes. The actual result for cricket,

Table 2. Object sports with a rating system (36)

Sport	Int. Fed.	Recognition	Type of Rating System	Accum. Years
Badminton	BWF	IOC Summer	Accumulative	1
Baseball	IBAF	IOC	Accumulative	4
Basketball	FIBA	IOC Summer	Accumulative	8
Beach Volleyball	FIVB	IOC Summer	Accumulative	1
Carom Billiards	WCBS(UMB)	IOC	Accumulative	2
Court Handball	USHA	Wikipedia	Accumulative	1
Curling	WCF	IOC Winter	Accumulative	6
Double Disc Court Frisbee	WFDF	IOC	Accumulative	1
Field Hockey	FIH	IOC Summer	Accumulative	4
Guts Frisbee	WFDF	IOC	Accumulative	1
Handball	IHF	IOC Summer	Accumulative	4
Ice Hockey	IIHF	IOC Winter	Accumulative	4
Korfball	IKF	IOC	Accumulative	4
Lawn Bowls	CMSB (World Bowls LTD)	IOC	Accumulative	4
Pool	WCBS (WPW)	IOC	Accumulative	1
Racketlon	FIT	Wikipedia	Accumulative	2
Racquetball	IRF(IRT)	IOC	Accumulative	1
Real Tennis	IRTPA	Wikipedia	Accumulative	1
Rugby Fives	RFA	Wikipedia	Accumulative	1
Rugby League	RLIF(RLEF)	Wikipedia	Accumulative	5
Rugby Sevens	IRB	IOC Summer	Accumulative	1
Snooker	WCBS (WPSBA)	IOC	Accumulative	2
Soft Tennis	ISTF	SportAccord	Accumulative	1
Table Hockey	ITHF	Wikipedia	Accumulative	2
Table Soccer	ITSF	Wikipedia	Accumulative	1
Table Tennis	ITTF	IOC Summer	Accumulative	4
Tennis	ITF (ATP[M], WTA[W])	IOC Summer	Accumulative	1
Ultimate Frisbee	WFDF	IOC	Accumulative	1
Volleyball	FIVB	IOC Summer	Accumulative	4
Water Polo	FINA	IOC Summer	Accumulative	4
Cricket	ICC	IOC	Adjustive	
Croquet	WCF	Wikipedia	Adjustive Elo	
Football (Soccer)	FIFA	IOC Summer	Adjustive (M) Adjustive Elo (W)	
Netball	IFNA	IOC	Adjustive	
Rugby Union	IRB	IOC	Adjustive	
Squash	WSF (PSA[M], WISPA[W])	IOC	Adjustive	

croquet, netball and rugby union are based on winning, tying and losing, where women's football and rugby union also include the affect of score difference and home advantage. For five of those rating systems, the target depends on rating difference. The systems for cricket and netball are identical since these were both developed by David Kendix for the two federations.

Croquet and women's football use the Elo probability function as the target, a probability function, which has the unique distinction of appearing in a movie. The Elo system was developed by Arpad Elo, a chess master, for rating chess players, Elo (1978). An actor in the movie *The Social Network* wrote the Elo probability equation on glass, which was viewed in reverse. If the ratings are called *RA* and *RB* for opponents A and B respectively, the Elo probability that A will beat B can be written

$1/[1 + 10^{(RB-RA)/400}]$. The actor multiplied by 10 instead of using 10 as a logarithmic base. There, we might say that poetic license became mathematical license.

For cricket, croquet, women's football, netball and rugby union, the opposing teams after each match exchange ratings points: what one team gains, the other loses. However, the adjustive systems for squash and men's football do not have that trait. For both squash and men's football, match points gained is the actual result where the average of past points serves as the target. For squash, match points depend on tournament finishing position and not on who was defeated. For men's football, fewer match points are gained by defeating a weaker opponent, but zero points are gained when losing, regardless of opponent.

In the 2011 Rugby Union World Cup, the higher ranked team won 91% of the matches. For the 2010 netball world championship and also for the 2011 Commonwealth Games, the higher ranked team won 90% of the matches. These adjustive systems can be quite accurate at rating competitors and predicting future results. For effective marketing:

- When referring to any of the adjustive rating systems, use terms like sophisticated, comprehensive, accurate, well-respected and discerning to let the reader know that these are especially well thought-out systems.
- The suggestions made above for accumulative systems hold here as well.

Table 3. Adjustive rating systems for 6 object sports

Sport	Federation	Actual Result	Target
Cricket	ICC	Win, tie, lose: (1, 0, -1)	*d/50*
Croquet	WCF	Win, tie, lose: (1, 0.5, 0)	Elo Probability: depends on *d*
Football (Soccer) Men Women	FIFA	- Match Points Fraction depending on score difference	- Average Match Points Elo Probability: depends on *d* and home adantage
Netball	IFNA	Win, tie, lose: (1, 0, -1)	*d/50*
Rugby Union (rating adjustment depends on margin of victory)	IRB	Win, tie, lose: (1, 0, -1)	*d/10*: includes home advantage
Squash	WSF (PSA[M], WISPA[W])	Match Points	Average Match Points

d = rating difference= team rating – opponent rating

MARKETING IMPLICATIONS FOR INDEPENDENT SPORTS

Table 4 contains the 56 independent sports with a rating system, most of which are individual sports. Independent sports outnumber object sports 74-63 among all 159 sports, but the gap is larger when it comes to rating systems where independent sports with a rating system outnumber object sports with a rating system 56-36. Given that teams and individuals compete without interaction, it is apparently easier to obtain a rating in independent sports. Further, 42 of the 56 sports are in the Olympics; hence this list contains many important sports. The 47 Olympic events of athletics plus the 34 Olympic events of swimming comprised 27% of all 302 2012 London Sumer Olympic events

Of the 56 sports in Table 3, 55 employ the simple accumulative system, giving points to a performance unimpeded by the opponent. Only golf uses an averaging system based on the most recent two years. However, the golf tour organizers know a marketing opportunity when they see it. The golf tour organizers use a seasonal FedEx point accumulation system for major tournaments. The last competitions are heavily marketed. The year's Tour Championship winner appeared prominently in the media, thus promoting the following season. Henrik Stenson won the $10 million bonus as Tour Champion in 2013. It is quite easy to locate a photo of him in major newspapers, a very effective example of free marketing. Here are some marketing implications.

- Of the 55 accumulative rating systems, 42 employ a one-year period, creating a seasonal champion, providing a significant marketing opportunity.
- All of the suggestions made regarding the effective marketing of object sports with accumulative systems should be applied here.
- There is an additional point to bear in mind. Many of the accumulative systems consist of taking one or more of the best performances from the most recent 52 week period. All athletics and swimming events are rated in that manner.
- Where rating values and differences of ratings are expressed in seconds and meters, those are much more tangible than using points.
- The marketer should be familiar with the exact performance gap existing among key competitors in terms of time, distance, etc. If the public realizes that a competitor is only 1 second from being best at a running distance; that is easily remembered.
- Similarly, if an additional two meters of distance in the javelin will move a thrower into the top five: that will be picked up by the media.

MARKETING IMPLICATIONS FOR COMBAT SPORTS

Table 5 contains the nine internationally-recognized combat sports having a rating system, six of which are in the Olympics. Five of the nine rating systems are accumulative and four are subjective. These sports are uniquely personal, as each competitor tries to overcome the opponent. A fencer may throw off a helmet in frustration with losing a point. A losing wrestler may hang the head in disappointment over losing to a stronger opponent. For effective marketing:

- A marketer should advertise an oncoming bout or tournament with very personal descriptions of the competitors: focus on personal background, major successes and obstacles overcome, for example.
- Sales will be enhanced when the potential audience identifies with a contestant.
- When marketing any of the four sports with a subjective rating system use terms like "as rated by the experts" and "as voted by the federation".
- Ensure that it is clear that the ordinal ranking position was done by those in the know.
- Look for athletes who have risen in the ranks. The up and coming athletes will catch the fancy of the media, which will provide free advertising.
- Be sure to honor the athlete that has had years of high ranking position. Again, the public needs to identify with the personal side of a competitor to become interested in the upcoming competition.

The five sports with accumulative system provide the same opportunities as mentioned above for sports with an accumulative system.

- Become familiar with the point table.
- Advertise competitors in personal terms and then indicate how that person can move up specifically in terms of position of finish in the next tournament.
- Indicate how many points the top ranked person leads by and then indicate first place points if it is clear that the ranking positions are in play.

These nine sports (and all the other in the tables) have in common that competition in tournaments, world championships and the Olympics are open to any qualified competitor. Not included here are other professional combat sports such as boxing and mixed martial arts which use a champion-challenger format. The challengers are ranked subjectively by the professional organization to form a list of contenders for a championship bout. Matches are arranged among the challengers. These one-off bouts can be marketed as to the possibility of the lower ranked challenger moving up and the higher ranked challenger moving closer to a title bout. As mentioned above, tout the personal side of each competitor.

MARKETING IMPLICATIONS FOR MIND SPORTS

Table 6 contains the four mind sports having a rating system. These four sports have been contested in the Mind Sports Games following the 2008 and 2012 Olympics. Another competition is scheduled in Rio flowing the 2016 Olympic Games.

Chess, draughts and GO federations use the same adjustive Elo system described in Table 3 for croquet and women's football. The actual result is (1, 0.5, 0) for a (win, tie, loss) respectively, or the fraction of such outcomes over a sequence of matches. If a player won three, tied once and lost once in five matches, the actual outcome would be recorded as (1 + 1 +1 +0.5 +0)/5 or 0.7. The target is the probability of winning one match, or fraction of a sequence of matches that should be won, based on the Elo probability function mentioned regarding object sports. The Elo system was developed by Arpad Elo specifically for chess. Since these four mind sport are intellectual in nature, most of those playing or those interested in attending a will likely be familiar with the Elo system.

Table 4. Independent sports with a rating system (56)

Sport	Int. Fed.	Recognition	Years for Accum System	Sport	Int. Fed.	Recognition	Accum. Years
Adjustive System							
Golf	IGF	IOC Summer					
Accumulative System							
Airsoft Practical Shooting	IAPS	Wikipedia	2	Modern Pentathlon	UIPM	IOC Summer	1
Alpine Skiing	FIS	IOC Winter	1	Motorcycle Racing	FIM	IOC	1
Archery	FITA	IOC Summer	1	Mountain Bike Cycling	ICU	IOC Summer	1
Athletics(Track and Field)	IAAF	IOC Summer	1	Mountain Running	WMRA	Wikipedia	1
Auto Racing	FIA	Wikipedia	1	Nordic Combined	FIS	IOC Winter	1
Biathlon	IBU	IOC Winter	1	Orienteering	IOF	IOC	1
BMX cycling	ICU	IOC Summer	1	Power Boating	UIM	IOC	1
Bobsled	FIBT	IOC Winter	1	Powerlifting	IPF	SportAccord	1
Bowling	FIQ	IOC	1	Rhythmic Gymnastics	FIG	IOC Summer	4
Canoe	ICF	IOC Summer	1	Rowing	FISA	IOC Summer	1
Cross County Skiing	FIS	IOC Winter	1	Sailing	ISAF	IOC Summer	2
Cycling-road	ICU	IOC Summer	1	Shooting	ISSF	IOC Summer	2
Cycling-Track	ICU	IOC Summer	1	Short Track Speed Skating	ISU	IOC Winter	1
Dance Sport	IDSF	IOC	1	Skeleton Sled	FIBT	IOC Winter	1
Darts	WDF	SportAccord	2	Ski Jumping	FIS	IOC Winter	1
Diving	FINA	IOC Summer	1	Ski mountaineering	UIAA	IOC	2
Equestrian	FEI	IOC Summer	1	Sled Dog Racing	IFSS	SportAccord	1
Figure Skating	ISU	IOC Winter	2	Snowboarding	FIS	IOC Winter	1
Freestyle Frisbee	WFDF	IOC	2	Speed Roller Skating	FIRS	IOC	1
Freestyle Skiing	FIS	IOC Winter	1	Speed Skating	ISU	IOC Winter	1
Frisbee Golf	WFDF	IOC	1	Sport Climbing	IFSC	IOC	1
Glider Racing	FAI	IOC	3	Surfing	ISA	IOC	1
Gymnastics	FIG	IOC Summer	1	Swimming	FINA	IOC Summer	1
Hang Gliding	FAI	IOC	3	Trampoline	FIG	IOC Summer	4
Ice Climbing	UIAA	IOC	1	Triathlon	ITU	IOC Summer	2
Kayak	ICF	IOC Summer	1	Water Skiing	IWSF	IOC	1
Luge	FIL	IOC Winter	1	Weightlifting	IWF	IOC Summer	1
Minigolf	WMF	SportAccord	3				

Table 5. Combat sports with a rating system (9)

Sport	Int. Fed.	Recognition	Type of Rating System	Accum. Years
Boxing	AIBA	IOC Summer	Accumulative	4
Fencing	FIE	IOC Summer	Accumulative	1
Judo	IJF	IOC Summer	Accumulative	2
Sumo Wrestling	ISF	IOC	Accumulative	1
Taekwondo	WTF	IOC Summer	Accumulative	3
Kickboxing	WAKO(WKF)	SportAccord	Subjective	
Mixed Martial Arts	ISCF	Wikipedia	Subjective	
Wresting- Greco Roman	FILA	IOC Summer	Subjective	
Wrestling-Freestyle	FILA	IOC Summer	Subjective	

Table 6. Mind sports with a rating system (4)

Sport	Int. Fed.	Recognition	Type of Rating System	Accum. Years
Bridge	WBF	IOC	Accumulative	7
Chess	FIDE	IOC	Adjustive Elo	
Draughts	FMJD	SportAccord	Adjustive Elo	
Go	IGF(EGF)	SportAccord	Adjustive Elo	

- A marketer should refer to the Elo rating system, using descriptions "sophisticated', "discerning," "well-respected," "widely-used" and "historic" to reinforce the importance of Elo ratings.
- The WBF bridge federation employs "master points" accumulated and aged.
- As with the other mind sports, anyone associated with bridge will already understand master points.
- The various suggestions marketing with an accumulative system hold here.

MARKETING IMPLICATIONS FOR SPORTS WITHOUT A RATING SYSTEM

Table 7 contains the remaining 54 sports which lack a rating system. Most of these sports have regional interest; but only modest international interest; hence no rating systems are available at present. American football is obviously popular in the USA. Some American football teams have played abroad with good attendance. What is mentioned here is the IFAF federation which has organized world cup competition for national teams in 1999, 2003, 2007 and 2011, an effort largely unknown in the USA. Australian Rules football has been played aboard. A set of International Rules are employed for Australian-Irish competition, combining Gaelic football with Australian Rules football.

Table 7. Sports without a rating system (54)

Sport	Int. Fed.	Recognition	Sport	Int. Fed.	Recognition
Combat Sports			**Object Sports**		
Aikido	IAF	SportAccord	American Football	IFAF	SportAccord
Ju-Jitsu	JJIF	SportAccord	Australian Rules Football	ARI	Wikipedia
Kabbadi	WFK	Wikipedia	Bandy	FIB	IOC
Karate	WKF	IOC	Bocci	CMSB (CBI)	IOC
Kendo	FIK	SportAccord	Broomball	IFBA	Wikipedia
Muaythai	IFMA	SportAccord	English Billiards	WCBS (IBSF)	IOC
Sambo	FIAS	SportAccord	Fistball	IFA	SportAccord
Savate	FISav	SportAccord	Floorball	IFF	IOC
Wushu	IWUF(IKF)	IOC	Gaelic Football	GAA	Wikipedia
Independent Sports			**Object Sports**		
Aerobatics	FAI	IOC	Hurling	GAA	Wikipedia
Apnea	CMAS	IOC	Inline Roller Hockey	FIRS	IOC
Artistic Roller Skating	FIRS	IOC	Lacrosse	FIL(IFWLA, ELF)	Wikipedia
Ballooning	FAI	IOC	Pelota Vasca	FIPV	IOC
Bodybuilding	IFBB	SportAccord	Pesapallo	PESIS	Wikipedia
Casting	ICSF	SportAccord	Petanque	CMSB(FIFJP)	IOC
Dragon Boats	IDBF	SportAccord	Polo	FIP	IOC
Finswimming	CMAS	IOC	Rock it Ball	IRIBF	Wikipedia
Fishing	CIPS	SportAccord	Roller Hockey	FIRS	IOC
Horseshoes	NHPA	Wikipedia	Rounders	NRA	Wikipedia
Life Saving	ILSF	IOC	Sepak Takrow	ISTAF	SportAccord
Practical Shooting	IPSC	Wikipedia	Shinty	CA	Wikipedia
Rafting	IRF	Wikipedia	Softball	ISF	IOC
Skibobbing	FISB	Wikipedia	Sport Bowls	CMSB(FIB)	IOC
Skydiving	FAI	IOC	Throwball	ITF	Wikipedia
Synchronized Swimming	FINA	IOC Summer	Tug of War	TWIF	IOC
Ultra-light Aircraft	FAI	IOC	Underwater Hockey	CMAS	IOC
Underwater Orienteering	CMAS	IOC	Underwater Rugby	CMAS	IOC

A number of the sports are lesser known. Kabbadi is popular in India. The players play a rough wrestling-like version of tag holding their breath. Dragon boats are very ornate crafts rowed by a large crew. Practical shooting simulates combat shooting. Sepek Takrow is popular in Indonesia: volleyball using only the feet. Underwater hockey is played by flicking a lead puck along the bottom of a pool. Underwater rugby involves trying to push a water-filled ball into a net at the bottom of the pool. Apnea is another underwater breath-holding sport, determined by swimming as deeply as possible in one event and far as possible horizontally in another event. Only one of the 54 sports is in the Olympics, synchronized swimming.

Many of theses sports have world championships. Those results can be used as a surrogate for a rating system. Advertise an upcoming competition as including certain medal winners, finalists, etc. from the recent international competitions. Bring visibility to a few improving competitors who may challenge for a medal at the next world championship. Advertise the specific accomplishments of top competitors. As mentioned above, attention is given by the media and to possible attendees whenever specific numbers are mentioned.

CONCLUSION

Recognized world sports federations appear to have chosen their official rating systems with marketing in mind. The profile of rating systems for each type of sport gives guidance as to the special features of each sport that should be exploited to enhance fan interest and therefore to enhance sales of tickets and sports paraphernalia. Accumulative systems encourage teams and individuals to enter as many competitions as possible and 55% of all rating systems involve an accumulative one-year window, in which a seasonal champion can be crowned. A marketer can chronicle the build up to that title among top contenders throughout the season, especially for the time preceding the final.

Combat sports such as wrestling, boxing and judo are intensely personal. A marketer should present top competitors in personal terms to the awaiting audience to draw them into the drama of the contest.

All but one of the independent sports has an accumulative rating system. Often that accumulative system amounts to that year's best performance. A rating in seconds and meters is more tangible than one in points. A marketer can illustrate the small gap between top competitors, making potential attendees realize each performance they will see could vault a challenger to the top for that season.

The rating systems for object sports have a mixture of point accumulators and the more sophisticated systems that self adjust, compensating for the relative strengths of the opponents. The accumulative systems provide information as to how close competitors are and which competitors are moving up. That information creates interest in an upcoming competition. The specific critical numerical values tend to be picked up by the media providing free advertising. The ratings gain credibility when the adjustive rating systems are described as being accurate, discerning, sophisticated and well-respected.

For mind sports, the rating systems are quite appropriately of the sophisticated self-adjustive type. A marketer must realize that players and audiences for mind sports are sophisticated and knowledgeable; hence, marketing must be equally sophisticated.

The tables covering the 159 sports and 105 rating systems are interesting in their own right. Readers may become interested in currently-obscure sports which await organized marketing efforts.

REFERENCES

Bloom, P.N., et al. (2006, January 1). How social-cause marketing affects consumer perceptions. *MIT Sloan Management Magazine: Opinion and Analysis.*

Kahle, L. R., & Close, A. G. (Eds.). (2011). *Consumer behavior knowledge for effective sports and event marketing*. London: Routledge.

Mittre, M., & Ordonez de Pablos, P. (2009). The power of sports marketing. *International Journal of Sport Management and Marketing*, *5*(3), 330–337. doi:10.1504/IJSMM.2009.023241

(1983). *Random House Encyclopedia*. New York: Random House.

Stefani, R. T. (1999). A taxonomy of sports rating systems. *IEEE Transactions on Systems, Man and Cybernetics. Part A*, *29*(1), 116–120.

Stefani, R. T. (2011). The methodology of officially recognized sports rating systems. *Journal of Quantitative Analysis in Sports*, *7*(4). doi:10.2202/1559-0410.1347

Stotlar, D. K. (1993). *Successful sport marketing. Brown and Benchmark. Official World Encyclopedia of Sports and Games. (1979)*. London: Paddington.

KEY TERMS AND DEFINITIONS

Accumulative Rating System: A rating system that converts performance to points with a non-decreasing running sum over a window of time. The points involve the result of the competition, importance and the year that competition occurred.

Adjustive Rating System: A rating system in which actual performance is compared to a target based on past performance such that a rating increases, decreases or remains the same depending on whether the actual result for the competitor or team is better, worse or the same, respectively, as the target.

Combat Sport: A physical sport in which the competitor comes in direct contact with the opponent in an effort to control the opponent.

Independent Sport: A physical sport in which contact is not allowed, as each competitor performs unimpeded by the opponent.

Mind Sport: A sport where a surrogate can make the play for the competitor, thus not requiring physical prowess.

Object Sport: A sport where contact occurs in an effort to control an object.

Physical Sport: A competition in which the competitor must make each play, as physical prowess is required.

Rating System: A system that creates a numerical value for each competitor or team. Each such competitor or team is then ranked in ordinal position based on the rating.

Sport: A competition with a set of rules for determining the winner.

Sports Federation: An international organization that organizes sports competition, as recognized by the International Olympic Committee, Sport Accord or as listed in Wikipedia for an internationally widely-played sport.

This research was previously published in Strategies in Sports Marketing edited by Manuel Alonso Dos Santos, pages 58-72, copyright year 2014 by Business Science Reference (an imprint of IGI Global).

Chapter 10
Social Media and Marketing:
The Evolution of Tottenham Hotspur Football Club

Ivan K. Cohen
Richmond, The American International University in London, UK

ABSTRACT

Tottenham Hotspur ("Spurs") Football Club were once the most entrepreneurial of English football teams, including being the first to obtain a stock market flotation and to attempt to diversify into other areas beyond their core. However, like many football clubs, they were slow to embrace the Internet including more recently the use of social media for marketing. This chapter investigates the history of Spurs' embrace of the Internet and social media and asks why a club traditionally renowned for its flair and enterprise on the pitch has been so slow to embrace modernity in the digital world.

INTRODUCTION

Association Football (football) is probably the world's most popular sport. Although fans of different clubs can often have a hostile relationship, football is one sport which globally unites people from all nations. It is beloved by every nationality on Earth. At the time of writing the world (with the possible exception of England fans!) is savouring the delights of the 2014 World Cup, hosted by Brazil. Both in-attendance at matches and via television, viewers of the World Cup continue to exceed those for that other worldwide sporting spectacle, the Olympic Games. According to AT Kearney (May 2011) the worldwide market for major sports events was worth €45 billion ($64 billion) in 2009. This includes revenues from ticketing, media and marketing. Football has the largest share of this market with global revenues of €20 billion ($28 billion) *per annum*. This is almost as much as the €23 billion ($32 billion) for all US sports on aggregate. European football is estimated as being worth €16 billion ($22 billion), with the five biggest leagues (English Premier League, Germany's Bundesliga, Italy's Serie A, Spain's La Liga and France's Ligue 1) taking half that share. It has long been acknowledged that top football teams attract a global following. One of the most popular football leagues around the world is the English

DOI: 10.4018/978-1-5225-5475-2.ch010

Premier League (EPL). Located in the historic home of football—the country in which the Laws of The Game were first promulgated—the EPL boasts one of the most cosmopolitan groups of players in this increasingly globalised sport. In order to compete English football clubs must constantly find new ways to increase revenues so that they can continue to attract the best players and provide stadia worthy of the fans who pay to attend. With an increasingly global audience it makes sense for EPL teams to pursue a global marketing strategy, to market their teams and associated merchandise in an attempt to boost revenues. In the modern world such a strategy needs to make full use of all forms of digital media, including the various forms of the Internet (websites, e-mail) and the more contemporary social media in its various guises. In this chapter our focus is on Tottenham Hotspur Football Club. Although football clubs have only turned to use social media in the past two to three years, we consider their use for marketing and other purposes, and consider the degree to which it has boosted club revenues.

Founded in 1882, Tottenham Hotspur Football Club (hereafter Spurs or THFC) is a professional Association Football team in north London. They play their home matches at "White Hart Lane" stadium, which is actually on the High Road N17, around the corner from White Hart Lane (the road). The club was named by its founders in respect for Sir Harry Hotspur (Sir Henry Percy, 1364–1463) partly due to his fame as a chivalrous and brave swashbuckling fighter, and also to recognise the association between the Tottenham area and the Percy family who lived locally during the 14th century and whose descendants owned land in the area. Sir Henry Percy is one of Shakespeare's best-known characters, making a strong appearance in *Henry IV, Part I*. Since it's founding, the club has always been renowned for playing attractive football with flair, something it's current supporters still demand. As former captain, the late Danny Blanchflower (1926–1993) argued:

The game is about glory. It's about doing things in style, with a flourish, about going out and beating the other lot, not waiting for them to die of boredom.

Blanchflower was echoing both the traditional spirit of the club and its Latin Motto "*audere est facere*", "to dare is to do". Spurs' history is replete with a large number of "firsts": they won the FA Cup in 1901, the only non-League club to do so since the Football League was formed. They were the first team in the 20th century to achieve the League and Cup "double", something considered almost impossible at the time (1960–1961). In 1963 they were the first British club to win a European competition, the European Cup Winners' Cup. They were the inaugural winners of the UEFA Cup in 1972, the first British team to win two major European trophies. Winning the League Cup a further time in 2008 meant that Spurs had won a major trophy in each of the last six decades, something matched only by Manchester United.

Given their renown for flair and enterprise on the field of play, one might imagine it should be reflected similarly in managerial performance by the Board of Directors. At the very least, it would make good commercial sense for a football club enjoying success—which can often be fleeting—to cash in on that success by improved marketing efforts. This assumes that a football club would have in place a properly devised marketing strategy, increasingly global in its outlook. The history of Spurs does not reflect that as a reality, the Boardroom often being a conservative bulwark to the on-pitch flair and entertainment. The only real exception to this in Spurs' history occurs in 1983, when new chairman Irving Scholar floated the club on the London Stock Exchange, the first English club to gain a stock market listing. It was Scholar who boosted the club's marketing efforts with the appointment of Edward Freedman, and diversified into leisure-wear (Hummel and Martex) and computer systems, the aim being that profits from these would boost the coffers of the football club. Freedman was Managing Director, Merchandising Division, Tottenham Hotspur Football Club between 1987 and 1992. When he left Spurs in 1992 (for Manchester United) it's football-merchandising turnover was the highest in England and 50% above that of Manchester United. During his time at Spurs, Freedman overhauled the retail operational structure, reviewed licensing, strengthened branding, and made Tottenham Hotspur a commercial force to be reckoned with. Freedman took his expertise and experience to Manchester United, and combined with the on-field success of the teams managed by Sir Alex Ferguson leveraged Manchester United to the most profitably and wealthy football club on Earth.

However, in the Internet age, sports teams, and especially football teams increasingly face new and increasing hurdles to get more fans through the turnstiles. Increasing competition from new leisure activities, both real and virtual, as well as the convergence of digital media and sports—so that sports can be viewed both on 'traditional' television and via the Internet—has meant that football fans can watch the game at the stadium or from the comfort of their own home. To compete stadiums need to offer more than simply a 90-minute game. The entire matchday experience counts, and with the uncertain English weather as a backdrop, football clubs must work harder than ever to bring supporters through the turnstiles. One of the avenues to which football (and other sporting) clubs have turned is a range of engagement initiatives. These are meant to provide supporters with a fuller matchday experience for their money thereby creating more lasting memories and, hopefully a bigger spend on merchandise. And there is no more important form of engagement than social media, which were designed for exactly that purpose: to bring people together!

SOCIAL MEDIA AND MARKETING

(For the origins of the Internet, and the use of social media for marketing see Salaber and Cohen in this volume)

Although the origins of the Internet began much earlier with ARPANET, the Internet for ordinary people began to appear in the early 1990s. The appearance of a new graphical interface, replacing the former menu-driven TELNET approach, began to make using the Internet a much more user-friendly experience, enabling access for non-technical members of the general public. By 1994 the Internet was showing clear signs of becoming of a commercial hub, primarily in the United States. Shopping malls and banks were among the first organisations to spot its commercial potential and establish a virtual presence. The switch from dial-up access (telephone access using a modem) to broadband simply accelerated the accessibility for the general public to the Internet. In the past 20 years the Internet has gone from being a haven for IT geeks and nerds to a communications medium for the general public all over the world. To say it has been transformative of lives sounds exaggerated, but remains a truth.

Despite its relative youth, the Internet has always been constantly reinventing itself. Although the concept of a website has now become firmly entrenched, the Internet more broadly continues to evolve and develop, thereby providing new and different opportunities for football clubs (Weeks *et al*, 2008). More recent Web 2.0 developments have offered a range of powerful new tools with which football clubs are able to market themselves (Seo and Green, 2008). Carlson and O'Cass (2012) have identified brand management and the optimisation of e-service platforms as a critical issue in sports management. In recent years this has been achievable via the increasing appearance of social media, providing new and ever-more accessible ways to join the virtual world. The names are well known throughout the world: Facebook, Twitter, LinkedIn, Instagram, Vine, Pinterest, and WhatsApp all provide media for social communication for both individuals and business. These names are even well known in countries where they are blocked, such as China. In such places other, homegrown, versions have been developed. Thus, in China Tencent's WeChat (a Twitter/Facebook amalgam) and are widely used, and have become especially popular with students. An interesting infographic of the various social media available, including suggestions for "best practice" is available at http://socialtimes.com/social-media-best-practices-marketers-2014-infographic_b148047.

In the past five years the development of smartphones and other mobile devices, such as iPads, has meant that Internet access has gone from being temporally available but also spatially available wherever there is a Wi-Fi or 3G/4G signal. The Internet no longer requires its users to be sat down at a desktop or laptop personal computer; mobile devices have taken over. A mobile device enables its user to know where they are (using a map app), what shops, restaurants, etc are nearby, and to make purchases on the move from shops which might be in any location. The use of mobile devices as a payments mechanism is in its infancy, but rapidly growing.

Modern social media have been subject to the same criticisms as were new channels of communication in previous generations—radio, cinema, and television—considered as a fad that would rapidly pass. History has proven all of the critics wrong, although it is probably still too early to pass final judgment on the success or otherwise of social media. According to a recent article in the *Financial Times* (Kuchler, 2014), social media may have initially emerged as a means of bringing teenagers and younger adults together, but they have long since become a key and integral element in the lives of billions of Earth's population across all demographics. Although Twitter does not resonate with all 'netizens' (citizens of the 'net), Facebook has become almost as ubiquitous as telephones and newspapers. LinkedIn has become an essential, a prerequisite for netizens of the virtual professional world. In China Tencent's WeChat has become equally as prevalent, and is the most popular app in Asia. Kuchler's article notes that twenty per cent of the top brands of 2014 are in the technology sector, but the fastest risers in the 'league table' are companies whose missions are to make social media as much of a common utility as electricity. Because social media are essentially global in their outreach (with the exception being one or two countries, such as China or Iran, which block Facebook or Twitter to prevent potentially subversive postings) they form the perfect tool for global marketing. The reach of social media increases daily.

Social media enables many objectives to be met by both individuals and companies (both for-profit and not-for-profit). In addition to being able to market themselves, social media also enables individuals and companies to build and enhance their online brand. LinkedIn, for example, is replete with examples from digital media gurus as to the best way to do this.

The use of social media to access global markets is available at relatively low cost, and often enables a company to target potential customers more narrowly than traditional advertising. Twitter and Facebook messages can be "liked" and also re-Tweeted or shared to reach an even wider audience. Although the core product of a football club is essentially local, there are peripheral products which naturally lend themselves to the broader global marketplace. Merchandise—such as replica shirts, other clothing, books, video recordings (DVDs), jewelry and household items—can easily be ordered online and shipped to overseas locations. However, with modern high-speed broadband, it is possible for overseas supporters to watch the streaming of live games, to subscribe to a club's online TV station, or to pay for and download recordings of contemporary or classic matches. There are eight primary reasons why a company might choose to pursue a global marketing strategy:

1. **Opportunistic Global Market Development (Diversifying Markets):** Modern telecommunications has enabled football clubs, including Spurs, to push into overseas markets. On the demand side there has been an increasing level of overseas support of English Premier League clubs due to the high profile gained from matches being televised almost globally. Additionally, global interest in English Premier League teams has been enhanced by the large and increasing numbers of overseas (non-English) players in the English Premier League. Spurs are renowned for being one of the first top-flight clubs to 'import' overseas players successfully when, in 1978, they brought two World Cup winning players, Osvaldo Ardiles and Ricardo Villa, to their ranks. The use of social media provides a cheap, yet effective way to engage both domestic and overseas fans, maintaining their interest and ultimately marketing club merchandise.
2. **Following Customers Abroad (Customer Satisfaction):** This may well have been the original factor pushing football clubs, including Spurs into digital marketing. Since the 1980s the fan base of football clubs has moved further away from the stadium geographically. There has been a phenomenon of increasing labour movement across countries, so that the current generation of Spurs' supporters overseas are often the offspring of previous generations from London or fans who themselves have found employment overseas. For a football club to maintain its connection with these fans requires use of modern telecommunications media. While this would have included websites and then e-mail in the late 20th and early 21st centuries, the use of social media has come increasingly to the fore in more recent years, as evidenced in Accepted Socially (2104).
3. **Pursuing Geographic Diversification:** Similar to 1, the objective here is more defensive, more about risk management. Geographic diversification helps to reduce the risk of domestic revenue uncertainty, stabilising revenues in the process. If there is reduced support (for whatever reason) in one region of the globe it may be offset by increased support elsewhere. However, the connection between team success on the pitch and support cannot be completely diversified away.
4. **Exploiting Different Economic Growth Rates (Gaining Scale and Scope):** It is a fact that the economies of Earth do not grow at the same rate. Indeed, while some economies are in recession others may be growing. The use of social media—as an extension of other digital media—enables Spurs to tap into growing economies and market its products more rapidly where the economic growth is more rapid.
5. **Exploiting Product Life Cycle Differences (Technology):** While the Internet has become a global phenomenon, it is more widely accessible in high-income economies. As social media becomes an older more established channel in those high-income economies the ability of a football club like Tottenham to leverage sales will reach a plateau. At the same time, growth in lower-income economies will enable their citizens to have greater and cheaper access to the digital world, including social media, enabling growth to continue for Spurs.
6. **Pursuing Potential Abroad:** There is a two-way relationship between having overseas players at Spurs and being able to reach (including convert) supporters overseas. For example, when Tottenham acquired Israeli international, Ronnie Rosenthal, in the 1980s, interest in Spurs from Israel increased significantly. The same with interest from Bulgaria when Tottenham acquired Bulgarian international, Dimitar Berbatov in 2006. Social media, both by Spurs itself, and by the individual players, enables the club to leverage its marketability beyond what is possible using more traditional marketing tools, including e-mail and websites.

7. **Globalising for Defensive Reasons:** Although most English football clubs are not renowned for their off-field spirit of enterprise, the prospect of being out-competed in overseas markets by other EPL clubs may force them to go global for defensive reasons
8. **Pursuing a Global Logic or Imperative (New Markets and Profits):** To a large degree this may be seen as an extension of 6. However, the strategy behind this objective is to increase the overall reach and access globally, based on more than the relationships between players and supporters of the same nationality. The success of the English Premier League in terms of TV viewing figures overseas enables clubs to pursue overseas markets on a wider basis.

It is easy to see that the use of online marketing, including social media, can be seen as one tool among a portfolio for pursuing any combination or all eight of these reasons.

There is an intriguing literature building in reviewing the impact of social media as a marketing tool. This includes Hoffman & Fodor (2010), Chiang, I-Ping & Hsieh (2011) and the fascinating Trattner & Kappe (2013). Barker, Barker, Borman & Neher (2013) note the following examples of successful returns from social media marketing efforts:

- "Dell generated $6.5 million dollars from its Twitter account.
- Marriott got over $500 million in bookings directly from its blog.
- Golden Tee saved tens of thousands of dollars running a contest on Facebook.
- VistaPrints sold $300,000 from social media marketing.
- Lenovo saved costs with a 20% reduction in customer service calls by using social media.
- Naked Pizza, a small regional pizza chain, had its highest-ever sales day from deals posted on Twitter."

MARKETING AND TOTTENHAM HOTSPUR

At first glance, the simplest way to generate additional revenues for any company is to reduce price. Whether or not this will increase revenues depends on the degree to which a given price drop increases sales volume: i.e. the elasticity of demand. A decade before the founding of the English Premier League, Bird (1982) using data between 1948 and 1980, calculated the price elasticity of demand as -0.2, and the income demand elasticity for football as -0.60, showing demand for football to be price-inelastic and an inferior good. Additionally, he found that the demand for league football was less elastic for higher divisions than lower. A similar study for the time period 1962–1992 was undertaken by Simmons (1996). One of his findings was that demand was more elastic for 'casual' spectators than for season-ticket holders. He discovered that the demand for football was short-term price inelastic, but more elastic in the longer-run. Other factors influencing demand for football include league position, goals scored, as promotion/relegation. However, empirically football clubs have been both to reduce prices to stimulate demand, partly based on the loyalty of their support base as evidenced by the low price elasticity of demand. This leaves them with one other option: marketing.

There are many people who would argue that modern-day football has become over-commercialised. Yet there is recognition of the importance of marketing and merchandising for football: supporters demand better and more iconic players for their teams, the funds for which have to come from somewhere in addition to the pockets of supporters. For many supporters the purchase of club merchandise is a statement of identity—albeit not a cheap statement—for the football clubs in England (and elsewhere) marketing and merchandising provides an additional revenue stream to pay for the ever-increasing salaries of professional footballers and their stratospheric transfer fees. Without this additional stream of revenue the cost of attending a football match would be even more prohibitive than it already is (the average cost per game at White Hart Lane in 2013–2014 was some £42 in the cheaper seats; this does not include the cost of transport, purchase of food, drink or a programme, or any other 'extras'). This is a far cry from the way things were before the foundation of the Premier League in 1992.

Back in the 1960s and early 1970s football clubs were slow to realise the possibilities of marketing. A football supporter wishing to wear the shirt of his (or occasionally her) favourite team would buy a T-shirt of the appropriate colour and then purchase the club badge, which they would usually cajole their mother into sewing onto the shirt. Scarves and bobble hats were usually homemade, knitted in the club colours by those self-same mothers! Things began to change in the 1973–1974 season, when sports manufacturer Admiral pioneered the introduction and development of the replica kit in the UK with its deal with Leeds United, then one of the top team in Europe. That season Leeds wore the first visibly branded kit in the top division of English football. On the heels of that deal, Admiral struck a five-year deal with the English FA in 1984 to produce the first commercially available England team shirt, with the Admiral logo evident. The success of commercial replica football kits has been such that there is almost no football team without one, and many change the design every other year to encourage supporters to provide ever-more revenues to their particular team.

It is usually the case that selling focuses on the needs of the seller, while marketing focuses on the needs of the customer or client. In order to achieve its primary objective (value maximisation) a company needs to acquire customers and keep them. The management guru, Peter Drucker, referred to this as creating and keeping a customer, usually though product differentiation and price competition. International marketing involves marketing products (goods and/or services) overseas, i.e. beyond the company's domestic market. Global marketing refers to activities which are coordinated and integrated across multiple markets. For a football club, in particular, this can be achieved using the same website, often available in multiple languages.

While many commercial organisations were quick to embrace the new technologies embodied in the Internet, some have always harboured doubts about its value for marketing. This has been even more marked with the advent of social media, whose profitable use for marketing purposes remains uncertain. Nonetheless, nowadays it is hard to find a football club which does not at least possess its own website, enabling the sale of match tickets and associated club merchandise in addition to providing news, views, and sometimes a forum for supporters' discussions. (In truth, club websites tend to be somewhat anaemic, providing propaganda, anodyne views and a moderated discussion to eliminate views not considered helpful to the club).

Most top-flight football clubs have had a website presence for some two decades. However, from a marketing perspective, a successful website needs to be quite interactive and it needs to be refreshed constantly to keep it's content interesting and (sometimes) surprising. A static unchanging website does not generate too many visitors. In other commercial organisations potential customers may not be aware of their website existence; for a football club's supporters a quick search via Google makes finding the website easy.

The advent of social media has turned this selection process around. A football club with a presence on Twitter or Facebook will easily be found and "Followed" or "Liked" by its supporters and other well-wishers. A well-placed small advertisement on Facebook or series of sponsored Tweets lets supporters know of news and any marketing efforts, as well as offering links to the club website for more information. Facebook, in particular, also offers a greater degree of targeted marketing, so that advertising for matches or some new merchandising can be sent only to those likely to be interested. Additionally, Facebook and Twitter provide uncensored forums for discussion of both on-field and off-field matters, which most supporters find more attractive than website forums. Many football clubs also direct their supporters to their website, or particular aspects of it, with the use of regular e-mailings, and postings to Facebook and/or Twitter.

It needs to be recognised that social media, like many new technologies, began largely as the preserve of teenagers and young 20s—the so-called Generations Y and Z. Although social media usage has spread more widely across the entire range of age groups, football supporters largely comprise people in their late teens and twenties: Generations Y and Z. Because social media are how young people prefer to communicate, then it makes good sense for football clubs to communicate with them via social media. As a marketing tool social media has largely been driven by the consumer. Producers have been a little slow to catch on to its potential, none more so than football clubs. Nonetheless, there still remains scepticism as to the effectiveness of social media in generating sales. Jeff Elder's (2014) *Wall Street Journal* article highlights evidence from a Gallup survey of 18,525 US adults conducted between December 2012 and January 2013 on the influence of social media on purchasing decisions. The general results of this survey were as follows:

The results shown in Table 1 came from a survey focusing mainly on Facebook and Twitter, to the exclusion of other forms of social media. With some 62% of respondents suggesting that social media extended no influence on their purchasing decisions, the notion of using social media as a marketing tool might well be decried. Of course, survey results can be notoriously spurious, and it may well be that many of the adults polled did not wish to admit to having been influenced by social media in their purchasing behaviour. There is also the possibility that companies have yet to find a way to make their use of social media effective as a means of generating revenues. Because social media are still in their infancy as a marketing tool companies are still trying to find the best way to utilise them. In the longer run the use of social media as a mechanism for creating and maintaining brand loyalty may be more optimal than their short-term direct use to try to generate sales. Comments about a particular brand by the general public via social media can be used by a company to improve their product offerings. In turn, this may generate improved sales in the longer term.

Table 1. The influence of social media on purchasing decisions: evidence from a Gallup survey

No influence at all	62%
Some influence	30%
A great deal of influence	5%
Don't know	3%

TOTTENHAM HOTSPUR AND THE INTERNET

In the early 1990s Spurs were both slow and reluctant to embrace the Internet age. This was despite the chairman of the club being Lord (then Sir Alan) Sugar, an entrepreneur who had made his name in the personal computer revolution of the 1980s and the satellite TV boom of the 1980s–1990s. Of course, entrepreneurs are fallible; in February 2005, Lord Sugar predicted that the iPod would be "dead, finished, gone, kaput" by the following Christmas. This topped a poll as one of the ten worst technology predictions ever! During several Annual General Meetings of THFC during the early 1990s (1993, 1994) myself and others asked Lord Sugar when THFC would be setting up a website, only to be brushed aside in his inimitable brusque manner, and the internet denounced as a passing fad (much like the iPod!). By 1995 someone at Spurs had decided that the Internet was more than passing fad, and that they required a web presence. Their first website was produced around 1995 by Jacqui Cawley, and was something of a bare-bones effort focusing almost solely on marketing merchandise. By 1997 Spurs were outsourcing their own website to a professional organisation, and it started to take the form from which it has evolved into today's slick professional tool. It is only in the past two years or so that Spurs have fully embraced social media, such as Facebook and Twitter. However, as we note in the next section, they have fully embraced these new tools to develop a greater rapport with supporters, both at home and overseas.

SOCIAL MEDIA AS A MARKETING TOOL

In today's world sport has become a global product (Ratten & Ratten 2011), none more so than football. However, sports marketing transactions contain different types of relationship marketing (Tower & Deery, 2006). Many sporting organizations, and especially football clubs have recognised the importance of their relationship with supporters, who regard themselves as the "true" long-term custodians of *their* club. Thus football clubs have focused on using social media for relationship programmes, with the twin aims of retaining supporters (consumers) over the longer term while also aiming for improved relationship quality. Hajli & Hajli (2013) have considered the use of social media as a means of establishing social interaction with supporters. Users of social media are a wide range of people, many of who integrate social media into their daily activities (Okazaki, 2009). Nambisan & Baron (2007) showed how social media provide new ways of communicating with consumers. Mangold & Faulds (2009) argue consider social media to be a hybrid element in the promotion mix, enabling companies to talk directly to their customers, and also for customers to communicate with each other. However, because this is outside of the direct control of marketing managers, unlike traditional marketing media, they need to learn to shape consumer attitudes differently. Managers need to learn to loosen the reins and shape consumer preferences in line with the company's mission and goals using networking platforms, blogs and social media to engage customers. The corporate inertia which prevents this from occurring was explored in McLean & Wainwright (2009), who examined the relationship between Newcastle United Football Club and its supporters. They found that:

Although steps to enable free communication have been made we are still a long way off supporters having a powerful enough voice to organise against the commercial power of the large football clubs and media conglomerates. The ideal speech situation remains elusive and the hegemonic state remains unchallenged. Football supporters are increasingly constructed as "consumers" and the ultimate power remains in mass media and broadcast rather than personal "narrowcast."

This is similar to the situation at Spurs and, in all probability, almost all EPL football clubs until it became obvious that the universe of social media could no longer be ignored. It is obvious that Spurs have made great strides to become more internet-savvy in the past couple of years, with a presence on all of the major social media. A recent report by Accepted Socially, marketing research and insights consultancy, based in London (acceptedsocially.com/social-media-in-the-premier-league) noted the following about Spurs' recent use of social media:

On the first day of looking at Spurs' social media activities, the North-London club hosted a Twitter Q&A with its contingent of Belgian players, Jan Vertonghen, Nacer Chadli and Mousa Dembele. Well promoted via its other channels, the #spursqa initiative trended in the UK (though inevitably this was partly down to 'ambush' questions submitted by fans of rival teams). However it demonstrates Spurs' commitment to social networks as a way of bringing the club and its players closer to its fans. It also regularly enters into dialogue with supporters on Twitter and frequently throws out questions to them, particularly around their matchday plans, retweeting photos and responses.

On Facebook, fans are encouraged to vote for their man-of-the-match by liking pictures of certain players while regular training galleries give fans that 'behind-closed-doors' access they appreciate.

Across both channels there's the usual news and activity around and during matches. There's also regular pushes for Spurs Connect, an interactive mobile game that fans can play while watching live matches.

Commercial messages aren't overdone

Spurs' does use its channels to raise awareness of certain products and services - like its soccer schools, merchandise stores and the usual tickets and programmes - as well as highlighting match odds through betting partner BetFred, but such posts are occasional.

The club does regularly push its Spurs TV online service though and it's on here that the vast majority of its video content is kept for paying customers.

Occasionally videos are available on YouTube but they are short and its clear the best content (including any interviews with Tim Sherwood) are kept for Spurs TV.

Instagram is regularly updated with the typical club and match pictures. Pictures of fans pre-game are also a regular feature (via FanCam), another way of making them feel part of the Spurs community. The club can also be found on Vine and Google+, where content is similar to that seen on Facebook.

Ranked according to four key criteria, Spurs notched up a score of 16.5, coming joint fourth in the social media league. The results table for all English Premier League Clubs is reproduced in Appendix 1, while that for Tottenham Hotspur is in Appendix 2.

The evidence for the success of social media as a marketing tool remains spurious. Table 2 (following) shows the revenue streams for Tottenham Hotspur in recent years:

Unfortunately, the reported data is very highly aggregated. Analysis of commercial revenues from direct vs. online sources would have been particularly helpful, but the pressures of time and distance (the author is currently in China, where internet access is sporadic and sometimes blocked) made it difficult to obtain more insightful information from Tottenham Hotspur. When contact has been made it has been rebuffed on the basis that such information is "price sensitive" and not available for the public domain. However, based on the available data we might note the following:

- Initially we might expect the increased use of social media to have a positive impact on commercial revenues. For example, both domestic and overseas supporters might be more inclined to purchase merchandise as a result of an increased sense of affiliation deriving from social media. Commercial revenues did increase between 2012–2013 by 5.44%, but this might also be accounted for by (i) increasing prices for season tickets and merchandise, and (ii) the initial euphoria over the purchase of seven new players with the money (£100m) from the sale of Gareth Bale to Real

Table 2. Tottenham Hotspur FC: revenue streams

	(£'000)						
	2013	***2012***	**2012**	**2011**	**2010**	**2009**	**2008**
Match receipts	33,491	*31,303*					
Gate receipts–Premier League			21,434	20,416	20,123	19,792	18,274
Cup competitions–Gate receipts and domestic prize money			6,225	9,962	6,726	8,065	10,341
UEFA solidarity and prize money			4,344	29,453			
Sponsorship and corporate hospitality			35,144	31,837	25,763	27,363	27,778
TV and media (Media and broadcasting)	57,347	*59,217*	59,217	54,016	51,519	44,811	40,329
Commercial	56,554	*53,636*					
Merchandising			9,211	9,553	7,793	6,960	9,723
Other			8,581	8,249	7,890	6,021	8,343
	147,392	***144,156***	**144,156**	**163,486**	**119,814**	**113,012**	**114,788**
European competition	EL	*EL*	EL	CL	–	UEFA Cup	UEFA Cup
EL =Europa League CL = Champions League							

Source: Tottenham Hotspur Football Club (various years) *Annual Report and Account*

Madrid. While some of this additional commercial revenue might be due to an increase in online sales, some would also come from direct purchases made in the Spurs' shops around London. Without additional disaggregated data this is impossible to ascertain.

- It might also be the case that social media increases the desire of supporters to attend matches, at which they might also purchase merchandise, etc. While there has been something of an increase (4.99%) in gate receipts in the past two years from which we can date Spurs' increased use of social media), it is in line with the previous upward trend and may be accounted for by increased cost of a seat or season ticket.
- Like other companies (including football clubs), Tottenham Hotspur are learning how to best use social media as a matter of trial-and-error. A typical daily Twitter feed from @SpursOfficial consists of some 20 Tweets, including photos of training sessions or matches, direct marketing of Spurs and affiliated companies and sponsors (e.g. UnderArmour) merchandise, competitions, details of match tickets, and real-time details of matches as they are being played. There are also re-Tweets from the Twitter-feeds of players and some ex-players. Spurs, in common with other EPL clubs, have yet to find the best way to use social media—which are still in their infancy—to generate additional revenues. This author believes that the optimal use of social media is as a mechanism for creating and maintaining brand loyalty, rather than as a short-term strategy to try and generate sales directly.

CONCLUSION AND FUTURE RESEARCH

In using Tottenham Hotspur as the basis for this research the author is certainly revealing his own affiliations and prejudices! However, as the Accepted Socially (2014) study reveals, the top-flight clubs in the English Premier League tend to do things in tandem. While many of the clubs in the upper echelons show flair and enterprise on the pitch, they are more loth to do so off-the-pitch, especially when it comes to the adoption of new (and hence untried) technologies. However, once one club makes the move others tend to follow for fear of being left behind. This has certainly been the case with all forms of online marketing, and especially social media. However, without a greater degree of disaggregation of the data it is difficult to ascertain whether or not social media have made a significant contribution to the club's revenue streams. It is also true that two or so years may not be an adequate length of time in which to make a judgment on the success or otherwise of social media as a marketing tool. Future research in this area may find access to data easy to come by, and perhaps for other football clubs as well as Tottenham Hotspur. Although EPL clubs are known for playing their cards close to their chests and not revealing too much more than mandated information. Perhaps counter-intuitively, the one thing the financial data of recent years does reveal is that Spurs' revenues have not been as adversely affected by their no longer being in the Champions League as one might have expected. Whether or not this can be seen as the result of increasing social media activity cannot be known without access to more complete data.

REFERENCES

Accepted Socially. (2104). *Social media in the Premier League*. Retrieved from http://acceptedsocially.com/social-media-in-the-premier-league

Barker, M., Barker, D., Borman, N., & Neher, K. (2013). *Social Media Marketing: A Strategic Approach*. Southwestern Cengage Learning.

Bird, P. (1982). The demand for league football. *Applied Economics*, *14*(6), 637–649. doi:10.1080/00036848200000038

Carlson, J., & O'Cass, A. (2012). Optimizing the online channel in professional sport to create trusting and loyal consumers: The role of the professional sports team brand and service quality. *Journal of Sport Management*, *26*(6), 463.

Chiang, I-P. & Hsieh, C-H. (2011). Exploring the impacts of blog marketing on consumers. *Social Behavior and Personality: An International Journal, 39*(9), 1245–1250.

Collignon, H. (May 2011). *The Sports Market*. AT Kearney. Retrieved from http://www.atkearney.com/paper/-/asset_publisher/dVxv4Hz2h8bS/content/the-sports-market/10192

Elder, J. (2014). Social media fail to live up to early marketing hype: Companies refine strategies to stress quality over quantity of fans. *The Wall Street Journal*. Retrieved from http://online.wsj.com/articles/companies-alter-social-media-strategies-1403499658

Hajli, M., & Hajli, M. (2013). Organizational development in sport: Co-creation of value through social capital. *Industrial and Commercial Training*, *45*(5), 283–288. doi:10.1108/ICT-01-2013-0001

Harris, L. C., & Ogbonna, E. (2008). The dynamics underlying service firm-customer relationships: Insights from a study of English Premier League soccer fans. *Journal of Service Research*, *10*(4), 382–399. doi:10.1177/1094670508314711

Hoffman, D., & Fodor, M. (2010, Fall). Can you measure the ROI of your social media marketing? *Sloan Management Review*, *52*(1), 40–49.

Kuchler, H. (2014). Global brands: Social media add value and become ever more mobile. *Financial Times*. Retrieved from http://www.ft.com/cms/s/0/bf30b140-cc7b-11e3-bd33-00144feabdc0.html?siteedition=uk#axzz35LSVKs4M

Mangold, W., & Faulds, D. (2009). Social media: The new hybrid element of the promotion mix. *Business Horizons*, *52*(4), 357–365. doi:10.1016/j.bushor.2009.03.002

McLean, R., & Wainwright, D. (2009). Social networks, football fans, fantasy and reality: How corporate and media interests are invading our lifeworld. *Journal of Information, Communication, and Ethics in Society*, *7*(1), 54–71. doi:10.1108/14779960910938098

Nambisan, S., & Baron, R. (2007). Interactions in virtual customer environments: Implications for product support and customer relationship management. *Journal of Interactive Marketing*, *21*(2), 42–62. doi:10.1002/dir.20077

Okazaki, S. (2009). The tactical use of mobile marketing: How adolescents' social networking can best shape brand extensions. *Journal of Advertising Research*, *49*(1), 12–26. doi:10.2501/S0021849909090102

Seo, W., & Green, B. (2008). Development of the motivation scale for sport online consumption. *Journal of Sport Management*, *22*(1), 5.

Simmons, R. (1996). The demand for English league football: A club-level analysis. *Applied Economics*, *28*(2), 139–155. doi:10.1080/000368496328777

Tottenham Hotspur Football Club. (various years). *Annual Report and Accounts*.

Tower, J., & Deery, M. (2006). Relationship marketing and partnerships in not-for-profit sport in Australia. *Sport Marketing Quarterly*, *15*(3), 167–180.

Trattner, C., & Kappe, F. (2013). Social stream marketing on Facebook: A case study. [IJSHC]. *International Journal of Social and Humanistic Computing*, *2*(1/2), 86–103. doi:10.1504/IJSHC.2013.053268

Weeks, C., Cornwell, T., & Drennan, J. (2008). Leveraging sponsorships on the internet: Activation, congruence, and articulation. *Psychology and Marketing*, *25*(7), 637–654. doi:10.1002/mar.20229

KEY TERMS AND DEFINITIONS

Facebook: A popular free social networking website that allows users to create personal profiles, upload photos and video, send messages and keep in touch.

Football: Association Football, known simply as football or soccer, is a game in which two teams of 11 players kick a ball and try to score more goals than their opponents. With both professional and amateur players, it is widely regarded as the world's most popular sport, with more than 250 million players in more than 200 countries.

Instagram: ("Instant Telegram") is an online mobile service that enables its users to take pictures and videos, and share them on a wide variety of social networking platforms.

Internet: A global system of interconnected computer networks: a network of networks. Consisting of millions of private, public, academic, business, and government networks, linked by an array of electronic, wireless, and optical networking technologies.

LinkedIn: A business-oriented social network service, primarily designed for professional networking.

Marketing: Refers to communication between producers and sellers and their customers (both potential and existing) using a wide range of advertising techniques.

Pinterest: A free website service which permits registered users to share photos and videos via 'pinboards'.

Social Media: An umbrella term referring to computer-based tools, both mobile and web-based, which permit users to create, share and exchange information, ideas and media (sound, pictures and video) in networks or virtual communities.

Tottenham Hotspur: A football club founded in 1882, currently playing in the English Premier League. Known also as Spurs.

Twitter: A free social networking microblogging service that allows members to broadcast short posts ("tweets") and direct messages (maximum of 140 characters) to other members.

Vine: A short-form (up to six seconds) video sharing social network service.

WeChat: A mobile text and voice messaging communication service developed by Tencent of China.

WhatsApp: An instant messaging app primarily for smartphones, available on a subscription basis.

This research was previously published in the Handbook of Research on Integrating Social Media into Strategic Marketing edited by Nick Hajli, pages 324-339, copyright year 2015 by Business Science Reference (an imprint of IGI Global).

APPENDIX 1

Table 3. The social media table

Pos	Club	Rel	Eng	Com	Cre	Total
1	Manchester City	5	5	4.5	5	19.5
2	Everton	4.5	5	4	4	17.5
3	Southampton	4	5	3.5	4.5	17
4 =	Arsenal	5	3.5	4	4	16.5
4 =	Tottenham	4	4.5	4	4	16.5
6	Chelsea	4	3.5	4.5	4	16
7 =	Manchester Utd	4	3.5	4.5	3.5	15.5
7 =	Liverpool	4	3.5	4.5	3.5	15.5
7 =	Sunderland	4	4.5	3.5	3.5	15.5
10	Swansea	4	4	3	4	15
11	West Ham Utd	4.5	3	4	3	14.5
12	Norwich City	4	3.5	3	3.5	13.5
13	Fulham	4	3	3	3.5	13.5
14 =	Cardiff City	4	3.5	2.5	3	13
14 =	Crystal Palace	3	3.5	3.5	3	13
16 =	Aston Villa	3.5	3	3.5	2.5	12.5
16 =	Hull City	3.5	2.5	3.5	3	12.5
18	West Brom	3	2.5	2.5	2.5	10.5
19	Newcastle Utd	3	2.5	2	1.5	9
20	Stoke City	2	2	2	2	8

Key: Rel = Relevance / Eng = Engagement / Com = Commercialisation / Cre = Creativity
Source: Accepted Socially (2014). *Social Media in the Premier League*. (Last accessed June 10th, 2014)

APPENDIX 2

Figure 1. Social media score: Tottenham Hotspur
Source: Accepted Socially (2104). Social Media in the Premier League. (http://acceptedsocially.com/social-media-in-the-premier-league. Last accessed June 10th, 2014)

Section 2

Management, Sponsorship, and Strategic Planning

Chapter 11
Branding Through Sponsorship-Linked Marketing:
A Case of Chinese Sports Apparel and Equipment Brand "Li Ning"

Luke Lunhua Mao
University of New Mexico, USA

James J. Zhang
University of Georgia, USA

ABSTRACT

The essence of sponsorship is reciprocity. Whereas sport organizations and event promoters have increasingly relied on sponsors' resources and financial support to stage their events, many companies have also been vigorously seeking sponsorship opportunities to actualize their marketing goals, such as enhancing brand equity. This research examines the impacts of sponsorship-linked marketing activities on perceived consumer-based brand equity elements (i.e., brand loyalty, perceived quality, and brand awareness/associations) of the sponsor. This was done through a case study of how sponsorship-linked marketing strategy has shaped the development of Li Ning Company Limited, a Chinese sports apparel and equipment company. Results show that the branding effectiveness of sponsorship directly depends on event quality, perceived event-brand congruency, and brand experience, but not level of sports involvement.

INTRODUCTION

Sponsorship-linked marketing is the "orchestration and implementation of marketing activities for the purpose of building and communicating an association (link) to a sponsorship" (Cornwell, 1995, p. 15). Research findings have suggested that most companies invest in sport sponsorships in an effort to achieve branding goals, such as increasing brand awareness and enhancing brand image (Cornwell & Maignan, 1998; Walliser, 2003). Many corporate marketing managers have perceived sponsorship as

DOI: 10.4018/978-1-5225-5475-2.ch011

an effective vehicle to enhance brand equity (Cornwell, Roy, & Steinard, 2001). In fact, corporate investments on sponsorship have increased rapidly over the past two decades. The number of U.S.-based companies spending more than $ 15 million on sponsorship grew from 85 in 2005 to over 100 in 2013 (IEG, 2014), with worldwide sponsorship expenditure projected at $ 53.3 billion in 2013 (IEG, 2013). Companies of various backgrounds have actively involved in sponsorship-linked marketing (IEG, 2014). The top U.S. based sponsors, among many others, include Anheuser-Busch, PepsiCo, General Motors, Coca-Cola, Nike, and Visa (IEG, 2014). The magnitude of sponsorship can also be manifested by The Olympic Partners (TOP) program. For instance, the twelve TOP sponsors of the Beijing Olympic Games contributed $866 million in cash, goods, and/or services for the 2008 Olympic Games (IOC, 2009). The average expenditure for each TOP sponsor exceeded $ 60 million.

With the prevalence of sponsorship-linked marketing, the evaluation of its effectiveness has attracted much scholarly interest. Researchers have proposed various theoretical explanations in an attempt to demystify the black box of the branding function of event sponsorship, including mere exposure (Zajonc, 1968), low involvement processing (Pham, 1991), image transfer (Gwinner, 1997), consumer inference (Pracejus, 1998), brand-event-dual-route (Martensen et al., 2006) and associative learning (Mao, Zhang, Connaughton et al. 2013). For instance, the central theme of mere exposure theory is that when an individual is repeatedly exposed to a stimulus, the mere exposure is capable of creating a positive attitude or preference for this stimulus, which is independent of cognition system (Zajonc, 1980). The image transfer theory, assuming that the cumulative interpretation of meanings or associations attributed to events is "transferrable" to sponsoring brands, by paring a brand with an event. Whereas mere exposure effects just take advantage of event as a vehicle for exposure, the effects of image transfer is typically moderated by the degree of function and/or image similarities between event and brand (Gwinner & Bennett, 2008; Kamins & Gupta, 1994; McDaniel & Heald, 2000). Therefore, sports apparel and equipment companies, such as Nike, Adidas, Wilson, and Speedo, have an innate advantage of using sports sponsorship and athlete endorsement to promote their brands due to their natural links (i.e., function and image similarities) with sports. Sponsorship resource is typically regarded by these companies as their distinct competitive advantage (Amis, Pant, & Slack, 1997).

Most existing studies on sponsorship have taken the prevailing effects-measurement perspective, which essentially are empirically driven (Olkkonen, 2001). A case study based on more detailed and longitudinal descriptions may offer an alternative approach to delineate the picture of the phenomenon. At issue is how a company may adopt sponsorship-linked marketing to enhance brand equity. The development of the Chinese sports apparel and equipment company, Li Ning (itself is also a brand), is a case that provides insight of how a company gradually learns to position and market its brand by using sponsorship-linked marketing. The goal of this case is to show how sports sponsorship-linked marketing has helped Li Ning to raise brand awareness and establish brand image in its domestic market—China during different stages of development, and how it plans to use sponsorship marketing strategy to gain entry into western markets that are predominated by international industrial leaders (e.g., Nike, Adidas, and others). The case is structured as follows. First, we briefly introduce the company (brand) of Li Ning. We then discuss the managerial dilemma confronted in current stage of development, followed by an investigation of its sponsorship practices in building its brand equity. Third, to corroborate the section on "Li Ning and its sponsorship-linked marketing practice", a survey study was also conducted and discussed. Finally, we summarize its successful experience and propose caveats and suggestions for future development.

LI NING AND ITS SPONSORSHIP-LINKED MARKETING

Theoretically sponsorship-linked marketing works for a company's branding strategy (Cornwell et al., 2001; Keller, 1993), it comes with costs. It often requires financial and human resources investment, as well as committed responsibilities. Empirically, it is very difficult to evaluate the true effects of sponsorship due to sponsorship contracts are always not publicly observable, and the effects are confounded by other marketing activities, such as advertising, sales promotion, or publicity (Pham, 1991). The case of Li Ning may shed light on how sponsorship-linked marketing strategy may work for a sport apparel company in an emerging market.

Development of Li Ning and Its Strengths

Li Ning Company Limited, is a major Chinese athletic company which makes athletic shoes and sporting goods. Li Ning, the major brand of the company, was founded in 1991 by and named after Mr. Li Ning, the Chinese legendary gymnast who won 6 medals at the Los Angles Olympic Games in 1984. Through over 20 years' development, the company underwent several rounds of reform (Yu, 2008). The company has seen an explosive growth in shoe sales in the past several years. In 2009, the company's total revenue broke the threshold of $1 billion for the first time and reached $1.25 billion. The company was listed in Hong Kong Stock Exchange Market in 2004. In January 2010, Li Ning opened its U.S. headquarters and flagship store in Portland, Oregon. The company manufactures and sells branded products targeting for consumers engaging in sporting activities such as running, basketball, badminton, football, tennis, and fitness. As of 2010, Mr. Li Ning remains the Chairman of the Board of Directors (Li Ning Company Limited, 2011).

The growth of Li Ning has a dynamic interaction with the strengths associated with its brand name. Firstly, Li Ning's branding strength lies with the name of its creator. Mr. Li Ning, as a heroic athletic star, has been known as the "prince of gymnastics" and recognized as one of the most influential athlete in China. The Li Ning brand was founded in 1991 when China was for the first time to host an international sporting event-- the 11th Asian Games. Taking advantage of Mr. Li Ning's reputation and the event, the Li Ning brand was able to be made known to the public expeditiously (Yu, 2008). In particular, in early 1990s, international brands such as Nike and Adidas had just begun to pilot China's market and had not fully assaulted the market. This gave Li Ning a golden opportunity to grow and it soon became the number one sports product brand in China in terms of reputation and sales (Cheng, 2002). The brand name "Li Ning" and the brand logo resembling the initials of "LN" therefore have been widely recognized in mainland China's market (Yu, 2008; Moore, 2008).

Secondly, the brand "Li Ning" has relative strong product category association due to the success and impact of Mr. Li Ning as an athletic icon. The brand itself has an innate link with sports performance and athletic spirit which many of Li Ning's competitors may have taken many years to forge and a substantive fortune to communicate to the market. In addition, Li Ning is also associated with the belief of "nationality", and has an emotional appeal of "kinship" or "affinity". In China, athletes are national assets because they have been traditionally financially supported by the country (Riordan & Jones, 1999). In a collectivism culture like China, a high performance athlete in the grassroots' mind represents the national pride and national spirit of excellence (Xu, 2006). Therefore, the association Li Ning has naturally embedded is a distinctive asset for the brand.

Branding Ling Ning: Weakness

Despite the advantages associated with the brand name, Li Ning has encountered many branding difficulties during its stages of development, such as establishing unique brand associations. Marketing gurus have advocated that each product must tirelessly communicate a single distinctive benefit to its consumers (Kotler & Keller, 2006). In a society where consumers are faced with overloading information, the brand must own a simple, focused position in the prospect's mind, usually a benefit associated with the product category (Aaker, 1996; Kotler & Keller, 2006; Shugan, 1980). Although Li Ning has pioneering advantage in the brand association of "athletic performance" in China, the association is not unique and has been undermined by company's unclear strategy during early period of development (Yu, 2008). First, the brand association is not distinctive. Most high profile sports brands, apparel brand Nike, tennis brand Wilson, or outdoor brand The North Face, share these associations. In addition, due to competitors' high spending on contracting high performance athletes to represent their products, Li Ning's brand associations have been overshadowed. Second, the social economic development stage of China's society overall has shaped Li Ning's development strategy. In early days, Li Ning had been selling clothes and shoes for casual wearing rather than for sports. At that time, sport was just a flamboyant concept rather than lifestyle. Chinese people used to wear Li Ning on any occasion. Further, due to the constraints of technology and expertise, Li Ning had not established the image of "professional sports products" brand (PwCC, 2002).

Li Ning understands the importance of youth market. However, the majority of youth in China nowadays are dreaming of the coolness of Nike. The brand personality Li Ning has been cultivating were "grassroots", "affinity", "national", but not "energetic", "coolness", or "rebellious" that most younger generations of Chinese want to be (PwCC, 2002). The story the Li Ning has been telling is no longer resonated in younger Chinese culture. Although Li Ning has a higher market share in 2nd and 3rd tier cities, we suspect that the brand loyalty is rather low among young consumers. Actually, it is reported that 50% of Li Ning's consumers are 35 years old or above (PwCC, 2002). They are more interested in international brands, but due to availability and affordability, they may have chosen Li Ning as a substitute. Given any opportunity, these consumers may switch to other brands.

Branding Ling Ning: Challenges

The global market for athletic footwear has grown in the last decades, but the market is cooling down with a reduced growth rate. From 2003 to 2004, the market for athletic apparel and footwear grew by almost $7.5 billion, 12%. Between 2004 and 2005, however, it grew by less than $4 billion; in percentage terms, the 6% growth was only half as high as growth a year earlier. Furthermore, in 2007, global footwear sales reached $44.4 billion, a mere 2% increase from 2006.The international market have been dominated by traditional high profile brands—Nike, Adidas, Reebok, Puma, etc. (Wikinvest, 2009).

In fact, Li Ning produces shoes and sportswear, largely for the Chinese market (Li Ning Company Limited, 2014). While the global and European athletic footwear market has been slowing down, the market for athletic footwear in China has grown at double-digit rates since 2000 (Wikinvest, 2009). China's increasing wealth and rising middle class led the Chinese market for retail goods to reach over $232 billion in 2006, with growth expected to be at least 15% annually (Wikinvest, 2014). For example, Nike's sales in China increased by 50% on a currency-neutral basis in 2008, particularly because of higher footwear sales (Nike, 2009). Li Ning also increased by over 50% in 2008, with total revenue reached

$983 million (Li Ning Company Limited, 2009). In China's sports apparel market, Li Ning takes a lead in second and third tier cities where consumers have limited accession to Nike and Adidas, and Li Ning has absolute distribution advantages (PwCC,2002). However, in the most profitable metropolitan markets, Li Ning can hardly compete with Nike and Adidas. Those international high profile brands have already established high entry barriers to defend their market share. These barriers include efficiency of global production, advanced channel management, innovation and designing, experience and expertise, and most importantly brand personality (PwCC, 2002). In second and third tier cities, Li Ning is facing fierce competition with other international brands, Chinese domestic brands, and unbranded products because in this market, the entry barriers are relatively easy to overcome.

Li Ning's Sponsorship-Linked Marketing Strategy

Since the birth of the brand, Li Ning has been active in sponsoring sports events in China, mainly by sponsoring national teams, individual athletes, the event organizers, or the event itself (li-ning.com, 2014). In fact, Li Ning made its début appearance through sponsoring the Beijing Asian Games in 1992. Li Ning applied to be the exclusive provider of sportswear for the Asia torch relay with five million yuan (less than one million US dollars) with the support of a state-owned enterprise, *jianlibao*, which the Li Ning brand was affiliated with. It is clear that in earlier years, Li Ning took a rather opportunistic approach to sponsorship (Yu, 2008). The purpose of the sponsorship activities was to raise brand awareness and notify the mass Chinese that Li Ning founded a brand under his name.

Over the years, Li Ning has aggressively used sponsorship deals, particularly with athletes and sports teams, both at home and abroad, to raise its profile. In 2006 the company signed "strategic collaborations" contracts with the National Basketball Association, the Association of Tennis Professionals, the China University Basketball Association, and the China University Football League. It also signed sponsorship deals with the Chinese national teams and the Sudan track and field team. The company provided apparel for the Argentina national basketball team at international events including the 2008 Summer Olympic Games and 2012 Summer Olympic Games (Li Ning, 2007). A similar deal was made with the Swedish Olympic Committee (China Daily, 2007). Since at least 2004, both the men's and women's Spanish National Basketball Team have been equipped by Li Ning. Li Ning is an official marketing partner of the American National Basketball Association and has sponsorship deals with at least six players: Baron Davis of the Los Angeles Clippers, Shaquille O'Neal of the Boston Celtics, Damon Jones of the Milwaukee Bucks, José Calderón of the Toronto Raptors, Evan Turner of the Philadelphia 76ers, and Dwyane Wade of the Heat (Li-ning.com, 2014). In 2006, O'Neal signed a five-year deal with Li Ning, reportedly worth US$1.25 million (China Daily, 2006). Six years later, Dwyane Wade signed a ten-year deal with Li Ning, reportedly worth US$60 million, the largest deal made by the company, and the highest profile signing of an American sports star by a Chinese company (Beam, 2014).

With the growth of company and accumulative experience in marketing, the company realizes that brand awareness is no longer as imperative an issue as it was in the earlier days. As discussed, the major difficulty lies with Li Ning's brand personality and acceptance by younger consumers. Since 2000, Li Ning has made tremendous efforts to promote their brands among the younger generation through sponsoring / initiating youth sports events, such as China University Football League, Chinese Youth Basketball Events, and etc. Besides sponsoring events, the company is also actively seeking for endorsement of athletic stars, in particular the NBA star players who have tremendous influences on the Chinese youth. For example, Shaquille O'Neal of the Boston Celtics has a personality that is inconsistent with traditional Li Ning brand personality. However, by aligning with the "Shark", it seems that Li Ning aimed at changing its brand image to catering the culture of the younger generation. The appeal of O'Neal to the younger generation is what Li Ning was missing. In 2010, Li Ning signed the Philadelphia 76ers rookie, Evan Turner, to represent its products. It is reported to be a 3-year deal worth around $12 million dollars (phillystylemag.com, 2010). How Li Ning will leverage the values of Evan Turner bringing to the brand is still an open question. Turner will wear Li Ning's shoes for both home and away games. It is expected that the signing of Turner will expose the brand to the world-wide NBA fans; and the publicity of Turner will bring "free" publicity to the brand. More importantly, by associating the brand with Turner, Li Ning would expect that sports fans will transfer their affection from their star player to the sponsored brand (Gwinner, 1997; Mao et al., 2013); the performance of Turner will enhance Li Ning's perceived brand quality in consumer's mind; and Turner's star power and personality can cultivate a preferable brand personality among younger consumers.

In summary, Li Ning has primarily relied on sponsorship-linked marketing strategy to brand its products. However, to evaluate the effects of these marketing efforts is a formidable task for professionals and researcher. In recent years, researchers have proposed various sponsorship communication theories or models to explain the effects of sponsorship, such as low-involvement communication model (Pham, 1991), image transfer model (Gwinner, 1997), and associative learning theory (Mao et al., 2013). In order to gain some insights into how consumers respond to Li Ning's sponsorship-linked marketing activities, a theoretical framework was firstly developed based on a review of literature and a survey study was subsequently conducted to test the findings from the first stage.

BRANDING AND BRAND EQUITY

Traditionally, two approaches or paradigms have been used to study brand equity. One is a financially based approach for estimating the value of a brand in terms of asset valuation (Kapferer, 2008; Keller, 1993). The other is strategy-based customer-oriented approach for improving marketing productivity (Keller, 1993), focusing on the relationship between customers and the brand (Kapferer, 2008). Following a customer orientation approach, frameworks developed by Aaker (1991, 1996) and Keller (1993) have often been adopted for studying brand equity. In Aaker's seminal brand equity framework, brand equity comprises five elements:

1. Brand awareness,
2. Perceived quality,
3. Brand associations,
4. Brand loyalty, and
5. Other proprietary brand assets.

Aaker (1996) later expanded the span of the concept and proposed the Brand Equity 10 as a systematic measure to evaluate brand equity across products and markets with both financial and distribution indicators. Keller's (1993) consumer-based brand equity, somewhat different from Aaker's model, is based on the premise that the brand resides in the minds of individual consumers as a cognitive construal (Heding, Knudtzen, & Bjerre, 2009) and focuses solely on the brand's relationship with its consumers (Batra, Myers, & Aaker, 1997). In Keller's conceptualization, consumer-based brand equity is "the differential effect of brand knowledge on consumer response to the marketing of the brand" (p. 2), and brand knowledge comprises brand awareness (e.g., brand recall and recognition) and brand image (i.e., a set of associations linked with the brand's attributes, benefits, or attitudes toward it). As such, consumers' familiarity and knowledge of a brand in terms of favorability, strength, and uniqueness determine a brand's equity. Comparatively speaking, Aaker's (1996) framework is essentially more comprehensive and incorporates a wide range of customer-based brand equity dimensions.

The awareness, associations, perceived quality, and loyalty dimensions represent consumers' perceptions of a brand. Awareness is related to the strength of a brand in consumer's memory reflected by consumers' ability to recall or recognize the brand under different conditions (Keller, 1993). Brand awareness plays an important role in consumers' decision-making as it can affect perceptions and attitudes, and in some context, it can drive brand choice and even loyalty (Aaker, 1996). Aaker divided brand associations into eleven categories, which include product attributes, intangibles, customer benefits, relative price, use/application, user/customer, celebrity/person, lifestyle/personality, product class, competitors, and country/geographic area. Brand associations lead to brand image and thus establish a solid network of brand knowledge (Keller, 1993). Perceived quality is consumer's subjective judgment about a product's overall excellence or superiority based on personal product experiences, unique needs, consumption situations, and other factors (Yoo et al., 2000; Zeithaml, 1998). As one of the key dimensions of brand equity, perceived quality provides a surrogate variable for other more specific elements of brand equity (Aaker, 1996). Brand loyalty is a deeply held commitment to purchase a preferred product or service in the future (Oliver, 1997) and is the core dimension of brand equity (Aaker, 1996). It is generally comprised of behavioral and attitudinal loyalty (Kaynak, Salman, & Tatoglu, 2008), suggesting that loyal customers hold favorable attitudes and thus routinely purchase a particular brand. Drawn from Aaker and Keller's conceptualizations of brand equity, Yoo and Donthu (2001) developed a multi-dimensional consumer-based brand equity scale (MBE). This measure was developed through rigorous measurement procedures, and it exhibited sound psychometric properties. Its generalizability has been examined across multiple samples drawn from Koreans, Korean American, and American populations (Yoo, Donthu, & Lee, 2000).

Factors Affecting Branding Effects

Martensen et al. (2007) proposed that two routes can influence the branding effectiveness of sponsorship-linked marketing, namely brand route and event route. Brand route represents the default psychological state of a consumer towards a brand; whereas, event route refers to the consumer's involvement, emotions, and attitude towards an event and their transfer into a sponsoring brand. Furthermore, as image transfer theory suggested, perceived brand-event congruence (Becker-Olsen & Simmons, 2002; McDaniel, 1999; Speed & Thompson, 2000) is a major factor that links event route and brand route and thus has a significant influence on branding effects.

The event route is a major concern of this study as it is under volitional control of sponsorship marketing managers. In particular, the quality of an event to be sponsored is crucial to the success of sponsorship-linked marketing and thus a major decision factor of marketing managers – the conceptual model accordingly highlights event quality as a core determinant. How to evaluate the quality of event itself is a formidable task for researchers, and is beyond the scope of this paper. We construe the quality of event as a subjective evaluation associated with consumers' event involvement, emotions intrigued by the event and event attitudes. Although all these three factors had been investigated in the regard of sponsorship effects evaluation (Hansen, Halling, & Christensen, 2006; McDaniel, 1999), they were not systematically conceptualized as indicators of event quality. In this paper, we have constructed a second order index called the Event Quality Index (EQI) which comprised involvement, emotions, and event attitude to measure event quality. Furthermore, we acknowledge the importance of brand route and perceived brand-event congruency in evaluating the branding effects. Without controlling the influence of existing brand experience and perceive brand-event congruency, we may commit omitted variables bias (Wooldridge, 2009). In this investigation, we have also included sports involvement, as it is a key characteristic of the target market of Li Ning's products, active sports participants and followers. The main purpose of the survey study was to investigate the influence of event quality, perceived brand-event congruence, prior brand experience, and sports involvement, on the branding effects of Li Ning's sponsorship-linked marketing.

METHOD

Based on a comprehensive review of literature, we developed a questionnaire including the following sections:

1. An index of event quality that consists of involvement, emotional responses, and attitude toward the event,
2. Prior brand experiences and perceived brand-event congruency,
3. Perceived branding effects of the event to be sponsored by Li Ning, and
4. Sport/event involvement and background information.

Stimulus

Three diverse sporting events of different magnitudes and market environments were purposefully selected as stimulus to measure the branding effects of Li Ning's sponsorship-linked marketing. They are a hallmark mega event (i.e., 2008 Beijing Olympic Games), a popular national major sport league with high achievement in international competitions (i.e., Chinese Basketball Association), and a notorious national major sport league with low achievement in international competitions (i.e., Chinese Soccer League). The two leagues and one event represented the primary sport properties in China at the time of data collections and they vary drastically in event magnitude, event participants, event spectators, television viewership, and national and social significance.

Branding Effects

The major dependent variable is branding effectiveness. It is operationalized in accordance with Aaker's conceptualization. Measurement of branding effectiveness was based on a modified application of the multidimensional brand equity measure (MBE) developed by Yoo and Donthu (2001). MBE contains 10 items on Likert five-point scale. This measure incorporates three dimensions of brand equity: brand awareness/associations, perceived quality, and brand loyalty. This section was preceded with the following statement: 'If Li Ning athletic shoe brand decides to sponsor Event X, to what extent will your evaluation of the following aspects of the brand be changed?'

The Yoo and Donthu's (2001) consumer-based brand equity scale was validated in literature. As the questions were modified and translated into Chinese in this study, exploratory factor analyses were executed to analyze the dimensionality of the perceived change of brand equity. The dimensions generated in this study generally matched with Yoo and Donthu's original dimensions: brand awareness/association, brand royalty, and perceived quality. 63.7% to 66.7% of total variances were explained by this three-factor extraction. The rotated component matrix is presented in Table 1. All dimensions except "perceived quality" in CBA data (0.65) were higher than the generally recommended lower threshold of .70 for Cronbach's alpha (Nunnally & Bernstein, 1994), and the perceived quality generally exceeded the minimum criterion 0.6 (Bagozzi & Yi, 1988; Malhotra and Birks, 2006) for satisfactory internal consistency reliability. Summary scores for each dimension therefore were used in further analysis.

Event Quality Index

Event Quality Index (EQI) was comprised of the following components: involvement, emotions, and event attitude. Zaichkowsky's (1994) Personal Involvement Inventory (PII) was adopted to measure the consumers' involvement with an event. This 10-item short version of PII contains items on a 7-point semantic-differential scale. PII and its revised versions have been repeatedly used in sport marketing studies (Martensen *et al.*, 2007; McDaniel, 1999). A measure of 20 statements assessing personal feelings developed by Hansen et al. (2005, 2006) was chosen to assess emotional responses to the broadcast viewing of Beijing Olympic Games. This measure had been tested in several sport event settings (Hansen et al., 2006; Hansen, Martensen, & Christensen, 2005; Martensen et al., 2007). The 20 items were measured on a 4-point Likert scale (4 = very strong feeling to 1 = no feeling). Attitude toward the event was measured by 3 items measured on a 7-point semantic-differential scale, which was adopted from Muehling and Laczniak (1988). The measures adopted in this study were context and domain free in nature; therefore, they could be used to measure the involvement with, attitudes towards, and feelings about other events and to compare different events.

For the involvement variables, an identical two-factor pattern emerged across all the three groups based on an eigenvalue equal to or greater than 1.0, explaining a total of 54.4% to 60.3% of variances (Table 1). An examination of content interpretability was conducted by comparing current results with Zaichkowsky's (1994) results. In Zaichkowsky's research, affective dimension included "interesting, exciting, appealing, fascinating, and involving", and cognitive dimension included "important, relevant, means a lot to me, valuable, and needed". Three items (important, interesting, and relevant) in the current study did not fit in with original conceptualization, hence were not used for further analysis. The 20 items of emotional responses first generated different patterns of dimensionality across three groups. Both Olympic Game and CSL data sets generated three factors, while CBA data set generated two factors, which is rather reasonable as emotions are not as simple as just positive and negative (Bagozzi et al., 1999; Richins, 1997). For the Olympic data, the item "worry" alone turned out to be the third factor, and the item "hope" had a tendency of double loading; and the item of "surprising" in CSL data had high loadings on all the three e factors. As mentioned, a two-factor solution to emotional responses has been commonly used by researchers (Martensent et al., 2004). Hence factor analyses fixing number of factors at two were conducted to further check the pattern congruency among three groups. A clear pattern of positive-negative emotions was then generated across all three groups, with 47.5% to 53.4% of total variances explained. The rotated component matrix is presented in Table 1. The internal reliability for positive involvement, cognitive involvement, positive emotions, negative emotions, and attitude construct

Table 1. Solutions of factor analyses of variables associated with branding effects

	Olympic (N=556)					CBA (N=615)					CSL (N=621)				
Variable	M	SD	Factor Loading			M	SD	Factor Loading			M	SD	Factor Loading		
			1	2	3			1	2	3			1	2	3
I consider myself to be loyal to X	.39	.68			.69	.40	.23	.83			.68	.13		.69	
X would be my first choice	.19	.81			.75	.31	.26	.79			.81	.18		.75	
I will not buy other brands if X is available at the store	.09	.75			.66	-.15	.17	.64			.75	.17		.66	
The likely quality of X is extremely high	.35	.23	.76		.24	.78	.19		.80		.23	.76			.78
The likelihood that X would be functional is very high	.23	.18	.86			.79	.26		.84		.18	.86			.79
I can recognize X among other competing brands	.53	.30		.66		.18	.57			.53	.30	.40	.66		
I am aware of X	.73	.12		.73		.11	.72			.73	.12	.30	.73		
Some characteristics come to my mind quickly	.82	.13		.66		.29	.72			.82	.13	.12	.66		
I can quickly recall the symbol or logo of X	.71	.24		.78		.22	.74			.71	.24	.26	.78		
I have difficulty in imagining X in my mind	.73	.31		.72		.07	.73			.73	.31	.23	.72		
Eigen value			2.88	2.02	1.77	2.79	1.69	1.68	2.69	2.02	1.66	2.88	2.02	1.77	2.79
% variance explained			28.70	2.20	17.70	27.90	16.90	16.80	26.90	2.10	16.60	28.70	2.20	17.70	27.90

were higher than the generally recommended lower threshold of .70 for Cronbach's alpha (Nunnally & Bernstein, 1994). As emotional responses are discrete in nature, we converted the positive emotions and negative emotions to a ratio scale based on the following equation – Emotional Ratio= (Summary of Positive Emotions)/ (Summary of Negative Emotions). To construct an event quality index, the cognitive involvement, affective involvement, emotional ratio, and attitude then model in a second order CFA model. The second order event quality model fits the data well (RMSEA=.094, CFI=.99, SRMR=.018).

Brand Experience, Perceived Brand-Event Congruence, and Sport Involvement

To measure prior brand experience, two follow-up questions about familiarity and likeability with the brand on a Likert 5 point scale were asked to those respondents who answered 'yes' to the question 'have you ever used/owned Li Ning product.' The perceived event-brand congruence of each brand with Olympic Games was also assessed by adopting 2 items adopted from Gwinner's (1999) representing functional-based similarity and image-based similarity, respectively. These items were "It is likely that (participants) in the (event name) use (brand name) during the (event name)," and "The (event name) and (brand name) have a similar image" (Gwinner & Eaton, 1999, p. 50). Three items of sports involvement was adapted from Orlick's (1974) Primary and Secondary Sport Involvement scale. Participants rated the frequency with which they take part in any sport activities, and the frequency with which they watch sport on television. They also reported how much they like sports on a Likert 5-point scale. In addition, a demographic information section included the following variables: gender, age, education level, and residency. These items were phrased in a multiple-choice response format.

Participants and Procedures

Research participants (N = 803) were students in two comprehensive universities that are located in a metropolitan coastal city and a mid-sized city of China respectively. Because both universities accept students from all over China, a wide range of geographical representations among the respondents were further ensured. Given that university students are a predominant segment of spectators and TV viewers of sporting events in China and they are also an important market segment of Li Ning's products, studying a student sample for the research questions was deemed relevant and appropriate.

Following the institutional approval for the conduct of this study, instructors of general physical education classes with the university was contacted and asked for support and cooperation with the data collection process. The physical education classes were a part of the general education curriculum of the university; thus, students in these classes represented a wide range of academic majors and disciplines. With the support of an instructor, test administration was usually conducted right before or during a class. Participation in the study was voluntary although a small notebook was used as an incentive for those who completed the questionnaire. Generally, it took an individual approximately 20 minutes to complete the questionnaire. All responses were anonymous and confidentiality was ensured.

A total of 1002 copies of questionnaires (i.e., 334 copies each set) were distributed to those who were willing to participate in the study and 803 copies were returned with completed responses, representing a valid response rate of 80.1%. The completion of each questionnaire was checked before rewarding a respondent with a notebook. Of all respondents, 63.6% were female and 36.4% were male. In terms of geographic locations where they mostly lived before 16 years old, 10% grew up in large size cities, 12.3% in medium size cities, 41.7% in small towns, 34.2% in countryside, and the remaining 1.8% in other countries or multiple urbanity settings.

Data Analyses

SPSS 17.0 was utilized to calculate descriptive statistics for variables in each of the sections and Cronbach's alpha coefficients for each construct. As most scales were adopted from existing literature, the validity and reliability of them have been tested. We confirm these psychological constructs (i.e., involvement, emotions, attitude, and brand equity) through a series of confirmatory factor analysis before we proceeded to construct a summary score for each variable. Items that were not loaded highly on the construct were eliminated for further analysis. To compare different variables, all summary data were mean-centered.

Mplus 5.21 (Muthén & Muthén, 2009) program was used to conduct an SEM analysis to examine the proposed structural relationships among sports involvement, event quality, perceived congruency, brand experience and the branding effectiveness variables. We have primarily used the robust maximum likelihood (MLR) method. Multiple Goodness-of-Fit (GOF) indices were chosen to evaluate model fit according to the suggestions made by several scholars (Hu & Bentler, 1998, 1999; McCallum & Austin, 2000), including chi-square per degree of freedom (or the scaled ML chi-square, Satorra-Bentler chi-square, when using MLR method), the Root Mean Square Error of Approximation (RMSEA), Tucker and Lewis Reliability Coefficient (TLI), Bentler's Comparative Fit Index (CFI), and the weighted root mean square residual (WRMR, or SRMR, the standardized root mean square residual when using MLR method). Hu and Bentler (1999) suggested that RMSEA values less than .05 indicate a close fit, between .05 and .08 indicate an acceptable fit, and greater than .10 indicate a poor fit. Because RMSEA has been identified as the best performing index for WLSMV estimate (Yu, 2002), it is our primary index to determine model fit. The TLI (Tucker & Lewis, 1973), also known as the non-normed fit index, penalizes for model complexity. The criterion for goodness of fit by TLI traditionally was .90 (Kline, 2005). A rule of thumb for the CFI index is that researcher's model has a reasonable fit when a value is larger than .90 (Hu & Bentler, 1999). Following the adequacy of the overall measurement model, we proceeded to examine the hypothesized relations among eight latent variables. This step allowed us to test the following:

1. Relationship between attitude toward event and the branding effectiveness of sponsorship (i.e., brand loyalty, perceived quality, and brand awareness/associations), and
2. Relationship among involvement, emotions, and attitude. Same GOF indices as the CFA were adopted in evaluating the structural model.

RESULTS

Descriptive Statistics

Among all 803 respondents, 244 completed the Olympic questionnaire, 278 completed CBA questionnaire and 281 completed CSL questionnaire. The sport involvement level overall did not differ among three groups (F=1.74, p=0.18). Their experience with Li Ning's products had some differences. The CSL group had a significantly higher percentage (48.1%) of respondents who had used Li Ning's products while the Olympic group (37%) had the least product usage rate. As a result, the three groups significantly differ in brand familiarity (F=18.11, p<.01). But brand favorability measure had no significant difference among three groups (F=2.38, p<.09). Descriptive statistics for the sport involvement, event quality, perceived congruency, brand experience and branding effects are presented in Table 2. As expected, all three sources for event quality differ significantly among three events, with Beijing Olympic Games having highest composite score and China Soccer League having lowest composite score. Both the perceived functional congruency and image congruency between event and the brand also differed cross three groups (F=6.02, p<.01, and F=82.99, p<.01 respectively). Not surprisingly, different events

Table 2. Descriptive statistics for sponsorship-linked marketing and perceived consumer-based brand equity variables

Variable	Olympic (N=244)		CBA (N=278)		CSL (N=281)		Pooled (N=803)	
	M	SD	M	SD	M	SD	M	SD
Sport Involvement	0.52	0.81	0.54	0.80	0.37	0.80	0.47	0.81
Love sports/exercise	-0.45	1.10	-0.39	1.08	-0.46	1.05	-0.43	1.08
Sports participation	-0.03	0.71	-0.15	0.76	-0.15	0.79	-0.11	0.76
Sports event fellowship								
Event Quality								
Event Involvement	1.95	1.11	0.19	1.09	-0.57	1.28	0.46	1.56
Emotional Surplus	2.80	1.02	1.46	0.72	0.99	0.64	1.70	1.10
Event Attitude	2.48	1.05	0.86	1.28	-0.23	1.49	0.97	1.69
Perceived Congruency								
Functional congruency	0.74	0.82	0.57	0.84	0.48	0.96	0.59	0.88
Image congruency	0.78	0.85	0.32	0.91	-0.28	1.05	0.25	1.04
Brand Experience								
Previous use (%)	37%		44.5%		61.8%		48.1%	
Familiarity	-0.14	1.05	0.17	0.93	0.37	0.97	0.15	1.00
Favorability	0.25	0.74	0.35	0.71	0.38	0.75	0.33	0.73
Branding Effect								
Brand Loyalty	0.21	0.66	0.19	0.64	-0.07	0.82	0.10	0.72
Perceived Quality	0.76	0.82	0.65	0.80	0.40	0.85	0.59	0.83
Brand Association/Awareness	0.71	0.74	0.62	0.72	0.39	0.74	0.57	0.75

showed significantly different branding effects. Beijing Olympic Games had the highest value to create brand equity while the CSL had the least value. Figure 1 presents the branding effects of sponsoring different sports properties. Sponsoring CSL even may cause a decrease of brand loyalty because consumer's negative emotional and attitudinal reaction to the event may have transferred to the sponsored brand. Sponsorship-linked marketing announcement had different effects on elements of brand equity, with perceived quality having the highest boosting effect and brand loyalty the least.

Data Screening and Reduction

To further examine the measurement property of the psychological state and brand equity variables, exploratory factor analyses (EFA) with principal component extraction and a varimax rotation technique were conducted for the 10 involvement, 20 emotions, and 10 brand equity variables, respectively. The Kaiser-Meyer-Olkin (KMO) measure of sampling adequacy (Kaiser, 1974) for the involvement, emotions, and brand equity across three groups were greater than .85, indicating that the samples were adequate for factor analyses. Bartlett Test for Sphericity was significant at .01 level, indicating that the hypothesis of variance and covariance matrix of the variables as an identity matrix was rejected; therefore, conducting the factor analyses was appropriate.

Figure 1. Branding effects of sponsoring different sports properties

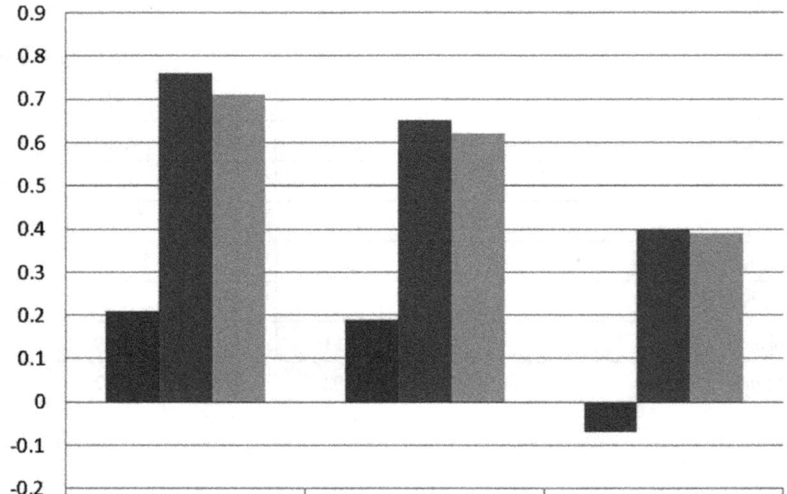

	Olympic	CBA	CSL
■ Brand Loyalty	0.21	0.19	-0.07
■ Perceived Quality	0.76	0.65	0.4
■ Brand Association/Awareness	0.71	0.62	0.39

For the involvement variables, an identical two-factor pattern emerged across all the three groups based on eigenvalue equal to or greater than 1.0, explaining a total of 54.4% to 60.3% of variances. An examination of content interpretability was conducted by comparing current results with Zaichkowsky's (1994) results. In Zaichkowsky's research, affective dimension included "interesting, exciting, appealing, fascinating, and involving", and cognitive dimension included "important, relevant, means a lot to me, valuable, and needed". Three items (important, interesting, and relevant) in the current study did not fit in original conceptualization, hence were not used for further analysis.

The 20 items of emotional responses first generated different patterns of dimensionality across three groups. Both the Olympic Game and CSL data sets generated three factors, while the CBA data set generated two factors, which is rather reasonable as emotions are not as simple as just positive and negative (Bagozzi et al., 1999; Richins, 1997). For the Olympic data, the item "worry" alone turned out to be the third factor, and the item "hope" had a tendency of double loading; and the item of "surprising" in CSL data had high loadings on all the three factors. As mentioned, a two-factor solution to emotional responses has been commonly used by researchers (Martensent et al., 2004). Hence factor analyses fixing the number of factors at two were conducted to further check the pattern congruency among three groups. A clear pattern of positive-negative emotions was then generated across all three groups, with 47.5% to 53.4% of total variances explained. The rotated component matrix is presented in Table 1.

Cronbach's alpha was calculated to measure internal consistency of obtained factors (Cronbach, 1951). A total of 11 items were eliminated for parsimony as they did not significantly contribute to the reliability. Table 5 depicted the results of internal reliability based on reduced items.

Path Modeling

To further explore the impacts of different variables on the branding effects. A structural model relating four independent variables to dependent variables were modeled through a path model based on the correlation matrix presented in Table 3. The model was assessed by using the Maximum Likelihood estimate in Mplus 5.21. Figure 2 presents the conceptual model. The values of Goodness-of-Fit indices suggested the resulting model has a close fit: $\chi 2/df = 2.02$, RMSEA=.036, CFI=.985, TLI=.969, SRMR=.024. Event quality, functional congruency, image congruency and brand favorability are significantly predictive of all three elements of the branding effects. Brand familiarity was only significantly predictive of brand loyalty while not predictive of brand quality and association. The sport involvement variable is not predictive of any of the three elements of branding effects. Table 4 summarizes the results of the path coefficients.

DISCUSSION

In today's extremely competitive and dynamic business climate, companies are striving to sustain long-lasting development by strategically positioning and differentiating themselves from competitors in the marketplace. Brands are one of the few assets available to a company that can provide a long-lasting competitive advantage (Bharadwaj, Varadarajan, & Fahy, 1993; Kapferer, 2008). Brands can distinguish products, provide legal protection for companies, signal a certain level of quality, increase the probability of brand choice, command premium price from loyal consumers, facilitate business forecasting, and gain greater market share (Kotler & Keller, 2006; Yoo, Donthu, & Lee, 2000). The power of a brand lies

Table 3. Correlation matrix for the sponsorship-linked marketing and perceived consumer-based brand equity constructs

	LS	SP	EF	EI	EM	EA	FC	IC	BU	Bfam	Bfav	Lo	Qu	As
Love Sport	1													
Sport Participation	0.264	1												
Event Followship	0.317	0.186	1											
Involvement	0.127	0.007	0.148	1										
Emotion	0.068	-0.048	0.034	0.643	1									
Attitude	0.087	0.015	0.056	0.779	0.617	1								
Functional Congruency	0.153	0.126	0.174	0.188	0.118	0.189	1							
Image Congruency	0.089	0.051	0.065	0.49	0.429	0.442	0.37	1						
Usage	-0.011	-0.026	-0.163	0.169	0.159	0.201	-0.027	0.098	1					
Familiarity	0.126	0.125	0.24	-0.191	-0.169	-0.184	0.197	-0.059	-0.336	1				
Favorability	0.185	0.14	0.23	-0.029	-0.059	-0.025	0.349	0.065	-0.266	0.475	1			
Loyalty	0.115	0.039	0.106	0.296	0.191	0.253	0.294	0.407	0.027	0.111	0.237	1		
Quality	0.132	0.03	0.109	0.257	0.184	0.238	0.254	0.311	0.044	0.042	0.202	0.433	1	
Association	0.148	0.004	0.074	0.279	0.159	0.301	0.295	0.339	0.044	0.075	0.202	0.522	0.526	1

Figure 2. Structural equation model

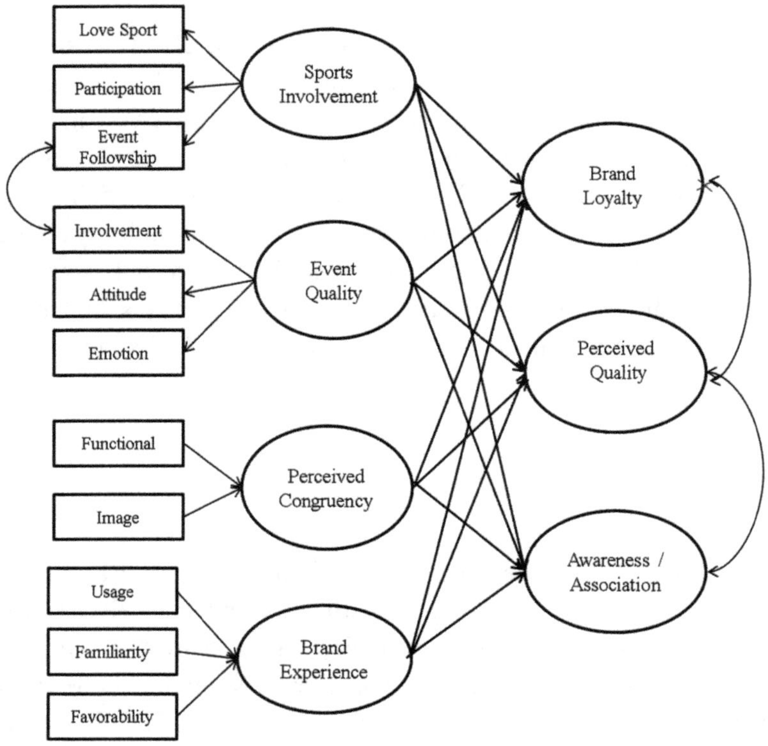

with its brand equity as well as customer's subjective and intangible assessment of the brand (Kotler & Keller, 2006). Therefore, branding effectiveness of sponsorship can be conceptualized as the influence of sponsorship related marketing on the enhancement of brand equity.

The purpose of this research is to examine the impacts of sponsorship-linked marketing activities on perceived consumer-based brand equity elements. It is done through an empirical investigation of how sponsorship-linked marketing strategy has influenced the positioning and branding of Li-Ning. This study firstly reviewed the history and strategy of Li-Ning's sponsorship-linked marketing practice. It shows how sports sponsorship-linked marketing has helped Li-Ning to raise brand awareness and establish brand image in its domestic market—China during different stages of development, and how it plans to use sponsorship-linked marketing strategy to gain entry into international markets that are predominated by international industrial leaders.

A conceptual framework linking factors of sponsorship effectiveness (i.e., event quality, brand experience, perceived event-brand congruency and sport involvement) to brand equity elements (i.e., brand loyalty, perceived quality, and brand awareness/associations) is then developed based on a comprehensive review of literature. As the quality of an event to be sponsored is crucial to the success of sponsorship-linked marketing and thus a major decision factor of marketing managers, the conceptual model accordingly highlights event quality as a core determinant. Accordingly, we have constructed a second order formative index called the Event Quality Index (EQI), which comprised the following reflective components: involvement, emotions, and event attitude. We further acknowledge the importance of brand experience, brand-event congruency, and sports involvement, which have been frequently addressed in literature,

Table 4. Summary of structural model including path coefficient values and model fit indices

Hypothesized Path	*β*	*se*	*t*	*p*
Brand Loyalty				
Sport Involvement → Brand Loyalty	0.01	0.05	0.21	0.83
Event Quality → Brand Loyalty	0.15	0.04	3.58	0.00
Functional Congruency → Brand Loyalty	0.08	0.04	2.28	0.02
Image Congruency → Brand Loyalty	0.28	0.04	7.16	0.00
Brand Usage → Brand Loyalty	0.04	0.03	1.20	0.23
Brand Familiarity → Brand Loyalty	0.08	0.04	1.94	0.05
Brand Favorability → Brand Loyalty	0.17	0.04	4.31	0.00
Perceived Quality				
Sport Involvement → Perceived Quality	0.07	0.05	1.37	0.17
Event Quality → Perceived Quality	0.15	0.04	3.38	0.00
Functional Congruency → Perceived Quality	0.09	0.04	2.26	0.02
Image Congruency → Perceived Quality	0.17	0.04	4.16	0.00
Brand Usage → Perceived Quality	0.05	0.04	1.26	0.21
Brand Familiarity → Perceived Quality	-0.02	0.04	-0.41	0.68
Brand Favorability → Perceived Quality	0.16	0.04	3.92	0.00
Association/Awareness				
Sport Involvement → Association / Awareness	0.02	0.05	0.34	0.73
Event Quality → Association / Awareness	0.20	0.04	4.52	0.00
Functional Congruency → Association / Awareness	0.13	0.04	3.46	0.00
Image Congruency → Association / Awareness	0.17	0.04	4.22	0.00
Brand Usage → Association / Awareness	0.04	0.04	1.24	0.21
Brand Familiarity → Association / Awareness	0.05	0.04	1.17	0.24
Brand Favorability → Association / Awareness	0.14	0.04	3.41	0.00

GOF indices: $\chi 2/df = 2.02$, RMSEA=.036, CFI=.985, TLI=.969, SRMR=.024.

thus have been included in the model. A questionnaire is developed and administered to college students (N=803) who are a major segment of sports products consumers.

The survey investigation reveals that sport involvement is not predictive in our model. It means that no matter you are a sport fan or not, sponsoring an event will have an impact on the perceptions of the consumers. However, sport involvement may still remain a relevant factor as it may well influence the frequency of brand exposure, which our model did not consider. Not surprisingly, quality of event as defined by its involvement and also emotional and attitudinal characteristics is significantly predictive of branding effects. Sponsoring a low quality event as CSL has double sided effects: on the one hand, it can raise brand awareness /associations or even perceived quality; but on the other hand, it may hurt brand loyalty. As low quality event is often less expensive; depending on the tactical purposes of the company (e.g., merely increase brand awareness), it may be appropriate for a company to sponsoring lower profile events. Conforming to previous study, congruency is also significantly predictive of branding effects.

The brand experience is also related to branding effects. Interestingly, however, brand familiarity is not significantly predictive of perceived quality. It may suggest that consumers rely on their cognition when they are familiar with brands.

There were several limitations in this study. Foremost, as a case study, an issue is how the practices by Li Ning Company will be generalizable to other companies. Mr. Li Ning had been an icon in Chinese society that goes beyond the realm of sport; and Li Ning brand was the very first brand created in China that named after a celebrity athlete. The political and economic climate in China had consequential influence on the development of the brand and the company. We suspect that the success of Li Ning can be replicated in today's China. On the other hand, the practices of sponsorship-link marketing of Li Ning proffer insights about how a company in emerging economy may utilize sponsorship to position or reposition its brand, and build its brand equity. Second, the dearth of research in China's sport markets and the lack of sound existing measures to evaluate the constructs proposed in this study were another limitation of this study. Although the measures, adopted from relevant disciplines, achieved adequate reliability and validity evidence after eliminating 15 items, it signals further efforts needed to tailor those existing measures from other disciplines or develop original measures focusing on the sport phenomenon. In summary, this study makes a first step in understanding China's sport marketplace for sponsorship. These findings invite future research on the relationship between the management of sponsorship marketing and the development of brand equity.

REFERENCES

Aaker, D. A. (1991). *Managing brand equity: Capitalizing on the value of a brand name*. The Free Press.

Aaker, D. A. (1996). *Building strong brands*. New York: Free Press.

Aaker, D. A. (1996). Measuring brand equity across products and markets. *California Management Review*, *38*(Spring), 102–120. doi:10.2307/41165845

Amis, J., Pant, N., & Slack, T. (1997). Achieving a sustainable competitive advantage: A resource based view of sport sponsorship. *Journal of Sport Management*, *11*(1), 80–96.

Batra, R., Myers, J. G., & Aaker, D. A. (1997). *Advertising management* (5th ed.). Prentice Hall.

Beam, C. (2012). Dwyane Wade and Li Ning: Can an American superstar save a Chinese sneaker company? *ESPN The Magazine*. Retrieved from http://espn.go.com/nba/story/_/id/10781332/miami-heat-dwyane-wade-new-face-chinese-sneaker-company-li-ning-espn-magazine

Becker-Olsen, K., & Simmons, C. J. (2002). When do social sponsorships enhance or dilute equity? Fit, message source, and the persistence of effects. *Advances in Consumer Research. Association for Consumer Research (U. S.)*, *29*(1), 287–289.

China Daily. (2006). *Li Ning goes global*. Retrieved from http://www.chinadaily.com.cn/bizchina/2006-08/15/content_664979.htm

China Daily. (2007). *Li Ning to sponsor foreign team.* Retrieved from http://www.chinadaily.com.cn/bizchina/2007-05/21/content_5415104.htm

Cornwell, T. (1995). Sponsorship-linked marketing development. *Sport Marketing Quarterly*, *4*(4), 13–24.

Cornwell, T. B. (2008). State of the art and science in sponsorship-linked marketing. *Journal of Advertising*, *37*(3), 41–55. doi:10.2753/JOA0091-3367370304

Cornwell, T. B., & Maignan, I. (1998). An international review of sponsorship research. *Journal of Advertising*, *27*(1), 1–21. doi:10.1080/00913367.1998.10673539

Cornwell, T. B., Roy, D. P., & Steinard, E. A. (2001). Exploring managers' perceptions of the impact of sponsorship on brand equity. *Journal of Advertising*, *30*(2), 41–51. doi:10.1080/00913367.2001.10673636

Gwinner, K. (1997). A model of image creation and image transfer in event sponsorhsip. *International Marketing Review*, *14*(2/3), 145–158. doi:10.1108/02651339710170221

Gwinner, K., & Bennett, G. (2008). The impact of brand cohesiveness and sport identification on brand fit in a sponsorship context. *Journal of Sport Management*, *22*(4), 410–426.

Gwinner, K. P., & Eaton, J. (1999). Building brand image through event sponsorship: The role of image transfer. *Journal of Advertising*, *28*(4), 47–57. doi:10.1080/00913367.1999.10673595

Hansen, F., Halling, J., & Christensen, L. B. (2006). Choosing among alternative parties to be sponsored for supporting brand strategies, based upon emotional responses. *Journal of Consumer Behaviour*, *5*(6), 504–517. doi:10.1002/cb.199

Hansen, F., Martensen, A., & Christensen, S. R. (2005). Modelling emotional and attitudinal responses as drivers of sponsorship value. *International Journal of Sports Marketing & Sponsorship*, *7*(1), 75–80.

Heding, T., Knudtzen, C. F., & Bjerre, M. (2009). *Brand management: Research, theory and practice.* Abingdon, UK: Routledge. doi:10.4324/9780203996171

Hu, L., & Bentler, P. (1999). Cutoff criteria for fit indexes in covariance structure analysis: Conventional criteria versus new alternatives. *Structural Equation Modeling*, *6*(1), 1–55. doi:10.1080/10705519909540118

IEG. (2013). *2013 sponsorship outlook: Spending increase is double-edged sword.* Retrieved from http://www.sponsorship.com/iegsr/2013/01/07/2013-Sponsorship-Outlook--Spending-Increase-Is-Dou.aspx

IEG. (2014). *Who spent the most on sponsorship in 2013: IEG's top spenders list.* Retrieved from http://www.sponsorship.com/IEGSR/2014/05/27/Who-Spent-The-Most-On-Sponsorship-In-2013--IEG-s-T.aspx

IOC. (2009). *International Olympic Committee marketing report Beijing 2008.* IOC.

Kamins, M., & Gupta, K. (1994). Congruence between spokesperson and product type: A matchup hypothesis perspective. *Psychology and Marketing*, *11*(6), 569–586. doi:10.1002/mar.4220110605

Kaynak, E., Salman, G. G., & Tatoglu, E. . (2008). An integrative framework linking brand associations and brand loyalty in professional sports. *Journal of Brand Management.*

Keller, K. L. (1993). Conceptualizing, measuring, and managing customer-based brand equity. *Journal of Marketing*, *57*(1), 1–22. doi:10.2307/1252054

Kotler, P., & Keller, K. L. (2006). *Marketing management* (12th ed.). Person Prentice Hall.

Kotler, P., & Keller, K. L. (2009). *Marketing management* (13th ed.). Upper Saddle River, NJ: Pearson Prentice Hall.

Li Ning Company Limited. (2007). *Li Ning forges cooperation with Argentina National basketball team makes further strides in brand internationalization.* Retrieved from http://www.lining.com/eng/media/press_popup.php?file=inside-3_1_24.html

Li Ning Company Limited. (2009). *2008 annual report.* Retrieved from http://www.irasia.com/listco/hk/lining/annual/

Li Ning Company Limited. (2011). *2010 annual report.* Retrieved from http://www.irasia.com/listco/hk/lining/annual/

Li Ning Company Limited. (2014). *About Li Ning.* Retrieved from http://www.li-ning.com.cn/english_test/news/about_intro2.html

Mao, L. L., & Zhang, J. J. (2013). Impact of consumer involvement, emotions, and attitude toward beijing olympic games on branding effectiveness of event sponsors. *Sport, Business, and Management International Journal (Toronto, Ont.), 3*(3), 226–245.

Mao, L. L., Zhang, J. J., Connaughton, D. P., Holland, S., & Spengler, J. O. (2013). An associative learning account of branding effects of sponsorship. *Journal of Customer Behaviour, 12*(1), 25–51. doi:10.1362/147539213X13645550618489

Martensen, A., Gronholdt, L., Bendtsen, L., & Jensen, M. J. (2007). Application of a model for the effectiveness of event marketing. *Journal of Advertising Research, 47*(3), 283–301. doi:10.2501/S0021849907070316

Martensen, A., & Hansen, F. (2004). *Modelling emotional and attitudinal evaluations of major sponsors.* Academic Press.

McCracken, G. (1989). Who is the celebrity endorser? Cultural foundations of the endorsement process. *The Journal of Consumer Research*, *16*(3), 310–321. doi:10.1086/209217

McDaniel, S. R. (1999). An investigation of match-up effects in sport sponsorship advertising: The implications of consumer advertising schemas. *Psychology and Marketing*, *16*(2), 163–184. doi:10.1002/(SICI)1520-6793(199903)16:2<163::AID-MAR6>3.0.CO;2-Y

McDaniel, S. R., & Heald, G. R. (2000). Young consumers' responses to event sponsorship advertisements of unhealthy products: implications of schema-triggered affect theory. *Sport Management Review*, *3*(2), 163–184. doi:10.1016/S1441-3523(00)70084-2

Muehling, D., & Laczniak, R. (1988). Advertising's immediate and delayed influence on brand attitudes: Considerations across message-involvement levels. *Journal of Advertising*, *17*(4), 23–34. doi:10.1080/00913367.1988.10673126

Muthén, L. K., & Muthén, B. O. (2009). Mplus user's guide (4th ed.). Los Angeles, CA: Muthén & Muthén.

Nike. (2009). *Nike 10-K 2009*. Retrieved from http://www.wikinvest.com/stock/Nike_(NKE)/Filing/10-K/2009/F46739126

Oliver, R. L. (1997). *Satisfaction: A behavioral perspective on the consumer*. New York, NY: McGraw-Hill.

Olkkonen, R. (2001). Case study: The network approach to international sport sponsorship arrangement. *Journal of Business and Industrial Marketing*, *16*(4), 309–329. doi:10.1108/EUM0000000005503

Orlick, T. D. (1974). An interview schedule designed to assess family sports environment. *International Journal of Sport Psychology*, *5*(1), 13–27.

Pham, M. T. (1991). The evaluation of sponsorship effectiveness: A model and some methodological considerations. *Gestion*, *2000*(4), 47–65.

Phillystylemag.com. (2010). *10 questions with Evan Turner*. Retrieved from http://phillystylemag.com/personalities/articles/10-questions-with-sixers-star-evan-turner

PwCC. (2002). *Strategic report on Li Ning Company Ltd*. Li Ning Company Limited Internal Report.

Riordan, J., & Jones, R. (1999). *Sport and physical education in China*. London: E & FN Spon.

Shugan, S. M. (1980). The cost of thinking. *The Journal of Consumer Research*, *7*(2), 99–111. doi:10.1086/208799

Speed, R., & Thompson, P. (2000). Determinants of sports sponsorship response. *Journal of the Academy of Marketing Science*, *28*(2), 227–238. doi:10.1177/0092070300282004

Tucker, L., & Lewis, C. (1973). A reliability coefficient for maximum likelihood factor analysis. *Psychometrika*, *38*(1), 1–10. doi:10.1007/BF02291170

Walliser, B. (2003). An international review of sponsorship research: Extension and update. *International Journal of Advertising*, *22*(1), 5–40.

Wikinvest. (2009). *Nike(NKE)*. Retrieved from http://www.wikinvest.com/stock/Nike_(NKE)/Asia_Pacific_Region

Wikinvest. (2014). *Rise of China's middle class*. Retrieved from http://www.wikinvest.com/concept/Rise_of_China%27s_Middle_Class

Wooldridge, J. M. (2009). *Introductory econometrics: A modern approach* (4th ed.). South-Western.

Xu, X. (2006). *Modernizing China in the Olympic spotlight: China's national identity and the 2008 Beijing Olympiad*. Oxford, MA: Blackwell Publishing.

Yoo, B., Donthu, N., & Lee, S. (2000). An examination of selected marketing mix elements and brand equity. *Journal of the Academy of Marketing Science*, *28*(2), 195–211. doi:10.1177/0092070300282002

Yu, C. (2002). *Evaluating cutoff criteria of model fit indices for latent variable models with binary and continuous outcomes*. Los Angeles, CA: University of California Los Angeles.

Yu, L. (2008). *Li Ning - The heart of the champion*. Beijing, China: China Citic Press.

Zajonc, R. (1980). Feeling and thinking: Preferences need no inferences. *The American Psychologist*, *35*(2), 151–175. doi:10.1037/0003-066X.35.2.151

ADDITIONAL READING

Amis, J., & Cornwell, T. (2005). *Global sport sponsorship*. Oxford: Berg.

Amis, J., Slack, T., & Berrett, T. (1999). Sport sponsorships as distinctive competence. *European Journal of Marketing*, *33*(3/4), 250–272. doi:10.1108/03090569910253044

Beck-Burridge, M., & Walton, J. (2002). *Sport sponsorship and brand development:The subaru and jaguar sotries*. Basingstoke: Palgrave Macmillan.

Becker-Olsen, K. (2003). Questioning the name game: An event study analysis of stadium naming rights sponsorship announcements. *International Journal of Sports Marketing & Sponsorship*, *5*(3), 181–192.

Chien, P. M., Cornwell, T. B., & Pappu, R. (2011). Sponsorship portfolio as a brand-image creation strategy. *Journal of Business Research*, *64*(2), 142–149. doi:10.1016/j.jbusres.2010.02.010

Close, A. G., Finney, R. Z., Lacey, R. Z., & Sneath, J. Z. (2006). Engaging the consumer through event marketing: Linking attendees with the sponsor, community, and brand. *Journal of Advertising Research*, *46*(4), 420–433. doi:10.2501/S0021849906060430

Close, A. G., & Kahle, L. R. (2011). *Consumer behavior knowledge for effective sports and event marketing*. New York: Routledge.

Cornwell, T. B. (2008). State of the art and science in sponsorship-linked marketing. *Journal of Advertising*, *37*(3), 41–55. doi:10.2753/JOA0091-3367370304

Cornwell, T. B., & Maignan, I. (1998). An international review of sponsorship research. *Journal of Advertising*, *27*(1), 1–21. doi:10.1080/00913367.1998.10673539

Cornwell, T. B., Weeks, C. S., & Roy, D. P. (2005). Sponsorship-linked marketing: Opening the black box. *Journal of Advertising*, *34*(2), 21–42. doi:10.1080/00913367.2005.10639194

Crompton, J. L. (2004). Conceptualization and alternate operationalizations of the measurement of sponsorship effectiveness in sport. *Leisure Studies*, *23*(3), 267–281. doi:10.1080/0261436042000183695

Drengner, J., Gaus, H., & Jahn, S. (2008). Does flow influence the brand image in event marketing? *Journal of Advertising Research*, *48*(1), 138–147. doi:10.2501/S0021849908080148

Henseler, J., Wilson, B., Götz, O., & Hautvast, C. (2007). Investigating the moderating role of fit on sports sponsorship and brand equity. *International Journal of Sports Marketing & Sponsorship*, *8*(4), 321–329.

Johar, G. V., & Pham, M. T. (1999). Relatedness, prominence, and constructive sponsor identification. *JMR, Journal of Marketing Research*, *36*(3), 299–312. doi:10.2307/3152078

Keller, K. L. (1993). Conceptualizing, measuring, and managing customer-based brand equity. *Journal of Marketing*, *57*(1), 1–22. doi:10.2307/1252054

Kotler, P., & Keller, K. L. (2006). *Marketing management* (12th ed.). New Jersey: Person Prentice Hall.

Lacey, R., Close, A. G., & Finney, R. Z. (2010). The pivotal roles of product knowledge and corporate social responsibility in event sponsorship effectiveness. *Journal of Business Research*, *63*(11), 1222–1228. doi:10.1016/j.jbusres.2009.11.001

Masterman, G. (2007). *Sponsorship: For a return on investment*. London: Butterworth-Heinemann.

Meenaghan, T. (2001). Sponsorship and advertising: A comparison of consumer perceptions. *Psychology and Marketing*, *18*(2), 191–215. doi:10.1002/1520-6793(200102)18:2<191::AID-MAR1005>3.0.CO;2-C

Pham, M. T. (1991). The evaluation of sponsorship effectiveness: A model and some methodological considerations. *Gestion*, *2000*(4), 47–65.

Skinner, B., & Rukavina, V. (2003). *Event sponsorship*. John Wiley & Sons.

Sneath, J. Z., Finney, R. Z., & Close, A. G. (2005). An imc approach to event marketing: The effects of sponsorship and experience on customer attitudes. *Journal of Advertising Research*, *45*(4), 373–381. doi:10.1017/S0021849905050440

Van Osselaer, S. J., & Alba, J. W. (2000). Consumer learning and brand equity. *The Journal of Consumer Research*, *27*(1), 1–16. doi:10.1086/314305

Yoo, B., & Donthu, N. (2001). Developing and validating a multidimensional consumer-based brand equity scale. *Journal of Business Research*, *52*(1), 1–14. doi:10.1016/S0148-2963(99)00098-3

Yoo, B., Donthu, N., & Lee, S. (2000). An examination of selected marketing mix elements and brand equity. *Journal of the Academy of Marketing Science*, *28*(2), 195–211. doi:10.1177/0092070300282002

KEY TERMS AND DEFINITIONS

Brand Association: Images and symbols associated with a brand in a sophisticated and interconnected fashion.

Brand Awareness: The extent to which a brand is recognized or recalled by consumers under different conditions.

Brand Loyalty: Consumer's behavioral and attitudinal commitment to purchase a preferred products or services in the future.

Branding Effects: Perceived enhancement of elements of brand equity as a result of sponsorship-linked marketing communication.

Event Quality: Event consumers' subjective evaluation associated with consumers' event involvement, emotions intrigued by the event, and event attitudes.

Perceived Event-Brand Congruency: Perceived relevance between a brand and an event based on consumer's judgment of the fit between the functions and images of both parties.

Perceived Quality: Consumer's subjective judgment about a product's overall excellence.

Sponsorship-Linked Marketing: Marketing activities designed and implemented by using sponsorship as an integrated communication platform.

This research was previously published in Emerging Trends and Innovation in Sports Marketing and Management in Asia edited by Ho Keat Leng and Noah Yang Hsu, pages 44-65, copyright year 2015 by Business Science Reference (an imprint of IGI Global).

Chapter 12
Predicting the Attentional Effect of Sport Sponsorship Information as an Innovative Evaluation Approach

Christopher Rumpf
German Sport University Cologne, Germany

Christoph Breuer
German Sport University Cologne, Germany

ABSTRACT

Most major sports events can no longer exist without the investments of sponsors. However, financially strong companies are increasingly adopting a critical attitude towards sponsorship since their strategic investments in a sports event cannot be evaluated sufficiently. Against this backdrop, the current approaches to the evaluation of sponsorship are discussed critically in this chapter before a more innovative approach is suggested. The new evaluation approach directs sports viewers' attention to sponsorship information, the central valuation object. At the core, it involves measuring the visual and cognitive attention in standardized experiments and using the identified patterns to predict sponsorship effectiveness. In this regard, the theoretical and methodological fundamentals of the new approach are introduced in the main part of the chapter before their applicability is illustrated based on three typical phases in sponsorship management. To close this chapter, the authors suggest topics for future research.

INTRODUCTION

In almost all relevant areas of professional sports, sponsors attempt to capture the viewers' attention by placing their brand logo on the jersey of a soccer team, on the press conference table at a Formula 1 race or on the shirt collar of a handball coach – to name just a few examples. If the sports event is broadcasted on TV channels reaching a large audience, companies are usually willing to invest high

DOI: 10.4018/978-1-5225-5475-2.ch012

amounts of money in order to be visible with their brand. While sponsorship mainly fulfills the function of a financing instrument from the point of view of sports events (Preuß, 2005), companies use sponsorship as a marketing instrument that should increase awareness of and sympathy for the brand (Olson & Thjømøe, 2003).

Even though sponsorship does not have a long tradition in comparison to other marketing communication instruments, the sponsorship market has reached an impressive level: Since 1992, global spending on sponsorships has more than quintupled and totaled $ 51.1 billion in 2012, of which 69% flew into the area of sports (IEG, 2013). In 2013 the sponsorship consultants of the International Events Group anticipate further growth of 4.2% in the global sponsorship market.

The rising expenditures for sponsorship have increased the pressure on sponsorship managers to prove the return on their sponsorship investment. In this regard, representatives from science and business have stated that the further growth of sponsorship will be closely tied to the development of adequate evaluation methods (Geach, 2007; Green, 2008; O'Reilly & Madill, 2009). Since a meaningful evaluation is always based on the understanding of the underlying interrelations, a scientific foundation is of critical importance.

However, research on sponsorship effectiveness has not been able to keep up with the rapid development of the sponsorship market. Elementary questions regarding the mental processing of sponsorship information in a viewer's mind have still not been explained. This could be due to the fact that the internal processes have not been addressed frequently in theoretical models so far (Cornwell, Weeks, & Roy, 2005). Furthermore, constructs in perceptual psychology such as sports viewers' attention is difficult to measure empirically, which is why viewers are regarded as a "black box" in most studies.

In order to strategically manage sponsorships, however, it is critical to have knowledge about the processing of information in the mind of a sports viewer. In this regard, the common practice to evaluate sponsorships based on sponsor logo exposure is not very far-reaching since it does not reveal to which extent the audience actually received and processed visible sponsorship information. Therefore, an analysis of attention can provide important insight into whether sponsorship information has found its way into the selective "black box" of a sports viewer and therefore becomes relevant with regard to the sponsor's marketing objectives.

Given that sponsorship investments grow in most global markets, the need to validly predict the effectiveness of sponsorship is increasing. To date, ex-ante evaluations have been based on vague estimations by experts and therefore offer no possibility of quantifying the effectiveness or efficiency of a sponsorship. This is the backdrop for the evaluation method that is presented in this chapter and will offer a strategic advantage for both sports properties and sponsors.

To put it in a nutshell, the chapter's goal is to critically discuss the current methods in sponsorship evaluation and to provide an alternative evaluation approach that makes sports viewers' attention the central valuation object.

SPONSORSHIP AS A STRATEGIC MARKETING TOOL

Before a new approach to sponsorship evaluation is presented in the next section, the current state of research and management practice will be discussed. To start with, sponsorship is briefly defined and its potential impact is described. This is then followed by the presentation of two different evaluation approaches from applied sponsorship management – the media-analytical and survey-based evaluation.

Sponsorship

After sponsorship was used only infrequently in business practice prior to the 1980s (Preuß, 2005), it has become such a firmly established marketing instrument in the meantime that it basically no longer requires a vast definition (Cornwell, 2008). Nonetheless, a short definition of the concept should be provided in order to establish a uniform understanding of sponsorship for this chapter. The further explanations relate solely to sponsorship in sports, even if the fundamental principle can also be applied to cultural, social, ecological or media sponsorship areas (Bruhn, 2007).

In the German critical literature on the subject, the most common definition is given by Bruhn (2010), who defines sponsorship as follows:

Sponsorship means the analysis, planning, implementation and management of all activities that are related to companies or institutions' providing money, material, services or know-how for the promotion of people and/or organizations [...] with the contractual arrangement of the sponsor's service and the sponsored party's consideration (service received) in order to achieve the objectives of marketing and corporate communication at the same time (Bruhn, 2010, pp. 6 f.).

In the English literature on sponsorship, a highly cited definition stems from Meenaghan (1983, pp. 9) according to which sponsorship means "the provision of assistance either financial or in-kind to an activity by a commercial organization for the purpose of achieving commercial objectives".

Bruhns (2010) and Meenaghans (1983) definitions differ to the extent that Bruhn (2010) describes sponsorship primarily as a management process, while Meenaghan (1983) understands it to be primarily an earmarked investment. Furthermore, Bruhn's (2010) definition allows for non-commercial institutions to act as sponsors, while Meenaghan (1983) limits the group of sponsors to commercial organizations. Nonetheless, the given definitions show substantial similarities: On the one hand, the two definitions stress the sponsor's self-serving purpose; on the other hand, both of them imply a two-sided relationship between an organization and a sponsored entity (e.g. sports event).

In her definition of "sponsorship-linked marketing" Cornwell (1995) makes a clear distinction between the investment into a sponsorship and the use of communication rights which come along with the contractual relationship between the sponsor and the sponsored entity. In this regard, Cornwell (1995) defines "sponsorship-linked marketing" as "the orchestration and implementation of marketing activities for the purpose of building and communicating an association to a sponsorship" (Cornwell, 1995, pp. 15). According to this definition, it is of central importance that the relationship between the brand and the sponsored entity is communicated to certain stakeholders by employing suitable marketing measures, i.e. that the sponsorship information is transmitted.

Generally, information is understood as a structure of symbols that can be perceived by a person and contain certain meaning (Mangold, 2007). In the sponsorship context, the concept of information stands for a visible signage (e.g. brand logo) at a sports event, which informs the viewer about the relationship between the sponsor and the sponsored entity. By communicating this associative information, which is described in the following as "sponsorship information," a sponsor pursues the strategic goal of producing a conceptual link between a brand and a sports entity in a viewer's mind (Humphreys et al., 2010; Meenaghan & Shipley, 1999).

Sponsorship Effectiveness

Although numerous studies address the effectiveness of sponsorship, the concept is not used uniformly in literature. The different understandings of the concept could be due, on the one hand, to the numerous synonyms (e.g. outcome, impact, result) and, on the other, to the lack of a definition in most research contributions. In the following, therefore, a clear definition of sponsorship effectiveness is provided for this chapter.

Even if the concept of effectiveness is not specified in more detail in most studies, it is generally possible to differentiate between sponsorship effectiveness on the individual level (e.g. Breuer & Rumpf, 2012; Olson & Thjømøe, 2009; Wakefield, Becker-Olsen, & Cornwell, 2007) and sponsorship effectiveness on the aggregate level (e.g. Clark, Cornwell, & Pruitt, 2009; Reiser, Breuer & Wicker, 2012).

On the individual level, effectiveness relates to the individual sport consumer and includes aspects such as memory of the sponsor or sensed sympathy for a sponsor's brand. On the aggregate level, effectiveness in relation to an entire company is considered, including changes in sales revenue or in share price. Independently of the level of effectiveness, all the understandings of the concept have in common that (1) effectiveness is interpreted as a change in a dependent variable and (2) there is causality to the use of sponsorship.

A conventional classification of sponsorship effectiveness on the individual level is provided by Cornwell, Weeks and Roy (2005). They differentiate between cognitive, affective and conative sponsorship effectiveness: Cognitive effectiveness is primarily characterized by a viewer's knowledge of a sponsor, while affective effectiveness reflects the sensed high regard for a sponsor and conative effectiveness describes a viewer's behavior (e.g. purchase, recommendation) with respect to a sponsor's brand. Furthermore, Cornwell et al. (2005) note that sponsorship effectiveness can also take place unconsciously, i.e. without the conscious processing of sponsorship information. Hence, in this chapter sponsorship effectiveness is defined as the conscious or unconscious reaction of a sports viewer to the exposure of sponsorship information.

It is noteworthy, that cognitive, affective and conative sponsorship effects have a complementary relationship to each other. Accordingly, in various studies, it was possible to prove that the memory of a sponsor precedes the transfer of image attributes (e.g. Grohs et al., 2004). Koo et al. (2006) also found that remembering a sponsor influences the intention to buy. Furthermore, it has been empirically proven that an intention to buy depends (among other variables) on a successful image transfer (e.g. Chavanat et al., 2009; Dees et al., 2008; Gwinner et al., 2009; Madrigal, 2001; Meenaghan, 2001).

With regards to the moderators of sponsorship effectiveness, the role of fit between the sponsor's brand and the sports event as well as prior brand familiarity have been examined in sponsorship research (e.g. Olson & Thjømøe, 2009; Pham & Johar, 2001; Wakefield et al., 2007). It can be assumed that a high level of fit benefits memory (Johar & Pham, 1999), the image transfer (Chien, Cornwell, & Stokes; Gwinner & Bennot, 2008) and the intention to buy (Lee & Cho, 2009). Concerning the influence of prior brand familiarity, it has been found that sponsor memory is more likely for prominent brands (Johar & Pham, 1999; Johar et al., 2006; Olson & Thjømøe, 2009; Pham & Johar, 2001; Wakefield et al., 2007).

Despite these numerous findings, fundamental questions in relation to sponsorship effectiveness remain unexplained. The most significant gap relates to the internal processes in sponsorship effectiveness, particularly the role of attention. In most studies on sponsorship effectiveness, the sports viewer is treated as a "black box" without analyzing the mechanisms of mental processing. This results in a lack of in-depth understanding about the complex process in sponsorship effectiveness, which is why the implications for theory and practice remain rather vague.

Sponsorship Evaluation

The evaluation of sponsorship effectiveness is described as the greatest challenge for sponsorship research (Crompton, 2004; O'Reilly & Madill, 2009). In this chapter, the term "evaluation" should be understood as the data-based measurement and evaluation of sponsorship effectiveness. In order to establish a better understanding for the evaluation practice in the sponsorship context, a brief outline of the two most common evaluation approaches – the media-analytical approach and the survey-based approach – will be provided firstly. Secondly, an overview of the current state of research on sponsorship evaluation will be given.

The principle of the media-analytical approach consists of monitoring the exposure of sponsorship information within sports broadcasts. In addition, the audience reach is analyzed by determining the number of households that turn on a given sports broadcast. The duration of exposure and the audience reach are multiplied with each other on the basis of each relevant broadcast and added up for an entire period (e.g. a season). On the basis of this total value (so-called sponsorship contact total), it is possible to compare different sponsorships with each other objectively (Felten, 2007).

Nonetheless, consideration is not given to whether the television viewer also mentally processed the corresponding sponsorship information, since only sponsor logo exposure and audience reach are measured. Consequently, it is only possible to make statements about the opportunities to be seen (Crompton, 2004), which is why the media-analytical approach, strictly speaking, does not represent a method for determining sponsorship effectiveness, but rather an evaluation of the potential effect.

Another form of evaluation that is used frequently in management practice is the survey-based approach. In phone interviews, on-site surveys or online surveys, the awareness of sponsors (cognitive effect), the sponsor sympathy (affective effect) or the intention to buy (conative effect) are determined. Such surveys can be conducted either as a pre-post design or take place with the aid of a control group, with the deviation between the pre- and post-measurement or between the control and test group being attributed to sponsorship effectiveness (Breuer, Rumpf & Kurz, 2013; Crompton, 2004).

Even if sponsorship effectiveness can be analyzed with the aid of the survey-based approach, different problems will occur, depending on the survey goal: In the collection of awareness data, it is necessary to consider that prominent and high-fit sponsor brands are systematically given an advantage (e.g. Pham & Johar, 2001). The measurement of the affective effectiveness is also problematic since the results are influenced by the survey situation and the mood of the test person (e.g. Hoyer & MacInnis, 2010). The measurement of the conative effectiveness is not regarded less critically in literature since external factors such as price or product packaging, for example, can influence the purchase behavior at the same time (e.g. O'Reilly, 2008).

To sum it up, it must be stated that there is an explicit gap in innovative approaches to the evaluation of sponsorship effectiveness. In this context, Walliser (2003) has found that the majority of scientific studies does not develop any new approaches, but rather primarily limit themselves to simple memory tests. O'Reilly and Madill (2009) add that there is primarily a need for evaluation approaches that are better suited for the associative character of sponsorship.

A widespread approach in sponsorship research consists of transferring existing evaluation approaches from general advertising research in a slightly adapted form to the evaluation of sponsorship (O'Reilly & Madill, 2009; Quester & Farrelly, 1998). For this reason, numerous studies do not record the characteristic association between the sponsor and the sports event in the process of sponsorship effectiveness and therefore might be misleading.

ATTENTIONAL EFFECT OF SPONSORSHIP INFORMATION

In this section, the underlying theoretical principle and the methodological requirements of an attention-based evaluation method will be introduced. To start with, the concept of attention is defined and applied to the sponsorship context. This is followed by a discussion on the method of measuring and predicting viewer-related attention for sponsorship information.

Viewer's Attention in a Sponsorship Context

Although James (1890) stated more than 120 years ago that actually everyone knows what attention is, attention in the sponsorship context will be briefly explained below.

Since a sports broadcast usually contains more information than a viewer can process, the human information processing system applies a selection mechanism that protects against information overload. This selection mechanism can be defined as attention and can be illustrated with the help of the "spotlight" metaphor (e.g. LaBerge, 1983). Hereby, attention is compared with a spotlight that directs its focus on certain objects in a person's field of vision and thereby facilitates their efficient processing, while other areas in the field of vision are processed less efficiently. As soon as an object has been mentally processed, the focus of the spotlight shifts again in order to illuminate another object in the field of vision (Palmer, 2002).

In the general marketing literature, attention is understood as a necessary requirement for successful communication with consumers (Davenport & Beck, 2001; Sacharin, 2001). Accordingly, the central challenge for marketing communication is to direct the target group's attention to its own brand message. In the sponsorship context, this specifically means that a viewer will only process sponsorship information which he or she has given a sufficiently large amount of attention to. Since both the visual and cognitive attention capacity of a sports viewer is limited, attention represents a chronically scarce resource from a sponsor's point of view (Breuer et al., 2013).

While sponsorship information in most cases is presented through sponsor signage, the visual system is responsible for the information intake. With regards to the intake of visual information, it is generally possible to differentiate between a controlled and an automatic form: In the controlled form, the viewer's attention is controlled intentionally with the consequence that only the most relevant information is processed and reaches the viewer's consciousness. Posner and Snyder (1975) assume that the controlled direction of attention leads to greater concentration as a result of which the processing of competing information is inhibited.

This form of intentional directing of attention is also described as a "strategy" or "top-down process" (e.g. Ansorge & Leder, 2010). Despite the increase in concentration, automatically activated mental processing may occur alongside the controlled directing of attention. Automatically activated mental processing is characterized by the fact that it occurs unconsciously without interrupting a top-down process. In contrast to conscious processing, no or very few cognitive resources are required, which is why automatically activated processing can occur relatively quickly. This form of attention is solely dependent on the physical properties of information stimulus, such as the color or size, and is also described as a "bottom-up-process" (Ansorge & Leder, 2010).

The primary intention of sports viewers is to follow a certain sport competition, which is why the cognitive resources are primarily dedicated to the sports event. On the basis of the preceding considerations, there are two possibilities for how sponsorship information can be processed. On the one hand, there is the possibility that the top-down process is interrupted (e.g. in a phase of less game action) and cognitive resources for the conscious processing of sponsorship information are therefore available.

The second possibility consists of the automatically activated processing (bottom-up processing) with the consequence that the sponsorship information is processed parallel to the sports event, but does not penetrate the consciousness of the sports viewer. A requirement for the automatic processing is the simplicity of the information stimulus (e.g. individual numbers or words) as well as the recipient's skill in processing such information (Posner & Snyder, 1975). Since only brand names or logos are exposed in the sponsorship context and most viewers are experienced in processing marketing information, the requirements for an unconscious and automatic form of processing can be seen as fulfilled.

Methods of Attention-Based Sponsorship Evaluation

The most frequently used instrument for measuring attention is the memory test (Milosavljevic, 2009). This is based on the assumption that memory for an object only occurs when attention has been given to this object beforehand (Moore, Stammerjohan, & Coulter, 2005). This assumption, however, is controversially discussed in literature since giving attention does not always take place consciously and therefore the object of mental processing cannot always be recalled (Rosbergen et al., 1997).

This problem can be taken into account by employing recognition tests where the previous appearance of an object is confirmed or rejected by a test person after the presentation of an illustration. As opposed to recall tests, recognition tests can also make subtle connections in memory accessible, assuming that the illustration in the test matches sufficiently well the object that is to be recognized (Tripodi et al., 2003).

An alternative instrument for the measurement of attention is eye-tracking, which is also increasingly used in the general marketing research (Duchowski, 2007). The fundamental principle of eye-tracking is to measure the direction of the gaze by recording the position of the pupils with high frequency as horizontal and vertical coordinate values.

Since the focus of the gaze can change not only through the movement of the eyeballs, but also through head movements, modern systems measure both the pupil position and the position of a reflection point on the cornea of the eye (Duchowski, 2007). On the basis of the relationship between the position of the pupils and the position of the corneal reflection on the eye, the eye tracking system can calculate the direction of the gaze independently of head movement. For this purpose, infrared light is beamed from a fixed lighting source onto the test person's face, while a special infrared camera records the reflected light (Mangold, 2007).

On the recorded video image, the eye tracking system can identify the test person's pupils as dark circles, since the beamed light is absorbed by the pupils. As opposed to the pupils, the cornea reflects the infrared light very strongly, which is why the corneal reflection appears as a bright point on the video image and is identified by the system (Holmqvist et al., 2011).

The application of the corneal reflection method allows for the precise recording of the direction of a sports viewer's eye. However, this method does not make it possible per se to determine whether a person's gaze falls on sponsorship information. In order to record gaze contact with sponsorship information, so-called areas of interest (abbreviated as AOI) must be marked within the sports broadcast. Due to the short length of fixation (100-400 milliseconds), this marking should be done frame by frame, whereby the manual work process can be supported by the automatic algorithms of modern computer programs.

After the complete marking of AOIs, it is possible to automatically evaluate how long and frequently a sports viewer's gaze enters into a certain AOI in order to draw conclusions about the attention for sponsorship information.

With regards to eye tracking, a differentiation can be made between table-mounted and head-mounted systems. Table-mounted systems offer the advantage that they record the direction of a person's gaze in a highly precise way without an additional scene camera since the video screen usually corresponds to a person's field of vision (Duchowski, 2007). Furthermore, a higher simulation of reality can be ensured with the table-mounted system since it is not necessary to attach an apparatus to a test person's head. However, table-mounted systems can only be used in laboratory situations and are therefore unsuited for field use in places such as a sports stadium.

The eye tracking system allows for the recording of fixations that fall on the sponsorship information and thus represent a gaze contact between the sports viewer and the sponsorship information. Furthermore, fixations that directly follow each other (and are all assigned to the same sponsorship information) are summarized as a single gaze contact. Figure 1 illustrates this understanding of fixation and gaze contact in the example of sponsorship information on a jersey. The five circles represent different fixations, and fixation 2, 3 and 4 fall on the sponsorship information and are therefore defined as a gaze contact.

Figure 1. Fixation and gaze contact

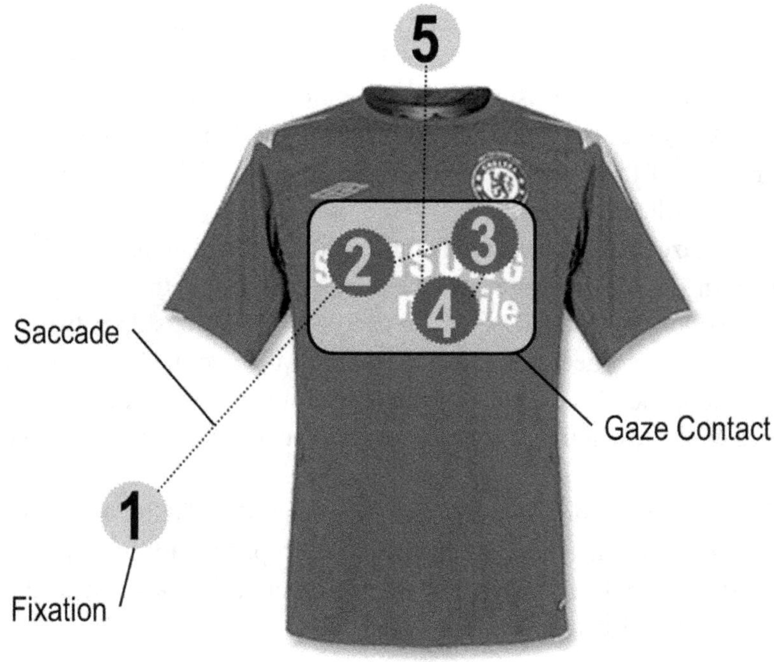

To develop an attention-based evaluation method, it is recommended that recognition testing and eye tracking are systematically combined with each other in order to best account for the complex construct of attention. This makes it possible to use the number of gaze contacts to determine the degree of visual attention for sponsorship information, while the recognition test pinpoints the sponsorship information that attracts the viewer's attention on a higher (cognitive) level.

To measure cognitive attention, the authors developed an electronic recognition test that is based on the "remember-know-guess" test from Sherman and Moran (2011) and contains two steps. In the first step, a sponsor's brand logo and the official logo of the sports event in question are shown next to each other on a screen. The following text appears directly above the two logos: "This brand is an official sponsor." The test person's task consists of confirming the statement by touching the "true" button on the screen or rejecting the statement by touching the "false" button. As soon as a test person has confirmed the statement, he or she is automatically forwarded to the second step in the test.

The second step serves to determine the cause of the sponsor recognition by asking the test person about the reason for his answer: "Did you see the brand during the sport broadcast, did you know about the sponsorship before or did you guess?". Three answer buttons appear below the text: By touching the "seen" button, the test person can state that he or she has processed the corresponding sponsorship information in the sports broadcast. If the "knew" button is touched, this means that the test person already knew about the sponsorship of the brand in question before the sports broadcast. Finally, by pressing the "guessed" button, the test person can indicate that the recognition is not based on actual memory, but by simply guessing.

The two step procedure is handled on a tablet PC for all visible sponsors. The produced dataset solely encodes as recognized those sponsors that the test person has reported as "true" in the first step and as "seen" in the second step.

Since the application of the eye-tracking method and the recognition testing requires a large amount of planning and time, it is recommended to test a suitable sample of sports viewers (n>100). While representative clippings from sports broadcasts are presented to the sample, the visual attention (eye tracking) and the cognitive attention (recognition test) is assessed. Multivariate statistics are used to identify and save the typical patterns in the collected data and ultimately apply them for predictive purposes. Depending on the application area, it is possible to build predictive models for specific types or certain groups of sports.

Prediction of Attentional Sponsorship Effects

In the following, the statistical method of neural network analysis is presented for the prediction of sponsorship effectiveness. The neural network analysis is based on the connectionism approach which deals with the functioning of the human brain and aims to produce a computer-based replication of a network made up of artificial neurons. Fundamentally, connectionism assumes that the human information processing results from the the interaction of numerous units (neurons) that have a restraining or activating impact on other units in the neural network. The replication of such a processing apparatus should include the most possible performance attributes of the human brain such as the ability to learn and adapt, a high tolerance for errors and the parallel processing of information (Haykin, 1999).

Since neural network models were originally developed from cognitive perception processes (Bishop, 1996), an analogy is frequently drawn in academic work between neural network models and the biological nervous system. Haykin (1999, pp. 2) defines a neural network as "a massively parallel distributed processor made up of simple processing units, which has a natural propensity for storing experiential knowledge and making it available for use." On the basis of this definition, neural networks can be understood as complex information processing systems that acquire knowledge in a learning process, save it in the form of weights and then use it for future estimation problems.

However, the term neural network analysis involves less a special analysis process than a collective expression for different network types. The following discussion concentrates on the multi-layer perception network[1] that is most frequently applied in social science research (Backhaus et al., 2011).

The basic unit in a multi-layer perception network (abbreviated: MLP network) consists of the individual neuron, which is described as a unit or processor. Within a neuron, the incoming signals are processed and forwarded to the next neurons. A signal is understood here as a permanent numeric value (Zander, 2001). A neuron receives signals from preceding neurons and aggregates them in the form of a one-dimensional net input value.

Depending on the net input value, the neuron's degree of activation is determined in the next step. To calculate the degree of activation, there are numerous activation functions discussed in literature, whereby the sigmoidal activation function is employed in most cases. In contrast to the linear activation function, the sigmoidal function offers the advantage that it can also form intrinsically non-linear relationships between input and output variables on the basis of its S-shaped curve. Sigmoidal functions can differ in terms of the logistical and tangent-hyperbolic function. Both functions have a similar curve and differ only with regard to their functional value: While the logistical function puts out values between 0 and 1, the values of the tangent-hyperbolic function are between -1 and 1 (Bishop, 1996).

After the information processing in the neurons has been explained, the structure between the neurons, the so-called configuration, is addressed. In an MLP network, the neurons are arranged step by step with a differentiation between at least three layers: In the (1) input layer, empirical information in the form of numbers is provided for the model, but no calculations are made. Only in the (2) hidden layer do matrix calculations take place on the basis of this information bundle, through which the weights in the network are adjusted. Finally, in the (3) output layer, the estimate of the neural network with regard to the problem input is produced in the form of a numeric value. Figure 2 shows a three-layer MLP network.

The number of input neurons (I1-I4) corresponds to the number of independent variables and should be based on logical considerations, i. e., only variables that make an explanatory contribution from a theoretical point of view should be included. In the sponsorship context, this involves the duration of sponsor logo exposure, optical features of the sponsorship information (e.g. the size) and sponsor-related variables (e.g. prior brand familiarity). The dependent variables are represented in the network as output neurons (O1 and O2) in the output layer and relate to either the number of gaze contacts or sponsor recognition. The hidden layer with three hidden neurons (H1-H3), which represents the "black box" of the sports viewer, is located between the input and output layer.

Typically, all the neurons in one layer are linked with all the neurons in the following layer, while the neurons in one layer fundamentally do not have any links. The goal of the analysis is to determine the weights for each link in the network in order to ensure the most precise estimate of the dependent variables (Backhaus et al., 2011).

Figure 2. Three layer MLP network

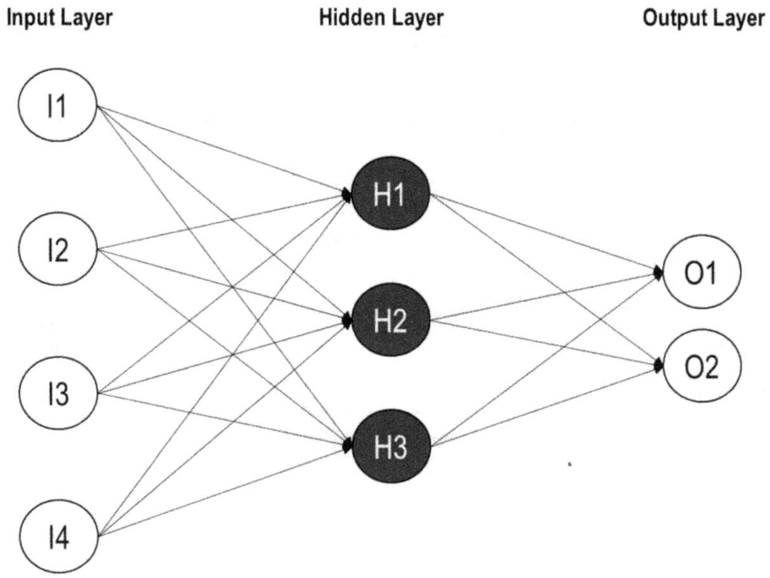

APPLICATION OF ATTENTION-BASED SPONSORSHIP EVALUATION

The described evaluation approach supports the strategic decision making of sponsorship managers by providing quantitative predictions on the attentional effect of a sponsorship. This allows for systematic evaluations of various sponsorship alternatives with regard to their effectiveness (gained attention) and their efficiency (costs per gained attention). Thus, the evaluation approach represents a functional tool to improve strategic decisions in sponsorship management.

The core of the evaluation approach consists of two neuronal network models that are interlinked. Thereby, the output in the two performance indicators of gaze contacts and likelihood of recognition are predicted. Figure 3 offers a schematic illustration of the attention-based sponsorship evaluation.

The application of this evaluation requires input data with regard to the exposure during sports broadcasts (exposure), the design of the sponsorship information (optical features) and the sponsor's brand (sponsor-related features). The reliability of this input data has a direct influence on the quality of predictions.

In the following, three characteristic phases are used to explain the extent to which the evaluation method contributes to the further professionalization of sponsorship management. A differentiation is made between the following three phases of sponsorship management:

1. In the *initiation phase,* a manager checks the sponsorship offer of a legal provider and compares it with alternatives.
2. In the *implementation phase*, the primary concern is to efficiently use the acquired communication rights.
3. In the *adjustment phase*, certain changes in the sponsorship agreement are negotiated.

Figure 3. Schematic illustration of the attention-based sponsorship evaluation

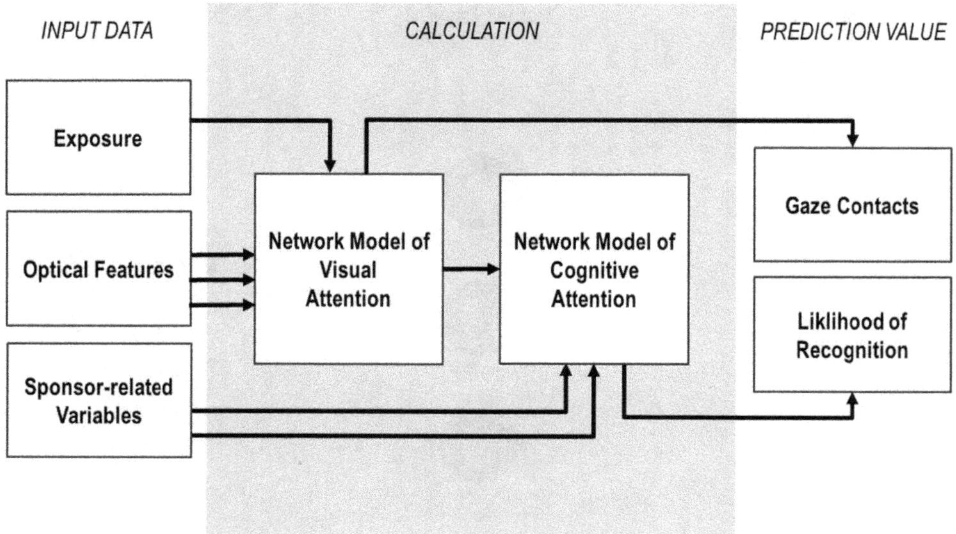

During the *initiation phase*, a company has the problem of selecting the most efficient offer from a number of options. After a pre-selection has been made on the basis of the ability to reach the specific target group of the brand, the sponsorship that offers the greatest amount of attention at the lowest cost needs to be identified. While the costs are provided in the sponsorship offer, the attention for the sponsor cannot be readily estimated. Therefore, it is recommended that a systematic ex-ante evaluation of the attentional effect to be made with the aid of the evaluation method. The option that offers the best ratio of predicted attention to cost is then to be selected.

In order to use the attention-based sponsorship evaluation method in this regard, it is necessary to obtain information about exposure, the design of communication tools and the company's own brand. The right holders usually have past-related exposure data on comparable sponsorship packages, while information on the optical properties of the offered communication tools can be obtained with the aid of video-analytical assessment. Furthermore, market research data is to be obtained which provides insight into prior brand familiarity and product knowledge within the sports target group in question. On the basis of this database, the evaluation method calculates a value for the anticipated gaze contacts and the average likelihood of recognition.

In order to be able to ultimately compare the efficiency of the sponsorship options, both the predicted gaze contacts and the likelihood of recognition must be considered with respect to the audience reach[2] and then put in relation to the costs of sponsorship. If one option offers the greatest efficiency with regard to gaze contacts, but another option provides the greatest efficiency with regard to the likelihood of recognition, the sponsorship manager has to decide which performance indicators is more important to the company's strategic goal.

If a company wants to make a new brand more well-known in the target group, the likelihood of recognition should be focused, since this performance indicator reflects the extent to which the sponsorship leads to an expansion of brand knowledge. If a brand is already established in the marketplace, gaze contacts represent the critical performance indicator since visual attention means the precondition for all types of sponsorship effectiveness (i.e. cognitive, affective, conative).

In the *implementation phase*, most sponsors rely on performance indicators from media analysis (e.g. exposure time) or from explicit market research (e.g. sponsor recall), although these indicators either cannot reflect sponsorship effectiveness or are subject to serious biases. In order to overcome the weaknesses of traditional sponsorship evaluation, it is recommended here to make the generated attention the central valuation object.

The attention-based sponsorship evaluation method takes the weaknesses into account by calculating the gaze contacts and the likelihood of recognition based on empirical models.

The shift to these new performance indicators is recommended for three reasons: First, as opposed to traditional sponsorship evaluation, it establishes a holistic basis for evaluation, since these indicators consider several success factors on multiple levels. Second, it is possible to discover effects that remain hidden from media analysis and explicit market research such as the direct influence of design features of sponsorship communication tools. Third, the attention-related performance indicators are easy to interpret, which is why they are particularly suited for practical use.

In the *adjustment phase*, a company must ultimately assess ex-ante the extent to which changes in certain communication conditions will be reflected in sponsorship effectiveness. On the one hand, most right holders adjust their marketing concept at regular intervals by changing, for example, the size of their sponsor pool or modifying the communication tools for their sponsors. On the other hand, sponsors try to achieve a high degree of effectiveness by adjusting the composition of communication tools or their design. In each case, this raises the question of whether the planned adjustments lead to a change in the value of the sponsorship. In order to obtain a clear answer, it is recommended that different scenarios are simulated with the aid of the attention-based evaluation method. On the basis of the respectively predicted attentional effect, it is possible to decide objectively whether an adjustment makes sense and a possible price increase is justified.

Even if the suggested evaluation method offers a series of advantages over traditional sponsorship evaluation, it is important to also address possible limitations. First, the predicted values are based on experimental data patterns and therefore it builds on the (unproved) assumption that the identified relationships are also valid in reality. This raises the question of the method's external validity which can be partly facilitated by the selection of random samples.

Second, there is a risk to the applicability of the evaluation method as a result of the lab situation. The artificial character of a lab situation leads in general to the criticism that the viewer behavior in a natural environment may deviate from the behavior in the lab.

FUTURE RESEARCH DIRECTIONS

The recommended evaluation method helps with the clarification of elementary questions regarding the attention-related effectiveness of sponsorship. Nonetheless, there is a need for additional research in relation to (1) long-term sponsorship effectiveness, (2) affective sponsorship effectiveness, (3) sponsorship effectiveness through new optical design possibilities and (4) the examination of sponsorship effectiveness under field conditions.

A starting point would be the expansion of the evaluation method to include the calculation of long-term sponsorship effectiveness. For sponsoring companies it would be of importance to receive reliable information about the effectiveness of a sponsorship in the long run. Empirical research on long-term effectiveness requires a longitudinal research design, the greatest challenge of which may lie in the control of external variables (e.g. marketing activities used in parallel to sponsorship). In addition, it is necessary to develop sophisticated measurement instruments that reliably detect consumers' knowledge structures.

Another critical point relates to the prediction of affective sponsorship effects. In this regard, neuro-scientific methods (e.g. EEG, fMRI) could help to discover the difficult-to-measure reactions on the emotional level. Specifically, it would be possible to examine in how far the frequency of gaze contacts during a sports broadcast produce an effect on the emotional perception of brands and the extent to which situational factors (e.g. phase of the game) play a moderating role.

Furthermore, in future research, other optical features of sponsorship information can be assessed with regard to their impact on attention. The use of electronic LED displays and virtual fade-ins give companies additional opportunities in the optical design of their sponsorship information (Tsuji et al., 2009). In this regard, it would be relevant both from a practical and a scientific point of view to predict the effect of animation or certain eye catchers (e.g. faces) on the attention of sports viewers. Since the new communication options bear the risk of being perceived by viewers as intrusive, possible reactance effects among sports viewers should be examined simultaneously (Sachse, 2010). In this way, animations could be set to a perfect level by considering the respective target group.

Finally, the external validity of the evaluation method could be strengthened by shifting the examination situation to the natural environment of sports viewers. By using mobile (i.e. head-mounted) eye tracking systems, it will be possible to conduct a valid examination of the attentional effect of sponsorship information under field conditions in the future.

CONCLUSION

The competition for sports viewers' scarce attention is a growing challenge for sponsorship managers. Fundamentally, companies can only benefit from a sponsorship if they are successful at drawing attention to their activity. Without attracting attention, the strategic goals in sponsorship (e.g. increasing the degree of awareness) cannot be achieved.

In particular with the management of cost-intensive sponsorships, companies are dependent on instruments that provide reliable information on the effectiveness and efficiency of gaining attention. In order to put companies in the position to evaluate their sponsorship on the basis of scientific evidence rather than subjective statements, an innovative evaluation method has been developed.

The application of the evaluation method supports companies in making decisions during all the important phases of sponsorship management. For example, sponsors can efficiently control their sponsorship budget by identifying relatively inexpensive sponsorship options or less effective communication tools early on. Overall, the application of attention-related performance indicators leads to greater transparency in the evaluation of sponsorship and contributes to a further professionalization of this marketing discipline.

REFERENCES

Ansorge, U., & Leder, H. (2010). *Wahrnehmung und aufmerksamkeit*. Wiesbaden, Germany: Springer VS.

Backhaus, K., Erichson, B., & Weiber, R. (2011). *Fortgeschrittene multivariate analysemethoden*. Berlin: Springer.

Bishop, C. (1996). *Neural networks for pattern recognition*. New York: Oxford University Press.

Breuer, C., & Rumpf, C. (2012). The viewer's reception and processing of sponsorship information in sport telecasts. *Journal of Sport Management*, *26*(6), 521–531.

Breuer, C., Rumpf, C., & Kurz, S. (2013). Entwicklung eines bewertungsmodells zur analyse von sponsoringalternativen. *Marketing Review St. Gallen*, *30*(1), 72–81.

Bruhn, M. (2007). *Kommunikationspolitik: Systematischer einsatz der kommunikation für unternehmen* (4th ed.). München, Germany: Vahlen.

Bruhn, M. (2010). *Sponsoring: Systematische planung und integrativer einsatz* (5th ed.). Wiesbaden, Germany: Gabler. doi:10.1007/978-3-8349-8563-7

Chavanat, N., Martinent, G., & Ferrand, A. (2009). Sponsor and sponsees interactions: Effects on consumers' perceptions of brand image, brand attachment, and purchasing intention. *Journal of Sport Management*, *23*, 644–670.

Chien, P. M., Cornwell, T. B., & Stokes, R. A. (2005). *Theoretical framework for analysis of image transfer in multiple sponsorships*. Paper presented at the ANZMAC 2005 Conference. Perth, Australia.

Clark, J. M., Cornwell, T. B., & Pruitt, S. W. (2009). The impact of title event sponsorship announcements on shareholder wealth. *Marketing Letters*, *20*, 169–182. doi:10.1007/s11002-008-9064-z

Cornwell, T. B. (1995). Sponsorship-linked marketing development. *Sport Marketing Quarterly*, *4*(4), 13–24.

Cornwell, T. B. (2008). State of the art and science in sponsorship-linked marketing. *Journal of Advertising*, *37*(3), 41–55. doi:10.2753/JOA0091-3367370304

Cornwell, T. B., Humphreys, M. S., Maguire, A. M., Weeks, C. S., & Tellegen, C. (2006). Sponsorship-linked marketing: The role of articulation in memory. *The Journal of Consumer Research*, *33*(3), 312–321. doi:10.1086/508436

Cornwell, T. B., Weeks, C. S., & Roy, D. P. (2005). Sponsorship-linked marketing: Opening the black box. *Journal of Advertising*, *34*(2), 21–42. doi:10.1080/00913367.2005.10639194

Crompton, J. L. (2004). Conceptualization and alternate operationalization of the measurement of sponsorship effectiveness in sport. *Leisure Studies*, *23*(3), 267–281. doi:10.1080/0261436042000183695

Davenport, T. H., & Beck, J. C. (2001). *Attention economy: Understanding the new currency of business.* Boston: Harvard Business School Press.

Dees, W., Bennet, G., & Villegas, J. (2008). Measuring the effectiveness of sponsorship of an elite intercollegiate football program. *Sport Marketing Quaterly*, *17*(2), 79–89.

Duchowski, A. (2007). *Eye tracking methodology, theory and practice* (2nd ed.). London: Springer.

Felten, J.-B. (2007). Defining industry standards for sponsorship performance: A German perspective. *Journal of Sponsorship*, *1*(1), 62–67.

Geach, N. (2007). Merits and pitfalls of developing standard guidelines for measurement in the sponsorship industry - What would they achieve? *Journal of Sponsorship*, *1*(1), 58–61.

Green, A. (2008). Planning for effective evaluation: Are marketers really doing it? *Journal of Sponsorship*, *1*(4), 357–363.

Grohs, R., Wagner, U., & Vsetecka, S. (2004). Assessing the effectiveness of sport sponsorships - An empirical examination. *Schmalenbach Business Review*, *56*(2), 119–138.

Gwinner, K., & Bennot, G. (2008). The impact of brand cohesiveness and sport identification on brand fit in a sponsorship context. *Journal of Sport Management*, *22*(4), 410–426.

Gwinner, K. P., Larson, B. V., & Swanson, S. R. (2009). Image transfer in corporate event sponsorship: Assessing the impact of team identification and event-sponsor-fit. *International Journal of Management and Marketing Research*, *2*(1), 1–15.

Haykin, S. (1999). *Neural networks: A comprehensive foundation*. Upper Saddle River, NJ: Prentice Hall.

Holmqvist, K., Nyström, M., Andersson, R., Dewhurst, R., Jarodzka, H., & van de Weijer, J. (2011). *Eye tracking: A comprehensive guide to methods and measures*. Oxford, UK: Oxford University Press.

Hoyer, W. D., & MacInnis, D. J. (2010). *Consumer behavior* (5th ed.). Mason, OH: South-Western.

Humphreys, M. S., Cornwell, T. B., McAlister, A. R., Kelly, S. J., Quinn, E. A., & Murray, K. L. (2010). Sponsorship, ambushing, and counter-strategy: Effects upon memory for sponsor and event. *Journal of Experimental Psychology. Applied*, *16*(1), 96–108. doi:10.1037/a0018031 PMID:20350047

International Events Group (IEG). (2013). *Sponsorship outlook: Spending increase is double-edged sword.* Retrieved February 14, 2013, from http://www.sponsorship.com/ IEGSR/2013/01/07/2013-Sponsorship-Outlook--Spending-Increase-Is-Dou.aspx

James, W. (1890). *The principles of psychology* (vol. 1). New York: Holt. Retrieved November 2, 2012, from http://archive.org/details/theprinciplesofp00jameuoft

Johar, G. V., & Pham, M. T. (1999). Relatedness, prominence, and constructive sponsor indentification. *JMR, Journal of Marketing Research*, *36*(3), 299–312. doi:10.2307/3152078

Johar, G. V., Pham, M. T., & Wakefield, K. L. (2006). How event sponsors are really identified: A (baseball) field analysis. *Journal of Advertising Research*, *46*(2), 183–198. doi:10.2501/S002184990606020X

Koo, G. Y., Quarterman, J., & Flynn, L. (2006). Effect of perceived sport event and sponsor image fit on consumers' cognition, affect, and behavioral intentions. *Sport Marketing Quarterly*, *15*(2), 80–90.

LaBerge, D. (1983). Spatial extent of attention to letters and words. *Journal of Experimental Psychology. Human Perception and Performance*, *9*(3), 371–379. doi:10.1037/0096-1523.9.3.371 PMID:6223977

Lee, H.-S., & Cho, C.-H. (2009). The matching effect of brand and sporting event personality: Sponsorship implications. *Journal of Sport Management*, *23*(1), 41–64.

Madrigal, R. (2001). Social identity effects in a belief-attitude-intentions hierarchy: Implications for corporate sponsorship. *Psychology and Marketing*, *18*(2), 145–165. doi:10.1002/1520-6793(200102)18:2<145::AID-MAR1003>3.0.CO;2-T

Mangold, R. (2007). *Informationspsychologie: Wahrnehmen und gestalten in der medienwelt*. München, Germany: Elsevier. doi:10.1007/978-3-642-37384-8

Meenaghan, J. A. (1983). Commercial sponsorship. *European Journal of Marketing*, *17*(7), 5–73. doi:10.1108/EUM0000000004825

Meenaghan, T. (2001). Understanding sponsorship effects. *Psychology and Marketing*, *18*(2), 95–122. doi:10.1002/1520-6793(200102)18:2<95::AID-MAR1001>3.0.CO;2-H

Meenaghan, T., & Shipley, D. (1999). Media effect in commercial sponsorship. *European Journal of Marketing*, *33*(3/4), 328–347. doi:10.1108/03090569910253170

Milosavljevic, M. (2009). *Computational modeling of visual attention and consumer research: Initial allocation of visual attention and its effects on consumer behavior*. Saarbrücken: VDM Verlag Dr. Müller.

Moore, R. S., Stammerjohan, C. A., & Coulter, R. A. (2005). Banner advertiser - Web site context congruity and color effects on attention and attitudes. *Journal of Advertising*, *34*(2), 71–84. doi:10.1080/00913367.2005.10639189

O'Reilly, N. (2008). Editorial: Sponsorship evaluation. *Journal of Sponsorship*, *2*(1), 8–10.

O'Reilly, N., & Madill, J. (2009). Methods and metrics in sponsorship evaluation. *Journal of Sponsorship*, *2*(3), 215–230.

Olson, E. L., & Thjømøe, H. M. (2003). The effects of peripheral exposure to information on brand preference. *European Journal of Marketing*, *37*(1/2), 243–255. doi:10.1108/03090560310453280

Olson, E. L., & Thjømøe, H. M. (2009). Sponsorship effect metric: Assessing the financial value of sponsoring by comparisons to television advertising. *Journal of the Academy of Marketing Science*, *37*, 504–515. doi:10.1007/s11747-009-0147-z

Palmer, S. E. (2002). *Vision science: Photons to phenomenology* (3rd ed.). Cambridge, MA: MIT Press.

Pham, M. T., & Johar, G. V. (2001). Market prominence biases in sponsor identification: Processes and consequentiality. *Psychology and Marketing*, *18*(2), 123–143. doi:10.1002/1520-6793(200102)18:2<123::AID-MAR1002>3.0.CO;2-3

Posner, M. I., & Snyder, C. R. (1975). Attention and cognitive control. In R. L. Solso (Ed.), *Information processing and cognition: The Loyola symposium* (pp. 55–85). Hillsdale, NJ: Lawrence Erlbaum.

Preuß, H. (2005). Sponsoring im Spitzensport. In C. Breuer & A. Thiel (Eds.), Handbuch sportmanagement (2nd Ed.), (pp. 274–291). Schorndorf: Hofmann.

Quester, P., & Farrelly, F. (1998). Brand association and memory decay effects of sponsorship-the case of the Australian formula one. *Journal of Product and Brand Management, 7*(6), 539–556. doi:10.1108/10610429810244693

Reiser, M., Breuer, C., & Wicker, P. (2012). The sponsorship effect: Do sport sponsorship announcements impact the firm value of sponsoring firms? *International Journal of Sport Finance, 7*(3), 232–248.

Rojas, R. (1993). *Theorie der neuronalen netze*. Berlin: Springer. doi:10.1007/978-3-642-61231-2

Rosbergen, E., Pieters, R., & Wedel, M. (1997). Visual attention to advertising: A segment-level analysis. *The Journal of Consumer Research, 24*(3), 305–314. doi:10.1086/209512

Sacharin, K. (2001). *Attention: How to interrupt yell, whisper, and touch consumers*. New York: Wiley & Sons.

Sachse, M. (2010). *Negative kommunikationseffekte von sponsoring und ambush-marketing bei sportgrossveranstaltungen*. Wiesbaden, Germany: Gabler. doi:10.1007/978-3-8349-8698-6

Sherman, S. M., & Moran, E. J. (2011). Creating false memories for brand names. *Applied Cognitive Psychology, 25*, 336–340. doi:10.1002/acp.1714

Tripodi, J. A., Hirons, M., Bednall, D., & Sutherland, M. (2003). Cognitive evaluation: Prompts used to measure sponsorship awareness. *International Journal of Market Research, 45*(4), 435–455.

Tsuji, Y., Bennett, G., & Leigh, J. H. (2009). Investigating factors affecting brand awareness of virtual advertising. *Journal of Sport Management, 23*(4), 511–544.

Wakefield, K. L., Becker-Olsen, K., & Cornwell, T. B. (2007). I spy a sponsor: The effects of sponsorship level, prominence, relatedness, and cueing on recall accuracy. *Journal of Advertising, 36*(4), 61–74. doi:10.2753/JOA0091-3367360405

Walliser, B. (2003). An international review of sponsorship research: Extension and update. *International Journal of Advertising, 22*(1), 5–40.

Zander, A. (2001). *Neuronale netze zur analyse von nichtlinearen strukturmodellen mit latenten variablen*. Wiesbaden, Germany: DUV. doi:10.1007/978-3-322-99297-0

KEY TERMS AND DEFINITIONS

Evaluation: Data-based measurement and evaluation of sponsorship effectiveness.

Eye-Tracking: Measuring the direction of the gaze by recording the position of the pupils as horizontal and vertical coordinate values.

Neural Networks: Complex information processing systems that acquire knowledge in a learning process, save it in the form of weights and then use it for future estimation problems.

Sponsorship: Two-sided relationship between an organization (e.g. company) and a sponsored entity (e.g. sports event), whereas the sponsoring organization has a self-serving purpose.

Sponsorship Effectiveness: Conscious or unconscious reaction of a sports viewer to the exposure of sponsorship information.

Sponsorship Information: Visible signage (e.g. brand logo) at a sports event, which informs the viewer about the relationship between the sponsor and the sponsored entity.

Viewers' Attention: Selection mechanism that protects against information overload.

ENDNOTES

1. With regard to alternative network types such as radial basis function refer to the basic literature (e.g. Bishop, 1996; Haykin, 1999).
2. If there are no substantial changes in the TV broadcasting, it is possible to rely on the data from the previous season when estimating the media coverage.

This research was previously published in Strategies in Sports Marketing edited by Manuel Alonso Dos Santos, pages 238-254, copyright year 2014 by Business Science Reference (an imprint of IGI Global).

Chapter 13 Views on Sports Sponsorship in Singapore

Lyon Lai Mun Wai
Republic Polytechnic, Singapore

ABSTRACT

Sports sponsorship is growing and this figure is projected to rise exponentially (Belzer, 2013). Hence, the sporting arena has approached a platform where sponsorship has become an intricate pillar in the sports industry (Hoye et al., 2012). Whilst it is widely acknowledged that sponsorship is able to advance the profit margins of sponsors (Boyle, 2001), there is little literature documenting the views of sports sponsorship in Singapore. This chapter seeks to identify the key stakeholders in the local sports sponsorship as well as the acknowledged elements in a successful collaboration. References are made to the local sporting scene based on qualitative feedback collected from relevant personnel and set against common practices worldwide based on the literature review of current papers. A model of how these factors are interlinked is finally proposed.

INTRODUCTION

Sponsorship is an alliance between those who market sport with those who market through sport. It is a business-to-business relationship that, when dealing across national borders, can benefit greatly from a tightly structured collaborative alliance. (Farelly & Quester, 2005)

There has been numerous literature expounding on constraints faced by athletes today. Most of them have identified financial constraint as one of the key factors that can possibly shorten or prolong one's athletic career. In Singapore, it is no different. The purpose of this chapter will seek to provide an overview coverage on the view of the sports sponsorship scene in Singapore, as well as an analysis on the concerns of main stakeholders in the process of sports sponsorship.

Due to the loose use of the terms "sport" and "sports" by academics and practitioners in the sports industry (Hoi, 1999), both will be utilized interchangeably for the purpose of this chapter. In the arena of sports sponsorship, an individual or organization issuing the form of sponsorship will be termed as

DOI: 10.4018/978-1-5225-5475-2.ch013

the "sponsor" while the recipient, be it an individual athlete, event, sports team or organization will be termed as the "sponsee" for ease of communicating the contents of this text. The playing level of the sponsee as well as the amount offered by the sponsor will not be part of the variable of the study so as to encapsulate as generic a base as possible. Even though there are initiatives and grants driven by the government (Ong, 2014) in Singapore, there will be an emphasis on corporate sponsorship in this chapter.

The chapter will start with a historical review of how sports sponsorship is practiced globally, its development through the years and what form it takes like today over the different processes. The chapter will then focus on the issues stakeholders involved in sports sponsorship face and the resultant essential elements of a successful sports sponsorship relationship in Singapore. The next part will discuss the onus of these elements on the various stakeholders and how they are interlinked. Finally, the chapter will provide a list of themes for future research and conclusion.

LITERATURE REVIEW

Definition of Sports Sponsorship

Commercial sponsorship is an investment, in cash or in kind, in an activity, in return for access to the exploitable commercial potential associated with that activity. (Meenaghan, 1991)

To date, many definitions of sports sponsorship have surfaced. Common variables include the acknowledgement of sports sponsorship as a form of relationship (Yang, Sparks & Li, 2008; Prantl & Andres, 2012), involving multiple parties (Yang, Sparks & Li, 2008; Farrelly & Quester, 2004; Ola, 2012) and with a pre-determined agreement to be carried out (Olsen, 2008; Sarli, 2010; Prantl & Andres, 2012; Ola, 2012). Such agreements are generally regarded with the purpose of commercial intent in mind (Farrelly & Quester, 2004; Sarli, 2010; Prantl & Andres, 2012; Ola, 2012).

For the purpose of this chapter, a relationship will be recognized as a sports sponsorship if the following elements are present:

- Contribution made by a party (sponsor).
- Contribution received by another party (sponsee).
- Agreed expectation of return in any form from the sponsee to the sponsor.

History of Sports Sponsorship

The concept of sport sponsorship reaches back to ancient Greece and Rome where wealthy members of the Greek society supported athletic and arts festivals with the purpose to enhance social standing, the Roman aristocracy supported gladiators for the same reasons. (Cornwell, 1995)

From sponsoring for altruistic reasons in the past (Farrelly, Quester & Burton, 2006), to the first form of commercial sponsorship by Kodak in the 1886 Olympic Games (Ola, 2012), to the inaugural nationalistic sports sponsorship by Spiers and Pond for the Australian Cricket Team in 1861, to the earliest record of professional sports sponsorship by Bovril for the UK football team Nottingham Forest in 1898 (Pope,

1998), the shape of sports sponsorship has indeed evolved over the decades and taken on a vastly different outlook from what the Greek aristocrats had portrayed in their time.

One residual similarity though, is the presence of a defining figurehead to effect the sponsorship. Be it the President, CEO or sales manager, there is an influencer of the outcome (Farrelly, Quester & Burton, 2006; Sarli, 2010). The reason for sponsoring was hardly ever about the commercial needs of the sponsor (Hill & Vincent, 2006) and went about in an unorganized manner (Farrelly, Quester & Burton, 1997).

Sports Sponsorship Today

From the tactical to the strategic, from the transactional to the relationship-oriented, from the short term to the long term, and from the periphery to the very core of corporate and brand positioning. (Farrelly, Quester & Burton, 2006)

Sports sponsorship has grown intricately inseparable from fundamental strategic planning (Santomier, 2008; Sarli, 2010; Ola, 2012). Sponsors are recognizing that in the context of current day technological advancements coupled with the reality of the world as a global village, sponsorship will be able to plug the gaps in communication with their customers (Olsen, 2008; Wiktor, Ilja & Ali, 2009; Sarli, 2010; Ola, 2012) as well as provide a substantial competitive edge over their rivals (Yang, Sparks & Li, 2008; Sarli, 2010).

In the context of sports sponsorship in Singapore, the findings from an interview with Glanbia Performance Nutrition supported that athletes are drivers at delivering the brand message of the company. It is much more convincing and credible when an athlete endorses a product as compared to traditional advertising platforms. This aids in plugging the gaps in communication with the company's target customers (Clarissa Then, personal communication, February 12, 2014).

It would seem preposterous then, to view sports sponsorship as something that is done only if there are leftover resources to utilize. Instead, sports sponsorship should be deemed as being part of any ambitious company's strategy to reach out to the global market and achieve broad corporate, marketing and media objectives (Sandler & Shanti, 1993).

Forms of Sports Sponsorship

Sport groups and agencies offer a wide variety of programs and services. These efforts are undertaken by a broad base of private and public sector groups operating at three basic levels: the grassroots (or community) level, the elite amateur level, and the professional level. Although many profound differences exist between these levels of activity, they all share a common need to generate funds. (McCarville & Copeland, 1994)

Whereas sports sponsorship in the past involves a direct capital outlay in return for an association with the sponsee, the scene in the present day is slightly more complicated. Today, the sponsor looks forward to investing in terms of financial resources, physical resources, human resources, technological resources, organizational resources and resources of reputation (Amis, Pant & Slack, 1997) in order to attain visual presence or promote demonstration of a product functionality (Carrillat & D'Astous, 2009). Be it naming rights (for events), endorsement rights (for athletes) or brand positioning (for sponsors), this "deliberate attempt to utilize sports sponsorship as the foundation for the selling proposition and the basis on which marketing activity is developed" (Farrelly, Quester & Burton, 1997) is growing rapidly to becoming a developed industry in its own right – evident from the increase in total global spending from $44 billion to $51.1 billion over 4 years from 2009 to 2012, representing an annual average growth of more than 5%. Out of this figure, the Asia-Pacific region is responsible for $12 billion of the spending with the main contributors coming from China, India and Russia (Insights Evaluation Guidance, 2013).

Process of Sponsorship

The closer sponsorship is to the marketing function, the more detailed and realistic the sponsorship objectives become, and the more stringent the evaluation criteria for judging its performance are. (Farrelly, Quester & Burton, 1997)

Identification

Sports sponsorship has taken on a whole new role in today's business strategic alignment. It had been akin to lottery in the past where the sponsor would be "spending large amounts of money on a shotgun approach or forging and developing links with as many high-profile athletes, teams or events as possible" (fiscal preponderance) in the hope that the sponsor will reap the returns of being associated with a world class athlete, team or event, or attempting to sign a young athlete, a low-profile event, team to a long-term contract" and then hope it will develop into something that can procure for the firm the kind of equity that amasses huge international following (serendipity) (McCarville & Copeland, 1994). Now, the approach has begun to become more business-like and structured, involving elements such as sponsorship management (Quester & Thompson, 2001), objective setting (Irwin & Sutton, 1994), evaluation (Cornwell, Pruitt, & Ness, 2001; Cornwell, Roy, & Steinard, 2001) and integration into their communications mix (Meenaghan, 1991).

Selection

Regardless of the initiator, be it the sponsor or sponsee, there needs to be considerable research conducted in order to decipher the requirements of the other party. Through this step, a shortlist of suitable candidates who are of the "best-fit" can be drawn up (Speed & Thomson, 2000). Though lengthy and more often than not, tedious, this has become mandatory so that an effective collaboration can be borne through this correct identification (Sandler & Shanti, 1993).

The next step will depend on the unique demands of each party. Some of the more common criteria oft-mentioned in literature included "increasing sales, building brand awareness, product positioning, reaching target markets, media coverage/publicity, enhancing company image, hospitality opportunities and VIP contacts" (Arthur, Scott, Woods & Booker, 1998; Blaise, 2000).

It is no different in Singapore as companies such as Tiger Balm, TYR, XBionic and Glanbia Performance Nutrition has indicated that the ability for athletes to build brand awareness amongst the general public, enhancing the company image and being an ambassador or spokesperson for the organization are keys in sponsorship. (AK Han, personal communication, March 4, 2014; Tan Li Jin, personal communication, 12 March, 2014; Clarissa Then, personal communication, February 12, 2014).

However, there were some who were clearly indicative of whom held the key to the selection. While Johnston & Paulsen (2007) focused on the managerial aspect in the decision-making, McCook et al.

(1997) chose to view the selection from a more holistic perspective starting from the pre to the post sponsorship journey. Turgeon & Colbert (1992) came up with an intricate model involving event-related, sponsored-organization related, market-related, sponsor-organization related and effect related.

Agreement

Once the selection is done, crafting of contractual terms in accordance to the service deliverables and methodology will follow. At this stage, presentations on the probable impacts and benefits of the partnership will have to be pitched with discussions made. Counter-proposals may ensue until an agreeable level of commitment and expectations is mutually set. It is important that there is an alignment in the direction of the sponsorship so as to reduce potential conflict over the proposed terms and conditions as much as possible.

Acknowledgment

Following the agreement, formal acknowledgement of the arrangement will be undertaken in the form of a contract, usually law-binding. This arrangement is akin to the "purchasing" of the "goods" by the "buyer" while the "seller" has to do their utmost to "deliver the goods", as per any normal business transaction. In most cases, especially where a long-term sponsorship is secured, there will be a follow up from both sides to evaluate the outcome of the partnership.

Delivery and Evaluation

The final step of evaluation in the process unfortunately "is rarely done at all or thoroughly enough because of the lack in knowledge on what methods to employ" (Ola, 2012). This oversight tends to place the risk of a partnership falling through as more often than not, both parties "do not consider risks as one of the most important criteria, and thereby they do not evolve any strategies to pre-empt risk" (Ola, 2012). Henceforth, to minimize the chances of a soured relationship and to reduce miscommunication, all areas of evaluation will have to be included in the previous step of agreement and linked to the objective setting (Pope, 1998).

To sum it up, in order for a sponsorship to work in today's context, the following steps of Identification, Selection, Agreement, Acknowledgement, Delivery and Evaluation will need to be present for a sustainable partnership to persist.

METHODOLOGY

The explorative nature of this topic requires a qualitative approach through the analysis and integration of in-depth literature review with interviews involving relevant personnel.

A qualitative approach has been employed for the purpose of this chapter as the purpose of this research aims to seek the rationalization behind human behavior and experiences (Silverman, 2000; Rugg & Petre, 2007), deriving at a valid generalization of explanation through subjective argument. Hence, the method of interview has been favoured as a deeper understanding on the topic (Legard, Keegan & Ward, 2003; Boyce & Neale, 2006) from the participants is sought after.

Sampling

All participants were identified through their respective expertise and experiences as well as the role they play in the Singapore sports sponsorship scene. Refer to Table 1.

Data Collection

Contact was established through the personal network of the writer in the form of electronic mail. The interview was conducted face-to-face at a neutral location and lasted between 1 to 2.5 hours. Interviews were voice recorded where possible. In 3 instances, a suitable schedule to meet was unsuccessful and the interview was conducted over the internet. In all instances, transcription verbatim was done.

Two lists of questions relating to finding out the views of the Singapore sports sponsorship scene from the participants were drafted, one each for the sponsor and sponsee. As far as possible, the wording and chronological order of the questioning was done similarly for all, depending on the responses outcome of individual participants.

The two lists of questions are as follows:

Questions for Sponsors

1. Background of Sponsor,
2. Background of Sports Sponsorship,
3. Conditions of Sports Sponsorship,
4. Type of Sports Sponsorship Relationship,
5. Condition/s (if any) for ending the contract prematurely,
6. Condition/s (if any) for not renewing the contract,
7. Reason(s) for engaging in Sports Sponsorship,
8. How the Sports Sponsorship started,
9. Expected benefits of the Sports Sponsorship,
10. Obstacles faced in Sports Sponsorship,

Table 1. List of interviewees for the purpose of this paper

Name	Organization/Sport	Stakeholder Role
AK Han	Tiger Balm	Sponsor
Clarissa Then	Glanbia Performance Nutrition	Sponsor
Tan Li Jin	TYR and X-Bionic	Sponsor
Amanda Lim	Swimming	Sponsee
Clement Lim	Swimming	Sponsee
Derek Wong	Badminton	Sponsee
Dipna Lim Prasad	Athletics	Sponsee
Kenneth Koh	Triathlon	Sponsee
Mervyn Foo	Singapore Bowling Federation	Sponsee

11. Comfortable range of Sports Sponsorship offered in cash and goods,
12. Views on potential growth of Sports Sponsorship locally.

Questions for Sponsees

1. Background of Sponsee,
2. Background of Sports Sponsorship,
3. Conditions of Sports Sponsorship,
4. Type of Sports Sponsorship Relationship,
5. Changes to life since embarking on the Sports Sponsorship,
6. Personal strategies to attract and seek Sports Sponsorship,
7. Reason(s) for seeking in Sports Sponsorship,
8. How the Sports Sponsorship started,
9. Expected benefits of the Sports Sponsorship,
10. Obstacles faced in Sports Sponsorship,
11. Comfortable range of Sports Sponsorship expected in cash and goods,
12. Views on potential growth of sports sponsorship locally.

Data Analysis

The findings from the Literature Review were coded into common themes and then sub-themes. The transcripts from the Interviews were put through a similar treatment after studying the responses line for line. Common grounds between both sets of data were then established to draw comparisons and differences in the view of sports sponsorship in Singapore.

FINDINGS

Sports sponsorship is a relationship between two direct parties, namely the sponsor and the sponsee. Hence, both play vital roles in ensuring the success of the partnership. However, external forces can play a role in affecting this collaboration, namely the environment and the industry. In this part of the chapter, the focus will only be on the two stakeholders in greater autonomy over the control of their actions i.e. that sponsor and sponsee. In the next part, in the portion on strategies to ensure a successful sports sponsorship relationship, onus on all four above-mentioned stakeholders will be discussed.

Stakeholders' Point of View (Sponsors)

So, what exactly do sponsors look out for? It is of no surprise that sponsors seek their own fair share of satisfaction in sports sponsorship which when attained, is likely to bring about "an incentive to collaborate" (Schul, Little, & Pride, 1985), to develop integrated management practices (Brown, Lusch, & Smith, 1991), or even as a "barrier to exit" (Hunt & Nevin, 1974).

Such satisfaction can generally fall into economic or non-economic terms (Dwyer & Gassenheimer, 1992; Mohr, Fisher & Nevin, 1996). A review of the literature revealed though that most sponsors are generally concerned with the economic terms, in other words, effects that are likely to affect the bottom-line earnings both in the long and short run (Wiktor, Ilja & Ali, 2009; Prantl & Andres, 2012; Sarli, 2010; Ola, 2012).

One of the most frequently mentioned concerns was the effect of product branding on the successful appreciation of sales. Sports sponsorship is primarily about the emplacing the brand within the awareness state of the consumers (Wiktor, Ilja & Ali, 2009; Sarli, 2010; Ola, 2012; Prantl & Andres, 2012) so that they are able to fully appreciate the authenticity (Wiktor, Ilja & Ali, 2009; Sarli, 2010; Ola, 2012) of the sponsor, establishing a positive image to go down in their mindsets. However, in order for this to be effective, the sponsor-sponsee fit has to be explicitly exposed (Farrelly, Quester & Burton, 2006) to get the message across (Pope, 1998; Wiktor, Ilja & Ali, 2009).

Another important outcome that sponsors look out for is the profile of the consumers associated with the sponsee. These consumers need to be the target market of the sponsor (Sarli, 2010; Ola, 2012; Prantl & Andres, 2012) who will attempt to transfer the emotional attachments of the consumers to the sponsee onto the sponsor themselves (Wiktor, Ilja & Ali, 2009; Ola, 2012).

Internally, sponsors do believe that sports sponsorship will be able to markedly stimulate employee morale and pride (Wiktor, Ilja & Ali, 2009; Prantl & Andres, 2012). Externally, sponsors see potential in sports sponsorship to engage in specific networking (Sarli, 2010; Prantl & Andres, 2012) with the result of achieving a competitive edge in the market (Wiktor, Ilja & Ali, 2009; Prantl & Andres, 2012; Ola, 2012). All these will have to be achieved though, with the calculated publicity that the sponsor will gain (Sarli, 2010; Prantl & Andres, 2012; Ola, 2012) to effectively communicate the desired image of the brand (Olsen, 2008; Yang, Sparks & Li, 2008; Prantl & Andres, 2012).

Quite a few authors have suggested that the perceived alignment of the sponsee with the overall strategic planning of the sponsor is key to a long-term sponsorship collaboration as well (Hultman & Lindgren, 2001; Ola, 2012) so that the image of the sponsor is positively regarded (Sarli, 2010; Prantl & Andres, 2012; Ola, 2012) among the consumers. One of these strategic outcomes hoped for is to improve community relations and societal goodwill (Wiktor, Ilja & Ali, 2009; Sarli, 2010; Prantl & Andres, 2012).

Many local sponsees are bounded contractually to participate in events organized by the sponsors. National shuttler Derek Wong explained that part of his obligations as a sponsored athlete requires him to turn up for marketing events by his sponsors (Derek Wong, personal communication, March 12, 2014). The involvement of a local sports hero in a marketing event will almost certainly boost the sponsor's community relations and societal goodwill.

Despite all of the above-mentioned factors, an interesting point to note would be how all those would count for naught if not for a well-positioned relationship (Farrelly & Quester, 2004; Sarli, 2010) between the sponsor and sponsee. Expectations are that both sides have their respective roles to play (Farrelly & Quester, 2004; Prantl & Andres, 2012), play it well (Farrelly, Quester & Burton, 2006; Olsen, 2008) and can be accorded the faith to do so to the best of their capabilities (Farrelly & Quester, 2004). This will then be likely to leave a positive impression on the decision-makers (Sarli, 2010; Ola, 2012) and prolong the longevity of the partnership.

Other noteworthy factors include past track record of the sponsee (Yang, Sparks & Li, 2008; Prantl & Andres, 2012), contractual terms and conditions (Farrelly & Quester, 2004). In the context of Singapore, Glanbia Performance Nutrition and Tiger Balm have indicated that if their sponsored athletes do not abide to their terms and conditions by engaging in irresponsible acts, the contract between the two parties would be terminated. This shows that sponsors take the contractual terms and conditions very seriously (Clarissa Then, personal communication, February 12, 2014; AK Han, personal communication, March 4, 2014).

In summary, the list of relevant factors that are of top priority for most sponsors are:

- **Economic Satisfaction:**
  - Brand equity.
  - Consumers' purchase intention.
  - Connection with target market.
- **Noneconomic Satisfaction:**
  - Boosting staff morale.
  - Corporate Social Responsibility (CSR).
  - Contract fulfilment.
  - Responsibility and Commitment.

Stakeholders' Point of View (Sponsees)

The role that sponsees play today has evolved from the past and is much more demanding. So what does this mean for the sponsees? First and foremost, there needs to be a recognition that they are a vital cog in the strategic planning of the corporate sponsors and that they are the gatekeepers to a powerful bridge between the sponsors and their target markets. Compounding this, sponsees have great influence on all parties due to their public recognition (Urrlolagoitia & Planellas, 2007).

However, sponsees have to play their part as well. As with any discerning commercial relationship, trust (Farrelly & Quester, 2004; Sarli, 2010) is integral to a successful collaboration. Sponsees can do so by pledging substantial resources (Farrelly & Quester, 2004) and sufficient manpower (Farrelly, Quester & Burton, 2006) to the cause and be proactive in looking out for the interests (Farrelly & Quester, 2004) and welfare (Farrelly, Quester & Burton, 2006) of the sponsor. In the first place, sponsees will have to do their homework and ensure that there is scope for potential sponsors to come in (Farrelly & Quester, 2004; Urrlolagoitia & Planellas, 2007). By doing so, sponsees will then be able to understand the needs of the sponsor and help them to understand how to utilize the sponsorship more meaningfully (Farrelly, Quester & Burton, 2006; Prantl & Andres, 2012). The baseline is that if they are found to be wanting in terms of commitment, it is unlikely the sponsorship will succeed. If they fulfill their obligations to the letter, chances of increasing the amount of sponsorship (Farrelly, Quester & Burton, 2006) or networking exposure to the athletes (Amanda Lim, personal communication, March 7, 2014) will be enhanced.

In the local context, national swimmer Amanda Lim attributed part of her success in securing sponsorships to her deep understanding of the objectives of the sponsors. She added that her successful relationship with her sponsors largely boils down to maintaining a reasonable level of commitment to the sponsors. "Sponsorship is a long-term commitment. Therefore, I have to be comfortable and confident with my sponsors." (Amanda Lim, personal communication, March 7, 2014).

Views of Sponsorship

When brand advertising is used during a sport event, it is more beneficial for the brand to either be the official sponsor of the event or to be the official provider of products that are integrated in the event than to apply these two sponsorship strategies at the same time. (Carrillat & D'Astous, 2009)

From the literature reviewed, seven elements of sports sponsorship have been found threading through most sports sponsorship issues. They are namely:

- Success through Competitive Advantage.
- Achieving the right sponsor-sponsee "fit".
- Consumers' experience.
- Symbiotic Growth through Sponsorship Credibility and Strategic Alliance.
- Effects of Exclusivity on Branding.
- New Media.
- Long-Term Commitment to Global Growth.

Success Through Competitive Advantage

It is heartening to note that sponsors today have evolved as they are gradually recognizing that sports sponsorship today is "capable of procuring a sustainable competitive advantage for the firm" (Amis, Pant & Slack, 1997). This competitive advantage depends on how the different firms can make a difference to the customer based on their utilization of resources. In other words, the firm must differentiate itself from its competitors. In order to be sustainable, the firm must ensure that this difference is capable of being replicated, and improved, in the long run (Bharadway et al., 1993). This is of paramount importance because sports today is held in higher esteem by people than ever before (Ola, 2012) so there is a recognition that communications to existing and potential markets cannot be viewed as overly "commercial" (Olsen, 2008). Thus, there have been great strides made in how sports sponsorship opportunities are assessed (Amis, Pant & Slack, 1997). Not surprisingly, doing well eventually in sales is a main driver locally as well for adopting the strategy of sports sponsorship (AK Han, personal communication, March 4, 2014; Mervyn Foo, personal communication, February 25, 2014).

Achieving the Right Sponsor-Sponsee "Fit"

By considering that the "consumer experience is playing a greater role on moulding brand perception" (Berry, 2000), attaining the right 'fit' between the image of the sport and the image of the firm will aid in the firm's image being enhanced by the transfer of the sport's image to the firm" (Martin, 1994). After all, "Sponsor-Fit has an impact on brand knowledge in a specific target group, which is emotionally connected to the sponsored field (sport sponsorship)" (Prantl & Andres, 2012). To reach out more effectively to the consumers, the firm has to position their products and services to the associated lifestyle images with the sport to enhance corporate image (Copeland et al., 1996) and this is usually achieved by identifying sponsees of positive attitude as well as a role model in the eyes of the public (Tan Li Jin, personal communication, 12 March, 2014).

Finding the sponsor-sponsee fit is currently practiced in Singapore. Tiger Balm, a sponsor of national hurdle runner, Dipna Lim Prasad, stated that " (Dipna) personally uses it (Tiger Balm products). She felt the benefit of it and so whatever she says on behalf as an ambassador for Tiger Balm, will be from the heart." In this case, Dipna is more than able to deliver the message that Tiger Balm wants to bring across to consumers because she uses the product and thus, there is the sponsor-sponsee fit (AK Han, personal communication, March 4, 2014).

Consumers' Experience

However, studies have found that the converse may be true as well. "Sponsorships and the along-side associations may not only generate a 'halo-effect' as well as a 'rub-off effect' but also the other way round to a negative perception is possible" (Meenaghan, 1991). What is of interest is that it seems to be easier to turn consumers off if they are rival fans though attracting supporting fans to be on the side of the sponsors is not as straightforward. This scenario can probably be attributed to the fact that rival fans tend to have a stronger negativity towards sponsors, although the probability of recalling the brand is higher as compared to supporting fans having less of an inclination towards the sponsor (Wiktor, Ilja & Ali, 2009).

Symbiotic Growth Through Sponsorship Credibility and Strategic Alliance

One way to navigate around this issue is to support a nonprofit organization (NPO) as findings have supported a positive relationship between the consumers' identification with an NPO and their intentions to purchase sponsors' products (Cornwell & Coote, 2005) because the sponsor's credibility can partially mediate the fan-identification-purchase link" (Wang, Jain, Cheng & Aung, 2012). Thus, sponsees of an NPO nature should take the initiative and attempt to seek relevance for the sponsor so as to gain an advantage at the negotiation table. After all, sponsorship relationships today should be viewed as a strategic alliance between both parties to unearth chances for bringing greater value to the partnership (Farrelly & Quester, 2005) rather than the outdated adage of one being overly reliant on the other.

Effects of Exclusivity on Branding

Eventually, a positive attitude to sports sponsorship of a particular target audience has a positive effect on the linked associations with a sponsor's brand (Prantl & Andres, 2012) because a brand can be "embedded with various information nodes and connection links" (Tripodi et al., 2003). Conversely, "negative implications will result in a negative image transfer endangering the success or even harming the sponsors' brand and reputation" (Aaker & Joachimsthaler, 2000).

This brand identification will have significant impacts on the purchase intent of the consumers as studies have noted that fans' identification with the brand positively correlates with purchase intent (Pentecost & Spence, 2009; Wang, Jain, Cheng & Aung, 2012; Prantl & Andres, 2012) which is most likely attributed to sponsorship today assuming the role of a "powerful and valuable communication element" (Prantl & Andres, 2012).

Once the messages of brand identification and perception are addressed, it will in turn help the firm to develop its brand equity and gain loyal consumers eventually (Henseler et al., 2011; Aaker, 2008) by differentiating their products from those of their rivals, thereby "serving as a proxy for quality and creates positive images in the minds of consumers, prevents erosion of market share during price and promotion wars, prevents market share from declining by giving the firm time to respond to environmental threats" (Bharadwaj et al., 1993).

Embracing New Media

One effective way to get this message through is the utilization of new media. Technological advancements in digital communications, resulting in new industries have drastically changed how a sport is "produced, delivered and consumed" (Santomier, 2008). Today, the new media "has become a vehicle for the expansion of synergistic marketing communication, which includes the integration of multiple media channels and publicity methods in order to sell products, services and ideas" (McAllister & Turrow, 2002). This change has even altered the face of many sports today by affecting the rules (such as Cricket, Table-Tennis) and presentation platform (such as F1 motorcar racing, UEFA Champions League). It can be said that the focus of attention has shifted from the live audience to the mediated audience because more viewers are supposed to lead to higher exposure, advertising and sponsorship funds or pay TV fees. This increasing reliance on new media works in the hand of sponsors as costs are rising to support this mode of communication coupled with the intention to draw away from the "increasing clutter in advertising messages in traditional media" (Nickell et al., 2011).

Long-Term Commitment to Global Growth

Despite the fickleness of sponsorship, sponsors should look long term because "discontinuation poses implications for the evaluation of sponsorships" (Copeland et al., 1996) as "it often takes time to build sponsor recognition with an event" (Pope & Voges, 1997). As Tan aptly puts it across, "we intend to be in the business for a very long time, hence we are fully prepared to invest resources into building a sound sponsorship deal if it is deemed to be worth it." (Tan Li Jin, personal communication, 12 March, 2014). Also, there is a general loyalty pledged to the sponsor if they were to stand by the athlete in both good times and bad as attested by national swimmer Clement when he revealed how he was grateful to his sponsors for supporting him when he was injured and it had helped him to make a comeback in his sporting career (Clement Lim, personal communication, March 17, 2014)

DISCUSSION

Value in the sponsorship exchange is intangible and subject to change and so requires a dynamic approach to management including distinct competencies. (Amis, Slack, & Pant, 1997)

Having a good game plan is important to enjoying a successful working partnership in sports sponsorship. Both sponsors and sponsees should aim to work towards addressing to the needs of the consumer and in turn making use of their goodwill to see to the progress in their own fields of concern. With effective strategies set in place, it will pave the way for a more conducive and successful working relationship.

Stakeholders' Point of View

Onus on Sponsees

One encouraging sign is how the image and attitude of sponsees today are being viewed as important determinants in the consideration before most sponsorship deals are signed (Ewing 2007; Conway 2014).

On one hand, this will serve to protect the interests of the sponsor's reputation while on the other; will send a strong signal out that sponsees have their role to play as well. Local urban racer Kenneth described a marked change in his attitude following his engagement with his sponsor "I am aware that I am more recognizable now. As such, I will make an effort to be polite and courteous as I am responsible for my sponsor's reputation." (Kenneth Koh, personal communication, March 7, 2014).

In fact, sponsors with undesirable image themselves, such as the alcohol companies in Australia (The Australian, 2012) are finding it difficult to leverage on sports sponsorship in their marketing plans despite understanding the benefits of doing so.

Onus on Sponsors

While the sponsees are expected to step up their game-plan to suit the needs of the sponsors, sponsors themselves should also recognize that, despite the huge amounts of money pumped into the industry as of the moment (Insights Evaluation Guidance, 2013; Wright, 2013), there is still a vast gap in the market waiting to be tapped. Athletes and sports everywhere are hungry for success and progressing in their respective areas but yet face the age-old issue of financial constraint even in countries such as the US (Killion, 2013) Australia (National Centre for Culture and Recreation Statistics, 2007), UK (Passy, 2012), the People's Republic of China (Hsu, 2013; Kuo, 2013), India (Anand, 2014) and Hong Kong (Yang, 2008). Being able to identify worthy sponsees and going in at the right moment with the right offer can plant the seed of loyalty within the sponsee and ensure a long-term commitment.

Onus on Environment

The environment is also proving to be a key influential factor in the development of the sports sponsorship scene in other countries. In most cases, the government is one of the strongest external forces. While some are fully supportive of sports development and even to the extent of making considerations for the ease of sponsorship (Keen, 2012), others have tried their best to fill in the gaps where corporate sponsors have not been forthcoming (Bond, 2013). Conversely, there are many others who simply have other priorities over sports development (Hsu, 2013; Anand, 2014).

Culture and societal mindset are other variables that may affect the support offered to sports development and which play on the mind of potential sponsors. In some cases, it can even lead to the discontinuation of the partnership (British Broadcasting Corporation, 2014) or a review of an existing one (Fields, 2014). With a supportive community behind the growth of their homegrown sports (Chiu, 2008), it will send out strong encouragement signals to sponsors on a higher possibility of reaping long-term rewards with their support. On a contrasting vein, a stifling culture will seem less appealing for sponsors to invest their resources (Adnkronos, 2013) as sports do enjoy the privilege of playing an influential role in shaping, as well as evoking, strong sentiments amongst the public (Hoi, 1999). It has also been initiated by Mervyn from the Singapore Bowling Federation that "support from the media" should also be present in order for the sports environment to develop (Mervyn Foo, personal communication, February 25, 2014).

Onus on Industry

One noteworthy result of a vibrant sports sponsorship scene is the level of the sports industry. With a more sophisticated network involving various stakeholders such as media coverage, retail presence, research & development (Mervyn Foo, personal communication, February 25, 2014), the environment tends to be friendlier towards new entrants and more welcoming to investors. Unfortunately, with the strong linkages that are forming between sports and the corporate world, it is perhaps inevitable that the strength of the country's economy will impact directly on the growth of the sports sponsorship scene (Tan Li Jin, personal communication, March 12, 2014; Anand, 2014).

Views of Sports Sponsorship

Success Through Competitive Advantage

What makes a successful sports sponsorship successful and what are some of the pitfalls? One of the key driving factors in most of the successful sponsorship case studies listed the probability of success (Farrelly & Quester, 2005; Yang, Sparks & Li, 2008; Sarli, 2010) when measured against the perceived efforts put in. There needs to be a reasonable amount of perceived value-add to the parties concerned in view of the sports sponsorship. Without seeing the expected forecasted impact, there is no point in furthering the relationship at the risk of incurring losses in terms of resources and man-hours where it can be better invested in other means of aiding the respective strategic goals.

Achieving the Right Sponsor-Sponsee "Fit"

The essential point is for both sponsor and sponsee to work closely together to portray their two brands as one (Farrelly, Quester & Burton, 2006) and allow the similar target market to see how both sides are able to connect more efficiently with the consumers (Olsen, 2008) for the benefit of the sport (McCarville & Copeland, 1994). This cooperation allows greater leverage into market penetration (Farrelly & Quester, 2005; Sarli, 2010; Ola, 2012) while at the same time diminishing potential entry by competitors (McCarville & Copeland, 1994) and limiting the ease of market development by the latter (Amis, Slack & Barrett, 1999).

Most importantly, the fit between the sponsor and sponsee has to be declared overtly to reassure the consumers that this form of partnership is not detrimental to the fundamental needs of the consumer (Pentecost & Spence, 2009; Prantl & Andres, 2012). Furthermore, with a successfully perceived fit, both sponsor and sponsee can latch onto each other's achievements and reputations, use it to enhance their operational capabilities (Amis, Slack & Barrett, 1999) for the heightening of their profiles and feed off the success of each other (Hill & Vincent, 2006).

It is of little surprise to find that all of the interviewees had noted "building relationships" as a key component in their respective dealings with sports sponsorship. They believe that building up a level of communication and trust between both parties will lead to a greater understanding which can only bode well for the collaboration (Clarissa Then, personal communication, February 12, 2014; AK Han, personal communication, March 4, 2014; Mervyn Foo, personal communication, February 25, 2014; Tan Li Jin, personal communication, 12 March, 2014; Kenneth Koh, personal communication, March 7, 2014; Dipna Lim Prasad, personal communication, March 7, 2014; Amanda Lim, personal communication, March 7, 2014; Derek Wong, personal communication, March 12, 2014; Clement Lim, personal communication, March 17)

Consumers' Experience

Henceforth, having the buy-in from consumers (Farrelly, Quester & Burton, 2006) should be the top of their priorities. By getting the consumers emotionally involved through the harnessing of their spectator experience (Santomier, 2008) during the sponsorship (Cliffe & Motion, 2005) will raise the subjective perception of the end-users. Through reaching out to the consumers as directly as possible (Santomier, 2008), their branding placement can be visible and the first strategy of marketing would have succeeded. Prolonged visibility, coupled with strategic placement, should enhance awareness as the consumers become accustomed to the presence of all parties via association. Eventually, with targeted marketing (Santomier, 2008), identification on the specificities of the product and/or service can be subtly projected into the imagery (Prantl & Andres, 2012) of the consumers. The next step of forming attitudes (Farelly et al., 1997) will be integral to the outcome of influencing consumers' intent (Prantl & Andres, 2012) because this will likely steer the appreciation (Santomier, 2008) of what is on offer. If there is a perceived alignment of wants or even needs with the marketed product, then chances of the consumer translating purchase intent into action becomes more plausible (Santomier, 2008). This alignment will then effectively improve the brand equity (Henseler et al., 2011) of both the sponsor and sponsee.

Symbiotic Growth Through Sponsorship Credibility and Strategic Alliance

There is also the notion of growth as part of a "natural process of advancement" (Farrelly, Quester & Burton, 2006) so as to develop the capabilities and set the targets higher each time (Farrelly, Quester & Burton, 2006; Sarli, 2010). This variable supports the ideology that time is required (Farrelly, Quester & Burton, 2006) for all concerned to learn, evolve and improve on their processes, resulting in a more robust modus operandi in the execution (Yang, Sparks & Li, 2008; Sarli, 2010; Ola, 2012). Open dialogue and a willingness to adapt accordingly to the market forces (McCarville & Copeland, 1994; Sarli, 2010) are some of the suggested means to reach this stage.

Through this interaction of knowledge (Farrelly, Quester & Burton, 2006) and exchange of information (McCarville & Copeland, 1994; Yang, Sparks & Li, 2008), critical decisions to improve on the current conditions to suit the dynamic landscape of the sport (Farrelly & Quester, 2004) will allow for an overall strengthening of the sponsorship relationship as well (Farrelly & Quester, 2005; Yang, Sparks & Li, 2008; Sarli, 2010). Conversely, a "lack of synergy between sponsorship partners severely limits the return on investment" (Farrelly & Quester, 2005).

Effects of Exclusivity on Branding

Once the momentum has kick-started, the integration of the sponsor within the sponsee has to be established in an un-imitable manner in order to weave the partnership stronger and ensure that both parties have as much in their favour to carry on with the sponsorship arrangement as possible. Exclusivity should be reserved to the advantage of the sponsor (Amis, Slack & Barrett, 1999) as much as possible so that there is a common goal (McCarville & Copeland, 1994) for both sponsors and sponsees to work towards – while the sponsor will enjoy undivided exposure, the sponsee can bask in its success to protect the interests of the sponsor thereby providing it with much credibility in negotiating improved future terms and conditions of contracts.

Embracing New Media

In order to extend the sporting experience of the consumer, the sponsor can look towards leveraging on new media (Milne & McDonald, 1999; Roberts, 2006/2007) as a means of an exchange (Wang, Jain, Cheng & Aung, 2012). In return for the enhancement of the consumer's leisure pursuit of sports (Santomier, 2008), a platform of indirect communication (Roberts, 2006; Kolah, 2006) can be set up to deliver messages across in a non-pervasive manner (Prantl & Andres, 2012) with projected cost-savings as well (Paul, 2007).

In an environment where the traditional media is not "pro-sports" and are seemingly wary of over-exposing the sponsors (Mervyn Foo, personal communication, February 25, 2014), turning to new media and dictating their own terms where they have greater autonomy over the quality and quantity of delivered content may well act as a suitable foil.

Tiger Balm had leveraged on new media when they used the social media platform Facebook to market their brand. A competition was launched on Facebook to sponsor a runner to the New York marathon. The person with the best reason and the most number of votes would be sponsored by Tiger Balm to participate in the marathon. With the public exposed to the brand name as they "like" the different posts, the awareness of the Tiger Balm brand would naturally go up (AK Han, personal communication, March 4, 2014).

Long-Term Commitment to Global Growth

If there are potential prospects of progressing further, both sponsors and sponsees should look towards global market development (Wang, Jain, Cheng & Aung, 2012). In today's context of the global village, time and distance have been rendered as no more than nominal and spatial definitions respectively (Kolah, 2006). If the resources and capabilities permit, why be contented with capturing one narrow segment of a potential global reach (Santomier, 2008)? This ambition not only enhances the value of sponsorship but also the reputations of all involved parties (Hill & Vincent, 2006).

Both the sponsors and the sponsees have to cooperate for mutual benefit. While the industry does affect the relationship, the sponsor has greater control over the industry. Likewise, the sponsee for the environment. Thus, the determinants of the relationship can be summed up in the mentioned seven elements in Figure 1.

FUTURE RESEARCH DIRECTIONS

Sponsorship effectiveness is directly related to the degree to which the sponsors are willing to leverage their investment with additional advertising and promotional activities and expenditure. (Quester & Thompson, 2001)

Differences in the views of sponsorship over different countries are to be expected. However, comparison can still be done. Reflecting on the experiences of others can help greatly in developing the operational capability of oneself. This reflection is deemed to be both true and necessary for both the sponsors and sponsees. Henceforth, it is suggested by the writer that greater research can be invested into comparing the state of Singapore's sports sponsorship scene with that of other comparable countries.

Figure 1. Relationship among the stakeholders and elements of a successful sports sponsorship

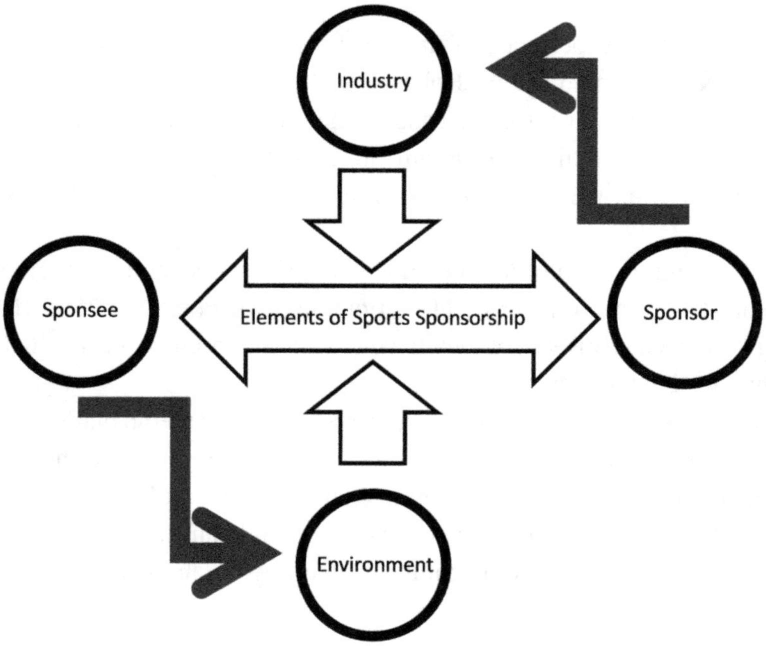

The increasingly influential role of new media in the sports industry is well documented. It has vast potentials to contribute to business development. Thus, the harnessing of new media to aid sports development practically can be further studied.

The direction of sports in Singapore is led by the Singapore Sports Council and the Singapore National Olympic Council. Even though there is a Strategic Planning & Marketing Group (Singapore Sports Council, 2013) helmed by the former to look into this aspect, the latter oversees operational issues (including sponsorship) for Team Singapore at International Olympic Committee-sanctioned events such as the Southeast Asian Games, Asian Games and Commonwealth Games (Singapore National Olympic Committee, 2014). A study of the effects of sponsorship on policy level decision making could also be done.

Although there are many studies that expounded on the benefits that sports sponsorship can bring to the sponsors and sponsees, there has never been a localized version done before to the knowledge of the writer. A research based on quantitative survey and historical data could reveal a picture of the longitudinal sports sponsorship scene in Singapore.

Finally, sports sponsorship will never be successful without a thriving sports scene which in turn depends greatly on the fan base. It will be interesting to find out the fans' perspectives on sports sponsorship in Singapore and what are their expectations of it.

CONCLUSION

Sponsorship is an alliance between those who market sport with those who market through sport. It is a business-to-business relationship that, when dealing across national borders, can benefit greatly from a tightly structured collaborative alliance. (Farelly & Quester, 2005)

Sports sponsorship today has come a long way since the Greek aristocrats invested for their personal indulgences and when Kodak agreed to emplace their logo next to a new multi-sports competition known today as the Olympic Games.

Despite the growing role of sports sponsorship not just in the sporting industry, but that of the corporate world as well, there is still little recognition given to the full extent of its impact both in academic research and everyday practice. It has morphed from a small-scale activity to one that is shaping into an industry in its own right, both in terms of financial responsibility and level of embrace by sponsors and sponsees.

This chapter has shown the correlations between an increased intimacy between sponsors and their (correctly emplaced) consumers through the use of sports sponsorship as a medium. A positive perception of the sponsee, by consumers, could indirectly create purchase intent of the sponsor's intended products.

In order for Singapore sports sponsorship to flourish further, sponsors should work hand-in-hand with sponsees through a rigorous process involving Identification, Selection, Agreement, Acknowledgement, Delivery and Evaluation. Both parties have to understand what the seven essentials (Success through Competitive Advantage, Achieving the right Sponsor-Sponsee "Fit", Consumers' Experience, Symbiotic Growth through Sponsorship Credibility and Strategic Alliance, Effects of Exclusivity on Branding, Embracing New Media, Long-Term Commitment to Global Growth) to a successful sports sponsorship entails and how they can structure the partnership. At the same time, sponsors have the greater influence on shaping and preparing the industry for sponsorship while sponsees can affect the overall climate in the environment of the sponsorship scene.

With a greater understanding on how the sports sponsorship process should work, sponsors and sponsees should be educated sufficiently on how to align their respective objectives together in a symbiotic relationship. No longer should sports sponsorship be viewed as a "good-to-have" but rather, a "need-to-have". Even though the inertia to remain status quo remains an easier option but without breaking free from the comfort zones, the sporting scene in any country will likely remain stagnant and fail to progress. Henceforth, an improvement in the sports sponsorship environment can only bode well for a healthier and more vibrant sporting scene.

REFERENCES

Aaker, D. A. (2008). *Strategic market management*. John Wiley & Sons.

Aaker, D. A., & Joachimsthaler, E. (2000). *Brand leadership*. New York: The Free Press.

Adnkronos. (2013, December 19). *Iran: Women excluded from sports in the name of Islam*. Retrieved from http://www.adnkronos.com/AKI/English/Sport/?id=1.0.1687961175

Amis, J., Pant, N., & Slack, T. (1997). Achieving a sustainable competitive advantage: A resource-based view of sport sponsorship. *Journal of Sport Management*, *11*, 80–96.

Amis, J., Slack, T., & Berrett, T. (1999). Sport sponsorship as distinctive competence. *European Journal of Marketing*, *33*(3/4), 250–272. doi:10.1108/03090569910253044

Anand, A. (2014, January 17). *India's winter games hopeful dogged by funding and official indifference.* Retrieved from http://www.theguardian.com/sport/2014/jan/17/india-winter-olympic-hopefuls-funding-shiva-keshavan

Arthur, D., Scott, D., & Woods, T. (1997). A conceptual model of corporate decision-making process of sport sponsorship acquisition. *Journal of Sport Management, 11*(3), 223–233.

Belzer, J. (2013, April 22). *The revolution of sports sponsorship.* Retrieved from http://www.forbes.com/sites/jasonbelzer/2013/04/22/the-revolution-of-sport-sponsorship/

Berry, L. (2000). Cultivating service brand equity. *Journal of the Academy of Marketing Science, 28*(1), 128–137. doi:10.1177/0092070300281012

Bharadwaj, S. G., Varadarajan, P. R., & Fahy, J. (1993). Sustainable competitive advantage in service industries: A conceptual model and research prepositions. *Journal of Marketing, 57*(4), 83–89. doi:10.2307/1252221

Blaise, D. (2000). *The dynamics of sport sponsorship: Understanding the sponsorship exchange process.* (Unpublished Ph.D. dissertation). University of Connecticut.

Bond, D. (2013, July 25). *Anniversary games: Olympic sports' sponsorship struggles.* Retrieved from http://www.bbc.com/sport/0/athletics/23458036

Boyce, C., & Neale, P. (2006). *Conducting in-depth interviews.* Pathfinder International.

Boyle, A. M. (2001). *The effectiveness of sports sponsorships: A study of the New Orleans Zephyrs.* (Unpublished doctoral dissertation). Louisiana State University.

British Broadcasting Corporation. (2014, January 20). *Nicholas Anelka: West Brom sponsor Zoopla to end deal.* Retrieved from http://www.bbc.com/sport/0/football/25810659

Brown, J., Lusch, R., & Smith, L. (1991). Conflict and satisfaction in an industrial channel of distribution. *International Journal of Physical Distribution & Logistics Management, 21*(6), 1517–1525. doi:10.1108/EUM0000000000390

Carrillat, F. A., & D'Astous, A. (2009). The sponsorship-advertising interface: Is less better for sponsor? *European Journal of Marketing, 46*(3/4), 562–574. doi:10.1108/03090561211202611

Chiu, W. H. (2008). *A study of motivation, satisfaction, and constraints of collegiate Chinese martial arts athletes engaged in leisure activities in Taiwan*. Proquest.

Cliffe, S.J., & Motion, J. (2002). Building contemporary brands: A sponsorship-based strategy. *Journal of Business Research, 58*(2005), 1068-1077.

Conway, C. (2014, February). *How to choose the right athlete to endorse your brand.* Retrieved from http://www.sportsnetworker.com/2011/02/15/athlete-brand-endorsements/

Copeland, R., Frisby, W., & McCarville, R. (1996). Understanding the sport sponsorship process from a corporate perspective. *Journal of Sport Management, 10*(1), 32–48.

Cornwell, T. B. (1995). Sponsorship-linked marketing development. *Sport Marketing Quarterly*, *4*(4), 13–24.

Cornwell, T. B., & Coote, L. V. (2005). Corporate sponsorship of a cause: The role of identification in purchase intent. *Journal of Business Research*, *58*(3), 268–276. doi:10.1016/S0148-2963(03)00135-8

Cornwell, T. B., Pruitt, S. W., & Ness, R. V. (2001). The value of winning in motorsports: Sponsorship linked marketing. *Journal of Advertising Research*, *41*(1), 17–31.

Cornwell, T. B., Roy, D. P., & Steinard, E. A. (2001). Exploring managers' perceptions of the impact of sponsorship on brand equity. *Journal of Advertising*, *30*(2), 41–52. doi:10.1080/00913367.2001.10673636

Coyne, K. P. (1985). Sustainable competitive advantage – What it is, what is isn't. *Business Horizons*, *29*(1), 54–61. doi:10.1016/0007-6813(86)90087-X

Dwyer, R., & Gassenheimer, J. (1992). Relational roles and triangle drams: Effects on power play and sentiments in industrial channels. *Marketing Letters*, *3*(2), 187–200. doi:10.1007/BF00993997

Ewing, J. (2007, June 7). *Sports sponsorship: A risky game.* Retrieved from http://www.businessweek.com/stories/2007-06-07/sports-sponsorship-a-risky-gamebusinessweek-business-news-stock-market-and-financial-advice

Farrelly, F., & Quester, P. (2005). Investigating large-scale sponsorship relationship as co-marketing alliances. *Business Horizons*, *48*(1), 55–62. doi:10.1016/j.bushor.2004.10.003

Farrelly, F., Quester, P., & Burton, R. (1997). Integrating sports sponsorship into the corporate marketing function: An international comparative study. *International Marketing Review*, *14*(3), 170–182. doi:10.1108/02651339710170249

Farrelly, F., Quester, P., & Burton, R. (2006). Changes in sponsorship value: Competencies and capabilities of successful sponsorship relationships. *Industrial Marketing Management*, *35*(8), 1016–1026. doi:10.1016/j.indmarman.2006.05.006

Farrelly, F.J., & Quester, P.G. (2004). Examining important relationship quality constructs of the focal sponsorship exchange. *Industrial Marketing Management, 34*(2005), 211-219.

Fields, L. (2014, February 8). *Olympic advertisers come out in support of gay rights.* Retrieved from http://abcnews.go.com/US/olympic-advertisers-support-gay-rights/story?id=22427888

Henseler, J., Wilson, B., & Westberg, K. (2011). Manager's perceptions of the impact of sport sponsorship on brand equity: Which aspects of the sponsorship matters most? *Sports Marketing Quarterly*, *20*, 7–21.

Hill, J. S., & Vincent, J. (2006). Globalisation and sports branding: The case of Manchester United. *International Journal of Sports Marketing & Sponsorship*, *7*(3), 213–230.

Hoi, N. Y. C. (1999). *Sport sponsorship in Singapore: A study of corporate sponsors' selection and evaluation criteria: Their implications for sports organizations and business corporations.* (Unpublished master thesis). Nanyang Technological University, Nanyang, Singapore.

Hoye, R., Smith, A., Nicholson, M., Stewart, B., & Westerbeek, H. (2012). *Sport management: Principles and application* (3rd ed.). New York: Routledge.

Hsu, J. W. (2013, July 9). *China beckons Taiwan tennis star.* Retrieved from http://blogs.wsj.com/chinarealtime/2013/07/09/china-beckons-taiwan-tennis-star/

Hultman, M., & Lindgren, O. (2001). *Sport sponsorship in Sweden.* (Unpublished bachelor thesis). Lulea University of Technology, Lulea, Sweden.

Hunt, S., & Nevin, J. (1974). Power in a channel of distribution: Sources and consequences. *JMR, Journal of Marketing Research, 11*(2), 186–193. doi:10.2307/3150557

Insights Evaluation Guidance. (2013). 2013 sponsorship outlook. *IEG Sponsorship Report.* Retrieved March 18, 2014, from http://www.sponsorship.com/IEG/files/6b/6bca0a93-47cc-4eb8-b514-c4cc3debc7d4.pdf

Irwin, R. L., & Sutton, W. A. (1994). A model for screening sport sponsorship opportunities. *Journal of Promotion Management, 2*(3/4), 53–69.

Johnston, N., & Paulsen, M. (2007). The relative importance of sponsorship selection criteria: A choice-based conjoint experiment using hierarchical Bayes analysis. In *ANZMAC 2007 Reputation, Responsibility, Relevance: Conference Proceedings: Australian and New Zealand Marketing Academy (ANZMAC) Conference 2007* (pp. 468-475). ANZMAC.

Kampitsch, K. N., & Liljehammar, S. (2012). *Sponsorship – Is it a double-edged sword?* (Unpublished bachelor thesis). Linnaeus University, Sweden.

Keen, L. (2012, July 27). *Australian Olympic athletes not draped in national pride.* Retrieved from http://www.afr.com/p/lifestyle/sport/olympics/australian_olympic_athletes_not_va5yqokdw2pIVhuu95aw7O

Killion, A. (2013, October 18). *Paying to play is normal for youth athletes.* Retrieved from http://www.sfgate.com/sports/article/Paying-to-play-is-new-normal-for-youth-athletes-4902034.php

Kolah, A. (2006, February 17). *The future of sport sponsorship.* Retrieved from http://ardikolah.blogspot.sg/

Kuo, L. (2013, July 17). *Taiwanese legislators and a beer company fight to keep national star athletes from defecting.* Retrieved from http://qz.com/105168/taiwanese-legislators-and-a-beer-company-fight-to-keep-national-star-athletes-from-defecting/#105168/taiwanese-legislators-and-a-beer-company-fight-to-keep-national-star-athletes-from-defecting/

Lavack, A. M. (2003). An inside view of tobacco sports sponsorship: An historical perspective. *International Journal of Sports Marketing & Sponsorship, 5*(2), 105–128.

Legard, R., Keegan, J., & Ward, K. (2003). In-depth interviews. In Qualitative research practice: A guide for social science students and researchers (pp. 138-169). London: Sage Publications.

Marshall, C., & Cook, G. (1992). The corporate sport sponsor. *International Journal of Advertising, 11*(4), 307–324.

Martin, J. H. (1994). Using a perceptual map of the consumer's sport schema to help make sponsorship decisions. *Sport Marketing Quarterly, 3*(3), 27–31.

McAllister, M. P., & Turrow, J. (2002). New media and the commercial sphere: Two interesting trends, five categories of concern. *Journal of Broadcasting & Electronic Media, 46*(4), 510–515. doi:10.1207/s15506878jobem4604_1

McCarville, R. E., & Copeland, R. P. (1994). Understanding sport sponsorship through exchange theory. *Journal of Sport Management, 8*, 102–114.

McCook, K., Turco, D., & Riley, R. (1997). A look at the corporate sponsorship decision-making process. *The Cyber-Journal of Sport Marketing*, *9*(2), 50–65.

McDonald, C. (1991). Sponsorship and the image of the sponsor. *European Journal of Marketing*, *25*(11), 31–38. doi:10.1108/EUM0000000000630

Meenaghan, J. A. (1991). The role of sponsorship in the marketing communications mix. *International Journal of Advertising*, *10*(1), 35–47.

Milne, G. R., & McDonald, M. A. (1999). *Sport marketing: Managing the exchange process.* Boston: Jones and Bartlett.

Mohr, J., Fischer, R., & Nevin, J. (1996). Collaborative communication in interfirm relationships: Moderating effects of integration and control. *Journal of Marketing*, *60*(3), 103–117. doi:10.2307/1251844

National Centre for Culture and Recreation Statistics. (2007). *Motivators and constraints to participation in sports and recreation.* Retrieved from http://sportsbusinessinsider.com.au/news/report-examines-the-impact-of-sport-sponsorship-in-australia-and-new-zealand/

Ngan, H. M. K., Prendergast, G. P., & Tsang, A. S. L. (2011). Linking sports sponsorship with purchase intentions. *European Journal of Marketing*, *45*(4), 551–566. doi:10.1108/03090561111111334

Nickell, D., Cornwell, B., & Johnston, W. J. (2011). Sponsorship-linked marketing: A set of research prepositions. *Journal of Business and Industrial Marketing*, *26*(8), 577–589. doi:10.1108/08858621111179859

Ola, S. (2012). *An analysis of the key criteria driving the selection process for Swedish firms investing in sports sponsorship.* (Unpublished master thesis). University of Wales, United Kingdom.

Olsen, E. L. (2008). Does sponsorship work in the same way in different sponsorship contexts? *European Journal of Marketing*, *44*(1/2), 180–199. doi:10.1108/03090561011008664

Ong, J. (2014, March 18). *Singapore athletes to get extra funding for SEA games 2015 and beyond.* Retrieved from https://sg.sports.yahoo.com/blogs/fit-to-post-sports/singapore-athletes-to-get-more-funding-for-sea-games-2015-and-beyond-024352628.html

Passy, C. (2012, September 8). *The cost of being an Olympic athlete.* Retrieved from http://www.huffingtonpost.com/2012/08/09/cost-of-being-an-olympic-athlete_n_1760687.html

Paul, A. (2007, October 17). *Sponsorships: Amplified with an interactive boost.* Retrieved from http://publications.mediapost.com

Pentecost, R. D., & Spence, M. T. (2009). Spill-over effects in multi-sponsored events: Theoretical insights and empirical evidence. *World Journal of Management*, *1*(1), 95–117.

Pope, N. (1998). Overview of current sponsorship thought. *Cyber Journal of Sport Marketing.* Retrieved March 18, 2014, from http://fulltext.ausport.gov.au/fulltext/1998/cjsm/v2n1/pope21/htm

Pope, N. K., & Voges, K. E. (1997). An exploration of sponsorship awareness by product category and message location in televised sporting events. *Cyber Journal of Sport Marketing*, *1*(1), 16–27.

Prantl, N., & Andres, S. (2012). *Impact of sport sponsorship on a brand.* (Unpublished master thesis). Karlstad University, Sweden.

Quester, P., & Thompson, B. (2001). Advertising and promotion leverage on arts sponsorship effectiveness. *Journal of Advertising Research*, *41*(1), 33–47.

Roberts, K. (2006, October). *Sponsorship strengthens its place in the mix.* Retrieved from http://www.sbrnet.com

Rugg, G., & Petre, M. (2007). *A gentle guide to research methods.* Open University Press.

Sandler, D. M., & Shani, D. (1993). Sponsorship and the Olympic games: The consumer perspective. *Sport Marketing Quarterly*, *2*(3), 38–43.

Santomier, J. (2008). New media, branding and global sponsorship. *International Journal of Sports Marketing & Sponsorship*, *10*(1), 15–28.

Sarli, E. (2010). *The selection process of sponsors and sponsees and the process of developing the sponsorship deal.* (Unpublished master thesis). University of Peloponese, Greece.

Schul, P. L., Little, T. E., & Pride, W. M. (1985). Influences on exchange process: Buyers preconceptions of a seller's trustworthiness and bargaining toughness. *The Journal of Consumer Research*, *11*(4), 939–953. doi:10.1086/209028

Silverman, D. (2000). *Doing qualitative research: A practical handbook.* London: Sage Publications.

Singapore National Olympic Council. (2014). *About SNOC.* Retrieved from http://www.singaporeolympics.com/about-us/about-snoc/

Singapore Sports Council. (2013, October 1). *Corporate structure.* Retrieved from http://www.ssc.gov.sg/publish/Corporate/en/about/corporate_structure.html

Sirgy, M. J., Lee, D. J., Johar, J. S., & Tidwell, J. (2008). Effect of self-congruity with sponsorship on brand loyalty. *Journal of Business Research*, *61*(10), 1091–1097. doi:10.1016/j.jbusres.2007.09.022

Speed, R., & Thompson, P. (2000). Determinants of sports sponsorship response. *Journal of the Academy of Marketing Science*, *28*(2), 226–238. doi:10.1177/0092070300282004

The Australian. (2012, June 23). *Sports ditch alcohol sponsorship.* Retrieved from http://www.theaustralian.com.au/sport/sports-ditch-alcohol-sponsorship/story-e6frg7mf-1226406509485

Tripodi, J. A., Hirons, M., Bednall, D., & Sutherland, M. (2003). Cognitive evaluation: Prompts used to measure sponsorship awareness. *International Journal of Market Research*, *45*(4), 435–455.

Turco, D. M. (1994). Event sponsorship: Effects on consumer brand loyalty and consumption. *Sport Marketing Quarterly*, *3*(3), 35–37.

Turgeon, N., & Colbert, F. (1992). The decision process involved in corporate sponsorship for the arts. *Journal of Cultural Economics*, *16*(1), 41–51. doi:10.1007/BF02275976

Urrlolagoitia, L., & Planellas, M. (2007). Sponsorship relationships as strategic alliances: A life-cycle model approach. *Business Horizons*, *50*(2), 157–166. doi:10.1016/j.bushor.2006.10.001

Wang, M. C. H., Jain, M., Cheng, J. M. S., & Aung, G. K. M. (2012). The purchasing impact of fan identification and sports sponsorship. *Marketing Intelligence & Planning*, *30*(5), 553–566. doi:10.1108/02634501211251052

Wiktor, J., Ilja, J., & Ali, M. (2009). *Attitudinal effects of sponsorship.* (Unpublished bachelor thesis). Jonkoping University, Sweden.

Wright, C. (2013, June 13). *Report examines the impact of sport sponsorship in Australia and New Zealand.* Retrieved from http://sportsbusinessinsider.com.au/news/report-examines-the-impact-of-sport-sponsorship-in-australia-and-new-zealand/

Yang, X. S., Sparks, R., & Li, M. (2008). Sports sponsorship as a strategic investment in China: Perceived risks and benefits by corporate sponsors prior to the Beijing 2008 Olympics. *International Journal of Sports Marketing & Sponsorship*, *10*(1), 63–78.

KEY TERMS AND DEFINITIONS

Elements of Sports Sponsorship: Factors that impact on the extent and scope of Sports Sponsorship.

Process of Sports Sponsorship: A 6-stage process involving the elements of Identification, Selection, Agreement, Acknowledgement, Delivery, Evaluation.

Sponsees: The recipient, be it an individual athlete, event, sports team or organization, of a sponsorship.

Sponsors: An individual or organization issuing the form of sponsorship.

Sponsorship: Contribution made by a party to another party with an agreed expectation of return in any form between both parties.

Sports Sponsorship: Contribution made by a sports-related party to another sports-related party with an agreed expectation of return in any form between both parties.

Stakeholders in Sports Sponsorship: Person or Persons directly or indirectly involved in the Process of Sports Sponsorship.

This research was previously published in Emerging Trends and Innovation in Sports Marketing and Management in Asia edited by Ho Keat Leng and Noah Yang Hsu, pages 22-43, copyright year 2015 by Business Science Reference (an imprint of IGI Global).

Chapter 14
Opportunities and Challenges in Wake Sports in Taiwan

Chiung-Tzu Lucetta Tsai
National Taipei University, Taiwan

ABSTRACT

The Chinese Taipei Waterski and Wakeboard Federation (CTWWF), founded in 1973, has actively trained and certified coaches and waterskiing boat drivers, increased public participation opportunities and security, and developed waterskiing experience standard processes, as well as safety advocacy. Using waterskiing mechanical equipment could help reduce the risk and allow the disabled to participate. The 2009 World Games in Taiwan were not easy to fight for. Taiwan took the opportunity to train waterskiing and wakeboarding athletes to enhance the strength of domestic water sports. For the people of Taiwan to understand the sports better requires taking time to watch them, learning to appreciate the beauty of water sports, and allowing water sports to integrate into people's leisure lives.

INTRODUCTION: SPORTS' DEVELOPMENT IN TAIWAN

The following is an attempt to examine the history of the involvement of the Taiwanese people in sport, from the period of the Japanese occupation (1895-1945), the time in which widespread involvement of the Taiwanese in sport began through to the period since 1945, a time of rapid transition within the country. The post war years are divided into three phases: The Early Post-War Years (1945-1969); The Foundation Years (1970-1984); and the Developing Years (1985-present).

The Period of the Japanese Occupation (1895-1945)

From the beginning of the nineteenth century, Taiwan was nominally controlled by the Chinese Ching Dynasty. In 1895, at the conclusion of the Sino-Japanese War, Taiwan was ceded to the Japanese in the Ma-Kuan Treaty (Taiwan History: Taiwan under the Japanese, 1895-1945, 2014), and the Japanese developed cultural and educational policies in Taiwan. Prior to the Japanese takeover, education had received little attention from the central government on the Chinese mainland. There was very little in

DOI: 10.4018/978-1-5225-5475-2.ch014

the way of any type of provision for higher learning (Epstein and Kuo, 1991). Along with education, the Japanese also introduced sport and games to Taiwan. While the Taiwanese were initially suspicious of these strange practices, they had won fairly wide acceptance among the islanders by the end of the first decade of the 20th century. The growth of public school sports and the holding of school meetings, competitive league games and displays of physical culture worked to help change this perception. Both sexes participated in sports such as track and field, lawn tennis, basketball, volleyball, and swimming and additionally boys played rugby, soccer, hockey, and baseball (Tsai, 2001).

The Early Post-War Years, 1945-1969

Following the Second World War Japan ceded rule of Taiwan and in 1945 the island was handed back to the Chinese. The lack of material resources and the poor conditions on the island meant that sport was afforded a low priority. Although, the government did form an unofficial "sports association" within the educational bureau from 1954 to 1958 and from 1961 to 1973 (Tsao, 1998). These organisations lacked funding, government support, and were very loosely structured. Their major purpose was to put together simple nationwide sports events that were mainly for students and only in the most popular events, such as track, baseball and basketball. Due to a very limited budget and an inadequate amount of public sport facilities almost all of the sports events that were staged were held on school grounds. However, most school sport facilities and fields were small and as such it was very difficult to stage any type of large scale sporting event. Generally speaking, the development of sport in this early post war period was constrained by the general economic and political conditions on the island (Winckler, 1994).

The Foundation Years, 1970-1984

The period between 1970 and 1984 was one of the most difficult political periods in the history of Taiwan and this had an impact on the development of sport on the island. In 1973, the government established a sports department within the education bureau. This was an official department with its own financing and it was responsible for all the nation's sport affairs. In 1974, the department enacted "the five year development plan" and, in 1979, "the complete citizen's sport education plan". This latter plan was initially decided by the central government and involved personnel in districts, cities and councils working with related departments to ensure the funding and implementation of the plan. The most important aspect of the project was to ensure that sports facilities were designed and built and to ensure opportunities for school sports, physical education, and sports for the general population were available. Programs were also developed at a national level to prepare athletes to compete internationally. In addition, several track and field areas, stadiums, gymnasiums, and swimming pools were built (Fourth Issue of the Taiwanese Educational Almanac, 1974). Schools were required to offer physical education as a mandatory class. Every grade at elementary school had to have three periods of physical education in the curriculum and each grade in middle school through to college had to have two periods (Fifth Issue of the Taiwanese Educational Almanac, 1974). Sport teachers were given the chance to learn and further their knowledge in the area. It was also an era in which increased understanding of the value and importance of sport by the Taiwanese government occurred (Sixth Issue of the Taiwanese Educational Almanac, 1974). This understanding would lay the foundation for the developments of the next twenty-five years (Wu, 1981).

The Developing Years, 1985-Present

From 1985 to 1999 the average economic growth rate maintained at around 7.28% and the GNP rose from US$3,993 to US$13,235. All of this provided a strong basis for the development of sport and the government decided to invest in this area. In 1989 it devised a plan called "The Mid-Term National Sports Construction Plan". The central focus of this plan was to invest in sport programs for schools, to organize nationwide sporting events, to increase the availability of sports equipment and facilities and to train athletes and sports professionals (Yahuda, 1998). Schools began to promote sport and, in 1987, 136 school teams competed with each other. The government's hope was that by sponsoring sports events among the student body this would provide a base of future athletes and also promote family interest in sport. It is important to note that sport was being developed in a climate where the primary objective of education for many Taiwanese students was to pass exams in order to increase their job prospects. For this reason, a number of "cram schools" were established. Such an emphasis obviously limits the time that children have for involvement in sport. However by 1994 the number of competitive school teams had risen to 2,678. The quality and number of sport facilities also improved; all of the twenty-three cities, districts and counties in Taiwan now have their own standard gymnasium, field, swimming pool, and other related sporting facilities. As a result, each takes turns sponsoring an event during the national games. One of the most significant developments concerning the development of sport in Taiwan that has taken place in recent years is the creation of the Sports Administration (Tsai, 2003).

EXPERIENCING WAKE SPORTS

For sports to flourish, requires the participation of the majority of the population, as well as excellent sports players. The Taiwanese government has been promoting domestic water sports in the last ten years and the island has a suitable climate and favorable conditions all year round for waterskiing. However, due to the Water Protection Act, waterskiing has encountered several obstacles. The president of the Chinese Taipei Waterski and Wakeboard Federation (CTWWF) has played an important role in managing to secure an appropriate venue for activities. The CTWWF is active in training athletes to participate in international events and to have excellent outstanding performances in those events. However, people in Taiwan lack familiarity with waterskiing. Therefore, this study attempts to explore the origins of waterskiing and the management of waterskiing clubs, as well as the strategic choice for future development for waterskiing and related sports in Taiwan.

The History of Waterskiing

Waterskiing is a sport in which boats are used for water taxiing. It can be traced back to June 28, 1922 when Ralph Samuelson, an 18-year-old, tried, to ski on the surface of Minnesota Lake City's Lake Pepin (Favret, 2010). On July 2, he succeeded. After this, many people began to mimic his gliding on the water's surface on wooden skis (Hickok Sports, 2014). The American Association of Waterski held its first official competition in Long Island, New York in 1939 (Hickok Sports, 2014). In Belgium, the sport is done in the same way as skiing around flagstaffs. Six buoys are put in the water to go around, this is called slalom. It has become one of the traditional waterskiing competitions. Some French water-skiers shorten and widen the board to do turns, spins and jumps on the water's surface and as a result, the second traditional waterskiing competition, tricks, has developed. The third traditional competition, jump, is also derived from skiing. Some waterskiers put up a wooden platform in the water, like a ski jump, then jump high and fall from the platform. The invention of waterskiing was deeply influenced by skiing, and the equipment design is similar too (Favret, 2010).

The International Waterski and Wakeboard Federation (IWWF)

In 1946, The World Water Ski Union (WWSU), the first international waterskiing organization, was established in Geneva, Switzerland. In 1988, the World Waterski Union changed its name to the International Waterski and Wakeboard Federation (IWWF) and it holds a contest every two years (IWWF, 2014). The traditional three tournament events are slalom, tricks and jump. Apart from these, barefoot waterskiing also exists, in which the athlete's feet are directly in contact with the water and slide to carry out the waterskiing movements in every event (Hickok Sports, 2014).

The IWWF is divided into five regions: Africa, the Americas, Europe, Asia and Oceania. The World Waterski Championship is held every other year with a total of ninety-two participating member federations. The Asian Championship and Asia, Australia and Oceania (AAO) Championships are also held every two years. These waterskiing competitions have created more than thirty million fans globally and fifty thousand competitors. The World Championship attracts contestants from more than forty countries with the number continuing to increase yearly. The development of waterskiing has brought about the generation of different projects, which now include tournaments, wakeboarding, barefoot, cable wakeboarding, cableskiing, racing and versions for the disabled (IWWF, 2014).

WATERSKIERS' AND WAKEBOARDERS' TRAINING IN TAIWAN

The number of trained athletes from the Chinese Taipei Waterski and Wakeboard Federation is quite small. The population of Taiwanese waterskiers may only be one hundred and fifty people; while Europe and the United States, especially the United States, has a population of two million waterskiers. Wakeboarding is an emerging leisure activity, and it has become more and more popular (Tsai & Hsieh, 2009). Wakeboarding is very similar to snowboarding, and even the equipment, clothing, action and scoring method are similar too. Athletes use a wide version of waterskies and stand in a suitable posture to make a variety of on-board fancy moves which are scored for difficulty.

Participation and Demand Trends in Taiwan

Many water sports lover in Europe and America participate in waterskiing. In Europe, America, Australia and New Zealand, almost everyone who likes water sports likes waterskiing as well (Favret, 2010). As a result, a lot of professional waterskiers have emerged. For example, during July, August and September in the United States, almost every week there are competitions providing professional contestants the opportunity to win prizes. The number of registered professional waterskiers in the world is about thirty million, most of them concentrated in Australia, the U.S and New Zealand (IWWF, 2014).

Accessibility and Gaps in Provision

There are few professional waterskiers in Taiwan, due to the promotion of waterskiing in Taiwan having several hindering factors. Waterskiing is an expensive sport, a boat, a coach and a driver are needed, in addition, the boat is very fuel consumptive and that increases the cost of engaging in the sport. High per capita income in Europe means that more people have the ability to participate in this sport. Most of the lakes in Taiwan are reservoirs, and after the Legislature passed the water protection law, all water source areas have not been allowed to host waterskiing boats. In the end, it is more difficult for Taiwan to promote wake sports and train athletes (Tsai & Hsieh, 2009). Taiwan's lunar Ghost Month in August happens to be in the summer vacation, as a result, most parents are reluctant to let their children come into contact with water. In Europe and America this superstition does not exist, and parents are willing to allow children to participate in water activities and therefore, the ratio of young people who can swim in Taiwan is less than in United States and Europe (Tsai & Hsieh, 2009). A golf course may allow up to seventy-two people to play the sport at the same time, however, a great body of water can only have one waterskiing boat on it at a time, it is not permitted to host a second or third boat, as it will cause a collision hazard. New Taipei City Breeze Canal, for example, can accommodate up to thirty to fifty waterskiers in one day. Furthermore, waterskiing has a high demand on the field. Suitable non-water source protected areas are not easy to find in Taiwan. Waterskiing requires calm waters and therefore, it is not suitable for the sea. In addition, waterskiers often need to soak in the water, it is not suitable to waterski in waters of poor quality. Currently in New Taipei City in Taiwan, enthusiasts can practice waterskiing and wakeboarding at Breeze Canal, which is one hundred and forty meters wide with a length of about one thousand meters. Very small waves caused by a ship's tail have caused waterskiers to fall and two boats will cause more tail waves. Coming across the waves from different directions greatly increases the probability of beginners falling, and it reduces the confidence of participants, enhancing the difficulty of promotion (CTWWF, 2014).

The Chinese Taipei Waterski and Wakeboard Federation has dedicated itself to train more wakeboarders and to increase the population of Taiwan engaged in wake sports. Due to waterskiing not being a competition event in the Asian Games and the Olympics, the Taiwan authorities are less concerned about it. As a result, budget allocation is often not focused on it and therefore, it is more difficult to train athletes. In fact, waterskiing is a sport in which Asian athletes may compete well with European and American ones. In China, for example, the number of people who engage in waterskiing is less than a thousand, however, the country won the world's gold medal in the 2004 Wakeboard Championships. Recently, China has also been facing a shortage of funds. The remaining four or five waterskiing teams must rely on artistic performances, such as human pyramids, double fancy and triple fancy to survive (Tsai & Hsieh, 2009). Taiwan participated in several international waterskiing competitions and its results were outstanding, including the bronze medal in the 1995, 9th Asian Waterski Championships. A gold medal was obtained in the 2002 Asia Pacific, 16th Asian Cup Waterski and Wakeboard Championships for Youth, moreover, a silver medal was obtained in the Waterski Championship in Hong Kong (CTWWF, 2014).

Issues, Controversies, and Problems

Waterskiing or wakeboarding is done by a speedboat pulling athletes on skis or barefoot producing the driving force to make a series of actions on the water's surface. Due to fluctuations on the water, it is not easy to balance the body. Slalom waterskiing requires changing direction in the process, rotating the body is required in wakeboarding, projectile motion in jump and wakeboarding requires rotation and jumping movements. Therefore, the center of gravity, stability, motion axis, parabolic, centrifugal force and other mechanical concepts are involved in the sports (Weber, 2000). Training focuses on front flip, back flip, straight backward, straight backward and rotation, straight backward rotation 720 degree and side flip. To make all actions be complete within the rule's time with ease in one breath, athletes must have good endurance and plenty of strength. An alternating and complex technique has very high requirements on the sensitivity of every part of the body, coordination and the feeling of time and judgment. The training puts focus on the following areas. Firstly, controlling the center of gravity. The center of gravity may be different due to change in positioning and weight. Controlling the center of gravity is one of the basic elements of waterskiing. Secondly, stabilizing the posture. The body needs to maintain stability following the impact of fluctuations of up and down, left and right, before and after. Although a lower center of gravity, and using two skis makes it easier to stabilize. However, when turning, rotating and accelerating, excessive body, stability will also affect the performance of the action. Thirdly, rotation. The center of gravity of the human body is X (left-to-right horizontal), Y (front-to-back horizontal), Z (top-to-the heel vertical lines) meet triaxial. The force applied to one side of the axis creates motion. Those around the left-right axis are front flip and backflips. Around the up and down axis are trick, waterskiing rotate and twist waterskiing. Around the front and rear axle are rollover, side flip, front flip, backflip, straight backward, straight back row, straight backward with a 720 degree side flip, and so on. Lastly, overseas training plans should be made in order to train athletes to respond and adapt to different environments and suitability of water. Experience of different coaches training and programs also helps to accumulate strength (Peterson, 2005).

A SPECIAL OPPORTUNITY: THE 2009 WORLD GAMES

When the US military advisory mission came to Taiwan in 1955, together with the Air Force Team 13 and the American Institute in Taiwan, they formed the Taipei Yacht Club and therefore, introduced waterskiing to Taiwan. It was rare to have waterskiing opportunities on the Dansui River in Taipei at that time. However, it became a very popular water sport among young people from 1966 to 1973. Waterskiing shows can be found very often at the grand opening of beach resorts and on national anniversaries. In 1973, the Japan Yacht Association donated thirty-three power boats to Taiwan and therefore, the Chinese Taipei Waterski Association was founded on February 28 of that year to promote waterskiing activities. The Chinese Taipei Waterski Association joined the Asia-Pacific Waterski Organization in the same year and it has been the only governing body officially to represent Taiwan to attend world waterskiing meetings and a variety of events. From 1977 to 1996, could be called the era of the sport's boom. Active international involvement, the holding of waterskiing youth camps and the demonstration of waterskiing shows in Taiwan attracted attention around the country. Extensive media coverage on site created a perfect carnival atmosphere for spectators in Taiwan. However, in 1990, there were several accidental deaths after a boat capsized on Sun Moon Lake, one of the most famous tourist attractions in Taiwan. Since then, the use of power boats has been prohibited on most of the water sites in Taiwan. There were barely any waterskiing activities developed in Taiwan for fifteen years, until a special opportunity came -the 2009 World Games.

The World Games, a non-Olympic sports events consisting mainly of large sport events, was held in Kaohsiung in 2009. Kaohsiung is the second biggest city in Taiwan and fought hard for its chance to host the World Games. There were thirty-one events which could be divided into six categories. Prior to the games, there had been other attempts to improve the popularity of waterskiing on the island. In order to strengthen the promotion of waterskiing and to gain experience hosting international tournaments, the Chinese Taipei Waterski and Wakeboard Federation held its first Asia invitational wakeboarding and waterskiing events for the Asia-Pacific region in 2006 (CTWWF, 2014).

Overall Strength of Wake Sports in Taiwan

In the preparation for the 2009 World Game in Taiwan, wakeboarding was introduced to the island in 2005, and soon after became even more popular than waterskiing among the young people. In the rest of the world, the manufacturers of wakeboard equipment have seen a business opportunity and have actively organized world and regional events and tournaments, offering cash prize to draw wakeboarders' attention. At the same time in Taiwan, a few wakeboarding schools and clubs were established, to help wakeboarders of different levels to improve and refine their skills in a more systematic and safer way.

In the 2009 World Games in Kaohsiung, watersports were scheduled to be held on the Lotus Pond, including traditional waterskiing (slalom, jumping and tricks), wakeboarding and barefoot classics (slalom, jump and tricks) with a total of seven items in the competition. Taiwan's men's and women's teams qualified for the wakeboarding events in the World Games. Asians compared with Westerners have an advantage in wakeboarding and therefore, Taiwan's primary training for the 2009 World Games was wakeboard based (CTWWF, 2014).

Plans for Waterskiing in the 2009 World Games

The 2009 World Games waterskiing competitions were divided into the traditional tournament, wakeboard and barefoot (IWWF, 2014). A Traditional Championship (Tournament) has three events including:

1. **Slalom:** Make meandering movement at a predetermined site. The competition focuses on rhythm. Starting speed is 58 km in the men's group, and 55 km in the women's group. Athletes must be behind a waterskiing boat towed by six corners buoys, each successful pass of a buoy will increase the speed and shorten the length of the waterskiing rope. All the athletes only have one chance.
2. **Tricks:** In the specified waterways and within twenty seconds, contestants make their choice of actions, including air stunts, flips foot across and hook the rope to score. The competition focuses on balance and flexibility. The athletes have second chances.
3. **Jump:** A ramp is placed in the water and then athlete's speed rush, leap into the water and glide down again. Distance is measured in this event. The men's group starting speed is 57 km, while for the women's group, it is 48 km. The jumping ramp is 4.2 meters wide and 1.65 meters high for the women's group, while for the men's group it is 1.8 meters high. All of the athletes have a second chance.

Water Sports Structure in Taiwan

Waterskiing is a sport which combines technology, speed, courage, and aesthetics, moreover, it is a sport with a high degree of excitements and therefore, it often attracts people's attention. As a result, there is never a lack of waterskiing competitions broadcast on sports channels in Europe. It has been considered a trendy watersport in Taiwan, in addition, waterskiing is considered one of the major watersports in Taiwan in the sports projects (Tsai & Hsieh, 2009). For example, on the Breeze Canal of New Taipei City, there are quite a few water sports lovers who engage themselves in wakeboarding every weekend. In terms of the strength and kinesiology of human bodies, Asians are more advantageous in wakeboard events than Westerners and therefore, the training for the 2009 World Games emphasized the wakeboard event with the slalom and the tricks as supplementary.

THE STRATEGIC CHOICE FOR SKIERS AND RIDERS: CABLE PARKS

Over the past decade, Switzerland and Germany have developed a new mechanism: cableskiing. In the middle of the waters, there is a cable machine which looks like a carousel, on which there are eight cables which pull the waterskiers. Waterskiers can slide without stopping and if five of the eight people fall, then the others can continue. The falling five people can simply swim to shore and there is no need to use a boat. This activity is relatively inexpensive because there are no boats and only one person is needed to control the machine. Eight people can use the same body of water at the same time and, most importantly, it does not need a 200 meter by 1000 meter body of water, even 150 meters by 150 meters bodies of water are suitable (Surhone, Timpledon & Marseken, 2010). If Taiwan wants to promote waterskiing, cable wakeboarding is a great opportunity to provide waterskiers in Taiwan an alternative choice.

The Marketing Strategy of Wakeboarding in Asia and the World

There are currently more than two hundred and fifty cable water systems worldwide. Wakeboarding is a great and fun-filled water sport. The sport is becoming increasingly popular around the world and is easy to learn. It is accessible to anyone of any age and ability and great for those wanting a new challenge in life (IWWF, 2014). More and more cable and system 2.0 parks are opening to the public. As a direct result wakeboarding is continuing to be one of the fastest growing action sports. Cable parks make wakeboarding more accessible for broad audiences who can find a lot of fun and new challenges in this fast growing sport. A full size cable can serve many people at once and hundreds a day, compared to the wakeboarding clubs in Taiwan that can accommodate up to ten wakeboarders in one boat a day.

It is nowadays a trend to build a community of wakeboarders, with locals coming back frequently since a wake park is a great place to hang out, make friends, and challenge oneself. It is highly attractive to one-time visitors and tourists as well because of the adventures one experiences at such a park. Some of the cable parks include restaurants, pro shops, accommodation for visitors, and events. The cable parks are highly efficient as they run with very little energy and are environmentally friendly (Larson, 2014). Besides low noise production and zero greenhouse gas emissions, they improve water quality through the constant oxygen contributions created by the wakeboarders. The 2014 Asian Beach Games will be held on Phuket Island in Thailand, which has Asia's first clockwise-cable. Another cablepark in Jakarta, Indonesia is brand new and has an interesting shape for the wakeboarding experience. Cable Wakeboard Worlds is a huge success, with more than thirty countries represented by over two hundred athletes, the entry level to these World Championships attracted the very best athletes in the sport of cable wakeboarding. As one of the sports shortlisted for entry to the 2020 Olympic Games, the level of interest in the event was extensive.

Analysis of Existing Strategies for Wakeboarding in Taiwan

The Chinese Taipei Waterski and Wakeboard Federation has attempted to develop and grow Taiwan's water sports community and industry by providing the best cable wake systems for wakeboarding. The CTWWF also introduced the manufacturing of cable wakeboard systems and wakeboard equipment to Taiwan. The scope of services extends from site planning, design, supply and installation of cable wakeboarding systems to the management, operation, maintenance and marketing of cable wake parks (CTWWF, 2014). A cable park on Lotus Lake in Kaohsiung, opened in April, 2014, is the first national project in Taiwan, and currently the CTWWF is actively negotiating more cable park projects with local governments (i.e. Taipei City, Hualien County), with lobbying of legislators and councilors.

SAFETY SOLUTIONS AND RECOMMENDATIONS

Waterskiing is a sport with a high degree of risk, because the boat's speed is pretty fast. In the beginning and even now, many insurance companies would state that coverage for waterskiing and skydiving was not included in their insurance. The main source of danger in waterskiing is the boat's propeller and when the body hits the water at high speed (Eck, 2001). The most dangerous place is the ship's propeller. Due to the powerful rotation force, if people hit the propeller it is just like stirring juice. This is something to which waterskiers must pay careful attention. Also, waterskiing involves fast movements. Waterskiers gliding on the water can normally reach speeds of 58 km per hour. When doing the pendulum swing they may even reach the speed of 70-80 km per hour (Goranson, 2004).

Water cannot make waterskiers break their heads, but it can cause their neck, vertebrae, or ribs to be fractured (Kalman, 2006). If the boat driver accidentally makes waterskiers hit the shore, it will result in greater harm. The most important factor in waterskiing safety education is the coaches. Waterskiing coaches should initially teach waterskiers about safety aspects, such as waterskiing safety gestures; how to avoid the propeller and the engine at the stern and letting go of the rope when falling to avoid the sprain or strain caused by the drag of the boat (Hayhurst, 2000). In addition, those who maneuver the boat also bear a heavy responsibility for safety. The boat cannot be sailed too close to the shore to avoid waterskiers hitting the shore in a situation beyond control. It is not difficult to learn to maneuver boats but a waterskiing boat's driver must be an excellent waterskier, and have adequate waterskiing experience, to properly carry out the function. The boat driver must fully understand the needs of the waterskier behind at any time, in order to appropriately maintain the safety of the waterskier. The CTWWF in Taiwan demands that the speedboat driver must be an excellent waterskiing athlete along with having the Ministry of Transportation's recognized power boat license, to enter the cockpit (CTWWF, 2014).

CONCLUSION: PRIORITIES FOR ENJOYING WATERSKIING

The Chinese Taipei Waterski and Wakeboard Federation is dedicated to promoting and growing competitive wake sports in Taiwan. It is the leading source for athletes, events and competitive standards and the undisputed sanctioning and governing body for the sport. For forty-one years the CWWF has been the island's premier provider of amateur and professional wakeboarding events, sanctioning and rules. Since its inception in 1973, the CTWWF has empowered the sport of wakeboarding to progress and evolve naturally by providing various amateur and professional sanctioning programs, protecting its athletes through extensive amateur and professional membership levels and allowing freedom and opportunities for organizers to grow the sport.

Wake sports were one of the key projects in the 2009 World Games in Taiwan. To be more effective in promoting waterskiing and wakeboarding, the government planned and opened more suitable lakes before then. Following wakeboarding's success in the 2009 World Games, with over 10,000 spectators attending, apart from the Asian Invitational Games events, the CTWWF is planning to host an international cable wakeboard event every year after the opening of a national cable park in Taiwan in 2014. This is guaranteed to create a unique festival atmosphere along the lake side. Moreover, the press conference for East Taiwan's annual water sports festival in July will be attended by most of Taiwan's major TV, radio and news organizations, and wakeboarding events will be hosted for the first time in Hualien County (CTWWF, 2014).

The success of a sporting movement depends on the majority of the population's participation, as well as outstanding athletes. There is a need for Taiwan to be more effective in promoting wake sports. The government needs to help out in creating more appropriate planning of lakes, to have more waterskiing clubs to provide proper training from qualified coaches and to increase public participation opportunities for waterskiing.

The Olympic Committee president Jacques Rogge, announced that eight sports were shortlisted for further review to be considered in the 2020 Olympic program, wakeboarding is up against seven other worthy sports for inclusion. The IWWF is the group behind the campaign and should be praised for all they are doing to boost the sport. According to their presentation, the IWWF counted three hundred and seventy-nine cableparks across the globe, although this number will have increased since they presented their "vision" - there are new parks popping up everywhere at the moment. They estimate there will be more than six hundred by the time the 2020 Olympics come around. With the sport growing that quickly, it surely goes to show the vast numbers of riders and skiers taking up the sports.

REFERENCES

Chinese Taipei Waterski and Wakeboard Federation. (2014). *The scientific analysis of attending 2009 world game: Wakeboarding*. Taipei: Chinese Taipei Waterski & Wakeboard Federation.

Corson, R. K. (1992). *IWSF tournament manual*. Retrieved March 15, 2014, from http://www.iwsf.com/tourman/Tourman00.htm

Corson, R. K. (2010). *2011 tournament water ski rules*. Retrieved March 15, 2014, from http://www.iwsf.com/rules/2011/2011WaterskiRulebook.pdf

Corson, R. K. (2012). *2012 tournament water ski rules*. Retrieved March 15, 2014, from http://www.iwsf.com/rules/2012/World%20rules%202012-3a.pdf

Corson, R. K. (2013). *2013 tournament water ski rules*. Retrieved March 15, 2014, from http://www.iwsf.com/rules/2013/World%20rules%202013%20-%203.pdf

Eck, K. (2001). *Wakeboarding: Check it out!* New York, NY: Rosen Publishing.

Epstein, E. H., & Kuo, W. F. (1991). Higher education. In D. C. Smith (Ed.), *The Confucian continuum: Educational modernization in Taiwan*. New York, NY: Praeger.

Favret, B. (2010). *Water skiing & wakeboarding*. Champaign, IL: Human Kinetics.

Fifth Issue of the Taiwanese Educational Almanac. (1974). Taipei: Department of Education.

Fourth Issue of the Taiwanese Educational Almanac. (1974). Taipei: Department of Education.

Goranson, C. D. (2004). *Danny Harf: Wakeboarding superstar extreme sports biographies*. New York, NY: Rosen Publishing Group.

Hayhurst, C. (2000). *Wakeboarding! Throw a tantrum*. Costa Mesa, CA: Saddleback Educational Publishing, Inc.

HickokSports. (2014). *Waterskiing*. Retrieved March 22, 2014, from http://www.hickoksports.com/history/waterskiing.shtml

Taiwan History. (n.d.). *Taiwan under the Japanese (1895-1945)*. Retrieved from www.mcauley.acu.edu.au/staff/andrewp/Taiwan_Pages/Taiwan_History_4.htm

International Waterski and Wakeboard Federation. (2014). *International Waterski and Wakeboard Federation website*. Retrieved March 22, 2014, from http://www.iwsf.com/

IWWF. (2009). *World rules 2009 cable wakeboard and wakeskate*. Retrieved March 15, 2014, from http://www.iwsf.com/13Wakeboard/Wakeboard%20World%20Rules%20Revised%20Categories%202013.pdf

IWWF. (2010). *World show ski technical rules*. Retrieved March 15, 2014, from http://www.iwsf.com/13Wakeboard/Wakeboard%20World%20Rules%20Revised%20Categories%202013.pdf

IWWF. (2011a). *2011 competition handbook water ski for the disabled*. Retrieved March 15, 2014, from http://www.iwsf.com/

IWWF. (2011b). *2011 racing rules*. Retrieved March 15, 2014, from http://www.iwsf.com/

IWWF. (2011c). *2011 technical rules for water ski for the disabled*. Retrieved March 15, 2014, from http://www.iwsf.com/

IWWF. (2011d). *2011 world cableski technical rules*. Retrieved March 15, 2014, from http://www.iwsf.com/13Wakeboard/Wakeboard%20World%20Rules%20Revised%20Categories%202013.pdf

IWWF. (2011e). *2011 world wakeboard rules*. Retrieved March 15, 2014, from http://www.iwsf.com/13Wakeboard/Wakeboard%20World%20Rules%20Revised%20Categories%202013.pdf

IWWF. (2011f). *Barefoot water-ski technical rules-2011*. Retrieved March 15, 2014, from http://www.iwsf.com/11Barefoot/2011%20Barefoot%20Rules.pdf

IWWF. (2011g). *Competition handbook water ski for the disabled addendum*. Retrieved March 15, 2014, from http://www.iwsf.com/

IWWF. (2012a). *2012 competition handbook water ski for the disabled*. Retrieved March 15, 2014, from http://www.iwsf.com/

IWWF. (2012b). *2012 technical rules for water ski for the disabled*. Retrieved March 15, 2014, from http://www.iwsf.com/

IWWF. (2012c). *2012 world cableski technical rules*. Retrieved March 15, 2014, from http://www.iwsf.com/13Wakeboard/Wakeboard%20World%20Rules%20Revised%20Categories%202013.pdf

IWWF. (2012d). *Wakeboard world rules 2013*. Retrieved March 15, 2014, from http://www.iwsf.com/13Wakeboard/Wakeboard%20World%20Rules%20Revised%20Categories%202013.pdf

IWWF. (2013a). *2013 competition handbook water ski for the disabled*. Retrieved March 15, 2014, from http://www.iwsf.com/

IWWF. (2013b). *2013 racing rules*. Retrieved March 15, 2014, from http://www.iwsf.com/

IWWF. (2013c). *2013 technical rules for water ski for the disabled*. Retrieved March 15, 2014, from http://www.iwsf.com/

IWWF. (2013d). *Environmental handbook for towed water sports: A guide to understanding and addressing environmental issues*. Retrieved March 15, 2014, from http://www.iwsf.com/EnvironmentalHandbook/IWWF%20Env.%20Handbook%20UpdateDec2013.pdf

IWWF. (2014a). *2014 competition handbook water ski for the disabled*. Retrieved March 15, 2014, from http://www.iwsf.com/

IWWF. (2014b). *Official safety manual*. Retrieved March 15, 2014, from http://www.iwsf.com/

Kalman, B. (2006). *Extreme wakeboarding (extreme sports-no limits!)*. New York, NY: Crabtree Publishing Company.

Kistler, B. (2014). *How to lay out a slalom course?* Retrieved March 15, 2014, from http://www.iwsf.com/slalomcourselayout/layout.htm

Larson, L. (2014). *Waterways education: What can we do for you?* Retrieved March 15, 2014, from http://www.iwsf.com/EnvironmentalHandbook/WaterwaysRequest.htm

Peterson, C. (2005). *Wakeboarding (blazers- to the extreme)*. North Mankato, MN: Capstone Press.

Sixth Issue of the Taiwanese Educational Almanac. (1974). Taipei: Department of Education.

Surhone, L. M., Timpledon, M. T., & Marseken, S. F. (2010). *Rash guard: Surfing, scuba diving, snorkeling, wakeboarding, body surfing, body boarding*. Betascript Publishing.

Tsai, C. L. (2003). The road to modernisation: Sport in Taiwan. *The International Journal of the History of Sport, 19*(2-3), 341-363.

Tsai, C. L., & Hsieh, L. (2009). Preliminary analysis of assessment on water-skiing in 2009 world game. *Journal of Sport Management Quarterly, 13*, 53–61.

Tsai, M. T. (2001). *Shadow foe-the legacy of Japanese culture in Taiwan*. Retrieved from http://etaiwannews.com?History/2001/11/26/1006740731.htm

Tsao, F. F. (1998). Postwar literacy programs in Taiwan: A critical review in sociolinguistic perspective. In Postwar Taiwan in historical perspective. Bethesda, MD: University Press of Maryland.

Weber, J. (2000). *Wakeboarding ...On the edge*. Phoenix, AZ: Sports on the Edge Llc.

Winckler, E. A. (1994). Cultural policy on postwar Taiwan. In Cultural change in postwar Taiwan. Boulder: CO: Westview Press.

Wu, W. C. (1981). *Chinese sports development history*. Taipei: Sanmin Publishing.

Yahuda, M. (1998). The international standing of the Republic of China on Taiwan. In D. Shambaugh (Ed.), *Contemporary Taiwan*. Oxford, UK: Clarendon Press.

KEY TERMS AND DEFINITIONS

Cable Wakeboarding: Cable wakeboarding is simply wakeboarding while being pulled not by a boat, but by an overhead cableski system.

Sports Policy: Sports policy and the sports environment are essential for the safety and wellbeing of athletes. Rules ensure fairness and order. Sport policy seeks to provide a holistic view of sport, what it is and why it is needed.

Strategy: Strategy is important because the resources available to achieve these goals are usually limited.

Taiwan: Taiwan is a state in East Asia and is ranked highly in terms of freedom of the press, health care, public education, economic freedom, and human development. Baseball is Taiwan's national sport.

Wake Sports: There are certain sports that involve water offering wakeboarding and waterskiing to experience the fun way to have a good time on lake or river.

Wakeboard: Wakeboarding is a surface water sport which involves riding a wakeboard over the surface of a body of water. It was developed from a combination of water skiing, snowboarding and surfing techniques. The rider is usually towed behind a motorboat.

Waterski: Waterskiing is a surface water sport in which an individual is pulled behind a boat.

This research was previously published in Emerging Trends and Innovation in Sports Marketing and Management in Asia edited by Ho Keat Leng and Noah Yang Hsu, pages 179-191, copyright year 2015 by Business Science Reference (an imprint of IGI Global).

Chapter 15
Driving Tourism Through Sport Event in the Lipno Region:
First Summer Olympic Park in the Czech Republic

Petr Studnička
The Institute of Hospitality Management in Prague, Czech Republic

Pavel Attl
The Institute of Hospitality Management in Prague, Czech Republic

ABSTRACT

Olympic Games have already been the top worldwide followed sporting event for 120 years. Until recently the Olympic Games were in terms of tourism associated exclusively with visitors' passive follow up. That status started to change with the emergence of an entirely new phenomenon called the Olympic parks. Based on this phenomenon is a research focusing on establishing an Olympic Park 2016 in Lipno nad Vltavou, Czech Republic. Part of the research was to analyze the impact of the Olympic Park it had on the region and the authors evaluated both positive and negative effects. The result of this research was to determine the main impacts of the Olympic Park on the destination, in the short and long terms. The authors concluded that the construction of the Olympic Park was a major impulse for the development of tourism in the area.

INTRODUCTION

The importance of tourism has increased in recent years and tourism activities have become an integral part of human life. Millions of people travel every year for the thrill of discovery, to relax, to take part in various sports and intellectual activities, to establish new contacts, or for personal fulfilment by at least short-term change in living environment and lifestyle. With the growth of population living standards and a simultaneous increase in leisure time, the tourism is one of the fastest growing sectors of the world economy. One of the forms of tourism is a sports-oriented tourism.

DOI: 10.4018/978-1-5225-5475-2.ch015

Sport and sports activities are increasingly becoming the way to spend free time of both individuals and groups of people. One of the reasons being people are more concerned about their health and want to be fit or want to relax actively. Here, sport is the best option to achieve not only composure but also a good physical condition. "We often talk about an approach called by English terms health and wellbeing" (Plzáková, 2015, p. 197). Sport, according to the European Sports Charter (2010) refers to all forms of physical activity, which aim, by casual or organized participation, at expressing or improving physical fitness and mental composure, and developing social relationships or obtaining results in competition at all levels.

Background

Standeven and De Knop (1999) state that "the relationship between sports and travel is symbiotic in the modern world. It is not so that the sport promotes tourism by offering an ever-increasing amount of valuable viewing experiences; tourism also helps sports" (p. 12). Tourism based on sporting activities is one of the specific forms of travel. Sports tourism is dynamically developing and has become a phenomenon of our time. The study of Hobza and Dohnal (2008) notes that, the focus of tourism motivated by sports is considered by professionals as one of the most promising developments. The primary reason for this statement is a demonstrable change in consumer habits, subject to long-lasting changes in lifestyle. Tourism motivated sport is an innovative product that offers to adapt existing products and services to new arising conditions for companies and entire regions, thus attracting new prospective clients (Preuss, 2004).

The Olympic Games, as the world's most prestigious sporting event, have since its inception in 1896 presented strong motivating factor for participation in tourism (Malfas, 2004). Olympic Games first took place in Ancient Greece in 776 BC. N. L. In modern history, the first Olympic Games were held in 1896. In 1924, the first Winter Olympic Games were organized. Until 1992, the Winter and Summer Olympics were held the same year after a four-year interval. Since 1994, the Summer and Winter Olympic Games alternate by a two-year period. Interest in the Olympics, was particularly accelerated with the development of communication technology and transport infrastructure. Passive participation in watching the Olympic Games in their place of venue or through the mass media undoubtedly contributed to increased motivation for active sports. The idea of direct connection of passive watching the Olympic Games with active sporting resulted in creation of so-called Olympic parks. This brought undoubtedly a shift in increased interest in sports especially among children, families with children and youth. Olympic Parks (KPMG, 2015) are a completely new phenomenon based on the combination of sports and tourism. Investigating this phenomenon and its implications in terms of regional development and destination management brings a whole set of interesting findings and experiences.

METHODOLOGY

The authors concluded that the construction of the Olympic Park was a major impulse for the development of tourism in the area, contributing to the building of primary and secondary infrastructure and that it could help mitigate regional disparities (Ogilvie, 1933). At the same time, it is necessary to recognize and eventually eliminate negative impacts that the construction of the Olympic Park might have.

Scientific goal is to identify opportunities for tourism development in addressing socio-economic disparities of the regions and propose recommendations for the development of Olympic Parks in the Czech Republic. Subject of investigation is addressing socio-economic disparities of regions through sport-oriented tourism and object of investigation is the Lipno cross-border region. The authors defined and tested two hypotheses:

H0: The process of preparation and setting up of an Olympic Park depends on cooperation among public, private and voluntary sectors.
H1: Building the Olympic park has a negative impact on the natural environment in a tourism destination.

When evaluating the impact of tourism on reducing inter-regional disparities are used basic statistical methods, results are interpreted using the methods of deduction and induction, as consequences of tourism in the municipal area are positive and negative. That tourism contributes to the reduction of regional disparities, it is essential that the regions and municipalities should formulating effective regional and municipal tourism policy. The Lipno Region is an ideal area with the 2nd highest tourism potential in the Czech Republic for the sport oriented tourism development and construction of the Olympic Park.

MAIN FOCUS OF THE CHAPTER

The relationship between sports and travel can already be found in ancient Greece. Ever since 776 BC. the Olympic Games had taken place regularly every four years, attended by athletes and spectators from all over Greece. The significance of the ancient Olympic Games is described by van Dalen and Bennett (1999). Athletes, peasants, nobles, politicians and prominent national diplomats from all parts of Greece gathered for the Olympic Games. A tent city extended up to Olympia. At the time of the Roman Empire a noteworthy situation occurred. Romans as spectators loved to watch gladiatorial contests, but as participants loved the thermal baths. Also during this period ball games gained popularity.

The situation in Egypt was similar. People have always enjoyed watching performances manifesting strength and skills. Among the most popular entertainments were ball games, hunting, fishing and shooting wild birds. Egyptians also enjoyed watching wrestling, boxing, and bullfights. Tug of war between two teams was also popular. Watching people taking part in games or wrestling was a form of entertainment well-liked by everybody (Zauhar, 2004).

In the Middle Ages, knightly tournaments, horse races and hunting were very popular among the nobility. During the Renaissance focus was mainly on intellectual activity but sports played also an important part of life, mostly among young men. During this period the top popular sports were dancing, soccer, tennis, archery and fencing. Further development of tourism and sports was brought by the Industrial Revolution in the 19th century, when the sports expanded from Europe to new colonized areas, such as colonies in Africa, Australia and New Zealand, and Canada. Urbanization, automation, fixed working hours and monotony in the workplace – all of these factors helped in the development of sports and tourism.

An important part of the sports-oriented tourism in the 19th century was hiking, demonstrated by rise of first tourist clubs and associations dedicated primarily to development of alpinism. In the Alpine countries mountaineering associations were gradually emerging. In 1862 the Austrian Alpine Association was founded, in 1863 it was the Swiss and Italian Alpine Club, with subsequent associations and clubs formed in Germany, France and other countries. The development of tourism in the Czech territory was sponsored by the physical education society Sokol, founded in 1862. But "the most significant association was the Club of Czech Tourists, founded in 1888 which at that time had about 4,000 members" (Plzáková & Studnička, 2014, p. 83).

A completely new impulse in developing of sports-oriented tourism was the organization of the first modern Olympics, held in Athens in 1896. Institutionally, the development of the modern Olympic Games is linked to the establishment of the International Olympic Committee. It was founded in Lausanne, Switzerland on June 23, 1894. At its birth there were three celebrities – Frenchman Pierre de Coubertin, the Greek Demetrius Vikelas, and Czech Jiří Guth-Jarkovský. Czechs were among the co-founders of the modern Olympic movement and were always significantly involved in it. The beginning of the 20th century saw a rapid growth the Olympic Movement, and the year 1924 saw the first Olympic Winter Games. Ever since, the Olympic Games have gradually become the world's most prestigious sporting event.

Since then, developments unfold very fast and sports-oriented tourism has taken to the front stage thus placing this phenomenon into scientific research and exploration. The impetus for this was the international conference "Sports and Tourism" organized by the International Olympic Committee together with the World Tourism Organization in Barcelona in February 2001. This conference represented recognition of sport and tourism by major sport and tourism international organizations. Its relationship is based on the demand for sporting experiences and growing number of academic research and publications in the field of sports tourism. Travel was for a long period of time influenced by sports, especially those having the criteria of major sporting events dating back to ancient Olympics. Nevertheless, a high percentage of today's tourists requires active and passive sports participation. It is becoming increasingly obvious that the scale, complexity and potential for sports tourism, as well as the expanding relationship between sport and tourism, which developed as a result of demand for academic and industrial expertise, is heading towards this area (Hinch & Higham, 2004).

Today there exist many definitions of sports-oriented tourism. Sports tourism is predominantly defined as the form of tourism, which includes sports activities. According Standeven & de Knop (1999, p. 12), sports tourism engulfs "all forms of passive and active involvement in sports activities, be it the participation of an individual or organized group for non-commercial or business reasons that require the departure from a place of residence or a place of work". The definition according to Hall (1999) states that sports tourism falls into two categories, namely traveling for participating in sport events, and traveling for merely watching sports. Sports tourism can thus be defined as traveling for non-commercial reasons by participating in or watching sports activities outside the place of residence. Gibson (2009) states that sports tourism is a travel of individuals in leisure time in order to participate in motional activities, to watch physical activities of others or to pay tribute to places associated with these activities.

There are two angles from which the participation in sports can be looked at. It is either an active or passive participation. Actively oriented sports tourism focuses on stays including sports activities. Passive form of sports-oriented tourism is associated with spectators visiting and viewing the sporting events (Pokorná, 2011). Individuals traveling to take part in specific sports are part of active sport tourism. In terms of active participation the individual participants can be divided into active participants who play sports within their holiday, amateurs for whom the sport is a hobby, and professional athletes who travel to participate in the races (Kortusová, 2006). Another category is a spectatorship involving passive participation in sporting events. People travel in order to watch some sporting events. Nostalgic sports tourism is a special type of tourism that involves traveling for sports or sightseeing attractions (e.g. museums, sports grounds) where major sporting events were held in the past (Weed & Bull, 2009).

Schwartzhoffová (2010) highlights the classification of six types of sport tourism, applied by Weed and Bull (2009):

1. **Sports Tourism With Sports-Related Content:** The sport is a secondary activity, and not the main purpose of the trip.
2. **Participatory Sport Tourism:** Could be a sporting holiday, including one-day trips.
3. **Sporting Holiday:** Including one-day trips.
4. **Training Sport Tourism:** Contains trips where the primary purpose is sports training or instructions.
5. **Sporting Events:** Is a tourism with primary focus of the trip being participation in the sports event, either as a direct participant (sportsman) or a viewer/visitor.
6. **Luxury Sports Tourism:** Includes luxury accommodation, sports facilities and equipment and is not defined by a specific type of activity.

An important component of sports-oriented tourism are sporting events, or events that often constitute the main reason for traveling to a specific destination. The term event is not easily definable. It is a complex and multifaceted expression, yet the definition by AIEST (*Association Internationale du Tourisme d'Experts Scientifiques*) is very concise. AIEST characterizes the events as a significant one-time or recurring events of limited duration to increase awareness, attractiveness and profits of tourism destination both in the long and the short term. These events base their success on uniqueness, prestige and timeliness in order to arouse interest and induce attention (Kotíková & Schwartzhoffová, 2008).

Events can be further characterized by a predetermined duration, joining a particular venue, uniqueness, originality, planning and local overreach. Every event requires personal presence of visitors and has a predetermined budget and a fixed schedule. Since the events come to the forefront of tourism and are the main reason for visiting the destination, this could establish a new trend in tourism, described as event tourism. There is a large diversity of sporting events not only with regard to the diversity of sports, but also with regard to the size and importance of individual actions with respect to the audience, participants, organization and other factors (Kotíková & Schwartzhoffová, 2008).

Vast quantities of sporting events organized annually attract the interest of spectators, media and sponsors. However, the media and sponsors pay more attention to major events such as the World Championships, the Olympic Games or the World Cup races in the world or domestic events (premier soccer league, hockey extra league). Nevertheless the category of sports events should also include events that are organized at a regional level.

The diversity of sporting events is large, so it is advisable to divide these events into more manageable parts. Kotíková (2008) divides the events from the point of view of sport performance and sport recreation. The first category consists of large sporting events and "mega" events. These actions have global significance with participation of a large number of athletes and spectators, require long-term and professional preparation which is often associated with building the necessary infrastructure, sports facilities, facilities for athletes, etc. Such "mega" events are characteristic in that they are held in a place which is the result of competitive tendering and are held usually once, or may be repeated only after a long period of time, and their long-term legacy must be planned and controlled by specifically managed institutions.

Other categories include visitor oriented events. These events relate to sports that have many fans and are popular – especially soccer, ice hockey, tennis. As their title suggest events focused on the participants, are aimed predominantly at participants and for spectators are not too attractive. The last category includes events in recreational sport that can be further divided into actions attractive for the audience and actions that require an active involvement of participants.

Sports tourism is not only an intentional activity during a holiday, as it may seem at first sight. An important component of this phenomenon is traveling to sporting events and actions. One of the most important events worldwide and the celebration of sports are the Olympic Games attracting millions of people around the world either to television sets or directly to the halls and sports grounds in the host city. To popularize and to boost the attractiveness of the Olympics, which often take place in remote destinations, the Czech Olympic Committee came up with the innovative idea of organizing Olympic parks in the Czech Republic. The first Olympic Park was organized at Prague's Letná plain on the occasion of the Winter Olympics in Sochi, Russia in 2014. The second main Olympic park was situated in Lipno region on the occasion of the summer Olympic Games held in Rio de Janeiro, Brazil in 2016. Auxiliary Olympic parks were located in Ostrava, Plzeň and Pardubice. Interestingly enough there was no Olympic Park in Prague, which is ironically the 2016 European Capital of Sports, due to political disputes and instability in Prague's municipal administration.

Issues, Controversies, Problems

Since its inception the Olympic games have grown into a very important event not only for the athletes but for the host country, as well. For the host country, the Olympic Games represent great opportunity and challenge, as much as the actual preparation of the Olympic Games represent substantial expenses associated with the reconstruction of old and construction of new sports facilities, building new infrastructure for athletes and media, car parks, not to mention marketing expenditures, safety measures etc. An anticipated positive fallout from all of this activity is the creation of new jobs, improving and boosting the image of the host city and the host country, increasing revenue from tourism. However, also the negative effects of the Olympic Games have been recently brought into attention, mostly concerning ecology.

The Olympic Games are economically a very challenging event. Their budgets range in hundreds of billions of dollars and their financing is usually shielded by the following four institutions: the government of the host country, the regional government, the city's municipality, and private sector (Preuss, 2004). Total costs and the ratio of public to private capital at the Olympics greatly vary (Dvořák, 2007). The lowest Olympic spending was recorded in organizing the Olympic Games in Atlanta in 1996 (2.2 bn. USD), Seoul in 1988 (3.1 bn. USD) and Sydney in 2010 (4.8 bn. USD). Conversely record high expenditures were spent on the Games in Beijing in 2008 (42 bn. USD). As a result of this in great effort is being made to reduce such monstrous amounts in the future. Consequently the London Olympics in 2012 cost roughly a third of Beijing's expenditures (14.2 bn. USD). To a certain degree a significant impact on rising costs is the continuously increasing number of athletes participating in the Olympic Games.

According to Preuss (2004) the most important part of the total costs is the construction of sports facilities and the Olympic Village. The total number of venues for the Olympic Games is around 35, with some of them have to be newly built and some, not entirely satisfactory, must be reconstructed. Another significant part of the costs is associated with building of a new infrastructure in the host city and its vicinity. Not always are all of the stadiums located within the city, many of them may be found in its vicinity. Therefore, it is necessary to build a proper transportation network or to modernize the existing one, from the improvement to municipal transportation (subway, buses, and pedestrian zones, etc.) to roads and railways, and the airport. Other expenses include organizing country marketing, security and much more.

On the other hand, the Olympic Games host country expects an economic benefit. The main sources of revenue are broadcasting rights to international and national sponsorship programs. Other sources include the traditional sale of licenses, lotteries, venue ticket sales, donations by companies and private individuals, and subsequent sale of estates and various facilities after the Games finish (Juranda, 2006). Not always is the Olympics hosting profitable (e.g. Montreal 1976) although a number of cities hosting the Olympic Games have managed to achieve profit (Los Angeles 1984, Seoul 1988, Barcelona 1992). An important source of revenue is the spending of foreign tourists. However, their arrival depends on many aspects, such as geographic location of the country, attractiveness of the region, political, economic and security situation in the country.

The scale of the Olympic Games has significant effects on the environment. The International Olympic Committee is aware of this particular issue and therefore in 1992 adopted an appeal by the World Conference on the Environment in Rio de Janeiro, which urged the world community to protect the environment and adopt a strategy for its sustainable development (Doležal & Pollert, 2004). Ecology has gradually become, alongside sports and culture, another pillar of the Olympiad, and in 1994 the commission of the International Olympic Committee's for "Sports and Environment" was established. For example, the Olympic Games held in Sydney were eco-designed in collaboration with Greenpeace, while the Olympic Games held in Athens were by Greenpeace criticized for not fulfilling environmental objectives.

The Olympic Games are not only demanding from the point of preparation, but also with respect to their actual implementation requiring enough human resources. The Olympic Games are an event that creates many jobs and business opportunities. It is not only about jobs related directly to the Olympics, but also about employment opportunities in tourism sector and in related trade fields, hotels and gastronomy (Malfas, 2004). To estimate the number of newly created jobs is according to experts rather problematic because the services are linked to the shadow economy (Studnička, 2013). Expert studies estimate that to the overall number of people employed in tourism must be added a further 20% actively engaged in tourism who are not officially registered and are part of the shadow economy (Freyer, 2009). It should be further noted that such work is rather of temporary nature, and is low-paid.

In social terms, the Olympic Games are beneficial for the citizens of the host country especially in that they boost their patriotic sentiment, develop better social relationships, strengthen the identity of the people living in the region and their self-confidence and their ability in providing enjoyable sporting venues. Bull and Lovell (2007) mention also the negative social impacts, among which rank crime, traffic congestion and driving infractions, disruption of local citizens' lives and their alienation, sometimes even displacement. Also, local culture and traditions are presented by means of the Olympic Games.

There are also significant political impacts because since its inception the Olympic Games have been influenced by politics. In times of war the Olympic Games were never held. Some countries boycotted their participation in the Olympics because of terrorist attacks or an attack on one State by another.

Statistics show that the Olympics are attended on the average by 400,000 to 800,000 foreign tourists with around 60,000 athletes and organizers taking part in the venues. Preuss (2004) classifies the tourists and residents during the Olympics in the following eight groups:

1. **Casuals:** Tourists who visit the city even without the Olympics.
2. **Time Switchers:** The tourists arriving in the city, but at a different time.
3. **Avoiders:** The tourists who stay at home but would come if the Olympics were not held.

4. **Extentioners:** The tourists who would have visited the city anyway, but are staying longer because of the Olympics.
5. **Olympians:** People who travel to the host city because of the Olympics.
6. **Home Stayers:** Residents who prefer to opt for a vacation home rather than going on vacation somewhere else at another time.
7. **Runaways:** Residents who leave the city and take their holidays elsewhere.
8. **Changers:** Residents who leave the city during the Olympic Games and spend their holidays at that time somewhere else.

These groups can be integrated into three groups from an economic point of view (namely according to their spending). The first group covers tourists, whose spending is not associated with the Olympics (Casuals, Time switchers, Changers). The second group covers tourists, whose expenses are associated with the Olympic Games (Extentioners, Olympians, Home stayers) and the third group includes tourists who would spend their money anyway, even if the Olympics were not held (Runaways, Avoiders). The number of tourists who visit the Olympic Games is limited by several factors. First and foremost, it is the capacity of hotels established prior to the Games. While during Olympics these capacities are full nearly by 100%, after the games their occupancy usually sharply drops down. Examples are hotels in Atlanta, whose availability during the Olympic Games in 1996 quickly changed.

This usual 100% occupancy for nearly two weeks has practically no significant influence on the overall annual occupancy rate of hotels, and the average occupancy rate of hotel rooms during the Olympic year in organizing cities is around 70% (e.g. Barcelona, Atlanta, Sydney, London). Another example of a limiting factor is the number of tourists who obtain visas to the destination. This problem surfaced particularly for tourists who were preparing for the Olympic Games in Beijing. The Chinese government had tightened rules for obtaining visas, the reason being to ensure security mostly for the athletes. In order to obtain visa the tourist traveling to the Games had to present an Olympic admission ticket. A number of tourists could have been discouraged by a very lengthy process of obtaining visas, security checks and also Beijing smog conditions.

Another important aspect of hosting the Olympics in terms of tourism is the image of the host city which extends to the image of the whole country. Tourists, even before visiting any city, have about the city certain preconceived idea which a personal visit may prove or disprove. In the case of the Olympics, all the host cities are trying to build the best possible image which could lure and attract new potential tourists to visit or encourage tourists for repeated visits. But if the Olympics would be hit by some tragic event endangering the safety of the athletes and tourists, or should there occur any other unpleasant circumstance, the overall image would be threatened and the tourists could perceive it rather negatively, creating consequently an uneasy situation for the host country (Montgomery, 2014).

Olympic parks should encourage public to an active lifestyle and are included in the project "the Czech Republic is sporting" as one of the main events of this project. The emphasis in Olympic parks is not only on TV broadcasts from the Olympics, but primarily on visitors' active involvement, especially that of young people, in a variety of Olympic and non-Olympic sports. These parks should also focus on identifying the population with the Czech Republic and Czech sports. When the Olympic games are held in remote destinations it is advisable that the Olympic parks be set up in Czech Republic.

The main motivation for establishing of the Olympic park (Stevenson, 2016) is:

- Development of regional tourism,
- Investments in sports infrastructure,
- Regional sports support,
- Healthy lifestyle promotion, and
- Motivation of youth to engage in sports activities.

The basic objectives of the Olympic parks project are: to introduce the Olympic and non-Olympic sports in cooperation with sports' clubs or associations with overlapping local successes and sports legends, to initiate programs for elementary school students, to emphasize the Olympic heritage, to support viewing of TV broadcasts from the Olympics, and to present and promote municipality/city, respectively region. On the implementation of the Olympic parks cooperate three entities: the Czech Olympic Committee and its official marketing agency "the Czech Olympic", the city and the county. Simultaneously an involvement of other sports organizations in the locality is expected.

Planning and Implementation

The Czech Olympic Committee already initiated the formation of the Olympic Park in 2013. This first such venue in Czech Republic took place at Letná in Prague, in February 2014, during the Winter Olympics in Sochi, Russia. Again, in Czech Republic, a similar project of Olympic parks was prepared to celebrate the Summer Olympic Games that would be held in 2016 in Rio de Janeiro, Brazil. The reason for this venue is not only the excitement of the Olympic Games, but also an emphasis on sports and physical activity. In November 2015, the Czech Olympic Committee issued a document entitled "Local Olympic Parks, a layout manual".

The Olympic Park at Letná had become a unique sports center. During 18 days, this event was attended by 409,184 people, one third of them children, and half of the visitors being from outside Prague. About 450 volunteers took part in ensuring smooth operation of the event. Also thanks to this Olympic Park, the Olympic Winter Games in Sochi became the Olympic Games with the greatest audience rating in history, totaling 7.2 million viewers. In 2016, the Summer Olympic Games were held for the first time in South America, and for the third time in the southern hemisphere. In the Czech Republic, total of four Olympic parks was established, with the largest one situated in the surroundings of the dam lake Lipno nad Vltavou, with an attendance reaching 350,000 people. Other parks were located in Ostrava, Plzeň and Pardubice. Compared with 2014, the aim was to propagate the concept of the Olympic parks to more cities in the regions of the Czech Republic. Unlike the Letná Olympic Park, which was a one-off event with nothing left after the park was dismantled, efforts were made at the Olympic Park in Lipno to keep all useful facilities even after the Games are over, in order for the park to continue its function.

The budget for building the Olympic Park at Lipno dam surroundings amounted to CZK 65 million (EUR 2.4 million), of which 15% was covered by the International Olympic Committee, 40% by commercial partners and 45% by the public sector (KPMG, 2015). The budget incorporated reconstructions of local sports grounds. Prerequisite for the investment was the commitment by the owners of the sports grounds to maintain the grounds for the future. The remaining three cities were given a franchise to allow building of the Olympic parks on its territory. An overall intention is to have a park similar the Olympic Park in every major Czech city by 2020, allowing visitors to experience the Olympic atmosphere.

SOLUTIONS AND RECOMMENDATIONS

Tourism, as one of the factors of regional development, is often considered to be the prime mover of economic development. District of Český Krumlov is made up of administrative districts of municipalities with extended powers for Český Krumlov and Kaplice. Český Krumlov region is considered a highly specific region from the perspective of tourism and its relationship to the regional development. It represents an area with extraordinary tourism potential (in Czech Republic placed second to the capital Prague). However, tourism in Český Krumlov region is distributed rather unevenly, including the city of Český Krumlov, tourist resorts Lipno nad Vltavou, Frymburk, Vyšší Brod, several sites or solitary objects (Zlatá Koruna, Rožmberk), and the Vltava river, a very busy waterway used by tourists. Remaining area is used for tourism only to a minimal extent, mainly because it contains a large area of the Boletice military domain.

Most interest in developing tourism in the mountainous areas and in proximity of water areas show primarily the providers of tourist services and the representatives of local authorities. Here the unambiguous necessity for cooperation between representatives of public and private sectors becomes clearly demonstrated. One of the most important goals is to eliminate inequalities in numbers of visitors arriving annually to the tourism destination. Lots of jobs become purely seasonal (e.g. water rescuers, towing operators) thus putting pressure on creation of off-season job opportunities. Thus in the mountainous regions emerges an integration of traditional winter activities with newly promoted attractions e.g. cycling, bobsleigh tracking, cable railway centers, parks for mountain bikes or in-line skates. Such a development is typical for Lipno nad Vltavou and its surroundings.

Tourism activities contribute to organizing events which are accessible not only to visitors/tourists but also to local residents. While during 2010 in the municipality of Lipno nad Vltavou were held about 20 events, five years later the number multiplied more than fivefold. The Lipno sports events are distributed rather evenly between winter and summer seasons. The realized events contribute to prolongation of summer and winter seasons, thereby primarily increasing revenues of business entities. Fallout of these events can be also seen through the application of marketing tools as a promotion of greater awareness of the region and the Lipno municipality itself. Some events have already achieved a supra-regional character (e.g. Summer Letná, the Lipno carousel). Several events also take into account inclusion in tourism activities of groups of people with disabilities (e.g. Lipno without barriers, Disability Day) thereby implementing the essence of promoting social tourism.

Lipno dam lake is the largest water area in Czech Republic and the Summer Olympic Games take place for the most part of it on the water. Moreover, this is an area in South Bohemia sought by visitors for other sports as well, i.e. cycling, inline skating or jogging. In Lipno nad Vltavou and its surrounding municipalities are available: a fully equipped beach, coastal promenade, a marina, a wild water track and a speed canoeing track, runners' and bikers' inline trails, a bike park, a soccer field, an athletic oval with jumping pits and a target range. Therefore, the Lipno nad Vltavou municipality has become the center of the Olympic Park. The individual sports events are being distributed to eight Lipno region municipalities, which are members of the Association of Lipno Municipalities to not only increase the tax yield, but also to ensure development of new accommodation capacities which thanks to a multiplication effect establish more jobs (Plzáková & Studnička, 2014).

FUTURE RESEARCH DIRECTIONS

Thanks to the Olympic Park many sports grounds were modernized that could serve the public in coming years. This also enhanced the image of the South Bohemian region as a major tourist destination, thanks to the project of the South Bohemian Olympic's official marketing agency. It was a long-term marketing campaign which ran since January 1, 2016, aimed at attracting tourists to South Bohemia and motivating them to participate actively. Despite a certain regional decline in paper or wood-processing industries there was recorded a positive development in leisure activities and tourism. The Olympic Park created a significant momentum of economic development in the region, in social policy and in protection of the territory environment.

The RIO-LIPNO 2016 Olympic Park was in operation August 5-22, 2016, and its center was the Lipno nad Vltavou municipality, which won the 2013 award of the European Commission EDEN (European Destinations of Excellence) themed "Travel without barriers" for a systematic approach to developing tourism for families with small children, the elderly, and especially disabled persons. A total of 91 collective accommodation facilities with 2,048 rooms and 6,573 beds were available to guests in eight municipalities. In order to improve tourism performance in South Bohemia region, the emphasis was put on cooperation with various entities.

Main identifiable potential development options of the RIO-LIPNO 2016 Olympic Park included:

- **For the Community:** Development of tourism superstructure and infrastructure with a priority on municipalities for planning their future development, from the regional perspective.
- **For Residents of Municipalities Involved in Organizing the Event:** New jobs, increased offer in social activities, prestige boost for the municipality.
- **For the County:** Region attractiveness improvement, luring the investors.
- **For Business:** Offer of additional leisure activities, accommodation and catering services development.

In terms of target markets and clientele segmentation the priority was the segment of families with children representing the core target market. Focusing on this segment, the Lipno nad Vltavou municipality got inspired by three Austrian municipalities acting under one marketing name "Serfaus-Fiss-Ladis – We are Family!". During summer, the clientele at Lipno region is usually created by more than 2/3 of the visitors/tourists aged 30-49 years arriving with their families, another 18% are young visitors/tourists of the age up to 29 years. The most important motive for visiting Lipno region is to have an active vacation (hiking, Nordic walking, cycling). Based on the experience of organizing the RIO-LIPNO 2016 Olympic Park we can evaluate the strengths, weaknesses, opportunities and threats.

CONCLUSION

Tourism presents, for a number of regions with limited resources for production activities, the only potential for infrastructure development, business and employment. When evaluating the relationship between tourism and regional development, the most important influence is the balancing function of tourism, by Ogilvie (1933). Its essence lies in the fact that visitors via tourism raise funds in place of their usual habitat, but spend them in places of temporary residence. By that the funds are moved from one place to another, usually from a place economically stronger to a place economically weaker which suffers from an economic malnutrition (Vorlaufer, 1984). Regional disparities reflect the degree of difference in which the development of the area differs from the level of the country as a whole. The cause of regional disparities can be differences in the intensity and level of human activity in different regions. Conversely the different natural conditions or other data of the given territory are not considered to be regional disparities. Consequence of regional disparities are such phenomena as a high unemployment rate, reduction of the number of permanent residents, long-term ecological burdens, the existence of brownfields, etc.

Two hypotheses were verified:

H0: Possibilities and forms of cooperation among public, private and voluntary sectors were analyzed. It is clear that a prerequisite for the successful realization of the Olympic Park project in a tourism destination are various forms and methods of cooperation among the entities mentioned above. Cooperation takes place primarily on the financial, marketing and management levels.

H1: The object of analysis was primarily the impact of building the Olympic Park on the natural environment. The scope and size of the Olympic Park in Lipno nad Vltavou required expansions of sports areas and consequently the sawing down of forest cover. Although the process of forest liquidation opened up the possibility for expansion of sports and leisure areas, by itself it created a controversial and long term risk activity.

Czech Republic is a world leader in organizing of Olympic parks (Sochi 2014 – Praha Letná, Rio de Janeiro 2016 – Lipno nad Vltavou, Ostrava, Plzeň, Pardubice) with a subsequent appraisal of the Czech Olympic Committee by the International Olympic Committee. This year, three similar parks will be built in other countries, namely in Netherlands, Finland and Israel. Organizers expected a total attendance of 200,000 visitors in the Czech Republic, only. The average attendance was estimated at 15,000 people per day, more on weekends and less during weekdays. During summer months of 2016, the South Bohemian Region made provisions for strengthening train and bus services from the České Budějovice to Lipno nad Vltavou and Černá v Pošumaví.

Lipno region possesses appropriate location and implementation of prerequisites and potential solutions for socio-economic disparities, by tourism development. It was important to distribute tourism activities in the whole of Lipno area and to alleviate the high intensity of tourism especially in Lipno nad Vltavou municipality. The most important factors for mitigating regions' disparities were considered the tax revenue and job creation. In order to tackle disparities, the endogenous factors (human factors, local actors, innovation) and the exogenous factors (subsidies, grants, fiscal relief posts) could have been applied. Economic and social effects of tourism on Lipno region demonstrated themselves due to coordination of activities through a strategic document with measurable indicators, where the fulfillment of these indicators would be the responsibility of destination management organizations.

REFERENCES

Bull, Ch., & Lovell, J. (2007). The Impact of Hosting Major Sporting Events on Local Residents: An Analysis of the Views and Perceptions of Canterbury Residents in Relation to the Tour de France 2007. *Journal of Sport & Tourism, 12*(3), 235.

Doležal, T., & Pollert, J. (2004). *Olympism and ecology.* Retrieved February 18, 2016, from http://www.olympic.cz/cz/olympismus

Dvořák, R. (2007). *Olympic Games and Chinese stocks.* Retrieved February 15, 2016, from http://www.investujeme.cz/clanky/olympijske-hry-a-cinske-akcie/

European Charter of Sport. (2010). Retrieved February 16, 2016, from http://www.msmt.cz/sport/evropska-charta-sportu

Freyer, W. (2009). *Tourism – Einführung in die Fremdenverkehrsökonomie.* München: Oldenbourgwissenschaftsverlag.

Hinch, T., & Hingham, J. (2004). *Sport tourism development.* Clevedon: Channel View Publications.

Hobza, V., & Dohnal, T. (2008). *Sport as a promising development potential of employment in the EU.* Retrieved April 14, 2016, from http://www.telesnakultura.upol.cz/index.php/telesnakultura/article/view/8/8

Juranda, Š. (2006). Main economic consequences of holding the Olympic Games in Prague in 2016. *Political Economy, 2006*(4), 498.

Kortusová, P. (2006). *Sports tourism as an area of scientific knowledge.* Prague: Czech kinantropology.

Kotíková, H., & Schwartzhoffová, E. (2008). *New trends in organizing activities and events in tourism.* Prague: Ministry for Regional Development.

KPMG. (2015). *The impacts of the project Olympic Park RIO-LIPNO 2016 in the project South Bohemia 2016 Olympic tourism.* Prague: KPMG.

Malfas, M. (2004). *Impacts of the Olympic Games as mega-events.* Retrieved March 20, 2016, from http://utsescholarship.lib.uts.edu.au/iresearch/scholarly-works/handle/2100/993

Montgomery, A. (2014). Lighting Olympic Park. In Design Week, p. 4.

Ogilvie, F. W. (1933). *The Tourist Movement: An Economic Study.* London: King & Son.

Paduchová, P. (2009). *Impact of the Olympics on tourism.* Retrieved March 21, 2016, from http://www.czechtourism.cz/files/statistiky/clanky/02_04_09_vliv_oh_na_turismus.pdf

Plzáková, L. (2015). New Conceptual Framework of Health and Well-Being Tourism Destinations. In *Proceedings of the International Scientific Conference Hospitality, Tourism and Education* (pp. 197-206). Prague: The Institute of Hospitality Management.

Pokorná, I. (2011). *Impact of Olympic Games on Tourism* (Master's Thesis). Prague: The Institute of Hospitality Management.

Preuss, H. (2004). *The Economics of Staging the Olympics: A comparison of the Games in 1972 – 2008*. Cheltenham, UK: Edward Elgar.

Schwartzhoffová, E. (2010). *Sports tourism*. Olomouc: Palacky University.

Standeven, J., & de Knop, P. (1999). *Sport Tourism*. Champaign: Human Kinetics.

Stevenson, N. (2016). Local festivals, social capital and sustainable destination development: Experiences in East London. *Journal of Sustainable Tourism*, *24*(7), 990–1006. doi:10.1080/09669582.2015.1128943

Studnička, P. (2013). *Effects of tourism on the local level – A case study of Lipno nad Vltavou*. Prague: Press21.

Vorläufer, K. (1984). *Ferntourismus und Dritte Welt*. Frankfurt am Main: M. Diesterweg.

Weed, M., & Bull, Ch. (2009). *Sports tourism – participants, policy and providers*. Oxford, UK: Elsevier.

Zauhar, J. (2004). Historical perspectives of sports tourism. *Journal of Sport & Tourism*, *9*(1), 27. doi:10.1080/1477508042000179348

ADDITIONAL READING

Beritelli, P., Bieger, T., & Laesser, C. (2007). Destination Governance: Using Corporate Governance Theories as a Foundation for Effective Destination Management. *Journal of Travel Research*, *46*(1), 96–107. doi:10.1177/0047287507302385

Cochrane, A. (1990). *Recent Developments in Local Authority Economic Policy*. London: Frank Cassel.

Gelan, A. U. (2003). Local economic impacts: The British open. *Annals of Tourism Research*, *30*(2), 406–425. doi:10.1016/S0160-7383(02)00098-1

Olympijské parky (2016). Retrieved June 15, 2016, from http://www.olympijskeparky.cz/

Olympijský park RIO-LIPNO 2016 finišuje (2016). Retrieved July 31, 2016, from http://www.olympic.cz/clanek/2357--olympijsky-park-rio-lipno-finisuje-podepsal-memorandum-s-np-a-chko-sumava

Plzáková, L., & Studnička, P. (2014). *Management of tourism in the Czech Republic – Past, Present, Future*. Praha: Wolters Kluwer.

Plzáková, L., & Studnička, P. (2014). Reducing regional disparities in unemployment tourism development at the local level. In *Proceedings reviewed contributions from the international scientific conference Hradec Economic Days 2014* (Part 2, pp. 432–444). Hradec Králové: Gaudeamus.

KEY TERMS AND DEFINITIONS

Lipno nad Vltavou: Lipno nad Vltavou is a municipality in South Bohemia which lies on the banks of the largest Czech dam lake.

Olympic Games: The Olympics represent the most important sporting event worldwide, unlike in other major sports events the Olympics are not a competition in a single sporting event but are a multidisciplinary sports event.

Olympic Park: Olympic Park is a sports and recreation complex built to support sports events related to the Olympic Games.

Regional Disparities: Regional disparities are defined as unjustified regional differences in the level of economic, social and environmental development of the regions.

Sport: Sport means a physical activity, the practice of which is linked to compliance with certain rules and customs.

Sports-Oriented Tourism: Sports oriented tourism is a form of tourism where the main motivation is the participation in sports competitions and activities.

Tourism Potential: The tourism potential is represented by a series of regional conditions and prerequisites for the development of tourism.

This research was previously published in Driving Tourism through Creative Destinations and Activities edited by Alžbeta Királ'ová, pages 245-259, copyright year 2017 by Business Science Reference (an imprint of IGI Global).

Chapter 16
Nature and Characteristics of the Sport Industry and Its Current Trends Impacting the Industry

Amber A. Ditizio
Texas Woman's University, USA

ABSTRACT

Global competition for fans and other stakeholders have caused increased pressures to maintain sport organizations' power and influence through e-commerce and social media. The ever evolving nature of sport managing research demands a reexamination of some of the major trends in the discipline that are impacted directly/indirectly by electronic mediation and its technology, especially social media. Although there are numerous trends that are occurring in sport management as a discipline, but this study concentrates on the role of ecommerce within organizations. The major trends examined are commercialization of sport, the role of mass communication to appeal to the needs of users, the need of engagement by fans, and the social needs for sports to deal with the epidemic of physical inactivity of the populace.

INTRODUCTION

General vs. Sport Management

There are many major similarities and major differences associated with sport management from general management. True, both general business management and the sport industries must deal with marketing forces in selling/advertising their products and/or services and, if possible, operate with a positive cash flow. However, sport industry and its associated research are rare unique, according to Pedersen (2013), since sport industry has an enviable position in that it has a universal significance, ubiquitous presence, and overall importance to its growth and viability in society. Only a few corresponding examples in the non-sport world comes to mind that have similar characteristics, but most are nonprofit entities, such

DOI: 10.4018/978-1-5225-5475-2.ch016

as healthcare and general public services. The major trend in sport management that is changing its characteristics is its research identity. Every academic discipline struggles with evolutionary changes in society attributes and how contemporary events may be framed in such a way that fits a predictive theory. The physical sciences generally have years of experimentation and active discourse on theory development to frame future research propositions and guide young scholars. However, in many of the social sciences, which do not lead itself to active experimentation in most cases, there is a trend to let current events, economic and political upheaval, and public opinion shape research agendas.

Sport management as an academic discipline is similarly struggling with establishing a sound theoretical framework to guide scholarly research. As research agendas are formulated in sport-related research, what are the theoretical underpinnings or paradigms that support and give credibility to such research? Unfortunately, this popularity greatly influences what is considered relevant themes or research threads, especially among doctorial students. Both Frisby (2005) and Pederson (2013) have commented that much research in sport management has been done at the micro-level, catering to new and emerging issues that have caught the attention of the public. Since American sports are becoming part of a global entertainment network, as noted by Helland (2007) and Lever & Wheeler (1993), all of its products and services, including cyberspace, are subjected to intensified commercialization.

Purpose of Present Study

The purpose of this present study is to explore the ever evolving nature of sport manage research, to make the case for the some of the major trends in the discipline that are impacted directly/indirectly by electronic mediation and its technology, especially social media. As there are numerous trends that are occurring in sport management as a discipline, but this study will concentrate on the following: Commercialization of sport, the role of mass communication to appeal to the needs of users, the need of engagement by fans, and the social needs for sports to deal with the epidemic of physical inactivity of the populace.

MAJOR TRENDS WITHIN SPORT MANAGEMENT IMPACTED BY ELECTRONIC MEDIATION

Commercialization in Sport

Although the beginning of commercialization in sport had humble beginning, now the astronomical costs associated with this new sports/media complex are being justified as part of giving valuable exposure to new series/entertainment specials through advertising spots and products. The great transformational changes in both technology and society's need for mass consumption (both services and goods), has led to an almost insatiable appetite sports to be treated as a consumable for the general commodification of leisure time. Many of the changes in global sports are the direct result and reflection of the existing pattern of growth through consumerism. In-other-terms, a growth of consumerism may over take the need for businesses to promote socially responsible behavior or citizenship. For example, one of the current trends in business is the opposite; there is a renewed call for ethical development among AACSB-accredited institutions to promote a more balance approach (e.g.; the 3Ps, profit, planet, and people). Unfortunately, it is natural for economic incentives to take over virtually all sectors of traditional life and turn them into methods for corporate growth. Hence, sport-related media have inevitably become commercialized with both positive and negative consequences.

This commercialization of sport, especially television and the broadcasting rights associated with it has manifested itself in the corporate world, where increased competition for audiences in a new media market has left a moral gap in the ideals of independent sports coverage and professionalism in news reporting. Helland (2007) and Szymanski (2006) suggested that this economic liberalism in sport broadcasting initially begin in the technological modernization of the sports/media complex, but soon moved to business processes founded in the principles of competitive marketplaces and promotions of sport products (e.g.; commercial sports, sponsorship, and media-product). As one relives the history of media development in sport coverage, what has happened to the broadcasting professionals' (e.g.; sports journalists, editors, and commentators) ideas of integrity, independence, and influence? As these ideals not worthy of protection from business interests and the mass appeal of sports; or are they the natural consequences of a successful integration of sports into society? Is it not natural for corporations that hold sport-related rights holders to actively use mass media to develop both image and product? These types of questions and their answers will have significant impacts on the ever evolving nature of the sport management discipline.

As highlighted by Szymanski (2006), the large capital flows from commercialization through the increase media accessibility of sports has become commonplace with sponsors, managers and teams. Unfortunately, as noted by Helland (2007), the growth and power of media is too weak to provide the journalistic safeguards that the general public needs to protect citizens' rights to fair coverage. Commercial interests will continue to dominate sports coverage, which threatens the social role of broadcasting and journalism. Commercialization is a double-edged sword; in that it provides for corporations' need for increased visibility and a place that may win the attention of fans. Many managers believe that the emotional meaning of the game or the team will be transferred to the sponsoring company. On-the-other-hand, the reverse may also be true; emotional meaning is just as easily transferred from the company to the club that it sponsors. Therefore, sports managers must be careful to find a good match before signing up with a sponsor. With these relationships, sport journalism may become simply a part of sport commercialism and its globalization (Zimmerman Clavio, & Lim, 2011).

Global sports organizations have grown to be part of big business in its scope and practices. Global competition for fans and other stakeholders have caused increased pressures to maintain its power and influence. Due, in part, to the extremely popular nature of sports in the media, many fans have elevated their sport organizations to a protected status. The author having come from the Pittsburgh, PA area, the radio and television media are full of "Steeler Nation" and "The Fan" programming. As pointed out by Foster (2006, p. 73), "Despite this the growing body of international sports law is concerned more with the governance of athletes' behaviour, and their relationships with their organisations and rules than with the organisations themselves." International law deals with ethical behavior of athletes, rarely with unethical business practices. As with large petroleum companies that have more wealth that most of the world's GDP (e.g.; gross domestic product), their lobbying and political powers are great and should not be underestimated. In essence, these companies, including GSOs, cannot be simply regulated or reduced. There are great market forces at work that both support and undermine GSOs. Strategic management activities that GSOs provide in the development a marketing plan of action to allure more fans to a sporting event, have placed a priority on the development and maintaining customer relationships with its fan base (Kerr & Gladden, 2008; Seguin, Richelieu, & O'Reilly, 2008).

So, there is little doubt that sport sponsorship is an essential and costly component in a company's strategic marketing plan. For example, the average price paid by corporate sponsors of the 2008 Beijing Olympic Games was US$78 million, with rights fees expected to increase by over 10% over the next four years ("Lenovo ducks out of Olympic …" 2010). Could such revenues be generated without such strategic planning, I doubt it. Business organizations and its fan base are married in a very symbolic relationship (e.g.; they need each other). From a theoretical perspective, these relationships may be explored by using Stakeholder Theory, where the needs of the various stakeholders in an organization are addressed via the efforts of an organization (Harrison, Bosse, & Phillips, 2010). Essentially, as true for general business, many important trends in the sport industry, such as further development and marketing brand loyalty efforts (Meyer-Waarden, 2007) in the professionalization, promotion, and commercialization of team-sport at all levels, have caused an increased emphasis on establishing a stable fan base. These trends all assume a relatively stable fan base, as in traditional brand marketing for consumer behavioral initiatives, having a stable fan and understanding its dynamics are essential for creating a driving force for market plans that enhances a firm's continued corporate profitability in the sport industry (Davis & Duncan, 2006).

As suggested by Foster (2006), even properly maintained governance monopolies in GSOs can have legitimate factors that allow such organizations exist in today's highly competitive marketplace. It takes accessibility to huge sums of financial and human capitals, as well as rights to media coverage and its various distribution channels in order to provide economies of scale to effectively competitive in the global sport industry. It is important that any commercial undertaking in sports requires an understanding the economic ramifications associated with developing a strong and loyal fan base for its team sports, regardless of competition level. In general, the fans must have the financial resources at its disposal as well as the propensity to spend those resources on its favorite team sport, as primarily measured through event ticket sales and related merchandise sold. The current global trend in the popularity of team sports, especially at the international competitive level, has resulted, according to Candemirır & Zalluhoğlu (2012), in a significant change in the importance given to economic and social role of team sports and its economic activities related.

This economic trend has been accelerated since sport activities have expanded to broader venues of sport clubs, associations, organizations and business-related organizations, where the implementation of detailed and purposed planned marketing promotions and strategies have become essential ingredients for success (Taks, Kesenne, Chalip, Green, & Martyn, 2011). Based on a recently published The Code of Sports Ethics, a Council of Europe's strategic documents, the organization tries to promote healthy sporting practices as a world-class standard. The document was adopted in 1992, revised 2001, but continues to evolve to reflect the new challenges of sports in society. In fact, the Council of Europe's Enlarged Partial Agreement on Sport (EPAS) has accepted a revised set of standards. Basically, the EPAS suggested a number of recommendations concerning the role of government in dealing with ethical considerations in sporting events ("The code of sports ethics …," 2013). Of particular interest to the governance monopolies in GSOs is the item that concerns maintaining the integrity of sport; which deals with the significant threats of match fixing, bribery, trafficking, and illegal betting to the overall integrity of the sporting industry.

The ability of a nation to improve oversight of the integrity and ethics of sports financing based on income from betting also applies to properly oversight of GSOs. It is not the case that would that GSOs go unregulated, as by this example, there are a number of regulatory bodies that provide such guidance. In conclusion, GSOs are an important element in the sport industry are worthy of scholarly inquiry.

Mass Media and the Need for Engagement

Another equally important trend is the inherent need for fans and other consumers of sport industry to become more engaged in their sport teams and/or activities. We are in a midst of a consumer-driven revolution as sport fans want to become more engaged in the activities that they deemed of value. The basic thesis expressed by several sport media researchers (Dees, 2011; Hutchins, 2011; Schirato, 2012; Weeks, Cornwell, & Drennan, 2008) is that increased trend of commercialization of the current "experience generation" requires a unique understanding of strategic leveraging sponsorship-linked marketing communications and activities in providing its intended audiences to become more interactive or involved with the sponsor and the sport. It is a symbolic and mutually beneficial relationship that allows all important stakeholders to use social networking and its various technical forms to strengthen and reinforce fan engagement via direct and accessible media and marketing opportunities (Dees, 2011). Hence, the term "spectator sport" has little meaning today as fans can develop a sense of belong with their beloved team, as many athletes are willing to directly communicate with fans via social networking platforms (e.g.; Facebook™ and Twitter™) in order to promote individual and organizational branding activities.

Even the physical entities associated with sporting events, such stadiums, are becoming more visually persuasive and engaging by the use of HD monitors (e.g.; StadiumVision and Mediamesh) that help place the fan in the midst of a personal experience with the game. The apparent goal of these communication-intensive technologies is to increase the activation leverage of corporate sponsorship with fan experiences. These trends assume a relatively stable fan base, based on providing value-added experiences, as in traditional brand marketing for consumer behavioral initiatives, having a stable fan and understanding its dynamics are essential for creating a driving force for market plans that enhances a firm's continued corporate profitability in the sport industry (Davis & Duncan, 2006). As the growth of telemediatization (e.g.; communications technologies and systems) has become more main stream and acceptable, so has what society considers what constitutes a routine flow of experience (Tomlinson, 2007).

Whether this new trend is part of "turbo-charged capitalism" that has reduced fans to layman rather than the connoisseur (Schirato, 2012) is a debatable point in the academic discussion of the associated issues of spectatorship and visual regimes. Examining this media-inspired sport engagement thesis from a theoretical perspective, regardless of the choice of theories (e.g.; Exchange, Technical Adoption Theory, Uses and Gratifications, and Social Learning, to name a few), the consumer is essentially exchanging their scare resources (e.g.; money, time, effort) for a value-added activity (e.g.; personalized experience) or product (merchandise, services). The exchange of these value-added activities may be driven by generational, technology savvy, disposable income, and/or changes in cultural norms. It is obvious that business will naturally take advantage of e-personalization innovations to given their audiences that value-added experience they desire. Technology, especially with mobile devices and greater and faster web-based accessibility, marketing and e-commerce has exponentially grown, promoting online betting as well.

As were the traditional ways of marketing in the past using a physical sales force, outlets (including retail branches, stores, kiosks), telephony (telephone, fax, call center contact), direct marketing (direct mail, radio, television) and mobile commerce (mobile phones, text messages), e-commerce and the Internet has since taken over in terms of cost valuation and customer attention. Many companies are now using the approach of a multichannel integration process which combines many channels in order to interact with a vast spectrum of customers (Frow & Payne, 2005). Despite these traditional, well-known ways, application service providers are promoting a variety of betting opportunities for sports-related gambling, ranging from fantasy sports to collegiate and professional athletic contests.

Social Responsibility and Its Role in Sport Management

There is little doubt that modern sports are directly tied to the media complex that promotes sport as entertainment. Helland (2007) regarded this complex relationship as the result of new technology and social developments. Just as in a business enterprise, the company's stockholders are not its only stakeholders. The sport industry has an important obligation to satisfy it various stakeholders by managing its entertaining function to promote a balance of exposure and exhibition of sport as a benefit for all ages, all stakeholders in society. "The realization of these strategies in the attraction process is through the contribution of significant other stakeholders such as development officers who assist with the implementation of programs, and sponsors in facilitating the smooth running of these programs and other strategies" (Sotiriadou, Shilbury, & Quick, 2008, p. 261). It is perhaps premature to state that entertainment is not as good of a function as improving the physical and mental wellbeing of children and senior adults, but to ignore these stakeholders would not be wise. Although stakeholders may not have equality in its strategic leverage abilities (e.g.; like powerful stockholders), they can still vote with his/her dollars. Undoubtedly, there is room for the sport industry to adequately, but not equally, the needs of its various stakeholders.

For example, there are many subtle as well as profound values of informal sport development that can be found in our increasingly global society. Regardless of an individual's value of sport development, such development may have large-scale implications for society as a whole. Rowe, Shilbury, Ferkins, and Hinckson (2013) provided insight to the value of an international dialogue on the value of sport development in combating the apparent rise of inactivity and obesity levels. The authors suggested that there is great gap or disconnect between the need for physical activity and sport management research, with suggestions of increased opportunities for collaboration and dialogue on the subject. Unfortunately, as a graduate student, I am often overly focused on some small aspect of issues and problems in sport management, which may lead me to ignore the bigger picture issues we all face in our society. Rowe, et al. pointed out that the sport management literature has mainly focused on sport as a form of entertainment with spectatorship outcomes. They suggested that sport developmental research has been less focus on organizational issues related to participation in sport and recreation. The extrinsic motivation for promoting sport development action may be based on promoting the value of community participation for health and social benefits.

The research on the socio-ecological models by Rowe, et al. (2013) suggested that environmental and policy considerations (macro-level) are important in addition to intrapersonal and interpersonal factors (micro-level) in the influence of participation in different forms of sport and recreation (e.g.; competitive cyclists). The conceptual study framed the global need for dealing with the many factors associated with physical inactivity as the leading cause of major non-communicable diseases (e.g.; cardiovascular disease, Type 2 diabetes, and some forms of cancer) with the complexity associated with elite sports (e.g.; strong club and competition structures, access to quality coaching and affordable, high quality equipment, and scholarship programs). Initially, it was doubtful on the surface that seeming two disparate sport concepts of pandemic and economic impacts of physical inactivity could be linked to elite sports participation. The links were theoretically imbedded in governmental policies, economic incentives, environmental factors, and attitudes of individuals. Only through an understanding of these complexities can a global policy be created and effective support to deal with physical inactivity. This research was a welcomed reminder of how important sport management as a discipline is to society and deserves to be treated seriously with other academic inquiries.

General Conclusions in New Trends in Sport Management

The driving force behind many of the new trends in the sport industry may be due in part to technological innovations have been created that greatly enhance social interaction among participants. This may be accomplished by exploiting the Internet's remarkable array of economic affordability and customer interaction, especially via social network sites. Many sports and related organizations have tapped into these aspects of social networking through blogs, texting, fantasy and betting cyber-communities, resulting in a current dialogue of the ethics of sports gambling, especially in the workplace environment (Filo, Funk, & Alexandris, 2008; Kerr & Gladden, 2008). The seeming chaos of complexity and violence now can be enjoyed by audience that what to inject the concepts of self and virtually create a sense of belong that was not technically feasible a relatively short time ago. New mobile and communication-intensive technologies allow the fan to watch and actively engage other fans during the real or virtual athletic contests. Such profound changes and trends in sport managements make one question what is your extrinsic motivation for doing sport development research in the first place. All of us have intrinsic reasons for pursuing an advanced degree in sport management (e.g.; career advancement, higher paying positions, personal accomplishment), but there must an extrinsic value to society that will result from such scholarly pursues. The following sections will discuss these trends in more detail in dealing with segmenting sport consumers, especially in fantasy sports and related office pooling and gambling.

SEGMENTING SPORT CONSUMERS

Theoretical Aspects

There are various means for segmenting sport consumers and how current and projected demographic variables may impact segmentation and marketing strategies for professional sport leagues regionally and nationally. Various theories at the marketing segment or individual level, such as Uses and Gratifications and Social Learning Theories, have been employed with various methodologies, such as experimental design studies, content analyses, and case studies) to investigate sport-related scientific inquiries. Both Frisby (2005) and Pederson (2013) have written their essays after the advent of the Internet and social networking have become main stream avenues for research in sport management. Pederson suggested that even contemporary studies in sport communication have used primarily content analysis to take mere snapshots of social media and its impact on sport. He suggested doing further research by examining the audience consumption and effects, framed by a strategic communication perspective.

Sport ticket sales and several components are essentially part of marketing campaign experience with the major functions of a successful business. It may be relatively easy to focus on the product when selling; but when the customer, not the product, is the focus of the sale, this is known as customer-focused selling. There are four main components of a sale, based on the STAR model proposed by Irwin, Sutton, and McCarthy (2008): Having a Sellable product, the Attitude of the salesperson, Leads identified by the salesperson, and the Equity, or value of the product to the customer. From a managerial perspective, this model is typically used to describe a product and the firm's your approach dealing with their customers. The SALE model is part of the basic training most salespersons receive in closing the sale procedures. Closing the sale, where it is face-to-face or online. The basic concepts is to develop some of the many skills and attitudes that contribute to developing a relationship with their customers (i.e. relationship marketing) and keeping track of product/sales performance (e.g.; customer relationship management) (Paas & Kuijlen, 2001; Woodcock, Green, & Starkey (2011). In the past, closing the sale usually came at the end of a sales visit, but this old definition only solved the current needs, not their continuing and evolving needs.

In order to do this, from a mangerial perspective, the organization must build a trusting relationship and partnership with their customers. You need to become a dependable resource that helps them solve their on-going problems and, hence, allows the organization to satisfy their continuing and evolving needs and desires. Management must understand that it is the lifetime value of a client is worth more than a single sale. So, the basic reasoning behind the SALE model is that managers need to take a future sales orientation in order to retain current customers, get new referrals, and get the sought after customer trust and loyalty. In terms of ticket sales, many fans may say they want low prices, but they are really saying they want low costs, nit value. Hence, if there is true value through customization unique to the fan's definition of value, it is easier to justify higher ticket prices and related sport products/services if there is true value. It avoids the problems of poor quality and many of the product/service problems.

For example, to illustrate fiscal responsibility, the current state of revenues and expenses in NCAA athletics have been the subject of much popular press articles, with the unflattering comments like cartels, big business, abuse of power, profits over concerns for students' well-being, are relatively commonplace. Managers oftentimes seem to focus on their physical assets, pushing to buy bigger and better equipment, machinery, and buildings, when really it is the intangibles that should be given equal if not more attention. Intangibles, such as reputation and culture, are often forgotten in the struggle to push out more widgets or make more sales. Yet, as demonstrated by the theoretical aspects of the Resource-based view of the Firm (RBV), it may be intangible strategic assets that do not necessarily show-up on a financial statement that really are driving a company's long-term success (Michalisin, Smith, & Kline, 1997, 2000).

To illustrate some of the concepts of corporate reputation as an intangible strategic asset from the theoretical assumptions of RBV, recently the Dallas Cowboys have become partners with AT&T and changed the name of the stadium from Cowboys Stadium to AT&T stadium. Typically, collegiate and professional athletic organizations generate revenue through many avenues, such as broadcasting rights, multimedia rights, stadium concessions, corporate sponsorships, individual donations, merchandise sales, and ticket sales (Leeds & Von Allmen, 2001; Gladden & Milne, 1999). It can be safely assumed that NFL Cowboys have become partners with AT &T sponsorship was transacted under similar commercial conditions and pressures. Since the sale of sport event tickets continues to be the foremost revenue stream over which collegiate and professional athletic organizations have direct control, management typically concentrates on developing ways to increase ticket sales revenue, especially through leveraging available media technologies.

To properly study this phenomenon of data capture and understanding the characteristics of their target market, one must look at management strategies. According to Bouchet, Ballouli, & Bennett (2011), some the most important issues that hindered ticket sales managerial issues. For example, frequent turnover at the senior leadership levels may lead to changes in priorities and tactics, which decreases stability in a plan for ticket sales. Strategic management may have limited experience in ticket sales at the collegiate/professional levels, which may result in a weak commitment to increasing ticket sales. There may poor and not properly developed lines of communication and reporting between senior athletic personnel and sales force. Another common problem in many organizations that it is difficult to find the most qualified sales staff if organizations do not pay competitive base salaries and sales commissions compared to other more successful professional sports organizations pay for the same type of work. This staffing expertise situation may prove especially challenging at the collegiate level, due not insufficient budgetary considerations. There concepts will be discussed in more detail in the following sections.

Importance of Marketing Plans in Sports

In the development a marketing plan of action to allure more fans to a sporting event, either professional, college, or international, such as the well-established Olympics, management has placed a priority on the development and maintaining customer relationships with its fan base (Kerr & Gladden, 2008; Seguin, et al., 2008). There is little doubt that sport sponsorship is an essential and costly component in a company's strategic marketing plan. For example, the average price paid by corporate sponsors of the 2008 Beijing Olympic Games was US $78 million, with rights fees expected to increase by over 10% over the next four years ("Lenovo ducks out of Olympic …," 2010).

Dees (2011) suggested that an application of Exchange Theory from an activational leverage of corporate sponsorship has been greatly influenced and accelerated by recent development in media-based technologies. Specially, these technologies are in-venue devices and smartphone applications, social media, and stadium technology, which serve to enhance branding of both the corporation and sport teams. As true for general business, many important trends in the sport industry, such as further development and marketing brand loyalty efforts in the professionalization, promotion, and commercialization of team-sport at all levels, have caused an increased emphasis on establishing a stable fan base. These trends all assume a relatively stable fan base, as in traditional brand marketing for consumer behavioral initiatives, having a stable fan and understanding its dynamics are essential for creating a driving force for market plans that enhances a firm's continued corporate profitability in the sport industry (Davis & Duncan, 2006).

Many professional and sponsored sporting events (e.g.; athletic contests, marathons, tournaments, to name a few) typically now include additional event entertainment meant to attract spectators and participants. In Green's (2001) study, the author addressed three separate events that include other event entertainment. One local Texas example of this was the Formula One Race, which includes Austin Fan Fest. Many celebrities and visitors travel to Austin, TX to attend the Fan Fest, but may not attend a single race. Initially, one may ask can these extra parties, seminars, concerts, broaden segments that might attend the actual athletic events. Can these events distract from the actual main event being hosted? How can a sport manager ensure the main event is not overshadowed by the side events? Should a manager even be concerned if such corresponding events attract fans, spectators, and interested parties? There is evidence that most researchers believe that sports leagues need to be current and provide relevance in their activities (Hutchins, 2011; Miloch & Lambrecht, 2006; Moorman, 2008; Paas & Kuijlen, 2001; Woodcock, Green, & Starkey, 2011). The present study's author, as a long-time Cleveland Browns fan, many times these additional activities were (and still are) welcomed relief from the dismissal showing of one's favorite professional football team's performance. Event planners need to cater and develop future as well as existing fans. To ignore attracting interested parties, regardless of their existing team localities, would not be good business practices. Positive word-of-month is a very powerful tool. There can be many strategies that attract future fans by having professional athletes do positive role modeling, community acts of charitable giving, and promote the sport franchises' branding in the local, regional, and national spotlights (Smith & Smith, 2008). The "main event" may not be the only important activity that provides entertainment and engagement that spectators crave.

College vs. Professional Sports Revenue Streams

There are other sources of revenue that illustrate the RBV aspects associated with intangible assets that can be directly tied to such championship participation, as in professional sports' championships typically have some of the highest ratings in terms of viewing, so can the case be made at the collegiate level. Die-hard fans to causal spectators are drawn to media coverage that, in turn, creates significant sources of revue for these athletic departments. Throughout this section, many comparisons between the professional leagues and NCAA member schools to highlight some fundamental differences in fiscal management can be made. For example, there is a Big 10 television network that requires a separate subscription in order to be viewed. Several cable networks will offer pay-on-demand to watch re-runs of these championship and bowl game appearances. Then there are advertising fees paid by commercial entities that add to the coffers of these teams for broadcasting and marketing rights. The officially licensed merchandise available before and after successful athletic contest dominates the retail and online stores. The list is almost endless. Burden, Li, Masiu, and Savini (2006), Pantuosco and Stone (2007), and Nagel, Amis, and Southall (2008) have cited that the commercial hype, commercialization, and advertising campaigns resemble the same coverage received by professional sport teams in term of their championships. From a strategic management viewpoint, although many of these items can be financially analyzed, it is very difficult to isolate to a single source, such as athletic programs. Hence, these assets may fall under the category of intangible strategic value.

Apparently, professional sport teams are better fiscally managed than NCAA-member organizations. They are also not hampered by the seemingly endless rules and regulations that plague collegiate teams (Baird, 2004). NCAA organization expenses for 2011-12 were US $800 million; with 63% were direct distributions to Division I conferences and institutions. In contrast, the professional NFL organization had total revenue over US $8 billion (Badenhausen, Ozanian, & Settimi, 2010), which dwarfs the revenues associated with the NCAA organization (Smith & Synowka, 2014).

Professional Sports Measures for Success

As Rishe (2010) discussed, although the NFL is very profitable, some teams are more cost-effective than others. There are lessons to be learned from dealing with the cost management approach for the NCAA. For example, the New England Patriots, having in the 2010 NFL league-best 14-2 record; they also rank as the league's most cost-effective team. The team had the third-lowest NFL payroll of about US $92.7 million and paid US $6.6 million in payroll per win. This is reported figure is surprising 58% more efficient than the league median cost per win. The second best cost-effective team was Atlanta Falcons, who won nine of their last 10, with a payroll of US $96.4 million, seventh-lowest in the league (US $7.4 million in payroll per win). It terms of least cost-effective, the Carolina Panthers (2-14 season), had US $56.1 million per win, with a 250% less efficient than the NFL median cost per win. It terms of revenue, as an indicator of changes in fans' prices, the average NFL ticket was US $78.38 in 2012, a 2.5% increase from last season. The overall change was 3.9% in traditional prices associated with attending a professional sport game (e.g.; beer, parking, hot dogs and food, and other consumables) ("NFL fan expenses," 2013). Fortunately, the NCAA reallocates financial resources back to its member (probably not in an equitable manner), while professional sport leagues like the NFL and NBA, for example, and use the revenue to increase profits to owners and, to some extent, its players.

Interestingly, from a professional sports perspective, Veeraraghavan and Vaidyanathan (2012) presented an analysis of perceived seat value in relation to several factors, including the location of the seat and the seats relation to the field or stage for professional sport events that deals with customer/fan perception of value. Their analysis yielded a measure of consumer satisfaction, referred to Seat Value Index. The Seat Value Index is then applied to a proprietary data set from a baseball franchise in Japan. The authors are able to quantify spectators' perceived value of the sporting event and derive subsequent seat valuations. The idea that all seats are created equal does not apply when examining the perceived experience and value of sporting events and theater presentations. The perceived by the patron is complicated further by the introduction of personal preference. Factors that are independent of the seat location may impact the value placed on the seat by the person sitting there. One such impact is the experience value. If that patron is attending for the first time, or has good or bad weather, can all drastically impact the perceived value. The consideration of Seat Value Index (SVI) on design of sporting and entertainment venues should allow management to maximize layout design and create a better experience and perceived value for a great amount of visitors, while simultaneously increasing gross margins by increasing the price of tickets. This is but one example of how professional sport leagues are more innovative in setting ticket prices with their fans than the NCAA-member institutions. As professional sport leagues are for profit organizations, they traditionally had to relieve on innovations to attract and hold its fan base and create new streams of potential revenue. It seems that the NCAA has lost its control on spiraling costs and has few solutions to its relatively flat sources of revenue. This makes the entire concept of a self-supporting NCAA athletic organization unsustainable from a financial standpoint.

Economic Ramifications of Successful Segmentation

It is important that any commercial undertaking in sports requires an understanding the economic ramifications associated with developing a strong and loyal fan base for its team sports, regardless of competition level. In general, the fans must have the financial resources at its disposal as well as the propensity to spend those resources on its favorite team sport, as primarily measured through event ticket sales and related merchandise sold. The current global trend in the popularity of team sports, especially at the international competitive level, has resulted, according to Candemirır & Zalluhoğlu (2012), in a significant change in the importance given to economic and social role of team sports and its economic activities related. This economic trend has been accelerated since sport activities have expanded to broader venues of sport clubs, associations, organizations and business-related organizations, where the implementation of detailed and purposed planned marketing promotions and strategies have become essential ingredients for success (Taks, et al., 2011). The authors empirically investigated the financial viewpoints between a traditional economic impact report analysis (EIA) and a cost-benefit analysis (CBA) and found several interesting results.

The authors conducted and EIA using an existing I-O (input-output) model, while the benefit side of the CBA included non-local visitor spending, the revenue of the local organizing committee (LOC), the consumer surplus, and public good value of the sporting event for the local residents. In the analysis, the cost side of the CBA was estimated based on the opportunity costs related to the construction of any faculties, such as a stadium (including labor costs and the cost of borrowing), imports, and ticket sales to locals. Their study on the factors affecting such sports-related consumer expenditures found that although both methods presented separate challenges and limitations, the CBA has the distinct advantage that it identifies the net benefits associated with the actual hosting sporting events. Empirical results obtained by Candemirır & Zalluhoğlu (2012) from a study in Turkey of the demographic and socioeconomic analysis of fans and their practices about sports-related activities and expenditures resulted in a factor analysis that revealed that such expenditures were based on their attitudes towards sporting events.

There are other financial considerations that are not directly related to spending behavior patterns of a sport's fans that are equally important, such as economic drivers and stimulus that are derived from hosting a sustainable team sporting events. For example, Walker and Mondello (2007) investigated the controversial issues associated with public investments in sporting facilities. These issues have received much attention in the popular presses as economists, politicians, and business owners debate the advantages and disadvantages of such investments at societal expense. Walker and Mondello provided empirical evidence that typically detailed the economic and strategic benefits derived from such public investments, such as whether team sport facilities or stadiums do serve as major economic drivers, such as increased revenues by fans in local business, or simply serve as means for corporate owners of sport teams to avoid investing their own financial resources to completely support such facilities. Although the authors have demonstrated empirically that typically such new stadiums and arenas have no significant direct financial impact on local economies, they do admit that such facilities and sport teams do generate both tangible and intangible benefits that may justify at some level for such public investment. Such benefits have been somewhat supported by academic works of Bartik (1998), Baade (1996), Baade and Dye (1990), and Coates and Humphreys (1999) as well.

Ticket Sale Revenues

In general, many collegiate athletic departments as well as professional sports organizations face issues in generating sufficient ticket revenue that helps supports teams' numerous expenditures. Typically, collegiate and professional athletic organizations generate revenue through many avenues, such as broadcasting rights, multimedia rights, stadium concessions, corporate sponsorships, individual donations, merchandise sales, and ticket sales (Leeds & Von Allmen, 2001; Gladden & Milne, 1999; Smith & Smith, 2009); can be safely assumed that professional team sponsorship is under similar pressures, although a number of opportunities exist for substantial governmental and monetary support systems for stadiums and related economic developments.

Since the sale of sport event tickets continues to be the foremost revenue stream over which collegiate and professional athletic organizations have direct control, management typically concentrates on developing ways to increase ticket sales revenue. According to Bouchet, et al., some the most important issues that hindered ticket sales managerial issues. For example, frequent turnover at the senior leadership levels may lead to changes in priorities and tactics, which decreases stability in a plan for ticket sales. Strategic management may have limited experience in ticket sales at the collegiate/professional levels, which may result in a weak commitment to increasing ticket sales. There may poor and not properly developed lines of communication and reporting between senior athletic personnel and sales force. Another common problem in many organizations that it is difficult to find the most qualified sales staff if organizations do not pay competitive base salaries and sales commissions compared to other more successful professional sports organizations pay for the same type of work. This staffing expertise situation may prove especially challenging at the collegiate level, due not insufficient budgetary considerations.

As an essential part of human resources and job design is providing maximum fan satisfaction within the financial and environmental constrains of the sports organization. Many salespeople thrive in a performance-based environment where there are incentives like commissions and bonuses for selling. However, many state-supported universities have bylaws that do not allow the administration to give any commissions or bonuses to employee staff. Private institutions are more able to give those incentives, but the best sales people will still come into these positions and realize the other flaws of the athletic organizational infrastructure that do not exist in a normal sales environment. There are job-design improvements that can offset these apparent flaws, primarily by creating more effective channels of communication and media support. The ultimate goal is to jointly maximize fans' satisfaction and profitability of the sales organizations. Maintaining good relationships, keeping ticket prices reasonably prices for the perceived value they obtain, enhancing media accessibility, and meet the motivational needs of the fan base (Smith & Smith, 2008; Swanson, Gwinner, Larson, & Janda, 2003; Taks, et al., 2011; Tobar, 2006; Walker & Mondello, 2007).

GENERAL CONCLUSION

Reputation, employee knowhow, and culture are all key strategic asserts based on the RBV theory that managers can specifically and intentionally seek to improve, but only if they recognize that these really are assets and that these factors are critical to profitability. Managers of athletic departments must realize that, without proper focus and intentional work of strategic managers, these assets can quickly become detriments, even in the initially most successful organizations. Being operationally lean is a basic requirement of management and, obviously, many sport organizations, including professional teams; need to perform better in that regard. However, financial analyses do not take proper accountability of the return on intangible assets will undoubtedly skew the financial analysis.

There is sufficient evidence that the customer-first sales approach works better in virtually all selling situations. People really do not want to be sold a product, but to engage in meaningful relationships that provide mutual benefit. True, coaches have to deal hand-on with their athletes, but so do most face-to-face selling. It is true in the world of e-commerce as well. Management needs to understand that it is the lifetime value of a client is worth more than a single sale. It is a matter of a value-added proposition. Marketing professionals basically want to retain current customers, get new referrals, and get the sought after customer trust and loyalty; all of which are long-term or strategic goals. Of course, the attitude towards the growth of the sports industry and its marketing can be greatly influenced by word-of-mouth (WOM) testimonials and success rates of existing websites and their associated customers' usage. Building relationships are the basic foundation to engage in our customers/fans on the long term, providing the needed services and products as only part of the traditional product-mix.

REFERENCES

Badenhausen, K., Ozanian, M., & Settimi, C. (2010). The most valuable NFL teams. *Forbes*. Retrieved from http://www.forbes.com/2010/08/25/most-valuable-nfl-teamsbusiness-sports-football-valuations-10-intro.html

Baird, K. (2004). Dominance in college football and the role of scholarship restrictions. *Journal of Sport Management, 18*(3), 217–235.

Bouchet, A., Ballouli, K., & Bennett, G. (2011). Implementing a ticket sales force in college athletics: A decade of challenges. *Sports Marketing Quarterly, 20*(2), 84–92.

Candemirır, A., & Zalluhoğlu, A.-E. (2012). Factors affecting the sport related consumer expenditures. *Ege Academic Review, 12*(1), 29–39.

Coates, D., & Humphreys, B. R. (1999). The growth effects of sports franchises, stadia and arenas. *Journal of Policy Analysis and Management, 14*(4), 601–624. doi:10.1002/(SICI)1520-6688(199923)18:4<601::AID-PAM4>3.0.CO;2-A

Dautzenberg, K. (2012). Gender differences of business owners in technology-based firms. *International Journal of Gender and Entrepreneurship, 4*(1), 79–98. doi:10.1108/17566261211202990

Davis, N. W., & Duncan, M. C. (2006). Sports knowledge is power: Reinforcing masculine privilege through fantasy sport league participation. *Journal of Sport and Social Issues, 30*(3), 244–253. doi:10.1177/0193723506290324

Dees, W. (2011). New media and technology use in corporate sport sponsorship: Performing activational leverage from an exchange perspective. *International Journal of Sport Management and Marketing, 10*(3/4), 272–285. doi:10.1504/IJSMM.2011.044795

Filo, K., Funk, D. C., & Alexandris, K. (2008). Exploring the role of brand trust in the relationship between brand associations and brand loyalty in sport and fitness. *International Journal of Sport Management and Marketing, 3*(1/2), 39–57. doi:10.1504/IJSMM.2008.015960

Foster, J. (2006). Global sports organisations and their governance. *Corporate Governance, 6*(1), 72–83. doi:10.1108/14720700610649481

Frisby, W. (2005). The good, the bad, and the ugly: Critical sport management research. *Journal of Sport Management, 19*(1), 1–12.

Gladden, J. M., & Milne, G. R. (1999). Examining the importance of brand equity in professional sport. *Sport Marketing Quarterly, 8*(1), 21–29.

Green, B. C. (2001). Leveraging subculture and identity to promote sport events. *Sport Management Review, 4*(1), 1–19. doi:10.1016/S1441-3523(01)70067-8

Green, B. C., Murray, N., & Warner, S. (2011). Understanding website useability: An eye-tracking study of the Vancouver 2010 Olympic Games website. *International Journal of Sport Management and Marketing, 10*(3/4), 257–271. doi:10.1504/IJSMM.2011.044793

Harrison, J. S., Bosse, D. A., & Phillips, R. A. (2010). Managing for stakeholders, stakeholder utility functions, and competitive advantage. *Strategic Management Journal*, *31*(10), 58–74. doi:10.1002/smj.801

Helland, K. (2007). Changing sports, changing media: Mass appeal, the sports/media complex and TV sports rights. *Nordicom Review*, *28*(Jubilee Issue), 105–119.

Hutchins, B. (2011). The acceleration of media sport culture. *Information Communication and Society*, *14*(2), 237–257. doi:10.1080/1369118X.2010.508534

Irwin, R., Sutton, W., & McCarthy, L. (2008). *Sport Promotion and Sales Management.2*[nd] (H. Kinetics, Ed.). Champaign, IL.

Kerr, A. K., & Gladden, J. M. (2008). Extending the understanding of professional team brand equity to the global marketplace. *International Journal of Sport Management and Marketing*, *3*(1/2), 58–67. doi:10.1504/IJSMM.2008.015961

Leeds, M. A., & Kowaleski, S. (2001). Winner-take-all in the NFL: The impact of free agency and the salary cap on skill position players. *Journal of Sports Economics*, *2*(3), 244–256. doi:10.1177/152700250100200304

Lenovo ducks out of Olympic sponsorship cost a factor. (2010). *Marketing Vox*. Retrieved from http://www.marketingvox.com/is-mass-marketing-dying-olympics-loses-second-big-sponsor-035097/

Lever, J., & Wheeler, S. (1993). Mass media and the experience of sport. *Communication Research*, *20*(1), 125–143. doi:10.1177/009365093020001006

Meyer-Waarden, L. (2007). The effects of loyalty programs on customer lifetime duration and share of wallet. *Journal of Retailing*, *83*(2), 223–236. doi:10.1016/j.jretai.2007.01.002

Michalisin, M. D., Smith, R. D., & Kline, D. M. (1997). In search of strategic assets. *The International Journal of Organizational Analysis*, *5*(4), 360–387. doi:10.1108/eb028874

Michalisin, M. D., Smith, R. D., & Kline, D. M. (2000). Intangible strategic assets and firm performance: A multi-industry study of the resource-based view. *The Journal of Business Strategy*, *17*(2), 91–117.

Miloch, K., & Lambrecht, K. W. (2006). Consumer awareness of sponsorship at grassroots sport events. *Sport Marketing Quarterly*, *15*(3), 147–154.

Moorman, A. M. (2008). Fantasy sports leagues challenged as illegal gambling. *Sport Marketing Quarterly*, *17*(4), 232–234.

NFL fan expenses. (2013). Retrieved from http://www.fancostexperience.com/pages/fcx/blog_pdfs/entry0000018_pdf000.pdf

Paas, L., & Kuijlen, T. (2001). Towards a general definition of customer relationship management. *Journal of Database Marketing*, *9*(1), 51–60.

Pedersen, P. M. (2013). Reflections on communication and sport: On strategic communication and management. *Communication and Sport*, *1*(1/2), 55–67. doi:10.1177/2167479512466655

Rowe, K., Shilbury, D., Ferkins, L., & Hinckson, E. (2013). Sport development and physical activity promotion: An integrated model to enhance collaboration and understanding. *Sport Management Review*, *16*(1), 364–377. doi:10.1016/j.smr.2012.12.003

Schirato, T. (2012). Fantasy sport and media interactivity. *Sport in Society: Cultures, Commerce, Media. Politics*, *15*(1), 78–87.

Seguin, B., Richelieu, A., & O'Reilly, N. (2008). Leveraging the Olympic brand through the reconciliation of corporate and consumers' brand perceptions. *International Journal of Sport Management and Marketing*, *3*(1/2), 3–22. doi:10.1504/IJSMM.2008.015958

Smith, A. A., & Synowka, D. P. (2013). Financial state of affairs for NCAA sports: A case for intangible strategic assets? *International Journal of Services and Operations Management*, *19*(1), 29–48. doi:10.1504/IJSOM.2014.064033

Smith, A. D., & Smith, A. A. (2008). Exploring the service location strategies behind super bowl venue selection. *Services Marketing Quarterly*, *29*(4), 66–84. doi:10.1080/15332960802218778

Sotiriadou, K., Shilbury, D., & Quick, S. (2008). The attraction, retention/transition, and nurturing process of sport development: Some Australian evidence. *Journal of Sport Management*, *22*(1), 247–272.

Swanson, S. R., Gwinner, K., Larson, B. V., & Janda, S. (2003). Motivations of college student game attendance and word-of-mouth behavior: The impact of gender differences. *Sport Marketing Quarterly*, *72*(3), 151–162.

Szymanski, S. (2006). The economic evolution of sport and broadcasting. *The Australian Economic Review*, *39*(4), 428–434. doi:10.1111/j.1467-8462.2006.00432.x

Taks, M., Kesenne, S., Chalip, L., Green, B. C., & Martyn, S. (2011). Economic impact analysis versus cost benefit analysis: The case of a medium-sized sport event. *International Journal of Sport Finance*, *6*(3), 187–203.

Tobar, D. A. (2006). Affect and purchase intentions of Super Bowl XL television spectators: Examining the influence of sport fandom, age, and gender. *Sport Marketing Quarterly*, *75*(4), 243–252.

Tomlinson, J. (2007). *The Culture of Speed: The Coming of Immediacy*. London, UK: Sage Publications.

Veeraraghavan, S., & Vaidyanathan, R. (2012). Measuring seat value in stadiums and theaters. *Production and Operations Management*, *21*(1), 49–68. doi:10.1111/j.1937-5956.2011.01249.x

Walker, M., & Mondello, M. (2007). Moving beyond economic impact: A closer look at the Contingent Valuation Method. *International Journal of Sport Finance*, *2*(3), 149–160.

Weeks, C. S., Cornwell, T. B., & Drennan, J. C. (2008). Leveraging sponsorships on the Internet: Activation, congruence, and articulation. *Psychology and Marketing*, *25*(7), 637–654. doi:10.1002/mar.20229

Woodcock, N., Green, A., & Starkey, M. (2011). Social CRM as a business strategy. *Database Marketing and Customer Strategy Management*, *18*(1), 50–64. doi:10.1057/dbm.2011.7

Yeh, J.-C., Hsiao, K.-L., & Yang, W.-N. (2012). A study of purchasing behavior in Taiwan's online auction websites: Effects of uncertainty and gender differences. *Internet Research*, *22*(1), 98–115. doi:10.1108/10662241211199988

Zimmerman, M. H., Clavio, G. E., & Lim, C. H. (2011). Set the agenda like Beckham: A professional sports league's use of YouTube to disseminate messages to its users. *International Journal of Sport Management and Marketing*, *10*(3/4), 180–195. doi:10.1504/IJSMM.2011.044789

This research was previously published in the Journal of Electronic Commerce in Organizations (JECO), 14(4); edited by Pedro Isaías, pages 13-27, copyright year 2016 by IGI Publishing (an imprint of IGI Global).

Chapter 17
Sport Management and Sustainability Innovation Challenges

Marco Tortora
University of Florence, Italy

ABSTRACT

In the first part of the book, the focus was on introducing the conceptual (Transition Studies) and first practical tolls (sustainable innovation) to set the scene to a deeper analysis of the effective role of grassroots innovation in sport for a sustainable future. This chapter opens the second part of the book by analyzing how sport management studies have analyzed the role of and relationship between innovation and sustainability. From a theoretical and practical perspective, the corporate social responsibility (CSR) function seems to be the area of study and application that could better create a relationship between sustainability and innovation in sport. Innovative CSR seems to be the managerial approach that from mainstream organizations and practices could give grassroots sports organizations practical guidelines to design and develop novel solutions for societal needs. The chapter concludes that a different approach (niche) should be considered for grassroots sport organizations.

INTRODUCTION

An organization can be defined as any group of people working together to achieve a common purpose or goal that could not be attained by individuals working separately. If the organization is the hardware, the software is composed of the set of managerial functions. These functions need the coordination of all human, material, technological, and financial resources that the organization exploits to achieve its goals. As introduced by (Covell, Walker, 2013), one way to look at the responsibility of the management, especially in sport industry, is the responsibility for performance. According to this perspective, sport managers are always responsible for the organization's realization of its goals that means that sport management is the responsibility for the performance and success of these organizations. The

DOI: 10.4018/978-1-5225-5475-2.ch017

continuous improvement of performances of sport organizations can depend on a multiple set of factors, especially functions and role as presented by classical studies. For Mintzberg (1980), the performance of the organization depends on how the managers perform their role, and indicate ten key managerial roles. Among these, on the base of the innovative organization definition as a dynamic and learning organization, the most prominent are the role of Liaison (interacting with other organizations); Monitor (receiving information critical for performance) and Disseminator (sharing information within the organization) and Spokesperson (presenting information outside the organization); Entrepreneur (initiating change to improve performance); Disturbance handler (dealing with issues and crises inside and outside of the organization).

Although these basic concepts are still valid today, the landscape for sport organizations has changed and accelerated a shift toward new business models and functions. The most important changes in the sport management landscape has affected the following areas: first, the shift from performance responsibility to shared responsibility for performance (internal vision, engagement of internal stakeholders). Second, the introduction of a dynamic and complex perspective on management and organization summarized in the concept of Sport Management in Transition. Third, the constant pressure to increase the performance though the delivery of better services and products according to evolving quality standard. Fourth, driving continuous improvements toward higher quality standards (compare to ISO 9001: 2015 for the latest two points). This implies that the focus on innovation is an essential need for contemporary sport organizations that want to innovate in terms of services, products and processes. Quality and innovation require flexibility to grow and stay competitive. Fifth, growth and competition depends on the capacity of the organization to stay sustainable, here intended as growing at a rate, and to a size that can be maintained over the long term. It refers to the economic and financial aspect of sustainability.

Finally, the sixth point is the development of integrity as the guiding principle by which all organizational decisions and actions are articulated and activated.

It is evident that, although some words refer to concepts of sustainability, here the approach is purely managerial.

Complexity, sharing and engagement, dynamicity, flexibility, quality and innovation, integrity all of these terms and concepts refer to the paradigm shift that occurred in the second half of the last century also in business and management sciences. Modern contributions to this management thinking came evidently from Systems theory (von Bertanlaffy, 1979), network theory, stakeholder theory (Freeman, 1984), Contingency theory and Learning organization theory (Senge, 1990). The main advantages of this new approach to the firm is that some important concepts guide the development of innovation policies and processes both at the political and business levels. In particular, Systems and network theories recognize the importance of factors and events occurring outside the organization and in the surrounding environment. Stakeholder theory focuses on firm's relationships with many constituent groups, or "stakeholders," that affect and are affected by its decisions. Contingency theory focuses on the firm's capacity to adapt to new situations and requirements. The Learning organization theory focuses on the investment on internal learning processes as the main resource for the growth of the organization and the exploitation or exploration of innovative solutions.

As such, the link between sustainability as the main normative goal also for sport organizations and sport management is not resolved. This perspective otherwise opens the field to the introduction of innovation as the main tool and goal for sport organizations and for the development of a specific research field.

INNOVATION IN SPORT MANAGEMENT STUDIES

In 2016 a special issue of Innovation: Management, Policy and Practice, was dedicated to the role of innovation in sport management (Potts, Ratten, 2016). The aim of the editors and authors was to offer a novel perspective about the role of innovation in sport. The starting conditions are first the recognition that sport is becoming an increasing area of interest to innovation management researchers due to the growth of the sports industry and its impact on other sectors of the economy at the global level. Yet there remains a lack of conceptual and applied analytical understanding of this research area. The second is that sport research can benefit from more attention to the work of innovation scholars in order to create a new sub-discipline of innovation management research. (Ratten & Ferreira, 2016).

In terms of geographical areas, the authors recognize that the majority of researches are from developed countries and that it would be helpful to study how international sport organizations can contribute to sports innovation in the developing world and the impact of resource constraints have on sports innovation. Studies about social innovations in developing countries in terms of sport programs would be interesting, as well as in the inner or internal areas of developed countries.

Thus, sport research can benefit from more attention to the work of innovation scholars in order to create a new sub-discipline of innovation management research. As for innovation management and innovation studies, innovation in sport can be analyzed from different perspectives. First in terms of products and processes. Then in terms of technological or not-technological innovation, or to-market or not-to-market innovation, or in terms of business innovation, sustainable innovation or social innovation.

Potts and Ratten cite many works that have discussed some aspects of innovation in sport, such as *technological innovation* (ICT for sport, social media) (Abeza et al., 2015), *service innovation* (end-user innovation, quality innovation) (Lüthje, Herstatt, & von Hippel, 2005; Damanpour & Aravind, 2012), *product innovation* (both technological and service) *and business model innovation* (professional sport organizations, non-profit organizations, community sport organizations) (Hoeber, Doherty, Hoeber, and Wolfe 2015). They conclude that despite the increased interest in sport innovation by businesses, the current state of research is underdeveloped.

In the special issue edited by Potts and Ratten, there are six papers that deal with sport innovation. The themes introduced in the special issue are theoretical as in the case of 'Sport innovation management: towards a research agenda' by Ratten. Here the author focuses on the future of the sport management and innovation management disciplines by *proposing a new theory called sport innovation*. The main themes found from the existing research are conceptualized as sport sociology, sports knowledge and sports research. This helps to understand how sport innovation is progressing in academia and the core literature about this theme. The other five articles bring to attention more empirical cases, focusing on innovation in service and in non-profit sport organizations like Sport Federations (Winand, Scheerder, Vox and Zintz, 2016); on technological innovation and the role of social media (Santomier, Hogan and Kunz, 2016); on innovation in branding (Brison, Baker and Byon, 2016); on Innovation in production (Gerke, 2016) and the role of clusters and networks to sport organizations; and finally on 'Innovation as clarifications: lessons from bat and ball sports' by Goorha (2016) who discusses the changing values and rules in sports suggesting four major types of innovation that stress the evolution and dynamic nature of sport.

Although there are references to social innovation and non-profit organizations, to dynamic and evolutionary characters of innovation, *there is no reference to innovation oriented towards sustainability*.

The progress on research about innovation and sport studies has been developed in 2017 with the publication on *sport, entrepreneurship and innovation* by the same authors (Ratten, Ferreira, 2017).

Sport innovation takes place in a variety of different forms depending on the context. They propose a useful theoretical framework for analyzing sport innovations to focus on usage, value, risk, psychology and image. This helps to understand the reasons why innovation takes place in a sport context and to evaluate how it adapts to the sport context. By focusing on each area (strategy, leadership, service, process), this approach provides a structure for future evaluation of sport innovations.

What emerges is extremely interesting for our purposes. The evolution of the field still have high levels of incremental development, especially if we consider the possibility to introduce sustainability and the role and positive effect of grassroots innovations for professional sports and for the sport context as a whole.

In fact, all the discourses about the innovation policy in sport and the innovation development proceed from the micro-firm perspective, that in this case it is not the one of the niche as in transition studies or innovation studies. It is, as clearly stated by the authors, the business and management perspective (as usual). From this reading, three implications descend and orient the approach to the topic. First, the role of sport innovation policy is essential for the development of a new agenda. Second, the micro perspective that focuses on usage innovation and related themes for management success such as reasons, value incentives, risk reasons, physiological factors, and image incentives. Third, innovation is essential for sport organizations to support their continued success in terms of growth and competitiveness.

Thus, the development of a theoretical framework in sport innovation could provide guidance to managers about identifying significant future avenues.

As the authors conclude, the growing recognition of the importance of innovation to society is a positive fact because it highlights the need for an agenda for sport innovation related research. These important works confirm that there is room for contributing to the development of the agenda and the related research field of sport innovation from the bottom up or, in academic terms, from other disciplines helping the field accrue its knowledge for future challenges.

The first opportunity to contribute comes from the level of sport innovation policy. This has been led by international government organizations that are concerned with sport in terms of how to monitor the integration of innovation into sport (Ratten, 2017), but they should also be concerned about how to support the role of sport in society for the creation and diffusion of more effective inclusive and responsible impacts. Cases like Vancouver and London Olympic games, and the Soccer world Cup in Rio 2016 are examples of the development of sustainable policies and strategies in global sport events.

These important and seminal contributions to the sport innovation's research field have found a confirmation by a recent search on Scopus *et similia* about the lack of research on some topics, especially on the key intertwining themes such as forms of sustainable innovation in sport management.

SUSTAINABILITY IN SPORT STUDIES

A latest search on Scopus in March 2017 showed that there were not so many articles citing at least one of the sustainability keywords chosen for the query (sustainability, sustainab*, CSR, corporate social responsibility, responsib+*). First, a search for articles on sport management using as keywords "Innovation" and "sport management" gave 20 results of which only one had the two keywords (Repo, 2012).

Then a search for "sustainable innovation" and "sport management" gave for abstract, keywords and title zero results. Then, a query for "sustainability" and "innovation" and "sport" gave no results. Then, the same search on ISI Web of Knowledge, limiting the search from 2011 on "Sustainability/le innovation" and "sport management" gave no results. Another query on "innovation" and "sport management" gave similar results to Scopus, while for "grassroots innovations" and "sport management" gave no results, and for "grassroots" and "sport management" gave not interesting results. This exercise was done just to have a quick overview of the key words discussed in this work. Although not scientific, it confirms in its way the recently growing and *expanding field of research on innovation and sport management, and the wide room for contributions from other fields and approaches interested in the topic.* The query was limited by the voluntarily general definition of innovation and related choice of words used for the query. More details in the search or different keywords should have probably given a wider perspective on the vast topic.

Anyhow, the scope here was to find academically relevant (mainstream) works citing these few key words. A search on Google Scholar and other websites (journals, publishers' web sites for articles and books or book chapters) gave a different perspective and a wider spectrum of results, much more interesting for our purposes. From the sustainability perspective, the link between sustainability and sport studies has developed in many research areas:

- Sport for development and sport for society (social capital, gender equality, social policies, volunteerism, sport organizations and citizenship, education, health issues, crime prevention, immigration) (Coalter, 2007; Edwards, 2015; Bruening et al., 2015),
- Culture politics and sport (immigration, racism, gender issues) (Whannel, 2008),
- Grassroots sports and elite sports (Donnelly, Kidd, 2015),
- Inclusive sports (Hums, Wolff, 2015)
- Sport and management: CSR, responsiveness and citizenship (Filizoz, Fisne, 2011; Walker, Parent, 2010); non-profit (Winand et al., 2016); environmental sustainability (Trendafilova et al., 2013); social entrepreneurship (Ratten, 2014); event-sport tourism and social impacts (Gibson et al. 2012; Richard et al., 2013)

For our purposes – to link sustainability, grassroots innovation and sport organizations - the following paragraphs will focus on the latest area, the relationship between Sport Management and Sustainability in order to analyze this relationship. It will emerge that the most comprehensive way sport organizations have tried to link empirically sustainability and (innovative) managerial practices is through the strategic and operational tool of (neo-classic) corporate social responsibility (CSR).

THE SPORT MANAGEMENT PERSPECTIVE ON SUSTAINABILITY: THE ROLE OF CSR

Sustainability in sport management has been especially studied from the strategic perspective of Corporate Social Responsibility (CSR). This approach introduces some questions: first, why CSR? What is the relationship between CSR and innovation? How do organizations contribute to sustainability transition through CSR? To answer these question is essential to introduce the main conceptual and practical aspects of the CSR concept.

The relationship between CSR and specific socially responsible actions has evolved in the last decades: from concepts like patronage to those of respect for the law, recognition and development of the rights of workers, improvement of the production cycle processes, stakeholder involvement and participation, up to compliance, transparency and accountability. The debate on CSR has consequently led to a progressive rethinking of the goals and objectives of a company in the attempt to integrate both environmental and social instances of stakeholders in corporate strategies and policies focusing on a re-conceptualization of enterprise value and relative mode of measurement. Various theories have had an impact on the development of the debate and following actions of CSR: from the Shareholder Value Approach (Friedman, 1970) - for which the firm creates value when maximizes the wealth of those providing the risk capital - to the Stakeholder Approach (Freeman, 1984, 2007) - for which the company creates value when is able to develop efficient interactions with multiple stakeholders and meet their expectations - up to the latest evolution of the CSR concept, that is Corporate Shared Value (Porter,Kramer, 2006 and 2011) – for which an organization creates value for all the stakeholders, and in doing so it also creates profits on a specific innovation designed and developed to respond to the needs of society.

The first definition of CSR was given by Bowen in 1953. Bowen referred to the social responsibilities of businessmen as the obligations to pursue those policies, to make those decisions, and to follow those lines of action desirable in terms of objectives and values to society. For Drucker (1954) Public Responsibility was part of the eight corporate objectives same: managers had to consider the impact of corporate actions on society. Carroll (1979, 1991) defined the concept of CSR as the continued commitment of businesses to behave ethically and contribute to economic development, while improving the quality of life of its employees and their families, of the local community and society as a whole. He elaborated the seminal concept of the CSR pyramid. According to this model, CSR is composed by four categories: 1) Discretionary-philanthropic responsibility: voluntary commitment to improve the well-being and quality of life of stakeholders; 2) Ethical responsibilities: respect for ethical values, doing what is right and fair, and avoiding harm to others; 3) Legal Responsibilities: obey the law and rules; 4) Economic Responsibility: to create profit. For Carroll the economic and social responsibilities are required or imposed by society, while ethical responsibilities are expected, and discretionary are desired.

In 1984, Freeman changed the approach with the introduction of the shared value concept with stakeholders. The stakeholders are those who can influence or are influenced by the company and that the company must take into account even if they do not directly affect profits. The scope of the theory was to offer to the government of the organization the support of the management of multiple relations that an organization must take into account in order to pursue its objectives (Tortora, Corsini, 2014). So the theory reaches a twofold goal: making the interests of the various stakeholders compatible, while proposing a method of governance for the multiple relations with them.

Since the beginning of the millennium, the scenario has evolved again towards a progressive redefinition of the relationship between businesses and organizations and the context in which they operate. It has developed a school of multi-stakeholder thinking, supporter of the balance among the reasons of profit/efficiency and fairness. In fact, between 2006 and 2011, Porter and Kramer pushed beyond the concept of CSR and introduced the Corporate Shared Value concept. According to the authors, the new competitiveness of enterprises is based on the value created by companies that respond to the needs and expectations of society. The shared value is a new and effective tool of economic success because social progress aligns with the economic value of firms. With CSR, therefore, the company exceeds government compliance to go into the territory of voluntary and transparent self-regulation forms. It is a volunteer and self-referential model that allows and is based on the multi-stakeholder approach for which the company is able to establish trust relationships and transparency towards the plurality of its stakeholders (ibidem).

The term stakeholder is a wider term than that of shareholder o stockholder, those who hold the shares of companies. It was introduced for the first time in 1963 in a research at the Stanford Research Institute. That definition referred to stakeholders as those groups without whose contribution the company could not survive. It is important to note that the term also encompasses the concept of risk. in fact, it is the presence of the business risk that introduces the idea of significant stakeholders, those who are exposed voluntarily or involuntarily to the risk that derives from the firm (Zamagni, 2013). Other definitions refer, for example, to individual or groups of individuals who can influence or be influenced by business activities and who have a legitimate interest or a legitimate claim on the company (Freeman, 1988). Clarkson (1995) categorized stakeholders into primary and secondary, according to different interests. The primaries are those whose involvement is critical to the survival of the organization (those who have a contractual relationship with the company). Secondary stakeholders are those that shall include those whose involvement is not essential to the survival but affect or are affected by the company itself. This includes also social stakeholders - those who, while not directly participating in the economic management of the company, are interested in the consequences on their environment and activities. In fact, firms and organizations are embedded in networks of social relationships (interactions and exchange relations) that should influence and impact, positively and negatively, directly and indirectly, their life and, in business terms, growth and competitiveness. This perspective requires an efficient management of this complex system of relationships strategically determinant for the continuation of its activities. It follows that if the term governance refers to the ability to lead an organization with an efficient management of resources and relationships, then CSR should be a form of extended governance to shareholders and stakeholders. Introduction to the efficient management of the external relationships is the identification of stakeholder, including the territory (Tortora, Corsini, 2014).

Innovative CSR

Management and economics approaches relegate innovation to the idea of main tool for reaching a competitive position in the market. Strategic CSR seems to move in that direction. Is CSR innovative? On the other hand, is there room for an innovative CSR? Porter and Kramer (2006) suggested that their concept of CSR - CSV, Corporate Shared Value - is a source of innovation as well as of competitive advantage and value creation. In the last years, there has not been too much attention paid to the fit between CSR and innovation (Louche et al., 2010; MacGregor et al., 2010) and it is still not clear how to derive value-generating activities from CSR. Anyhow, it seems that the CSR concept, still debated, has developed till the point to embrace the concept of 'innovation driver', showing the passage from a risk management approach to a more progressive and entrepreneurial one oriented toward the identification of strategic opportunities for all the stakeholders (MacGregor et al., 2010).

Hockerts and Morsing (2007) identify four themes that link innovation to CSR. The first is *corporate social innovation* (Kanter, 1999) for which companies use social issues as the learning laboratories for identifying unmet societal needs and for developing new solutions for potential new niches of the market. The second is the *Bottom of the Pyramid (BoP)*, for which it is possible to create value satisfying the needs of the poor living in developing countries, thus creating profits and contributing to the development of the poor (Prahalad and Hart, 2002). Third is *social entrepreneurship* that regards the exploration and exploitation of opportunities to create public goods. Fourth is eco- or *environmental innovation*.

Although contributions like this show the many relationships there are and that there should be between innovation and CSR, there is evidence that only a minority of firms consider CSR solutions as innovative (Louche et al., 2010; Hockerts 2008), ad that there is not a clear definition of innovative CSR. Preuss (2010) defined innovative CSR as an alternative conceptualization of strategic CSR. It consists of technological and organizational CSR innovation. Innovative CSR differs from other definitions because it can address external stakeholder demands, offering an opportunity to play an active role in the innovation process. Thus, while strategic CSR (innovation) built on the business case for sustainability can be defined as conducting existing business operations in a more responsible fashion (exploitation more than exploration), CSR innovation develops new business models (exploration more than exploitation) for solving social and environmental problems.

From our perspective, it is interesting to find the areas in which the potential link with society and communities or territories enter in the debate. As in the case of innovation in sport studies in the previous paragraphs, communities enter the management/ business debate on CSR as external stakeholders that are positioned in the society area. These stakeholders, usually defined as secondary stakeholders, such as schools, sport teams, cultural and sport associations, are engaged in activities such as charity/ donations, corporate volunteerism, sponsorships, time banking, social auditing, local employment, community engagement programs and community projects. The policies of engagement are usually values-driven in the sense that the organization's CSR strategy and policy is set on the sharing of values with its community more than on the creation of value (customer-oriented or supply chain). It also means that the CSR strategy (formal or informal, explicit or implicit) drives innovation. MacGregor et al. (2010) propose a model for Small Medium Enterprises (SMEs) in which CSR is an innovation process to develop along four areas: the *process and organization spheres*, which relate to the firm's structure and actions, and *the relationship and social spheres*. The two latter are the most interesting for our analysis. The relationship represents the degree of interactions of an organization with its stakeholders, and it is important because the degree of innovation closely links to existing good relationships with the (local) stakeholders. Good relationships open communication channels that are essential for the dissemination of ideas and the selection of potential innovations. The *social sphere* represents areas of opportunities for the development of societal innovations. Moreover, the social sphere or context can impose change on organizations. This approach (Lam, 2000; Preuss, 2010), although limited to the institutional context (national institutional frameworks that surround businesses), has the advantage to focus on three aspects:

1. The social embeddedness of the firm,
2. The relationships with firm's stakeholders defined as CSO - Civil Society Organizations, as those actors who can impact through dialogue the direction for an innovative CSR,
3. The process of diffusion of innovation, where differences in societal expectations may make forms of innovative CSR suitable for a few societies, not for all.

In conclusion, organizations might develop an innovative CSR strategy if they are oriented toward resolving societal problems emanating from society and usually expressed by unmet needs of secondary stakeholders. These stakeholders are located in specific territories and belong to local communities that surround those organizations and with which they develop a continuous dialogue or program of engagement for an efficient delivery of novel solutions.

INNOVATIVE CSR AND GRASSROOTS SPORT INNOVATIONS

What is the role of sport in society? If sport does have a role to play to resolve in an innovative way unmet societal needs, then sport organizations and sport management should develop their strategies in accordance to CSR in both theoretical and practical ways. Since the role of sport in society is growing as well as its direct and indirect effects on people and places, CSR's concepts such as responsibility, transparency, accountability become key managerial concepts to manage effectively organizations, resources and processes while at the same time creating value for all the stakeholders. Thus, sport organizations have to develop CSR and try to implement it in many ways (Babiak and Wolfe, 2006, 2009; Walker and Kent, 2009). Smith and Westerbeck (2007) have identified seven unique characteristics of sport CSR that descend from the consideration of sport organizations identity and role as unique in society. The first is the *media distribution and communication power of sport* and the following capacity to communicate CSR activities to a wide audience. Second, sport has a *youth appeal* so that it can engage easily children and young people. Third, sport CSR can deliver *positive health impacts* through events and programs. Fourth, sport CSR *help group participation and social interaction*. Fifth, sport CSR improve *cultural understanding and integration*. Sixth, it enhances *environmental and sustainability awareness*. Seventh, participation in CSR programs provides *immediate gratification*.

These seven points for sport CSR highlight the wide extension of sport social impact and the potential benefits of novel solutions sport organizations could develop and deliver for the societal unmet needs.

As in the case of strategic CSR and innovative CSR for businesses, CSR in sport organizations develop especially in formal and explicit ways in professional sports on the pressing instances of the International Olympic Committee or National Olympic Committee and then of National Federations or by the proactive and voluntary activity of established professional sport teams with a wide international audience. This the case for examples of Italian Federations that started considering CSR strategies and related toll such as sustainability reporting or social balance after the Italian Olympic Committee developed its first sustainability reporting in 2014. On the opposite, global sport teams and brand such as the Italian soccer team FC Juventus has been the first to report on their CSR strategies and sustainability impacts, as the Manchester United in UK. These examples are exception to a general underestimation of the potentialities of sport and sport CSR as innovation drivers for the benefits of society.

Grassroots Sport Innovations as Niches for Societal Innovations

A completely different experience is the one of grassroots sport organizations. In the following paragraphs, three cases from the Italian grassroots sport system will be introduced to report on the innovative solutions for society from the bottom.

Before analyzing in detail the three cases, a presentation of the potential benefits of developing innovative solutions with grassroots sport organizations is essential for the continuity of the analysis.

The sport sector is unique, as unique are its organizations and their roles. Because of this, in this complex and evolutionary landscape, sport is influenced and affected by trends of change at different levels. These transformations affect the profile and operatively of sport organizations, both professional and grassroots. The growth of competitiveness or new members or supporters, the shrink of private and public finances at many levels, the need for a professionalization of volunteers and investments in education and training for all the personnel, the reduction of volunteers, the aging of the population, and so on are all factors that influence structure, behaviors and results of sport organizations, especially nonprofit and grassroots organizations. Beyond these risks and challenges, the responsible function of sport for society and its social and environmental impacts constitute a capital to build new opportunities of development for both grassroots sport organizations and the community and the territory. The supply of services to communities in education, social integration, prevention, health, social inclusion pass through the organization and management of sport activities in a professional way. To make these functions strategic for their growth and beneficial for society, grassroots sport organizations have to develop new management tools to effectively apply their sustainability principles and communicate their social quality to all their stakeholders. In this sense, grassroots sport organizations need to acquire, include and develop sustainability management principles and tools to create and diffuse social innovation for the social value of all. CSR principles, strategies and tools (e.g. the social balance) or managerial tools like sustainability guidelines (ISO 26000) or responsible innovation certification schemes, can help grassroots sport organizations (GRSO) plan, manage, control their complex system of relationships with their stakeholders (the community) and the territory. GRSO as the main actors of the civic economy should search for their development path sharing their sustainability principles and practices especially in innovative participatory processes. GRSO should transmit and disseminate values of social inclusion, integrity, integration, fairness, loyalty, solidarity. They should be able to engage and involve their stakeholder not only in the physical or sport activity, but also in the active participation to the organization and programs, with a special interest for those aimed at creating positive impacts. The realization of positive impacts requires a strong cultural identity, clear vision and mission both oriented toward sustainability, an effective coherence and management of decisions and behaviors. These are the basic pillars to build on a positive transformation of the organization and of its processes. The sustainability transition of GRSO, to be effective requires a profound transformation and transition of the organization, structure and processes. A sport innovative CSR system (strategies, tools) may support GRSO. The investment on new organizational models and processes should not be sufficient to create the conditions for innovative solutions for the benefits of all. The style of the management should be marked by collaboration and cooperation with all internal and external stakeholders. Developing partnerships with other actors such as local governments, sport federations, third sector's agents, firms, banks and so on will increase the possibilities for novel solutions to scale up and create more impact through learning opportunities and networking. Innovative CSR could provide GRSO with the right means to reduce the weight of financial constraints and costs in order to free resources in support of those value utilities that are necessary for the creation of social value. The capacity to scale up novel solutions and the opportunity to disseminate them through networking should be amplified by the unique role of sport as driver of contaminating the values of equality, integration, and fairness in society.

CONCLUSION

The relation between sustainability, as the main normative goal for sport organizations aimed at developing positive impacts in society, and innovative sport management studies is not resolved yet. The latest developments and progress show that there is room for different contributions coming from other disciplines, referring to different theoretical frameworks and applying different but complementary approaches. This perspective otherwise opens the field to the introduction of sustainable grassroots innovation as the main tool and goal for sport organizations (profit and nonprofit) and for the development of a specific research field that is grassroots innovation in sport. If grassroots innovation is a dynamic, complex process that needs to be managed in order to drive innovation, growth and diffusion for the benefits of society from the bottom, a possible solution to link grassroots sport organizations novel solutions to the latest development in sport management and sustainability is to focus on the specific innovative character and identity of CSR, that is innovative CSR as a values-driven innovative process and strategic management tool.

REFERENCES

Abeza, G., OReilly, N., Seguin, B., & Nzindukiyimana, O. (2015). Social media scholarship in sport management research: A critical review. *Journal of Sport Management*, *29*(6), 601–618. doi:10.1123/JSM.2014-0296

Bowen, H. R. (1953). *Social Responsibility of Businessman*. New York: Harper.

Carroll, A. B. (1979). 1979, A three-dimensional conceptual model of corporate social performance. *Academy of Management Review*, *4*(4), 497–505.

Carroll, A. B. (1991). 1991, The pyramid of corporate social responsibility: Toward the Moral Management of Organization Stakeholders. *Business Horizons*, *34*(4), 39–48. doi:10.1016/0007-6813(91)90005-G

Clarkson, M. B. (1995). A stakeholder framework for analyzing and evaluating Corporate Social Responsibility. *Academy of Management Review*, *20*(1), 92–117.

Coulter, F. (2007). *A Wider Social Role for Sport. Who's keeping the score?* London: Routledge.

Covell, D., & Walker, S. (2013). *Managing sport organizations. Responsibility for performance*. London: Routledge.

Damanpour, F., & Aravind, D. (2012). Managerial innovation: Conceptions, processes and antecedents. *Management and Organization Review*, *8*(02), 423–454. doi:10.1111/j.1740-8784.2011.00233.x

Donnelly, P., & Kidd, B. (2015). Two Solitudes: grass-roots sport and high-performance sport in Canada. In R. Bailey & M. Talbot (Eds.), *Elite Sport and Sport-for-All. Bridging the Two Cultures?* London: Routledge.

Drucker, P. F. (1954). *The Practice of Management*. New York: Harper and Row Publishers.

Freeman, R. E. (1984). *Strategic Management: A stakeholder Approach*. Boston: Pitman.

Freeman. (2007). *Managing for Stakeholders*. University of Virginia, Darden School of Business.

Friedman, M. (1970, Sept. 13). The social responsibility of business is to increase its profits. *New York Times Magazine*, 32-3, 122-6.

Hoeber, L., Doherty, A., Hoeber, O., & Wolfe, R. (2015). The nature of innovation in community sport organizations. *European Sport Management Quarterly*, *15*(5), 518–534. doi:10.1080/16184742.2015.1085070

Hums, M. A., & Wolff, E. A. The Paralympic Movement and sport-for-all: elite, recreational and inclusive sport for development. In R. Bailey & M. Talbot (Eds.), *Elite Sport and Sport-for-All. Bridging the Two Cultures?. Academic Press.*

Louche, C., & Idowu, S. (Eds.). (2010). *Innovative CSR: From risk management to value creation.* Greenleaf Publishing.

Louche, C., Idowu, S. O., & Leal Filho, W. (2010). Innovation in corporate social responsibility: how innovative is it?. *Innovative CSR: From Risk Management to Value Creation*, 284

Luthje, C., Herstatt, C., & von Hippel, E. (2005). User-innovators and local information: The case of mountain biking. *Research Policy*, *34*(6), 951–965. doi:10.1016/j.respol.2005.05.005

MacGregor, S. P., Fontrodona, J., & Hernandez, J. (2010). *Towards a sustainable innovation model for small enterprises. In Innovative CSR: From Risk Management to Value Creation* (pp. 305–330). Sheffield, UK: Greenleaf Publishing. doi:10.9774/GLEAF.978-1-907643-26-2_16

Mintzberg, H. (1980). Structure in 5's: A Synthesis of the Research on Organization Design. *Management Science*, *26*(3), 322–341. doi:10.1287/mnsc.26.3.322

Porter, M. E., & Kramer, M. (2011, Jan.). Creating Shared Value. *Harvard Business Review*, 62–77.

Porter, M. E., & Kramer, M. R. (2006). Strategy and Society: The link between competitive advantage and CSR. *Harvard Business Review*, *84*(12). PMID:17183795

Potts, J., & Ratten, V. (2016). Sports innovation: Introduction to the special section. In Innovation: Management. *Policy & Practice*, *18*(3), 233–237. doi:10.1080/14479338.2016.1241154

Preuss, L. (2011). Innovative CSR: A framework for anchoring corporate social responsibility in the innovation literature. *Journal of Corporate Citizenship*, *2011*(42), 17–33. doi:10.9774/GLEAF.4700.2011.su.00004

Ratten, F. (2017). *Sport, Entrepreneurship and Innovation.* Routledge.

Ratten, V. (2010). Developing a theory of sport-based entrepreneurship. *Journal of Management & Organization*, *16*(04), 573–582. doi:10.1017/S1833367200001930

Ratten, V. (2011). Sport-based entrepreneurship: Towards a new theory of entrepreneurship and sport management. *The International Entrepreneurship and Management Journal*, *7*(1), 57–69. doi:10.1007/s11365-010-0138-z

Ratten, V. (2011a). Social entrepreneurship and innovation in sports. *International Journal of Social Entrepreneurship and Innovation*, *1*(1), 42–54. doi:10.1504/IJSEI.2011.039811

Ratten, V. (2011b). Sport-based entrepreneurship: Towards a new theory of entrepreneurship and sport management. *The International Entrepreneurship and Management Journal*, *7*(1), 57–69. doi:10.1007/s11365-010-0138-z

Ratten, V. (2012). Sports entrepreneurship: Towards a conceptualisation. *International Journal of Entrepreneurial Venturing*, *4*(1), 1–18. doi:10.1504/IJEV.2012.044814

Ratten, V. (2016). Sport innovation management: towards a research agenda. In Innovation: Management. *Policy & Practice*, *18*(3), 238–250. doi:10.1080/14479338.2016.1244471

Ratten, V., & Ferreira, J. J. (Eds.). (2016). *Sport entrepreneurship and innovation*. Routledge.

Repo, P. (2012). Users as innovators of new sports equipment and services. *Innovation Vision 2020: Sustainable growth, Entrepreneurship, and Economic Development - Proceedings of the 19th International Business Information Management Association Conference*, *4*, 2219-2225.

Senge, P. (1990). *The fifth discipline: the art and practice of the learning organization*. Academic Press.

Senge, P. M., & Sterman, J. D. (1992). Systems thinking and organizational learning: Acting locally and thinking globally in the organization of the future. *European Journal of Operational Research*, *59*(1), 137–150. doi:10.1016/0377-2217(92)90011-W

Tortora, M., & Corsini, F. (2013). From society to communities: new geopolitical scenarios for sustainable business strategies. In J. M. Munoz (Ed.), *Handbook on the Geopolitics of Business*. Northampton, MA: Edward Elgar. doi:10.4337/9780857939753.00026

Walters, G. (2012). Managing social responsibility in sport. In *Managing Sport Business. An introduction*. London: Routledge.

Winand, M., Vos, S., Claessens, M., Thibaut, E., & Scheerder, J. (2014). A unified model of nonprofit sport organizations performance: Perspectives from the literature. *Managing Leisure*, *19*(2), 121–150. doi:10.1080/13606719.2013.859460

Winand, M., Vos, S., Zintz, T., & Scheerder, J. (2013). Determinants of service innovation: A typology of sports federations. *International Journal of Sport Management and Marketing*, *13*(1/2), 55–73. doi:10.1504/IJSMM.2013.055194

Winand, S., Scheerder, J., Vos, S., & Zintz, T. (2016). Vox and Zintz, 2016. Do non-profit sport organisations innovate? Types and preferences of service innovation within regional sport federations. Innovation: Management. *Policy & Practice*, *18*(3), 289–308. doi:10.1080/14479338.2016.1235985

Zamagni, S. (2013). *Impresa responsabile e mercato civile*. Bologna: Il Mulino.

This research was previously published in Grassroots Sustainability Innovations in Sports Management edited by Marco Tortora, pages 57-76, copyright year 2018 by Business Science Reference (an imprint of IGI Global).

Chapter 18
Perceived Importance and Extent of Implementation of Volunteer Management Practices:
Comparison Between National Sports Associations and Event Management Companies

Huijing Huang
Nanyang Technological University, Singapore

Wai Cheong Eugene Chew
Nanyang Technological University, Singapore

Koon Teck Koh
Nanyang Technological University, Singapore

ABSTRACT

Effective volunteer management practices have been shown to be linked to performance, commitment, satisfaction, and retention of volunteers. In addition, it has been shown that organisational contexts are crucial to successful implementation of such practices. Using a volunteer management framework comprising four main stages of management practices (concept, planning, implementation, review), the volunteer management practices of non-profit national sports associations are examined against those of for-profit event management companies. Findings reveal some differences in the level of perceived importance, and the extent of implementation between non-profit national sports associations and for-profit event management companies. Themes that emerged from the content analysis of the interviews conducted with key management staff in the organisations support the notion that the reasons underlying the perceived importance of volunteer management practices are associated with volunteer retention, and with support organisations' objectives. Implications for decision-makers are discussed.

DOI: 10.4018/978-1-5225-5475-2.ch018

INTRODUCTION

The launch of the Committee on Sporting Singapore (CoSS) Report in 2001 was a critical milestone in the development of sport in Singapore, and the current vibrancy of the sport industry and the growth in sport volunteers can arguably be attributed to it. The committee added the strategic thrust of sports industry development to the existing two strategic thrusts of promoting sports to the masses (sports for all), and grooming elite athletes to achieve accolades in the international sports arenas (sports excellence). Initially focusing on the hosting of marque sports events, the economic spinoffs generated by the sport industry are expected to contribute to the gross domestic product of the nation. For almost one and a half decade after the launch of the CoSS Report in 2001, sport in Singapore has gain greater prominence and popularity. This is evidenced by the number of marquee events hosted by Singapore. These include the inaugural Youth Olympic Games 2010, Hongkong and Shanghai Banking Corporation Women's Champions, Barclays Singapore Open, Aviva Ironman 70.3 Singapore Triathlon, and the Li-Ning Singapore Open. With the upcoming official opening of the new S$1.33 billion Singapore Sports Hub in the second half of 2014, more world class events are set to be featured. For example, Singapore won the right to host the prestigious 2014-2018 Women's Tennis Association Championships under a record-setting five-year agreement (World Sport Group, 2012). The World Club 10s Rugby, and the Asean Football Federation Suzuki Cup will also be held in the Singapore Sports Hub. In addition, participation in sporting events such as the Standard Chartered Singapore Marathon, Sundown Marathon, Vertical Marathon, Singapore International Triathlon, and Overseas Chinese Banking Corporation (OCBC) Cycle Singapore has grown over the years. For example, the OCBC Cycle Singapore event began in 2009 with 5,400 riders, attracted more than 10,000 riders in 2011 (Channel NewsAsia, 2009; TODAY, 2010). With the number of riders rising to 11,500 in 2013, the organizer decided to cap the number of participants at 12,000 for the 2014 edition for safety reasons and to ensure that riders have an enjoyable race experience (Channel NewsAsia, 2013). Another event that has seen phenomenal growth is the Standard Chartered Singapore Marathon which was started in 2002 with 6,000 runners, grew to 21,000 runners in 2005, attracted 60,000 participants in 2010, and recorded 54,000 participants in 2013 (Singapore Sports Council, 2006, 2011, 2013).

The contribution of volunteers towards the success of such sporting events, and to sport in general, is getting more substantial and crucial. At the 2010 Singapore Youth Olympic Games, over 45,000 volunteers were engaged to help ensure that the world-class event run smoothly (MyPaper, 2010). The involvement of over 4,000 volunteers in staging the 2013 edition of the Standard Chartered Singapore Marathon also signified the importance of volunteers in sport. The increasing need for volunteer means that sport organisations (e.g., national sports associations which are the national governing bodies of their respective sports) and sport-related companies (e.g., events management companies) that engage volunteers face the challenge of attracting, managing and retaining volunteers. At the same time, it is important that they ensure that volunteers have a positive experience. Recognising the need to better manage volunteers in sport, and to make the best use of this pool of human capital, Sport Singapore (formerly known as Singapore Sports Council) and the Ministry of Culture, Community and Youth (formerly known as Ministry of Community Development, Youth and Sports) included developing a sports volunteer framework as one of the recommendations in the Vision 2030 Report (Singapore Sports Council, 2012). The aim is to create a high standard in sport volunteerism as part of the capabilities development plan supporting the Vision 2030 by working with the National Volunteer & Philanthropy

Centre (NVPC) and other relevant organisations. Vision 2030 is a joint project led by Sport Singapore and the Ministry of Culture, Community and Youth with active participation from the public, people and private sectors. It sought to set policy directions for sport through an "exploration of public thinking on the value that sport brought to their lives, what they would change in our sports system and how sport could best serve Singapore" (Singapore Sports Council, 2012, p. 1).

In sports organisations, volunteers can be seen as an asset in supporting organisational objectives. Sport volunteers make up for more than one quarter of the total volunteers in Australia (in 2000) and England (in 2002), and one-fifth in Canada (in 2000), with 130 million, 1.2 billion and 167million total volunteer hours contributed to sport in each of these countries respectively. This is equivalent to 77,000 to 720,000 full-time paid job, representing a significant savings in manpower costs for sports (Cuskelly, Hoye, & Auld, 2006). For Singapore, sport volunteers made up 8% of the total number of volunteers in 2002 (National Volunteer Centre, 2002). However, the latest available information from the study conducted by NVPC in 2004 showed that although the overall volunteer participation rate has increased to 15.2% from 14.9% in 2002, sport volunteers only accounted for 3% of the total number of volunteers contributing 1.05 million hours to sport or S$22.38 million in economic value (National Volunteer & Philanthropy Centre, 2005). Compared to 2002, there is a shift away from volunteering in activities for sports/recreation. The study also found that dissatisfaction in volunteering, on the whole, arises from volunteer management issues and poorly organized activities and the lack of adequate appreciation. In a subsequent study on Institutions of a Public Character (IPCs) conducted by the NVPC (National Volunteer & Philanthropy Centre, 2007b), IPCs that engaged volunteers responded that the top two management issues faced by them were the lack of commitment from volunteers, and the inability to sustain volunteering interest and retaining volunteers. IPCs are organisations approved by the Commissioner of Charities to receive tax-deductible donations (i.e., donors are given tax deduction for donations made to these organisations), and half of the national sports associations in Singapore are approved IPCs. One of the main recommendations from the study was to pay more attention to volunteer management. With more large-scale sports events coming on stream coupled with the drive towards higher levels of sports participation, a corresponding increased need for sport volunteers in Singapore is anticipated. In addition, a more informed public expects organisations to be more professional in the way they manage volunteers. Therefore, this present study aimed to examine volunteer management practices in organisations that engage sport volunteers to understand better the state of volunteer management in sports organisations and sport-related private enterprises, and how sport volunteer satisfaction as well as volunteer retention can be enhanced.

To manage volunteers effectively, the human resource management (HRM) approach to managing employees in large for-profit organisations to attain operational excellence and improve business outcomes has been promoted by government agencies such as those in Australia, England and New Zealand (Cuskelly et al., 2006). The Australian Sports Commission's Volunteer Management Programme, and Sport England's Volunteer Investment Programme, and Running Sport programme developed by Sport England and Sport and Recreation New Zealand (SPARC) all employ a HRM system of planning, recruitment, selection or screening, orientation, training, support and supervision, and recognition practices in the management of volunteers. In Singapore, the NVPC (formerly known as National Volunteer Centre) adopts a four-stage volunteer management system—concept, planning, implementation and review—that incorporates all the HRM practices mentioned above with the addition of "performance review and appraisal" and "assessment of programme" in the review stage (see Table 1).

Table 1. NVPC volunteer management framework

Stages	Volunteer Management Practices
1) Concept Stage (CS)	a) Has clearly defined vision, mission and goals for the volunteers
	b) Assessed volunteer needs
	c) Designed a budget for volunteer involvement
2) Planning Stage (PS)	a) Has written job description & policies
	b) Has a recruitment plan and procedure for volunteers
	c) Designed database and record keeping system for managing volunteers'information, activities, hours etc
	d) Identified potential risks faced by volunteers and ensuring that these risks are minimised
3) Implementation Stage (IS)	a) Has a screening procedure to identify suitable volunteers
	b) Conducted orientation and training for volunteers
	c) Supervised volunteers
	d) Has recognition activities for volunteers
4) Review Stage (RS)	a) Reviewed performance/ reasons for exit of volunteers
	b) Assessed impact of volunteer programme

It is modeled after the Investing in Volunteers standard which is the United Kingdom quality standard for organisations that involve volunteers (Investing in Volunteers, 2005). The adoption of such practices are linked to performance, commitment, satisfaction of volunteers and hence, retention of volunteers (Cuskelly et al., 2006). Hager and Brudney (2004) found that specific practices such as training, development and screening of volunteers to ensure suitability have an impact on retention rates. In major sporting events, volunteer management practices have an impact on volunteer satisfaction, in particular in relation to communication with, and recognition of, volunteers (Johnston, Twynam, & Farrell, 2000).

The NVPC defined a volunteer as one who makes a considered personal choice to offer, share and commit one's time, energy, skills, talents, experiences and/or expertise to programmes that benefit/serve the community or society (National Volunteer Centre, 2002). Volunteers may differ in participation on the basis of free choice, remuneration, structure in which volunteering occur and intended beneficiaries (Cnaan, Handy, & Wadsworth, 1996). Cnaan et al. developed a continuum for each of these four dimensions in order to distinguish between what they termed as 'pure' and broadly defined volunteers. Pure volunteer tend to be narrowly defined (e.g., has free choice to be involved; no remuneration; conducted within a formal organisational, no connection to the beneficiaries). The NVPC defines volunteer more broadly, and is cognizant that volunteers are often provided with reimbursements for out-of-pocket expenses such as transport, refreshments, and that certain costs and resources such as training and development, work space, staff time, and recognition gifts are required (National Volunteer & Philanthropy Centre, 2012). Sports volunteers are defined as those taking part in roles undertaken to support, arrange and/or run organised sport and physical activity. This definition is extended to coaches, instructors, referees or umpires, committee members or administrators, scorers or timekeepers, medical personnel and other roles (Australian Bureau of Statistics, 2002).

Organisational context has been identified by extensive research in HRM as an important factor in determining effective HRM practices. For example, findings of a research by Purcell (1999) indicated that the organisational context is crucial to the successful implementation of strategic management practices, and that certain practices are only effective in particular environments. Hence, to test whether HRM practices found to be successfully implemented in large for-profit organisations are applicable in different organisations, researchers (Fenwick, 2005; Wright & McMahan, 1992) have advocated that more studies need to be conducted outside of the typical context of large for-profit organisations in which majority of research were situated. Research on the effective implementation of HRM-based volunteer management practices in non-profit and volunteer-dependent organisations has received scant attention. In one such studies, apart from other investigations conducted, senior management of 220 non-profit IPCs from various sectors were asked by the NVPC to rate the extent of implementation of the thirteen volunteer management practices (National Volunteer & Philanthropy Centre, 2007b). These IPCs were mostly small and medium sized organisations classified by their total receipts reported for that year. It was found that the extent of implementation of volunteer management practices vary among various organisations, and the greater emphasis was placed on the practices under the *implementation stage* compared to other stages. However, as the focus of the study was to investigate whether IPCs with and without a volunteer coordinator differed in the extent of implementation of their volunteer management system, the findings pertained to comparison between IPCs with versus those without volunteer coordinators. Results comparing sports organisations and other types of organisations in relation to the volunteer management practices were not available. In a follow-up study, the NVPC investigated the barriers to effective volunteer management that employed HRM practices among 121 IPCs from various sectors of which less than 7% were sport organisations (National Volunteer & Philanthropy Centre, 2007a). It was found that one of the three main barriers to effective volunteer management was that top management did not see volunteer management as important. In sum, there are some preliminary evidence suggesting that the extent to which volunteer management practices are implemented, and the level of importance accorded to volunteer management practices by the management of organisations vary between organisations. But empirical findings on how non-profit sports organisations differ from for-profit enterprises in these aspects are lacking.

To enhance understanding of differences in the management of sport volunteers in different types of organisations that engage sport volunteers, the present study focused on two types of organisations; non-profit national sports associations (NSAs) and sport-related for-profit events management companies (EMCs). These two types of organisations were chosen because they engage substantial number of volunteers in organising marquee or large-scale events for the public. In Singapore, the popularity of a number of mass sport events (e.g., Standard Chartered Singapore Marathon, Sundown Marathon, Vertical Marathon, Singapore International Triathlon, and OCBC Cycle Singapore) discussed earlier provide an opportunity for the volunteer management practices of NSAs and EMCs that are associated with these sport events to be studied. Having effective volunteer management practices in these organisations is critical to volunteer satisfaction and retention. How these two types of organisations differ in their volunteer management practices has not been addressed by past studies. The aim of the study was to examine differences in the perceived importance of volunteer management practices held by the management, and the extent of implementation of volunteer management practices between non-profit NSAs and for-profit sport-related EMCs in Singapore. Based on the findings from the earlier mentioned

NVPC study that top management of the surveyed non-profit IPCs does not see volunteer management as important, it was expected that the management of the selected non-profit NSAs compared to those of the for-profit EMCs would perceived volunteer management practices to be of lower importance. As HRM practices are commonly used in for-profit organisations and can be easily deployed to manage volunteers besides salaried staff, it was also hypothesised that the extent of implementation of volunteer management practices in the for-profit sport-related EMCs to be greater than those in the non-profit NSAs.

METHOD

To answer the research questions, two methods were used. First, a questionnaire was used to assess the relative importance accorded to each of the thirteen volunteer management practices by the management of the NSAs, and those of the EMCs. Second, semi-structured interviews were employed to (a) gain a more in-depth understanding of why some volunteer management practices are perceived as more important than others, (b) assess the extent of implementation of the four-stage volunteer management system comprising the thirteen volunteer management practices in the organisations, and (c) gain insights into the factors that are associated with the successful implementation or incomplete implementation of the volunteer management practices. Face-to-face interviews were used because of their usefulness in facilitating the exploration and investigation into a thought or idea expressed. It allows the interviewer to probe an answer further to gain a more complete picture. The on-site interviews also enabled the examination of evidence that were relevant for demonstrating actual implementation of the practices.

Participants

Six organisations participated in this study. Three NSAs and three EMCs were selected as case studies using purposive sampling. Using the identified key mass sport events that engage sizable number of volunteers as a criterion, NSAs and EMCs that have been associated with these mass sport events were invited to participate in the study. These organisations have engaged volunteers in these events, other similar events or in voluntary roles in various capacities. To derive meaningful data, responses were obtained from representatives who possess relevant experience in volunteer management from each organisation. They were all management executives with 2 to 5 years (M = 2.76) working experience in volunteer management.

Instruments

Perceived importance of volunteer management practices questionnaire. Using the NVPC Volunteer Management Framework (see Table 1), a questionnaire incorporating the 13 volunteer management practices was designed to assess how management staff regard the relative importance of volunteer management practices. Respondents were asked to rate the importance of each of the practices to their organisation using a Likert scale of 1 to 7 with 1 being " not important at all" and 7 being " very important".

Interview guide. An interview guide was developed to investigate the extent of implementation of volunteer management practices. The Volunteer Management System Implementation checklist (National Volunteer & Philanthropy Centre, 2012) which is a document developed by the NVPC for organisations to guide and evaluate their implementation of volunteer management practices was used to generate the set of interview questions. The questions were a combination of 37 closed and open-ended questions. There were 5 questions on background information on the organisation and also on the designation and experience of the interviewee, 28 questions (3, 9, 11, and 5 questions for Concept, Planning, Implementation and Review stages respectively) were to elicit information pertaining to the extent of implementation of volunteer management practices, 2 questions were on the reasons why the particular volunteer management practices were rated as important or not as important, and 2 questions were to understand factors that may have influenced the implementation or non-implementation of volunteer management practices even though they were rated as important.

Procedure

The present study was approved by the institutional review board. Thereafter, organisations were invited to participate in the study. Once the approvals to participate in the study were obtained, separate interviews were scheduled for each representative of the organisations. The interview was conducted at the office of the organisation. Prior to the interview, participants were informed of the purpose of the study. They were assured confidentiality of information provided and anonymity of their identity, and then were asked to sign the consent form.

First, the questionnaire on the importance of the volunteer management practices was administered. The participants rated the importance of each of the practices to his or her organisation. Once the participants completed the questionnaire, preparation for the semi-structured interview to understand the extent of implementation of the volunteer management practices was made. Permission to make an audio recording of the interview was sought from each of the participants before commencing the interview. The interviews were conducted using the interview guide. The participants were also asked to provide any documentation or any form of evidence of the volunteer management practices that were implemented.

Data Analysis

The interviews were transcribed verbatim for further analysis purposes. An average of 11.67 pages of transcriptions was recorded for the interviews. Transcripts for the background information, volunteer management practices, reasons for the ratings of perceived importance of volunteer management practices, and factors associated with either successful or non-implementation of volunteer management practices were analysed separately.

Perceived importance of volunteer management practices. Mean ratings, and the standard errors, of the respondents' perceived importance for each of the 13 volunteer management practices for the NSAs and the EMCs were derived. Standard errors were reported as they take into account the small sample sizes, and to indicate the degree of uncertainty of the estimated means. Using SPSS (version 21), a one-way ANOVA was conducted to determine if these mean ratings for NSAs differ from those for the EMCs. The average scores for each of the four stages were obtained by calculating the mean scores for perceived importance of the volunteer management practices classified under each respective stage. A one-way ANOVA was conducted to examine if the mean scores for each of the four stages for EMCs differs from those for the NSAs.

Reasons for relative perceived importance of volunteer management practices. For the interview transcripts related to the reasons for the ratings of perceived importance of volunteer management practices, thematic analysis was conducted to examine the reasons underlying the perceived importance.

All of the interview transcripts were read and re-read to gain an overall impression, before returning to focus on specific passages and coded in the style of a grounded theory approach. Basic units of analysis were identified, and those with similar meanings were labelled with descriptive codes. The constant comparative technique employed in grounded theory method (Glaser & Strauss, 1967), and in earlier social research (Urquhart, 2013) was used to ensure that data coded into the concepts and categories were distinct and unique. Descriptive codes were merged and redefined where necessary. This process is repeated for the rest of the transcripts. Those codes with common meanings were then classified under higher-order interpretive codes. Overarching themes were derived from the data set by drawing references from the interpretative codes. The development of the descriptive codes, interpretive codes and themes resulted from open coding, selective coding and theoretical coding steps in accord with the grounded theory method (Glaser, 1978; Urquhart, 2013).

Extent of implementation of volunteer management practices. The extent of implementation by each organisation was assessed based on the interviewee's account pertaining to the implementation or non-implementation of the volunteer management practices. Guided by the Volunteer Management System Implementation checklist, the participants' accounts were then cross-examined with the evidence of implementation such as volunteer policies or guidelines, forms, annual reports, newsletter, and webpages provided by the interviewee. An ordinal scale was used to quantify the extent to which each of the volunteer management practices were implemented. A scale of 0 to 4 was used; 0 for no indication of practice, 1 for practice implemented to a small extent, 2 for practice implemented to a moderate extent, 3 for practice implemented to a large extent, 4 for practice implemented to a large extent with supporting evidence. The ratings were then recoded to a scale of 1 to 5, and then using simple proportional transformation, each 5-point score was multiplied by 7/5 to scale up it up to an equivalent 7-point score (Colman, Norris, & Preston, 1997). This was done to enable comparison to be made with the perceived importance scores. The extent of implementation of the volunteer management practices was analysed according to the four stages of the system (concept stage [CS], planning stage [PS], implementation stage [IS], review stage [RS]). For each of the four stages, the average scores were calculated by summing the scores of each of the questions on volunteer management practices, and then dividing the total score by the number of questions within each respective stage. Using SPSS (version 21), a one-way ANOVA was conducted to examine if the average scores for each of the four stages for EMCs differs from those for the NSAs.

RESULTS

Perceived Importance of Volunteer Management Practices

The mean ratings and standard errors of perceived importance of volunteer management practices for both EMCs and NSAs are presented in the bar chart (Figure 1). Compared to those in the NSAs, participants in the EMCs accorded higher level of importance to all of the volunteer management practices except "Budget for volunteer involvement" and "Orientation and training for volunteers". A one-way ANOVA conducted to determine if the mean ratings for NSAs differ from those for the EMCs showed that differences in perception were significant only in the practices of "Recruitment plan and procedure for volunteers", $F(1,4) = 18.00$, $p = .013$, "Risk management system", $F(1,4) = 25.00$, $p = .007$, "Screening procedure to identify suitable volunteers", $F(1,4) = 8.00$, $p = .047$, and "Assess impact of volunteer programme", $F(1,4) = 25.00$, $p = .007$.

*Figure 1. Mean ratings and standard errors of perceived importance of volunteer management practices for both EMCs and NSAs (Note: * p < .05)*

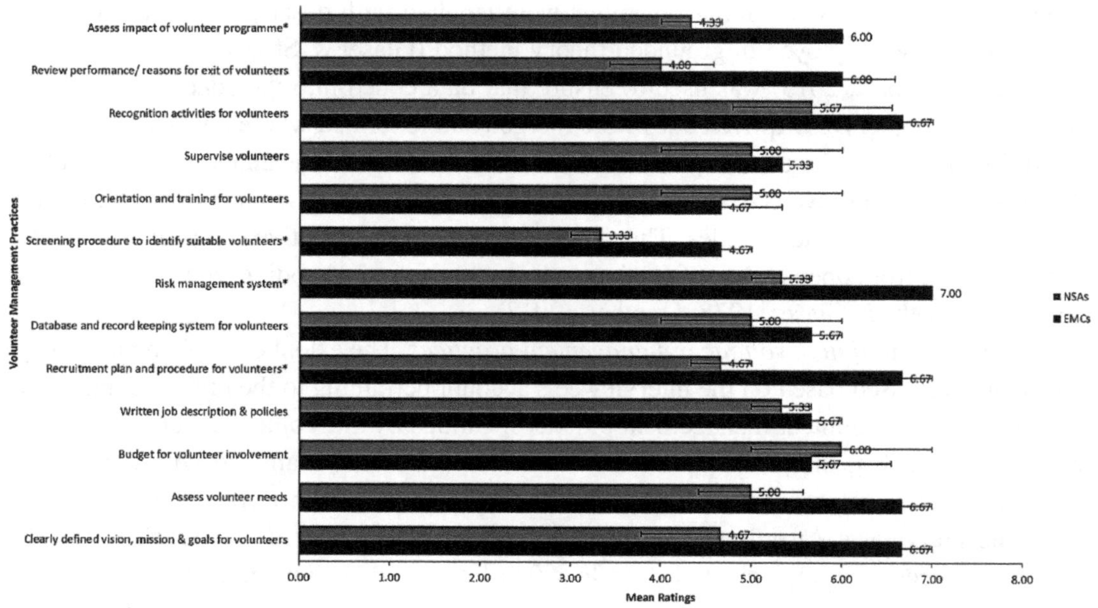

Reasons for Relative Ratings of Perceived Importance of Volunteer Management Practices

To understand the underlying reasons for the perceived importance of volunteer management practices cited by participants from both EMCs and NSAs, their responses to the two questions on the reasons why particular volunteer management practices were rated as important or not as important were analysed. As the reasons given by participants from both types of organisations were similar, their accounts were analysed together. Several descriptive codes that were found to represent the participants' views are shown in Figures 2. For example, the code *garner support for resources* characterised the effort by the management in garnering support for resources that will ensure that they are able to recruit and retain volunteers, and the following quotes from the participants fall under this descriptive code: "Unless we get the support of everybody, especially the management, it is very hard to have enough resources to gather the volunteers." (EMC1), and "... especially for the volunteer's budget, the management must acknowledge the importance of volunteer if not they might try to lower the cost. That's why I always tell them it is important, I will tell them to give standard rates." (NSA 1). Other examples of participants' quotes and the associated descriptive codes are (a) *clarity in volunteer's involvement* – "Because we need to know specific areas how many people we need, what kind of jobs that needs to perform. So we need to assess it before the event." (NSA1); (b) *appreciation of volunteers* – "So for every event, we will send a 'thank you email' email to the EXCO. We also present certificates of appreciation. I think these are just very small ways of just acknowledging their contributions and we can always do more. It is always good to feel acknowledged." (EMC1); and (c) *emphasis on importance of building relationships* – "As we always mention, we need to be friends and keep a good relationship with volunteers as well." (EMC3). Four interpretive codes were found to categorise descriptive codes that were closely linked. These were *operational efficiency* (entail attributes which ease the smooth running of events and enhance the volunteer management process), *achieving effectiveness* (relate to characteristics that aid in the achievement of goals), *building rapport* (about establishing good relationships with volunteers), and *well-being of volunteers* (about maintaining physical, emotional, mental well-being and interests of volunteers and developmental opportunities). From these four interpretive codes, two overarching themes emerged (Figures 2). The first was *support organisation's objectives*. Under this theme, the two interpretive codes were *operational efficiency* and *achieving effectiveness*. The second theme, *volunteer retention*, encompasses the two interpretive codes of *building rapport* and *well-being of volunteers*. As depicted in Figure 2, it is posited that these two themes represent important elements that are associated with the accomplishing organisation's mission.

Extent of Implementation of Volunteer Management Practices by Each Stage

The average scores of the extent of implementation of each stage of the volunteer management system for the six organisations are shown in Figure 3. For the purpose of comparison, the average scores for perceived importance of volunteer management practices of each stage for the six organisations are also presented in Figure 3. Visual inspection of the chart revealed that the averages scores for extent of implementation for all stages of the volunteer management system are below those for the level of im-

Figure 2. Reasons for relative importance of volunteer management practices

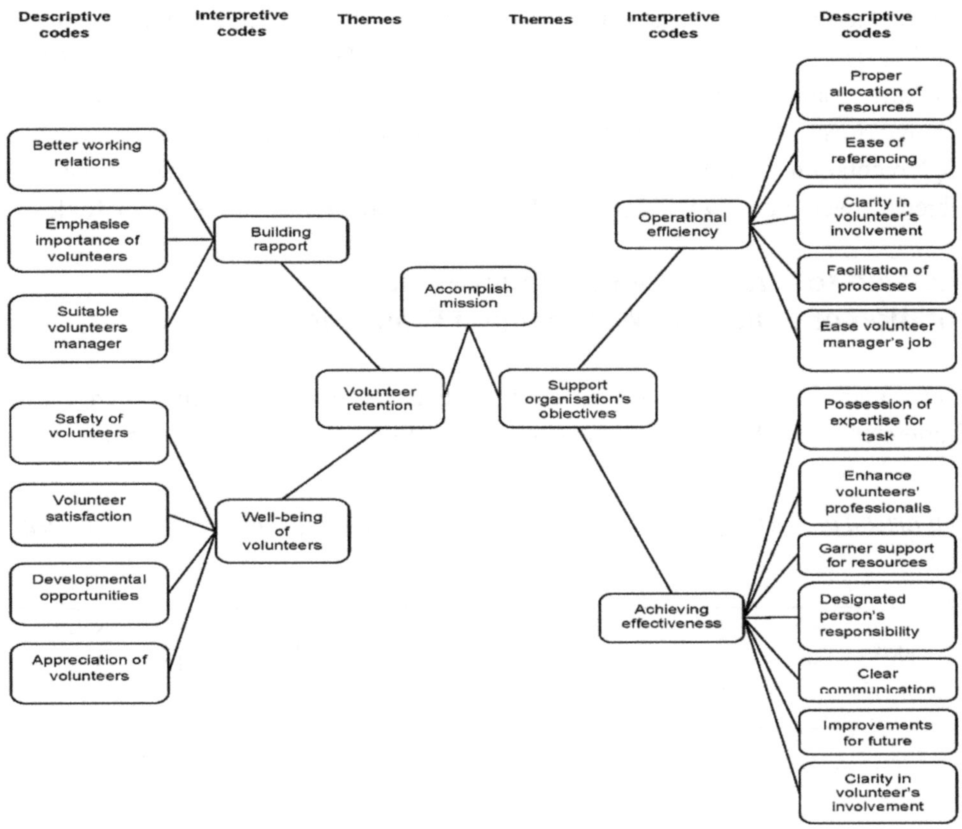

Figure 3. Average scores for perceived importance and extent of implementation of each stage volunteer management system for each organization (Note: CS = concept stage, PS = planning, IS = implementation stage, RS = review stage; with and without prefix "Imp" denote scores for perceived importance and extent of implementation respectively)

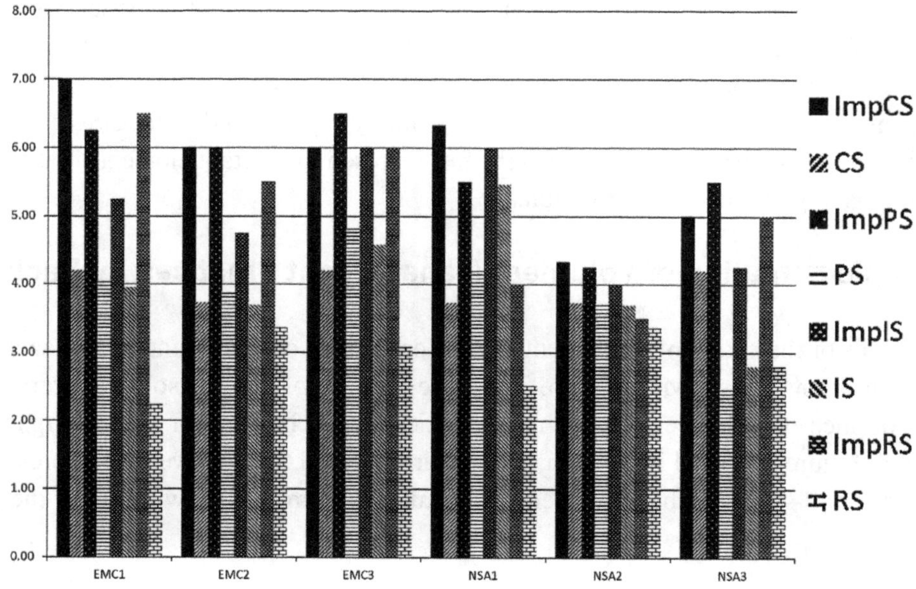

portance accorded to them by all organisations. A paired sample t-test showed that the differences were significant, CS: $t(5) = 4.79, p = .005$; PS: $t(5) = 5.18, p = .004$; IS: $t(5) = 5.11, p = .004$; RS: $t(5) = 3.89$, $p = .012$. In addition, all organisations, except NSA3, scored lowest on the extent of implementation of the Review Stage. Results of the one-way ANOVA conducted to examine if the average scores for the extent of implementation of each of the four stages for EMCs differ from those for the NSAs showed that the differences were non-significant. The descriptive statistics are presented in Table 2.

Factors Related to Successful or Unsuccessful Implementation of Volunteer Management Practices

Results from the interviews revealed that the common reasons cited by participants from EMCS for the successful implementation of volunteer management practices were management support, constant review

Table 2. Comparison of extent of implementation of volunteer management system stages between EMCs and NSAs

Stages	EMCs			NSAs		
	M	SD	SE	M	SD	SE
Concept stage	4.04	.27	.16	3.89	.27	.16
Planning stagee	4.25	.50	.29	3.47	.88	.51
Implementation stage	4.07	.46	.26	3.99	1.36	.79
Review stage	2.89	.58	.34	2.89	.43	.25

of practices, and education of staff and volunteer. As for the NSAs, good communication, and recognising the importance and need for such practices were highlighted. Reasons cited for the unsuccessful implementation by both EMCs and NSAs were lack of time, lack of resources, and lack of proper procedures.

DISCUSSION

Based on the previous findings that the top management of non-profit IPCs does not see volunteer management as important and that volunteer management practices are widely employed in the private sector, we expected that the participants from the NSAs would perceive the 13 volunteer management practices to be of lower importance than those from the EMCs .In general, this hypothesis was supported. Participants from EMCs rated almost all of the practices higher in importance than those from NSAs with significant differences in the practices of "Recruitment plan and procedure for volunteers", "Risk management system", "Screening procedure to identify suitable volunteers", and "Assess impact of volunteer programme". To better understand why such differences were found, we looked at the reasons expressed by the participants. For example, with regard to "Assess impact of volunteer programme", participant from one of the NSAs cited that this practice is not important because "... normally, the staff are busy with event-related stuff; they wouldn't really put volunteers in the highest priority." In contrast, one of the EMCs revealed that it is important to "evaluate and make sure that it [volunteer programme] is interesting." It seems that the EMC view this practice as important because it entails volunteers' satisfaction, which falls under interpretive code of *well-being of volunteers* and overarching theme of *volunteer retention.* Another example illustrating the differences found pertains to the "Risk management system". One participant from a NSA said: "We have organised a lot of events. For this [risk management], we don't really assess. It is only meant for certain roles such as for kayakers or critical points." On the contrary, a participant from a EMC cited that: "This is how we assure that volunteer will have a safe environment to work. Usually, we will make sure that safety plan, medical plan are shared with them, all volunteers are covered by insurance." In alignment with the management thinking of this EMC, good risk management practices is an important legal consideration for sport-related organisations where there exist a need to protect the interest of various stakeholders including volunteers (Cuskelly et al., 2006). It is argued that the organisation must not allow time, attention and resources to be diverted to less critical areas. And that a well-conceptualised risk management plan when communicated to stakeholders can potentially assist in volunteer recruitment and retention (Martinez, 2003).

Only two of the practices—"Budget for volunteer management" and "Orientation and training for volunteers"—were rated higher in importance (the differences were non-significant), by the NSAs than by the EMCs. The participant from one of the NSAs explained that the volunteers that were engaged also included coaches and officials, and why this practice is important: "The courses that we are running, they are important. They [the volunteers] have to go through the course to carry out their job." On the other hand, this practice may not be as highly important to the EMCs where the volunteers were mainly event crew performing simpler roles, as evidenced by the interview accounts of participants from two EMCs. One of them mentioned that: "For general simple volunteer work, if there is no chance for rehearsal, they will only be briefed on event day". Another said that: "I would say this is important not to every level of volunteers, but definitely not as important to the ground crew because there is just way too many." Overall, the findings indicate that, when benchmarked against for-profit companies, the levels of importance placed on volunteer management practices by NSAs were lower. They also provide a yardstick for comparison and a fuller picture of some of the reasons why certain practices were considered more or less important,. Hence, these findings add to what was previously reported by NVPC (National Volunteer & Philanthropy Centre, 2007a) where it was found that one of the three main barriers to effective volunteer management was that top management does not see volunteer management as important.

The overarching themes of *support organisation's objectives* and *volunteer retention* were derived from the thematic analysis on the reasons cited on the relative importance of volunteer management practices revealed the pragmatic and strategic inclinations of these organisations. These two themes are posited to contribute to the successful accomplishment of the organisation's mission. While one theme emphasises *operational efficiency* and *achieving effectiveness*, the other focuses on volunteer-related matters that go toward *building rapport* with volunteers and enhancing the *well-being of volunteers*. Researchers in HRM practices have argued that human resources can provide a source of sustained competitive advantage. (Huselid, 1995; Wright & McMahan, 1992). Others have pointed out that HRM practices can enhance individual employee performance productivity through their influence over employee skills and motivation, and through organisational structures that enable employees to determine how their roles are performed (Bailey, 1993). Intermediate outcomes such as lower turnover and higher productivity which in turn enhance corporate financial performance were shown to result from investment in high performance work practices based on HRM (Huselid, 1995).Hence, through well implemented HRM-based volunteer management practices, one can expect that the organisation has a higher chance of accomplishing its mission.

It was also hypothesised that the extent of implementation of volunteer management practices in the for-profit sport-related EMCs to be greater than those in the non-profit NSAs. This hypothesis was not supported. Although the average scores for the extent of implementation of each of the four stages for the EMCs were either slightly higher or the same as those for the NSAs, the differences between these scores were non-significant. It seems that HRM practices that are usually found in private enterprises have yet to be fully adopted by the EMCs included in this study to make a significant difference as was expected. The observed disparity between the perceived importance of the volunteer management system accorded by the management of both the EMCs and NSAs and the extent of implementation for all stages of the volunteer management system may perhaps shed some light on the issue. Although they considered that the volunteer management practices were important, the actual practices were not fully carried out. Osterman (1987) argued that there should be an underlying logic to an organisation's system of HRM practices and that certain policies and practices fit together. For example, it was found that organisations that value employee commitment are more likely to invest in skills training (Osterman, 1994). The translation from thinking to policies and then to practices is critical to the successful implementation of HRM practices. This was not the case for all of the organisations studied.

The identified factors contributing to the successful or unsuccessful implementation of volunteer management practices in this study provide an insight into what might be some enablers and barriers to developing effective volunteer management practices. The management of organisations would do well to focus on management support that recognise the importance and need for such practices, constant review of practices, good communication, and education of staff and volunteer. On the other hand, concerted attention and effort are required to remove the identified barriers of lack of time, lack of resources, and lack of proper procedures.

CONCLUSION AND FUTURE RESEARCH DIRECTIONS

In conclusion, while adding a cautionary note that this study only examined six organisations as case studies and hence the findings may not be generalised to all such organisations, we surmise that the observed use of HRM practices in volunteer management in Singapore mirrors what other organisations that engage volunteers in other countries are already doing. The extent of implementation of volunteer management practices in both EMCs and NSAs lags behind the level of importance accorded by the management of these organisations. It points to a gap in volunteer management practices that might explain what was found in the NVPC study that volunteers shifted away from the sports/recreation sector to other areas. The findings also may be indicative of the nascent nature of HRM-based system advocated by the National Volunteer & Philanthropy Centre in Singapore. It also signals the important role played by lead organisations such as the National Volunteer & Philanthropy Centre and Sport Singapore in raising the standards of volunteer management practices.

Future research can include a larger and more representative sample size to enable the findings to be applied to the relevant context. Other than NSAs and EMCs, various pertinent types of sport-related organisations can be included. In addition, obtaining the perspective of the volunteers with regard to how they perceived the volunteer management practices as well as their volunteering experience (e.g., satisfaction) can enhance our understanding of the state of volunteer management practices.

REFERENCES

Australian Bureau of Statistics. (2002). Involvement in organised sport and physical activity. Author.

Bailey, T. (1993). *Discretionary effort and the organization of work: Employee participation and work reform* (Working paper). Columbia University.

Channel NewsAsia. (2009). *OCBC Bank will return as title sponsor for Cycle S'pore event in 2010.* MediaCorp News Pte Ltd.

Channel NewsAsia. (2013). *OCBC Cycle 2014 organisers to cap participants at 12,000.* MediaCorp News Pte Ltd.

Cnaan, R. A., Handy, F., & Wadsworth, M. (1996). Defining who is a volunteer: Conceptual and empirical considerations. *Nonprofit and Voluntary Sector Quarterly*, *25*(3), 364–383. doi:10.1177/0899764096253006

Colman, A. M., Norris, C. E., & Preston, C. C. (1997). Comparing rating scales of different lengths: Equivalence of scores from 5-point and 7-point scales. *Psychological Reports*, *80*(2), 355–362. doi:10.2466/pr0.1997.80.2.355

Cuskelly, G., Hoye, R., & Auld, C. (2006). *Working with volunteers in sport: Theory and practice.* New York: Routledge.

Fenwick, M. (2005). Extending strategic international human resource management research and pedagogy to the non-profit multinational. *International Journal of Human Resource Management*, *16*(4), 497–512. doi:10.1080/09585190500051480

Glaser, B. (1978). *Theoretical sensitivity: Advances in the methodology of grounded theory*. Mill Valley, CA: The Sociology Press.

Glaser, B., & Strauss, A. (1967). *The discovery of grounded theory: Strategies for qualitative research*. Hawthorne, NY: Aldine.

Hager, M. A., & Brudney, J. L. (2004). *Volunteer management practices and retention of volunteers*. Washington, DC: The Urban Institute.

Huselid, M. A. (1995). The impact of human resource management practices on turnover, productivity, and corporate financial performance. *Academy of Management Journal*, *38*(3), 635–672. doi:10.2307/256741

Investing in Volunteers. (2005). *Investing in volunteers: UK quality standard for organisations that involve volunteers*. London: Volunteering England.

Johnston, M. E., Twynam, G. D., & Farrell, J. M. (2000). Motivation and satisfaction of volunteers for a major youth organization. *Leisure, 24*(1-2), 161-177.

Martinez, J. M. (2003). Liability and volunteer organisations: A survey of the law. *Nonprofit Management & Leadership*, *14*(2), 151–169. doi:10.1002/nml.27

MyPaper. (2010). *More than 45k YOG certs to be reprinted and redistributed*. Retrieved 28 March, 2014, from http://news.asiaone.com/News/AsiaOne+News/Singapore/Story/A1Story20100924-238846.html

National Volunteer & Philanthropy Centre. (2005). *The state of giving: Inaugural study of Singapore's giving landscape*. Singapore: National Volunteer & Philanthropy Centre.

National Volunteer & Philanthropy Centre. (2007a). *Barriers to effective volunteer management*. Singapore: National Volunteer & Philanthropy Centre.

National Volunteer & Philanthropy Centre. (2007b). *Study on institutions of a public character (IPCs)*. Singapore: National Volunteer & Philanthropy Centre.

National Volunteer & Philanthropy Centre. (2012). *Doing good well: Volunteer manangement system - A guide for non-profit organisations*. Retrieved from http://www.nvpc.org.sg/knowledge/research_publications.aspx

National Volunteer Centre. (2002). *Survey on volunteerism in Singapore*. Singapore: National Volunteer Centre.

Osterman, P. (1987). Choice of employment systems in internal labor markets. *Industrial Relations*, *26*(1), 46–57. doi:10.1111/j.1468-232X.1987.tb00693.x

Osterman, P. (1994). How common is workplace transformation and how can we explain who adopts it? Results from a national survey. *Industrial & Labor Relations Review*, *47*, 173–188. doi:10.2307/2524415

Purcell, J. (1999). Best practice and best fit: Chimera or cul-de-sac. *Human Resource Management Journal*, *9*(3), 26–41. doi:10.1111/j.1748-8583.1999.tb00201.x

Singapore Sports Council. (2006). *Record participation expected for 5th year of Standard Chartered Singapore Marathon*. Retrieved 11 March, 2012, from http://www.ssc.gov.sg/..._media_releases/Record_Participation_Expected_for_5th_Year_of_Standard_Chartered_Singapore_Marathon_.html

Singapore Sports Council. (2011). *Standard Chartered Marathon Singapore receives S$9.75 million in funding over three years*. Retrieved 11 March, 2012, from http://www.ssc.gov.sg/...ED_MARATHON_SINGAPORE_RECEIVES_S_9_75_MILLION_IN_FUNDING_OVER_THREE_YEARS.html

Singapore Sports Council. (2012). *Live better through sports: Vision 2030 steering committee report*. Singapore: Singapore Sports Council.

Singapore Sports Council. (2013). *World's elite runners headline the Standard Chartered Marathon Singapore 2013*. Retrieved 28 March, 2014, from http://www.ssc.gov.sg/publish/Corporate/en/news/media_releases/2013/WORLD_S_ELITE_RUNNERS_HEADLINE_THE_STANDARD_CHARTERED_MARATHON_SINGAPORE_2013.html

TODAY. (2010). *A race to get bigger and better: OCBC event draws record number of cyclists, now organisers eye expanded schedule*. MediaCorp Press Ltd.

Urquhart, C. (2013). *Grounded theory for qualitative research: A practical guide*. London: Sage Publications Ltd.

World Sport Group. (2012). *WTA Championships awarded to Singapore in 2014-2018 record deal*. Retrieved 27 March, 2014, from http://www.wsgworld.com/wta-championships-awarded-to-singapore-in-a-2014-2018-record-deal/

Wright, P. M., & McMahan, G. C. (1992). Theoretical perspectives for strategic human resource management. *Journal of Management*, *18*(2), 295–320. doi:10.1177/014920639201800205

KEY TERMS AND DEFINITIONS

Human Resource Management Practices: Business practices targeted at deriving optimal performance from human resources within an organization.

Marquee Events: Events that has an international following and are considered to be large and prestigious.

Non-Profit Organisations: Organisations where their profits generated are not distributed as dividends but are used to achieve the organisational goals.

Private Enterprises: Commercial business units that are own by private investors.

Sports Organisations: Governing bodies of sport(s) at various levels (e.g., national, state or provincial, club).

Volunteer Management Practices: Organisational practices employed for managing volunteers.

Volunteer Management System: A host of volunteer management practices that are organised in some manner that enable it to be implemented effectively.

This research was previously published in Emerging Trends and Innovation in Sports Marketing and Management in Asia edited by Ho Keat Leng and Noah Yang Hsu, pages 258-274, copyright year 2015 by Business Science Reference (an imprint of IGI Global).

Section 3

Spectatorship and Consumerism

Chapter 19
The Passion That Unites Us All:
The Culture and Consumption of Sports Fans

Brandon Mastromartino
University of Georgia, USA

Wen-Hao Winston Chou
University of Georgia, USA

James J. Zhang
University of Georgia, USA

ABSTRACT

Sports fans are individuals who are interested in and follow a sport, team, and/or athlete. These fans reinforce their identity as a fan by engaging in supportive and repetitive consumption behaviors that relate to the sport or team they are so passionate about. This chapter will provide an overview of the history and cultural heritage of sports fandom, discuss the significance and functions of fandom, underline what motivates individuals to consume sports, examine the consequences and results of fandom, and highlight contemporary research and developmental trends. This chapter will allow for a good understanding of where research on sports fandom is headed and the important issues affecting sports fans.

INTRODUCTION

This is a true story about a sport fan. Wertheim and Sommers (2016) noted the experience of Dennis Doyle, a season ticket holder for the 2014-15 New York Knicks:

A thirty-something recovering lawyer, Doyle left his job, withdrew $25,000 from his savings, and devoted the next year to attending every New York Knicks game. Not every home game. Every game. That meant venturing as far as London to watch his team. ...The Knicks weren't merely bad. They were putrid, wretched, miserable...Doyle endured it all. The blowouts and the blown leads. The thousands of shots that clanged off the rim. The missed defensive switches. The failure to grasp the Triangle Offense. He dutifully watched every moment of every game (p. 4).

DOI: 10.4018/978-1-5225-5475-2.ch019

This chapter is about sport fandom, and the aforementioned anecdote is a typical story of a sport fan — a loyal, enthusiastic, but somehow understandable admirer — who spends a significant amount of his or her time and money on following a sport, a team, or athlete. Understanding sport fans is important because of the large role sports play in modern society. An example of this is shown in the dramatic increase in media time allotted to sport programming. Between 1960 and 1988, the total number of hours allotted to sport programming on the three major TV networks, American Broadcasting Company (ABC), Columbia Broadcasting System (CBS), and National Broadcasting Company (NBC), increased by 600%, from 300 hours to over 1,800 hours (Wenner, 1989). Since the introduction of the Entertainment and Sports Programming Network (ESPN) in 1979, sports-only channels have gathered increased viewership and revenues. In 2014, ESPN made $10.8 billion in revenue (Gaines, 2015).

Consuming sports has become a part of the American way of life. Compared to the early 1900s when professional sports began to rise, people now have more discretionary money and time to spend on leisure activities and commercial sports have steadily attracted more and more fans. With the availability of sports via television and the Internet, sport fans can watch different kinds of televised sport games or follow their favorite teams and athletes from anywhere in the world. As sport fandoms grow, the money generated from advertising, sponsorship, and sporting good sales has increased considerably. A prominent example of this economic growth is the rising cost of advertisements during the NFL's Super Bowl. In 1967, 30-second commercials for the first Super Bowl cost a measly $42,000; that amount broke the $1 million barrier in 1995 and hit a record high of $4.5 million per commercial in 2015. CBS is now charging $5 million for ads in 2016, which equals to $166,666 per second (Schwartz, 2016).

The evolution of sport fandom is closely related to the changes in the contemporary sport industry. Despite the amazing growth in production of modern sports, fans are harder to reach, attract, and retain now because fans are now confronted with an array of sport and non-sport options like never before (Rein, Kolter, & Shields, 2007). Sports are increasingly in danger of losing their fans. Dominant sports like the NFL, NBA, and MLB are under pressure to maintain market shares because an entire group of emerging sports are gaining new fans and fragmenting the market even further. As the global marketplace becomes more accessible, sports that were formerly national or regional in scope are now seeking opportunities to conquer new overseas markets. In a market so crowded with sports and entertainment options, why and how sport fans connect, disconnect, or reconnect to a sport is often overlooked. Thus, it is important for researchers and practitioners look deep into the realm of sport fandom. The huge economic and cultural impact has led many people to wonder: Who are these people and why are they so passionate about sports? This chapter examines who sports fans are, how they become a sports fan in the first place, and what motivates them to continuously consume sports. As well, we further inquire about some of the unique elements that make up a sports fan, the ways in which sport fans engage in their fandom, and how sport organizations market their products to meet the needs of their fans. Finally, we touch on some current trends in sport fan research and what the future might hold for sport fans.

BACKGROUND

Who are sports fans? For the purpose of this chapter, it is especially important to define the difference between a sport fan and a sport spectator. Wann, Melnick, Russel, and Pease (2001) described sport fans as "individuals who are interested in and follow a sport, team, and/or athlete. Sport spectators are those individuals who actively witness a sporting event in person or through some form of media". Oftentimes, the two terms are used interchangeably when they should not be. They should not be confused because some sport fans rarely witness sporting events in person, while some spectators do not have any interest in identifying with one specific team. Wann et al. (2001) used the example of a person who received a free ticket to go to a basketball game, who might attend the game even though he/she had no interest in the event itself; the person might be just going along with friends. Thus, this chapter will use 'sport fans' as a generic term to describe individuals with an abiding interest in sports. In reality, the terms 'fan' and 'spectator' are not mutually exclusive as a majority of people who witness a sporting event are also fans of that sport or team involved; meanwhile, most fans do attend sporting events as spectators, at least occasionally. This chapter is primarily concerned with sport fans and their long-term, even lifelong commitment that can be developed.

Previous researchers have found that certain sociodemographic variables are highly related to the level of game consumption, such as gender, age, ethnicity, occupation, education, and household income. In the 2008 Survey of Public Participation in the Arts done by the National Endowment for the Arts, it was found that 30.6% of American adult population attended at least one sport event in the past 12 months. Among these sport attendees, 54.9% were male while 45.1% were female. Younger adults from age 18 to 24 were most likely to attend a sporting event. Furthermore, these sporting event attendees were more likely to be higher educated and of higher income than the non-attendees, and were more likely to be white than Hispanic or African-American. Similarly, another survey done by the Pew Research Center in 2006 indicated that about one half of all Americans claimed to follow sports, and more than twice as many males as females followed sports very closely. Data from previous studies revealed that more spectators come from households of two to four people with higher than average incomes (Williamson, Zhang, Pease, & Gaa, 2003). In some specific sports, previous research findings also revealed that the sociodemographic backgrounds of fans and spectators might vary. For example, young to middle-aged Caucasian males are most likely to attend professional basketball games (Zhang et al., 1995), and they also represent close to 50% of the audience at major league professional sporting events (Simmons Market Research Bureau, 2010). As for the professional and amateur female sporting events, the fan base is young to meddle-aged Caucasian females (Kerstetter & Kovich, 1997). As previous research findings have shown, sport fandom can come from a diverse background of sociodemographic categories.

HOW DOES SOMEONE BECOME A SPORTS FAN?

Socialization

A sport fan's identification formation starts with socialization and those factors that contribute to an individual's identity formation are called socialization agents. Socialization is the process of learning to live in and understand a culture or subculture by internalizing its values, beliefs, attitudes, and norms. A sport subculture may include learning the jargon, the history, player statistics, and the history of the team. Early sport exposure and participation can begin one's affiliation with a sport and lead to a long-term commitment to a sport, league, and/or team. One of the earliest studies on identification formation was McPherson's (1976) study on Canadian adolescents to find out the reasons they became sport fans, which found that there were four main factors responsible for teaching the values, beliefs, attitudes, and norms of sport fandom to individuals, including an individual's family, peers, school, and community. The researcher further discovered the impact of these agents on adolescents' sport consumptions and differences existed between males and females. The four socialization agents continue to be prominent in more recent investigations (e.g., Mastromartino, 2016). It appears apparent that these are influential in how one becomes a sport fan and lead into fan identity formation.

Identity

Wakefield (2007) defines identification in sport fandom as when 'when an individual reacts to events that occur to the team or player as if the events happened to him or her. Highly identified fans will internalize or adopt the team or player's attitudes and behaviors as their own. If you are highly identified with a team, you feel good when the team wins and bad when the team loses. You believe the team is a representation of who you are to yourself and to others. You practically feel as though you are part of the team' (p. 37). Identification leads to an emotional attachment, which then leads to consumer behaviors and responses to team performance and marketing activities. Support behaviors include going to games and events, buying team related merchandise, and consuming team media, which are the primary sources of revenue for sport organizations. As there are varying levels of identification, various factors may influence the degree to which one identifies as a sport fan, especially a particular sport and team. The more identified fans are, the more they would consume, and consequently, the more the organization would profit.

Identity as a sport fan means being attached to a particular team, player, or some aspect of sport. This identity is often confirmed and showcased with an individual purchasing and wearing apparel of that team, consuming that team's media, and engaging others in conversation about that team. In early social psychology, McCall and Simmons (1978) suggested identity would derive from the idea that individuals might base their actions on how they would like to see themselves and how they would like to be seen by others. Their research in combination with the Social Identity Theory gives a theoretical base for what it means to be a sport fan and why individuals engage in that culture. Social Identity Theory (Trajfel, 1978) has been a widely accepted concept to guide studies on sport fan's identification with teams. According to Turner and Trajfel (1986), social identity is a part of an individual's self-concept deriving from knowledge of his or her membership in a social group in addition to the emotional and value significance attached to the membership. Individuals create a shared social identity through membership in a social group (such as a sport team's fan base) and internalize the values and beliefs of the social group as their own. With a desire to develop and maintain a positive social identity, sport fans identify strongly with the team they support. Wann and Schrader (2000) suggest that positive social identity is usually derived in three ways: first through a strong association with the city, state, or college the team is based in, second through intergroup differentiation from rival teams, and third through becoming a part of the team and sharing in victory and defeat. A fan's perceived connection to a team and feeling with the team's success and failures is what it means to identify with a team (Ashforth & Mael, 1989).

Funk and James (2001) suggest that sports fans form a social identity by going through stages of their Psychological Continuum Model, the first stage being awareness. This stage is often brought about through the influence of the significant people in one's life. For instance, at a young age, often the most significant people in one's life are his/her parents and can make a large impact in forming one's social interests, including sport fandom. Parents can have this influence through having games on television at home, purchasing merchandise, or enrolling their children to participate in that sport. Once the identity as a sport fan is solidified, sports fans experience various motivations to consume sports. The next section will look at what motivates sport fans to continue to consume their favorite sport, team, or athlete once they have been socialized into fandom.

WHAT MOTIVATES SPORT FANS TO CONSUME SPORTS?

Sport fan motivation and satisfaction theories can provide significant insight into sport fan culture and lead to an understanding of how sport marketers develop a relationship with their fans. One of North America's leading researchers in fan psychology and behavior, Wann (1995) developed the Sport Fan Motivation Scale (SFMS). Through a series of questions, this scale determines the level of investment an individual has in a team and what specifically motivates an individual to consume that sport. The scale identified eight motivational factors for individuals to participate in spectator sport, including eustress (feeling of excitement), benefits to self-esteem, diversion from everyday life, entertainment, aesthetics, economic value (gambling), need for affiliation, and family needs. In the original study it was noted that motivations could vary by sociodemographic status and by a specific sport or activity. Although these are the main overlying themes that come up in sport fandom research, there are many subsections within them.

Internal and External Motivations

In a constantly evolving sport landscape, sport marketers have to find ways to meet the changing needs and wants of their consumers. They need to understand the motivations of their fans and market their product in a way that is appealing to the consumers. When considering the motivation of sport fans, their needs can be largely divided up into two categories: internal or external motivations. Needs may be of human nature (internal factors), or formed through societal construction (external needs) (Zhang et al., 1995). Internal factors are innate, unconscious, latent, non-specific, uncertain of satisfier, and contribute to the fundamental motivations for human behavior (Maslow, Frager, & Cox, 1970). Sloan (1989) and Wann *et al.,* (2001) explained that sport fans are self-pushed and internally motivated to attend sport events as social outings to fulfill their personal and social needs. According to Sloan (1989), there are five theoretical categories that can be used to explain the social motivations of sport fans: (a) salubrious effect theories (recreation theory and diversion theory), (b) stress and stimulation seeking theories, (c) catharsis and aggression theories (catharsis theory, frustration-aggression theory, and social learning theory), (d) entertainment theories, and (e) achievement seeking theories. Salubrious effect theories suggest that spectators are attracted to a game for its pleasure and benefits of physical and mental well-being. By attending sport events, fans can relieve their fatigue and boredom and become recharged. Sport attendance can also be used as an escape from work and other tedium of life. Based on stress and stimulation seeking theories, sport games are seen as stressors. Fans are attracted to a game for the stressful, risky, arousing, and stimulating experiences in socially acceptable ways. Positive stress and arousal allows for the expenditure of excess energy by being involved with the crowd. Catharsis and aggression theories propose that fans are attracted to a game for its violence and aggressive actions. Some believe that the aggression levels of spectators will be reduced by watching the acts of aggression of others (i.e., athletes), while others believe aggression levels are increased. According to entertainment theories, fans are attracted to a game to seek pleasure, sensation, satisfaction, and happiness. The aesthetic nature of movement skills makes sport an art form for spectators. Achievement seeking theories emphasize that spectators are attracted to a team to identify with the achievement of others, share success, gain knowledge, and satisfy their own needs. These internal motivations can be referred to as 'push' factors since they are motivations that come from within a sport fan and push him/her toward consuming the product.

On the opposite spectrum, external needs are motivations that are cultivated from environmental factors that surround the sport fan. These external motivates can be learned and nurtured from past experiences, social environment, and exposures to promotional schemes, and are contingent on specific situations and product categories. They can be manifested with 'pull' factors initiated by a sport organization to 'pull' the customers in by meeting their needs through offering various marketing initiatives (Zhang et al., 1995). For example, Zhang *et al.* (1995) developed the Spectator Decision Making Inventory (SDMI) with four pull factors (game promotion, home team, opposing team, and schedule convenience) and these factors were found to be predictive of sport event consumption variables. In a sport game event setting, pull factors are related to the actual game features as the core product itself, often times the quality of which is outside the control of sport marketers. Apparently, sport organizations need to look for ways to enhance the quality of the game's core product; in the meantime, enhancing the quality of event operation and enchant the consumer's game experience are also necessary to meet those external needs of sport fans.

Based on the Expectancy Disconfirmation Theory (Oliver, 1980), service quality can be defined as the comparison of a consumer's evaluation of the service performance to his/her pre-expectation of the service. Numerous researchers have suggested that a focus on service quality enhances customer satisfaction and in turn earns loyal fans. Zhang *et al.* (2004) argued that services in relation to a sporting event are usually manifested through game support and operation programs, which are considered extensions of the core game product. Game support programs includes the organizational or operational aspects of the game, such as ticket services, stadium accessibility, promotional activities, arena staff courtesy, and intermission entertainment. Zhang et al. (1995) remarked that various event amenities (e.g., singing, music, dance, and mascot) may also heighten the entertainment value of the game for sports fans.

WHAT ELSE MAKES A SPORTS FAN?

Building a strong fan base is one of the most imperative elements of operating a successful sport team, thus management dedicates a great deal of effort, time, and money in the development and promotion of their team. Despite the overall growth of attendance and revenues in spectator sports, various scholars have noted that sports are increasingly in danger of losing their fans as rapid changes and competition are occurring in a crowded marketplace (e.g., Rein *et al.,* 2007). In addition to the main motivation factors mentioned earlier, more and more scholars and practitioners are looking into other conceptual ideas and seek for practical ways that might make sport consumers become a fan. Surely, efforts should also be made to finding constraining or even negative causes that might prevent people from developing strong and long-standing sport fandom.

Socioeconomics

It is pervasively believed that socioeconomic status affects the nature of sport fandom (Woods, 2016; Zhang et al., 2001). One instance can be evident by observing the demographics of college sport team fans. Many college sport fans hold a college degree from the school they cheer for, and their role as alumni led them to loyally support that team. Such loyalty may even drive them to donate money for many years after graduation. For fans of professional sports, class and economic status may impact their fandom of certain sports. For example, polo, sailing, and golf may not interest middle class or the blue-collar crowd since they may not have the means to access those sports and related events. These organizations may choose to look into more affluent groups to market their product to and build a fan base with.

History and Culture

History and culture are a factor that creates different sport fandom in various countries. Although modern sport is commonly traced back to the ancient Greece, Great Britain had a large impact by introducing traditional English sports to its colonies in Africa, India, Asia, Australia, Canada, and the United States. During the 17th and 18th centuries, the British spread cricket, horse racing, and boxing to their colonies. In the next century, soccer, rugby, tennis, and track and field emerged as the next wave of popular sports (Elias & Dunning 1986; Woods, 2016). Certain sports are more popular in some areas of the world than others, a factor that sport organizations should consider when building a fan base. If the International Ice Hockey Federation is looking for a place to host their annual World Hockey Championship event, it is likely that they will host it in a country like Canada, Finland, or Russia where they know hockey has a deep rooted history in that country.

Team Ownership

A unique aspect of sport fandom is the relationship between ownership and fans. The ownership can influence sport fandom, but it runs both ways. For example, George Steinbrenner, the former principal owner of Major League Baseball's New York Yankees, purchased and then rebuilt a declining team into a world powerhouse by starting a wave of high spending for star players in the free agency market. In 2009, the year before his death, the Yankees' payroll was $210 million and was referred to as the 'evil empire' by fans of rival teams. During his 37-year ownership, the Yankees earned seven World Series championships, and increased the organization's value up to $1.6 billion (Goldstein, 2010). Other owners such as the Dallas Maverick's Mark Cuban is beloved by Dallas Mavericks fans and Jeff Vinik is often credited for the organizational turn-around for the Tampa Bay Lightning. Despite the owner's positive contribution and winning over fans, some critics point out the negative impact team owners might have. Zirin (2010) asserts that many owners, including the Colorado Rockies' Charlie Monfort, and the Oklahoma Thunder's Clay Bennett, abuse their ownership by relying on public funds to stay afloat. There were 78 stadiums or arenas either newly built or substantially renovated in the United States between 1991 and 2004, and 61% of the total cost of $2 billion came from public funds (Fischer-Baum, 2012). As of 1950, only 12 of the 46 facilities in which major professional sport teams played were publicly owned. Today, about 70% of the franchises from the big four leagues (i.e., NFL, NBA, MLB, and NHL) play in venues constructed since 1980, and almost all of these have utilized significant amount of public funds (Quinn, 2009). From 1992 to 2006, new stadiums and arenas in the United States have been built at an unprecedented rate (Baade & Matheson, 2006). Team owners are often public figures that have a large influence of team decisions, impacting the attitudes of fans and ultimately playing a large role in their fandom than that in the history.

Physical Space

The physical space (stadium) where sport fans congregate is a unique aspect of sport fandom and also contributes to one's identity as a sports fan. Having a physical space for a fan community to congregate is essential in a sport fan community. For many brands, a physical space exists as a core brand association. Let us think of the Apple Store for Apple or theme parks for Disney. These brand associations characterize the product symbols the brand wants to portray, with which consumers have the strongest associations. The physical space can showcase the brand, as well as create meaning for consumers. For sports, famous stadiums such as Lambeau Field, Fenway Park, and Madison Square Garden carry meaning beyond just being a location where sporting events take place. In Chicago Magazine, writer Bill Veeck described the meaning of Wrigley Field for Chicago Cubs fans: "The bleachers aren't just concrete and steel, cheap seats, and concession stands; they're a state of mind, a way of life, the best of summer" (Veeck, 1984). Examples such as the Michigan Wolverines and the 'Big House', Baltimore Orioles and the 'Camden Yards', and the Florida Gators and the 'Swamp' are all examples of linking the stadium and the brand. This has direct implications on the fan community as that association between team and facility becomes more salient; the impact it has on team and community identification is paramount (Underwood *et al.,* 2001). Aside from creating the association between stadium and brand, the physical space also functions to create an atmosphere that is conducive to fans forming a group identity. Sport facilities should provide more than a clean place with accessible amenities and they should work to foster a strong sense of group affiliation and identity. Increasingly, more stadiums are designed to create an intimate and nostalgic feeling. The 'Dawg Pound' for Cleveland Browns fans at FirstEnergy Stadium (formerly Cleveland Municipal Stadium) is a good example of this practice. "Physical facilities should be designed to both communicate a unique brand identity and facilitate shared experience among consumers" (Underwood *et al.*, 2001, p. 10). The idea that a stadium can keep fans coming back regardless of team performance shows how integral this physical space is to the fan community.

Fantasy Sports

New media and technology also affect the development of sport fandom, the most prominent being fantasy sports. According to the Fantasy Sports Trade association (FSTA), there are 57.4 million people playing fantasy sports in North America in 2015, generating more than $1 billion in revenue per year. Fantasy sports participants spend an average of 17 hours per week consuming sport entertainment, of which 8.5 hour involve fantasy sports, which means fantasy sports have cornered a significant share of the time that sport fans spend on other sports (Woods, 2016). Starting in 2012, the NFL started the 'NFL.com Fantasy Player of the Year' award to salute the best fantasy sport participant. While the experience of fantasy sports can enhance engagement of sport fans, playing fantasy sports may also change the nature of sport fandom. For fantasy sport participants, the key concept is rooting for individual players regardless which team they belong to, rather than supporting their hometown teams, adding another perspective to their fandom.

In brief, there are many ways consumers become fans and various factors that contribute to sport fandom. As the identity of a sports fan is gradually formed and strengthened, sport fans engage in their fandom in various ways. The next section looks at the significance and functions of sports fandom.

SIGNIFICANCE AND FUNCTIONS OF SPORTS FANDOM

Sport fans reinforce their identity as a fan by engaging in supportive and repetitive consumption behaviors that relate to the sport or team they are so passionate about. Consumption behaviors can include, but are not exclusive to, buying tickets to games, purchasing team merchandise, engaging in social media, reading printed media, watching games on television, and even listening to radio broadcasting. For a sport organization, developing and maintaining a diehard fan base is much more efficient than constantly having to recruit new fans. These organizations are much more interested in developing lifelong fans as opposed to one time spectators as it results in more repetitive consumption and therefore profit over time. As well, sport fandom can be generational and fandom of a team can be passed down from parent to child with little to no efforts made by the organization.

Sport Fan Loyalty

Sport organizations and their managers cannot always guarantee a winning product. The nature of sports is that there are ebbs and flows over the years, and only one team can win the championship at the end of the year. General managers can do their best to get top quality players, which may still result in a losing season or tournament. Despite a sometimes below average core game product, diehard sport fans are usually not sensitive to price increases when it comes to game tickets and team merchandise. For the most part, sport fandom is a lifelong attachment and a few down seasons will not alter one's consumption behaviors in large ways. For example, research by Calabuig *et al.* (2014) found that although price increases hurt the satisfaction of sport fans at times, they have a low direct effect on predicting future intentions of sport consumers. Win or lose, sport organizations are able to gradually increase prices and it will not change their fans' consumer behaviors in the long run. The lack of sensitivity to failure is similar to sport fans' tolerance to controversy. An example of this is labor disputes between owners and players that have resulted in partial or full cancelation of a professional sport league's season. The general thought would be that a labor dispute would upset fans and hurt revenues coming out of the strike, but research has shown attendance and consumption rebounds once the league returns to business (Schmidt & Berri, 2004). This kind of brand loyalty is important to sport organizations because they can leverage it to increase revenues and offset costs where expenses are increasing in such areas as player salaries or building new stadiums (Gladden and Funk, 2001).

Achieving Through Others

In sport fandom, a unique aspect of 'achieving vicariously' through athletes contributes to a strong brand loyalty (Trail, Fink, & Anderson, 2003). This allows for new marketing opportunities for organizations to capitalize on. Sport fans feel as though they are living through athletes and feel like they are part of the team. By consuming the sport product, a fan can feel that they are contributing and they play an integral role in the team's success. Sutton, McDonald, Milne, and Cimperman (1997) developed a framework for different levels of fan identification and the motivations and benefits of such identification. They divided fans into three groups with key characteristics associated with each level: Low, Medium, and High identification. Low identification is for social fans that are low on emotion, financial commitment, and involvement, but a relationship does exist. These fans may be more attracted to sport entertainment than the sport or team itself. Medium identification is a fan's association based on some attributes or elements found to be attractive. They have some achievement developing desires and may be mostly attracted to the 'big event', which can sometimes lead to higher levels of identification but could also fade away if there is poor team performance or a star player is traded. The fans in the high identification classification are vested fans who have the strongest, most loyal and long term relationship a fan can have with his/her team. The success of the team reflects personally upon these fans as well as on the collective identity of the community. Their study concluded that community affiliation is the most significant correlate of fan identification. It is potentially the most important factor in building fan identification and can have the strongest long term effects.

Rivalries

Every sport team has at least one rival team, a team that fans cannot stand seeing their team lose to and often have a long and bitter history with. When two rival teams play each other, it enhances a sport fan's fandom and creates a special event for fans. Some of the most prominent rivalries in sports include the Los Angeles Lakers vs. Boston Celtics, Toronto Maple Leafs vs. Montreal Canadiens, New York Giants vs. Philadelphia Eagles, and the Boston Red Sox vs. New York Yankees. As much as fans want to see their own team do well, they often want to see failure come to their rival teams, a function of their fandom that means almost as much as their team winning. This was scientifically proven using functional magnetic resonance imaging (fMRI), where researchers can monitor changes in blood flow to different regions of the brain in real time. Cikara, Botvinick, and Fiske (2011) recruited two groups of baseball fans – one who were fans of the New York Yankees and the other who were fans of the rival Boston Red Sox. The researchers scanned the participants' brains while playing clips of baseball games in front of them. The fMRI results of the experiment proved that the excitement or discouragement a sport fan claimed to experience is authentic. One of the obvious observations is the reaction of the participants' ventral striatum, the region being referred as the pleasure center of the brain. The activity in their ventral striatum increased when the participants saw their own team performing well. On the contrary, their anterior cingulate cortex, the brain region associated emotional responses to pain, had greater reaction when their team failed. Another observation came from the participants' responses to the performance of their rivals. According to the fMRI data, the Yankees fans experienced great joy when they saw a Red Sox player make an error. Not surprisingly, the researchers observed the same pattern when analyzing the brain activities of the Red Sox fans who were witnessing a Yankees player's failure. Rivalries are a unique function of sports fandom, not often found in consumers of other industrial products.

Community Affiliation

Community affiliation is derived from friendship and bonding motivations and is highlighted in the Cialdini et al (1976) study of college students and the phenomenon of "BIRGing" (Basking in Reflective Glory). In this study, respondents used the term 'we' to describe a team victory but would use the term 'they' to describe their team's loss. Also, it was revealed there was an increase in students wearing school-related apparel after team victories. Sutton et al (1997) identified four ways in which teams could increase fan identification. They are to increase team/player accessibility to the public, increase community involvement activities, reinforce the team's community history and tradition, and create opportunities for group affiliation and participation.

Underwood, Bond, and Baer (2001) highlighted areas in which sport franchises could build brand awareness, image, and loyalty to have financial success regardless of the team's win-loss record. An example is how the Chicago Cubs have been an enduring brand for decades without winning a championship. They identify the group experience, history and tradition, the role of the physical facility, and ritual as the four characteristics the sport environment promotes social identity. The group experience in sport can be a unique motive characterized by a sense of belonging that spectators feel and an inherent bias against out-group members. As it relates to building a brand, being a season ticket holder, a member of the booster club, and a participant in other scheduled events develop strong consumer relationships. Many organizations integrate the team's community history into their core branding strategies. These teams have unique traditions and play on the nostalgia of days in the past to promote the current team. Typically, this is associated with teams who have long established roots in the community and have celebrated championships. Rituals are patterns of behavior that are social in nature and where things can be shared together. Things such as chants in the stands, pre-game ceremonies, and even unique traditions with friends or family all contribute to ritual significance in sport fandom. In order to be most effective, rituals must be different than one's every day routine in order to invoke past experiences, be automatic behavior but have the awareness of its meaningful presentations, and have a strong sense of community as a foundation. Combining these characteristics, sport organizations can build strong fan communities leading to more brand awareness and loyalty from consumers.

ISSUES, CONTROVERSIES, PROBLEMS

The world of sports is constantly evolving; with that, issues, controversies, and problems are regularly emerging. Specifically, the way in which fans consume sports is changing in the new age of communication and technology; without a doubt, sport organizations need to respond to these shifts. As such, sport organizations need to have a heavy focus on the impact of televised sports, the game experience at the stadium, and new technologies. These developmental trends are a direct result of the ever changing landscape of modern society that goes much beyond the world of sports itself.

Sports and Television

Sport and media have long been connected. As technology rapidly changes, sports and the media are increasingly a major interacting point of sport fan research (Bernstein & Blain, 2002). Television specifically has played a large role in sport fan consumption behavior. The TV viewing experience is different for sports fans than viewers of other TV programming. In a new age with large screen televisions being affordable and accessible, high definition technology to bring the game to life better than ever, and the increasing production volume in sport broadcasting can create a very unique experience for sport fans. Research from Gantz, Wang, Paul, and Potter (2006) found that when compared to fans of other TV programs, sport fans were more likely to engage in pregame planning and information searching. Sport TV viewing is more purposive and content oriented as sport fans were more emotionally involved and caring about the game outcomes. Comparatively, viewers of other TV genres were not as active or invested. For many, watching the sport game on TV has become a ritual amongst members of a family or groups of friends, and has led sport fans to gain social and cultural empowerment (Eastman & Riggs, 1994). What is seen on TV is widely considered a part of everyday culture. Being aware of what happened in the sport world allows individuals to participate in 'water cooler' talks with friends, family, and co-workers. Beyond the impact of television itself, the way fans consume sports on television is changing.

For many years, advertisers would pay big dollars to air their ads during popular sitcoms, dramas, and reality shows on network cable as they knew millions of people would be watching at a specific time and could target their ads on the viewers according to the viewing audience for a specific program. However, as technology has changed and the DVR was introduced, television viewers were able to record their favorite shows, watch it at their leisure, and fast forward through commercials. This caused advertisers to cut back on spending because they could not guarantee that people were watching their commercials (Loebbecke & Radtke, 2005). However, one genre of television is immune to that, and that is live sports. Sport fans want to watch the game live as the excitement and suspense reduces significantly if the game is watched later on a recording. This has led to advertisers making live sport programming a priority. Revenues for professional sports have skyrocketed, significantly impacting how sport leagues operate and are consumed (Cave & Crandall, 2001). In this sense, sport fans have had a direct impact on the presentation of their favorite sport programming. Due to this changing landscape of television broadcasting, it has allowed for sport fans to consume more of their favorite sports, or be exposed to sports from all over the world that was unimaginable when sports first began broadcasting on TV. Due to cable packages offering sport channels from all over the world, online streaming becoming more prevalent, and social media growing rapidly, sport organizations and researchers are kept on their toes in researching the effects of these developments in sport fan consumption behavior (Hutchins & Rowe, 2012). In addition to the technology behind sports television consumption, sports on television have led to many subsequent developmental trends including topics in gender and sexuality in televised sports (Cooky, Messner, & Hextrum, 2003; Duncan *et al.*, 1990; Whiteside & Hardin, 2011), racial representations in sport media (Bruce, 2004; Grainger, Newnian, & Andrews, 2006), and the role of violence in sports broadcasting (Cummins & Hahn, 2013; Young, 2013). Media, television especially, have played a large role in sport fandom and how a sport fan consumes the sport product and is a constantly evolving topic for researchers to examine.

Enhancing the Stadium Experience

When considering the impact of sport media, especially television, sport organizations have found that fans prefer to stay at home and watch the game instead of paying for tickets to attend a game live. With crystal clear television broadcasting and the ability to watch in the comfort of one's own home, fans often choose to watch a game on TV over paying the high price of tickets and dealing with other inconveniences such as traffic, parking, and expensive concessions. With this in mind, sport organizations have had to become creative in finding new ways to attract consumers to the stadium. Many sport teams have opened new stadiums over the past decade and sport fan research has been following this new rend. Wakefield and Sloan (1995) acknowledged that while strong team loyalty affects attendance, stadium design and stadium services also directly influence spectator's desire to stay and attend more games. Through making improvement in such areas as food service, event quality, fan behavior control, crowd control, stadium parking, and stadium cleanliness, a sport organization can improve fan attendance experience regardless of how successful a team is when it comes to wins and loses. They also concluded that these results could be especially important for teams in small markets, as stadium factors are something within their control. Factors such as market size, competitors, and team performance are out of control of the sport managers and marketers; however, enhancing the stadium experience is important to building a loyal fan base that keeps coming back. Of these, building team loyalty is crucial, which can be accomplished through promotions that reinforce spectator's involvement in the team, making team members accessible to the general public, and offering discounted first time tickets as ways to begin that loyal relationship.

In order to deter people from staying at home to watch the game and get them to come to the stadium, sport organizations have begun constructing stadiums that offer interactive, connected, and instantaneous services. In recent years, Levi's Stadium in San Francisco, California, AT&T Stadium in Arlington, Texas, and Suntrust Park in Atlanta, Georgia have been constructed and are considered part of this new wave of 'smart' stadiums. Services such as ordering food via mobile phone or 'second screen' experiences offering data and games for fans to engage in on mobile phone or tablet while the game is occurring are examples of creative services being offered in this new age of sport stadiums. Bal and Fleck (2016) examined the impact of these smart stadiums on the future of sport fans in France and discussed the various stakeholders impacted by these new stadiums. These new game experiences have the door for new ways for corporate sponsors to engage their consumers and enhance relationship marketing in sports (Dees, 2011). This type of connectedness at sporting events is only one of many new initiatives to develop a unique relationship with the fans. Sport organizations want their brand to extend beyond attendance at just one game and want to form a community where their fans have a lifelong connection with the organization.

New Technologies

In addition to television and stadium technology, other technology is rapidly rising and making an impact on the sport scene. E-sport represents another factor influencing modern sport fandom, especially since e-sports has attracted more than 70 million viewers in 2013. The average e-sport viewer watches 19 times per month for a session lasting 2.2 hours (Llamas, 2014). These competitions are so popular on college campuses that Robert Morris University in Chicago even created an official video game team in their athletic department where scholarships are awarded to their e-sport athletes. E-sports have emerged as a brand-new form of entertainment by watching other people play video games competitively around the world. The year of 2016 marked the inaugural season of the ELEAGUE, a professional e-sport organization, which was formed in partnership between the Turner Broadcasting System (TBS) and the William Morris Endeavor-International Management Group (WME-IMG). This new league has delivered strong audience consumption since beginning broadcasting in summer 2016 on TBS. During its inaugural season, the ELEAGUE's televised events delivered 897 million gross minutes of video consumption across TBS and Twitch, and a reach of 19 million total viewers on TBS (Hofer, 2016). Since the fandom composition consists greatly of millennial viewers falling between 18 and 34 year-old men, e-sports will surely impact the development of sport fandom by gaining more new fans and adding to the rapidly fragmented sport market.

FUTURE RESEARCH DIRECTIONS

In emerging sport fandom research, various aspects of fan community formation is becoming a significant developmental trend. Stemming from Muniz and O'Guinn's (2001) concept of brand community, it is now being applied to sport fans and 'fan nations.' Brand community is a large collection of individuals that is formed on the basis of attachment to a product. In the case of sport, it is a particular sport, team, and/or athlete. Muniz and O'Guinn highlighted three integral elements of forming brand communities: (a) consciousness of kind, (b) shared rituals and traditions, and (c) moral responsibility to the brand. This concept suggests that a company's brand can grow stronger based on interactions consumers have with each other and the community they build within themselves that is centered on their common identification with a company or product. Since the brands of sport organizations have boomed over the past three decades, the concept of brand community can be applied to sport fandom research. For example, Yoshida, Heere, and Gordon (2015) found that attachment to the fan community explained the largest amount of variance within team identity for a group of fans. As well, the research highlighted that fan community attachment was the only significant predictor of continued attendance at the games of a sport team throughout the year. The related theories and studies on brand communities show that how fans build a community amongst themselves is just as important as actions taken by the organization when it comes to having a strong fan base. Without a doubt, the aspect of fan community continues to evolve due to increasingly more interactive technology. Internet hubs such as message boards and social media have led to fan communities no longer having geographic restrictions. Foster and Hyatt (2008) believe that the building of a fan base should not be limited to just within the city where the team is located. With today's growth technology, sport franchises should target a more global audience and build a fan community of both local and distant loyal fans. The Real Madrid of the Spanish Primera Division in European football is a good example that has an estimated 150 million supporters worldwide. Developing these 'fan nations' is more important than selling out one game, or maximizing concession stand purchases. A study by Mastromartino (2016) found that many NHL fans said the community aspect was the most important part of their fandom and connecting with other fans online is their favorite part of being a fan. The unpredictability of sport will often lead to peaks and valleys in team revenues; but, it is those who remain strongly connected to a team that help generate the most revenue for the team in the long run. With new global opportunities available to sport marketers, it is in their best interests to expand their fan communities and create more consumption opportunities.

The contemporary trend in forming fan communities has led to further investigations into how they operate by utilizing such theories as the stakeholder theory and network analysis theory. Early research findings have already shown that sport fans play a clear and influential role within how the organization operates; when given the status and opportunities to be 'co-producers' of sport events, fan communities strengthen fan identifications. For example, Zagnoli and Radicchi (2010) examined the fan community of ACF Fiorentina in the Italian Seria A soccer league and found that fans were crucial actors in how the organization implements its service and more importantly, they play a large role in influencing the choices and behaviors of the sport organization and other stakeholders involved. Other research from Katz and Heere (2013) conducted social network analysis among fans of a newly formed sport team and found that the leader of each group of fans was crucial in the long term attachment of other fans toward the team. Their research noted, "The findings signify that not all members are created equal. A newly formed community is not a homogenous or random network of individuals but rather a network where a select few persons have many more connections, and thus a heightened importance, than the average consumer" (p. 283). This suggests that in a sport fan context, 'fan nations' are not a collection of hundreds of thousands of individuals, they are made up of a few thousand highly invested individuals that have many connections to others whom they bring along to consume the team's product. In a follow up study, Katz and Heere (2015) found that the leaders who empowered other members of their group led to a stronger and better balanced fan group, contributing to stronger team identification. With new technologies emerging and the uniqueness of sport competitions where the organization cannot control the final outcome of the product, it is important for the organization to develop and understand its fan communities for long term revenue generation. Sport fandom is a constantly evolving phenomenon and contemporary research helps sport organizations understand the developmental trends of sport fans.

CONCLUSION

There's no denying the passion and dedication of sports fans. The sports landscape has changed over the decades but the commitment these fans have to their teams has not. Sports fans have a significant emotional attachment to sports, teams, and players and invest valuable time and money into supporting their team. The rush a fan gets when their team wins and the defeat they feel when their team loses is all part of the up and down rollercoaster ride that being a sports fan is. In current times with more sports media, products, and events available; sports fans are able to express their fandom in many ways. Often an attachment to a sports team is a lifelong allegiance, something that is not easily broken. As the importance of sports rises in modern society, sports fans will continue to be the driving force that keeps sports in the spotlight.

REFERENCES

Ashforth, B. E., & Mael, F. (1989). Social identity theory and the organization. *Academy of Management Review*, *14*(1), 20–39.

Baade, R. A., & Matheson, V. A. (2006). Have public finance principles been shut out in financing new stadiums for the NFL? *Public Finance & Management*, *6*(3), 284.

Bal, C., & Fleck, N. (2016). Connected stadium: A pillar for football clubs' marketing development? In Making a difference through marketing (pp. 43-58). Singapore: Springer.

Bernstein, A., & Blain, N. (2002). Sport and the media: The emergence of a major research field. *Sport in Society*, *5*(3), 1–30.

Bruce, T. (2004). Marking the boundaries of the normal in televised sports: The play-by-play of race. *Media Culture & Society*, *26*(6), 861–879. doi:10.1177/0163443704047030

Calabuig, F., Núñez-Pomar, J., Prado-Gascó, V., & Ano, V. (2014). Effect of price increases on future intentions of sport consumers. *Journal of Business Research*, *67*(5), 729–733. doi:10.1016/j.jbusres.2013.11.035

Cave, M., & Crandall, R. W. (2001). Sports rights and the broadcast industry. *The Economic Journal*, *111*(469), 4–26. doi:10.1111/1468-0297.00596

Cialdini, R. B., Borden, R. J., Thorne, A., Walker, M. R., Freeman, S., & Sloan, L. R. (1976). Basking in reflected glory: Three (football) field studies. *Journal of Personality and Social Psychology*, *34*(3), 366–375. doi:10.1037/0022-3514.34.3.366

Cikara, M., Botvinick, M. M., & Fiske, S. T. (2011). Us versus them social identity shapes neural responses to intergroup competition and harm. *Psychological Science*, *22*(3), 306–313. doi:10.1177/0956797610397667 PMID:21270447

Cooky, C., Messner, M. A., & Hextrum, R. H. (2013). Women play sport, but not on TV: A longitudinal study of televised news media. *Communication & Sport*, *1*(3), 203–230. doi:10.1177/2167479513476947

Cummins, R. G., & Hahn, D. (2013). Re-presenting sport: How instant replay and perceived violence impact enjoyment of mediated sports. *Mass Communication & Society*, *16*(6), 787–807. doi:10.1080/15205436.2013.779719

Dees, W. (2011). New media and technology use in corporate sport sponsorship: Performing activational leverage from an exchange perspective. *International Journal of Sport Management and Marketing*, *10*(3-4), 272–285. doi:10.1504/IJSMM.2011.044795

Duncan, M. C., Messner, M. A., Williams, L., Jensen, K., & Wilson, W. (1990). *Gender stereotyping in televised sports*. Los Angeles, CA: Amateur Athletic Foundation of Los Angeles.

Eastman, S. T., & Riggs, K. E. (1994). Televised sports and ritual: Fan experiences. *Sociology of Sport Journal*, *11*(3), 249–274. doi:10.1123/SSJ.11.3.249

Elias, N., & Dunning, E. (1986). *Quest for excitement: Sport and leisure in the civilizing process* (Vol. 288). Oxford, UK: Blackwell.

Fischer-Baum, R. (2012, December 4). Animated infographic: Watch as America's stadiums pile up on the backs of taxpayers. *Deadspin*. Retrieved from http://deadspin.com/5964116/animated-infographic-watch-as-americas-stadiums-pile-up-on-the-backs-of-taxpayers

Foster, W. M., & Hyatt, C. G. (2008). Inventing team tradition: A conceptual model for the strategic development of fan nations. *European Sport Management Quarterly*, *8*(3), 265–287. doi:10.1080/16184740802224183

Funk, D. C., & James, J. D. (2006). Consumer loyalty: The meaning of attachment in the development of sport team allegiance. *Journal of Sport Management*, *20*(2), 189–217. doi:10.1123/jsm.20.2.189

Gaines, C. (2015, November 30). More than 60% of ESPN's revenue comes from their dwindling subscriber base. *Business Insider*. Retrieved from http://www.businessinsider.com/espn-revenue-subscriber-fees-2015-11

Gantz, W., Wang, Z., Paul, B., & Potter, R. F. (2006). Sports versus all comers: Comparing T sports fans with fans of other programming genres. *Journal of Broadcasting & Electronic Media*, *50*(1), 95–118. doi:10.1207/s15506878jobem5001_6

Gantz, W., & Wenner, L. A. (1995). Fanship and the television sports viewing experience. *Sociology of Sport Journal*, *12*(1), 56–56. doi:10.1123/ssj.12.1.56

Gantz, W., Wilson, B., Lee, H., & Fingerhut, D. (2008). Exploring the roots of sports fanship. *Sports mania: Essays on fandom and the media in the 21st century*, 63-77.

Gladden, J. M., & Funk, D. C. (2001). Understanding brand loyalty in professional sport: Examining the link between brand associations and brand loyalty. *International Journal of Sports Marketing & Sponsorship*, *3*(1), 54–81. doi:10.1108/IJSMS-03-01-2001-B006

Goldstein, R. (2010, July 13). George Steinbrenner, who built Yankees into powerhouse, dies at 80. *New York Times*. Retrieved from http://www.nytimes.com/2010/07/14/sports/baseball /14steinbrenner.html?_r=0

Grainger, A., Newnian, J. I., & Andrews, D. L. (2006). *Sport, the media, and the construction of race.* Academic Press.

Hofer, B. (2016, August 1). ELEAGUE's first season delivers strong audience across all platforms. *Gaming Target*. Retrieved from http://www.gamingtarget.com/

Hutchins, B., & Rowe, D. (2012). *Sport beyond television: The Internet, digital media and the rise of networked media sport* (Vol. 40). London: Routledge.

Katz, M., & Heere, B. (2013). Leaders and followers: An exploration of the notion of scale-free networks within a new brand community. *Journal of Sport Management*, *27*(4), 271–287. doi:10.1123/jsm.27.4.271

Katz, M., & Heere, B. (2015). Empowerment within brand communities: Overcoming the Achilles Heel of scale-free networks. *Sport Management Review*, *18*(3), 370–383. doi:10.1016/j.smr.2014.10.001

Kerstetter, D. L., & Kovich, G. M. (1997). An Involvement Profile of Division I Womens Basket-ball Spectators. *Journal of Sport Management*, *11*(3), 234–249. doi:10.1123/jsm.11.3.234

Llamas, S. (2014, September 9). eSports brief by SuperData Research. *Slide Share*. Retrieved from http://www.slideshare.net/StephanieLlamas/esports-brief-by-superdata-research

Loebbecke, C., & Radtke, S. (2005). Business models and programming choice: Digital video recorders shaping the TV industry. *AMCIS 2005 Proceedings*, 20.

Maslow, A. H., Frager, R., & Cox, R. (1970). Motivation and personality (Vol. 2; J. Fadiman & C. McReynolds, Eds.). New York: Harper & Row.

Mastromartino, B. (2016). *Skating in the sun: Examining the identity formation of national hockey league fans in the sunbelt states* (Unpublished master's thesis). The University of Georgia, Athens, GA.

McCall, G. J., & Simmons, J. L. (1978). Identities and interactions: An examination of human associations in everyday life (Rev. ed.). New York: Academic Press.

McPherson, B. D. (1976). Socialization into the role of sport consumer: A theory and causal model. *Canadian Review of Sociology/Revue canadienne de sociologie, 13*(2), 165-177.

Muniz, A. M. Jr, & OGuinn, T. C. (2001). Brand community. *The Journal of Consumer Research*, *27*(4), 412–432. doi:10.1086/319618

Oliver, R. L. (1980). A cognitive model of the antecedents and consequences of satisfaction decisions. *JMR, Journal of Marketing Research*, *42*(4), 460–469. doi:10.2307/3150499

Quinn, K. G. (2009). *Sports and their fans: The history, economics and culture of the relationship between spectator and sport.* McFarland.

Rein, I., Kotler, P., & Shields, B. R. (2007). *The elusive fan: Reinventing sports in a crowded marketplace*. McGraw Hill.

Schmidt, M. B., & Berri, D. J. (2004). The impact of labor strikes on consumer demand: An application to professional sports. *The American Economic Review*, *94*(1), 344–357. doi:10.1257/000282804322970841

Schwartz, N. (2016, February 6). Stunning infographic charts the skyrocketing cost of as Super Bowl ad. *USA Today*. Retrieved from http://ftw.usatoday.com/2016/02/how-much-does-super-bowl-ad-cost

Sloan, L. R. (1989). The motives of sports fans. *Sports, Games, and Play: Social and Psychological Viewpoints*, *2*, 175–240.

Sutton, W. A., McDonald, M. A., Milne, G. R., & Cimperman, J. (1997). Creating and fostering fan identification in professional sports. *Sport Marketing Quarterly*, *6*, 15–22.

Tajfel, H. E. (1978). *Differentiation between social groups: Studies in the social psychology of intergroup relations*. Academic.

Trail, G. T., Fink, J. S., & Anderson, D. F. (2003). Sport spectator consumption behavior. *Sport Marketing Quarterly, 12*(1).

Turner, J. C., & Tajfel, H. (1986). The social identity theory of intergroup behavior. *Psychology of Intergroup Relations*, 7-24.

Underwood, R., Bond, E., & Baer, R. (2001). Building service brands via social identity: Lessons from the sports marketplace. *Journal of Marketing Theory and Practice*, *9*(1), 1–13. doi:10.1080/10696679.2001.11501881

Veeck, B. (1984). Don't Call Us Bums. *Chicago Magazine.*

Wakefield, K. L. (2007). *Team sports marketing*. Elsevier.

Wakefield, K. L., & Sloan, H. J. (1995). The effects of team loyalty and selected Stadium factors on spectator attendance. *Journal of Sport Management, 153*, 172.

Wann, D. L. (1995). Preliminary validation of the sport fan motivation scale. *Journal of Sport and Social Issues*, *19*(4), 377–396. doi:10.1177/019372395019004004

Wann, D. L., Melnick, M. J., Russell, G. W., & Pease, D. G. (2001). *Sport fans: The psychology and social impact of spectators*. New York: Routledge.

Wann, D. L., & Schrader, M. P. (2000). Controllability and stability in the self-serving attributions of sport spectators. *The Journal of Social Psychology*, *140*(2), 160–168. doi:10.1080/00224540009600455 PMID:10808638

Wenner, L. A. (1989). Media, sports, and society. *Sage (Atlanta, Ga.).*

Wertheim, L. J., & Sommers, S. (2016). *This is your brain on sports: The science of underdogs, the value of rivalry, and what we can learn from the T-shirt cannon*. New York: Crown Archetype.

Whiteside, E., & Hardin, M. (2011). Women (not) watching women: Leisure time, television, and implications for televised coverage of womens sports. *Communication, Culture & Critique*, *4*(2), 122–143. doi:10.1111/j.1753-9137.2011.01098.x

Williamson, D. P., Zhang, J. J., Pease, D. G., & Gaa, J. P. (2003). Dimensions of spectator identification associated with women's professional basketball game attendance. *International Journal of Sport Management*, *4*, 59–91.

Woods, R. (2016). *Social issues in sport* (3rd ed.). Champaign, IL: Human Kinetics.

Yoshida, M., Heere, B., & Gordon, B. (2015). Predicting behavioral loyalty through community: Why other fans are more important than our own intentions, our satisfaction, and the team itself. *Journal of Sport Management, 29*(3), 318–333. doi:10.1123/jsm.2013-0306

Young, K. (2013). *Sport, violence and society*. London: Routledge.

Zagnoli, P., & Radicchi, E. (2010). The football-fan community as a determinant stakeholder in value co-creation. *Sport in Society, 13*(10), 1532–1551. doi:10.1080/17430437.2010.520941

Zhang, J. J., Pease, D. G., Hui, S. C., & Michaud, T. J. (1995). Variables affecting the spectator decision to attend NBA games. *Sport Marketing Quarterly, 4*(4), 29–39.

Zhang, J. J., Pease, D. G., Smith, D. W., Wall, K. A., Saffici, C. L., Pennington-Gray, L., & Pitts, B. G. et al. (2004). Spectator satisfaction with the support programs of professional basketball games. *Inaugural Sport Marketing Association Conference*, 207-229.

Zirin, D. (2010). *Bad sports: How owners are ruining the games we love*. Simon and Schuster.

KEY TERMS AND DEFINITIONS

Identity: Identity is a part of an individual's self-concept deriving from knowledge of his or her membership in a social group in addition to the emotional and value significance attached to the membership. Individuals create a shared social identity through membership in a social group (such as a sport team's fan base) and internalize the values and beliefs of the social group as their own.

Socialization: The process of becoming a fan through learning the culture and history of a particular sport, team, and/or athlete.

Socialization Agent: Factors that contribute to an individual's identity formation as a fan are called socialization agents. Examples of these include parents, friends, peers, and media.

Socioeconomic Status: An individual's or group's position within a hierarchical social structure. Socioeconomic status depends on a combination of variables, including occupation, education, income, wealth, and place of residence. Sociologists often use socioeconomic status as a means of predicting behavior.

Sports Fans: Individuals who have an emotional attachment to a particular sport, team, or athlete.

Sports Marketing: Sports marketing is a subdivision of marketing which focuses both on the promotion of sports events and teams as well as the promotion of other products and services through sporting events and sports teams.

Sports Spectators: Sport spectators are those individuals who actively witness a sporting event in person or through some form of media.

This research was previously published in Exploring the Rise of Fandom in Contemporary Consumer Culture edited by Cheng Lu Wang, pages 52-70, copyright year 2018 by Business Science Reference (an imprint of IGI Global).

Chapter 20 Rationalizing Sport Spectatorship: Analysis of Fan Behaviour in S-League

Shankar Selvam
Asia Pacific School of Sports and Business, Singapore

ABSTRACT

This chapter aligns itself with spectatorship theories to identify possible causes for the poor spectatorship numbers observed at S-League matches. Taking into account club affiliations among spectators and how such relationships affect the fortunes of a club's following, relevant theories are discussed in the context of the sports situation in Singapore. Qualitative and quantitative components pertaining to S-League spectatorship are analysed, which serve as the basis for the recommendations presented on improving attendance at local football matches.

INTRODUCTION

The S-League is the premier football league in Singapore, commissioned by the Football Association of Singapore (FAS) in 1996. It has struggled with poor match-day attendances (spectatorship) and has shown no improvement over the years, noticeably dwindling in recent times. Little attention has been given to the factors that influence spectators in the decisions they make with regard to their support for professional sports in Singapore and this paper argues that such fundamental understanding forms the critical foundation on which the FAS (as well as other local football organizations) can enact measures that will lead to improved spectatorship.

The sport spectator is a curious specimen since he may support a particular team but yet not care for the sport itself (Branscombe & Wann, 1991, p. 116). However, instead of exploring the problem of non-attendance and what encourages fans to make themselves present at sports events, it is noted (Dominic, Ian & Ivan, 2000) that much of the research on sports spectatorship, even in the case of a popular sport such as football, has been on hooligan behavior. As there is a dearth of study on the aver-

DOI: 10.4018/978-1-5225-5475-2.ch020

age attendance of football spectators, there is a need for papers such as this to shed light that facilitates informed decision-making at the policy level.

ROLE OF SPORTS IN SOCIETY

Sport spectator involvement is defined as forms of unobservable motivation, arousal, or interest toward a sporting event (Rothschild, 1984; Laverie & Arnett, 2000), and spectators play a significant economical role as they end up becoming consumers of sports events (Milne & McDonald, 1999). A number of empirical studies have also shown that there is a link between sports spectatorship and active sports participation (Anderson 1979: Godbey & Robinson, 1979: Guttmann, 1986: Snyder & Spritezer 1983). In addition, fans fulfill their personal desire to be a sports celebrity or player by identifying with their chosen team, resulting in a feeling of strong attachment (Fink et al., 2002b; Trail et al., 2000; Trail et al., 2003). Individuals who are inclined towards sport typically have a need for vicarious achievement which can be satisfied through association with a successful other – such as being a fan of a successful club – and seeks to retain membership where there is positive contribution to his identity, thereby strengthening their own self-esteem (Posten, 1998).

Based on the concept of functionalism, people have shared values and cooperatively work for the benefit of all, and sport is viewed as one of those constructive forces with regard to the needs of the society (Troutman, 2003). In a stressful society such as Singapore (Channel NewsAsia, 2012), sport can also be an outlet for the release of tension, where the socio-cultural 'rituals' that take place at a football game allows an individual to become a part of the match (Cohen, 1974) and thus psychologically experiences real emotions (Funk et al., 2004). People in society generally look for a connection through sport and a purpose behind the activity (Troutman, 2003), and extensive research has shown that team identification can be a strong perception of social identity (Fink, Trail & Anderson, 2002; Madrigal, 2001; Wann, 2000; Wann, 1993; Wann, Brewer & Royalty, 1999).

Social Identity Theory suggests that an individual feels committed or attached to a specific group as well as the status and characteristics of this group relative to other social categories (Tajfel & Turner, 1986). In addition, participants become more resilient when they feel a sense of shared identity with other individuals (Haslam & Reicher, 2006), and feel more attractive and likeable (Posten, 1998) which can lead to positive relationships. Naturally, fans attempt to associate themselves with successful teams and in the process appear more positive as a result (McDonald, Milne & Hong, 2002). The economic interest invested by sports fans is not insignificant, evidenced by the wide range of sports-specific television networks, radio stations, and magazines in Europe (Johnsen & Solwell, 2007), for example.

SPORTS SPECTATORSHIP AND ATTENDANCE

Factors affecting whether a spectator attends a sports event can be divided into consumer preferences (crowd effect), economic factors (price of tickets, cost of travel, fan income unemployment level), stadia experiences, weather conditions, event characteristics (team success, match quality, uncertainty of match outcome, opponent characteristics) and supply scarcity (stadium capacity) (Borland & MacDonald, 2003). Wann's (1995) Sport Fan Motivation Scale (SFMS) similarly draws eight motivational constructs to assess sport spectator motive – namely, *eustress, self-esteem benefits, escape, entertainment, economic factors, aesthetic qualities, group affiliation, and family needs.*

Singapore's sports culture is promoted by the Singapore Sports Council (SSC), with the view to helping build the nation's identity through sports and bringing people from various walks of life and culture together (SSC, 2012). Its research efforts include studying sports participation trends over the past decade (from 2002 to 2011) which shows that only 38% of Singaporeans had any sports participation in 2005 while more recent figures show 42.2% of all Singaporeans do some form of sports activity once a week.

The S-League is the only professional domestic football league in Singapore, and comprises local teams supplemented by a handful of foreign teams. Currently, Brunei DPMM FC (Brunei Darussalam), Albirex Niigata FC (Japan) and Harimau Muda (Malaysia) are the foreign teams participating in the league. Before the S-League, local club teams were amateur, semi-professional outfits having little spectator interest, with a Singapore team (comprising of the best local footballers and professional foreign players) separately competing in the Malaysia Cup and Malaysian Football League, largely supported by the majority of Singapore football fans.

After a victorious campaign that ended with this team winning the league and cup double in 1994, the FAS decided to pull out of the competition to the shock and anxiety of the local supporters (Palakrishnan & Malathi, 1996). Citing participation in the Malaysia Cup as a severe restriction to talent growth in the country, the S-League was an alternative avenue operated on strict criteria, such as fiscal sustainability and management competence of clubs. There was no promotion/relegation concept adopted by the league management committee and participating teams had to get approval from the FAS selection committee to register and participate (Palakrishnan & Malathi 1996).

The implementation of tight criteria led to the exit of several local teams, which was then quickly balanced by inviting foreign clubs into the league. This move was explained as vital to ensuring quality and raising the standard of football in the S-League. Thus, Chinese club, Sinchi FC, became the first foreign club in the S-League (Kunju, 2009) with the addition of the Singapore National U-23 side (renamed as the Young Lions). Since inception, several foreign teams have participated in the S-League, including fellow Chinese teams Dalian Shide Siwu FC and Liaoning Guangyuan FC; Japanese team, Albirex Niigata FC (still participating in the league as of 2012); African team, Sporting Afrique FC; and, Super Reds FC from Korea (Kunju, 2009). Etiole FC, a French team which became the first foreign club to win the league, eventually went the way of other clubs before them by failing to meet the criteria set by the S-League committee and consequently withdrawing from the next installment of the campaign (Channel NewsAsia, 2012).

SPECTATORSHIP IN THE S-LEAGUE

The S-League has averaged about 1,090 spectators since inception in 1996 to 2012 (16 years), but in recent years has been erratic – with 2,050 in 2009 followed by a dismal 944 in 2011 (TODAY, 2012). It appears clubs are resigned to the fact that sale proceeds from ticket sales are not going to contribute much to their budget, since the attendance "figures provided by clubs include complimentary tickets, regardless of the presence of the ticket holders at the stadium" (TODAY, 2010), with the actual paying spectators making up just 10%.

In spite of these modest attendance figures, it was shortlisted as one of the top 10 leagues by the Asian Football Confederation (AFC) in 2007 – the only football league in Southeast Asia to be selected

Table 1. S-League average attendance figures

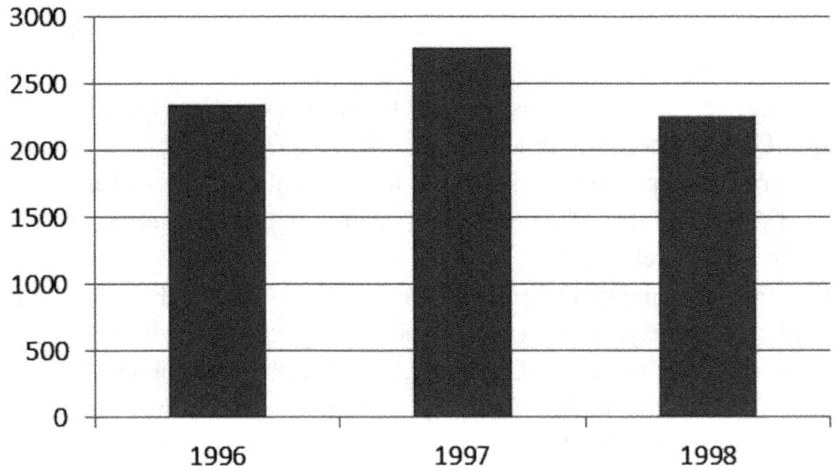

Number of spectators attending each S-League match on average for the first three years

Table 2. S-League average attendance and average sales figures

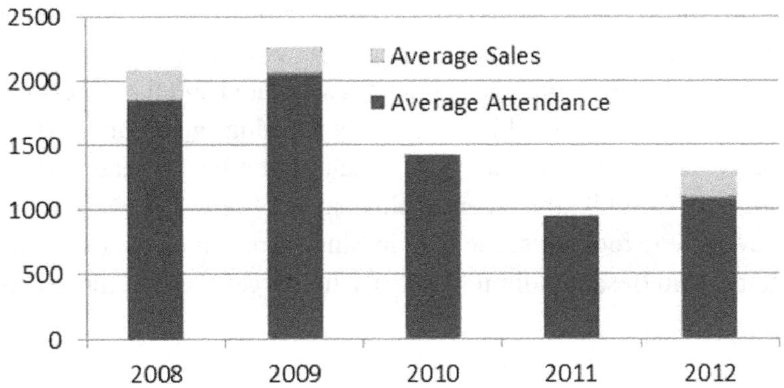

Number of spectators attending each S-League match on average in recent years, including the proportion of tickets as a result of sales

**Data on ticket sales was not available for the years 2010 and 2011.*

for this prestigious honour (AsiaOne, 2007). Attendance figures that year were registered at an average of 2,700, up from the 2,526 for 2006, with television viewership rising to an average of 80,000, up from 37,000. The market feasibility of the S-League translated into more sponsorship opportunities where non-sports related brands such as Levi's and Nokia came on board to sponsor the league and Nike's $1 million a year sponsorship over five years demonstrated its strength.

But currently, the S-League management committee's target is to attract just 2,000 fans per match as attendance figures have continued to plummet. Generally, poor sales is a problem faced by every club in the S-League, with the better attendance figures in 2005 and 2006 attributed to the Singapore National Team doing well at the time. Various clubs have resorted to different tactics to encourage more spectators to attend matches – for example, in 2010, players of Sengkang Punggol (which has since been renamed as Hougang United) went to the streets to hand out a list of upcoming fixtures and tickets. For most clubs, it is their community outreach programme that is the main platform of promoting the S-League (TODAY, 2010) – Balestier Khalsa Football Club for instance went door to door to try and establish a bond with the community (Reuters, 2013). Another club, Woodlands Wellington, relies on food, beverage and item giveaways to draw in the crowds.

The S-League organizing committee meanwhile, has resorted to cheerleading in an effort to boost attendance – an 'S-League Super Gals' concept where female cheerleaders from Singapore, Australia, Indonesia and Argentina were recruited to perform at S-League matches, in the hopes of upping the excitement level at the stadiums (Yahoo Sports, 2012). However, such initiatives did not sit well with some local fans likening it to "using sex to sell stuff".

Former international, R Sasikumar and Singapore Armed Forces Football Club (SAFFC) coach Kok believe that raising the quality of foreign players in the league is the way forward, which echoes the sentiments of international pundits – for example, Jamie Carragher, a former Liverpool player mentioned that the English Premier League (EPL) needed the best foreign players in order to be the best league in the world (The Telegraph, 2012) while another England international, Matthew Le Tissier, also agreed that the EPL is more exciting because of the foreign imports (The Mirror, 2013).

Most of the S-League clubs have stadiums that offer in excess of over 2,500 seating capacity but are hardly filled up during matches. Shahril Jantan, a current player and goalkeeper with Home United, mentioned in an interview that "seeing the crowds spilling out of the stadiums was the only reason why I want to be a professional footballer. But for the past four to five years, the crowds have dwindled and the interest has shifted to the Malaysian Super League (MSL)," (kallangroar.com, 2012).

Former SAFFC coach Vincent Subramaniam feels that the league has stagnated and the dependence on subsidies from the FAS is a sign that the current model is not entirely working (goal.com, 2012) as reiterated by another former S-League coach, R. Vengadasalam, who said that after 17 years the state of league attendance is poor (goal.com, 2013). While the recent inclusion of a Lions XII team into the Malaysian Super League (MSL) has revived the football scene here in Singapore somewhat (thousands have been packing into the 8,000 capacity Jalan Besar Stadium weekly), it has largely been at the expense of the S-League (TODAY, 2012).

CRITICAL ANALYSIS OF THE S-LEAGUE MODEL

Using a SWOT analysis (Mullins, 2010), the S-League model was analysed based on press reports and other local website sources, as not much information was available in academic literature at the time of writing.

Strengths

Professional League Set-Up

The S-League is the platform to promote football excellence and raise the quality of football to full professional standards while promoting the ideals of sportsmanship and fair play. It is also the stage to provide a rich and fulfilling environment to enable football players and coaches to build a strong base of quality talent to compete internationally as well as gain recognition for the sport as a worthwhile career. The League also aims to raise, encourage and nurture community awareness and participation by providing high quality football worthy of community pride and loyalty, supporting the regional football clubs in their youth development programmes with a commitment to promote budding footballers and honing their skills and knowledge of football (sleague.com, 2013)

Prestige

Despite the formation of a professional league only in 1996, Singapore was ranked 13th (out of the top 25 leagues in the Asian region) in the Asian Football Confederation (AFC) list of 2010. The ranking system is determined by the top five clubs of each country which scored the highest in the Club World Ranking during that calendar year, determined by the International Federation of Football History & Statistics (www.iffhs.de, 2013). In fact, the S-League is widely regarded as the best league in South East Asia, and has been shortlisted by the AFC in 2007 as among the top ten leagues in Asia (sleague.com).

Sustained Community Engagement

Clubs are continuously encouraged to do their part in community engagement – an example would be the pledge by Geylang International Football Club (GIFC) and NTUC Club in February 2013 to work together and co-organize football-related events and activities for community engagement and talent development. Mr. Leong Kok Fann, Chairman of GIFC and Mr. Yeo Khee Leng, Chief Executive Officer of NTUC Club, both agreed to share their resources and facilities to achieve this community bonding aim (kallangroar.com, 2013).

Continued Efforts by Organising Committee

The S-League Business Unit (SBU) has engaged the assistance of Sports Business Group (Deloitte, UK) to carry out a strategic review of the S-League in time for changes to be implemented for the new season. The SBU intends to bring the S-League model forward and ensure clubs become self-financed entities through commercial development frameworks. A strategic blueprint has been formulated to guide this development, including recommendations on league's vision and mission, structure and organization, commercial operations, expenditure and funding, and facilities and stadia (Deloitte, UK), in addition to the $430,000 in annual cash subsidies received by clubs from the FAS (AsiaOne, 2013).

The efforts of the S-League organizing committee can be evidenced by the memorandum of understanding signed with MINDEF (Singapore Armed Forces) and Ministry of Home Affairs (MHA) that commits each full time National Serviceman (NSF) to attend at least one S-League match annually with his company/platoon. In addition, NSFs attending the games would be given off-in-lieu if the team they are representing wins (3 days off) or draw (1 day off). NSFs are also required to sit for a test that poses questions about the match attended and compels the NSF to attend another match (and one extra duty) should he answer three or more questions wrongly. Finally, NSFs are required to cheer loudly for their team and produce at least one banner to demonstrate their support, and are bound to fulfill these requirements before they are officially released from service (The League News, 2012).

Weaknesses

Poor Club Finances

Clubs reportedly need about $1.2 million annually to run an S-League club, inclusive of player and staff salaries and the costs of renting stadiums and training facilities from the Singapore Sports Council (The Straits Times, 2011). In some instances, clubs have been forced by their funding situation to withdraw from the competition altogether – e.g. Gombak United withdrew from the current season's competition (Liga Singapura, 2012), marking the second time it has had to do so (it was out from 2003 to 2005).

Lack of Quality Foreign Players

The monthly salary cap for a 'Star Player' is fixed at S$85,000, with the caveat that he must have featured prominently in any of the elite leagues in Europe (sleague.com, 2012). This salary though is not fully borne by the clubs but by sponsors and the league authorities, which indicates a lack of spending power and lack of independent financial strength of the clubs. While this concept was drawn from similar systems employed by other countries such as Japan, Australia and the United States, fans still point out that the poor crowd figures are due to the lack of quality foreigners (Mediacorp, 2009), which is echoed by former players such as national team player Egmar Goncalves who observes a sharp drop in attendance numbers since the league's inception (redsports.sg, 2010).

To a large extent, Singapore's experience with the marquee player system has not been good with only one player big enough to fit such a billing (Cameroonian Emile Mbouh Mbouh who had featured in the World Cup editions of 1990 and 1994). Local fan-inspired group 'Lions All The Way' (LATW) suggests that the foreign players were better in the early days of the S-League than what we are seeing now (lionsatw.com, 2011).

Negative Impact of Lions XII's Participation in MSL

The reality is that Singapore football is divided across two camps – one seeking local league growth while the other rooting for Lions XII, a U-23 side comprising of local footballers, playing in the Malaysian football league (known as the Malaysian Super League, or MSL). Balestier Khalsa vice-chairman S Thavaneson suggested that the S-League will suffer falling attendance levels depending on how the LionsXII team fares in the MSL, Malaysian FA Cup and Malaysia Cup (TODAY, 2012), with the current observation being thousands of fans packing the stadium to watch the Lions XII while local S-League clubs struggle to get even 250 paying fans.

Media's Preference in Promoting Lions XII Over S-League

The media has helped in the promotion of the Lions XII matches with social media platforms being used intensively to spread awareness and create interest. This enables the reach to go beyond the actual crowd attendance at the stadium of about 8,000 through mobile phone applications offered by StarHub (which is the Official Broadcaster and Principal Sponsor of LionsXII) (kallangoroar.com, 2012) – something that has not been extended much to S-League matches.

Poor Attendances

Sports events (such as football matches) offer the chance to spend time with family members, friends and business associates, and a healthy sports setting builds and motivates players' performances as well (McDonald, Milne & Hong, 2002). Players like Noh Alam Shah (an ex-international player for Singapore) cited the poor crowd turnout as one of the factors that led him to move abroad to the Indonesian Super League because the fanatical crowd support was motivating.

For the 2013 edition, the league format had been changed such that twelve teams were set to play a total of 27 league matches, an increase of three games coming through the introduction of a split-group, half-round, after two full rounds are completed, with the teams divided into two mini-leagues of six each. According to S-League Director of Operations Kok Wai Leong, such a format will present a good compromise in enhancing the competitiveness of the 18-year-old professional league (sleague.com, 2012), however, such efforts come across as desperate efforts to raise attendance numbers.

High Stadium Rental Fees

Another drawback for clubs and even other National Sports Associations (NSAs) is the substantial increase in leasing facilities from the SSC that "reflect the market valuation of these community facilities" (AsiaOne, 2013). In Singapore, stadiums are not owned by the clubs and thus renting sets them back by more than $80,000 annually. While the SSC subsidises $3.5 million of the rental cost (i.e. clubs pay $1.2 million of the $4.7 million bill), the annual cash subsidy of $430,000 is still a far cry from offsetting the actual financial impact of the rental (AisaOne, 2013).

Unrecognised Club Affiliation and Identity

Humans are social beings and thus have the desire to develop and sustain associations or relations with others (Handy, 1993) but the poor entertainment level of the S-League does not provide a conducive environment for this to occur. As Holt (2002) mentioned, fans can be both consumers and actors at the sporting event or game, and their desire to be part of the event is the actualization of the event (Keyes, 1998).

Another major influence on fan attendance is the degree of identification the spectator has with the team (Lagace, 1996), and those who identify highly with a team tend to more involved with team players, more tolerant of ticketing issues, view fellow spectators as special and feel the need to be with fellow fans (Wann & Branscombe, 1993), thus building team fan bases and promoting solidarity through sports and leisure activities (Wakefield, Blodgett & Sloan, 1996). There have been informal sprouting of S-League club supporters' groups and the issue seems to be that such clubs remain as unofficial supporters' groups. Despite their contributions being acknowledged by the club's management and the players themselves, there has been minimal effort to make them a part of the marketing strategy.

While there is talk of making 'Black Sheep' supporter groups into official fan clubs, the implementation will have to wait because such measures are not the immediate concern of the clubs, though this attitude is strange considering the fact that attendance figures have been very poor at stadiums and the clubs face the particular issue of how to grow revenue.

No Promotion/Relegation Format

The poor state of S-League clubs and even poorer state of National Football League (NFL) clubs make the prospect of any promotion/relegation system unfeasible, but the alternative idea hitting bottom teams with fines could be detrimental, bearing in mind that clubs are already struggling financially to stay afloat. Media reports have mentioned talk of a penalty of around S$50,000 each to the bottom two teams in the 2013 season, which is certainly unwelcomed by clubs, who presently make very little through ticket sales and merchandising (sleague.com, 2012).

No Income From TV Rights

The FAS announced a deal to have Great Eastern-YEO's S-League matches broadcast by StarHub and MediaCorp, the league's broadcast partners (starhub.com, 2011) where one 'live' match would be telecast every Friday. Employing segments of the football audience by Merkel (1994) and Rubin and Windhal's (1986) dependency model, the S-League fan base largely comprises consumers whose interest in football is rather sensitive – with the other two segments being fans whose demand for the game and support remains very strong and those whose interest in the game is moderate (Johnsen & Solwell, 2007). However, the TV broadcasting approach does not seem to allow for the growth of spectatorship in the S-League as the limited number of matches telecast requires a fan to subscribe to a 12-month package that includes many other things other than the main focus.

With regard to TV broadcast money, in England, increased TV rights will benefit all clubs in the EPL (Solanki, 2012), with the entire deal worth billions. Contrasted against the S-League, the televised game every Friday on MediaCorp, Singapore's only free-to-air broadcaster, probably generates little revenue (if any at all) and is more likely an initiative funded by the FAS – as opposed to most countries where the local football association is paid by sports broadcast markets. Ultimately though, the fact remains that Singapore's tiny domestic market will never extend the viewership numbers to be of any significant impact (redsports.sg, 2009).

Opportunities

Revenue Through Merchandising

A professional sports team typically harnesses the potential to build brand equity by capitalizing on the emotional relationship it shares with its fans (Underwood, Bond, & Baer, 2001) which in turn generates income through the sale of a variety of goods and services (Burton & Howard, 1999; Gustafson, 2001; Mullin, Hardy & Sutton, 2000). The SBU is looking into how outreach programmes such having activities in the heartland malls (Liga Singapura, 2013) can connect with the 'heartlanders', such that better branding can be achieved. Loyalty is a 'deeply held commitment to re-buy or patronize a preferred product/service consistently in the future, thereby causing repetitive same-brand or same brand-set purchasing' (Oliver, 1999), and in order for such loyalty to be ingrained and developed further, merchandising remains an important outlet. The store at Jalan Besar Stadium (home stadium of Courts Young Lions) in Singapore will open soon and fans will be able to purchase jerseys of their favourite teams.

Foreign Stints for Promising Players

The S-League offers players the chance to move abroad and play in a different setting – such as Ridhuan, who started his career with the Young Lions in before moving to Tampines Rovers and eventually joining former Singapore international Noh Alam Shah at Arema in Indonesia (Yahoo Sports, 2013). Similarly, there are people in the industry such as Frenchman Gouttefangeas who are actively trying link top local players with clubs abroad for training stints, attachments and even playing contracts (TODAY, 2012).

Possible Football Tie-Ups With Other Leagues

The inclusion of foreign clubs in the S-League has increased diplomatic relations – for example, Japan and Singapore signed a Memorandum of Understanding (MOU) in June 2013 (aseanfootball.org, 2013) which will see Asia's top professional football league provide assistance and guidance to the S-League on enhancing the latter's overall management, while strengthening its influence and reach in the region.

Increased Prize Money

There will be an increase of S$100,000, S$50,000 and S$20,000 in prize money awarded to the teams finishing first, second and third respectively for the 2013 edition of the S-League. Tampines Rovers received S$150,000 as S-League champions in 2012, runners-up DPMM S$75,000, and third-placed Albirex S$40,000. There will be also rise in excess of S$20,000 for each of the top three teams in the 2013 edition of the RHB Singapore Cup (Sleague.com, Nov 2012).

Threats

Competing Against the English Premier League

While there are many fans worldwide for the major football leagues around the world, it is possible that the large population base in countries like Indonesia and Malaysia ensure their local leagues remain unaffected (Travel CNN, 2010). This not the case for Singapore where poor spectatorship numbers can be consistently linked to the preference of Singaporeans to watch English Premier League (EPL) matches live on TV instead of going to the stadium of an S-League match (Reuters, 2013). Singaporeans tend to affiliate themselves better with EPL teams such as Liverpool and Manchester United than local teams.

A case in point would be when the Singapore National Team played Liverpool at the National Stadium which was filled with Liverpool fans – i.e. Singaporeans there to support Liverpool over the national team (Travel CNN, 2010). There are currently more than 300,000 subscribers for the sports package on StarHub, resulting in fans paying $96.3 million in cable fees, which is five times the 2007 operating income of the FAS (redsports.sg, 2009).

Foreign Club Inclusion May Dilute Local Talent Pool

Teams from Europe, Africa and Asia have already expressed an interest in joining Singapore's S-League next season (AsiaOne, 2010). While foreign clubs are invited to participate in lieu for local clubs that pull out, opinion is divided if this brings positive or negative influence. Former Woodlands Wellington and

Tampines Rovers official R. Vengadasalam pointed to Sinchi (poor discipline) and Liaoning Guangyuan FC (match-fixing scandal) as examples of the trouble they bring (goal.com, 2013). Former Singapore international Malek Awab similarly suggests that the future of the S-League lies with local teams and that the foreign sides are not helping local football (AsiaOne.com, 2010).

End of Sponsorships and Media Attention

The S-League is struggling to attract significant cash injection from sponsors. Great Eastern, an insurance firm has come on board since 2009 with $1.8 million to co-sponsor with local beverage company Yeo's (redsports.sg, 2009). Local mainstream media hardly reports on the S-League and The Straits Times, the main English broadsheet, does not cover the S-League on a sustained basis, but instead devotes more attention to European leagues such as the EPL and other international sports. Unfortunately, the limited reach that the S-League has (as compared to the EPL) will mean that it is likely to continue grappling with this.

RESEARCH METHODOLOGY

Based on the SWOT analysis, there is a clear worry on league attendances at matches, and the following broad questions were drawn to guide this explorative study, which includes both qualitative (focus group discussion, face to face interview & observation) as well as quantitative (pilot study and survey findings) methodologies.

1. Has Lions XII participation in the MSL (a Singapore team in the neighbouring Malaysian Super League) led to poor attendance figures in the S-League since 2011?
2. Do local fans prefer to watch the English Premier League (EPL) on TV than watch S-League matches (live at stadium or on TV)?
3. Is media promotion in favour of the Lions XII than the S-League?
4. Has the non-existence (or low strength) of club affiliations and identification with local clubs in the S-League resulted in poor spectatorship?

Qualitative Exploration

The qualitative research is a field that intersects many fields of study (Glenn, 2010) and is aimed at providing more thorough information and inquiring a comprehensive and deeper understanding of the entire situation (Ross, 1999) that results in an in-depth presentation of facts not found in qualitative analysis (Jha, 2008). Thus the "blending of qualitative and quantitative methods of research can produce a final product which can highlight the significant contributions of both" (Nau, 1995, p.1) where "qualitative data can support and explicate the meaning of quantitative research" (Jayaratne, 1993, p.117).

Focus Group Discussion

Focus groups involve the use of in-depth group interviews in which participants are selected because they are a purposive, although not necessarily representative, sampling of a specific population, this group being 'focused' on a given topic (Thomas et al., 1995). Participants in this qualitative research mechanism would probably have something to say on the topic, are within the age-range, have similar socio-characteristics and would be comfortable talking to the interviewer and each other (Richardson & Rabiee, 2001).

A fan group (Ultras Eagles) which was established in 2012 by a group of enthusiasts of Geylang International Football Club was invited to this focus group discussion. The questions were drawn based on Wann's (1995) Sport Fan Motivation Scale (SFMS), a research developed to assess sport spectator motives using eight motivational constructs.

Face-to-Face Interview

The in-depth interview pursues a respondent's subjective interpretation of a subject and allows researchers to gather detailed attitudinal and experiential information from respondents, which is elicited through broad, open-ended, exploratory questions (Powell & Single, 1996). In-depth interviews are a useful qualitative data collection technique and are most appropriate for situations in which you want to ask open-ended questions that elicit depth of information from relatively few people, unlike surveys which is a quantitative approach (Guion, Diehl & McDonald, 2001).

The questions used in this study (Appendix A) were drawn to elicit answers on the S-League playing experience of players and eventually moved onto the current S-League model where players were queried on the attendance situation and ways to improve it. This approach was to complement the earlier focus group discussion process and to compare the perceptions of a fan group with players to see whether both sets of participants have differing or similar views of the research study.

Observation

The observation method is employed in this research study as a means to collect data in qualitative methodology. Observation can be used as a research method in two distinct ways – structured and unstructured (Pretzlik, 1994). Observation methods provide researchers with ways to check for nonverbal expression of feelings, determine who interacts with whom, grasp how participants communicate with each other, and check for how much time is spent on various activities (Schmuck, 1997). This research tool was employed in this study alongside the focus group discussions and interviews with players to further enhance the validity of the research.

Tomlinson's (1995) classification of influences is perhaps one of the more prominent approaches, where factors are categorized into controllable and uncontrollable. The revised influence factors chosen for the research study on New Zealand sportscape and rugby union by Garland, Macpherson and Haughey (1994) was employed in this study as most of the factors are relevant. Certain factors were omitted in view of the scope of this study (e.g. planned special events, testimonials/benefits, childcare facilities, fan income/catchment area size).

Quantitative Exploration

Quantitative methods such as surveys and questionnaires allow the researcher to remove biases of the respondents (Kothari, 2004). In addition, quantitative methods enhance research validity and accuracy especially when numerical expression is included (Colwell, 2006). A quantitative research design, ac-

Table 3. Fan attendance influences

Controllable Influences	Uncontrollable Influences
General atmosphere/party atmosphere Game live on television Food & beverage availability & quality Star players/team quality Stadium sportscape – capacity, toilets etc. Opportunities for social interaction Parking availability/proximity/access Other fans' behaviour (especially offensive) Pricing – tickets/parking/"whole" day" Location of available seats Ease of access to stadium Entertainment - pre & post-match/off-field Time of game (weekend/evening)	Good weather Unplanned special events – semifinals/finals Recent performance (slumps/winning) Quality of opposition Time in the season Team position in the league Chance of winning Live sport action/family outing/other games Other competing entertainment Unplanned special events – semifinals/finals Recent performance (slumps/winning)

cording to Jones (1997), enables the researcher to have the "flexibility in the treatment of data, in terms of comparative analyses, statistical analyses, and repeatability of data collection in order to verify reliability" as well.

Survey

Using Hansen and Gauthier's (1989) study of factors affecting attendance at professional sport events, forty variables (classified into economic, personal demographics, entertainment and residual factors) were identified and questionnaires drawn based on these. Using the mass reach and cost effectiveness of an online survey, respondents were directed to the survey site (Survey Monkey) through the high traffic Facebook page of *The Online Citizen.*

The original survey included 44 questions to help understand the awareness levels of the S-League model, as well as the fan and club identity football fans have in general. A pilot study was then done on 13 participants, which identified several limitations of the questions and the possible erroneous answers that might be drawn out. Based on the information gained from the pilot test, several changes were made to the survey. The final draft of the survey included items measuring respondent demographics, sports preferences, establishing their interest in football, football match attendance (local), football match non-attendance and the reasons behind both attendance and non-attendance preferences (e.g. stadia experience, team identity, preference to watching foreign football over local football, Lions xi match viewing preferences, etc.).

FINDINGS

Focus Group Discussion

Five out of seven participants (one did not respond) in the focus group discussion agreed that situations of sports, either through reading, watching or discussing it enabled one to temporarily escape life's problems. This raises the possibility of the fact that Singapore is a stressful society. Betting was not a reason for involvement in sports for most participants of this discussion process. The group/family following were again primarily important for most participants, relating to the theories of club affiliation and following, which was primarily lacking in the S-League.

Generally, all focus group members agreed that the marketing and branding of the S-League was bad and this area needed lots of improvement, including lack of merchandising (as referenced in the SWOT analysis). With regard to the spectatorship issues in the league, a variety of reasons were offered by the participants, with the general view being a lack of marketing, branding (again) and the lure of the EPL as reasons for the poor spectatorship numbers at stadiums. A few participants attributed to the spectatorship numbers at stadiums to the economic gains of betting. Despite betting not being a reason for the fan group participants' spectatorship at matches, they felt that the older generation (those over 50) could be watching matches live at the stadiums for this purpose.

Stadia experience, entertainment and the availability of food and beverages were cited as very important by the participants and they reiterated that these were sorely lacking at local stadiums. Most encouraged the creation of group/family-friendly events to be included as match-day entertainment. The lack of food and beverage accommodation was seen as an important aspect neglected by the clubs especially for working adults who attend midweek matches. Ticketing and the availability of multiple locations for ticket purchases was not a major concern as low average attendance figures meant that tickets were most likely available at the venues directly.

Fan identity, with regard to supporting a winning team was mentioned as being a strong motivational factor but generally was not that decisive according to the responses of the participants. As for the support for the league based on its players' quality and entertainment, it drew mixed responses and there was no clear evidence of what the respective individuals clearly wanted. Some were critical of the player quality and were citing the lack of match day experience (referring to the atmosphere at the stadium), while others sounded more like hardcore fans who stick with a particular club no matter what. Generally, most of the participants agreed that sports spectatorship was indeed a form of recreation but as clearly pointed out, the S-league was lacking in numbers and awareness of the league.

Face-to-Face Interview

Both interviewees were from different backgrounds – one is primarily a local footballer while the other is a well-travelled player. The first question was more about their background and links to the S-League, followed by a discussion on their respective football development in relation to the S-League. While the local player agreed that the S-League helped develop his footballing career, (Shahril Jantan), the other (Fabio Fanticelle Da Silva) spoke about his development back in Brazil.

The more relevant questions for this study were from questions three to six where each player was probed on the S-League model and his perceptions of its success and credibility in recent years. Both players agreed that the start of the professional league was good but in recent years has not been very successful. Fabio, being a foreigner, was impressed with the project in the early years in 1996 and was attracted to become a foreign player then while Shahril spoke about how the league is suffering with the limited budgets of the clubs and the lack of sponsorship.

Both interviewees agreed that the league can only thrive with prominent and well-known foreign players and the entertainment factor suffers as a result of poor quality in foreign imports. Shahril spoke about how the marquee signing concept by the S-League organizing committee has failed to attract big stars to Singapore (reflected in SWOT analysis) while Fabio mentioned that S-League players – both local and abroad – are merely waiting for opportunities to move to other leagues. According to him, poor foreign players and the low entertainment factor lead to poor crowd turnouts which, in the end, leaves the league suffering.

Shahril brought up the point that fans being brought together in support of the national team without any relation to local football. The problem of the English Premier League and its big lure in drawing viewership away from local football was mentioned by both players as well. Fabio generally lamented the lack of national emphasis for sports and the lack of club identification amongst fans. Also, the issue about the lack of marketing was mentioned several times, as was the problem of the existence of the Lions XII team. Fabio found it amusing that a team playing in a foreign league was given priority over homegrown local clubs of the country. Shahril added that Singaporeans preferred to follow football on TV and in the comfort of their homes where the availability of cable TV, the EPL and La Liga (Spanish football league) was just a click away. He also mentioned that segregating fan loyalty based on geographical locations in Singapore is not possible as he observes there is no immediate connection.

Both interviewees gave suggestions to improve the league such as increasing the overall operating budget to bring in better players, and enhancing club rivalries in collaboration with fan groups. They felt coaches ought to be given more flexibility and press freedom (a point brought by ex-manager Vengadasalam, as mentioned earlier) to express themselves better and promote the league in their own way, as current press reports are not informative enough to draw the fans and thus the excitement factor is largely absent. Shahril mentioned fan expectations must be fair in the sense that S-League clubs cannot be expected to perform like European clubs and the fans must be realistic enough in this aspect.

Observations Made at S-League Matches

During live observation, stadium appearance, food and beverage availability, and entertainment factors were noted – which appear under the list of controllable influence factors. The social environment and atmosphere of a sporting event is shown to have an impact on fan spectatorship decisions (Guttmann, 1986; Hall et al., 1991; Hocking, 1982; Melnick, 1993: Rothenbuhler, 1988: Smith, 1988). The S-League league needs more than the followers; in fact, they need the casual fans to form the bulk of the attendance. Such casual fans who have little interest in team affairs are influenced by "various forms of advertising that promote specific attributes of the sport product" (Ross et al., 2006, p.262) including discounts and promotional inducements (Allen, 2007). Casual fans decisions are based on "the consumer's decision to attend a game was typically a choice among entertainment alternatives" (Robertson & Pope 1999).

In the S-League, based on match-day observations, half-time entertainment was basically the employment of student groups from ITE College East (a tertiary technical education institute), as percussionists. While non-relevant performances may be effective (Bruce Springsteen's halftime show in a Super Bowl game is an example), it was observed at the Bedok Stadium that the crowd actually left the stadium quickly for smoke breaks and hurried to get food and beverages at nearby coffee joints in close proximity of the stadium during halftime. Therefore, the percussion performance by the ITE students did not deliver the desired effect in the entertainment aspect. The poor economic structure of S-League clubs does not allow for better entertainment events to be arranged. The half-time entertainment proceedings looked decisively on a voluntary basis at no cost.

The regular Singapore football fan is likely a working adult and the availability of food and drinks is a crucial aspect. A significant number of spectators at stadiums are of this type (Johnsen & Solwell, 2007) who will not be satisfied with just watching the match and will look what other stadium 'perks' are available – usually in the form of food and beverage. Based on Maslow' Hierarchy of Needs (1954), an individual's primary need (i.e. food) must be met before the exploration of secondary, tertiary and quaternary necessities are satisfied. Upon observation at two stadiums in the S-League, the aspect of food and beverage is seriously neglected – the availability is basically provisional tables, temporarily set up to sell drinks on match-days. The range of food items available to fans were basically hotdogs, burgers and a local favouritessuch 'nasi lemak' (coconut rice with chicken, chilli paste and cucumber pieces).

Recent studies show that the facility and its service elements play a critical role in fan behaviour and satisfaction (e.g., O'Neill, Getz, & Carlson, 1999; Wakefield & Sloan, 1995). Packed stadiums bring a variety of surreal experiences to fans that lead to continuous interest in the sport, much like for a player who thrives on playing in packed stadiums (a point illustrated in the SWOT analysis). Of course, such association at packed stadiums brings an added excitement to the paying fans and the eventual formation of fan subcultures, which in turn creates identification with the team (Holt, 1995; Melnick, 1993).

The stadium experience in the case of the S-League is extremely crucial, in view of poor spectatorship numbers. Usually, the clubs look to the growth and sale of corporate boxes, members' stands, and season ticket packages to bring fans to the game, increasing gate takings and revenue (Harper, 1993; Howard & Crompton, 1995). Ownership of stadiums allows clubs and owners to look into improving the match-day experience for fans such as incorporating larger screens for replays, computer graphics, and other messages; luxury boxes; a full range of food and beverage services from sit down restaurants in ice-cream stands; improved seating; pre-game, halftime, and post-game entertainment; and amenities such as in-seat television screens and even cup-holders (John & Sheard, 1999; Swearingen, 1986).

Observations were done both at the Bedok Stadium (home of S-League club Geylang International FC) and at the Toa Payoh stadium (home of S-League club Balestier Khalsa FC). Both stadiums were poorly prepared to host a professional football league game, with only minimum security. Both stadiums also did not display enough vivacity to indicate that they were proper football stadiums. As discussed earlier, the non-ownership by clubs has resulted in poor maintenance of the stadiums with clubs merely using the stadium facilities to play matches and do nothing else further to bring a sense of exclusivity or attach identity to the venue.

Survey Results

The attendance and non-attendance aspects took precedence in this research study as the four research questions were brought into perspective. A total of 282 respondents responded to the survey, with 93% (263) indicating that they were football fans. 93% (262) of the survey participants were males and 7% (20) were females. All participants had completed at least a secondary school education and over 77% (206) were employed either on a full-time or part-time basis. The financial status of the participants showed that 64% (177) were earning more than S$30, 000 a year, and 99% (280) were able to access the internet from home, with 46% (129) being StarHub subscribers.

A portion of the survey questionnaire (questions 9-18) attempted to discover the perceptions of the participants, with questions targeting their views on Singapore being a sports nation and how sports events in Singapore generated interest. The results indicated that 79% (224) disagreed that Singapore is a sports nation and generally sports events attracted little interest or interest was generated only for selected events (86% or 242). This was followed up with another question where survey respondents were asked about the efforts of sports associations on sports spectatorships; with over 81% (228) illustrating that sports spectatorship promotion either was absent or caused a state of uncertainty amongst sports fans.

Figure 1. Respondent perception of Singapore as a sports nation

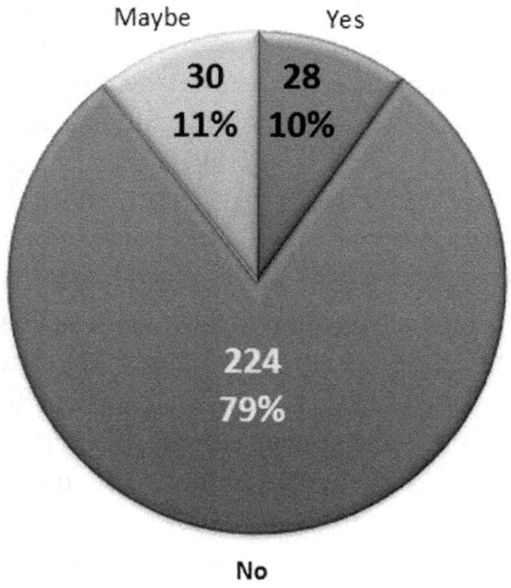

Is Media Promotion in Favour of the Lions XII Than the S-League?

Addressing one of the research questions explored in this paper, 57% (162) of the respondents agreed that there was little promotion or marketing (media) efforts were generally done at the start of an event and were only for selected events. 50% (141) gave the efforts to promote Lions XII as an example where media marketing was present. 31% (87) participants disagreed or indicated that they were unsure whether any marketing done in the first place.

The research study focused on local football spectatorship and the S-League in particular. As a result, out of the 263 survey participants who watched football in various media platforms, 66% (135) mentioned that they are regular spectators at football stadiums (S-League matches alone) while 34% (71) reported that they did not watch football matches regularly at stadiums. Thus non-attendance questions were directed at these 71 respondents while the 135 regular S-League spectators were queried on the aspects associated with S-League in general. The preference for the EPL and Lions XII was investigated by directing relevant questions at the 135 regular S-League spectators. 85% (115) of these agreed that they must support the local football fraternity but only 48% (65) agreed that watching the S-League matches made them happy.

Has Non-Existence of Club Affiliations in the S-League Resulted in Poor Spectatorship?

Only 36% (49) of the 135 regular S-League spectators agreed with the notion that team identity was linked to a club's success, while 46% (62) agreed that S-League matches provided a platform for meeting and forming friendships. Research does suggest that fan identity does not necessarily associate itself with team success though this aspect could change over time due to evolving circumstances. Only 36% (49) agreed that S-League matches gave them a sense of belonging to clubs.

Figure 2. Respondent perception of marketing efforts

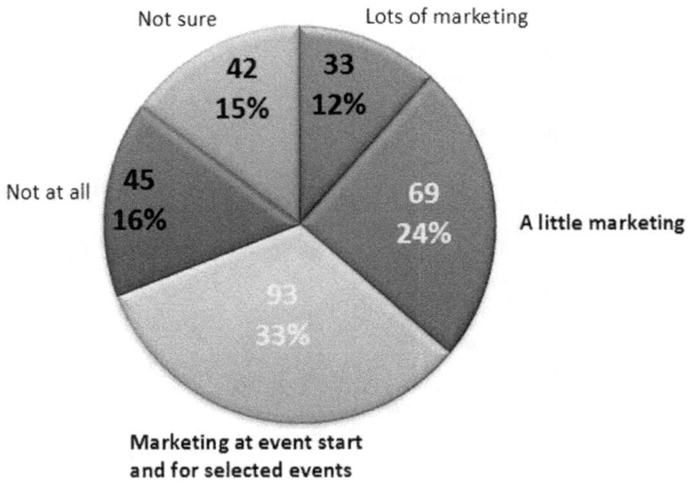

Figure 3. Reactions on whether watching S-League matches leads to happiness

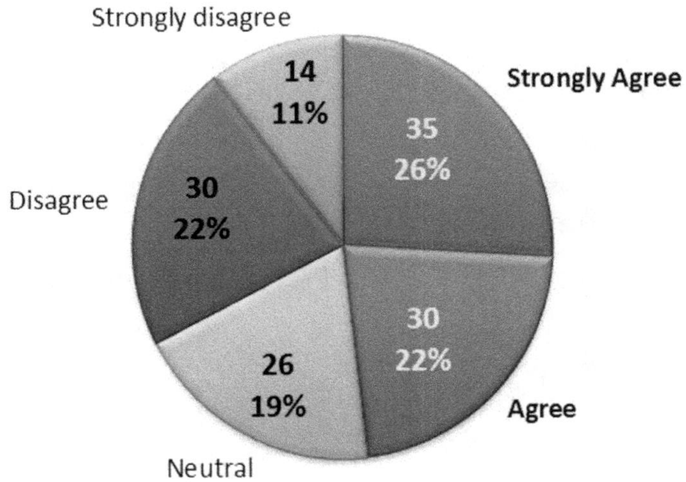

Do Local Fans Prefer to Watch the EPL on TV Than Watch S-League Matches?

62% (44) of the 71 respondents who indicated that they do not watch matches live at stadiums attributed it to a lack of time to physically attend matches. The majority of this group 90% (64) also flatly rejected the notion that they had any club affiliation through the S-League. In addition, 88% (63) indicated that S-League matches are boring and did not excite them. On the other hand, 96% (68) of the same set of respondents quoted the EPL as having the upper hand in football viewership here in Singapore and 86% (61) agreed that other football leagues were receiving more attention in Singapore (than the local league).

Figure 4. Feeling of club affiliation

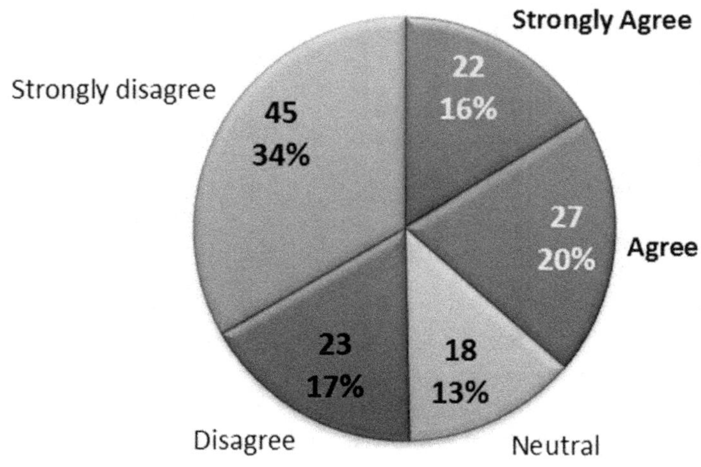

Figure 5. Respondent perception on more interest in other major leagues

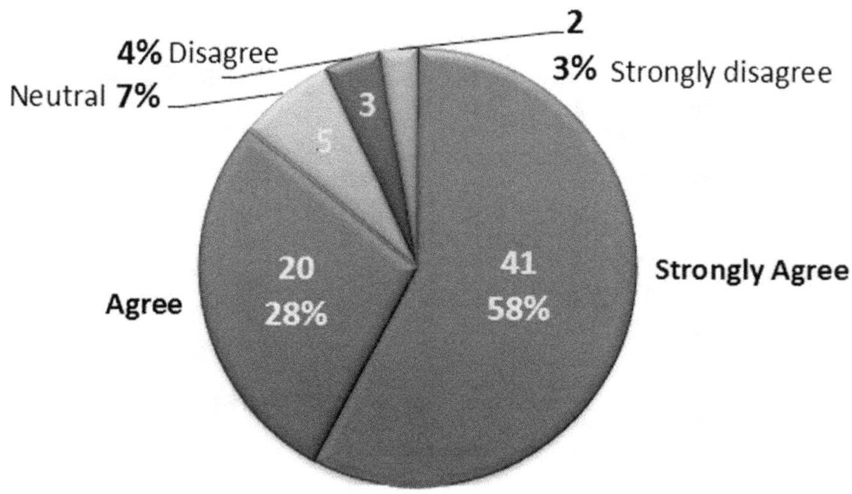

As to the possible reasons for the lack of interest in the S-League, 84% (60) of the respondents mentioned that it lacked quality players, and 78% (58) felt that the advertising and promotion was lacking. Perhaps most worrying is the revelation that there seems to be no interest in S-League matches even when that is the only football available to the individual – 61% (43) of the respondents admitted that usually there was no competing football match such as those telecast live from major European leagues when an S-League match is being played. The preference to watch matches in the comforts of one's home was also illustrated by 62% (44) who indicated that an S-League match of their preference had not been shown 'live' on TV.

Has Lions XII Participation in the MSL Led to Poor AttendWance Figures in the S-League?

Looking at the involvement level of those who did not attend football watches at stadiums, 83% (59) reported that they generally did not have time to support local football. Despite this, 59% (42) indicated that they preferred the causeway rivalry (in response to the Lions XII team playing in the Malaysian league) and 84% (60) clearly preferring to support the Lions XII team rather than any S-League club.

Looking at other incidental factors such as release from stress, the association of vicarious achievement of team success and interest of S-League matches because of the placement of bets (from an attending fan's perspective), 90% of survey respondents mentioned that food and beverages were the key aspect to increase sports spectatorship with 57% (77) suggesting pre-match entertainment and 9% (12) suggesting post-match entertainment as key components in increasing sports spectatorship. Other significant figures include wanting match booklets to be part of the match-day programme (46%) and choice seating (17%) as an important aspect of sports spectatorship.

CONCLUSION

As the findings show, the major issues amongst the S-League clubs include poor marketing, branding and revenue income which lead to poor spectatorship numbers during S-League match days. The following recommendations could therefore be adopted by S-League clubs to promote their league structure further and increase numbers of the games.

Figure 6. Respondent preference for Lions XII to S-League

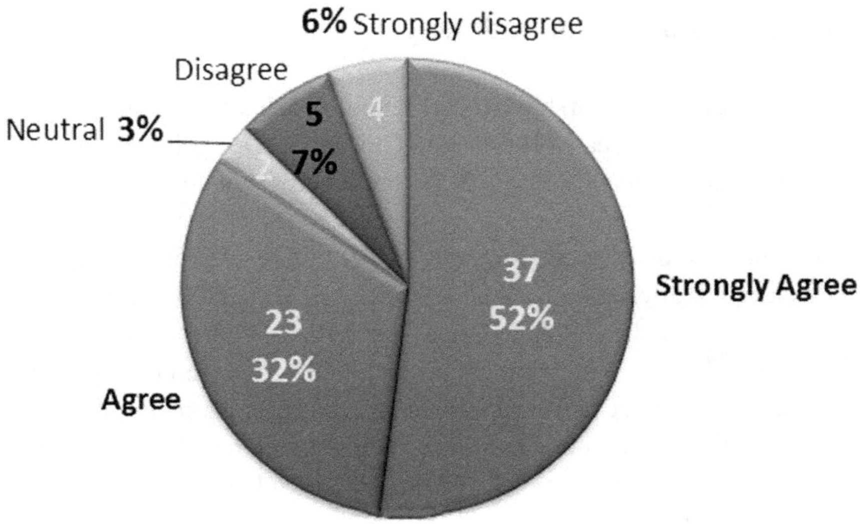

Inspiring the Nation

The Vision 2030 Committee aims to raise public awareness and interest towards sports, in particular local sports by developing sport-centric media channels to elevate local sports coverage in television, print, internet and new media. However, there is only a handful of existing online media coverage portals such as "Vox-sports and Red Sports". Another approach to inspire the local football fraternity could be to promote our S-League players as inspiring heroes and positive role models. There is also a need to have more 'airtime' for S-League matches to be shown and ideally, matches must be telecast from other stadiums, apart from the Jalan Besar Stadium to promote more clubs at their respective home grounds. Another day (besides Friday) should also be used to be telecast matches 'live' from selected stadiums.

Building a Flourishing Sports Ecosystem

The organising committee aims to generate high levels of community involvement, with market-driven initiatives to support sports clubs, programmes and infrastructure. This includes setting up an NSA Advisory Council to discuss issues and strategy, identify areas of collaboration, fortify NSAs' sports management capabilities so that NSAs can become world-class, and encourage the private sector to manage sports facilities and programming for the public to enjoy more varied and accessible playing opportunities.

Ratify MCYS Sporting Culture Committee Recommendations

Areas of synergy could include greater community involvement by our elite athletes to build up sports participation at the grassroots level. A 'many helping hands' approach would encompass rallying key stakeholders in the government and non-government sectors – such as NSAs, grassroots groups and sports clubs – to help drive sports awareness and participation.

Deploy Short-Term Measures Immediately

The 'Youth Olympics Games Spectatorship Model' relied on schools and military forces to fill up a certain percentage of the spectator seats (The Online Citizen, 2010). Although this is not a long-term solution, major S-League games featuring top of the table clashes and cup competitions can accommodate such measures.

Schools adopted countries to represent during the 2010 YOG and promoted them through various activities (www.chungchenghighyishun.moe.edu.sg). The same strategy could be employed to promote S-League clubs, with more than 80 schools in Singapore, especially at primary level, offering football as a Co-Curricular activity (CCA). A specific S-League could be adopted by a school and its students given concession passes to encourage active support on match-day at the stadium. S-League clubs could also visit schools in their geographic neighbourhood and do assembly shows to promote their brand, players and upcoming matches. These are small steps in getting our local populace, especially the young, to appreciate our footballing fraternity.

Currently, the monthly salary cap for a 'Star Player' is capped at S$85,000 with player required to have featured prominently in any of the elite football leagues in Europe. This salary cap should be raised to a more realistic S$100,000 to attract the necessary marquee quality. As fans here are huge followers of EPL, necessary effort should be made to get players from this popular who are in the twilight of their careers to consider joining one of the S-League clubs.

Another possible angle could be Singapore Pools – the country's major gaming operator that includes collecting bets on S-League matches, offering free tickets to those who place bets through its platform on local league matches as inducement for punters to attend those matches.

At the present moment, some stadiums do not have a proper food & beverage stalls operating on match-days, which has been repeatedly surfaced through the various analyses contained in this study. This is indeed an important aspect which has been neglected, bearing in mind that most spectators of S-League matches do so on a weekday after the end of their workday. The availability of beer (in cups) is another consideration (though controversial due to a large Malay/Muslim representation among spectators) that might help in this regard – with the added possibility of sponsorship from beer companies (an area which can provide rich material for further research).

RECOMMENDATIONS FOR FUTURE RESEARCH

Most of the information sourced in this study has come from newspaper articles and websites. There are virtually no local academic journals or articles which have investigated the attendance situation of games, in general. FAS also declined to provide data on crowd attendances (attendance and sales figures presented in this paper are from 2008, sourced from a newspaper report). The local football federation should take interest in this and work with academic institutions in sport management to develop areas of attendance research and other aspects further. Research on fan groups and the neighbourhood affiliation should be investigated as well. It is hoped that this study wills serve as a catalyst for such further research.

REFERENCES

Armstrong, G. (1998). *Football hooligans*. Oxford, UK: Berg. Architectural Press.

Armstrong, M. (2006). *A handbook of human resource management practice* (10th ed.). London: Kogan Page.

Aseanfootball.org. (2013). *FAS sign MOU with Japan professional football league*. Retrieved from http://www.aseanfootball.org/v2/?p=13147

Asiahoreca.com. (2011). *S-League clubs stand to get $1m*. Retrieved from http://www.asiahoreca.com/Singlenews.aspx?DirID=107&rec_code=717012&title=S-League%20clubs%20stand%20to%20get%20$1m

Asiaone.com. (2007). *Thumbs up to the Super S-League*. Retrieved from http://news.asiaone.com/News/The%2BNew%2BPaper/Story/Thumbs%2Bup%2Bto%2Bthe%2BSuper%2BS-League.html

Asiaone.com. (2010). *Opinion split over foreign teams in S'pore league*. Retrieved from http://www.asiaone.com/News/Latest%2BNews/Sports/Story/A1Story20101008-241295.html

Asiaone.com. (2013). *Clubs may face stadium rental hike*. Retrieved from http://www.asiaone.com/print/News/Latest%2BNews/Sports/Story/A1Story20130120-396692.html

Axrosstheline.com. (2012). *Gombak United to sit out 2013 S-League*. Retrieved from http://axrosstheline.com/2012/11/gombak-united-to-sit-out-2013-s-league.html

Axrosstheline.com. (2013). *SBU task force begins work, Singapore football merchandise store to follow*. Retrieved from http://axrosstheline.com/2013/01/sbu-task-force-begin-work-singapore-football-merchandise-store-to-follow.html

Bennett, R. (2013). *Can you call yourself a U.S. soccer fan if you don't support MLS?* Retrieved from http://espnfc.com/blog/_/name/relegationzone/id/728?cc=4716

Bernard, H. R. (1994). Research methods in anthropology: Qualitative and quantitative approaches (2nd ed.). Walnut Creek, CA: AltaMira Press.

Borland, J., & Macdonald, R. (2003). Demand for sport. *Oxford Review of Economic Policy*, *19*(4), 478–502.

Boyce, C., & Neale, P. (2006). *Conducting in-depth interviews: A guide for designing and conducting in-depth interviews for evaluation input*. Retrieved from http://www.pathfind.org/site/DocServer/m_e_tool_series_indepth_interviews.pdf?docID=6301

Branscombe, N., & Wann, D. (1991). The positive social and self-concept consequences of sports team identification. *Journal of Sport and Social Issues*, *15*(2), 1. doi:10.1177/019372359101500202

Branscombe, N., & Wann, D. (1992). Role of identification with a group, arousal, categorisation processes and self-esteem in sports spectator aggression. *Human Relations*, *45*(10), 1013–1033. doi:10.1177/001872679204501001

Brian Troutman September. (2003). *Sport in society: An inspiration or an opiate?* Retrieved from http://www.briantroutman.com/features/engl030s/papers/essayreview.html

Burca, S., Brannick, T., & Meenaghan, T. (1996). Spectators as consumers: A relationship marketing approach. In *Proceedings Fourth European Congress on Sport Management*. Academic Press.

Burrows, D., & Kendall, S. (1997). Focus groups: What are they and how can they be used in nursing and health care research? *Social Sciences in Health*, *3*, 244–253.

Channelnewsasia.com. (2012b). *Etoile FC will not participate in 2012*. Retrieved from http://www.channelnewsasia.com/stories/singaporelocalnews/view/1177048/1/.html

Channelnewsasia.com. (2012a). Retrieved from http://www.channelnewsasia.com/stories/sportsnews/view/1185686/1/.html

Channelnewsasia.com. (2012c). *Singaporeans overworked, more stressed.* Retrieved from http://www.channelnewsasia.com/stories/singaporelocalnews/view/1225811/1/.html

Channelnewsasia.com. (n.d.). *Football attendance: Not all bad news.* Retrieved from http://www.channelnewsasia.com/stories/sportsnews/view/1185686/1/.html

Choi, Y., Martin, J. J., Park, M., & Yoh, T. (2009). Motivational factors influencing sport spectator involvement in NCAA Division II basketball games. *Journal for the Study of Sports and Athletes in Education, 3*(3), 265–284. doi:10.1179/ssa.2009.3.3.265

Chungchenghighyishun.moe.edu.sg. (n.d.). *We celebrate YOG 2010.* Retrieved from http://www.chungchenghighyishun.moe.edu.sg/cos/o.x?c=/wbn/pagetree&func=view&rid=1040749

Correia, A., & Esteves, S. (2007). An exploratory study of spectators' motivation in football. *International Journal of Sport Management and Marketing, 2*(5), 572–590. doi:10.1504/IJSMM.2007.013968

Creswell, J. (1994). *Research design: Qualitative and quantitative approaches.* London: Sage.

Deloitte.com. (n.d.). *Sports business group case studies - Football money league.* Retrieved from http://www.deloitte.com/view/en_GB/uk/industries/sportsbusinessgroup/967b046ec7583210VgnVCM200000bb42f00aRCRD.htm

DeWalt, K. M., & DeWalt, B. R. (1998). Participant observation. In H. R. Bernard (Ed.), *Handbook of methods in cultural anthropology* (pp. 259–300). Walnut Creek, CA: AltaMira Press.

DeWalt, K. M., & DeWalt, B. R. (2002). *Participant observation: a guide for fieldworkers.* Walnut Creek, CA: AltaMira Press.

Douvis, J. (2007). A review of attendance and non-attendance studies at sporting events. *Department of Sports Sciences, 3*, 2007.

Duke, V. (1991). The sociology of football: A research agenda for the 1990's. *The Sociological Review, 39*(3), 627–645. doi:10.1111/j.1467-954X.1991.tb00870.x

Dunning, E., Murphy, P., & Williams, J. (1988). *The roots of football hooliganism.* London: Routledge.

Facebook.com. (2013a). *WWFC.* Retrieved from https://www.facebook.com/unofficial.wwfc.supporters.club

Facebook.com. (2013b). *Photo 1.* Retrieved from https://www.facebook.com/photo.php?fbid=296116553854740&set=o.288804197796354&type=3&theater

Facebook.com. (2013c). *Photo 2.* Retrieved from https://www.facebook.com/photo.php?fbid=529809290389089&set=pb.479634648739887.-2207520000.1371709871.&type=3&theater

Facebook.com. (2013d). *Photo 3.* Retrieved from https://www.facebook.com/photo.php?fbid=443392372418505&set=pb.283555658402178.-2207520000.1371710592.&type=3&theater

Fink, J.S., Trail, G.T., & Anderson, D.F. (2002b). An examination of team identification: Which motives are most salient to its existence? *International Sports Journal, 6*(Summer),195-207.

Gary Armstrong and Richard Giulianotti. (1997). Entering the field: New perspectives on world football. Berg Publishers.

Goal.com. (2012). Retrieved from http://www.goal.com/en-sg/news/3880/singapore/2012/04/06/3016407/well-probably-struggle-now-with-the-lionsxii-tampines-rovers

Goal.com. (2013a). *Singapore speakeasy.* Retrieved from http://www.goal.com/en-sg/news/3883/features/2013/01/31/3695119/goalcom-singapore-speakeasy-we-must-get-sleague-right-says

Goal.com. (2013b). *Eagles soar comfortably over Young Tigers*. Retrieved from http://www.goal.com/en-sg/match/104235/geylang-international-fc-vs-harimau-muda-b/report?

Goal.com. (2013c). *Woodlands Wellington.* Retrieved from http://www.goal.com/en-sg/match/103313/woodlands-wellington-fc-vs-hougang-united-fc/report

Guion, L. A., Diehl, D. C., & McDonald, D. (2001). *Conducting an in-depth interview*. Academic Press.

Guttman, A. (1986). *Sports spectators*. New York: Columbia University Press.

Hall, J., O'Mahony, B., & Vieceli, J. (2010). An empirical model of attendance factors at major sporting events. *International Journal of Hospitality Management, 29*(2), 328–334. doi:10.1016/j.ijhm.2009.10.011

Hansen, H., & Gauthier, R. (1989). Factors affecting attendance at professional sport events. *Journal of Sport Management, 3*(1), 15–32.

Harper, G. B. (1993, Fall/Winter). An emerging new market. At the university level, the Haslam, S.A. & Reicher, S.D. (2006). Stressing the group: Social identity and the unfolding dynamics of responses to stress. *The Journal of Applied Psychology, 91*, 1037–1052.

Hill, B., & Christine Green, B. (2000). Repeat attendance as a function of involvement, loyalty, and the sportscape across three football contexts. *Sport Management Review, 3*(2), 145–162. doi:10.1016/S1441-3523(00)70083-0

Hirt, E., Zillman, D., Erickson, G., & Kennedy, C. (1992). The costs and benefits of allegiance: Changes in fans self-ascribed competencies after team victory versus team defeat. *Journal of Personality and Social Psychology, 63*(5), 724–738. doi:10.1037/0022-3514.63.5.724

Hogg, A. (2003). *"Web efforts energize customer research", electric perspectives, Holt, D.B. (1995). How consumers consume: A typology of consumption practices*. Journal.

Horna, J. (1994). *The study of leisure*. Oxford, UK: Oxford University Press.

Howard, D. R., & Crompton, J. L. (1995). *Financing sport*. Morgantown, WV: F.I.T.

Iffhs.de. (2013). *Asia's strongest league in the 1st decade of the 21st century (2001-2010)*. Retrieved from http://www.iffhs.de/?20fa3002f73816ff3854a46817f7370eff3702bb1c2bbb6e13

Iso-Ahola, S. (1980). Attributed determinants of decisions to attend football games. *Scandinavian Journal of Sport Science*, *2*(2), 39–46.

Jayaratne, T. (1993). Quantitative methodology and feminist research. In M. Hammersley (Ed.), *Social research: Philosophy, politics and practice* (pp. 109–123). London: Sage.

John, G., & Sheard, R. (1999). *Stadia: A design and development guide*. Retrieved from http://www.nova.edu/ssss/QR/QR3-4/jones.html

Kallangroar.com. (2012a). *'LionsXII Live' app by StarHub*. Retrieved from http://kallangroar.com/news/lionsxii/lionsxii-live-app-by-starhub/

Kallangroar.com. (2012b). Retrieved from http://kallangroar.com/news/exclusive-interviews/exclusive-hard-hitting-interview-with-saffcs-shahril-jantan/

Kallangroar.com. (2013). *Geylang International FC fans bash*. Retrieved from http://kallangroar.com/news/s-league/geylang-international-fc-fans-bash/

Kawulich, B. (2005). Participant observation as a data collection method. *Forum Qualitative Sozial Forschung*, *6*(2). Retrieved from http://www.qualitative-research.net/index.php/fqs/article/view/466/996

King, A. (1997). The lads: Masculinity and the new consumption of football. *Sociology*, *31*(2), 329–346. doi:10.1177/0038038597031002008

Kitzinger, J. (1995). Qualitative research: Introducing focus groups. *British Medical Journal*, *311*(7000), 299–302. doi:10.1136/bmj.311.7000.299 PMID:7633241

Kunju, B. (2009). *Singapore League (S. League)*. Retrieved from http://infopedia.nl.sg/articles/SIP_1572_2009-09-26.html

Lagace, D. (1996). *Sports spectatorship theories and spectator views of LPGA golf product*. Dissertation.

Lazar, J., & Preece, J. (1999). Designing and implementing web-based surveys. *Journal of Computer Information Systems*, *39*(4), 63–67.

Lee, A., & Zeiss, C. (1980). Behavioural commitment to the role of sport consumer: An exploratory analysis. *Sociology and Social Research*, *64*(3), 405–419.

Lee, M. (1985). Self-esteem and social identity in basketball fans. *Journal of Sport Behavior*, *8*(4), 210–223.

Lionsatw.com. (2011). *A look into our foreign players in the S-League*. Retrieved from http://www.lionsatw.com/2011/01/look-into-our-foreign-players-in-s.html

Macpherson, T., Garland, R., & Haughey, K. (2000). *Attracting fans to the game*. Facing the Challenge.

Madrigal, R. (1995). Cognitive and affective determinants of fan satisfaction with sporting event attendance. *Managing Service Quality*, *9*, 158–166.

Malcolm, D., Jones, I., & Waddington, I. (2000). The people's game? Football spectatorship and demographic change. *Soccer & Society*, *1*(1), 129–143. doi:10.1080/14660970008721254

Marsh, P., Rosser, E., & Harre, R. (1978). *The rules of disorder*. London: Routledge and Kegan Paul.

Marshall, C., & Rossman, G. B. (1989). *Designing qualitative research*. Newbury Park, CA: Sage.

Maslow, A. (1954). *Motivation and personality*. New York: Harper & Row.

Maurer, T. J., & Pierce, H. R. (1998). A comparison of Likert scale and traditional measures of self-efficacy. *The Journal of Applied Psychology*, *83*(2), 324–329. doi:10.1037/0021-9010.83.2.324

Maykut, P., & Morehouse, R. (1994). *Beginning qualitative research: A philosophic and practical guide*. London: Falmer Press.

Mediacorp.com.sg. (2010). *Low numbers, falling standards? Empty seats force S-League clubs to rethink branding*. Retrieved from http://imcms2.mediacorp.sg/CMSFileserver/documents/006/PDF/20100705/0507SPC021.pdf

Melnick, M.J. (1993). *Searching for sociability in the stands: A theory of sport spectating*. Academic Press.

Melnick, M. J., & Wann, D. L. (2011). An examination of sport fandom in Australia: Socialization, team identification, and fan behaviour. *International Review for the Sociology of Sport*, (December): 46, 456–470. doi:10.1177/1012690210380582

Miller, S. (1976). Personality correlates of football fandom. *Journal of Human Behaviour*, *13*(4), 7–13.

Mirror.co.uk. (2013). Retrieved from http://www.mirror.co.uk/sport/football/news/england-cannot-win-trophies-because-1937130

Mnzava, B. (2011). *Financial plight in English Premiership football: An impact of recent global recession*. Retrieved from www3.unileon.es/pecvnia/pecvnia2011/2011_179_189.pdf

Mullins, L. J. (2010). *Management & organisational behaviour* (9th ed.). Prentice Hall-Financial Times

Murrell, A., & Dietz, B. (1992). Fan support of sports teams: The effect of a common group identity. *Journal of Sport & Exercise Psychology*, *14*, 28–39.

Nau, D. (1995, December). Mixing methodologies: Can bimodal research be a viable post-positivist tool? *The Qualitative Report*, *2*(3). Retrieved from http://www.nova.edu/ssss/QR/QR2-3/nau.html

O'Neill, M., Getz, D., & Carlson, J. (1999). Evaluation of service quality at events. *Consumer Research*, *22*, 34–38.

Palakrishnan & Das. (Eds.). (1996). S. League: The kick-off. Singapore: Singapore Professional Football League. (Call no.: RSING 796.33406095957 S)

Patton, M. (1987). *How to use qualitative methods in evaluation*. London: Sage Publications.

Pooley, J. (1978). *The sports fan: A social psychology of misbehaviour*. Calgary, Canada: CAPHER Sociology of Sport Monograph Series.

Posten, M. (1998). *Social identity theory: Sports affiliation and self-esteem.* Living in a Social World Psy 324: Advanced Social Psychology, Spring, 1998.

Powell, R. A., & Single, H. M. (1996). Focus groups. *International Journal for Quality in Health Care, 8*(5), 499–504. PubMed

Rabiee, F. (2004). Focus-group interview and data analysis. *The Proceedings of the Nutrition Society, 63*(4), 655–660. doi:10.1079/PNS2004399 PMID:15831139

Ratner, C. (2002, September). Subjectivity and objectivity in qualitative methodology. *Forum Qualitative Sozialforschung, 3*(3), Art.16. Retrieved from http://www.qualitative-research.net/fqs-texte/3-02/3-02ratner-e.htm

Ray, N. M., & Tabor, S. W. (2003). Cyber surveys come of age. In *Marketing research.* Chichester, UK: John Wiley and Sons.

Redsports.sg. (2010). *Singapore is always in my heart.* Retrieved from http://www.redsports.sg/2010/08/05/egmar-goncalves-interview/

Redsports.sg. (2009). *SLeague sponsorship – A good marketing play or national service?* Retrieved from http://www.redsports.sg/2009/02/17/sleague-sponsorship-football/

Reuters.com. (2013). *Singapore players go door-to-door to bring in crowds.* Retrieved from http://in.reuters.com/article/2013/02/25/soccer-singapore-crowd-idINDEE91O09Z20130225

Richardson, C.A., & Rabiee, F. (2001). *A question of access' – An exploration of the factors influencing the health of young males aged 15–19 living in Corby and their use of health care.* Academic Press.

Schensul, S. L., Schensul, J. J., & LeCompte, M. D. (1999). *Essential ethnographic methods: Observations, interviews, and questionnaires.* Walnut Creek, CA: AltaMira Press.

Schmuck, R. (1997). *Practical action research for change.* Arlington Heights, IL: IRI/Skylight Training and Publishing.

Scholl, N., Mulders, S., & Drent, R. (2002). Online qualitative market research: Interviewing the world at a fingertip. *Qualitative Market Research, 5*(3), 210–223. doi:10.1108/13522750210697596

Schurr, K., Wittig, A., Ruble, V., & Ellen, A. (1987). Demographic and personality characteristics associated with persistent, occasional, and non-attendance of university male basketball games by college students. *Journal of Sport Behavior, 11*, 3–17.

Schwarz, N. (1999). Self-reports: How the questions shape the answers. *The American Psychologist, 54*(2), 93–105. doi:10.1037/0003-066X.54.2.93

Sheehan, K. B., & Hoy, M. B. (1999, March). Using e-mail to survey internet users in the United States: Methodologyand assessment. *Journal of Computer-Mediated Communication.*

Singapore Sports Council. (2012a). *Participation.* Retrieved from http://www.ssc.gov.sg/publish/Corporate/en/participation/participation.html

Singapore Sports Council. (2012b). *Sport as strategy opportunities for all.* Retrieved from http://www.ssc.gov.sg/publish/Corporate/en/news/media_releases/2012/SPORT_AS_STRATEGY__OPPORTUNITIES_FOR_ALL.html

Singapore Sports Council. (2012c). *Annual report.* Retrieved from http://www.ssc.gov.sg/publish/etc/medialib/sports_web_uploads/gc/annual_report.Par.0006.File.tmp/SSC%20Annual%20Report%20 2011%2012.pdf

Singapore Sports Council. (2013). *Rates & charges.* Retrieved from http://www.ssc.gov.sg/publish/Corporate/en/participation/hotspot/rates___charges.html

Singstat.gov.sg. (2013). Retrieved from http://www.singstat.gov.sg/publications/publications_and_papers/reference/monthly_digest/mdsmay13.pdf

Sleague.com. (2012a). *Black sheep- Who are they?* Retrieved from http://www.sleague.com/news-features/news/2012/april/black-sheep-who-are-they-

Sleague.com. (2012b). *CEO Lim hints at need for realism.* Retrieved from http://www.sleague.com/news-features/news/2012/november/ceo-lim-hints-at-need-for-realism

Sleague.com. (2013a). *Ticket info.* Retrieved from http://www.sleague.com/ticket-info

Sleague.com. (2013b). *Financial info.* Retrieved from http://www.sleague.com/about/financial-info

SNCCFR. (1996). *F. A. Premier League surveys.* Leicester, UK: Sir Norman Chester Centre for Football Research, University of Leicester.

SNCCFR. (1997). *F. A. Premier League surveys.* Leicester, UK: Sir Norman Chester Centre for Football Research, University of Leicester.

Solanki, S. (2012). *New premier league TV rights: How will they affect the clubs?* Retrieved from http://hereisthecity.com/2012/10/15/premier-league-tv-rights-how-will-they-affect-the-big-clubs/

Starhub.com. (2012). *'Live' great eastern – YEO'S SLeague matches now shown on StarHub TV.* Retrieved from http://www.starhub.com/corporate/newsroom/2011/02/_live_great_easternyeossleague-matchesnowshownonstarhubtv.html

Swearingen, D. L. (1986). Spectator seating: Get them into the stadium and out of theliving room. *Athletic Business, 10*(1), 70–74.

Tajfel, H., & Turner, J. C. (1986). The social identity theory of intergroup behaviour. In S. Worchel & W. G. Austin (Eds.), *The psychology of intergroup relations* (pp. 7–24). Chicago: Nelson-Hall.

Telegraph.co.uk. (2012). Retrieved from http://www.telegraph.co.uk/sport/football/competitions/euro-2012/9370755/Premier-League-needs-more-top-class-foreign-players-if-it-wishes-to-be-regarded-as-the-worlds-best.html

The New Paper. (2013). *S-League clubs to share homes*. Retrieved from http://www.tnp.sg/content/s-league-clubs-share-homes

Theleagueneus.blogspot.sg. (2012). *New guidelines implemented for national serviceman*. Retrieved from http://theleagueneus.blogspot.sg/2012/04/new-guidelines-implemented-for-national.html

Thomas, L., MacMillan, J., McColl, E., Hale, C., & Bond, S. (1995). Comparison of focus group and individual interviewmethodology in examining patient satisfaction with nursingcare. *Social Sciences in Health*, *1*, 206–219.

Today. (2012). Retrieved from http://imcmsimages.mediacorp.sg/CMSFileserver/documents/006/PDF/20120107/0701SPC033.pdf

Trail, G. T., Anderson, D. F., & Fink, J. S. (2000). A theoretical model of sport spectatorconsumption behavior. *International Journal of Sport Management*, *1*, 154–180.

Trail, G. T., Fink, J. S., & Anderson, D. F. (2003). Sport spectator consumption behavior. *Sport Marketing Quarterly*, *12*, 8–17.

URA Lifestyle survey 2009 and Concept Plan 2011 Online Survey. (2010). *High public satisfaction with Singapore's quality of life*. Retrieved from http://www.ura.gov.sg/pr/text/2010/pr10-51.html

Van Teijlingen, E., & Hundley, V. (2001). The importance of pilot studies. *Social Research Update*, (35): 1–4. PMID:11328433

Wakefield, K., & Sloan, H. (1995). The effects of team loyalty and selected stadium factors on spectator attendance. *Journal of Sport Management*, *9*, 153–172.

Wakefield, K.L., Blodgett, & Sloan. (1996). Measurement and management of the sportscape. *Journal of Sport Management.*, *10*, 15–31.

Wann, D., & Branscombe, N. (1993). Sports fans: Measuring degree of identification with their team. *International Journal of Sport Psychology*, *24*, 1–17.

Wann, D., & Dolan, T. (1994). Influence of spectator's identification on evaluation of past, present and future performance of a sports team. *Perceptual and Motor Skills*, *78*(2), 547–552. doi:10.2466/pms.1994.78.2.547

Wann, D., & Hamlet, M. (1995). Author and subject gender in sport research. *International Journal of Sport Psychology*, *26*, 225–232.

Weible, R., & Wallace, J. (1998). The impact of the Internet on data collection. *Marketing Research*, *10*(3), 19–23.

Yahoosports.com.sg. (2012). Retrieved from http://sg.sports.yahoo.com/news/former-singapore-international-muhammad-ridhuan-joins-arema-205417886--spt.html

KEY TERMS AND DEFINITIONS

Attendance: The act or state of attending an event.

Club Affiliation: The act of becoming formally connected or joined to clubs with regards to fans in a competition.

Fan Behaviour: Manner of behaving or conducting oneself, from a fan perspective.

FAS: Formed in 1966, the Football Association of Singapore is responsible for developing and advancing the game at all levels. FAS also ensures that the Laws of the Game are adhered to, from the professional S. League to amateur leagues.

S. League: Singapore's professional football league, started in 1996.

Sport Spectatorship: Attendance of spectators at an event which features sports.

Stadia Experience: Direct personal participation or observation gained from stadia. It also refers to the different experiences the individual obtains while attending an event in stadia.

This research was previously published in Emerging Trends and Innovation in Sports Marketing and Management in Asia edited by Ho Keat Leng and Noah Yang Hsu, pages 130-160, copyright year 2015 by Business Science Reference (an imprint of IGI Global).

APPENDIX A: SURVEY QUESTIONS

Q1: May I ask your age? ___________

(Subject must be 18 or older.)

Q2: Do you attend S-League matches? (Please tick)

Yes □ No□
(If the response is a "No", go to Q3. If the response is a "Yes", skip to Q4.)

Q3: Did you attend S-League matches in the past?

Yes □ No□
(Please proceed to non-attendance factors column)

Q4: Do you attend more than 5 matches per season?

Yes □ No□
(Please proceed to the attendance factors column.)

Attendance Factors Column

***Now I would like to ask you some questions about the reasons that might lead you to attend to attend S-League matches. On a scale from 1 to 5, with 1 being unimportant and 5 very important, please rate the following in terms of what would motivate you *to attend S-League matches.*

Q5: I am a local football fan and I feel the need to support our own S-League 1 2 3 4 5
Q6: S-League matches give you pleasure and makes you feel good 1 2 3 4 5
Q7: S-League matches are stimulating and exciting 1 2 3 4 5
Q8: S-League matches helps you to relieve your frustrations and anxiety 1 2 3 4 5
Q9: S-League matches entertain you and make you less stressful 1 2 3 4 5
Q10: S-League matches helps you to identify with the success of the team 1 2 3 4 5
Q11: S-League matches give you the opportunity to meet other people and make friends 1 2 3 4 5
Q12: S-League matches make you feel important and successful 1 2 3 4 5
Q13: S-League matches gives you a sense of belonging (e.g. Club affiliation) 1 2 3 4 5
Q14: S-League matches help you to escape from the routine of everyday life 1 2 3 4 5
Q15: S-League matches allows you to watch, read and/or discuss football so that you can bet on the match 1 2 3 4 5

***Now I would like to ask you some questions about yourself.

Q16: Which of the following best describes your educational status?

Primary Secondary Tertiary Bachelor's degree holder Post Graduate diploma and above

Q17: What is your marital status? Are you…

Married Single Divorced Separated Widowed

Q18: Which or the following best describes your professional status?

Employed full-time Employed part-time Homemaker Student Retired Unemployed
(If employed please proceed to Q19)

Q19: What kind of work do you do? ______________________________
Q20: Your annual income is

Less than 30,000 a year, 30,000- 50,000 a year, 50,000 - 70,000 a year, 70,000 - 90,000 a year, More than 100,000 a year

Q21: Male Female

Non-Attendance Factors (Not Interested in Attending League Matches)

***Now I would like to ask you some questions about the reasons that you don't attend S-League matches. On a scale from 1 to 5 with 1 being unimportant and 5 very important, please rate the impact of the following factors in your decision *NOT to attend S-League matches.*

Q22: I have no time to support local football 1 2 3 4 5
Q23: I cannot relate to the S-League clubs because there is no affiliation with them 1 2 3 4 5
Q24: S-League has a long way to go to match/garner EPL kind of following 1 2 3 4 5
Q25: There is not enough coverage on S-League matches in Singapore 1 2 3 4 5
Q26: Too much attention is given to other leagues' football in Singapore (e.g. EPL, La Liga)
Q27: Quality of players on show in S-League is not good enough 1 2 3 4 5
Q28: Unattractive advertising of the S-League1 2 3 4 5
Q29: Some other game is live on TV at the same time (e.g. English Premier League) 1 2 3 4 5
Q30: I prefer Lions XII team, the Malaysian Super League and the causeway rivalry that entails 1 2 3 4 5

Non-Attendance Factors (Interested in Attending League Matches)

***Now I would like to ask you some questions about the reasons that you don't attend S-League matches. On a scale from 1 to 5 with 1 being unimportant and 5 very important, please rate the impact of the following factors in your decision *NOT to attend S-League matches.*

Q32: I don't know the S-League and players
Q33: The S-League game you are interested in is live on TV 1 2 3 4 5
Q34: I prefer Lions XII team, the Malaysian Super League and the causeway rivalry that entails 1 2 3 4 5
Q35: Cost of ticket is a concern 1 2 3 4 5
Q36: Difficulty of access to stadium 1 2 3 4 5
Q37: Lack of parking facilities in around of stadium 1 2 3 4 5
Q38: Inappropriate behavior of the fans 1 2 3 4 5
Q39: Lack of stars and quality amongst teams 1 2 3 4 5
Q40: Poor quality of services at stadium 1 2 3 4 5
Q41: Poor public transportation to get to stadium 1 2 3 4 5
Q42: Poor quality of pre match and off field entertainment 1 2 3 4 5
Q43: Low team league position 1 2 3 4 5
Q44: Predictable game results 1 2 3 4 5
Q45: You prefer other forms of entertainment rather than watching football at stadiums 1 2 3 4 5
Q46: Low quality of competition and spectacle 1 2 3 4 5
Q47: Poor quality of the league's promotional campaign 1 2 3 4 5
Q48: Players difficult to approach and interact with 1 2 3 4 5
Q49: Are there any other reasons for not attending that you can think of?

____

General Perceptions of the Sports and the S-League in Singapore

Q50: What was your favorite sport to play while you were growing up?

____

Q51: Do you follow football on TV? Yes No

(If the response is a "Yes", proceed to Q52. If the response is a "No", skip to Q55.)

Q52: Do you follow European football leagues (e.g. EPL) on TV? Yes No
Q53: Do you follow the S-League matches on TV? Yes No
Q54: Do you think that the S-league pales in comparison to foreign football leagues in general? Yes No

Reason: ______________________________

Q55: Do you think the Lions XII matches are more exciting than S-League matches than the S-League? Yes No

Reason: ______________________________

Q56: Do you follow any other sport on TV? Yes No

(If the response is a "Yes", proceed to Q57 If the response is a "No", skip to Q)

Q57: What other sports do you follow on TV? ____________
Q58: Do you attend games of any other sports? Yes No

(If subject responds "Yes", ask Q59. If subject responds "No", skip to Q60.)

Q59: Games of what other sports do you attend? ____________
Q60: Do you have Internet at home? Yes No
Q61: Do you have cable TV at home? Yes No

APPENDIX B: FACE-TO-FACE INTERVIEW QUESTIONS

Player: Shahril Jantan
Current Club: Home United (S-League)
Q1: How did you get associated with the S-League as a player?
Q2: Has the S-League helped you in your development as a footballer? If not, why?
Q3: Do you think the S-League model (current) is working? If not, why?
Q4: What is the local football scene like, in your opinion, in Singapore? How can it get better?
Q5: Football is a great participatory sport in Singapore but doesn't always translate to devoted fan bases here, especially spectators? Why do you think this is the case?
Q6: What do you think we need to do to increase football interest in this country? How do we get fans to the stadium to watch the S-League?

Player: Fabio Fanticelle Da Silva
Playing History in S-League: 2001 – 2003, Jurong FC, Singapore; 1999 – 2001, Balestier FC, Singapore; 1998 – 1999, Tanjong Pagar FC, Singapore; 1996 – 1997, Home United FC, Singapore
Q1: How did you get associated with the S-League as a player?
Q2: Has the S-League helped you in your development as a footballer? If not, why?
Q3: Do you think the S-League model (current) is working? If not, why?
Q4: What is the local football scene like, in your opinion, in Singapore? How can it get better?
Q5: Football is a great participatory sport in Singapore but doesn't always translate to devoted fan bases here, especially spectators? Why do you think this is the case?
Q6: What do you think we need to do to increase football interest in this country? How do we get fans to the stadium to watch the S-League?

Chapter 21
Those Who Rarely Attend Alone: Tribal Sport Fans

David P. Hedlund
St. John's University, USA

Rui Biscaia
Coventry University, UK

Maria do Carmo Leal
Universidade Europeia, Portugal

ABSTRACT

Sport fans rarely attend sporting events alone. While traditional consumer and sport fan behavior research frequently segmented fans based on demographic characteristics, recent advances in understanding how sport fans co-create and co-consume sporting events provides substantial evidence that sports fans should be examined as tribal groups. In this chapter, seven dimensions of sport fan tribalism are proposed and tested (membership; geographic sense of community; social recognition; shared rivalry; and shared knowledge of symbols, rituals and traditions, and people) with samples from top-level American college football (Division I American football) and the top level of professional Portuguese soccer (Primeira Liga). The results provide reliability and validity evidence in support of the seven-dimension scale. In addition, the structural testing of the scale highlights differences between tribal fans and their teams (relative to other teams) in terms of five behavioral intentions and two commitment- related outcome variables. The implications of labeling sports fans at tribal, the use of the seven-dimension scale and the structural results are all discussed.

INTRODUCTION

In today's world, from fans of music and movies to fans of particular types of food to fans of specific geographic places, fans are everywhere. Perhaps, however, there is no part of the current human existence that has more fans than sport teams, athletes and sporting competitions. From globally-known sports teams such as Real Madrid (Spanish soccer/football), the Dallas Cowboys (American football) and the

DOI: 10.4018/978-1-5225-5475-2.ch021

New York Yankees (American baseball); to athletes such as Cristiano Ronaldo (soccer/football), Serena Williams (tennis), Phil Mickelson (golf), LeBron James (basketball), Ronda Rousey (mixed martial arts), Floyd Mayweather Jr. (boxing), Yuna Kim (figure skating), and Usain Bolt (track and field); and to sports such as football (soccer), American football, rugby, tennis and golf; each team, athlete and sport respectively boasts of millions of fans watching competitions in-person or through media. For example in 2009 when Cristiano Ronaldo was signed by Spain's Real Madrid football club, approximately 80,000 fans attended a brief introduction ceremony at the Bernabéu stadium (The Guardian, 2009). More recently for the National Football League's Super Bowl 50 on February 7, 2016, more than 71,000 people attended the game at Levi's Stadium in Santa Clara, California (Breech, 2016). In addition, according to the San Francisco Bay Area Super Bowl 50 Host Committee, more than 1.1 million people visited the surrounding San Francisco Bay area in the week leading up to the game specifically because of the game; total television viewership was estimated at 167 million people, and 3.96 million people live-streamed the event (2016). Clearly, athletes, teams and sporting events are watched by millions of fans.

Being a fan is generally not an individualistic pursuit. Sports fans, for example, rarely attend sporting events alone (Hedlund, 2014). After arriving at the sporting event location, often as a group, sport fans interact with each other, cheer on athletes and teams in the venue, and co-create and co-consume the sporting event with other fans. For many sport fans, it is the simultaneous process of co-creating and co-consuming the fan experience with other fans at sporting events that holds the most significant meaning and value (Woratschek, Horbel, & Popp, 2014). While the volume and propensity of cheering and yelling can provide an advantage for the home team (Jamieson, 2010; Schwartz & Barsky, 1977), generally speaking, fans have little effect on the outcome of the competition because they are not directly involved in the on-field/court play. Without fans in attendance, however, professional sporting events would be immensely different and more akin to recreational activities. Thus, the process of creating, developing, maintaining and motivating a large fan base, comprised of tens of thousands of individuals who come together at a sporting event to be part of a unique experience is a challenge for all sporting event owners and managers.

Over the past 25 years, experiential consumer researchers have identified a multitude of different types of groups that co-create (i.e., the process of sports fans, the teams, coaches and athletes coming together and creating a unique experience at the event location) and that co-consume (i.e., the process of actually experiencing the game and related activities with other fans) (Schau, Muñiz, & Arnould, 2009). While many consumption groups provide substantial value to a variety of business and entertainment-related goods and services (e.g., users of Apple products, bikers who ride Harley-Davidson Motorcycles, fans of the Tom Petty and the Heartbreakers rock band, viewers of the "Xena: Warrior Princess" television show) (Schau et al., 2009), little research has been undertaken to attempt to label consumption groups and to create a tool that can be used to measure and compare groups. Because athletes and teams have the power to draw large numbers of fans to a sporting event, examinations of sports fans and their relationship to one another and their favorite team may bring some clarity and insight to fan group and consumer (community) behavior research. Thus, the purpose of this research is to identify and measure components of tribal sport fans and to examine empirically the relationship between these fans and important outcomes such as being committed to the team, attending future games, buying merchandise in the future, telling others about the team's games and reading about and watching games through media.

BACKGROUND

While becoming and identifying oneself as a fan has historically been considered a choice for the individual, recently greater understanding of several processes such as socialization and peer pressure have expanded inquiry into how and why individuals become fans of an athlete, team, sport or event (e.g., fan consumption communities). Research first focused on individuals identifying with particular sport teams (see Branscombe & Wann, 1991; Wann & Branscombe, 1993), and other authors began to identify and examine experiential group consumption of leisure and sport activities such as surfing, skydiving, river rafting and attending baseball games (Arnould & Price, 1993; Celsi, Rose, & Leigh, 1993; Holt, 1995). What began as research about why individuals became sport fans transformed quickly into research on groups of fans who shared a preference for the same sport team or athlete. More recently, research has been undertaken regarding how groups of fans co-create and co-consume sporting events (Hedlund, 2014; Woratschek et al., 2014).

In business, strong brands are frequently built by creating an emotional connection between the organization and its consumers, and one path to fostering this type of desirable relationship is the formation of a passionate and loyal user community around the brand (Muniz & O'Guinn, 2001; Underwood, Bond, & Baer, 2001). Couvelaere and Richelieu (2005) indicated that professional sport teams also have the potential to build strong brands by capitalizing on the emotional bond shared among fans. Recent studies have increasingly acknowledged the importance of fan communities for professional sport teams (Grant, Heere, & Dickson, 2011; Hedlund, 2014; Katz & Heere, 2015). The purpose behind sport fan communities is to provide opportunities for like-minded fans to engage in collaborative consumption activities, including simultaneously creating and consuming the event experience with other fans (Hedlund, 2014). The authors of recent research have provided evidence that when fans have the opportunity to come together at a sporting event and participate in the creation and consumption of the event, then they tend to feel of a sense of community with other fans based on shared knowledge they have of the coaches and athletes, the competing teams, and the sporting event (Grant et al., 2011; Hedlund, 2014; Heere, Walker, Yoshida, Ko, Jordan, & James, 2011).

One of the most important aspects of fan groups is the creation and maintenance of a sense of community (Devasagayam & Buff, 2008). For many years, researchers in numerous disciplines have espoused the benefits of a strong sense of community among individuals. The benefits include bringing order to people's lives, resistance to the advance of personal and social problems, improved physical and mental health, and enabling individuals and groups to achieve their maximum potential (Chavis & Newbrough, 1986; Puddifoot, 1996). In sport contexts, fans often seek out and are able to recognize other fans of the team with whom they identify based on a multitude of characteristics, including where they are from, which team(s) they support, and what they know about various sports, teams and players (Dionísio, Leal & Moutinho, 2008; Lai & Yang, 2013), thus creating a sense of community.

Another of the most important aspects of fan groups is the notion that its members are devoted to the team and have similar feelings about the symbolic features of the common object which brings them together (e.g., the sport team) (Cottingham, 2012). There are multiple symbols known and understood by fans within a team's fan group that are associated with the team and convey meanings beyond their tangible and physical characteristics, such as the colors, logos and important coaches and players on the team (DeSarbo & Madrigal, 2011). If an individual feels like a member of a sport fan community, then he/she will likely learn a multitude of information about the team and its fans, including the symbols which represent the team (Holt, 1995). Similarly, Belk and Tumbat (2005) noted that devoted fans tend to ennoble their teams and associated symbols with strong meaning and importance, while Dionísio et al. (2008) indicated that individuals within fan communities often consume team-related products because of their symbolic meaning rather than their material utility.

Previous studies have also suggested that fans with a strong sense of community tend to wear the logo and colors of the team with pride (Apostolopoulou, Papadimitriou, Synowka & Clark, 2012; Papadimitriou & Apostolopoulou, 2015). Moreover, these fans engage in a number of rituals and traditions exemplify their commitment to the team and showcase a solid knowledge of the most important people linked to the team's history (Belk & Tumbat, 2005). The wearing of the logo and colors, the continued participation in rituals and traditions, and the knowledge of team-related personalities reinforces feelings of fans' membership in the community and increases their collaboration and integration in these fan groups (Dionísio et al., 2008; Holt, 1995). Thus on the basis of previous research, feelings of membership in the team's fan group, recognition by others that fans are members and shared knowledge of the symbols of the team and the rivals of the team represent important markers that characterize tribal sport fans.

Tribal Sports Fans

A consumer tribe is a group of people who are emotionally connected based on similar consumption values and usage; and through their consumption of goods and/or services, they create a community and express a shared identity (Cova, 1997). At the fan group level, teams become the link that connects diverse fans and acts as a type of social aggregator (Yngfalk, 2013). Furthermore, sporting events bring fans together in a type of ceremonial ritual where passionate members gather around the event and cheer on their favorite athletes or team. While fan groups are comprised of heterogeneous and diverse individuals, unlike other types of consumer groups that prefer only those members who will be totally and completely loyal, fan groups are open to new members as long as they are not fans of rival athletes or teams (Cova & Cova, 2002). Cova and Cova (2002) further suggested that these consumer groups can be held together based on shared emotions (i.e., a liking of the same team). Because fan groups can include a multitude of diverse individuals, traditional types of demographic segmentation are ineffective at identifying them (Cova & Cova, 2002; Goulding, Shankar & Canniford, 2013; Mitchell & Imrie, 2011).

While it may be easy to recognize "true" fans based on a number of different observable characteristics and/or behaviors at a sporting event, researchers still struggle to identify different types of fans (Heere & James, 2007; Tapp & Clowes, 2002). In previous research, an extensive and overlapping list of frequently used terminology, such as consumption communities (Boorstin, 1973), cultures of consumption (Kozinets, 2001), subcultures of consumption (Celsi et al., 1993; Schouten & McAlexander, 1995), consumer tribes (Cova & Cova, 2002; Maffesoli, 1996), brand communities (McAlexander, Schouten, & Koenig, 2002; Muniz & O'Guinn, 2001), and brand cults (Belk & Tumbat, 2005) have all been used to describe various types of consumer groups. Relative to sport fans and the co-creation and co-consumption of sporting events, a growing amount of research suggests that one of the most appropriate ways to describe and label sports fans is as sport tribes (Canniford, 2011; Dionísio et al., 2008; Morris, 1981; Smith & Westerbeek, 2004).

Cova (1997) described consumer tribes as a way to organize and facilitate members co-creating and co-consuming experiences. In an effort to differentiate tribes from other consumer groups, Canniford (2011) listed three unique aspects of tribes. First, individuals can be members of multiple tribes, and membership in one or more tribes does not require an all day, every day commitment (Goulding, Shankar, Elliott, & Canniford, 2009). Second, through the process of what Cova, Kozinets and Shankar (2007) call "active play," members of the sport tribe interact with one another face-to-face or online about the team and athletes' performance, expectations about upcoming events, how they feel about or their expectations of the team and athletes' performance, and their plans for attending the event and cheering for their team and athletes. Third, if members of the sport tribe move to different geographic areas, they can maintain their connection with other members of the tribe through online or social media. Alternatively, they may find like-minded fans of the team in their new area and create a new "branch" of the tribe. In local branches of the tribe, members may recreate the same types of tribal activities and events as occur in other locations.

Thus while a tribal sport fan is not bound by geographic limitations, the shared nature of being a fan of the same team can bring members together face-to-face and online. In addition, members of tribal sport fan groups feel a sense of community with others who share similar feelings and attitudes toward the team (Huang, 2014). In other words when generally unrelated fans of the same team come together online or face-to-face, a social link can be created among them based on their shared support of the same sport team, and the co-creation and co-consumption experiences they feel can be enhanced. As a result, the initial dimensions to consider for tribal sports fans are the shared feelings and attitudes that underpin whether or not they feel like members of the community and sense the connection to the people and geographic area represented by a particular team.

Psychological and Geographic Sense of Community

In 1974, Seymour Sarason wrote "The psychological sense of community: Prospects for a community psychology," in which he stated that "a community is more than a political or geographical area. It contains a variety of institutions which may be formally or informally related to each other – or not related at all. It is made up of myriads of groups, transient or permanent, which may have similar or different purposes and vary in size, power, and composition" (p. 131). In other words, the members of a community can be connected based on their geographic and psychological commonalities. Geographic communities refer to neighborhoods, towns, cities, and regions, while psychological, sometimes called "relational" communities, refer to connections based on common interests or activities without specifying any specific geographic locale (McMillan & Chavis, 1986; Obst, Smith, & Zinkiewicz, 2002). In sport, the distinction between psychological and geographical communities is important because the name of a sport team usually includes a geographic place, and the name or nickname of the team is frequently derived from some type of symbol of that geographic area (e.g., Dallas Cowboys, Japan Samurai Blue, Italy Azzurri). On the other hand, some fans of a team may just simply share an interest in a particular sport and no connection or feeling of commitment to the team. It is important to note that psychological and geographic communities are not mutually exclusive terms, as communities based on interests or activities do not need to be based in a certain geographic area (i.e., sport fans of a local "home" team). Thus, members of a sport fan group may be connected due to geographic considerations such as close physical proximity to home stadium or arena, or they can be based on some type of shared feeling of connection among fans that is not bound by territorial limitations or boundaries.

For at least the last four decades, one of the most important ways in which a feeling of connection or relatedness has been understood is through the notion of sense of community. McMillan (1976) defined sense of community as "a feeling that members have of belonging and being important to each other"

(McMillan & Chavis, 1986, p. 9). When applied to sport fans of the same team, they come together based on shared liking of and experiences with the same team. With today's technology, while it is not necessary that sport fans physically can connect in the geographic region of the team they support, it is more likely that if an individual lives in the particular geographic area in which the team is located, then these individuals will likely be fans of the local team. An exception frequently occurs when individuals move to a new geographic area where a different, sometimes rival team exists.

When examining the notion of sense of community, one of the most important aspects is the feeling of membership. McMillan and Chavis (1986) defined membership as "the feeling of belonging or of sharing a sense of personal relatedness" (p. 9). In a sport setting, fans who feel that they have invested in or contributed to the team and fan community may consider themselves to be members. For example if fans expend resources (e.g., time, energy, money) to attend a sporting competition, cheer on the team, and buy the team's merchandise, then they feel like they are a member of the team's fan community, as distinct from those who are not part of the group (Rein, Kotler, & Shields, 2006). Based on feelings of membership in the group, fans will engage in the process of co-creating and co-consuming the sporting event and related offerings with other fans of the team.

Within tribal sport fan groups, both the psychological sense of community based on feelings of membership in and with the group and its members, and the geographic sense of community based on a connection to the geographic area in which the team is located, are essential aspects. Without feelings of connection to others in group, there would be no need to expend one's resources on maintaining that relationship. At the same point in time, sports teams frequently engender the characteristics of the local community (Cova & Cova, 2002; Mitchell & Imrie, 2011); thus when considering the importance of sense of community and tribal sport fans, both psychological and geographic considerations should be included.

Social Recognition

While both psychological and geographic senses of community relate to how individuals perceive themselves relative to the group and the geographic area inhabited by fans of the team, it is also important to examine the relationship among members, specifically how they recognize and assess other potential members (Heere & James, 2007). For example in sport, just because a fan attends a game while wearing a replica jersey of a team does not mean that the fan is a "real" fan of that team or a member of that team's fan tribe. In order to be member of a fan group, the individual needs to receive some type of social recognition (Dionísio et al., 2008). Based on criteria such as displaying certain characteristics (e.g., wearing team-branded merchandise), engaging in certain activities (e.g., attending a home game, sitting in the fan section, and cheering loudly for the team), and/or reaching certain achievements (e.g., attending every home and away game), fans can receive social recognition from other fans regarding their status as a "true" fan of the team (Bennet & Sani, 2004; Vallerand, 2007). Within the broader identity theory focus of social recognition scholars, researchers have discussed similar processes such as social identification, classification and evaluation (i.e., who is a member of the "in-group" or not, and thus a member of the "out-group") (see Ashforth & Mael, 1989; Hogg, Terry, & White, 1995; Tajfel & Turner, 1979, 1985). Social recognition is a three-part phenomenon including positive, neutral, or negative recognition (Pettigrew, 1967). It can be based on how individuals evaluate those they encounter based on a general understanding about how someone should behave, characteristics they should engender, and belongings they should have based on the role they are playing (Bennet & Sani, 2004). Depending on how one is perceived based on these expectations, the resultant social recognition can be positive, neutral, or negative (Rottiers, 2010). In the process of striving to achieve social recognition, individuals will usually attempt to avoid negative and instead attempt to gain positive social recognition. Such social recognition can also provide an individual with externally validated information about themselves, based on others' perceptions (Forgas & Williams, 2002).

Additionally, social recognition may act as a motive for people's behavior. According to Becker (1996), the value of certain goods and services depends on their recognition within their own social environment. For example, some sports fans may only buy and wear a cotton t-shirt with the name and logo of their favorite team, while many tribal fans may dress in head-to-toe authentic, team-licensed merchandise that makes them completely unique in how they look compared to other fans. Frequently, dressing in head-to-toe team merchandise provides social recognition from others that the fan is without a doubt a passionate fan of the team and a member of the tribe that supports the team. As such, tribal sports fans may seek to be socially recognizable by fans of the team, rival fans and society in general.

Shared Rivalry

Rivalry is considered as an important characteristic of many sports and sporting events. Rivalry has been described as "a fluctuating adversarial relationship existing between two teams, players, or groups of fans, gaining significance through on-field competition, on-field or off-field incidences, proximity, demographic makeup, and/or historical occurrence(s)" (Havard, Gray, Gould, Sharp, & Schaffer, 2013, p. 51). Havard, Eddy and Ryan (2016) suggested that rivalry plays an important role to sport fans and has been used by organizations to promote and market their on- and off-field goods and services to consumers. In addition, when fans feel the same sense of rivalry toward the same opponent, these shared feelings can add a level of excitement and suspense to the sporting event (Kimble & Cooper, 1992).

While rivalries can bring sports fans together who share similar characteristics, attending sporting events where two rivals are competing often engenders symbolic meaning (Mueller & Sutherland, 2010). For example, an effective method of motivating fans to attend or watch sporting events is by turning competitors into heroes and villains, while also creating potential storylines within the competition that heighten the experience and value of the event itself. Similarly, Trail, Robinson, Dick, and Gillentine (2003) documented the benefits of giving fans teams to cheer for and against. Because sports are a fertile domain for ritualized behaviors (Dionísio et al., 2008), sporting events have become metaphors for good versus evil, or heroes versus villains (Mueller & Sutherland, 2010). Anker (2005) referred to sporting events as popular culture melodramas.

Marketers and the media create and perpetuate the importance of rivalries, and tribal sports fans are expected to know about and understand the importance of the rivalry games to their team. Moreover, many teams do not just have one single rival because successful teams often face the same team(s) year after year during championship competitions, thus adding importance, meaning and history each year (Havard, 2014; Tyler & Cobbs, 2015). For example in the Spanish soccer League (La Liga), Real Madrid, Barcelona and Atlético Madrid are historic rivals that compete every season for the league championship. During the last 10 years, only these three teams have been champions of La Liga; and since the 1928-29 season (not including 1936-37, 1937-38 and 1938-39 when the Spanish Civil War occurred), 62 of the 85 champions have been won by one of these three teams, with Real Madrid winning a total of 32 national championships to date (La Liga, 2016). Year after year, the drama and history of the rivalries grows, while important moments from games can be used to symbolize or summarize some aspect of the rivalry. In Major League Baseball (MLB) in the United States, the New York Yankees and the Boston Red Sox have an historic rivalry that many believe began in 1919 when Red Sox owner Harry Frazee sold Babe Ruth to the New York Yankees for $125,000 (SoxAndPinstripes.com, 2016). Until 2004 when the Red Sox won MLB's World Series championship, stories related the "Curse of the Bambino" epitomized the intense rivalry between Boston and New York. Throughout the world, it is not difficult to find similar stories and histories of intense rivalries between teams. Thus for tribal sport fans, it is important that they know which teams are their rivals and the stories and history that accompany and epitomize these rivalries. Because they know all of these aspects (e.g. symbols and history), they are more likely to connect with other tribal fans of the team, which reinforces feelings of being a member of the team's fan group (i.e., the "in-group").

Shared Symbols

In sport research, Morris (1981) was one of the first scholars to catalogue many of the important symbols for tribal sport fans. After extensive research, he categorized the symbols into seven different types:

- Tribal roots (e.g., as a battle, religious ceremony, business, theater, etc.),
- Tribal rituals (e.g., laws and punishments, territories, taboos, strategies and tactics, victory celebration, etc.),
- Tribal heroes (e.g., skills, superstitions, stories, displays, gamesmanship, etc.),
- Tribal trappings (e.g., costumes, colors, emblems, trophies, etc.),
- Tribal elders (e.g., owners and managers, leagues and referees, coaches, etc.),
- Tribal followers (e.g., ranks, adornments, displays, souvenirs, mascots, etc.), and
- Tribal tongue (e.g., language and chants).

From this array of potential symbols tribal fans might share, eight have been earmarked for inclusion in this research due to their importance in modern day sports: team-related logos, colors, songs, rituals, traditions, players, coaches and heroes.

Logos, colors and songs of the team (and its fanbase) refer to identifiable deployed symbols that can represent a team. Prior studies have commonly acknowledged logos, colors and songs of a sport team as important, especially for areas such as developing a team-brand association between the team and its fans (Bauer, Stokburger-Sauer, & Exler, 2008; Biscaia, Correia, Ross, Rosado, & Marôco, 2013; Gladden & Funk, 2002; Ross, Russell, & Bang, 2008). The logo and colors often act as the primary visual representation of a team's or brand's image (Park, Eisingerich, Pol, & Park, 2013). Knowledge and understanding of the meaning of the team's colors, logos and songs are also important to the fans, especially because these symbols all may characterize and represent the history of the team (Cottingham, 2012). For example, it is well-known that fans of Liverpool FC sing "You'll never walk alone," a communal anthem of triumph over adversity, often before and after a (victorious) match (FourFourTwo.com, 2016).

Bishop (2001) reported that, in many cases, the connection between fans and their favorite team is built on the colors and logos. He further suggested that when fans know and understand the meaning of the logo, this can signify a turning point in the relationship with the team and other members of the fan group because the fan has learned enough and earned the "right" to cheer for and represent the team. Dionísio et al. (2008) noted that the display of a team's logo and colors is a symbolic action of fans' affiliation with other team supporters. Apostolopoulou and colleagues (2012) found that wearing licensed team merchandise with the logo and colors serves as a connector of the fans with their favorite team and other team followers.

Wearing branded merchandise with a team's logo and colors conveys a visible message that the fan is a member of the tribe (Richardson, 2013). Moreover, knowledge of the logo, colors and songs allows tribal fans to identify each other (both fellow members and rivals) (Healy & McDonagh, 2013). For many tribal members, displaying merchandise and paraphernalia emblazoned with a team's logo and colors indicates an individual's connection to the team, while such a display also creates immediate relationships with other members of the tribe for dialogue, activities, rituals and traditions (Giulianotti, 2002). As such, knowledge of the logo, colors and songs of a team (and the team's history) are important to tribal sport fans.

Shared Rituals and Traditions

The rituals and traditions associated with a team can be a powerful source of brand associations (Biscaia et al., 2013; Gladden & Funk, 2002). Richelieu (2003) referred to rituals as important mechanisms for a sport team to develop its unique brand, enhance the ambiance of the games, and help create excitement and value at the game for fans. The members of tribal fan groups often engage in specific rituals and traditions at the venue, such as songs to support the team and its players before, during and after games.

Rituals and traditions (1) serve to recreate the intense emotions experienced in the past, (2) should have a repetitive nature through an automatic and meaningful behavior for the individuals of a given community, and (3) must be built based on a strong sense of continuity to have maximum effect (Underwood et al., 2001). It is also important to note that rituals and traditions frequently take place as a way to celebrate the history of the brand allowing members to share stories about the brand/club (Madupu & Krishnan, 2008). Sharing rituals and traditions related to the team is also important for reinforcing the fans' sense of community in the sense that rituals and traditions are related to each specific team, hold an explicit meaning and should represent a differentiation point from other teams and fan groups (Crawford, 2004). Biscaia, Ross, Yoshida, Correia, Rosado, and Marôco (2016) also found that fans within team supporter groups tend to have greater knowledge of the team traditions.

Overall, rituals and traditions can be shared among members of a team's fan group, and on game days, participation in these activities contributes to the co-creation and co-consumption of the sport event and thus create value for members of the fan group (Belk & Tumbat, 2005; Mullin, Hardy, & Sutton, 2014). As a result, one can say that rituals and traditions contribute to a win-win situation in which fans create and participate in their own event experience, reinforce their sense of community with other tribal fans of the team who also know the rituals and traditions, and the supporter's team can benefit from and participate in these activities with the fans (often at the end of the competition). For tribal sport fans, it is essential for them to know and share one's knowledge of the rituals and traditions in which fans and sometimes even players participate.

Shared Knowledge of People

Technological advancements in types of communication have increased the popularity of sports as cultural spectacles around the world, and athletes and coaches are considered some of the most visible aspects of modern day sports (Bolsmann & Parker, 2007). Due to the popularity, importance and relevance of sport, when athletes or coaches achieve milestones or have an extraordinary performance, they are frequently recognized and have their status elevated (Hasaan, Kerem, Biscaia, & Agyemang, in press). Often, knowledge of players' and coaches' achievements are shared, and over time that knowledge becomes part of the larger historical record of the team and (future) heroes can be created.

As evidence that one is a real fan of a team, it is essential that one knows the history of the team including its coaches and athletes (Gwinner & Swanson, 2003; Sutton, McDonald, Milne, & Cimperman, 1997). Over time, understanding the importance of historical events and how players have been elevated to the role of a hero is also important to tribal sport fans. Stories of the team's heroes have the power to convey important history and act as a reminder of important events for fans (Fetcho, Roy, & Clow, 2013).

A fan's knowledge about important people linked to the team is often an indicator of his/her relationship to the team and other fans of the team. When tribal fans all know the historical events of their team, it is likely that the common knowledge can also result in increases in sense of community. Giulianotti (2002) noted that committed fans often refer to their heroes by first name, discuss their private lives and traits, collect biographical snippets, and perhaps even fantasize relationships with their objects of affection. Sport heroes are a fundamental element in the sports landscape and their accomplishments are often found in the club archives, museums, halls of fame and webpages around the globe; yet their qualities are difficult to pin down (Gammon, 2014). Holt and Mangan (1996) indicated that sport heroes should demonstrate prowess but also exude character in moments whether in fortune or adversity. Gammon (2014) further noted that sport heroes can act as symbols of nostalgia, and the interpretation of heroism depends on the context and may vary depending on cultural values and the extent of fan's link to the team.

The extent to which a hero is valued is dependent on cultural indicators, but also on the degree of fandom attached to the hero and its team (Gammon, 2014). Individuals within tribal fan groups have been recognized as devoted fans exhibiting great knowledge of team-related symbols such as rituals, logos and important people (Belk & Tumbat; 2005; Hedlund, 2014; Grant et al., 2011). Thus, the shared knowledge among fans of the team of the important people (past, present and even future) represents an important aspect of tribal sport fans.

In summary, sport fans tend to be tribal in nature with either or both geographic and psychological connections with other members who together engage in co-consumption of sporting events. Tribal sport fans share psychological feelings of membership and belonging (Hedlund, 2014; Dionísio et al., 2008), geographic connections (Brown, Crabbe & Mellor, 2006; Kraszewski, 2008), understanding of the importance of rivalries (Giulianotti, 2002; Mael & Ashforth, 2001), and a variety of common symbols understood by members of the tribe including colors, logos, songs, heroes and other ritual and traditions (Smith & Westerbeek, 2004). In order to gain a better understanding of tribal sport fans and how one tribe may compare to another, a tribal sport fan scale is proposed consisting of seven constructs:

1. Membership (Psychological Sense of Community)
2. Geographic Sense of Community
3. Social Recognition
4. Shared Rivalry
5. Shared Symbols (team colors and logos)
6. Shared Rituals and Traditions
7. Shared Knowledge of People (heroes, players and coaches)

Using diverse samples from the United States and Portugal, a description of the development and testing of a tribal sport fan scale is provided in the following section.

METHODOLOGY

Participants and Procedures

In order to undertake the development and testing of a tribal sport fandom scale, in addition to maximizing the potential generalizability of the findings, data were collected in two different countries (the United States and Portugal), at two different sport levels (university and professional), and from two different sports (American football and soccer). In Portugal, an agreement was reached with the sport section managers at the "Sapo Desporto" sports news website (desporto.sapo.pt) to place an advertisement on their website recruiting responses from members of the fan bases of all 20 teams in the "Primeira Liga," the top soccer league in Portugal. In the United States, fans of the Florida State University's football team were recruited via announcements placed on the most populous and "liked" social media groups and blogs (e.g., Warchant.com, Facebook groups).

For the data collection in Portugal, 2080 people entered the online survey and 2063 respondents agreed to take the survey. In order to limit common method bias, the survey was separated into multiple pages. After examining all responses, 707 respondents were removed due to the incompleteness of their responses (i.e., less than 50% of the survey questions were answered) or potentially biased responses (i.e., clicking the same number for all responses), that resulted in 1356 analyzable responses and a 65.73% completion rate. Based on the valid responses, 86.50% were male and the mean age of the respondents was 33.48 years old (SD=11.70). Club membership used extensively in European sports clubs requires that fans can pay to be a member of the team's (fan) club and derive benefits such as the ability to vote on club management personnel; as such, 42.92% of respondents indicated that they pay to be "voting rights" members of the club, and on average these individuals have been members of the fan club for 15.17 years (SD=12.18). Moreover, 19.50% of respondents are season ticket holders, and these individuals have been season ticket holders, on average, for 7.20 years (SD=6.17). As for respondents' relationship status, 54.10% are single and 40.57% married. In terms of respondents' education level, 41.14% have a high school education or below, 41.71% have earned an undergraduate college/university degree, and 17.15% have at least obtained a graduate, masters and/or doctoral degree. Finally, regarding their employment status, 18.58% are students, while 71.60% are either employed or self-employed.

For the data collection in the United States, 974 respondents entered the online survey, and 973 agreed to participate in the data collection. In exactly the same manner as the Portuguese data collection, the American online survey was separated into multiple pages to minimize the effect of common method bias. After reviewing all the responses, using the same methods as those utilized with the Portuguese data, 266 respondents were removed based on the incompleteness of their responses or questions about the truthfulness of their responses. The remaining data included 707 responses, which resulted in a 72.66%, completion rate. These respondents' mean age is 43.81 years old (SD=13.02) and 60.23% are male. On average, they have been fans of the Florida State University's football team for 29.05 years (SD=11.54). In American sports, many educational institutions (e.g., high schools, colleges and universities) have "booster" clubs composed of parents, alumni and/or local individuals who support the athletics department and sports teams through raising or donating money, organizing events, etc. In total, 49.37% of respondents indicated that they are "boosters," and on average, they have spent 14.26 years (SD=12.23) in this role. In addition, 28.41% of respondents are season ticket holders, and on average they have been season ticket holders for 15.00 years (SD=12.69). In terms of some basic demographics, 26.39% are single and 63.89% are married, while 90.28% classify themselves as white/Caucasian, while 3.66% are black/African-American and 3.16% are Hispanic/Latino/a. Finally in terms of their level of education, 58.56% have earned an undergraduate or bachelor's degree, while 27.97% have completed a graduate, masters, doctoral or terminal degree.

Measures

After a thorough review of the literature, the four items used to measure "Membership" were taken from Hedlund (2014), the four items for "Geographic Sense of Community" were previously used by Hedlund and Perricone (2013), and five items for "Shared Rivalry" were adapted from Havard et al. (2013). Because "Social Recognition" has never been tested in the context of sport fans, five new items were specifically created for this research. In terms of the items to be used to measure "Shared Knowledge of the Symbols" for fans of a sport team, Morris' (1981) more than 30 different types of symbols are summarized in these categories: team's colors, logos, songs, rituals, traditions, heroes, players and coaches of the team. These eight types of symbols were selected to be included, based on review of the literature. In addition, five of the most common "Behavioral Intentions" outcome measures were collected: intentions to attend games in the future, intentions to buy team merchandise in the future, intentions to recommend to other that they attend the team's games in the future, intentions to watch the team's games on television in the future, and intentions to read stories in the media about the team in the future (Biscaia, 2016; Hedlund, 2014). Because behavioral intentions can be affected by whether or not a team wins games and championships (Trail, Fink & Anderson, 2003), one item representing the degree to which respondents felt like a true fan of the team, and a second item related to the degree to which respondents felt connected to the team were also collected. All items were measured using 11-point (0-10) Likert-type scales.

Because all of the items would be tested in two separate countries in which two different native languages are spoken, all items were originally written in English. Two sport marketers familiar with this research examined all of the items for face validity. As suggested by Banville, Desrosiers and Genet-Volet (2000), after a reconciliation process ensured the wording of all items was appropriate, a process of translation into Portuguese and back-translation occurred. The results of this process indicated that the English- and Portuguese-language surveys are equivalent.

DATA ANALYSIS AND RESULTS

For the seven proposed constructs, 28 total items were analyzed. Additionally, the five single-item behavioral intentions and two single-item commitment-related outcome variables were also included. In order to identify the constructs and items that best fit the model, exploratory factor analysis (EFA), confirmatory factor analysis (CFA) and structural equation models (SEM) were all employed. Before undertaking any analyses, the data collected from the United States and Portugal were randomly split into two separate datasets ("Dataset 1" for EFA and CFA and "Dataset 2" for SEM). While the data collected in the United States only included respondents who were fans of Florida State University's (FSU) football team, the data from Portugal included responses from 19 of the 20 current teams in the Primeira Liga. Further examinations showed that three teams (known as the "Big Three" in Portugal), FC Porto (n=270), SL Benfica (n=682), and Sporting CP (n=423) had the highest number of responses, and the remaining responses (n=130) came from 16 other teams. Therefore, Dataset 1 was created with randomly selected cases (n=500) included 251 responses from Florida State University and 249 from FC Porto, SL Benfica, and Sporting CP. The remaining data were separated by team into four distinct data sets labelled Dataset 2a (FSU, n=456), Dataset 2b (Benfica, n=625), Dataset 2c (Porto, n=229), and Dataset 2d (Sporting, n=372). As indicated above, Dataset 1 was used for the EFA and CFA procedures, while Datasets 2a, 2b, 2c and 2d were used to test the structural models for each of the four samples.

Based on the literature review and Morris' (1981) thorough cataloguing of tribal sport fan symbols, eight items were selected and included to measure fans' shared knowledge of the team's symbols. EFA procedures were utilized to identify the factor structure of the data regarding shared knowledge of symbols of the team because no previous research had examined such a large number of items measuring this concept. The results of the EFA are shown in Table 1, Figure 1 and Table 2.

The results of the EFA, using Principal Components Analysis (PCA) as the extraction method and Direct Oblimin (DO) as the rotation method, indicate that based on evidence from the Eigenvalues (Table 1), scree plot (Figure 1) and pattern matrix (Table 2), three components could be extracted that cumulatively represent 75.87% of the variance. Based on the commonalities of the items that load on each of the three components, new labels were given (see Table 2). Component 1, including shared knowledge of the colors, logos and songs of team was labelled as "Symbols." Component 2, which included shared knowledge of the rituals and traditions of the team, was labelled as "Rituals and Traditions." Finally, Component 3 was labelled as "People," because it includes items related to the shared knowledge of the heroes, players and coaches of the team.

After separating the eight items measuring shared knowledge of the symbols of the team into three separate constructs, all 28 items measuring seven total constructs (membership, geographic sense of community, social recognition, shared rivalry, shared knowledge of symbols, shared knowledge of rituals and traditions, and shared knowledge of people) were tested using CFA procedures in Mplus. In order to determine the best fit of the model to the data, the items and constructs were examined using (1) model fit indices, including the chi-squared value, degrees of freedom (df), p-value (significance) for the chi-square test, comparative fit index (CFI), Tucker–Lewis index (TLI), root mean square error of approximation (RMSEA), and standardized root mean square residual (SRMR); (2) standardized loadings; (3) modification indices; and (4) the theoretical justification for removing an item or construct (Anderson & Gerbing, 1988; Bagozzi & Yi, 1988; Bollen, 1989; Kline, 2005).

Table 1. Exploratory Factor Analysis Total Variance Explained (Dataset 1, n=500)

Component	Eigenvalues		
	Total	% of Variance	Cumulative %
1	3.385	42.318	42.318
2	1.669	20.861	63.180
3	1.015	12.685	75.865
4	.574	7.180	83.045
5	.448	5.594	88.639
6	.392	4.903	93.543
7	.332	4.152	97.695
8	.184	2.305	100.000

Figure 1. Exploratory Factor Analysis Scree Plot (Dataset 1, n=500)

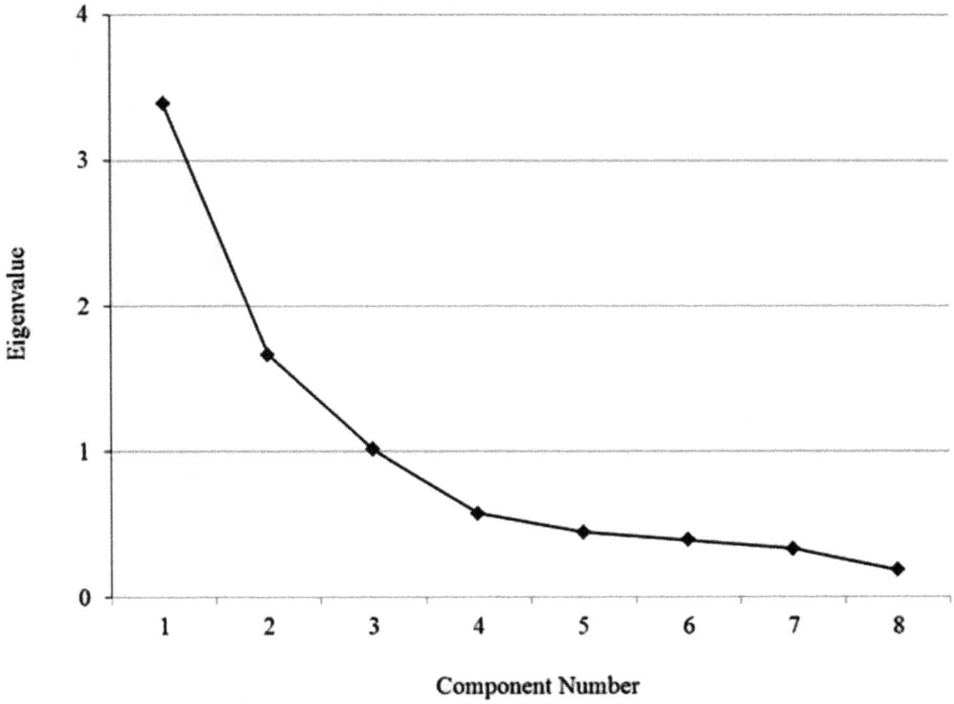

Table 2. Exploratory Factor Analysis Pattern Matrix (Dataset 1, n=500)

Item	Components		
	Symbols (1)	Rituals & Traditions (2)	People (3)
The colors of <team name> mean something important to fans of <team name> and I.	.90		
The logo(s) of <team name> have important meanings to fans of <team name> and I.	.91		
Fans of <team name> and I know the <team name> songs which are sung at games.	.44	.31	
Fans of <team name> and I know the rituals of <team name>.		.96	
Fans of <team name> and I know the traditions of <team name>.		.96	
Fans of <team name> and I know the heroes of <team name>.	.40		-.55
Fans of <team name> and I know the players on <team name>.			-.94
Fans of <team name> and I know the coaches of <team name>.			-.85

Notes: Principal Components Analysis was used as the extraction method; Direct Oblimin was used as the rotation method; Values below ±.30 were suppressed

The results of the analyses of the 28 items (see Table 3) suggest that one item each should respectively be removed from the constructs of membership, geographic sense of community and shared knowledge of symbols. Additionally, two items should be removed from the construct of social recognition; and for shared rivalry, three items should be removed. Based on the combinatorial rules for model fit proposed

Table 3. CFA Results (Dataset 1, n=500)

Construct	Item		Loading (γ)	SE	CR	AVE
Membership (Psychological Sense of Community)					0.95	0.87
	1.	I consider myself to be a member of the <team name> fan community.	0.89	0.02		
	2.	I am a part of the <team name> fan community.	0.94	0.02		
	3.	I am a member of the <team name> fan community.	0.96	0.01		
	4.	I belong to the fan community of <team name>.	Removed	N/A		
Geographic Sense of Community					0.88	0.71
	1.	As a fan of <team name>, I feel ties to <city name>.	0.77	0.03		
	2.	I feel like I belong in <city name> because of <team name>.	0.83	0.02		
	3.	Being a fan of <team name> helps me to feel connected to <city name>.	0.92	0.02		
	4.	<Team name> helps to improve my opinion about <city name>.	Removed	N/A		
Social Recognition					0.84	0.64
	1.	I like others to know that I am a fan of <team name>.	0.70	0.04		
	2.	I receive recognition from others for being a fan of <team name>.	0.76	0.04		
	3.	In general, people recognize me as a fan of <team name>.	0.93	0.02		
	4.	In general, <team name> recognizes me as a good fan.	Removed	N/A		
	5.	Being a fan of <team name> makes me feel socially valued.	Removed	N/A		
Shared Rivalry					0.78	0.64
	1.	Fans of <team name> and I feel a sense of satisfaction when <team name> beats their biggest rival.	Removed	N/A		
	2.	Fans of <team name> and I feel a sense of accomplishment when <team name> defeats their biggest rival.	Removed	N/A		
	3.	Fans of <team name> and I have bragging rights when beats their biggest rival.	Removed	N/A		
	4.	Fans of <team name> and I are happy when <team name> is victorious over their biggest rival.	0.73	0.06		
	5.	Fans of <team name> and I celebrate when <team name> defeats their biggest rival.	0.86	0.05		

by Hu and Bentler (1999), the CFA results for the revised seven construct, 18 item model fit the data well ($\chi 2$ (df)=199.95 (114), $p<.001$, CFI=0.97, TLI=0.96, RMSEA=0.04, SRMR=0.04).

To establish evidence of reliability, the composite reliability (CR) value was calculated for each of the seven constructs and the items that measure each construct (see Table 3). The calculated CR values range from 0.78-0.95. Composite reliability values over 0.70 are desirable, though values closest to 1.00 are most preferable (Raykov, 1997). In addition, evidence of convergent and discriminant validity was established through comparisons between the average variance extracted (AVE) values (see Table 3) and the correlations for the seven constructs (see Table 4). Evidence of convergent validity is established when each construct's AVE value is greater than 0.50, while evidence of discriminant validity is found when a construct's AVE value is greater than the squared multiple correlation for any two related constructs (Fornell & Larcker, 1981). The results of the CFA provide evidence of construct reliability and both convergent and discriminant validity with Dataset 1.

Table 4. Correlations and Descriptive Statistics (Dataset 1, n=500)

	MEM	GSOC	SREC	RIVL	SYM	R&T	PEOP	ATT	PUR	WOM	TV	MEDI	TRUE	COMM
MEM	1.00													
GSOC	0.34	1.00												
SREC	0.57	0.36	1.00											
RIVL	0.58	0.36	0.62	1.00										
SYM	0.55	0.35	0.60	0.60	1.00									
R&T	0.22	0.14	0.24	0.24	0.23	1.00								
PEOP	0.57	0.36	0.61	0.62	0.59	0.24	1.00							
ATT	0.16	0.10	0.17	0.17	0.16	0.06	0.17	1.00						
PUR	0.20	0.13	0.22	0.22	0.21	0.08	0.21	0.65	1.00					
WOM	0.19	0.12	0.21	0.21	0.20	0.08	0.20	0.59	0.62	1.00				
TV	0.18	0.11	0.20	0.20	0.19	0.08	0.19	0.28	0.32	0.25	1.00			
MEDI	0.18	0.11	0.20	0.20	0.19	0.08	0.19	0.27	0.33	0.33	0.49	1.00		
TRUE	0.60	0.38	0.65	0.65	0.63	0.25	0.64	0.17	0.24	0.16	0.22	0.17	1.00	
COMM	0.49	0.31	0.53	0.54	0.51	0.21	0.53	0.21	0.20	0.20	0.17	0.09	0.52	1.00
Mean	8.81	7.47	8.99	9.64	9.25	8.82	8.84	8.90	8.39	8.63	9.13	9.39	9.43	9.40
SD	2.17	2.98	1.68	1.07	1.54	2.05	1.78	2.07	2.55	2.27	2.10	1.54	1.32	1.39

Notes: MEM=Membership, GSOC=Geographic Sense of Community, SREC=Social Recognition, RIVL=Shared Rivalry, SYM=Shared Knowledge of Symbols, R&T= Shared Knowledge of Rituals and Traditions, PEOP= Shared Knowledge of People, ATT=Intention to Attend Future Games, PUR=Intention to Buy Merchandise in the Future, WOM=Intention to Tell Others to Attend the Team's Games in the Future, TV=Intention to Watch the Team's Games on Television, MEDI=Intention to Read about the Team in the Media, TRUE=Feel like a true fan of the team, COMM=Feel committed to the team, SD=Standard Deviation

These results with Dataset 1 also provide evidence that the seven construct, 18-item model fit the data well. Based on the CFA model results, four SEM models (with Dataset 2a, 2b, 2c and 2d), each including the relationships between the seven-dimension tribal sport fan scale and the seven total outcome variables were tested using Mplus (see Figure 2). The results for the four structural models are shown in Table 5.

Using Dataset 2a, the results based on responses from the Florida State University fanbase show that all seven constructs measuring tribal sport fans are positively and significantly related to attendance intentions ($\gamma=0.58$, SE=0.08, $p<0.001$), team merchandise purchase intentions ($\gamma=0.63$, SE=0.07, $p<0.001$), intentions to recommend that others attend the team's games ($\gamma=0.61$, SE=0.08, $p<0.001$), intentions to watch the team's games on television ($\gamma=0.69$, SE=0.13, $p<0.001$), intentions to read stories about the team in the media ($\gamma=0.69$, SE=0.11, $p<0.001$), feeling like a true fan of the team ($\gamma=0.93$, SE=0.03, $p<0.001$), and feeling committed to the team ($\gamma=0.77$, SE=0.05, $p<0.001$). For the fanbase of SL Benfica (Dataset 2b), while the seven tribal sport fan scale dimensions all have positive and significant relationships, the relationships with the five behavioral intentions variables are much weaker than those for the Florida State University fanbase, though the relationships with the outcome variables measuring two forms of commitment are comparably high. For the behavioral intentions variables, only four relationships are significant: attendance intentions ($\gamma=0.13$, SE=0.04, $p<0.01$), team merchandise purchase intentions ($\gamma=0.17$, SE=0.5, $p<0.001$), intentions to recommend that others attend the team's games ($\gamma=0.16$, SE=0.05, $p<0.001$), and intentions to read stories about the team in the media ($\gamma=0.11$, SE=0.04, $p<0.05$). The relationship with intentions to watch the team's games on television ($\gamma=0.08$,

Figure 2. Structural Model of Tribal Sport Fandom

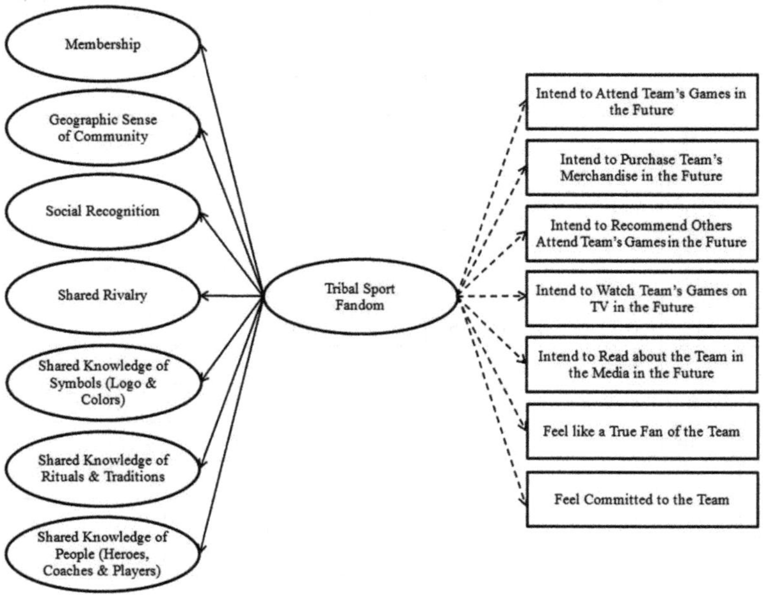

SE=0.05, p>0.05) is not significant. The relationships with the two variables measuring commitment are both positive and significant: feeling like a true fan of the team (γ=0.75, SE=0.03, p<0.001) and feeling committed to the team (γ=0.69, SE=0.05, p<0.001). While more similar to SL Benfica than Florida State University, the results for the FC Porto fanbase (Dataset 2c) show first that shared knowledge of rituals and traditions have an insignificant loading on the tribal sport fan scale (γ=-0.02, SE=0.07, p>0.05), and all five relationships with the behavioral intentions outcome variable are also insignificant: attendance intentions (γ=-0.03, SE=0.06, p>0.05), team merchandise purchase intentions (γ=-0.04, SE=0.07, p>0.05), intentions to recommend that others attend the team's games (γ=-0.07, SE=0.07, p>0.05), intentions to watch the team's games on television (γ=-0.05, SE=0.07, p>0.05), and intentions to read stories about the team in the media (γ=0.02, SE=0.07, p>0.05). In contrast, the relationships between the tribal sport fan scale and both commitment-related outcome variables are positive and significant: feeling like a true fan of the team (γ=0.80, SE=0.04, p<0.001), and feeling committed to the team (γ=0.69, SE=0.04, p<0.001). Unlike the SL Benfica and FC Porto fanbase and more similar to results from Florida State University fans, all the relationships in the model for Sporting CP fans are positive and significant: attendance intentions (γ=0.57, SE=0.06, p<0.001), team merchandise purchase intentions (γ=0.57, SE=0.05, p<0.001), intentions to recommend that others attend the team's games (γ=0.53, SE=0.05, p<0.001), intentions to watch the team's games on television (γ=0.29, SE=0.09, p<0.01), intentions to read stories about the team in the media (γ=0.43, SE=0.09, p<0.001), feeling like a true fan of the team (γ=0.81, SE=0.03, p<0.001), and feeling committed to the team (γ=0.79, SE=0.05, p<0.001). The model fit results for all four models provide evidence of near acceptable or good fit to the data. For the five behavioral intentions outcome variables, the amount of variance explained by the results for the Florida State University model (34.1%-48.1%) and Sporting CP model (8.6%-32.2%) is much higher than the amount of variance explained for the same five outcome variables for SL Benfica (0.6%-2.8%) and FC Porto (0.1%-0.5%) models (see Table 5). For all four models, however, positive and

Table 5. Structural Model Results (Datasets 2a, 2b, 2c, and 2d)

				FSU SEM (Dataset 2a, n=456)	**Benfica SEM (Dataset 2b, n=625)**	**Porto SEM (Dataset 2c, n=229)**	**Sporting SEM (Dataset 2d, n=372)**
Construct				*Loading (SE)*	*Loading (SE)*	*Loading (SE)*	*Loading (SE)*
Tribal Sport Fandom	←	1.	Membership	0.67 (0.09) ***	0.71 (0.03) ***	0.75 (0.04) ***	0.74 (0.04) ***
	←	2.	Geographic Sense of Community	0.40 (0.05) ***	0.53 (0.03) ***	0.60 (0.06) ***	0.39 (0.04) ***
	←	3.	Social Recognition	0.86 (0.04) ***	0.78 (0.03) ***	0.76 (0.05) ***	0.84 (0.03) ***
	←	4.	Shared Rivalry	0.98 (0.03) ***	0.64 (0.06) ***	0.73 (0.08) ***	0.60 (0.09) ***
	←	5.	Shared Knowledge of Symbols	0.84 (0.06) ***	0.79 (0.40) ***	0.77 (0.04) ***	0.79 (0.06) ***
	←	6.	Shared Knowledge of Rituals & Traditions	0.64 (0.70) ***	0.27 (0.05) ***	-0.02 (0.07)	0.73 (0.04) ***
	←	7.	Shared Knowledge of People	0.49 (0.08) ***	0.75 (0.05) ***	0.82 (0.04) ***	0.91 (0.03) ***
Tribal Sport Fandom	→	1.	I will attend <team name>'s games in the future.	0.58 (0.08) ***	0.13 (0.04) **	-0.03 (0.06)	0.57 (0.06) ***
	→	2.	I will buy <team name>'s merchandise in the future.	0.63 (0.07) ***	0.17 (0.05) ***	-0.04 (0.07)	0.57 (0.05) ***
	→	3.	I will recommend to others that they attend <team name>'s games in the future.	0.61 (0.08) ***	0.16 (0.05) **	-0.07 (0.07)	0.53 (0.05) ***
	→	4.	I will watch <team name>'s games on television in the future.	0.69 (0.13) ***	0.08 (0.05)	-0.05 (0.07)	0.29 (0.09) **
	→	5.	I will read stories in the media about <team name> in the future.	0.69 (0.11) ***	0.11 (0.04) **	0.02 (0.07)	0.43 (0.09) ***
	→	6.	I am a true fan of <team name>.	0.93 (0.03) ***	0.75 (0.03) ***	0.80 (0.04) ***	0.81 (0.03) ***
	→	7.	I am very committed to <team name>.	0.77 (0.05) ***	0.69 (0.05) ***	0.69 (0.04) ***	0.79 (0.05) ***
		Model Fit:	χ^2 (*df*) *p* CFI (TLI) RMSEA (SRMR)	518.00 (247) < 0.001 0.91 (0.89) 0.05 (0.09)	741.48 (247) < 0.001 0.93 (0.91) 0.06 (0.09)	467.48 (247) < 0.001 0.91 (0.89) 0.06 (0.09)	468.92 (247) < 0.001 0.95 (0.93) 0.05 (0.05)
		R^2:	Attendance	34.1%	1.7%	0.1%	31.9%
			Merchandise	39.1%	2.8%	0.2%	32.2%
			Recommend	37.0%	2.6%	0.5%	28.2%
			Watch on TV	47.7%	0.6%	0.2%	8.6%
			Read in the Media	48.1%	1.1%	0.1%	18.8%
			True Fan of Team	87.0%	56.3%	64.1%	65.8%
			Committed to Team	58.7%	47.8%	47.3%	62.1%

Notes: Loading=Path coefficient (γ), SE=Standard Error, χ^2 = chi-squared value, *df*=degrees of freedom, *p*=significance test value, CFI=comparative fit index, TLI=Tucker-Lewis index, RMSEA=root mean square error of approximation, SRMR=standardized root mean square residual

*p<.05, **p<.01, ***p<.001

significant relationships are found between the tribal sport fandom scale and both feeling like a true fan of the team (the amount of variance explained ranges from 56.3% to 87.0%) and feeling committed to the team (the amount of variance explained ranges from 47.3% to 62.1%) for all four models.

DISCUSSION

Many labels can be used to describe groups of sports fans who engage in the co-creation and co-consumption of sporting events. In previous research, consumer groups have been labelled as consumption communities (Boorstin, 1973), cultures of consumption (Kozinets, 2001), subcultures of consumption (Celsi et al., 1993; Schouten & McAlexander, 1995), brand communities (McAlexander et al., 2002; Muniz & O'Guinn, 2001), brand cults (Belk & Tumbat, 2005), and consumer tribes (Cova & Cova, 2002; Maffesoli, 1996). Because every group of consumers – or in this case, group of fans – is organized and works in different manners, it is possible that groups of sports fans could be labelled with all of the preceding terms, as the label is often dependent on the focal object of group and the relationships among members. Based on the unique factors which epitomize "true" and "committed" sports fans (e.g., continuing to support the team regardless of the win-loss record), however, sport tribes and tribal sport fans may be the most accurate labels.

For tribal sport fans, there are two important aspects that can be used to define and identify them, including a sense of community (a psychological feeling of belonging others, a feeling of connection to the geographic area the team represents, and a social recognition from others of their connection to the team) and shared knowledge (with other fans) of the rival teams and the symbols (e.g., logos, colors, rituals, traditions, players, coaches and heroes) of the team. It is the sport team, its athletes, and the games that are played that provide reason(s) for these fans to connect online or face-to-face. In the same ways that human beings came together and occupied distinct geographic areas in early human history and created human tribes, a similar process continues with the relationship between sports fans and the team they support. For important events early in human history, members of the tribes would come together to co-create their culture. Today on games days, tribal sport fans come together in the same way to co-create and co-consume sporting events.

Over the years, numerous researchers have reported that the need to belong to some type of group is important for sports fans (Branscombe, Schmitt & Harvey, 1999; Gwinner & Swanson, 2003; Wann, 2006; Wann, Melnick, Russell, & Pease, 2001). Theodorakis, Wann and Weaver (2011) also note that the need to belong is positively correlated with the level of identification with a local sport team, but not identification with a distant team or mere sport fandom. Baumeister and Leary (1995) succinctly summarized the need to belong when they defined it as a "need to form and maintain strong, stable interpersonal relationships" (p. 497). As Wann and Grieve (2005) state, by viewing the in-group positively or perceiving out-groups negatively, individuals are able to boost or restore their collective (i.e., group or social) self-esteem. For tribal sport fans, the need to feel a sense of belonging with others based on, in many cases, a shared liking of the local sport team is an important process which lays the foundation for these fans to co-create and co-consume sporting events.

Social recognition also plays a significant role for tribal sport fans. While anyone can engage in behaviors linked to being a fan of a team (i.e., wear the team's jersey, cheer for the team), there are additional ways in which tribal sport fans can be recognized by others. The process of social recognition assists with identifying who are real members and who are either temporary or not actual fans of a team. The process of social recognition also reinforces fans' feelings of connection and integration into the larger tribe. For example while many owners of Harley Davidson motorcycles display their jackets and "hogs" and large numbers of "Mac Users" proudly show their multiple Apple devices (e.g., Macbook, iPhone), sport team fans similarly are often found wearing a multitude of team merchandise on the day before, day of, and day after a game (especially if their team wins) (Fisher & Wakefield, 1998; Sutton et al., 1997; Wann & Branscombe, 1993).

In order to facilitate the growth of a sport tribe, it is also important to emphasize how that tribe is different from others, and one of the best ways this can be done is to share and highlight rivalries (Rein et al., 2006). Due to the competitive nature of sport and fans' strong connections to their team and other fans, sometimes tribal fans may "go to war" with other fans and engage in potentially fanatical and negative behaviors toward rivals (Bristow & Sebastian, 2001; Kelley & Tian, 2004). Even though most fans usually demonstrate their devotion to their favorite team through socially acceptable behaviors (Dalakas, Melancon, & Sreboth, 2015), in some instances fanaticism can become extreme and lead to inappropriate or dangerous behaviors (Dalakas et al., 2015; Wakefield & Wann, 2006). Often such behaviors entail some form of aggression or willingness to engage in aggressive behavior toward one's rivals and/or their fans (Wann, 1993). Tribal fans can become violent, but because these negative behaviors are undertaken by a small subsection of the tribal members, such a group might be more properly labelled as a sport fan cult. On an almost weekly basis, one can find news reports across the world describing violence and fighting between these small groups of supporters of different teams.

In terms of the symbols that tribal sports fans know and share, research has shown that logos and colors are primary visual representations of a brand or team's meaning (Biscaia et al., 2016; Park et al., 2013). To illustrate this idea, a renowned supporter of the Sporting Lisbon team once suggested that the solution to a crisis in Portugal could be solved by removing the red color from Portugal's national flag (Jornal de Notícias, 2013). By removing the red color, the flag would look like Sporting Lisbon's flag (which is green and white); and as a result, the country as a whole would prosper just like recent Sporting Lisbon teams had done (Jornal de Notícias, 2013). Tribal sport fans often wear the logo and colors of their sports team and engage in a number of rituals and traditions showing their support of the team, while also exhibiting a solid knowledge of the most important people in the team's history such as players, coaches or even managers. Tribal sport fans also tend to ennoble their teams and associated symbols (Belk & Tumbat, 2005). Sport teams and the leaders of the fan tribes can establish and/or build on their unique history and traditions, and initiate meaningful rituals involving the consumption process. For example, Florida State University football fans share many rituals and traditions such as singing the FSU fight song, engaging in the "warchant" (i.e., extending one's right arm in front of the body and bending the arm at the elbow in a 90-degree motion in a 'chopping' type of motion), putting four fingers from one hand in the air during the break between the third and fourth quarters of the game that symbolizes to players that their mental toughness will prevail in the fourth and final quarter of the game, and engaging in FSU-related chanting (Lonzo, 2011; Seminoles.com, 2016a). Underwood and colleagues (2001) also acknowledge the importance of rituals and traditions as characteristic of consumer groups, and including that tribal fans tend to know almost everything about the history of the team and its players and coaches (Gladden & Funk, 2002). Knowledge of the team's symbols provides evidence of the strong relationship between the sport fan and the team (Holt, 1998; Schouten & McAlexander, 1995). Thus, tribal sport fans often recognize coaches and players, mascots, rituals (e.g., cheers and chants), and other symbolic representations of the team. For example, in addition to keeping track of former players who currently play in the National Football League (NFL), Florida State Football fans know the history and stories related to legendary coaches (e.g., Bobby Bowden) and renowned former players (e.g., Deion Sanders, Warrick Dunn, Charlie Ward) (Seminoles.com, 2016b).

Overall, the sense of community tribal fans feel towards their teams is paramount due to its impact on consumer behavioral patterns, such as attendance, media consumption, merchandise purchase, and loyalty (Fisher & Wakefield, 1998; Gwinner & Swanson, 2003; Madrigal, 2000; Wann & Branscombe, 1993). The stronger the link with the team, the more willing a fan will be to adopt positive behaviors such as merchandise and media consumption, and game attendance or positive word-of-mouth behaviors (Heere et al., 2011). This idea is supported in the current study as behavioral intention items are significantly related to sport tribal fandom in some cases. Due to the reinforcing nature of the unique co-creation and co-consumption activities of tribal sport fans of a specific team, members form strong preferences for the team's goods (e.g., merchandise) and services (e.g., event experiences) (Dionisio et al., 2008). Moreover, participation in the sport tribe can result in positive attitudes and emotions toward the team and positive word-of-mouth behaviors (Hedlund, 2014; Holt, 1995). The two teams included in this study that have recently achieved high levels of either success (Florida State University) or increased performance over the last years (Sporting CP) both produced results that show positive and significant relationships to the tribal sport fandom scale; however, the other two teams included in this research (SL Benfica and FC Porto) indicate much weaker or no significant relationships with the behavioral intentions outcome variables. FC Porto, in particular, recently may not have reached the expectations of their fanbase; therefore, fans may not be as willing to indicate that they intend to attend games or buy merchandise in the future – unless the team gets back on the right track and wins championships. Previous researchers have indicated that behavioral intentions can be affected by winning (or a lack thereof) (Trail et al., 2003). To counter this circumstance, two variables representing feelings of commitment as a fan and to the team were both also included as outcomes variables. The results in all four models are positive and significant for both of these variables, and the amount of variance explained is relatively high. Thus, the results of this research provide further evidence that winning (or a lack thereof) may affect how fans respond when asked about whether or not they intend to support a team in the future. The amount of variance explained in all four models for feeling like a true fan of a team and feeling committed to the team also provides additional evidence that this new tribal sport fandom scale is indeed tapping into some of the important dimensions that constitute tribal sport fandom.

FUTURE RESEARCH DIRECTIONS

In this research, a scale to measure tribal sport fans has been created, developed and tested in multiple settings with different types of sports teams at different levels of sport. There can be many types of fan groups, but based on recent evidence one of the most appropriate labels for groups of sports fans is a sport tribe. While the current research was strongly quantitative, additional ethnographic research similar to Morris' (1981) can and should be conducted in order to better understand how and why fans become tribal, and to determine if there are other important factors or dimensions that could be included in future measurements of tribal sport fans. Because this research is one of the first quantitative forays into establishing a better understanding of tribal sport fans and how to measure them, only eight of more than 30 tribal symbols identified by Morris (1981) were included. Moreover, when subjected to quantitative (EFA) analysis, those symbols were further culled down into only three separate constructs. It is likely that, based on the cultural norms of different fans in different countries, there will be additional shared symbols that members of the sport tribes share. Further identification and understanding of potential symbols is warranted. Finally, while cross-sectional data methods were used in the current research, a more longitudinal perspective would also be helpful. Through such methods, the causes of why fans are tribal can be identified and if any specific tribal-only outcomes exist.

CONCLUSION

The authors of this research created, developed, tested and validated a reliable scale to measure aspects that constitute sport fan tribes. In testing the scale with four separate samples, the Florida State University and Sporting CP datasets showed strong evidence of tribal sport fandom, as exhibited by the strong empirical relationships with desirable behavioral outcomes such as attending games, buying merchandise, telling others to attend games, watching games on television, and reading about the team in the media. In two separate data sets, while both sets of results produce evidence of the reliability and validity of the scale, relationships with those same behavioral outcome variables show positive and significant (although very weak) results in the case of SL Benfica fans, and no significant results are found for the FC Porto fans. These findings indicate that the dimensions of membership, geographic sense of community, social recognition, shared rivalry, shared knowledge of symbols, shared knowledge of rituals and traditions, and shared knowledge of people are important factors that can be used to measure tribal sport fandom. In addition, these dimensions produce positive and significant relationships with behavioral intentions towards some of the teams examined. For all four data sets, positive, significant results, in addition to relatively large amounts of accounted for variance in the relationships between the tribal sport fandom scale and the outcome variables "Feeling Like a True Fan" of the team and "Feeling Committed to the Team" provide initial evidence of the strength of the current research. Understanding tribal sport fandom is important for managers, practitioners and academics because understanding the process of how fans may move from the early stages of being a (new) fan of a team to eventually (and possibly) becoming a strongly committed tribal sport fan can help sport teams develop and implement marketing programs which create opportunities for fans to come together in face-to-face and online opportunities and co-create event experiences which can strengthen and enhance the relationships between fans, other fans and the team.

REFERENCES

Anderson, J. A., & Gerbing, D. W. (1988). Structural equation modeling in practice: A review and recommended two-Step approach. *Psychological Bulletin*, *103*(3), 411–423. doi:10.1037/0033-2909.103.3.411

Anker, E. (2005). Villains, victims and heroes: Melodrama, media and September 11. *Journal of Communication*, *55*(1), 22–37. doi:10.1111/j.1460-2466.2005.tb02656.x

Apostolopoulou, A., Papadimitriou, D., Synowka, D., & Clark, J. S. (2012). Consumption and meanings of team licensed merchandise. *International Journal of Sport Management and Marketing*, *12*(1/2), 93–110. doi:10.1504/IJSMM.2012.051266

Arnould, E. J., & Price, L. L. (1993). River magic: Extraordinary experience and the extended service encounter. *The Journal of Consumer Research*, *20*(1), 24–45. doi:10.1086/209331

Ashforth, B. E., & Mael, F. (1989). Social identity theory and the organization. *Academy of Management Review*, *14*(1), 20–39.

Bagozzi, R. P., & Yi, Y. (1988). On the evaluation of structural equation models. *Journal of the Academy of Marketing Science*, *16*(1), 74–94. doi:10.1007/BF02723327

Banville, D., Desrosiers, P., & Genet-Volet, Y. (2000). Translating questionnaires and inventories using a cross-cultural translation technique. *Journal of Teaching in Physical Education*, *19*(3), 374–387. doi:10.1123/jtpe.19.3.374

Bauer, H. H., Stokburger-Sauer, N. E., & Exler, S. (2008). Brand image and fan loyalty in professional sport team: A refined model and empirical assessment. *Journal of Sport Management*, *22*(2), 205–226. doi:10.1123/jsm.22.2.205

Baumeister, R. F., & Leary, M. R. (1995). The need to belong: Desire for interpersonal attachments as a fundamental human motivation. *Psychological Bulletin*, *117*(3), 497–529. doi:10.1037/0033-2909.117.3.497 PMID:7777651

Becker, G. S. (1996). *Accounting for tastes*. Cambridge, MA: Harvard University Press.

Belk, R. W., & Tumbat, G. (2005). The cult of Macintosh. *Consumption Markets & Culture*, *8*(3), 205–217. doi:10.1080/10253860500160403

Bennet, M., & Sani, F. (2004). Introduction: Children and social identity. In M. Bennet & F. Sani (Eds.), *The Development of the Social Self* (pp. 1–26). New York, NY: Psychology Press. doi:10.4324/9780203391099_chapter_1

Biscaia, R. (2016). Revisiting the role of soccer spectator's behavioral intentions and its antecedents. *The Open Sports Sciences Journal, 9*(Suppl-1), 3-12.

Biscaia, R., Correia, A., Ross, S., Rosado, A., & Marôco, J. (2013). Spectator-based brand equity in professional soccer. *Sport Marketing Quarterly*, *22*(1), 20–32.

Biscaia, R., Ross, S., & Yoshisda, M. (2016). Investigating the role of fan club membership on perceptions of team brand equity in football. *Sport Management Review*, *19*(2), 157–170. doi:10.1016/j.smr.2015.02.001

Bishop, R. (2001). Stealing the signs: A semiotic analysis of the changing nature of professional sports logos. *Social Semiotics*, *1*(1), 23–41. doi:10.1080/10350330125030

Bollen, K. A. (1989). *Structural equations with latent variables*. New York, NY: John Wiley & Sons, Inc. doi:10.1002/9781118619179

Bolsmann, C., & Parker, A. (2007). Soccer, South Africa and celebrity status: Mark Fish, popular culture and the post-apartheid state. *Soccer and Society*, *8*(1), 109–124. doi:10.1080/14660970600989442

Boorstin, D. J. (1973). *The Americans: The democratic experience*. New York, NY: Vintage.

Branscombe, N. R., Schmitt, M. T., & Harvey, R. D. (1999). Perceiving pervasive discrimination among African Americans: Implications for group identification and well-being. *Journal of Personality and Social Psychology*, *77*(1), 135–149. doi:10.1037/0022-3514.77.1.135

Branscombe, N. R., & Wann, D. L. (1991). The positive social and self-concept consequences of sports team identification. *Journal of Sport and Social Issues*, *15*(2), 115–127. doi:10.1177/019372359101500202

Breech, J. (2016). *Fans at Super Bowl 50 spent nearly $11 million, bought 8K glasses of wine*. Retrieved on January 9, 2017 from http://www.cbssports.com/nfl/news/fans-at-super-bowl-50-spent-nearly-11-million-bought-8k-glasses-of-wine/

Bristow, D. N., & Sebastian, R. J. (2001). Holy cow! Wait 'til next year! A closer look at the brand loyalty of Chicago baseball fans. *Journal of Consumer Marketing*, *18*(3), 256–275. doi:10.1108/07363760110392976

Brown, A., Crabbe, T., & Mellor, G. (2006). English professional football and its communities. *International Review of Modern Sociology*, *32*(2), 159–179.

Canniford, R. (2011). A typology of consumption communities. *Research in Consumer Behavior, 13*, 57-75.

Celsi, R. L., Rose, R. L., & Leigh, T. W. (1993). An exploration of high-risk leisure consumption through skydiving. *The Journal of Consumer Research*, *20*(1), 1–23. doi:10.1086/209330

Chavis, D. M., & Newbrough, J. R. (1986). The meaning of community in community psychology. *Journal of Community Psychology*, *14*(4), 335–340. doi:10.1002/1520-6629(198610)14:4<335::AID-JCOP2290140402>3.0.CO;2-T

Cottingham, M. D. (2012). Interaction ritual theory and sports fans: Emotion, symbols, and solidarity. *Sociology of Sport Journal*, *29*(2), 168–185. doi:10.1123/ssj.29.2.168

Couvelaere, V., & Richelieu, P. (2005). Brand strategy in professional sports: The case of French soccer teams. *European Sport Management Quarterly*, *5*(1), 23–46. doi:10.1080/16184740500089524

Cova, B. (1997). Community and consumption: Towards a definition of the "linking value" of product or services. *European School of Management*, *31*(3/4), 297–316.

Cova, B., & Cova, V. (2002). Tribal marketing: The tribalisation of society and its impact on the conduct of marketing. *European Journal of Marketing*, *36*(5/6), 595–620. doi:10.1108/03090560210423023

Cova, B., Kozinets, R., & Shankar, A. (2007). Tribes, Inc.: The new world of tribalism. In B. Cova, R. Kozinets, & A. Shankar (Eds.), *Consumer tribes* (pp. 3–26). New York, NY: Routledge.

Crawford, G. (2004). Consuming sport: Fans, sport and culture. *International Journal of Sports Marketing & Sponsorship*, *6*(2), 47–62. doi:10.1108/IJSMS-06-02-2004-B007

Dalakas, V., Melancon, J. P., & Sreboth, T. (2015). A qualitative inquiry on schadenfreude by sport fans. *Journal of Sport Behavior*, *38*(2), 161–179.

DeSarbo, W. S., & Madrigal, R. (2011). Examining the behavioral manifestations of fan avidity in sports marketing. *Journal of Modelling in Management*, *6*(1), 79–99. doi:10.1108/17465661111112511

Devasagayam, P. R., & Buff, C. L. (2008). A multidimensional conceptualization of brand community: An empirical investigation. *Sport Marketing Quarterly*, *17*(1), 20–29.

Dionísio, P., Leal, C., & Moutinho, L. (2008). Fandom affiliation and tribal behaviour: A sports marketing application. *Qualitative Market Research: An International Journal*, *11*(1), 17–39. doi:10.1108/13522750810845531

Fetcho, M., Roy, D., & Clow, K. E. (2013). *Sports marketing*. New York, NY: Prentice Hall, Pearson Education.

Fischer, R., & Wakefield, K. (1998). Factors leading to group identification: A field study of winners and losers. *Psychology and Marketing*, *15*(1), 23–40. doi:10.1002/(SICI)1520-6793(199801)15:1<23::AID-MAR3>3.0.CO;2-P

Forgas, J. P., & Williams, K. D. (2002). The social self: Introduction and overview. In The social self: Cognitive, interpersonal, and intergroup perspectives (pp. 1-18). New York, NY: Psychology Press.

Fornell, C., & Larcker, D. F. (1981). Evaluating structural equation models with unobservable variables and measurement error. *JMR, Journal of Marketing Research*, *18*(1), 39–50. doi:10.2307/3151312

FourFourTwo.com. (2016). *Why Liverpool fans sing 'You'll Never Walk Alone'*. Retrieved on September 16, 2016 from http://www.fourfourtwo.com/features/why-liverpool-fans-sing-youll-never-walk-alone

Gammon, S. (2014). Heroes as heritage: The commoditization of sporting achievement. *Journal of Heritage Tourism*, *9*(3), 246–253. doi:10.1080/1743873X.2014.904321

Giulianotti, R. (2002). Supporters, followers, fans and flaneurs: A taxonomy of spectator identities in football. *Journal of Sport and Social Issues*, *26*(1), 25–46. doi:10.1177/0193723502261003

Gladden, J. M., & Funk, D. C. (2002). Developing an understanding of brand associations in team sport: Empirical evidence from consumers of professional sport. *Journal of Sport Management*, *6*(1), 54–81. doi:10.1123/jsm.16.1.54

Goulding, C., Shankar, A., & Canniford, R. (2013). Learning to be tribal: Facilitating the formation of consumer tribes. *European Journal of Marketing*, *47*(5), 813–832. doi:10.1108/03090561311306886

Goulding, C., Shankar, A., Elliott, R., & Canniford, R. (2009). The marketplace management of illicit pleasure. *The Journal of Consumer Research*, *35*(5), 759–771. doi:10.1086/592946

Grant, N., Heere, B., & Dickson, G. (2011). New sport teams and the development of brand community. *European Sport Management Quarterly*, *11*(1), 35–54. doi:10.1080/16184742.2010.537364

Gwinner, K., & Swanson, S. R. (2003). A model of fan identification: Antecedents and sponsorship outcomes. *Journal of Services Marketing*, *17*(3), 275–294. doi:10.1108/08876040310474828

Hasaan, A., Kerem, K., Biscaia, R., & Agyemang, K. (in press). A conceptual framework to understand the creation of athlete brand and its implications. *International Journal of Sport Management and Marketing*.

Havard, C. T. (2014). Glory out of reflected failure: The examination of how rivalry affects sport fans. *Sport Management Review*, *17*(3), 243–253. doi:10.1016/j.smr.2013.09.002

Havard, C. T., Eddy, T., & Ryan, T. (2016). Examining the impact of team identification and gender on rival perceptions and consumption intentions of intercollegiate athletics fans. *Journal of Applied Sport Management*, *8*(2), 33–49.

Havard, C. T., Gray, D., Gould, J., Sharp, L., & Schaffer, J. (2013). Development and validation of the sport rivalry fan perception scale (SRFPS). *Journal of Sport Behavior*, *36*(1), 45–65.

Healy, J. C., & McDonagh, P. (2013). Consumer roles in brand culture and value co-creation in virtual communities. *Journal of Business Research*, *66*(9), 1528–1540. doi:10.1016/j.jbusres.2012.09.014

Hedlund, D. P. (2014). Creating value through membership and participation in sport fan consumption communities. *European Sport Management Quarterly*, *14*(1), 50–71. doi:10.1080/16184742.2013.865775

Hedlund, D. P., & Perricone, D. (2013). *Measuring sport fans' sense of community*. Presented at the *11th Annual Sport Marketing Association Conference, Albuquerque*, NM.

Heere, B., & James, J. D. (2007). Sports teams and their communities: Examining the influence of external group identities on team identity. *Journal of Sport Management*, *21*(3), 319–337. doi:10.1123/jsm.21.3.319

Heere, B., Walker, M., Yoshida, M., Ko, Y. J., Jordan, J. S., & James, J. D. (2011). Brand community development through associated communities: Grounding community measurement within social identity theory. *Journal of Marketing Theory and Practice*, *19*(4), 407–422. doi:10.2753/MTP1069-6679190404

Hogg, M. A., Terry, D., & White, K. (1995). A tale of two theories. *Social Psychology Quarterly*, *58*(4), 255–269. doi:10.2307/2787127

Holt, D. B. (1995). How consumers consume: A typology of consumption practices. *The Journal of Consumer Research*, *22*(1), 1–16. doi:10.1086/209431

Holt, D. B. (1998). Does cultural capital structure American consumption? *The Journal of Consumer Research*, *25*(1), 1–25. doi:10.1086/209523

Holt, R., & Mangan, J. A. (1996). Prologue: Heroes of a European past. *The International Journal of the History of Sport*, *13*(1), 1–13. doi:10.1080/09523369608713921

Hu, L., & Bentler, P. M. (1999). Cutoff criteria for fit indexes in covariance structure analysis: Conventional criteria versus new alternatives. *Structural Equation Modeling*, *6*(1), 1–55. doi:10.1080/10705519909540118

Huang, H. C. (2014). A study of tribe sport tourism products planning: Case by Smangus in Taiwan. *Journal of Global Business Management*, *10*(2), 36–44.

Jamieson, J. P. (2010). The home field advantage in athletics: A meta-analysis. *Journal of Applied Social Psychology*, *40*(7), 1819–1848. doi:10.1111/j.1559-1816.2010.00641.x

Jornal de Notícias. (2013). *Bruno de Carvalho sugere sugere retirada do vermelho da bandeira de Portugal*. Retrieved on May 21, 2016 from http://www.jn.pt/desporto/interior/bruno-de-carvalho-sugere-retirada-do-vermelho-da-bandeira-de-portugal-3554781.html

Katz, M., & Heere, B. (2015). Empowerment within brand communities: Overcoming the Achilles Heel of scale-free networks. *Sport Management Review*, *18*(3), 370–383. doi:10.1016/j.smr.2014.10.001

Kelley, S. W., & Tian, K. (2004). Fanatical consumption: An investigation of the behavior of sports fans through textual data. In L. R. Kahle & C. Riley (Eds.), *Sports marketing and the psychology of marketing communication* (pp. 27–65). Mahwah, NJ: Lawrence Erlbaum Associates Publishers.

Kimble, C., & Cooper, B. (1992). Association and Dissociation by Football fans. *Perceptual and Motor Skills*, *75*(1), 303–309. doi:10.2466/pms.1992.75.1.303

Kline, R. B. (2005). *Principles and practices of structural equation modeling*. New York, NY: The Guilford Press.

Kozinets, R. V. (2001). Utopian Enterprise: Articulating the meanings of Star Treks culture of consumption. *The Journal of Consumer Research*, *28*(June), 67–88. doi:10.1086/321948

Kraszewski, J. (2008). Pittsburgh in Fort Worth football bars, sports television, sports fandom, and the management of home. *Journal of Sport and Social Issues*, *32*(2), 139–157. doi:10.1177/0193723508316377

La Liga. (2016). *Historical Statistics: Standings*. Retrieved on October 29, 2016 from http://www.laliga.es/en/statistics-historical/standings

Lai, M., & Yang, S. (2013). The influence of IBC to brand community equity: The mediation effect of brand community identity and brand community commitment. *Marketing Review/Xing Xiao Ping Lun*, *10*(3), 293-321.

Lonzo, K. (2011). *Toughness. Effort. Discipline. Nole Pride.* Retrieved on October 29, 2016 from http://www.seminoles.com/ViewArticle.dbml?DB_OEM_ID=32900&ATCLID=209553381

Madrigal, R. (2000). The influence of social alliances with sports teams on intentions to purchase corporate sponsors products. *Journal of Advertising*, *29*(4), 13–24. doi:10.1080/00913367.2000.10673621

Madupu, V., & Krishnan, B. (2008). The relationship between online brand community participation and consciousness of kind, moral responsibility, and shared rituals and traditions. In A. Y. Lee & D. Soman (Eds.), *Advances in consumer research* (Vol. 35, pp. 853–854). Duluth, MN: Association for Consumer Research.

Mael, F. A., & Ashforth, B. E. (2001). Identification in work, war, sports, and religion: Contrasting the benefits and risks. *Journal for the Theory of Social Behaviour*, *31*(2), 197–222. doi:10.1111/1468-5914.00154

Maffesoli, M. (1996). *The time of the tribes: The decline of individualism in mass society*. London: Sage Publications.

McAlexander, J. H., Schouten, J. W., & Koenig, H. F. (2002). Building brand community. *Journal of Marketing*, *66*(1), 38–54. doi:10.1509/jmkg.66.1.38.18451

McMillan, D. W. (1976). *Sense of community: An attempt at definition* (Unpublished manuscript). Nashville, TN: George Peabody College for Teachers.

McMillan, D. W., & Chavis, D. M. (1986). Sense of community: A definition and theory. *Journal of Community Psychology, 14*(1), 6–23. doi:10.1002/1520-6629(198601)14:1<6::AID-JCOP2290140103>3.0.CO;2-I

Mitchell, C., & Imrie, B. C. (2011). Consumer tribes: Membership, consumption and building loyalty. *Asia Pacific Journal of Marketing and Logistics, 23*(1), 39–56. doi:10.1108/13555851111099989

Morris, D. (1981). *The soccer tribe*. London: Jonathan Cape.

Mueller, T. S., & Sutherland, J. C. (2010). Heroes and villains: Increasing fan involvement in pursuit of "the elusive fan". *Journal of Sport Administration & Supervision, 2*(1), 20–30.

Mullin, B. J., Hardy, S., & Sutton, W. A. (2014). *Sport marketing* (4th ed.). Champaign, IL: Human Kinetics.

Muniz, A. M. Jr, & OGuinn, T. C. (2001). Brand community. *The Journal of Consumer Research, 27*(March), 412–432. doi:10.1086/319618

Obst, P., Smith, S. G., & Zinkiewicz, L. (2002). An exploration of sense of community, Part 3: Dimensions and predictors of psychological sense of community in geographical communities. *Journal of Community Psychology, 30*(1), 119–133. doi:10.1002/jcop.1054

Papadimitriou, D., & Apostolopoulou, A. (2015). Capturing the meanings of sport licensed products. *Journal of Marketing Communications, 21*, 1–17. doi:10.1080/13527266.2015.1065900

Park, C., Eisingerich, A., Pol, G., & Park, J. (2013). The role of brand logos in firm performance. *Journal of Business Research, 66*(2), 180–187. doi:10.1016/j.jbusres.2012.07.011

Pettigrew, T. F. (1967). Social evaluation theory: Convergences and applications. In D. Levine (Ed.), *Nebraska Symposium on Motivation* (pp. 241-311). Lincoln, NE: University of Nebraska Press.

Puddifoot, J. E. (1996). Some initial considerations in the measurement of community identity. *Journal of Community Psychology, 24*(4), 327–336. doi:10.1002/(SICI)1520-6629(199610)24:4<327::AID-JCOP3>3.0.CO;2-R

Raykov, T. (1997). Estimation of composite reliability for congeneric measures. *Applied Psychological Measurement, 21*(2), 173–184. doi:10.1177/01466216970212006

Rein, I., Kotler, P., & Shields, B. (2006). *The elusive fan: Reinventing sports in a crowded marketplace*. New York, NY: McGraw-Hill.

Richardson, B. (2013). *Tribal marketing, tribal branding: An expert guide to the brand co-creation process*. London, England: Palgrave Macmillan. doi:10.1057/9781137349101

Richelieu, A. (2003). A brand new world for sports teams. In B. G. Pitts (Ed.), *Sharing best practices in sport marketing: The Sport Marketing Association's inaugural book of papers* (pp. 3–21). Morgantown, WV: Fitness Information Technology.

Ross, S., Russell, K., & Bang, H. (2008). An empirical assessment of spectator-based brand equity. *Journal of Sport Management*, *22*(3), 322–337. doi:10.1123/jsm.22.3.322

Rottiers, S. (2010). *The sociology of social recognition: Competition in social recognition games*. CSB Working Paper No. 10/04. Retrieved on October 4, 2016 from http://www.centrumvoorsociaalbeleid.be/index.php?q=node/2025/en

Sarason, S. B. (1974). *The psychological sense of community: Prospects for a community psychology*. San Francisco, CA: Jossey-Bass, Inc. Publishers.

Schau, H. J., Muñiz, A. M. Jr, & Arnould, E. J. (2009). How brand community practices create value. *Journal of Marketing*, *73*(5), 30–51. doi:10.1509/jmkg.73.5.30

Schouten, J. W., & McAlexander, J. H. (1995). Subcultures of consumption: An ethnography of the new bikers. *The Journal of Consumer Research*, *22*(June), 43–61. doi:10.1086/209434

Schwartz, B., & Barsky, S. F. (1977). The home advantage. *Social Forces*, *55*(3), 641–661. doi:10.2307/2577461

Seminoles.com. (2016a). *Seminole Traditions*. Retrieved on October 29, 2016 from http://www.seminoles.com/ViewArticle.dbml?ATCLID=209576825&DB_OEM_ID=32900&DB_OEM_ID=32900

Seminoles.com. (2016b). *Retired Numbers/Jerseys*. Retrieved on October 29, 2016 from http://www.seminoles.com/ViewArticle.dbml?DB_OEM_ID=32900&ATCLID=209577365

Smith, A., & Westerbeek, H. (2004). *The sport business future*. New York, NY: Palgrave Macmillan. doi:10.1057/9780230513693

SoxAndPinstripes.com. (2016). *Red Sox Yankee Rivalry – The Greatest Rivalry in Baseball?* Retrieved on October 29, 2016 from http://www.soxandpinstripes.com/

Super Bowl 50 Host Committee. (2016). *Super Bowl 50 Sets Records Across the Board*. Retrieved on January 9, 2017 from http://www.sfbaysuperbowl.com/super-bowl-50-sets-records-across-the-board

Sutton, W. A., McDonald, M. A., Milne, G. R., & Cimperman, J. (1997). Creating and fostering fan identification in professional sports. *Sport Marketing Quarterly*, *6*(1), 15–22.

Tajfel, H., & Turner, J. C. (1979). An integrative theory of intergroup conflict. In W. G. Austin & S. Worchel (Eds.), *The social psychology of intergroup relations* (pp. 33–47). Monterey, CA: Brooks.

Tajfel, H., & Turner, J. C. (1985). The social identity theory of group behavior. In S. Worchel & W. G. Austin (Eds.), *Psychology of inter-group relations* (pp. 15–40). Cambridge, UK: Cambridge University Press.

Tapp, A., & Clowes, J. (2002). From carefree casuals to professional wanderers: Segmentation possibilities for football supporters. *European Journal of Marketing*, *36*(11/12), 1248–1269. doi:10.1108/03090560210445164

The Guardian. (2009). *Cristiano Ronaldo welcomed by 80,000 fans at Real Madrid unveiling*. Retrieved on December 17, 2016 from https://www.theguardian.com/football/2009/jul/06/cristiano-ronaldo-real-madrid-bernabeu

Theodorakis, N. D., Wann, D. L., & Weaver, S. (2011). The team identification–social psychological health model: Sport fans gaining connections to others via sport team identification. *Group Dynamics*, *15*(1), 75–89. doi:10.1037/a0020780

Trail, G., Fink, J. S., & Anderson, D. F. (2003). Sport spectator consumption behavior. *Sport Marketing Quarterly*, *12*, 8–16.

Trail, G. T., Robinson, M. J., Dick, R. J., & Gillentine, A. J. (2003). Motives and points of attachment: Fans versus spectators in intercollegiate athletics. *Sport Marketing Quarterly*, *12*(4), 217–227.

Tyler, B. D., & Cobbs, J. B. (2015). Rival conceptions of rivalry: Why some competitions mean more than others. *European Sport Management Quarterly*, *15*(2), 227–248. doi:10.1080/16184742.2015.1010558

Underwood, R., Bond, E., & Baer, R. (2001). Building service brands via social identity: Lessons from the sports marketplace. *Journal of Marketing Theory and Practice*, *9*(1), 1–13. doi:10.1080/10696679.2001.11501881

Vallerand, R. J. (2007). Intrinsic and extrinsic motivation in sport and physical activity: A review and a look at the future. In G. Tenenbaum & R. E. Eklund (Eds.), *Handbook of sport psychology* (3rd ed.; pp. 49–83). New York, NY: John Wiley. doi:10.1002/9781118270011.ch3

Wakefield, K. L., & Wann, D. L. (2006). An examination of dysfunctional sport fans: Method of classification and relationships with problem behaviors. *Journal of Leisure Research*, *38*, 168–186.

Wann, D. L. (1993). Aggression of highly identified spectators as a function of their need to maintain a positive social identity. *Journal of Sport and Social Issues*, *17*(2), 134–143. doi:10.1177/019372359301700207

Wann, D. L. (2006). The causes and consequences of sport team identification. In Handbook of Sports and Media (pp. 331-352). Mahwah, NJ: Erlbaum.

Wann, D. L., & Branscombe, N. R. (1993). Sports fans: Measuring degree of identification with their team. *International Journal of Sport Psychology*, *24*(1), 1–17.

Wann, D. L., & Grieve, F. G. (2005). Biased evaluations of in-group and out-group spectator behavior at sporting events: The importance of team identification and threats to social identity. *The Journal of Social Psychology*, *145*(5), 531–545. doi:10.3200/SOCP.145.5.531-546 PMID:16201677

Wann, D. L., Melnick, M. J., Russell, G. W., & Pease, D. G. (2001). *Sport fans: The psychology and social impact of spectators*. New York, NY: Routledge.

Woratschek, H., Horbel, C., & Popp, B. (2014). The sport value framework–A new fundamental logic for analyses in sport management. *European Sport Management Quarterly*, *14*(1), 6–24. doi:10.1080/16184742.2013.865776

Yngfalk, A. F. (2013). Its not us, its them! Rethinking value co-creation among multiple actors. *Journal of Marketing Management*, *29*(9/10), 1163–1181. doi:10.1080/0267257X.2013.796318

KEY TERMS AND DEFINITIONS

Co-Consumption: The process of fans experiencing an event with other fans.

Co-Creation: The process of fans coming together and creating a unique experience.

Consumption Groups: Fans who shared a preference for and consumption of a particular good or service. Examples of consumption groups include: consumption communities, cultures of consumption, subcultures of consumption, consumer tribes, brand communities, and brand cults.

Geographic Sense of Community: A feeling of belonging to a specific geographic locale and/or people from that particular area.

Psychological Sense of Community: A feeling of belonging with other people based on common interests or activities without specifying any specific geographic locale.

Rivalry: A fluctuating adversarial relationship existing between two or more groups.

Sense of Community: A feeling that people have of belonging to a group and being important to one another.

Social Recognition: The ability to be identified by other members of a group based on discernable characteristics.

Tribal Fans: A group of people who are emotionally connected based on similar consumption patterns and preferences.

Tribal Symbols: The representations and cultural aspects which denote a group.

This research was previously published in Exploring the Rise of Fandom in Contemporary Consumer Culture edited by Cheng Lu Wang, pages 71-101, copyright year 2018 by Business Science Reference (an imprint of IGI Global).

Chapter 22
Automatic Live Sport Video Streams Curation System From User Generated Media

Kazuki Fujisawa
Nara Institute of Science and Technology, Japan

Yuko Hirabe
Nara Institute of Science and Technology, Japan

Hirohiko Suwa
Nara Institute of Science and Technology, Japan

Yutaka Arakawa
Nara Institute of Science and Technology, Japan

Keiichi Yasumoto
Nara Institute of Science and Technology, Japan

ABSTRACT

Emerging Internet of Things (IoT) technologies will allow spectators in a sport game to produce various video streams from various angles. With existing technologies, however, it is difficult to process massive and various data streams for multi-channel contents in real-time. To solve this problem, we aim to construct a software agent (called "Curator") that compiles video contents automatically according to his/her values. In this paper, we propose a system to automatically switch multiple video streams that general sports spectators have taken using Random Forests classifier. Meta data such as image feature data and game progress data is extracted for each video scene as the input of the classifier. For evaluation, we constructed a camera switching timing estimation model using the live TV broadcast of some baseball game data. A video of another baseball game was curated with the constructed model. As a result, our system predicted the camera switching timing with accuracy (F-measure) of 85.3% on weighted average for the base camera work and 99.7% for the fixed camera work.

DOI: 10.4018/978-1-5225-5475-2.ch022

INTRODUCTION

Emerging Internet of Things (IoT) technologies will allow spectators in a sport game to produce various data streams including videos from various angles and zoom-levels, audios, Social Networking Service (SNS) messages, and so on. Recently, live video streaming applications such as Meercat[1] and Periscope[2] have been available. Such real-time Consumer Generated Media (CGM) will receive increasing attention. Besides, new frameworks for processing various media streams in real-time are emerging. For example, Jubatus[3] enables real- time machine learning from massive media streams.

In this paper, based on the idea of Information Flow of Things (IFoT) (Yasumoto, K. et al., 2016), we aim to develop a method to create personalized and high-presence multi-channel contents through real-time compilation of various media streams captured/created by spectators. Here, we target baseball games because it is one of the most popular sports. With existing technologies, however, it is difficult to process massive and various data streams for multi-channel contents in realtime. Thus, existing services assume human curators who compile contents by selecting necessary data streams. Curator creates a content by compiling it from various data streams according to his/her values and streams the created content in real time as his/her own channel. Here, curation is the process of compiling a content according to the curator's own values from various information available from different sources. In this paper, curation means creation of a video consisting of scenes extracted from various different videos recording a baseball game. Our final goal is to automatically construct a software agent corresponding to a human curator. To this goal, in this paper, we use the live TV broadcast as a ground truth data and construct a machine learning-based model to conduct curation from multiple videos which spectators captured from different angles and zoom levels.

The live TV broadcast of a baseball game has some curation rules which select a specific angle camera for some specific scenes (e.g., a pitcher throwing a ball). Our proposed method uses machine-learning to learn these rules for different scenes. Random Forests algorithm (Breiman, 2001) is used for learning since this algorithm is fast and suitable for real-time processing. As inputs for constructing a model, we use meta data such as image feature data (e.g., a pitcher is on the screen) in each interval of baseball videos and game progress data (e.g., the number of the innings is top of the third inning). Output is the camera ID (among multiple cameras of spectators) at each point of time.

RELATED WORK

In this section, existing studies are first explained on content curation to show the difference from our proposed method. Then, other related studies are described such as automatic camera control and pattern recognition for sports video and automatic live-sport broadcast summarization.

Existing Studies for Content Curation

Some applications are introduced on a content curation. SmartNews (2012) and FlipBoard (McCue, 2012) are one of major mobile apps for curating news. These apps generate a curated content by collecting huge news from the Internet and analyzing both collected contents and user preferences. Chirpstory (2010) and Togettor (2009) are web-based curation services that help curators generate a summarized web page of tweets. Also, Naver Matome (2009) is a web-based curation service that can deal with not only tweets but also web pages and images. The target of curation in the above mentioned applications is static contents such as news texts, images, tweets and published videos. On the contrary, our target contents are real-time video streams, i.e., dynamic contents.

As related work on manipulating dynamic contents, Yonezawa (Yonezawa, & Tokuda, 2012) has proposed a remote video control system for NicoNico Live Video (2007). It is not a content curation but it allows viewers over the Internet to control the angle and zoom level of camera according to their preferences. VDMX5 (2007), a commercial software for a video jockey, can mix multiple video streams for creating and distributing a curated video content. However, it is not supposed to deal with many video streams like our target environment where many cameras including user's smartphones are capturing the same event. In such a case, some support systems for selecting a suitable video stream is needed. To solve these problems, we implemented a video curation support system for real-time video streams where videos are scored based on a curator's preference. In this system, the curator sets his demands such as "want to create a downward view video," "want to focus on a certain player," and so on. Based on these settings, some recommended video streams are selectively shown on the user interface. However, a curation itself must be done manually by a curator. To reduce human labor, this paper aims to realize automatic content curation based on a curator's demand.

Other Related Work

There are many studies on automatic camera control. For example, references (Wulff, & Fecke, 2012; Viel, et al., 2013) and reference (Ranjan, et al., 2008) aim to realize an automatic video recording for a lecture and a meeting respectively. The former system (Wulff, & Fecke, 2012) includes a lecturer tracker module based on moving foreground detection and silhouette analysis to drive a single PTZ camera. The latter (Ranjan, et al., 2008) proposes to control a camera automatically based on a motion tracking sensor, microphone and principle techniques of TV broadcasting. Soloshot3 (2015) is a stand-alone-robot camera that tracks a person wearing a certain wristband. It can automatically track a person and identify highlights. It is suitable for focusing on a certain player. However, it does not assume that multiple self-shot videos are compiled into one content in real time.

Pattern recognition for sports video has also been studied widely. For example, references (Lu. et al., 2011; Xing, et al, 2011) have proposed a system that can track and recognize multiple players in real time. However, it does not consider multiple cameras and their switching.

Automatic summarization is proposed as a method to automatically compile only what is needed from a large video stream. There are some existing studies on automatic summarization of the video. Video summarization is divided into highlights and digests roughly. References (Jai-Andaloussi, S. et al., 2014; Rui, Y. et al., 2000; Hsieh, L. C. et al., 2012) have proposed the method to analyze the video content, voice and twitter, to detect the highlights of TV sports broadcast. References (Ekin, A. et al., 2003; Nichols, J. et al., 2012) have proposed the method to digest of sports video by using the image processing and twitter automatically and efficiently. These studies have made it possible to extract only the exciting scenes and to summarize only the important scenes from several videos. However, these studies are different from our study because these studies are not suitable to redistribute the curation results to others in real-time.

Ursu (Ursu, M. F. et al., 2015) presents an experimental investigation into automatically-orchestrated, video-mediated communication within various social group interaction settings such as friends playing social games, chatting and having fun, from two separate living rooms, using the TV as the communication conduit to the other room. This system generates one video stream from multiple cameras automatically based on predefined orchestrated logic. However, this technique cannot apply to curation of sporting events which require a wide range, and it takes a lot of effort to define orchestrated logic in our target environment where many cameras are capturing the same event.

Wang (Wang, X. et al., 2014) has proposed a camera agent that evaluates the video quality of each camera view by the combination of image features. In addition, Wang proposed and implemented two type producer agents that recommend the most appropriate viewpoints by evaluated video quality, consecutive selected duration, and variation of viewing angle. The purpose of this system is similar to our system, but it did not consider to learn an appropriate switching timing of multiple cameras.

AUTOMATIC SPORT VIDEO CURATION

Figure 1 shows an overview of our proposed system. The system switches automatically among multiple video streams based on their meta data in real time. Policy of content curation can be various. We develop a system that can create a real-time sport video content similar to the high-value video from multiple video streams captured by game spectators. The system consists of 4 steps.

Details of these steps are described in the following subsections.

Collection and Processing of Multiple Video Streams

In Step 1, the system collects multiple video streams captured by general sport spectators using different devices. In this paper, we use only digital video cameras (including wearable cameras, smartphone cameras, etc.). The collected streams are divided into segments with a fixed interval (e.g., three seconds).

Figure 1. Overview of the proposed system

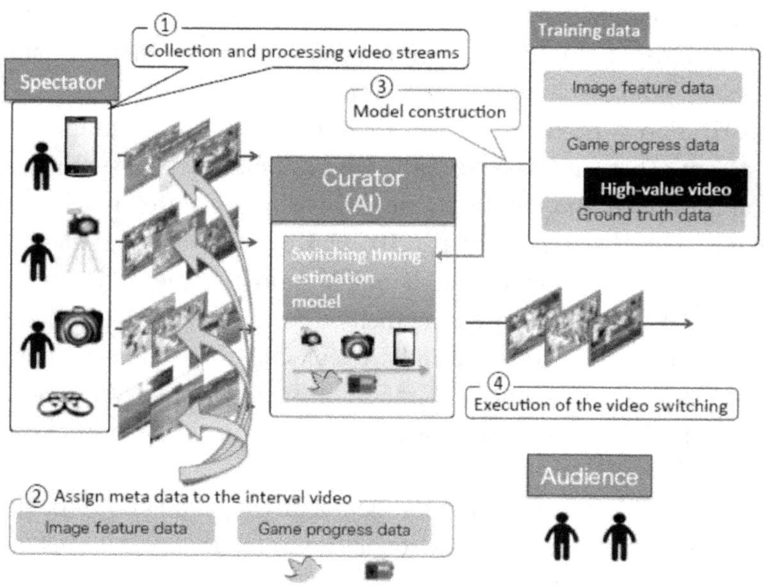

Assignment of the Meta Data to the Video Segments

In Step 2, meta data consisting of image feature data and game progress data is assigned to each segment.

Image feature data includes specific object (e.g., players, ball about baseball, goal about soccer etc.), zoom level, and so on. In this paper, the image feature data is manually assigned by human. However, it can be assigned automatically by using a special camera (Suzuki, et al., 2015), a special wearable device (Plötz, et al, 2012), or using existing annotation techniques (Yonezawa, et al., 2014; Sarvas, et al, 2004; Xu, et al., 2008). The proposed system will support the above automatic image feature data assignment in the future.

Game progress data includes the condition of the game such as elapsed time, the inning number about baseball, and loss time about soccer. We also assume that this data is manually assigned in this paper. However, it can be assigned from the voice data or closed caption data of the TV or radio broadcast through voice recognition (Duxans, et al., 2009) or from the text data of the SNS like Twitter using natural language processing (Nguyen, & Jung, 2015).

Meta data is manually assigned by the human. We didn't use the mentioned algorithms and techniques to automatically assign the information. This is why we assume that annotation is done both manually and automatically in real time and it is thought that the accuracy of manual annotation is higher than automatic annotation in the present circumstances. Also, while meta data will be annotated automatically in the future, manual annotation is selected as first step.

Construction of Camera Switching Timing Estimation Model

In Step 3, to extract the camera switching timing, the camera switching timing estimation model is constructed by supervised machine learning. The model is constructed by Random Forests algorithm. Random Forests is a machine-learning algorithm based on ensemble learning. It uses multiple decision trees as weak classifiers and obtains the classification result by integrating the results by the weak classifiers. It is said to have higher performance with shorter computation time to particular targets than other algorithms. Expecting video curation in real time, this algorithm has been selected. The algorithm is implemented using Weka[4]. Weka is a data mining tool which has many machine learning algorithms.

We use a video stream that was curated based on some specified values as the ground truth data. The attributes are two kinds of meta data assigned to each segment. The correct output data is the camera position (ID) selected in the high-value video, that is the camera switching timing.

Automatic Switching Among Multiple Cameras

In Step 4, we estimate a camera position (ID) which should be selected at each time point by inputting the meta data (Step 2) assigned to the current segments captured by all cameras to the model (constructed in Step 3). By estimating the camera position every point of time, it becomes possible to switch to the camera at each point of time and thus conduct real-time automatic video curation. If there is no camera to be selected, the system randomly selects a camera or does not switch the camera.

APPLICATION TO HIGH SCHOOL BASEBALL

For application of the proposed method, spring-selection high school baseball games was selected as a target content, because it is popular and has 100 years' history from 1915.

The overview of application to high school baseball is shown in Figure 2. In the following subsections, it is described how to acquire and process videos of the game, how to add meta data such as image feature data and game progress data labeling, and how to acquire ground truth data.

Video Acquisition and Processing

All the video streams used in this paper are recorded by ourselves in two actual game. The target game are the two championship games (semifinal and final). The semifinal game was between Tsuruga Kehi high school in Fukui prefecture and Osaka Toin high school in Osaka prefecture, which was held on March 31 (Thu), 2015. The final game was between Tsuruga Kehi high school in Fukui prefecture and Tokaidaiyon high school in Hokkaido, which was held on April 1 (Wed), 2015. Videos were captured using seven handy cameras. The videography environment is shown in Figure 3.

Ten participants (consisting of seven males and three females in twenties to thirties), who are unfamiliar with baseball and cameras, were asked to capture the videos. At this time, the participants were indicated some shooting policies based on their recording target and positions.

The cameramen at Points A and B recorded the pitcher. The cameraman at Point C shot the area around the first base if a runner got to the first base. Otherwise, the cameraman at C focused on the batter in the batter's box when there was no first base runner. The cameramen at Points D and E shot a video freely based on their preference and the conditions of the game and ball. During interviews after the game, the cameraman at Point D said, "In the semifinal game, I focused on the pitcher or the batter

Figure 2. Overview of application to high school baseball

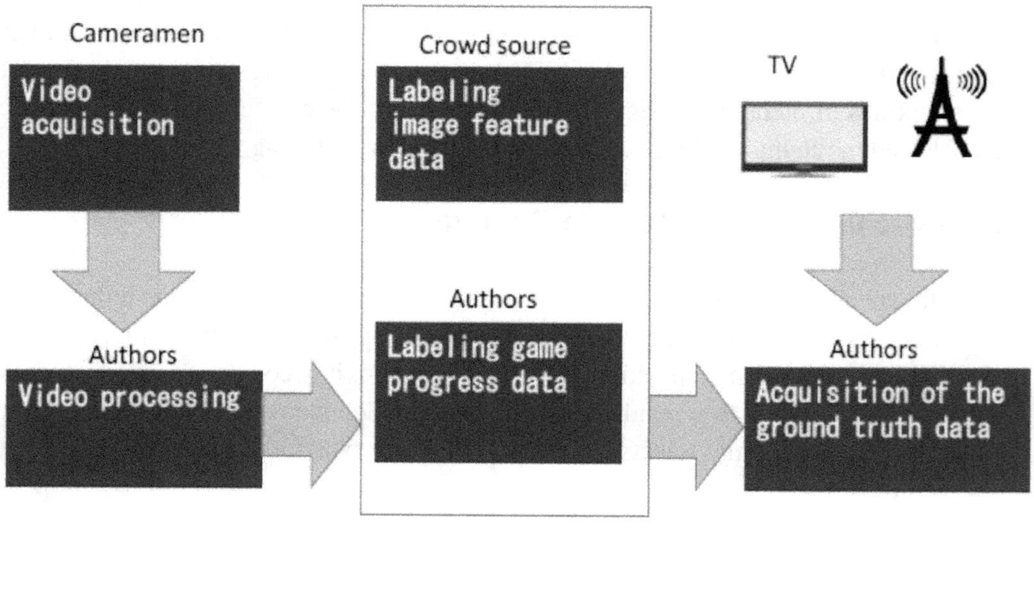

Figure 3. Videography environment

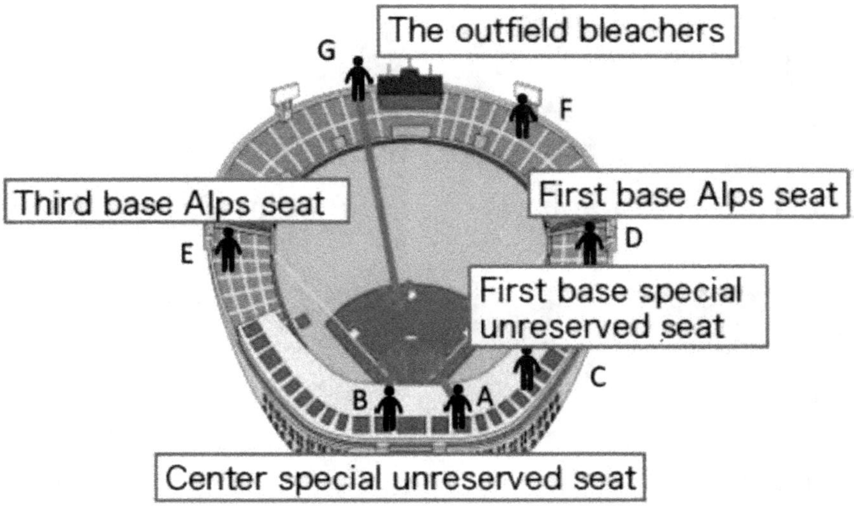

or the overall diamond randomly. In the final game, I focused on the pitcher during the first inning, and on the batter during the second inning. I zoomed in on the players individually during the third inning." The cameraman at Point E said, "I captured video of the overhead of the entire diamond, but I also sometimes focused on the bleachers in both the semifinal game and the final games." If there was a person to sell a beer, the cameraman at Point F recorded the person, otherwise he shot freely. The cameramen at Point F of both the semifinal game and the final game said that "if there were no beer sellers, I shot the audience around myself." The cameraman at Point G captured the back of a pitcher and a batter and a catcher. Screenshots of the videos are shown in Figure 4[5].

All the videos were divided into segments with three seconds (called "3 seconds videos", hereafter), and were uploaded to our server.

Labeling Meta Data

The innings to be labeled in each game are listed in Table 1.

1. **Labeling Image Feature Data:** The candidate labels of image feature data are the following 12 labels: *pitcher, catcher, batter, umpire, ball, supervision, runner, fielder, bench, seat, vendor, overlook degree.*

Since it takes much time to assign labels for all the 3 seconds videos, we employed to use a commercial crowdsourcing for assigning image feature labels. The crowd workers were asked as follows. Crowd workers are people who do simple task anonymously on the Internet. If an item (label) appeared in a 3 seconds video, please give a value of "1" for the item (label). Otherwise, please give a value of "0" for the item (label).

Figure 4. Example of videos which are captured by each cameraman

(a) Point A (b) Point B (c) Point C (d) Point D

(e) Point E (f) Point F (g) Point G

Table 1. Innings to be labeled in each game

Game	Inning
Semifinal	from top of the first inning to top of the second inning, from top of the forth inning to top of the fifth inning, from top of the eighth inning to bottom of the eighth inning
Final	First to third innings

For the overlook degrees: "low" means that the face or the upper body of a player is shown, "middle" means that the whole body of a player is shown, "high" means that multiple players are scattered on the screen. One of them are labeled manually.

2. **Labeling Game Progress Data:** The labels and examples of game progress data are listed in Table 2.

Table 2. Item and the example of game progress data to be labeled

Item	Example
Dominant team	Tsuruga Kehi, Osaka Toin, Tokaidaiyon, draw
The inning	top of the third inning, bottom of the eighth inning etc.
Out count	0,1,2
The batting order of the batter	1,2,3,4,5,6,7,8,9
Base situation	bases loaded etc
The situation of the pitcher	pitching phase, waiting phase

In this experiment, game progress data was labeled manually by the authors. As shown in Figure 5[6], the situation of the pitcher is switched, cued by audio information radio commentators, such as "Here comes the pitch." The phase from the time a pitcher puts up a glove to the time a bat hits a ball, or a pitcher receives a ball from a catcher without a bat hitting a ball is defined as the *pitching phase*. The other phase is defined as the *waiting phase*.

Acquisition of the Ground Truth Data

In this paper, assuming that the live TV broadcast is one of the curation results with high values, an actual live TV broadcast content was used as the ground truth data. Similar to the videos captured by ourselves, the recorded broadcast content was divided into 3 seconds videos, and assigned the camera position (ID) which is the closest to that at each cameraman's point manually and objectively without referring to image feature data and game progress data. If the camera work is switched during 3 seconds video, the camera ID appeared for the longest time is used as the ground truth data. If it is difficult to determine the ground truth data, it was labeled with "not applicable."

In this paper, assuming that the live TV broadcast is one of the curation results with high values, an actual live TV broadcast content was used as the ground truth data. To avoid wrong learning, 3 seconds videos when a commercial or replay video are broadcasted are not taken into consideration. The ground truth data are classified to one of A– G and "not applicable." The classification result of the ground truth data which is labeled is shown in Table 3. Each game was broadcast by two different TV companies: M and N. In the TV broadcast of the semifinal game by M and N, the number of the 3 seconds videos which were taken from point G was the largest, and the number of the videos which were classified to "not applicable" was the second largest. On the other hand, the video captured from Point F never appeared in the TV broadcast. In the final game broadcast by M, the number of the 3 seconds videos which were classified to "not applicable" was the largest, and the number of the videos which were taken from point G was the second largest. On the other hand, the video captured from Point F never appeared in the TV broadcast.

EVALUATION EXPERIMENT

We experimentally evaluate the recognition accuracy of the camera switching timing estimation model developed by machine learning. We use the Random Forest classifier implemented by Weka. Optimal parameters are extracted by the grid search in the 10-fold cross-validation. The number of trees used is

Figure 5. Transition of the situation of the pitcher

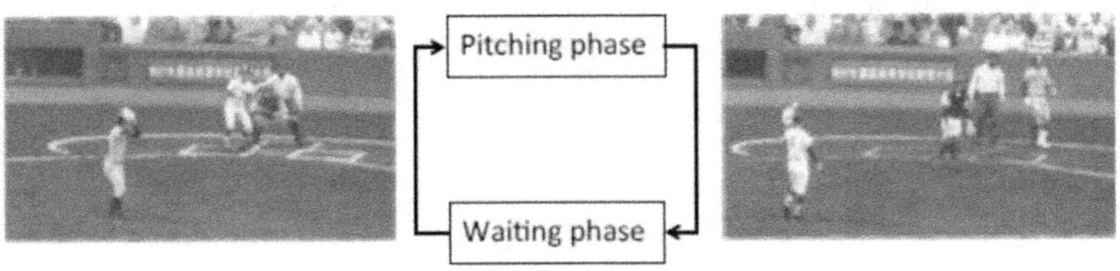

Table 3. Classification result of ground truth data

Camera ID		A	B	C	D	E	F	G	not applicable	Sum
Count	semifinal game (company N)	47	31	69	31	24	0	229	124	555
	semifinal geme (company M)	70	27	50	19	24	0	194	114	498
	final game (company M)	54	47	73	22	11	0	182	202	591

1000, each constructed while considering 25 random features. In this evaluation, Precision, Recall, and F-measure are used as the evaluation metrics. Our model is evaluated using two methods. One method is 10-fold cross-validation. Another method is hold-out method. Spring-Selection high-school baseball games were targeted. As training data, we used image features, game progress data, and the camera ID at each point of time which records the scene closest to that of the TV broadcast. We used videos of two baseball games (semifinal and final) captured from 7 different points in stadium using handy video cameras. We generated sample data set using crowdsourcing to put image features to scenes of exciting innings of the semifinal game and first to third innings of the final game, and manually putting game progress data. Here, each scene (sample) has a 3-second interval video. In the following, we evaluate the third inning which is recognized by the model learned with the first two innings as a representative. Moreover, we evaluate the one game which is recognized by the model learned with different game as a representative. Because the instructions to the cameramen at Points A and B were the same (focusing on the pitcher), Point A and Point B were unified to one camera work about evaluation. Tables 4 and 5 show the recognition results of 10-fold cross-validation and hold-out method. The results of 10-fold cross-validation are diagonal area, the results of hold-out method are the other area. In the confusion matrix in Table 4, the rows show the correct camera ID while the columns show the camera ID predicted by our model. Table 5 shows the Precision, Recall, and F- measure for each of the camera IDs.

As shown in Table 4, in case of 10-fold cross-validation for M's final game, majority of the 3 seconds videos from Point D and Point E were not estimated with the correct camera IDs, but were estimated as "not applicable".

From Table 5, F-measure of 66.2% with weighted average (considering the number of 3 seconds videos classified to each camera ID) was attained in case of 10-fold cross-validation method for M's final game. The weighted average F-measure is calculated as follows. In case of the F-measure in the camera work *i* is *Fi*, The percentage of the number of classification results of ground truth of the camera work *i* to the total number of ground truth is *Wi,* the number of camera works is *N*,

$$\text{Weighted average F-measure} = \sum_{i=1}^{N} W_i \cdot F_i$$

Among the individual F-measures of the IDs of each camera, Point G has the highest with 92.4%, and "not applicable" is the second highest with 68.6%. On the other hand, Point D and Point E has the lowest F-measure of 0%. It was confirmed that F-measure was uneven between all the points.

As shown in Table 4, in case of hold-out method about learning M's final game and testing M's semifinal, majority of the 3 seconds videos from Point A or B, Point D and Point E were not estimated with the correct camera IDs, but were estimated as "not applicable".

From Table 5, F-measure of 65.2% with weighted average was attained in case of hold-out method about learning M's final game and testing M's semifinal. Among the individual F-measures of the IDs of each camera, Point G has the highest with 99.7%, and "not applicable" is the second highest with 55.2%. On the other hand, Point D and Point E has the lowest F-measure of 0%. It was confirmed that F-measure was uneven between all the points.

Tables 6 and 7 show the recognition results of the hold-out method (in case that the third inning is recognized by the learning model constructed from the first two innings of M's final). From Table 6, it can be confirmed that, among all the videos, the videos from Point A to Point D are not estimated with the correct camera IDs, but are estimated as "not applicable". From Table 7, F-measure value of 59.3% is obtained with weighted average. Among the individual F-measure of the ID of each camera,

Table 4. Confusion matrix

Learning		N's Semifinal						M's Semifinal						M's Final					
		A or B	C	D	E	G	Not Applicable	A or B	C	D	E	G	Not Applicable	A or B	C	D	E	G	Not Applicable
N's semi final	AorB	50	6	1	1	2	18	44	10	3	0	2	38	14	20	2	1	9	55
	C	1	48	2	2	1	15	5	34	3	1	0	7	9	30	2	1	8	23
	D	5	1	8	6	2	9	0	0	18	0	0	1	0	3	3	3	2	11
	E	1	1	6	13	0	3	2	0	0	20	0	2	1	4	0	1	1	4
	G	2	3	2	0	216	6	1	0	1	0	190	2	1	0	0	0	179	2
	not appli cable	20	12	3	3	10	76	27	7	6	0	5	69	14	17	7	6	12	146
M's semi final	AorB	45	6	0	2	1	24	46	5	2	2	0	42	37	15	1	2	9	37
	C	18	41	0	0	0	10	9	33	0	2	0	6	16	35	1	2	6	13
	D	6	1	19	0	1	4	4	0	2	6	0	7	7	0	4	4	2	5
	E	0	2	0	22	0	0	3	0	5	8	0	8	5	4	0	1	0	1
	G	4	4	0	0	213	8	0	0	0	0	194	0	2	0	0	0	179	1
	not appli cable	38	8	0	1	8	69	42	12	3	5	1	51	59	22	5	14	12	90
M's final	AorB	19	12	0	0	1	46	25	11	0	0	0	61	42	10	0	1	8	40
	C	18	30	0	0	0	21	5	23	0	0	0	22	12	36	0	3	2	20
	D	2	1	0	0	1	27	1	0	0	0	0	18	5	0	0	0	2	15
	E	2	2	0	0	0	20	2	1	0	0	0	21	1	3	0	0	0	7
	G	3	3	0	0	214	9	0	0	0	0	194	0	2	0	1	0	176	3
	not appli cable	12	10	0	0	8	94	18	5	0	0	1	90	22	14	3	2	11	150

Table 5. Evaluation results

Camera ID		N's semifinal			M's semifinal			M's final		
		Precision	Recall	F-measure	Precision	Recall	F-measure	Precision	Recall	F-measure
N's semi final	A or B	56.6	55.1	55.8	55.7	45.4	50.0	35.9	13.9	20.0
	C	67.1	68.1	67.6	66.7	68	67.3	40.5	41.1	40.8
	D	37.5	29.0	32.7	58.1	94.7	72.0	21.4	13.6	16.7
	E	48.0	50.0	49.0	95.2	83.3	88.9	8.33	9.09	8.70
	G	91.6	94.8	93.1	96.4	97.9	97.2	84.8	98.4	91.1
	not appli cable	58.5	58.1	58.3	58.0	60.5	59.2	60.6	72.3	65.9
	Weighted average	71.3	72.1	71.7	75.2	75.3	75.2	58.9	63.1	59.8
M's semi final	A or B	40.5	57.7	47.6	44.2	47.4	45.8	29.4	36.6	32.6
	C	66.1	59.4	62.6	66.0	66.0	66.0	46.1	47.9	47.0
	D	100	61.3	76.0	16.7	10.5	12.9	36.4	18.2	24.2
	E	88.0	91.7	89.8	34.8	33.3	34	4.35	9.09	5.88
	G	95.5	93.0	94.2	99.5	100	99.7	86.1	98.4	91.8
	not appli cable	60.0	55.6	57.7	44.7	44.7	44.7	61.2	44.6	51.6
	Weighted average	76.1	73.7	74.4	66.6	67.1	66.8	59.6	58.5	59.0
M's final	A or B	33.9	24.4	28.4	49.0	25.8	33.8	50.0	41.6	45.4
	C	51.7	43.5	47.2	57.5	46.0	51.1	57.1	49.3	52.9
	D	0	0	0	0	0	0	0	0	0
	E	0	0	0	0	0	0	0	0	0
	G	95.5	93.4	94.5	99.5	100	99.7	88.4	96.7	92.4
	not appli cable	43.3	75.8	55.1	42.5	78.9	55.2	63.8	74.3	68.6
	Weighted average	60.3	64.3	61.2	63.8	66.7	65.2	64.7	68.4	66.2

Table 6. Confusion matrix with the third inning based on model that is constructed from 1-2 innings

	A or B	C	D	E	G	Not Applicable
A or B	0	5	0	0	2	34
C	0	8	0	0	0	11
D	0	0	0	0	1	8
E	0	1	0	0	0	0
G	0	0	0	0	67	0
not applicable	2	5	1	0	5	78

Table 7. Evaluation results with the third inning based on model that is constructed from 1-2 innings

Camera ID	Precision	Recall	F-measure
AorB	0	0	0
C	42.1	42.1	42.1
D	0	0	0
E	0	0	0
G	89.3	100	94.4
not applicable	59.5	85.7	70.3
Weight average	53.5	67.1	59.3

Point G is the highest with 94.4% of F-measure, and "not applicable" is the second highest with 70.3% of F- measure. On the other hand, Point A or B and Point D and Point E have the lowest F-measure of 0%. It was also confirmed that F-measure was uneven between all the points.

DISCUSSION

We interviewed persons who actually worked as a switcher in TV station, and reviewed our obtained results.

Study on the Camera Work by Interview

Based on interviews, we learned that the camera work of the sports video was divided into two types. First, the camera work that requires the cameraman to follow set rules and does not allow any originality. We call it "base camera work." Second, the camera work that does not require the cameraman to follow set rules and allows originality on the side of the cameraman. We call it "context camera work." In addition, we learned that among base camera work, absolutely-fixed camera work which always follows the basic pattern exists.

1. **Base Camera Work:** The base camera work conforms to the decided rules without being influenced by the ideas of the director. Therefore, the camera to be used is limited. The base camera work was done in this experiment. For example, the videos from Point A, Point B, Point C and Point G had to follow rules like "I continue to take a pitcher." The videos from Point G correspond to the fixed camera work. The F-measure of the videos of Point A or B, Point C and Point G about M's final game model that are the base camera work are relatively high (i.e., 45.4%, 52.9%, and 92.4% respectively). An accuracy of 76.0% was attained when F-measure of the weighted average was calculated only for these.

The F-measure of the video from Point G was high because it was captured from the same point as the TV station's cameraman and the object which was captured is the same. The F-measure of the video of Point G was improved because the timing that the switcher of the TV station selects the video of the Point G was learned using the game progress data (the situation of the pitcher), such as pitching phase or waiting phase. The precision of Point G is not 100% because while the pitcher was in the pitching phase, but there were some scenes in which the switcher of the TV station chose the video of a different camera.

2. **Context Camera Work:** The context camera work is based on the feeling of the cameraman and external situations and circumstances (e.g., the ideas of the director, which team is favored, or when statistical records are broken during the game). In this experiment, the videos that were captured freely from Point D, Point E and Point F are examples of this camera work. The context camera work from Point D and Point E about M's final game model had both low F-measures of 0%. The cameramen of TV station captures videos while predicting what videos the director and the switcher want. In this study, the videos of Point D and Point E were captured based only on the ideas of the cameramen, so their F-measures are expectedly low. F-measures are expected to increase if it is possible to know what the director and the switcher want and the theme of the game.

Study on the Influence of Labeling Ground Truth Data

From Table 4, it was found that the accuracy of semifinal game model is higher than final game model about from Point A to Point G. This is because the number of the 3 seconds videos which were classified to not applicable as the ground truth data is large in the final game compared to the semifinal game from Table 3. In this study, one camera ID is selected with the longest duration in case that 3 seconds time interval video includes multiple correct data (multiple camera IDs). In this labeling process, "not applicable" label is often assigned as the ground truth data about final game, because it is hard to distinguish which cameras are selected for the longest duration. Through the experiment, we noticed that each video stream should be divided based on the switching timing in the TV broadcast (i.e., the ground truth data) or we need to prioritize.

Study on the Different Game Curation Result and Same Game Curation Result Using Different Company's Video

Table 8 is a result of re-summarized the curation results of the evaluation in Chapter EVALUATION EXPERIMENT, in the framework of base camera work and fixed camera work which is discussed in Section A.

From Table 8, regardless of the TV station's company, it was found that the accuracy in case of learning final game and testing semifinal game is higher than the accuracy in case of learning semifinal game and testing final game. This is because the data set of the final game included larger noise than the data set of the semifinal game from Table 3. Similarly, in the base camera work and the fixed camera work, it was found that the accuracy using the same TV station's company's video is higher than using the different TV station's company's video, in case of both the final game recognition by using semifinal game data and the semifinal game recognition by using final game data. In addition, even if the game is the same, it was found the accuracy in case of learning N's broadcast video and testing M's broadcast video is higher. This is because the accuracy of the base camera work and fixed camera work of M's semifinal game model is higher than those of N's semifinal game model from Table 8. Therefore, it is important to increase the performance of each model in order to increase the curation accuracy of unused game for learning. Also, accuracy is not changed too much by changing the TV station's company. Therefore, it is found that there is not too much difference in curation pattern by the company of TV stations.

Table 8. Re-summarized evaluation results

		N's semifinal			M's semifinal			M's final		
		Precision	Recall	F-measure	Precision	Recall	F-measure	Precision	Recall	F-measure
N's semifinal	base camera work	82.0	84.1	83.1	84.4	83.6	83.9	69.3	74.9	71.0
	fixed camera work	91.6	94.8	93.1	96.4	97.9	97.2	84.8	98.4	91.1
	all camera work	71.3	72.1	71.7	75.2	75.3	75.2	58.9	63.1	59.8
M's semifinal	base camera work	81.7	81.5	81.6	84.8	85.7	85.2	66.9	76.2	71.2
	fixed camera work	95.5	93.0	94.2	99.5	100	99.7	86.1	98.4	91.8
	all camera work	76.1	73.7	74.4	66.6	67.1	66.8	59.6	58.5	59.0
M's final	base camera work	82.0	78.1	79.9	87.9	83.8	85.3	75.0	77.0	75.8
	fixed camera work	95.5	93.4	94.5	99.5	100	99.7	88.4	96.7	92.4
	all camera work	60.3	64.3	61.2	63.8	66.7	65.2	64.7	68.4	66.2

Study on the Different Inning Curation Result

F-measure of the weighted average is 59.3% in case of the third inning recognition by using first two innings data about M's final game. This F-measure is lower than the result of the 10-fold cross-validation method. Similarly, F-measure of the weighted average is 55.7% in case of recognizing the first inning by the second and the third innings data. F-measure of the weighted average is 69.4% in case of recognizing the second inning by using the first inning and the third inning data. It was found that F-measure was uneven in a different inning. This is because the editing of the TV station varies in each inning. For example, in the actual M's final game's TV broadcasting, the first inning began with the camera zooming in on the players for their introductions. In contrast, the third inning began by showing the Alps seat cheering for the offense.

Difference From Existing Automatic Video Curation Research and the Effect of Annotation Technology on the Evaluation Results

We compare our proposed method with the existing automatic video curation research to demonstrate its effectiveness. Ortis (Ortis, et al., 2015) presented a system that automatically creates a single video from multiple video sources by taking into account the popularity of the acquired scenes. The frames composing the final popular video are selected from the different video streams by considering the visual scenes that are pointed and recorded by the highest number of users' devices. The point of generating one video stream from multiple video streams is same. But, switching timing of multiple video streams is different. Ortis' system selects the video based on the number of users' devices. Our system selects the video by supervised learning using meta data which is assigned to each stream, and correct data. Ortis' system generates a high value video stream for most viewers. But, it is not suitable for personalization and multi-channel video. In addition, it is difficult to generate a consistent value video stream. But, it is possible for our system to generate a consistent value video. Moreover, our system is suitable for realizing next generation live which satisfies personalized and high-presence multi-channel.In this paper, meta data is manually assigned by the human. This is why we assume that it is thought that the accuracy of manual annotation is higher than automatic annotation in the present circumstances. We didn't compare with the results using automatic annotation in this paper. But, the accuracy of manual annotation by crowd workers is high and our methods predicted the camera switching patterns with accuracy (F-measure) of 85.3% on weighted average for the base camera work and 99.7% for the fixed camera work in learning a game and testing another game. Using the baseball games data, our proposed method curated the camera switching time with the good performance results. Moreover, when looking at the output video from our system, it was confirmed that the video was switched as same as TV video without feeling uncomfortable. So, I thought manual annotation led to good results.

CONCLUSION

In this paper, we developed a system for automatic curation from multiple video streams captured by general sports spectators using machine learning. For machine learning, as inputs, we used image feature data (e.g., players shown in the scene) and game progress data (including the inning number and the batting order) for each scene of videos captured by sport game spectators. As ground truth data, we used the live TV broadcast of the same game. The output is the camera ID at each point of time which captures the video closest to that of the live TV broadcast. That is, timings of camera switching are output.

We applied our method to videos captured from 7 different locations at Hanshin Koshien Stadium when Spring-Selection high-school baseball games were held. As a result, our method curated the camera switching timings of a game by learning another game with the F- measure of 85.3% on average for the base camera work and of 99.7% on average for the fixed camera work.

As part of future work, we will improve recognition accuracy by increasing the number of training samples and we will use a feature reduction and selection algorithm (such as PCA, IG and so on) to remove redundant features and improve the performance of the classification. Moreover, we will propose the method to annotate meta data automatically. Also, to realize curation of multiple channels contents for personalization and high presence, we plan to construct models using ground truth data extracted from TV broadcast of different style baseball games (e.g., major league baseball games) or compiled by tasteful human curators. In addition, we will extend the proposed method to be applied for other sports (e.g., basketball or soccer) or live concerts by musicians.

ACKNOWLEDGMENT

This study is partly supported by JSPS Grant in Aid for Scientific Research 25280031 and 26220001. We would like to thank Hiroshi Saito and Shin Hamaguchi of Mainichi Broadcasting System, Inc. who gave us precious suggestions.

REFERENCES

Breiman, L. (2001). Random forests. *Machine Learning*, *45*(1), 5–32. doi:10.1023/A:1010933404324

Chirpstory. (2010). Retrieved from http://chirpstory.com/

Duxans, H., Anguera, X., & Conejero, D. (2009). Audio based soccer game summarization. *Proceedings of the IEEE International Symposium on Broadband Multimedia Systems and Broadcasting BMSB '09* (pp. 1-6). IEEE. doi:10.1109/ISBMSB.2009.5133759

Ekin, A., Tekalp, A. M., & Mehrotra, R. (2003). Automatic soccer video analysis and summarization. *IEEE Transactions on Image Processing*, *12*(7), 796–807. doi:10.1109/TIP.2003.812758 PMID:18237954

Hsieh, L. C., Lee, C. W., Chiu, T. H., & Hsu, W. (2012). Live semantic sport highlight detection based on analyzing tweets of twitter. *Proceedings of the 2012 IEEE International Conference on Multimedia and Expo (ICME)* (pp. 949-954). IEEE. doi:10.1109/ICME.2012.135

Jai-Andaloussi, S., Mohamed, A., Madrane, N., & Sekkaki, A. (2014). Soccer Video Summarization Using Video Content Analysis and Social Media Streams. *Proceedings of the 2014 IEEE/ACM International Symposium on Big Data Computing* (pp. 1-7). IEEE Computer Society. doi:10.1109/BDC.2014.20

Lu, W. L., Ting, J. A., Murphy, K. P., & Little, J. J. (2011). Identifying players in broadcast sports videos using conditional random fields. *Proceedings of the 2011 IEEE Conference on Computer Vision and Pattern Recognition (CVPR)*, Providence, RI, USA (pp. 3249-3256). doi:10.1109/CVPR.2011.5995562

McCue, M. (2012). Flipboard Launches World's First Social Magazine.Flipboard.com. Retrieved from http://flipboard.com/press/flipboard-launches-worlds-first-social-magazine

Naver matome. (2009). Retrieved from http://matome.naver.jp/

Nguyen, D. T., & Jung, J. J. (2015). Real-time event detection on social data stream. *Mobile Networks and Applications*, *20*(4), 475–486. doi:10.1007/s11036-014-0557-0

Nichols, J., Mahmud, J., & Drews, C. (2012). Summarizing sporting events using twitter. *Proceedings of the 2012 ACM international conference on Intelligent User Interfaces* (pp. 189-198). ACM. doi:10.1145/2166966.2166999

Nicovideo. (2007). Retrieved from http://live.nicovideo.jp/

Ortis, A., Farinella, G. M., D'amico, V., Addesso, L., Torrisi, G., & Battiato, S. (2015). RECfusion: Automatic video curation driven by visual content popularity. *Proceedings of the 23rd Annual ACM Conference on Multimedia Conference* (pp. 1179-1182). ACM. doi:10.1145/2733373.2806311

Plötz, T., Chen, C., Hammerla, N. Y., & Abowd, G. D. (2012). Automatic synchronization of wearable sensors and video-cameras for ground truth annotation-a practical approach. *Proceedings of the 2012 16th International Symposium on Wearable Computers (ISWC)* (pp. 100-103). IEEE. doi:10.1109/ISWC.2012.15

Ranjan, A., Birnholtz, J., & Balakrishnan, R. (2008). Improving meeting capture by applying television production principles with audio and motion detection. *Proceedings of the SIGCHI Conference on Human Factors in Computing Systems* (pp. 227-236). ACM. doi:10.1145/1357054.1357095

Rui, Y., Gupta, A., & Acero, A. (2000). Automatically extracting highlights for TV baseball programs. *Proceedings of the eighth ACM international conference on Multimedia* (pp. 105-115). ACM. doi:10.1145/354384.354443

Sarvas, R., Herrarte, E., Wilhelm, A., & Davis, M. (2004). Metadata creation system for mobile images. *Proceedings of the 2nd international conference on Mobile systems, applications, and services* (pp. 36-48). ACM. doi:10.1145/990064.990072

Smartnews. (2012). Retrieved from https:www.smartnews.com/en/

Soloshot3. (2015). Retrieved from http://shop.soloshot.com/

Suzuki, R., Sakamoto, D., & Igarashi, T. (2015). AnnoTone: Record-time Audio Watermarking for Context-aware Video Editing. *Proceedings of the 33rd Annual ACM Conference on Human Factors in Computing Systems* (pp. 57-66). ACM. doi:10.1145/2702123.2702358

Togetter. (2009). Retrieved from http://togetter.com/

Ursu, M. F., Falelakis, M., Groen, M., Kaiser, R., & Frantzis, M. (2015). Experimental enquiry into automatically orchestrated live video communication in social settings. *Proceedings of the ACM International Conference on Interactive Experiences for TV and Online Video* (pp. 63-72). ACM. doi:10.1145/2745197.2745211

VDMX5. (2007). Retrieved from http://vidvox.net/

Viel, C. C., Melo, E. L., Pimentel, M. D. G., & Teixeira, C. A. (2013). Multimedia multi-device educational presentations preserved as interactive multi-video objects. *Proceedings of the 19th Brazilian symposium on Multimedia and the web* (pp. 51-58). ACM. doi:10.1145/2526188.2526211

Wang, X., Muramatu, Y., Hirayama, T., & Mase, K. (2014). Context-dependent Viewpoint Sequence Recommendation System for Multi-view Video. *Proceedings of the 2014 IEEE International Symposium on Multimedia (ISM)* (pp. 195-202). IEEE. doi:10.1109/ISM.2014.44

Wulff, B., & Fecke, A. (2012). Lecturesight-an open source system for automatic camera control in lecture recordings. *Proceedings of the 2012 IEEE International Symposium on Multimedia (ISM)* (pp. 461-466). IEEE. doi:10.1109/ISM.2012.94

Xing, J., Ai, H., Liu, L., & Lao, S. (2011). Multiple player tracking in sports video: A dual-mode two-way bayesian inference approach with progressive observation modeling. *IEEE Transactions on Image Processing*, *20*(6), 1652–1667. doi:10.1109/TIP.2010.2102045 PMID:21189238

Xu, C., Wang, J., Lu, H., & Zhang, Y. (2008). A novel framework for semantic annotation and personalized retrieval of sports video. *Multimedia. IEEE Transactions on*, *10*(3), 421–436. doi:10.1109/TMM.2008.917346

Yasumoto, K., Yamaguchi, H., & Shigeno, H. (2016). Survey of Real-time Processing Technologies of IoT Data Streams. *Journal of Information Processing*, *24*(2), 195–202. doi:10.2197/ipsjjip.24.195

Yonezawa, T., Ogawa, M., Kyono, Y., Nozaki, H., Nakazawa, J., Nakamura, O., & Tokuda, H. (2014). Sensetream: Enhancing online live experience with sensor-federated video stream using animated two-dimensional code. *Proceedings of the 2014 ACM International Joint Conference on Pervasive and Ubiquitous Computing* (pp. 301-305). ACM. doi:10.1145/2632048.2632104

Yonezawa, T., & Tokuda, H. (2012). Enhancing communication and dramatic impact of online live performance with cooperative audience control. *Proceedings of the 2012 ACM Conference on Ubiquitous Computing* (pp. 103-112). ACM. doi:10.1145/2370216.2370234

ENDNOTES

1. https://meerkatapp.co/
2. https://www.periscope.tv/
3. http://jubat.us/en/
4. http://www.cs.waikato.ac.nz/ml/weka/
5. Right of likeness is considered, and the resolution is lowered.
6. The image resolution is purposely reduced by considering the players' right of publicity.

This research was previously published in the International Journal of Multimedia Data Engineering and Management (IJMDEM), 7(2); edited by Shu-Ching Chen and Yonghong Tian, pages 36-52, copyright year 2016 by IGI Publishing (an imprint of IGI Global).

Chapter 23
Exploring Factors That Lead to People Watching Professional Soccer on Television

Alan D. Smith
Robert Morris University, USA

Steve R. Clinton
Robert Morris University, USA

ABSTRACT

The purpose of this study is to examine and determine factors that lead to increased television ratings for soccer in the U.S. The study primarily focuses on fantasy soccer participation, involvement in soccer, presence of a local professional team, and social media interaction. After providing a brief history of soccer television ratings in the U.S., a conceptual model based on these factors is developed and explained. The factors of this conceptual model are tested through statistical analysis. Based on these results, the model provides recommendations and conclusions for soccer decision makers to increase television ratings in the future, which ultimately will drive and increase the bottom line of all parties involved.

INTRODUCTION

Growth of Soccer in the U.S.

There is little doubt that when Major League Soccer (MLS) played its initial 1996 season, it could not expect in the short-term to compete with the advertising budget and player-related expenses with its big business professional football. As the 2014 World Cup games played on, many spectators hope for a strong competitive showing of the young U.S. soccer team. During this time, the Internet was taking a foothold in the general public and allowed an avenue or communication channel for sport organizations to directly create relationships and influence the hearts and minds of its potential fan base. The MLS handles the initial contracts for individual players to help owners take on a lesser financial burden that had crippled previous attempts at professional sport organizations such as the North American Soccer

DOI: 10.4018/978-1-5225-5475-2.ch023

League (NASL) and the USA Football League. These organizations mainly failed due to excessive expenditures in the largest markets (Zimmerman, Clavio, & Lim, 2011).

In general, soccer in the U.S. has had an interesting history, but not since the golden days of the NASL has soccer ever been reaching a level that it is at today in the U.S. ("It has been a good year …" 2011). Although soccer's relevance in the American sports landscape is not something completely new, soccer's relevant presence in the American television production and broadcasting has been rapidly approaching new territory. The market is a vast one, with an ever-growing domestic league in MLS, an increase in viewing of foreign leagues such as the English Premier League, and rapidly increasing ratings in both the World Cup 2014 in Brazil) and other major soccer tournaments. Researchers have always tried to pinpoint what exactly fuels television ratings and how they can increase ratings, but soccer in the U.S. has not been covered very much by research, likely due to MLS's infancy and only the recent surge in television ratings. This study explores a few areas, from fantasy sports to involvement in sports, which may or may not contribute to increased television ratings in the soccer market. By understanding these aspects, decision makers can increase their e-commerce approaches or target specific viewers to increase television ratings in the U.S. Increasing television ratings can generate many forms of increased revenues including online streaming and advertisement revenue.

When discussing television ratings, it is probably best to first take a look at where MLS has come in such a short time. MLS, the U.S.' top flight domestic league, is a vital sign of how soccer has grown in the past 20+ years, but most importantly in the past decade. MLS, an infant in the American sports scene and in the global soccer market at just seventeen years of age, is currently rounding out its largest expansion in history. Within a six-year span from 2007-2012, MLS grew over 50% from 12 teams to 19 teams. This period of expansion is shown in Table 1. Expansion in recent years has been well executed into popular markets and helped improve everything league-wide from global exposure to a bigger salary cap to superb attendance figures. With MLS's young age and the recent upswing overall of soccer in the U.S., very little research has been done on why Americans are now tuning into soccer at a higher rate than ever before. With the domestic league now spanning so many large cities and the increased availability for Americans to watch foreign soccer, research on how and why television ratings increase for soccer is vital to decision makers in the global marketplace.

MLS has a niche market in the U.S. with per-game attendance figures surpassing both the National Hockey League (NHL) and the National Basketball Association (NBA). These two leagues are generally referred to as the arena leagues because they are played indoors with smaller capacity stadiums. None of these three leagues (e.g.; MLS, NBA, or NHL) play in venues nearly as big as Major League Baseball (MLB) or the National Football League (NFL). With proper expansion, MLS broke above the

Table 1. Expansion 2007-12 in MLS

Year	Expansion Team(s)
2007	Toronto FC
2008	San Jose Earthquakes
2009	Seattle Sounders FC
2010	Philadelphia Union
2011	Portland Timbers, Vancouver Whitecaps
2012	Montreal Impact

Table 2. MLS attendance vs. major sport leagues

League	Average Attendance per Game
NFL	67,358
MLB	31,368
MLS	18,732
NBA	17,273
NHL	17,455

arena leagues and sits nicely in the middle of the pack in per-game attendance. Most recent per-game season attendance figures are listed in Table 2. Although these numbers are great for soccer in the U.S., it is important to note that MLS teams do not play as many games as any other U.S. major sport league, except for the NFL.

However, revenues and salaries are not near the other major sports in the U.S. television ratings, including streaming video online for revenue, could help increase both of these aspects for the league and other leagues and competitions. But, as mentioned, MLS is just one piece of a much larger picture in the global soccer market. Unlike other professional sports in the U.S., viewers can choose to watch one of many leagues around the world along with numerous other competitions throughout the year. While those leagues and tournaments will compete against one another for television ratings, this research paper just focuses on soccer as a sport and combines all of the leagues/competitions into a single group. This research looks to fill a specific void in examining a set of characteristics and determining if these items have any effect on whether or not a person decides to watch soccer on television. If the decision makers of soccer programming can pinpoint these characteristics, they may be able to focus their broadcasts better or increase ratings in the long-term through better preparation of a few topics including various e-commerce opportunities.

The former first-division soccer league of the U.S. was the North American Soccer League. With similar characteristics to MLB (i.e.; unlimited spending for large market teams, little parity, minimal revenue sharing), the league quickly failed. MLS from its beginning planned and promised to never follow the business structure of the former NASL, but rather a slow-and-steady growth approach to avoid failure of the league. Overexpansion was a huge reason for the failure of NASL and must be avoided in MLS. Average attendance of the NASL never broke 15,000 and while some teams were very successful because of their big market ability to spend, others were left with horrible teams in poor stadiums with barely any people watching. To avoid this and past problems of the NASL, MLS has achieved a relative parity. With a salary cap, individual player cap, revenue sharing, and single-entity business structure, MLS has created one of the most competitive league structures in the world. Most recently, Columbus Crew became the best team in the league in 2008 after being one of the worst teams in both 2006 and 2007. This parity is a unique attribute to MLS that provides an opportunity for all firms to maximize their potential both on and off the pitch.

Looking for Parity With Other Professional Team Sports

The parity found in MLS is one of the items that helps make this study so interesting. Not only are there numerous leagues and tournaments for fans to watch on television, their local team always has the opportunity to be competitive and bring attention to their city. Everything in this survey directly ties back to an e-commerce concept of online television viewership. Streaming of soccer matches is one of the most-used forms of streaming on the Internet, because it is impossible to show every team's games throughout the year. So, if managers and executives can drive up soccer television ratings, they will ultimately drive up the page views on their websites and the views of online matches. This study also focuses on a few other concepts of e-commerce like social media interaction and participation in fantasy sports. It is important to determine whether any of these items truly increase television ratings or if they are not a cause of an increase television ratings.

RECENT TRENDS IN SOCCER TELEVISION RATINGS AND CONTRACTS

Domestic Acceptance and Growth Trends

Soccer television ratings in the U.S. have been improving in recent years, especially in major tournaments, including the World Cup, which is the largest sporting event in the world. On a smaller scale, teams in the U.S. and MLS have also signed more lucrative television contracts. Improving television ratings is really the last major step MLS needs to compete with the other major sports in the U.S. As mentioned earlier, gate revenue from attendance, one of the biggest revenue drivers in any sport, is already at a great level for the league and surpasses some of the other major sports in the U.S. Simon Evans explained after speaking with MLS Commission Don Garber that "breaking through on television remains the missing link" (Evans, 2012). To increase ratings, MLS released an iPad/iPhone app that allows its users to watch the league website's live games and highlights on their mobile devices (Dure, 2011). With a mixture of increased television partnerships and the availability to stream over 200 matches each year online, MLS is combating their television ratings in a couple different ways.

Other tournaments, such as the World Cup and the European Championship, have seen drastic increases in television ratings during the two most recent tournaments. The average viewing attendance for all 31 matches at Euro 2012 was 1.3 million viewers, which represented a 51% increase on the numbers from the 2008 edition of the tournament (Matchett, 2012). These numbers are even more impressive when realizing when the games were broadcast. The majority of the games were shown during weekday working hours in the U.S. as the tournament was played live during peak times in Poland and Ukraine. Similarly, television ratings for the most recent World Cup in 2010 were just impressive, even though they faced a similarly bad time slot for American viewing audiences. It was the most-watched World Cup ever in the U.S., with more than 3.2 million average viewers per game. This total resulted in an increase of 41% over the previous World Cup in 2006 (Seidman, 2010). The U.S. will likely continue this trend and crush the record in 2014, as the tournament will be hosted in Brazil and many games will start during a more lucrative television timeslot. Not only did television ratings increase in the U.S., but American online websites who covered the tournaments also posted record numbers (Tidey, 2012).

Similarly, companies have begun to pay more for these tournaments' broadcast rights. ESPN is now paying US$100 million for the rights for two World Cups and two women's World Cups through 2014, which is up significantly from US$11 million in 1994 and US$22 million in 1998 (Sandomir, 2010). Soccer has quickly become a major player in sports, television deals, and online revenue, which have all attributed to its place in the forefront of this study.

Internet and Spectator Engagement

MLS has significantly benefited from the immediacy and engaging nature of the Internet; hence allowing fans to become more engaged in their favorite sports. These trends allow fans to become a more active spectator rather than a passive one. The Internet has a vast variety of tools and channels for this enhanced interaction to occur. The almost universal acceptance of YouTube has become a significant tool in measuring how users display an individual clip and allowing input from its users. Such information can be used to collect fans' thoughts on the individual video and the effects of brand marketing and team logos on game attendance and team-related merchandising behaviors. As suggested by Zimmerman, et al., 2011. The communication and marketing channels created by YouTube was become the industrial standard among newly created websites in terms of options, engagement, and collecting users' feedback on company-based initiatives in such popular social media as Facebook, Tweeter, and Wikipedia. The exponential growth of social media and its various communication channels makes it an excellent platform to increase the exposure and fan loyalty without the huge financial and marketing budgets of more traditional professional sport organizations. Many well-known professional sports leagues have just begun to explore the power of social media, it is interesting to note that management of MLS teams have more embraced YouTube and social media platforms, allowing the MLS as a lesser known sports league to maximized its regular use of essential free websites to become more competitive in attracting a loyal fan base.

On top of these significant contracts and increases for major tournaments, the U.S.' domestic product, MLS, has also benefited recently from big contracts. The most significant of these new contracts, and a big headline grabber for the league, was the recent three-year contract signed with NBC and the NBC Sports Network. This contract was formerly with the Fox Soccer Channel (FSC), but NBC bid and won the contract for US$30 million over three years to broadcast 45 league matches. In just half a season since obtaining this contract, NBC Sports has nearly doubled the ratings from FSC on their networks attracting roughly over 120,000 viewers per match. In addition to this national contract, local teams have also signed many new lucrative contracts (many of those amounts are undisclosed due to league policies) that will help increase television ratings. The Los Angeles Galaxy signed a ten-year US$55 million deal with Time Warner to broadcast their matches locally (Becker, 2011). Similarly, Columbus Crew signed a contract with Fox Sports Ohio to broadcast all 32 of their non-nationally televised games in high-definition ("Fsohio and Columbus," 2012). Each of these contracts, slightly smaller in games to NBC's contract and only locally, gives the league and soccer in general more exposure in the country and will likely lead to higher television ratings. Figure 1 displays a conceptual model or map of the major trends indirectly/directly impacting domestic soccer TV ratings that will be examined in the present study.

Figure 1 highlights some of potential driving factors and/or importance of soccer television ratings. This survey addresses the four potential factors that could lead to higher soccer television ratings: fantasy sports, social media interaction, involvement in soccer, and the presence of a local professional team. The importance of improved soccer television ratings is emphasized by the four outward points (i.e., television contracts, online streaming, advertisement revenue, and merchandise and ticket sales). This entire group of outward points drive up the bottom line for the various soccer party entities involved in increasing soccer television ratings. A few of these were mentioned in the preceding sections, including the increased revenue from television contracts and ticket sales, both of which have skyrocketed in recent years.

Figure 1. Conceptual model

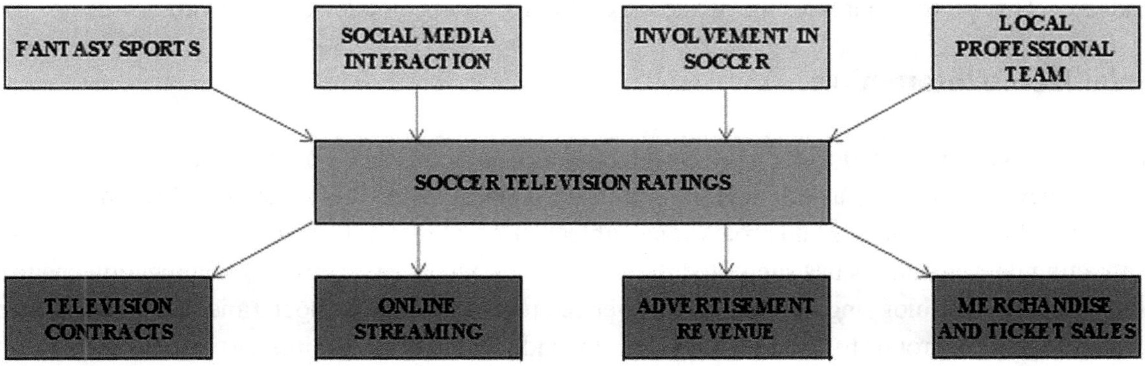

Growth of Fantasy Sports and Its Relation to Professional Sports

Fantasy sports have the ability to drive up interest in a sport and increase people's willingness to watch or attend sporting events. Fantasy sports are activities that allow fans to activity engage as owners to order to create and manage competitive teams. The complexities begin in that fantasy owners directly compete based on the actual athletic performances of existing professional sports via statistics generated by the players and/or teams of a professional sport. There has been much controversy concerning who actually owns those statistics or are they part of the public domain (Schirato, 2012). While fantasy sports are extremely popular for some professional leagues in the U.S., such as the NFL or MLB, other sports have not found the success or popularity of these games in the U.S. MLS falls into one of the leagues who have struggled to make their fantasy sports games popular among the masses. MLS's current fantasy game, MLS Fantasy Manager, has just around 15,000 current participants. While there are other smaller and independent leagues, this is by far the largest for MLS. In comparison to other sports, this is barely a fraction of some of the largest leagues a person can find on the Internet. In 2009, for example, it was estimated that over 25 million people in the U.S. participated in some form of fantasy sports, with 80% of those people participating in an NFL league and 40% participating in a MLB league ("The reality of," 2009). Not only do fantasy sports have the ability to drive up television ratings (as discussed further in the next paragraph), fantasy sports also have the ability to increase advertisement revenue to league websites where players run their leagues, track games, and check statistics.

Nesbit and King (2010) found interesting results relating to fantasy sports and television ratings. Overall, they found that participants who participate in fantasy sports are very likely to watch more games per week in the sport of their fantasy game than non-participants. For MLB, participants were estimated to watch 1.12 to 2.85 more games per weeks than those who did not participate. For the NFL, participants were estimated to watch 0.59 to 1.07 more games per week (Nesbit & King, 2010). These estimated equated to a 73% and 35% increase in viewership of MLB games and NFL games, respectively, for fantasy sports participants.

Similarly, Fortunato (2010) agreed and found that fantasy football participation can be a variable that influences viewership of NFL games. He suggests that the NFL should use the attraction of fantasy football and the appeal of certain players in helping construct and put together their TV schedule. Another initiative he suggests that all broadcast partners adapt is some form of scrolling statistics and live updates for big fantasy plays. These same suggestions could be used for MLS and all other soccer broadcasts. This survey addresses the influence of fantasy sports on television viewing.

Social Media Interaction

Social media is a powerful tool that has grown in importance significantly over recent years. Twitter and Facebook have taken nearly a daily role in millions of peoples' lives. It is a way to follow your favorite things, including sports teams and professional athletes. Recent research on social media and its impact on attracting new customers has suggested that Facebook, Twitter, and active communication channels created through live-blogging have fueled viewer interest in television. Social media has encouraged many demographic groups to comment, participate, and engage in a real-time virtual chat rooms, with million, if not billions, of global watchers (Pookulangara & Koesler, 2011; Smith, 2012; Wu, Wang, & Tsai, 2011). Although there may have some fears that these social media sites and other websites would actually hurt television ratings, but it appears they help increase TV ratings as people enjoy interacting with one another along with following their favorite television programs and celebrities ("Internet enhances TV for viewers ..." 2010; Seidman, 2010). Laura Wood, Senior Manager at Research and Markets, for example, agreed that the Internet has become television's best friend because Americans are watching more television than ever before, but they are watching television while engaging online at the same time (Wood, 2012). In the present study, it was examined if respondents' opinions on whether following their favorite sports teams has any effect on their television viewing of those teams as they see updates related to live sporting events.

Involvement in Sports

It is often thought that a specific sport's biggest fans are those fans who have participated in that sport throughout their life. Very little prior research has been done on this topic so it would be interesting in determining if people who have been involved in soccer are more likely to watch soccer on television. Is this truly a driving factor that soccer business people should be concerned with? Similarly, it was just as important to understand if people are willing to watch a sport that they have never been involved in. Do people only watch sports that they once played or coached? If this is not a factor, it allows soccer, or any sport, to be open to every potential viewer. If involvement does affect soccer television ratings, then the market for soccer shrinks, but it actually remains one of the biggest markets in the U.S. as soccer is one of the most popular youth sports among both men and women.

The Internet has become a prominent tool in sport management because it provides sport content, e-commerce, and video clips. But now is it evolving into more than that. The ESPY (Excellence in Sport Performance Yearly Award) presented by ESPN, for example, is a creation where sport clips are selected and broken into categories by ESPN and then fans go online and vote for a winner. The awards show is then broadcasted similarly as other award shows such as the EMMYS and OSCARS. It would be an interesting academic exercise to analyze the ESPYS based on the seven key Internet Strategy Themes presented in Evans & Smith (2004): leadership, managers' perceptions of online commerce, IT assimilation theory, internet vision statements, project trams, partnership/alliances, and online communities. ESPY Award winners were initially chosen only through direct voting by fans. Based on Evans & Smith (2004), this strategy ignored most of seven key Internet-bed strategy themes by taking advantage of only online communities and IT assimilation. By 2004, the other interested expert stakeholders in the process, such as sportswriters, broadcasters, sports executives, and sportspersons. Hence, future award winners were selected via online fan balloting from a list of candidates selected by the ESPY Select Nominating Committee. This additional step brought the other important strategic elements discussed by Evans & Smith. A future study on the strategic process of incorporating all the major elements of Internet strategy would be best served by an application of the Stakeholder Theory (Harrison, Bosse, and Phillips, 2010; Husted & Allen, 2011), which deals with the expectations of the various stakeholders involved in satisfying the mission of the firm. Since ESPN management is directly responsible for forming a dialog with the various stakeholder groups concerning their needs. These needs are usually based on a prescribed laundry list of delineating factors. To ensure a high-level of quality of this communication link, online voters should vote on the criteria to judge potential candidates, not just the candidates that ESPN choose. Determining this list would be a good basis for a research study, based on the theoretical aspects of Stakeholder Theory.

Local Professional Teams

MLS currently has 19 teams in 15 U.S. markets (Los Angeles has two teams) and three Canadian markets. This is a little less than two-thirds of the market coverage found in other professional sports leagues (NHL, NFL, NBA, and MLB) in the U.S. While this lower market coverage likely leads to lower television ratings as people do not have a team in as close of proximity to follow as other sports, the idea is an interesting component of my study. Not only does this mean less markets have soccer teams, it also means less markets have interest in the league overall as parts of the U.S. do not have a team anywhere nearby (i.e.; Southeast). The map shown in Figure 1 shows the markets covered by MLS in the U.S. and Canada. A key component in this study is whether people are willing to follow sports teams outside of their market, but maybe even more importantly it is determining whether people follow leagues that are not represented in their market (which includes MLS and foreign leagues).

As explained by Tainsky and McEvoy (2011), it is extremely important for leagues such as the NFL to attract television viewers from large markets without professional teams. The importance of television ratings from markets without professional teams because television contracts are a huge revenue source, but are not as valuable when the only market interested is the local market. They found that "demand is positively associated with team age as well as the presence of select franchises or the closest team geographically, suggesting that familiarity with the teams featured is especially important to these fans" (Tainsky & McEvoy, 2011). If these results carry to MLS, they likely work against the league for a few key reasons. First, the league is very young and does not have the history of other sports. Leagues from around the world are much older (along with specific franchises in MLS) so this may not necessarily impact soccer television ratings completely. Second, local teams are far away from some major markets. Some states, such as Florida, Georgia, and Alabama, do not have teams anywhere nearby.

Television Contracts

Television contracts is one of the first positive impacts felt from increases soccer television ratings and the first of four result items of the conceptual model. Television contracts and their growing revenues were discussed earlier in this paper. These included significant revenue increases for television contracts relating to the World Cup, Euro Championship, and MLS. All of these contracts have significantly increased year-over-year or competition-over-competition. MLS is poised for what is likely another increase in their bargaining power during the next round of television contract negotiations. During the 2012 season, MLS was on pace for their best season ever on ESPN, up 12% during the same period in 2011, and is off to a great start during their first year with NBC and the NBC Sports Network (Karp, 2012). Fox Soccer had the same contract as NBC last year, and NBC was having 78% better ratings during the same time period. Both of these statistics, along with the increased viewership for the Euro Championship and World Cup, mean larger and more profitable television contracts in the future for soccer.

Online Streaming

With the availability of live broadcasts to be shown online, it is likely that as interest grows towards a program online (in this case, soccer) that the corresponding ratings of online streaming will increase as well. Online streaming provides companies the ability to make advertisement revenue online and increase viewership overall when a television is not available or the market is not covering a specific channel or program (Smith, 2013; Smith & Rupp, 2013; Smith, Synowka, & Smith, 2014). Online streaming is on the rise and becoming just as important to companies as the traditional television market. Generally, a firm or program should see online viewing increase in stride with television ratings. This survey asks people about their willingness and tendency to stream sports and stream soccer online, but the focus is not to prove whether the characteristics of a person increase either of the two. To understand the new importance of online streaming, it is easiest to look at the growth of Netflix. For example, subscribers watched more than one billion hours of video in June, 2012, which made the service more popular than any traditional U.S. cable network ("Netflix just became," 2012). The same demand functions that possibly lead to increased soccer television ratings may lead to increased online streaming ratings. However, the characteristics of users of the traditional television market in comparison to online streaming users may be vastly different.

Advertisement Revenue

An increase in soccer television ratings can relate directly to an increase in advertisement revenue for all parties involved in soccer on television. Soccer, as it is unique in many aspects, is also unique in advertising opportunities. Besides commercial revenue and online advertisements, soccer teams also have very lucrative sponsorship deals for advertisements on their jerseys. Like other sports, they also receive revenue for stadium sponsorships. All of these forms of advertisement can generate more revenue when the various leagues and teams can prove that their reach to a television audience is greater. Bloxsome, Voges, and Pope (2011) suggested that the rewards of sport sponsorship are relatively clear via audience reach, which is specifically measured through attendance and television rating metrics. When these metrics improve, the revenue generated through sponsorships increases with it. Another unique aspect to soccer television advertisements is a running advertisement that runs alongside the scoreboard graphic during each half of play, as soccer has no television breaks or timeouts during the two halves of the match. If television ratings improve, the audience grows, and this advertisement space increases significantly in value.

Merchandise and Ticket Sales

An increase in television ratings also relates to a heightened interest in merchandise and ticket sales. As a focal point of where soccer currently sits in the U.S., there has been considerable growth of MLS, especially in terms of increased attendance numbers. This is a bit of an anomaly in the conceptual model because it is uncertain whether attendance drives television ratings or television ratings drive attendance. In the present research study, the possibility of both and the general relationship between the two is explored in some detail. But in 2011, as soccer television ratings increased for the league at 16% and 26% on Fox Soccer and ESPN, respectively, merchandise sales increased 35% year-over-year ("It has been," 2011). This indicated that the two may not relate to one another, but they definitely correlate with one another. Each of the two brings soccer new exposure and open the door to more revenue.

Sports have been traditionally viewed as an entertainment economy, where consumer decisions are heavily driven by the infusion of entertainment (Irwin, Sutton & McCarthy, 2008). By placing greater emphasis on the entertainment value of the team's performance and product extensions rather than interest in sport as a product in and of itself, the sport industry has seen a decline in sport consumption while seeking entertainment has increased. In the sport promotion mix, advertising, personal contact, atmospherics, sponsorship and publicity are all tactics employed interdependently to achieve sport marketing goals. With a shift in the demand for greater entertainment elements as part of the sport product, will there be a need for a shift in the sport promotion mix? A quick review of some of the important sport promotion literature reveals a strong view that online success would be improved with active involvement by senior management in setting sport marketing goals (Zimmerman, Clavio, & Lim, 2011). Although there are many tactics that can be interdependently employed to achieve sport marketing goals, it should be recognized that if management who determine organization-wide strategies should be actively involved in sport-related websites and its marketing strategies. The Internet is basically unorganized and chaotic, so sport promotion on related websites should be more closely aligned to overall strategies. Sport organizations need to be actively involved in their website development in order to consistently develop higher quality. Evans and Smith (2004) commented that such care to detail on websites are often considered a standard service rather than a source of potential competitive advantage.

Therefore, with the reach and range of the Internet, fans are constantly raising the bar of standards for information access and degree of engagement. Just be reactive to customers instead of being proactive is not a competitive strategy. The lack of an official Internet vision statement represents a significant weakness in organizational strategy. Zimmerman et al. (2011) proposed an application of agenda-setting theory, which allows management actively manipulating the messages the public receives, or learns about the organization. Since local TV outlets have lost much of their importance in the face of online media's ability to spread news to fans on a more immediate basis, should not management allow its stakeholders (i.e. athletes, fans, product merchandisers, and corporate sponsors) communicate in very thought-out ways. The Internet is always characterized as an unorganized mess. Should not marketing managers try to organize and direct from the sidelines by actively promoting the agenda of the sport organization though social media and its YouTube channel?

METHOD

Specific Research Hypotheses

The three hypotheses presented in this paper dealing with the interplay of online social networking, work assignments, and office layouts, as derived from the review of relevant operations literature and from applying the basic tenants of Uses and Gratification Theory are as follows:

H1: Participation in online fantasy soccer leads to increased television ratings for soccer.
H2: A local professional soccer team leads to increased television ratings for soccer.
H3: Respondents who are more athletically or programmatically involved in soccer are more likely to watch soccer on television.

The basic conceptual model, Figure 1, was designed to serve as an aid to display the interplay of the three major areas of focus and how they relate to firms dealing with productivity and job satisfaction issues. It is further research assumption that management needs to properly manage these elements in order to promote a more satisfying and productive work environment. The conceptual model found in Figure 1 and the sport management literature were used to describe the relative importance of the three hypotheses of the present study. It is hoped that the results of the study should help management to more effectively promote the domestic soccer industry by understanding fans' increasing desire to become more engaged with their league by understanding various impacts of media choices and their potential interactions. Media choices, it is assumed in the present study, help fans with their skill set and technologies available to promote self-identity and user gratification.

Sample and Statistical Techniques

A basic survey instrument was developed for exploratory purposes. The survey instrument consists of items that were developed from the sport business literature and media applications. Through personal and confidential connections on the part of the researcher, a focused stratified sample of employed professional management (typically at the lower to middle-levels) was created and collected. The sample chosen was representative of the service industry located in the metropolitan section of Pittsburgh, PA. Pittsburgh was chosen as the site of the study as a classic rebirth urban area that historically a low unemployment, technically advanced, and economically strong within an area of declining manufacturing, but a very strong professional sport following.

This procedure resulted in 129 submitted useable questionnaires from an initial sampling frame of approximately 500+ professional personnel from several large area marketing and financial service firms. The surveyed personnel, primarily service representing marketing and financial services, were conducted over a three-month period. The rationale for selecting employed and relatively well-educated people was to gauge the sense of the impact of communication technology in a knowledge-based environment on television of MLS ratings theme. The following section on results will address the previously mentioned hypotheses and also considers a few other interesting results that came out of the 25 question survey. The primary goal of the survey and these tests was to find any useful media interconnection for soccer business decision-makers in regards to television ratings and increase the dividends these ratings create, as discussed in the earlier conceptual model.

Mostly scale (interval) measurements, with a few nominal-based questions, were used to develop graphs and perform the relevant statistical analyses; the actual instrument is available upon request. Most perceptual questions were based on a 5-point scale (i.e., 5 = strongly disagree, 1 = strongly agree). The dominant statistical techniques used in the present study were descriptive statistics, means testing, and regression analyses. The following survey questions that were used in the analysis may be at least partially derived from the descriptive statistics and the cross-tabulations found in Table 1 and the resulting cross-tabulations.

RESULTS AND DISCUSSION

Descriptive Comparisons

Table 3 displays the descriptive statistics of the 129 management professionals' responses to the survey instrument. As evident from an inspection of the table, the majority of respondents were relatively frequent users of social media websites, view social media at the workplace regardless of management's approval, and ranked cell phone as the preferred technology to access social media (followed by tablet, MP3, and other). There was moderate agreement on the use of social networking sites streamline com-

Table 3. Basic descriptive statistics of the major scaled variables in the present study

Variable Description and Coding Schema	N	Mean	Std. Deviation	Skewness	Kurtosis
Age of respondent (years) (1 = less than 20, 6 = 60+)	129	3.16	1.372	.822	-.641
I'm more likely to watch sports on TV if personally involved in a fantasy sports league (5 = strongly disagree, 1 = strong agree)	129	3.16	1.247	-.250	-.891
Regularly follow sports teams from different cities (5 = strongly disagree, 1 = strong agree)	128	3.20	1.358	-.170	-1.239
Regularly follow sports leagues not represented in my local city like following the NBA in Pittsburgh (5 = strongly disagree, 1 = strong agree)	128	2.96	1.416	.138	-1.357
Watch the majority of my local sports teams' games on television (if not attending in person) (5 = strongly disagree, 1 = strong agree)	128	3.91	1.157	-1.193	.630
Regularly stream sports matches online like ESPN3 (5 = strongly disagree, 1 = strong agree)	129	2.26	1.289	.644	-.877
Regularly stream soccer matches online (5 = strongly disagree, 1 = strong agree)	129	1.79	1.273	1.510	.993
Involvement in soccer throughout your life (e.g., player, coach) (1 = never, 5 = lifetime)	129	2.47	1.490	.658	-1.007
Involvement in ALL sports throughout your life (e.g., player, coach) (1 = never, 5 = lifetime)	129	3.90	1.211	-.903	-.101
Based on sports teams' social media updates, more likely to turn on TV and watch a live sporting event (5 = strongly disagree, 1 = strong agree)	129	2.75	1.173	-.005	-.849
Valid N	128				

munication in the workplace, somewhat split on whether social media sites at work positively affect worker productivity, and generally felt that social networking sites increase expertise/information sharing.

There were lower levels of acceptance among employees (including management) that engaging in meaningful, value-adding activities social networking sites within workplace was productive, unless properly monitored. Considerable agreement among respondents about the positive influence on productivity was found on innovative technologies, such as social networking sites, ultimately increase workplace productivity, work assignments involve communication technologies motivate employees to be more efficient and effective, employee satisfaction with increased access to communication technologies improves productivity, challenging work tasks involve greater understanding of communication technologies increase productivity, routine work tasks that can be standardized increase productivity, and office layout positively affects worker productivity, even if current office layout is not ideal.

In terms of management's perceived degree of strong personal face-to-face communication with co-workers cross-tabulated with strong personal electronic communication with co-workers, Figures 2 through 9 illustrate a strong relationship among the various cross-tabulation of customer preferences of television and social media programming options with age. As expected, younger age groups have a greater affinity for social media and fantasy league inactions/engagements than older groups that have greater preferences for fan-based face-to-face skills/sport participation to more electronic forms of communication/social networking.

Hypothesis-Testing Results

Results of Specific Hypothesis (H1)

H1: Participation in online fantasy soccer leads to increased television ratings for soccer.

Figure 2. Cross-tabulation of selected customer preferences of television and social media programming options with age: Fantasy soccer

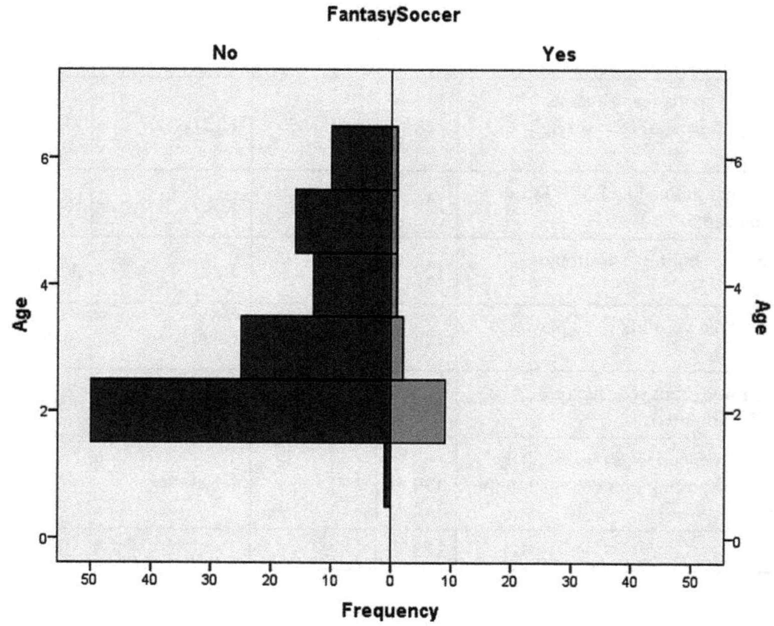

Figure 3. Cross-tabulation of selected customer preferences of television and social media programming options with age: Soccer on TV

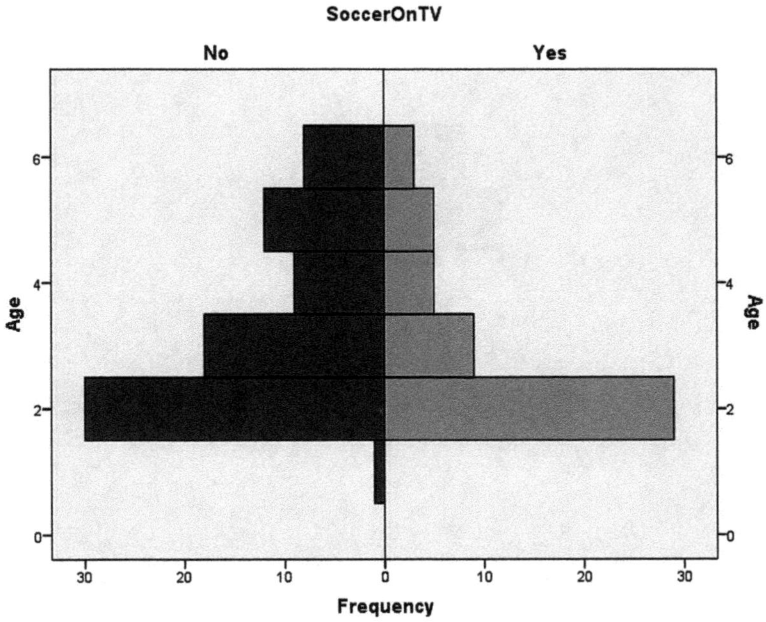

Figure 4. Cross-tabulation of selected customer preferences of television and social media programming options with age: Sports on TV

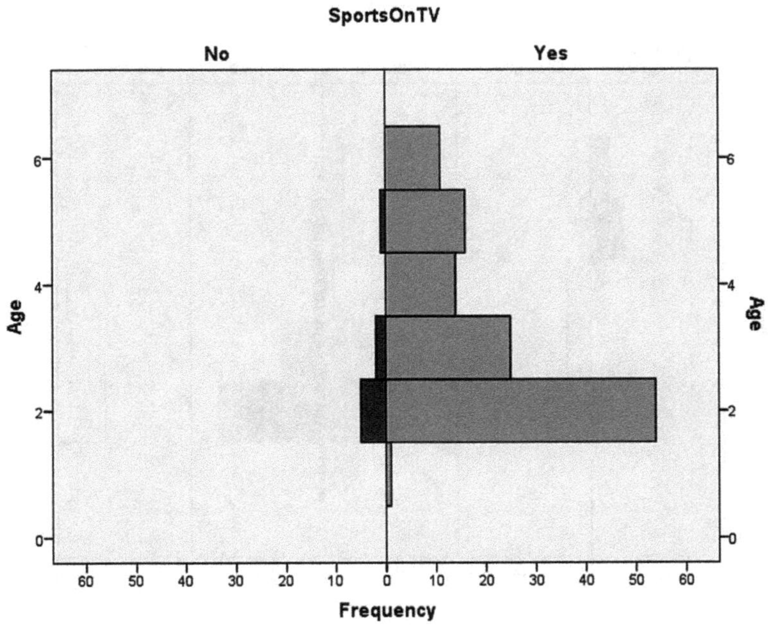

Figure 5. Cross-tabulation of selected customer preferences of television and social media programming options with age: Fantasy sports

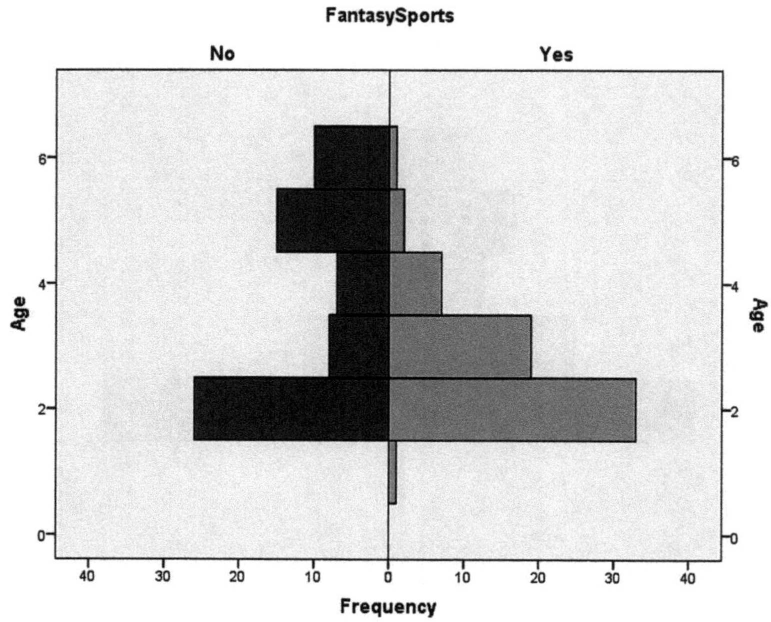

Figure 6. Cross-tabulation of selected customer preferences of television and social media programming options with age: Fantasy sports viewed on TV

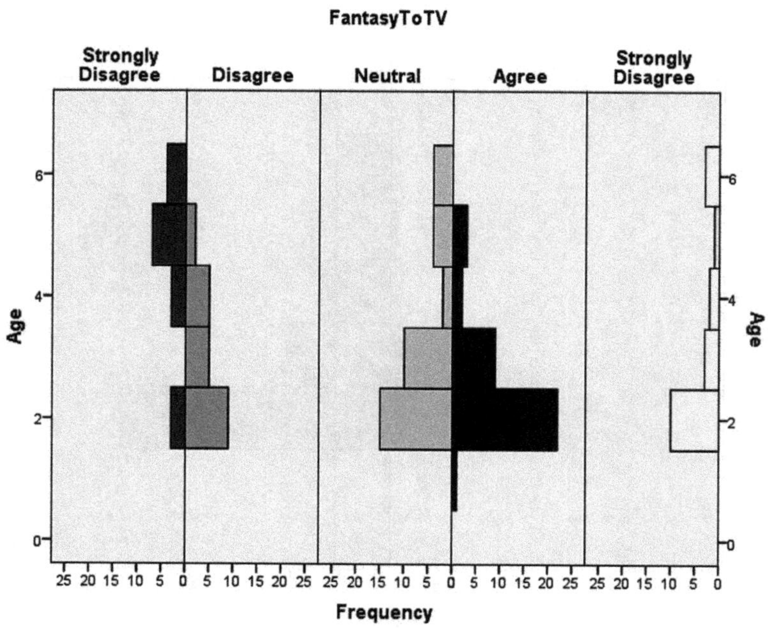

Figure 7. Cross-tabulation of selected customer preferences of television and social media programming options with age: Fantasy sports

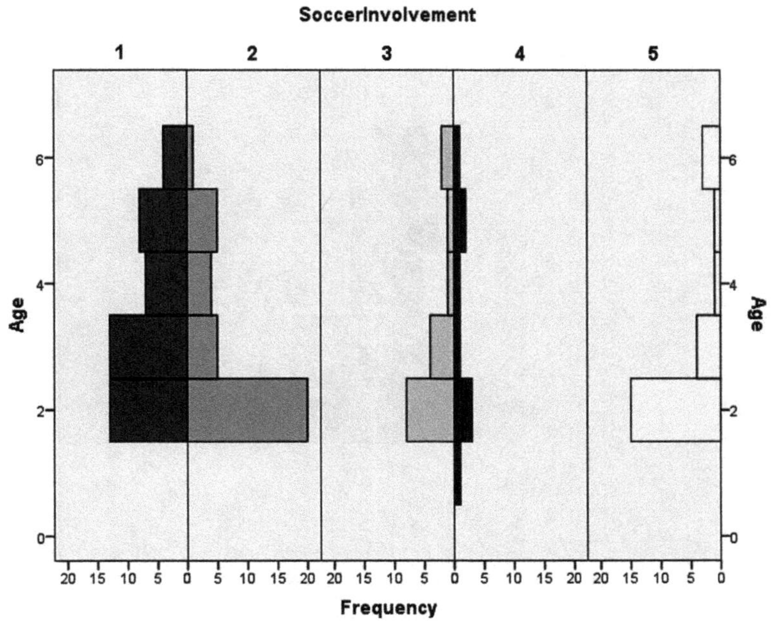

Figure 8. Cross-tabulation of selected customer preferences of television and social media programming options with age: Sports involvement

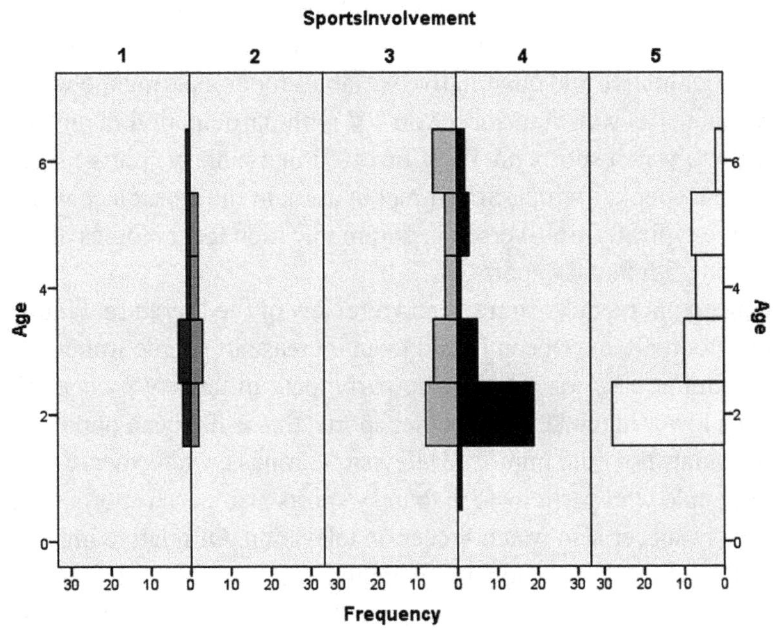

Figure 9. Cross-tabulation of selected customer preferences of television and social media programming options with age: Use social media

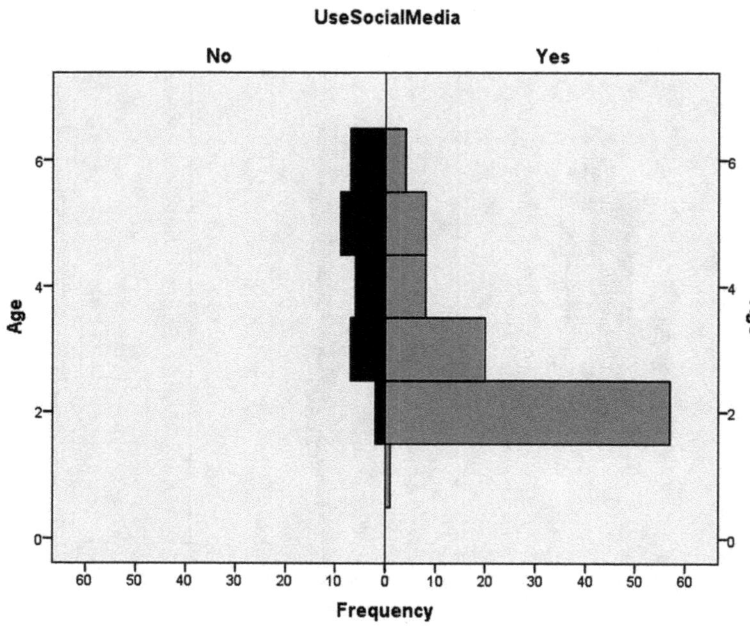

The first stated hypothesis is that managerial employees with greater access to mobile and online social media technologies, as measured in various forms of passive/active participation with fantasy soccer leagues generally leads to increased ratings for televised soccer participation/viewing. In order to properly test this hypothesis, a series of Chi-square tests were decided as a legitimate option to inspect these apparent differences of qualitative and quantitative variables for comparing the willingness to engage in these efforts. Such variables as watching soccer on TV with participation in any soccer fantasy sports games with more likely to watch sports on TV if involved in a fantasy sports league, as well as use of social media sites like Facebook, Twitter. Social media users in the workplace were investigated in the present study, as they are typically well-versed in communication technologies and have the propensity to become more engaged with fantasy sports.

As noted in the conceptual model, Figure 1, and a review of the literature, fantasy sports, especially participation in fantasy football, have been linked to an increase in people watching the NFL on television. There may be a similar case for people who participate in fantasy soccer. While fantasy soccer participation is so much lower in the U.S. than other sports, this is likely an opportunity for soccer decision makers to help stimulate new and improved television ratings even further in the U.S. It is important to determine whether people who participate in fantasy sports also watch sports on television and those who participate in fantasy soccer also watch soccer on television. Of relative importance would also be finding the correlation between those who participate in fantasy soccer and attend live soccer matches. Without monitoring the amount of games a person watches, the survey simply asks if people are more likely to follow sports when they are involved in fantasy sports.

Fantasy sports and fantasy soccer was discussed in three specific questions in the survey determining whether people participate in fantasy soccer, other fantasy sports, and if their participation in fantasy sports leads them to watch more sports on television. Nearly half of the people surveyed participate in some form of fantasy sports. However, only about 10% of those surveyed participate in fantasy soccer. Generally, people who participate in fantasy sports believe that they do watch more sports and are more interested in tuning into sports on television because of fantasy sports. Those that do not participate in fantasy sports may not share the same feelings. With this knowledge, it is likely that those who do not participate decided to participate in fantasy sports, they would end up watching more sports on television. Figure 10 illustrates the cross-tabulation between watching sports on television because of fantasy sports with participation with fantasy sports.

As illustrated in Tables 4 through 9, a cross-tabulation statistics associated with watching soccer on TV with participation in any soccer fantasy sports games with more likely to watch sports on TV if involved in a fantasy sports league (H1), factoring degree of social media usage. It is realtively clear that people who participate in fantasy sports feel they are more likely to watch television because of of their participation. With such low fantasy soccer participation, this trend may suggest a significant opportunity for the soccer industry to help improve overall television ratings. As the results point to roughly 28% of those who watch soccer on television also participate in fantasy soccer. With only 14 people participating in fantasy soccer, it was harder to get sufficient data results, so it is just as important to look at television viewing of those who participate in all fantasy sports. Overall fantasy sports participation is extremely important to look at when predicting the success of increasing fantasy soccer participation. Only one person did not watch sports on television that participates in fantasy sports, but over 50% of those who watch sports on television participate in fantasy sports (Chi-Square = 24.018, $p < .000$).

Participating in fantasy sports has a significant relationship with people watching sports on television. With low fantasy soccer participation, this is a significant opportunity for soccer (or any sport) to increase their television ratings. These results provided support for the hypothesis that online fantasy

Figure 10. Watching sports on television because of fantasy sports with participation with fantasy sports

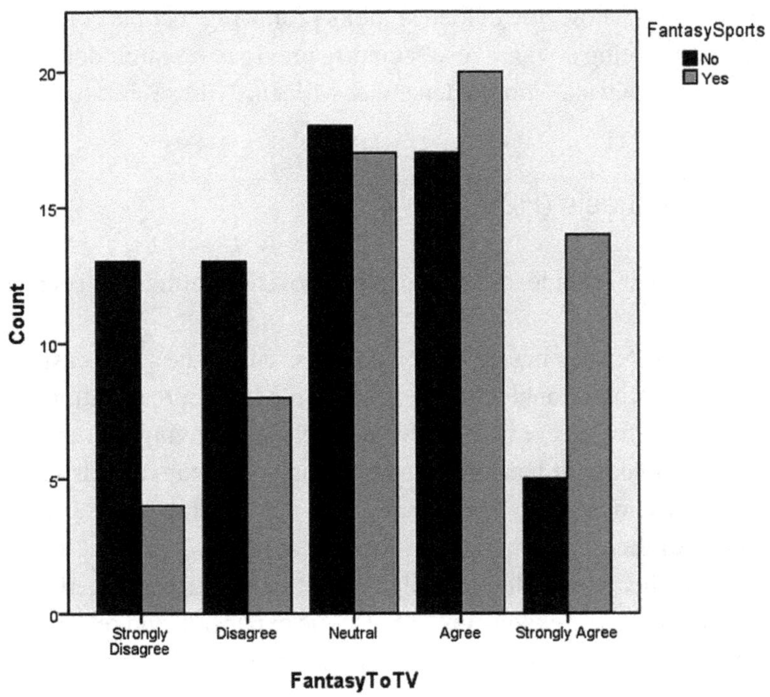

Table 4. Cross-tabulation statistics associated with watch soccer on TV with participate in any soccer fantasy sports games with more likely to watch sports on TV if involved in a fantasy sports league (H1): Actual count

I'm more likely to watch sports on TV if Personally involved in a fantasy sports league			Participate in any soccer fantasy sports games		Total
			No	Yes	
Strongly Agree	Watch soccer on TV	No	12		12
		Yes	5		5
	Total		17		17
Agree	Watch soccer on TV	No	11	0	11
		Yes	8	2	10
	Total		19	2	21
Neutral	Watch soccer on TV	No	25	0	25
		Yes	7	3	10
	Total		32	3	35
Disagree	Watch soccer on TV	No	18	0	18
		Yes	12	7	19
	Total		30	7	37
Strongly Disagree	Watch soccer on TV	No	12	0	12
		Yes	5	2	7
	Total		17	2	19
Total	Watch soccer on TV	No	78	0	78
		Yes	37	14	51
	Total		115	14	129

sports participation leads to increased television ratings. However, the low number of people surveyed participating in fantasy soccer makes it difficult to confirm (or deny) if this is currently going on with soccer television ratings. On a whole, the evidence looks promising that participating in fantasy soccer leads to increased television ratings, which also supports previous research done in other major sports (Davis & Duncan, 2006; Lee, Kwak, Lim, Pedersen, & Miloch, 2011; Schirato, 2012). Hence, H2 was accepted.

Results of Specific Hypothesis (H2)

H2: A local professional soccer team leads to increased television ratings for soccer.

As previously mentioned, MLS only has 15 major markets within the U.S., easily the lowest number of markets among the major professional sports leagues. This low representation will likely result in a negative impact on TV ratings for soccer in the U.S., since each marketing segment is further away from other sport-related markets, making it harder to find coverage on a team and drive interest in a positive direction. It would be equally interesting to determine if a relationship existed if people are following leagues and teams outside of their local market. By looking at people's interest in teams outside of their local market and looking at whether people generally follow their local teams, perhaps useful insights can be made on the importance of league expansion. U.S. league expansion and relocation have traditionally been an important topic in all professional leagues, as picking the right locations can mean success or failure for a league and its bottom line.

Table 5. Cross-tabulation statistics associated with watch soccer on TV with participate in any soccer fantasy sports games with more likely to watch sports on TV if involved in a fantasy sports league (H1): Actual count (Chi-square test results)

I'm more likely to watch sports on TV if Personally involved in a fantasy sports league		Value	df	Asymptotic Significance (2-sided)	Exact Sig. (2-sided)	Exact Sig. (1-sided)
Strongly Agree	Pearson Chi-Square	.[c]				
	N of Valid Cases	17				
Agree	Pearson Chi-Square	2.432[d]	1	.119		
	Continuity Correction[b]	.664	1	.415		
	Likelihood Ratio	3.201	1	.074		
	Fisher's Exact Test				.214 (NS)	.214 (NS)
	Linear-by-Linear Association	2.316	1	.128		
	N of Valid Cases	21				
Neutral	Pearson Chi-Square	8.203[e]	1	.004		
	Continuity Correction[b]	4.822	1	.028		
	Likelihood Ratio	8.258	1	.004		
	Fisher's Exact Test				.018 (S)	.018 (S)
	Linear-by-Linear Association	7.969	1	.005		
	N of Valid Cases	35				
Disagree	Pearson Chi-Square	8.179[f]	1	.004		
	Continuity Correction[b]	5.954	1	.015		
	Likelihood Ratio	10.885	1	.001		
	Fisher's Exact Test				.008 (HS)	.005 (HS)
	Linear-by-Linear Association	7.958	1	.005		
	N of Valid Cases	37				
Strongly Disagree	Pearson Chi-Square	3.832[g]	1	.050		
	Continuity Correction[b]	1.399	1	.237		
	Likelihood Ratio	4.411	1	.036		
	Fisher's Exact Test				.123 (NS)	.123 (NS)
	Linear-by-Linear Association	3.630	1	.057		
	N of Valid Cases	19				
Total	Pearson Chi-Square	24.018[a]	1	.000		
	Continuity Correction[b]	21.265	1	.000		
	Likelihood Ratio	28.659	1	.000		
	Fisher's Exact Test				.000 (HS)	.000 (HS)
	Linear-by-Linear Association	23.832	1	.000		
	N of Valid Cases	129				

a. 0 cells (0.0%) have expected count less than 5. The minimum expected count is 5.53.
b. Computed only for a 2x2 table
c. No statistics are computed because Participate in any soccer fantasy sports games is a constant.
d. 2 cells (50.0%) have expected count less than 5. The minimum expected count is .95.
e. 2 cells (50.0%) have expected count less than 5. The minimum expected count is .86.
f. 2 cells (50.0%) have expected count less than 5. The minimum expected count is 3.41.
g. 2 cells (50.0%) have expected count less than 5. The minimum expected count is .74.

NS denotes not statistically significant at the 0.05 level for a two-tailed test; S denotes statistically significant at the 0.05 level for a two-tailed test; HS denotes significant at the 0.01 level for a two-tailed test.

With MLS being such a new league in the U.S., one of the biggest issues holding television ratings back may well be the under-presence of teams in local markets. As mentioned earlier, MLS has teams located in few markets in the U.S., easily the least of any professional sports league and well below leagues like the NFL, NBA, and NHL. However, and despite this fact, ratings for soccer in the U.S. are growing. Potentially, one way to create higher television ratings is just to expand the league further, as they have done over the past few years. The survey focused on a few key questions surrounding local teams and people's willingness to follow teams and leagues that are not locally represented. Since that

Table 6. Cross-tabulation statistics associated with watch soccer on TV with participate in any soccer fantasy sports games with more likely to watch sports on TV if involved in a fantasy sports league (H1): Symmetric measures

I'm more likely to watch sports on TV if Personally involved in a fantasy sports league			Value	Approximate Significance
Strongly Agree	Nominal by Nominal	Phi	.[c]	NA
	N of Valid Cases		17	
Agree	Nominal by Nominal	Phi	.340	.119 (NS)
		Cramer's V	.340	.119 (NS)
		Contingency Coefficient	.322	.119 (NS)
	N of Valid Cases		21	
Neutral	Nominal by Nominal	Phi	.484	.004 (HS)
		Cramer's V	.484	.004 (HS)
		Contingency Coefficient	.436	.004 (HS)
	N of Valid Cases		35	
Disagree	Nominal by Nominal	Phi	.470	.004 (HS)
		Cramer's V	.470	.004 (HS)
		Contingency Coefficient	.425	.004 (HS)
	N of Valid Cases		37	
Strongly Disagree	Nominal by Nominal	Phi	.449	.050 (S)
		Cramer's V	.449	.050 (S)
		Contingency Coefficient	.410	.050 (S)
	N of Valid Cases		19	
Total	Nominal by Nominal	Phi	.431	.000 (HS)
		Cramer's V	.431	.000 (HS)
		Contingency Coefficient	.396	.000 (HS)
	N of Valid Cases		129	

NS denotes not statistically significant at the 0.05 level for a two-tailed test; S denotes statistically significant at the 0.05 level for a two-tailed test; HS denotes significant at the 0.01 level for a two-tailed test.

Table 7. Cross-tabulation statistics associated with watch soccer on TV with participation in any soccer fantasy sports games with more likely to watch sports on TV if involved in a fantasy sports league by use of social media sites like Facebook, Twitter (H1): Actual count

Use social media sites like Facebook, Twitter			Participate in any soccer fantasy sports games		Total
			No	Yes	
No	Watch soccer on TV	No	21	0	21
		Yes	9	1	10
	Total		30	1	31
Yes	Watch soccer on TV	No	57	0	57
		Yes	28	13	41
	Total		85	13	98
Total	Watch soccer on TV	No	78	0	78
		Yes	37	14	51
	Total		115	14	129

Table 8. Cross-tabulation statistics associated with watch soccer on TV with participation in any soccer fantasy sports games with more likely to watch sports on TV if involved in a fantasy sports league by use of social media sites like Facebook, Twitter (H1): Chi-square test results

Use social media sites like Facebook, Twitter		Value	df	Asymptotic Significance (2-sided)	Exact Sig. (2-sided)	Exact Sig. (1-sided)
No	Pearson Chi-Square	2.170[c]	1	.141 (NS)		
	Continuity Correction[b]	.149	1	.700 (NS)		
	Likelihood Ratio	2.334	1	.127 (NS)		
	Fisher's Exact Test				.323 (NS)	.323 (NS)
	Linear-by-Linear Association	2.100	1	.147 (NS)		
	N of Valid Cases	31				
Yes	Pearson Chi-Square	20.837[d]	1	.000 (HS)		
	Continuity Correction[b]	18.173	1	.000 (HS)		
	Likelihood Ratio	25.493	1	.000 (HS)		
	Fisher's Exact Test				.000 (HS)	.000 (HS)
	Linear-by-Linear Association	20.625	1	.000 (HS)		
	N of Valid Cases	98				
Total	Pearson Chi-Square	24.018[a]	1	.000 (HS)		
	Continuity Correction[b]	21.265	1	.000 (HS)		
	Likelihood Ratio	28.659	1	.000 (HS)		
	Fisher's Exact Test				.000 (HS)	.000 (HS)
	Linear-by-Linear Association	23.832	1	.000 (HS)		
	N of Valid Cases	129				

a. 0 cells (0.0%) have expected count less than 5. The minimum expected count is 5.53.
b. Computed only for a 2x2 table
c. 2 cells (50.0%) have expected count less than 5. The minimum expected count is .32.
d. 0 cells (0.0%) have expected count less than 5. The minimum expected count is 5.44.

Table 9. Cross-tabulation statistics associated with watch soccer on TV with participation in any soccer fantasy sports games with more likely to watch sports on TV if involved in a fantasy sports league by use of social media sites like Facebook, Twitter (H1): Symmetric measures

Use social media sites like Facebook, Twitter			Value	Approximate Significance
No	Nominal by Nominal	Contingency Coefficient	.256	.141 (NS)
	N of Valid Cases		31	
Yes	Nominal by Nominal	Contingency Coefficient	.419	.000 (HS)
	N of Valid Cases		98	
Total	Nominal by Nominal	Contingency Coefficient	.396	.000 (HS)
	N of Valid Cases		129	

NS denotes not statistically significant at the 0.05 level for a two-tailed test; S denotes statistically significant at the 0.05 level for a two-tailed test; HS denotes significant at the 0.01 level for a two-tailed test.

vast majority of the respondents are located within or around Pittsburgh, it is unlikely that most people have a local MLS team. The closest teams to Pittsburgh are Columbus, OH, Philadelphia, PA, and Washington, DC. However, the results are a fairly good indicator to show the difference between people with a local team and people without one. As evident from the descriptive statistics, 22 respondents who have a local MLS team. To be consistent, it is important to understand the difference between people with a local professional soccer team and local sports teams in general. Overall, the majority of people surveyed have local sports teams (119/128). The question really now is whether the people with a local professional soccer team are more likely to watch soccer on television. A simple Chi-square (Tables 10, 11, and 12) test should provide evidence to accept/reject H2. As shown in the previous hypothesis (H1) test, 51 respondents watch soccer on television (while only 21 have a local MLS team) so it may be safe to assume that that a local team is not necessary for a person to watch soccer on television. However,

Table 10. Cross-tabulation statistics associated with having a local professional soccer team (MLS) with watching the majority of local sports teams' games on television (if not attending in person) (H2): Actual count

Independent Variables		Watch the majority of my local sports teams' games on television (if not attending in person)					Total
		Strongly Agree	Agree	Neutral	Disagree	Strongly Disagree	
Have a local professional soccer team (MLS)	No	6	10	5	47	39	107
	Yes	2	2	2	10	6	22
Total		8	12	7	57	45	129

Table 11. Cross-tabulation statistics associated with having a local professional soccer team (MLS) with watching the majority of local sports teams' games on television (if not attending in person) (H2): Chi-square test results

Statistics	Value	df	Asymptotic Significance (2-sided)
Pearson Chi-Square	1.465	4	.833 (NS)
Likelihood Ratio	1.371	4	.849 (NS)
Linear-by-Linear Association	.756	1	.385 (NS)
N of Valid Cases	129		

Note, 3 cells (30.0%) have expected count less than 5. The minimum expected count is 1.19. NS denotes not statistically significant at the 0.05 level for a two-tailed test.

Table 12. Cross-tabulation statistics associated with having a local professional soccer team (MLS) with watching the majority of local sports teams' games on television (if not attending in person) (H2): Symmetric measures

Statistics		Value	Approximate Significance
Nominal by Nominal	Contingency Coefficient	.106	.833 (NS)
N of Valid Cases		129	

NS denotes not statistically significant at the 0.05 level for a two-tailed test.

it is also reasonable to expect that the ratio of people who watch soccer on television with a team in a local market to be higher. Figure 11 graphically displays this cross-tabulation as well.

Surprisingly, the presence of a local team does not have a significant relationship to people watching soccer on television (Chi-square = 1.465, P = .833). Only 11 of 21 (52%) people with a local professional soccer team watch soccer on television. Comparatively, 40 out of 107 (37%) people without a local professional soccer team watch soccer on television. While the percentage of people watching in local markets is higher than the ratings in markets without local teams, the results of the current study does not find this to be a significant factor in increasing television ratings. Of course, if this hypothesis would be tested on a larger population, perhaps the results would have been more positive. In sports, local television markets are often the highest rated markets for any particular contest, but these results were not replicated in the present study. However, when looking at fan's willingness to watch their local teams' games, it was shown that was very likely for a person to watch their local professional sports teams on a regular basis. The majority of people agreed that they followed most of their local teams on television, which contradicts the findings that a local professional team is not important to television ratings. A local team and that market is extremely important to television ratings.

Therefore, as illustrated in Figure 11, many sport fans had mixed opinions on whether they would follow a team outside of their local market. Similarly, respondents are also mixed in whether they would follow a league not represented in their local market. Both of these findings, relating to non-local teams and non-local leagues, show support to the hypothesis that a local professional team would increase television ratings. Overall, it appears respondents enjoy following their local teams, but some are willing to follow teams and leagues outside of their local markets. An overarching premise for MLS and soccer

Figure 11. Watching majority of local sports teams on television with having a local professional soccer team

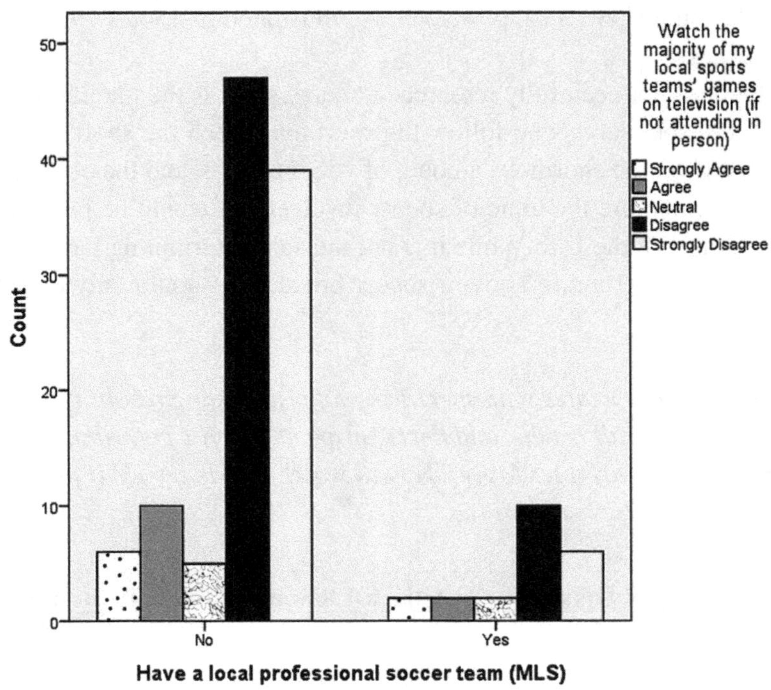

in the U.S. would be to continue to grow and develop the domestic league to increase television ratings. This seems to work in other sports as the sport is greater represented throughout the nation and opens more eyes to the sport and the league, which will drive other leagues and other major competitions. Hence, H2 was rejected.

Results of Specific Hypothesis (H3)

H3: Respondents who are more athletically or programmatically involved in soccer are more likely to watch soccer on television.

Many respondents in the U.S. follow sports that they have never participated in or been involved in, especially the NFL. However, respondents often have interesting reasons for not following soccer, which includes not understanding the game. These same reasons are often given for reasons why respondents do not follow the National Hockey League (NHL), as well (Fortunato, 2011; Nesbit & King, 2010). The purpose of testing H2 was to determine respondents' willingness to follow sports that they never participated in and understand aspects of whether respondents who watch soccer on television are primarily those fans who have been involved in soccer throughout their life. This is an important concept for decision makers to understand, since it could theoretically help marketers target an audience, whether involvement in soccer matters or not and how they can attract new viewers to soccer programming. Of course, being physically involved in a highly competitive and demanding sport like soccer would be relatively rare for most fans of soccer; therefore, engagement in fantasy soccer was also analyzed in the formal testing of H3 (Tables 13, 14, and 15), and basically the same test with selecting only those respondents that also watch soccer on television (Tables 16, 17, and 18). As evident from both tables, only the independent variable involvement in soccer throughout one's life (e.g., player, coach) was statistically significant ($t = 2.297$, $p = .023$), but not statistically significant when the population was limited to those fans who also watched soccer on television ($t = 1.112$, $p = .272$). As illustrated in Tables 19, 20, and 21, the results of the Chi-square analysis.

An observation that has not been fully researched on any sport is the likelihood that direct involvement in sports leads to respondents who follow the sport and watch the sport on television. With the infancy of soccer in the U.S., the enormous amount of youth players, and the complexities of any sport, it would be interesting to explore the topic of soccer involvement would be beneficial research to the subject of television ratings in the U.S. While it is not the sole determining factor, as we will see later in the survey results, it is important to know if soccer broadcasts should only be targeted at a market

Table 13. Relevant statistics associated with specific hypothesis-testing results (H3). Part A displays the model summary, Part B the overall results, and Part C inspects specific contributions of each component in the hypothesis (Dependent variable: More likely to watch sports on TV if personally involved in a fantasy sports): Model summary.

R	R Square	Adjusted R Square	Std. Error of the Estimate
.354	.125	.067	1.209

Table 14. Relevant statistics associated with specific hypothesis-testing results (H3). Part A displays the model summary, Part B the overall results, and Part C inspects specific contributions of each component in the hypothesis (Dependent variable: More likely to watch sports on TV if personally involved in a fantasy sports): ANOVA results.

Source of Variation	Sum of Squares	df	Mean Square	F-ratio	Significance
Regression	24.944	8	3.118	2.133	.038 (S)
Residual	173.931	119	1.462		
Total	198.875	127			

Dependent Variable: I'm more likely to watch sports on TV if personally involved in a fantasy sports league. Predictors: (Constant), Regularly stream soccer matches online, Watch the majority of my local sports teams' games on television (if not attending in person), Involvement in ALL sports throughout your life (e.g., player, coach), Follow favorite sports teams on social media sites, Regularly follow sports leagues not represented in my local city, Involvement in soccer throughout your life (e.g., player, coach), Regularly follow sports teams from different cities, Regularly stream sports matches online like ESPN3. S denotes statistically significant at the 0.05 level for a two-tailed test.

Table 15. Relevant statistics associated with specific hypothesis-testing results (H3). Part A displays the model summary, Part B the overall results, and Part C inspects specific contributions of each component in the hypothesis (Dependent variable: More likely to watch sports on TV if personally involved in a fantasy sports): Coefficients-testing results.

Independent Variables	Unstandardized Coefficients		Standardized Coefficients	t-test	Significance
	B	Std. Error	Beta		
(Constant)	2.559	.555		4.613	.000
Involvement in soccer throughout your life (e.g., player, coach)	.206	.090	.246	2.297	.023 (S)
Involvement in ALL sports throughout your life (e.g., player, coach)	-.096	.105	-.093	-.913	.363 (NS)
Follow favorite sports teams on social media sites	.197	.233	.079	.845	.400 (NS)
Regularly follow sports teams from different cities	.069	.129	.075	.539	.591 (NS)
Regularly follow sports leagues not represented in my local city	.197	.117	.223	1.688	.094 (NS)
Watch the majority of my local sports teams' games on television (if not attending in person)	-.088	.096	-.081	-.914	.363 (NS)
Regularly stream sports matches online like ESPN3	.102	.138	.105	.741	.460(NS)
Regularly stream soccer matches online	-.291	.138	-.297	-2.118	.036 (NS)

Dependent Variable: I'm more likely to watch sports on TV if personally involved in a fantasy sports league. NS denotes not statistically significant at the 0.05 level for a two-tailed test; S denotes statistically significant at the 0.05 level for a two-tailed test.

Table 16. Relevant statistics associated with specific hypothesis-testing results (H3). Part A displays the model summary, Part B the overall results, and Part C inspects specific contributions of each component in the hypothesis (Dependent variable: More likely to watch sports on TV if personally involved in a fantasy sports, when Watch soccer on TV = Yes Selected): Model summary.

R Watch soccer on TV = Yes (Selected)	R Square	Adjusted R Square	Std. Error of the Estimate
.358	.128	-.038	1.237

Table 17. Relevant statistics associated with specific hypothesis-testing results (H3). Part A displays the model summary, Part B the overall results, and Part C inspects specific contributions of each component in the hypothesis (Dependent variable: More likely to watch sports on TV if personally involved in a fantasy sports, when Watch soccer on TV = Yes Selected): ANOVA results.

Source of Variation	Sum of Squares	df	Mean Square	F-ratio	Significance
Regression	9.449	8	1.181	.772	.629 (NS)
Residual	64.238	42	1.529		
Total	73.686	50			

Dependent Variable: I'm more likely to watch sports on TV if personally involved in a fantasy sports league, selecting only cases for which Watch soccer on TV = Yes.
Predictors: (Constant), Regularly stream soccer matches online, Involvement in ALL sports throughout your life (e.g., player, coach) , Watch the majority of my local sports teams' games on television (if not attending in person), Involvement in soccer throughout your life (e.g., player, coach), Follow favorite sports teams on social media sites, Regularly follow sports leagues not represented in my local city , Regularly follow sports teams from different cities, Regularly stream sports matches online like ESPN3. NS denotes not statistically significant at the 0.05 level for a two-tailed test.

who is full of soccer knowledge or if respondents need to learn and understand the game, as the NFL explains during many of their broadcasts and shows. Recently reported by ESPN analyses (Karp, 2012; Matchett, 2012; Sandomir, 2010), soccer has the youngest average age of fans in the U.S. among major professional sports. It may be an indicator that the sport is continuing to grow. Involvement in soccer, as shown in Tables 19, 21, and 21, is relatively high for this group of respondents. This may be a possible reason that the previous hypothesis, H2, which dealt with local teams was not found to be statistically significant. If one inspects in further detail at soccer involvement's ability to increase soccer television ratings, respondents involved in soccer (e.g., player or coach) may be more likely to watch soccer on television. To test this assumption, hypothesis, Tables 19, 20, and 21 inspects the distribution of those who are involved in soccer and whether they watch soccer on television.

Even by viewing this relatively simple table, it is very easy to see that respondents who are moderately to highly involved in soccer are more likely to watch soccer on television. The target audience for soccer television is respondents very familiar with the sport. However, pulling new viewers in may require the networks to educate and make the sport attractive to respondents who were not highly involved in soc-

Table 18. Relevant statistics associated with specific hypothesis-testing results (H3). Part A displays the model summary, Part B the overall results, and Part C inspects specific contributions of each component in the hypothesis (Dependent variable: More likely to watch sports on TV if personally involved in a fantasy sports, when Watch soccer on TV = Yes Selected): Coefficients-testing results.

Independent Variables	Unstandardized Coefficients		Standardized Coefficients	t-test	Significance
	B	Std. Error	Beta		
(Constant)	.444	1.434		.310	.758
Involvement in soccer throughout your life (e.g., player, coach)	.151	.136	.186	1.112	.272 (NS)
Involvement in ALL sports throughout your life (e.g., player, coach)	.229	.202	.170	1.136	.262 (NS)
Follow favorite sports teams on social media sites	.447	.387	.178	1.154	.255 (NS)
Regularly follow sports teams from different cities	.181	.205	.201	.885	.381 (NS)
Regularly follow sports leagues not represented in my local city	-.019	.200	-.021	-.095	.925 (NS)
Watch the majority of my local sports teams' games on television (if not attending in person)	.058	.168	.052	.343	.734 (NS)
Regularly stream sports matches online like ESPN3	.127	.246	.149	.518	.607 (NS)
Regularly stream soccer matches online	-.266	.228	-.339	-1.167	.250 (NS)

Dependent Variable: I'm more likely to watch sports on TV if personally involved in a fantasy sports league, Selecting only cases for which Watch soccer on TV = Yes. NS denotes not statistically significant at the 0.05 level for a two-tailed test.

Table 19. Cross-tabulation statistics associated with soccer involvement (e.g., player, coach) with watching soccer on television (H3): Actual count

Independent Variables		Watch soccer on TV		Total
		No	Yes	
Involvement in soccer throughout your life (e.g., player, coach)	never involved	39	6	45
	little involvement	26	9	35
	somewhat involved	10	6	16
	more involvement	2	7	9
	lifetime involvement	1	23	24
Total		78	51	129

Table 20. Cross-tabulation statistics associated with soccer involvement (e.g., player, coach) with watching soccer on television (H3): Chi-square test results

Statistics	Value	df	Asymptotic Significance (2-sided)
Pearson Chi-Square	53.076	4	.000 (HS)
Likelihood Ratio	58.876	4	.000 (HS)
Linear-by-Linear Association	50.649	1	.000 (HS)
N of Valid Cases	129		

a. 1 cells (10.0%) have expected count less than 5. The minimum expected count is 3.56.

Table 21. Cross-tabulation statistics associated with soccer involvement (e.g., player, coach) with watching soccer on television (H3): Symmetric measures

Statistics		Value	Approximate Significance
Nominal by Nominal	Contingency Coefficient	.540	.000 (HS)
N of Valid Cases		129	

cer throughout their life. This table supports H3, namely that respondents involved in soccer are more likely to watch soccer on television, although not necessarily those engaged actively in fantasy sports, especially fantasy soccer (Tables 16, 17, and 18). Overall, respondents are more likely to watch soccer when they are involved in soccer as a player or a coach. Hence, H3 was formally accepted.

GENERAL CONCLUSION AND RECOMMENDATIONS

As suggested by Hutchins (2011), there is little doubt that communication via networked personal computers as well as mobile devices has become the dominate form of communication, domestically and globally. With Internet-connected devices, particularly mobile devices and smart phones, social networking via Facebook and Tweeter has added chaotic and highly unpredictable consequences of how fans enhance a sense of engagement in terms of expression and promotion associated with spectator sport and its media coverage. This has certainly been the case with U.S. soccer. Soccer in the U.S. has made great strides over the past decade, as evident by the massive showing on television viewing the of 2014 World Cup in Brazil. One of the most important and often most overlooked areas of profitability when discussing MLS and other professional soccer is what drives and can increase soccer television ratings. As discussed in the conceptual model, increased soccer television ratings can lead to significant profit increases through sponsorships, advertisements, and increase merchandise sales. While the empirical evidence presented in the present study explored a number of areas and driving factors of soccer television ratings, the hypotheses focused on a few main areas that may present opportunities to decision makers in the professional soccer industry.

First, fantasy sports have had a significant impact on respondents watching sports on television. Soccer appears to have a significant following of fantasy fans, although still dwarfed by fantasy football, and remains a large opportunity for a way to increase television ratings for both MLS and other leagues looking to gain significant inroads in the domestic marketplace. With MLS fantasy soccer being the lowest participated fantasy sport of the major sports, MLS should look to promote their fantasy league efficiently and deliberately over the next season and throughout the season. Management should find that there are abundant opportunities for players to join late, constantly create new contests that reward players on a regular basis and keep them motivated, and offer some great prizes that the league will clearly get a return on from advertisements and site views. By increasing fantasy soccer participation, soccer probably will drive television viewers up, and increase their financial investments.

Second, local professional teams are a driving force that increase and virally promote a sport in big markets on a regular basis. MLS is definitely behind other professional sports leagues in the U.S. when it comes to acquiring a large number of major television markets. While overexpansion and too quick of expansion can be costly and ruin a league, MLS would be wise to look at some other large markets in the U.S. that may be smart investments for the league. Although the results of empirical section were mixed, but the overwhelmingly positive response of respondents who regularly watch and follow their local professional sports teams should show the significance of having as many local teams as possible for a league. MLS has some very large and important markets of the U.S. without a local team, which ultimately may be keeping television ratings relatively low. Respondents in these areas typically do not hear viral campaign messages in relation to the league and can likely put their interest to many other sports that are local enough to be involved in. It is recommended that MLS continue to expand at its current pace with a new team every 1-2 years until reaching a size that is equivalent to other professional sports in the U.S. While leagues in Europe are much smaller, the U.S. has a significantly different market in terms of size and remaining too small will keep soccer's presence only within a niche market.

Third, respondents heavily involved in soccer tend to watch soccer on television more than those who have never been involved in the sport in their life. With one of the largest youth sport programs in the country, soccer in the U.S. has the ability to turn many casual viewers into regular viewers. Perhaps, a factor that might be keeping ratings lower in comparison to other sports is the ability for all of these players/coaches to watch numerous soccer leagues and competitions on television, compared to other major sports which generally only have one major league in the world. With expansion and an increase in fantasy soccer participation, another way to help increase television ratings is to keep respondents involved in soccer after the youth ages. A recommendation would be for the league to setup hubs throughout the country of recreational leagues for teenagers and adults. Unfortunately, unlike many other countries, the U.S. does not have the club and organizational support that would allow most serious players after high school to continue their athletic development it they decide if they want to pursue soccer in a competitive fashion. If they do not want to pursue it competitively anymore, there is generally no league for teenagers to just enjoy the game and play. MLS could promote to its benefit with free promotion and make money from small fees by setting up a national non-competitive youth league. Keeping players involved will likely increase television ratings throughout adulthood. In most areas, there are already adult leagues, both recreational and competitive so this would not be as big of an area to improve ratings, but an adult league in underrepresented areas would also be a smart move.

Finally, there were a few other areas of the results that produced interesting results, but were not focused on throughout the three hypotheses. These areas certainly warrant further research. For example, it appears that social media sites and accounts help drive respondents' interest in live sporting events. Teams and leagues should constantly look to grow and adapt their social media presence. A simple statistic to increase is followers on Twitter and Facebook. A team and league should look to double their followers through competitions and promotions every couple months. Most of these followers will stay on for the long-term and help drive interest and ratings for the television matches. Second, a high proportion of respondents in the survey who watch sports and soccer on television also stream sports online. A recommendation for soccer and MLS would be to have matches available online through their television partners and allow for matches to be watched after completion online through television partners. These help increase television ratings for other shows as this is a new way respondents get their television time in around a busy schedule. It would also allow respondents to follow a team more easily and generate revenue and advertisements for the league and partners.

Soccer has a lot of room for growth in television ratings, but prior research and the results of the present study illustrate that the ratings are already becoming significant. MLS and other leagues and tournaments have opportunities in the U.S. to increase television ratings through fantasy sports, social media interaction, soccer involvement, and smart expansion. All of these items lead to increases in soccer television ratings, which will help increase television contracts, online streaming revenue, advertisement revenue, and merchandise and ticket sales. The empirical results are just a starting point for exploring the many aspects of driving soccer television ratings in the U.S. The journey is still a bit unclear, but these results can help. Undoubtedly, recent data and television revenue for soccer show one thing is clear: soccer in the U.S. is here to stay and it is important for decision makers to capitalize on this quickly growing market.

ACKNOWLEDGMENT

The authors wish to thank most heartedly for the valuable contributions by the reviewers for their input into the final paper. Peer reviewing and editing are often tedious and thankless tasks.

REFERENCES

Becker, J. (2011). La galaxy announces $55 million TV contract. *SBNation.* Retrieved from http://losangeles.sbnation.com/los-angeles-galaxy/2011/11/15/2565118/la-galaxy-55-million-TV-contract-time-warner

Bloxsome, E. L., Voges, K. E., & Pope, N. K. (2011). Sport sponsorship: Appeal and risks. *The International Journal's Research Journal of Social Science and Management, 1*(8), 133–145.

Davis, N. W., & Duncan, M. C. (2006). Sports knowledge is power: Reinforcing masculine privilege through fantasy sport league participation. *Journal of Sport and Social Issues, 30*(3), 244–253. doi:10.1177/0193723506290324

Dure, B. (2011). Getting bigger, major league soccer seeks better TV ratings: New clubs add buzz, but getting more viewers to tune in is trick. *USA Today*. Retrieved from http://www.usatoday.com/SPORTS/usaedition/2011-03-14-mls14_st_U.htm

Evans, D. M., & Smith, A. C. T. (2004). The Internet and competitive advantage: A study of Australia's four premier professional sporting leagues. *Sport Management Review*, *7*(1), 27–56. doi:10.1016/S1441-3523(04)70044-3

Evans, S. (2012). Soccer-television ratings missing link for growing major league soccer. *Reuters*. Retrieved from http://www.reuters.com/article/2012/03/09/soccer-mls-television-idUSB67913220120309

Fortunato, J. (2011). The relationship of fantasy football participation with NFL television ratings. *Journal of Sport Administration ad. Super Vision*, *3*(1), 74–90.

FSOhio and Columbus crew announce television agreement. (2012). Retrieved from http://www.foxsportsohio.com/02/22/12/FSOhio-and-Columbus-Crew-announce-televi/landing_crew.html?blockID=671512

Harrison, J. S., Bosse, D. A., & Phillips, R. A. (2010). Managing for stakeholders, stakeholder utility functions, and competitive advantage. *Strategic Management Journal*, *31*(10), 58–74. doi:10.1002/smj.801

Husted, B. W., & Allen, D. B. (2011). *Corporate Social Strategy: Stakeholder Engagement and Competitive Advantage*. Cambridge, UK: Cambridge University Press.

Hutchins, B. (2011). The acceleration of media sport culture. *Information Communication and Society*, *14*(2), 237–257. doi:10.1080/1369118X.2010.508534

Internet enhances TV for viewers; social media, liveblogs bolster TV ratings; watchers connect in 'virtual living room'. (2010). *National Post*. Retrieved from http://www.financialpost.com/todays-paper/story.html?id=2718763

Irwin, R., Sutton, W., & McCarthy, L. (2008). *Sport Promotion and Sales Management* (2nd ed.). Champaign, IL: Human Kinetics.

It has been a good year for major league soccer: Looking at the numbers. (2011). *TigerDroppings.com*. Retrieved from http://www.tigerdroppings.com/rant/p/29701823/It-Has-Been-A-Good-Year-For-MLS--Looking-At-The-Numbers.aspx

Karp, A. (2012). Final ratings: Major League Soccer on pace for best season on ESPN; Strong first year on NBCSN. Retrieved from http://m.sportsbusinessdaily.com/Daily/Issues/2012/07/20/Media/Final-Ratings.aspx

Lee, W.-Y., Kwak, D. H., Lim, C., Pedersen, P. M., & Miloch, K. S. (2011). Effects of personality and gender on fantasy sports game participation: The moderating role of perceived knowledge. *Journal of Gambling Studies*, *27*(3), 427–441. doi:10.1007/s10899-010-9218-9 PMID:20865303

Matchett, K. (2012). ESPN TV ratings for Euro 2012: New record viewings in US for soccer final. *BleacherReport.com*. Retrieved from http://bleacherreport.com/articles/1244834-espn-TV-ratings-for-euro-2012-new-record-viewings-in-us-for-soccer-final

Nesbit, T. M., & King, K. A. (2010). The impact of fantasy sports on television viewership. *Journal of Media Economics*, *23*(1), 24–41. doi:10.1080/08997761003590721

Netflix just became cable's biggest TV network. (2012). *Textually.org*. Retrieved from http://www.textually.org/TV/archives/2012/07/030853.htm

Pookulangara, S., & Koesler, K. (2011). Cultural influence on consumers' usage of social networks and its impact on online purchase intentions. *Journal of Retailing and Consumer Services*, *18*(4), 348–354. doi:10.1016/j.jretconser.2011.03.003

Sandomir, R. (2010). For ESPN and Univision, the US is a soccer country. *The New York Times*. Retrieved from http://www.nytimes.com/2010/06/08/sports/soccer/08sandomir.html

Schirato, T. (2012). Fantasy sport and media interactivity. *Sport in Society: Cultures, Commerce, Media. Politics*, *15*(1), 78–87.

Seidman, R. (2010). World cup ratings: Out of home viewing adds 14%, non-TV platforms add 32%. *TVbythenumbers.zap2it.com*. Retrieved from http://TVbythenumbers.zap2it.com/2010/07/18/world-cup-ratings-out-of-home-viewing-adds-14-non-TV-platforms-add-32/57429/

Smith, A. A., Synowka, D. P., & Smith, A. D. (2014). E-commerce quality and adoptive elements of e-ticketing for entertainment and sporting. *International Journal of Business Information Systems*, *15*(4), 450–487. doi:10.1504/IJBIS.2014.060397

Smith, A. D. (2012). Social media and online dating service providers: Re-examining the new face of romance in the current global economic recession. *International Journal of Business Information Systems*, *9*(2), 127–148. doi:10.1504/IJBIS.2012.045166

Smith, A. D. (2013). Online social networking and office environmental factors that affect worker productivity. *International Journal of Procurement Management*, *6*(5), 578–608. doi:10.1504/IJPM.2013.056173

Smith, A. D., & Rupp, W. T. (2013). Data quality and knowledge/information management in service operations management: Regional supermarket case study. *International Journal of Knowledge-Based Organizations*, *3*(3), 35–52. doi:10.4018/ijkbo.2013070103

Tainsky, S., & McEvoy, C. D. (2011). Television broadcast demand in markets without local teams. *Journal of Sports Economics*, *13*(3), 250–265. doi:10.1177/1527002511406129

Tidey, W. (2012). ESPN ratings for Euro 2012 demonstrate soccer's growing reach in America. *BleacherReport.com*. Retrieved from http://bleacherreport.com/articles/1245475-us-audience-for-euro-2012-demonstrates-soccers-growing-reach-in-america

Wood, L. (2012). Research and markets: Social TV. *Business Wire*. Retrieved from http://www.businesswire.com/news/home/20120711006070/en/Research-Markets-Social-TV-Marketers-Reach-Engage

Wu, J. H., Wang, S. C., & Tsai, H. H. (2011). Falling in love with online games: The uses and gratifications perspective. *Computers in Human Behavior*, *26*(6), 1862–1871. doi:10.1016/j.chb.2010.07.033

Zimmerman, M. H., Clavio, G. E., & Lim, C. H. (2011). Set the agenda like Beckham: A professional sports league's use of YouTube to disseminate messages to its users. *International Journal of Sport Management and Marketing*, *10*(3/4), 180–195. doi:10.1504/IJSMM.2011.044789

This research was previously published in the Journal of Electronic Commerce in Organizations (JECO), 14(4); edited by Pedro Isaías, pages 66-95, copyright year 2016 by IGI Publishing (an imprint of IGI Global).

Chapter 24
The Effect of E-Service Quality on Football Fan Satisfaction and Fan Loyalty Toward the Websites of Their Favorable Football Teams

Javad Khazaei Pool
University of Isfahan, Iran

Ali Dehghan
California Lutheran University, USA

Hadi Balouei Jamkhaneh
University of Mazandaran, Iran

Akbar Jaberi
University of Tehran, Iran

Maryam Sharifkhani
University of Isfahan, Iran

ABSTRACT

The purpose of the current study was to examine the effect of electronic service quality on fan satisfaction and fan loyalty in the online environment. Selection of three hundred and fifty-six fans of a famous sports club was through random sampling using the club's website. AMOS used structural equation modeling for data analysis. Results provided strong support on the effect of electronic service quality (E-S-QUAL) on fan satisfaction and fan loyalty toward the website of their favorable football teams. Business enterprises have well researched e-service quality and loyalty. However, limited research exists in the sports context. This paper provides valuable insight into the measurement of e-service quality and fan loyalty in the sport and offers a foundation for future marketing research.

DOI: 10.4018/978-1-5225-5475-2.ch024

1. INTRODUCTION

In recent years, the growing development of the internet in Iran has provided an opportunity for online purchases. Therefore, e-services and their unique characteristics have become a new area of interest. A number of organizations use internet as a profitable channel to distribute goods and to deliver services (Akinci et al., 2012; Barrutia and Gilsanz, 2013). They are trying to satisfy their customers and create great relationships with them. Recent marketing studies have assessed the importance of perceived quality variables on customer satisfaction and customer loyalty, with all leading to evaluate marketing success and efficiency. This is even more critical in service companies (Finn, 2011).

Today, services are widely expanded, and no business can survive without service. Club managers have to retain customers and provide better service, paying the most attention to the needs, opinions, and complaints that customers make in relation to service. Reviewing the problems and addressing the comments and the level of satisfaction with regard to the quality and speed enhancement of service can be a huge help to preserve them.

Service quality has a close relationship with customer satisfaction in the sports service industry; nowadays, sports organizations understand that providing service quality to customers is essential for success and is a key to survival in today's competitive environment. Customer retention and creating a basis for the return of their vital task requires special tools and tricks. The most important tools for sports clubs are constant communication with people, providing appropriate services, and being aware of the competitive market. Loyalty maintains and strengthens customers for organizations concerned to maintain and develop their competitive position in the market, and seen as a strategic challenge.

To create a loyal fans base, sports clubs must be in direct contact with their fans and create a mental picture where the fans feel informed about the activities of the club, that the club hears the voice of fans, and they are given importance; the club then goes on to meet their needs and day-to-day quality of service improved. In this case, making satisfactory changes in activity can turn them into loyal fans and one of the methods is by means of communication, use of the website.

The rapid growth of the internet as a low-cost facilitator tool for businesses and consumers has made customer satisfaction a critical component in marketing. To attract online customers, websites should be well designed and deliver proper services. To gain competitive advantages, it is important to understand factors influencing electronic service quality and customer satisfaction (Craig-Lees et al., 2013; Allameh et al., 2012).

Sports clubs should design their websites to provide information in a user-friendly manner, to satisfy their fans and customers. The better the website, the more customers are attracted. Satisfaction and loyalty are strong mediators for facilitating customers' purchasing behaviors.

Weathers and Makienko (2006) believe that online service quality provides organizations with remarkable success through online satisfaction and online loyalty. Because of its critical impact on customers' behavioral intentions, customer satisfaction has attracted remarkable attention in marketing literature (Theodorakis et al., 2013).

Previous studies have discussed the importance of understanding the various attributes of service quality and purchasing, often in the area of e-services delivery (Rezaei Dolatabadi and Khazaei Pool, 2013).

There have been a large number of studies conducted regarding the role and importance of service quality during the past twenty years (Rezaei Dolatabadi et al., 2012; Shaemi et al., 2012). In 2005, Parasuraman et al. developed a dual scale for measuring service quality in an electronic context. The main scale of E-S-QUAL consisted of 22 items that involved four dimensions: efficiency, system availability, fulfillment, and privacy. The next scale is E-RecS-QUAL, which mainly scales the service of goods exchange or withdrawal when the goods have some problems. The second scale (E-RecS-QUAL) consisted of 11 items classified into three dimensions: responsiveness, compensation, and contact (Akinci et al., 2010). Both scales have been found to be both valid and reliable. Previous studies regarded satisfaction as a critical indicator of increasing loyalty among customers.

Satisfied customers are more interested in repurchasing goods and services, and they also suggest the products and services to other people. A large number of previous studies have confirmed the positive effect of online satisfaction on online loyalty in an online context (Gera, 2011). Based on previous studies, it can be proposed that satisfaction has a positive relationship with loyalty.

Previous studies have also defined satisfaction as a functional consequence of service quality. The general satisfaction reflects the effect of organization's service quality on customers' perceptions, and satisfaction can be a better indicator for loyalty (Yang & Peterson, 2004).

Researchers have also investigated the mediating effect of satisfaction on loyalty in a comprehensive model of loyalty or a behavioral intention model (Butt & Aftab, 2013). General impact of organization service on customer perception results in customer satisfaction, and this satisfaction, in turn, leads to customer loyalty (Theodorakis et al., 2013).

The conduct of this study is to identify the electronic service quality factors that are influencing satisfaction and loyalty among football fans in Iran based on E-S-QUAL.

Today, the sports industry plays a key role in the global economy. With the growth of living standards and attention to sports and sports' facilities, the use of sports facilities is increasing. In addition, the stresses of life have caused the people to participate in sports clubs' activities for peace of mind and to drain their energy. Sports' entertainment centers are places where people can achieve their health goals. By increasing the number of sports centers, competition in attracting customers and providing better services is growing. Sports recreation centers sometimes draw unfavorable criticisms from consumers and gradually lose customers to other competitors. With regard to this issue and future customer behavior toward sports entertainment, important variables include customer satisfaction, customer loyalty, and improvement in perceived value.

Websites offering professional sports content have a remarkable potential to offer an expansion of e-commerce opportunities. Despite an increasing rate of internet technology and website utilization by sports teams and organizations, such as a marketing communication tools and a distribution channel in Iran, limited research has assessed how sport fans evaluate e-services and discerned appropriate dimensions of the quality of e-service delivery in the context of sports team.

The current study can be the first study conducted to investigate this issue in a professional football league context in Iran. The goal is to examine the effect of electronic service quality on football fans' satisfaction and loyalty toward the websites of their favorable football teams. The findings of the current study can be applicable for sports managers and sports marketers to design their websites more properly as well as to provide desired services, in order to attract more loyal and satisfied fans.

In this study, there is proposal of a conceptual model according to the literature review in which there will be examination of the casual relationships among electronic service quality, e-satisfaction, and e-loyalty. Figure 1 presents the conceptual model.

Figure 1. The study model and hypotheses

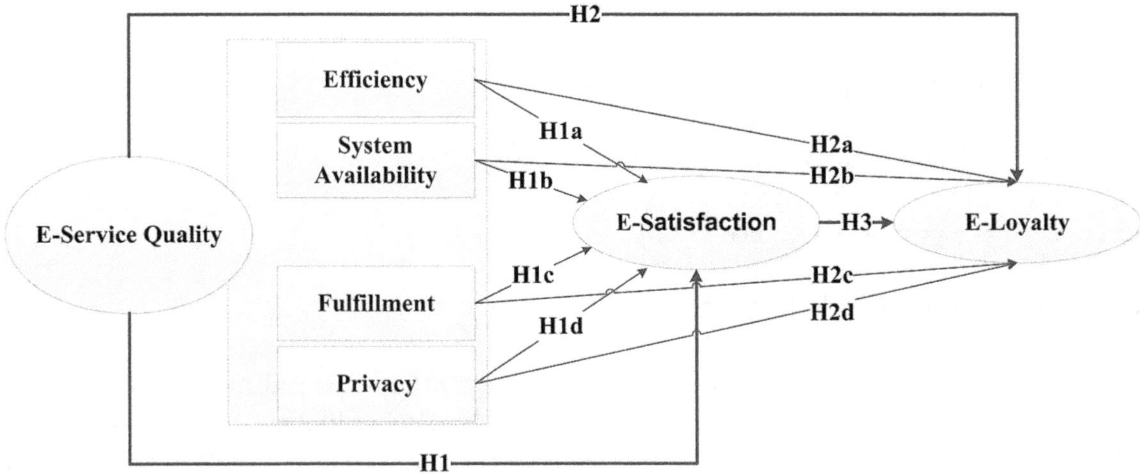

1.1. E-Service Quality and E-Satisfaction

In the consumer context, previous research has supported a significant relationship between e-service quality and e-satisfaction (Giovanis and Athanasopoulou, 2014). E-business research does indicate that e-service quality characteristics influence consumer satisfaction with a web site (Chang and Wang, 2011). Thus, once a customer makes a judgment or appraisal of e-service quality derived from the total experience offered by the website (e.g. efficiency, system availability, fulfillment, and privacy) then satisfaction should result if the assessment procedure is positive. That is, the way in which the e-service is delivered through a web site plays a significant and positive role in driving consumer e-satisfaction (Kim and Kim, 2010; Carlson and O'Cass; 2010; Vos et al., 2014). Hence the corresponding hypotheses are:

H1: E-service quality has a positive effect on e-satisfaction.
H1a: Efficiency has a positive effect on e-satisfaction.
H1b: System availability has a positive effect on e-satisfaction.
H1c: Fulfillment has a positive effect on e-satisfaction.
H1d: Privacy has a positive effect on e-satisfaction.

1.2. E-Service Quality and E-Loyalty

Prior research in e-marketing settings across a variety of services has found a significant positive relationship between perceived e-service quality and e-loyalty (Gera, 2011). In the context of the e-business environment, perceived e-service quality can potentially increase behavioral intentions such as e-loyalty (Carlson and O'Cass; 2010).

Giovanis and Athanasopoulou (2014) indicated that e-service quality influences consumer e-loyalty. According to Pearson et al. (2012), perceived e-service quality and perceived information quality similarly influence e-loyalty intentions. Marimon et al. (2012) mentioned that e-service quality dimensions such as efficiency of a website and responsiveness to complaints have a positive influence on e-loyalty.

Therefore, it is argued that a consumer's positive assessment of e-service quality is directly related with e-loyalty. Hence this research tests the following hypotheses:

H2: E-service quality has a positive effect on e-loyalty.
H1a: Efficiency has a positive effect on e-loyalty.
H1b: System availability has a positive effect on e-loyalty.
H1c: Fulfillment has a positive effect on e-loyalty.
H1d: Privacy has a positive effect on e-loyalty.

1.3. E-Satisfaction and E-Loyalty

Several studies have shown that e-satisfaction lead to e-loyalty (Giovanis and Athanasopoulou, 2014; Sheng and Liu, 2010). Previous research on the web indicates similar findings to studies in e-service settings, in that a direct relationship exists between e-satisfaction with a web site and e-loyalty (Kim et al., 2009). E-satisfaction has emerged as a major predictor of e-loyalty in the context of the new information technologies (Gera, 2011). Bringing the current work into the context of e-business, it could be argued that consumers who are e-satisfied might be likely to exhibit e-loyalty (Kim and Kim, 2010; Audrain-Pontevia et al., 2013). Thus the literature review leads to the following hypothesis:

H3: E-satisfaction has a positive effect on e-loyalty.

2. THEORETICAL BACKGROUNDS

2.1. Customer Loyalty

E-loyalty has been defined as a customer's favorable attitude toward an electronic business leading to repurchasing behavior (Anderson and Srinivasan, 2003). Thus, e-loyalty's identification is as a consumer's intention to revisit a website in the future and use it to make a purchase (Cyr, 2008; Cheng et al., 2008). Relevant studies on e-loyalty have greatly applied such a definition.

Customer retention and reduced cost of attracting new customers in the long-term are some of the advantages of e-loyalty (Reichheld et al., 2000). Marketing scholars have given different definitions to define loyalty. Largely, the basis of the delivery of these definitions is on two basic approaches. The first approach to loyalty is behavioral, and the other is emotional (Buttle & Burton, 2002; Oliver, 1999). According to the emotional approach, emotional feeling is important to understand loyalty (Kim et al., 2006; Jih et al., 2010). However, to have a proper understanding of loyalty, both behavioral and emotional approaches are necessary.

Developing fan loyalty can provide sports teams with significant profits and advantages. Loyal customers have a low level of sensitivity to the prices of goods and services, and often recommend the brand to others (Reichheld and Schefter, 2000). Loyal customers have a greater intention to purchase something, and they also provide positive word of mouth, which has been found to positively influence others' purchasing behavior. As a process, many scholars emphasized the importance of loyal customers in online contexts (Fuentes-Blasco et al., 2010; Marimon et al., 2010; Meng, 2010; Sousa, 2012; Lu et al., 2013). It seems that understanding the factors influencing the development of electronic loyalty among customers can certainly result in business improvement in competitive sports contexts.

2.2. Customer Satisfaction

Oliver (1980) defined customer satisfaction as customers' assessment of a product or service according to their needs and expectations (Oliver, 1980). Customer satisfaction leads to repurchasing behaviors, positive word of mouth, and brand loyalty (Lee et al., 2010; Nam et al., 2011; Ha and Im, 2012). Satisfied consumers have positive brand attitudes and brand preference (Bolton, 1998; Oliver, 1980; Roest and Pieters, 1997) toward the goods, services, or sports brands with which they have had a positive experience. In addition, customer satisfaction increases trust, and trust increases the level of loyalty. There are reports that higher levels of perceived quality in the online arena are associated with customer satisfaction, trust, and loyalty (Ribbink et al., 2004). Cristobal et al. (2007) found that increased satisfaction leads to increased website traffic. Also, increase in consumer satisfaction with the features and content of the website prompts the formation of positive attitudes toward that website.

A large number of scholars have shown the critical role of satisfaction in securing loyal consumers (Bloemer et al., 1999; Baida et al., 2005; Al-Hawari and Ward, 2006). Cristobal et al. (2007) showed a direct and significant relationship between satisfaction and loyalty in electronic contexts.

2.3. Electronic Service Quality

Santos (2003) defined electronic service quality as customers' overall evaluation and judgment regarding the excellence and quality of e-service delivery in the virtual marketplace (Santos, 2003, p. 235). Parasuraman et al. (2005, p. 217) defined electronic service quality as the "extent to which a website facilitates efficient and effective shopping, purchasing and delivery of products and services."

In the context of online shopping, there was identification of various e-service quality factors to be positively affected by consumer attitudes toward the website (Lee et al., 2006; Wolfinbarger and Gilly, 2003; Springer et al., 2013).

Previous electronic shopping research found that there was a direct relationship between e-service quality and a variety of behavioral intentions. Studies illustrated that electronic service quality was positively related with purchase intention and site revisit (Collier and Bienstock, 2006; Cristobal et al., 2007; Francis and White, 2002; Loiacono et al., 2002).

These findings reveal that sports managers and sports marketers can use the profitable advantages of their team's website to manage the purchasing behaviors of sports fans.

3. METHODOLOGY

The findings of this study can practically help managers to design proper strategies in the areas of sport management; therefore, there is consideration of this kind of study as a practical one.

Conduct of a review and librarian study was first for the literature review to collect proper theoretical content. Books, articles, and dissertations were the most important resources at this stage.

A questionnaire was sent to target samples via electronic mail. Once respondents agreed to take part in the survey, we gave them informed consent forms emphasizing that their responses would remain confidential. To persuade the sample to reply, respondents who completed the questionnaire were eligible for a prize draw and had a chance to win a shirt of their favorable team (Persepolis).

3.1. Questionnaire Design

For testing the hypothesis in the current study, there was conduction of a field study by incorporating sample fans ascribed to the Persepolis football team in Iran. The survey was designed to collect required data for this study. The survey measured the following concepts:

1. **Electronic Service Quality:** E-S-QVAL measured this concept and Parasuraman et al. (2005) developed it. According to Akinci et al. (2010), there was omission of three items (ful2, ful4, and ful5) of the original E-S-QVAL scale because these three items were relevant to physical goods. Thus, they were not proper for the purpose of this study. The modified scale consists of 19 items; they were categorized across four key constructs: efficiency (8 items), system availability (4 items), fulfillment (4 items), and privacy (3 items). (The original scale included 22 items) As suggested by Parasuraman et al. (2005), modification of scale and its items has been according the nature of electronic sports services;
2. **Electronic Loyalty:** A 4-item scale developed by Sheng and Liu (2010) with the least modification measured this concept;
3. **Electronic Satisfaction:** The four-item scale of electronic satisfaction was adapted from Ribbink et al. (2004) with the least changes.

All scales are in a 5-point Likert-type scale ranging from 5 being "strongly agree" to "1" being "strongly disagree."

The survey form, two pages in length, consisted of three sections. The first section included demographic items that asked respondents to list their age, gender, education level, and monthly income (including four items). The second section of the questionnaire filtered items to ensure the researchers that all respondents had used the electronic services of the Persepolis football team in Iran. The third and final section of the questionnaire contained the measures of electronic service quality, electronic satisfaction, and electronic loyalty (including 27 items).

3.2. Sample and Data Collection Procedure

The study sample included Persepolis fans who had visited the website of their favorable club in the last 12 months. The sample was taken from a Persepolis football club database. According to the Asian Football Confederation, Persepolis is the most popular football club in Asia. Only Dalian Shide and Al-Hilal come anywhere near having such an enormous amount of support in Asia.

The use of fans as the research sample was found to be suitable because they are the main consumers of sports services, and the use of fans as the research population is common in marketing research and relevant issues. Selection of the subjects was through random sampling. A sample of 600 users was recognized, and we sent an e-mail to each user asking him or her to participate in the research process. Overall, 446 users agreed to participate. Finally, the researchers collected a total of 432 surveys, and 356 of them were used in data analysis. Discard of some surveys was because they were incomplete. Overall, 356 valid questionnaires were retrieved, which provided an acceptable retrieval rate. Collection of research data was in December 2012. Sports professionals were then asked to test the questionnaire to clarify the subjects' responses to the questions and to edit the questionnaire accordingly.

3.3. Measure Reliability and Validity

After completing the initial draft of the questionnaire, we invited nine academics and experts from sports-related fields (sports management, management experts, and e-business) to help ratify the validity of the questionnaire (expert validity). The panel of experts ensured that the survey had good content validity (Esmaeili, 2014, p. 40). In addition, there was revision of the wording of items to ensure the items were clear and unambiguous. In a pilot study, there was then a random draw of 38 questionnaires as test samples for item analysis and reliability analysis.

Conduction of confirmatory factor analysis was to determine if the indicators for each construct loaded as predicted on the respective construct. Confirmatory factor analysis showed that all the items were loaded meaningfully on the underlying constructs. Thus, it confirmed the validity of the survey. We also used Cronbach's alpha to determine the reliability of the questionnaire. Table 1 shows the results of confirmatory factor analysis and reliability of the variables.

Table 1. Results of factor analysis and reliability tests

Variable	Items	Factor Loading	Alpha
Efficiency	EFF1 EFF2 EFF3 EFF4 EFF5 EFF6 EFF7 EFF8	0.82 0.81 0.76 0.91 0.82 0.64 0.81	0.91
System Availability	SYS1 SYS2 SYS3 SYS4	078 0.91 0.62 0.77	0.82
Fulfillment	FUL1 FUL2 FUL3 FUL4	0.81 0.88 0.91 0.80	0.93
Privacy	PRI1 PRI2 PRI3 PRI4	0.69 0.81 0.92 0.84	0.88
E-satisfaction	ESA1 ESA2 ESA3 ESA4	0.82 0.77 0.86 0.88	0.84
E-loyalty	ELO1 ELO2 ELO3 ELO4	0.91 0.83 0.78 0.92	0.87

3.4. Data Analysis

The sample profile was provide by usage of the descriptive statistics. Structural equation modeling (SEM) technique AMOS 20.0 tested the relationships of e-service quality, e-satisfaction, and e-loyalty. There can be usage of structural equation modeling to examine the path coefficient value and test the hypotheses in the proposed model (Esmaeili and Eydgahi, 2014).

4. RESULTS

Thirty-four percent of respondents were female, and 66 percent of them were men. Findings showed that the respondents were relatively young, from 26 to 30 years old. The sample seemed to be a highly educated group, with the majority of the respondents holding a college degree. Most of the respondents' monthly income was between $700 and 1000. Table 2 summarizes the demographic breakdown of the respondents.

To ensure that the indices are acceptable for the conceptual model, there was investigation of the measurement models. Table 3 shows the fitness indices of the conceptual model.

Findings show that the measurement model fits the study well; in other words, overall indices showed that the collected data properly support the model.

After investigating and confirming the measurement model, there was usage of structural equation modeling to test the hypotheses. Figure 2 shows the structural equation modeling, along with the regression coefficients.

After investigating and confirming the proposed model, we used the critical ratio (C.R.) and P value to test the significance of the hypotheses. The critical ratio is computed through regression weight divided by the standard error. Based on the significance level of 0.05, C.R. should be higher than 1.96. Those values under 1.96 are not considered an important parameter in the model. In addition, the P values lower

Table 2. Demographic data of the main survey

Demographic Object	The Valid Items	Percent %
Gender	Female Male	0.34 0.66
Age	<=25 26–30 31–35 36–40 41–45 >=46	0.19 0.36 0.15 0.14 0.10 0.05
Education	General secondary College Bachelor Master Doctoral	0.01 0.18 0.32 0.37 0.11
Monthly income	<= $400 $ 401–700 $ 701–1000 >= $ 1001	0.12 0.28 0.39 0.20

Table 3. Fit indices for the conceptual model

Indices Name	Cmin/df	GFI	AGFI	NFI	CFI	RMSEA
study model	2.12	0.92	0.91	0.94	0.92	0.017
Recommended value	<3	>٪90	>٪90	>٪90	>٪90	**<10٪**

Figure 2. Structural model results

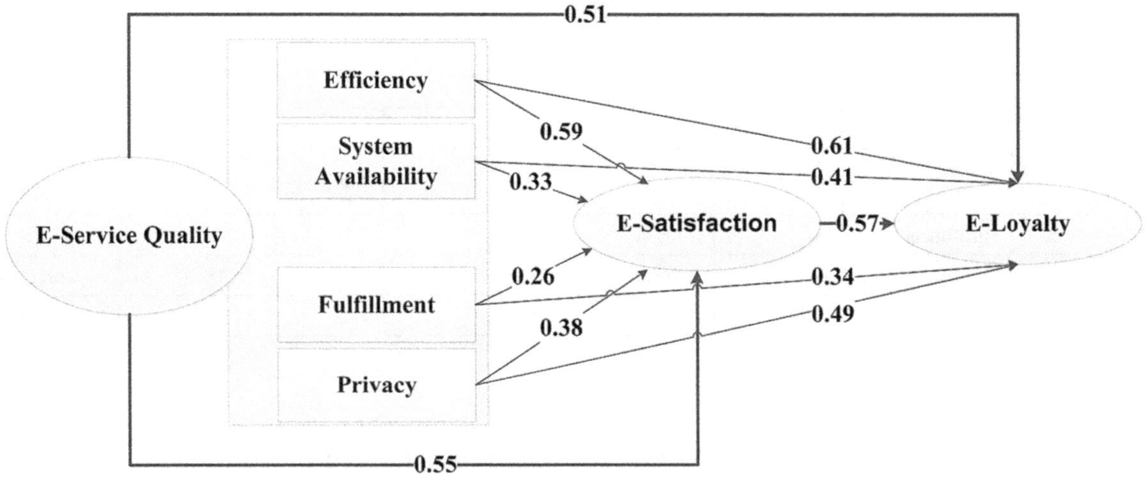

than 0.05 show a significant difference of the computed values for regression weights of zero at 0.95 of confidence level. Table 4 shows the hypotheses, regression weights, and the index of each hypothesis.

Table 4 showed that there was confirmation for all hypotheses.

5. CONCLUSION AND DISCUSSION

Understanding fans' demands and behavior outcomes can be very useful for sports marketing managers to effectively and efficiently determine e-marketing strategies that will lead to long-term relationships. Previous studies in the traditional commercial environment related to conventional marketing have argued the importance of various attributes of service quality that drive consumer satisfaction and associated consumer behavior outcomes. An intensive literature review shows that there have been limited attempts to understand the various attributes of e-service quality in sports fandom. Limited research has also simultaneously assessed e-service quality and satisfaction in conjunction with fan loyalty. This study can be critical in holistically understanding fans' e-service experiences across websites of sports clubs.

The modified E-S-QUAL designed for this study has been reliable enough for measuring electronic service quality. According to the relationship between satisfaction, electronic service quality, and loyalty, electronic service quality is a strong indicator of both e-satisfaction and e-loyalty among Persepolis fans in Iran.

Table 4. Hypothesis-testing results

Hypothesis		Path		Regression Weights	C.R.	P	Result
H1	E- service quality	→	E-satisfaction	0.55	9.25	***	Supported
H1a	Efficiency	→	E-satisfaction	0.59	10.15	***	Supported
H1b	System Availability	→	E-satisfaction	0.33	4.56	***	Supported
H1c	Fulfillment	→	E-satisfaction	0.26	4.01	0.006	Supported
H1d	Privacy	→	E-satisfaction	0.38	5.32	***	Supported
H2	E- service quality	→	E-loyalty	0.51	8.72	***	Supported
H2a	Efficiency	→	E-loyalty	0.61	12.82	***	Supported
H2b	System Availability	→	E-loyalty	0.41	7.68	***	Supported
H2c	Fulfillment	→	E-loyalty	0.34	4.71	***	Supported
H2d	Privacy	→	E-loyalty	0.49	9.01	***	Supported
H3	Satisfaction	→	E-loyalty	0.57	9.43	***	Supported

*** $p < 0.001$.

All dimensions of electronic service quality had significant and positive effects on e-satisfaction as well as on e-loyalty. Among all four dimensions of E-S-QUAL, "efficiency" influenced e-loyalty the most. The results revealed that electronic satisfaction has a positive and significant effect on electronic loyalty. Electronic satisfaction also has a mediating role between electronic service quality and electronic loyalty. The research outcomes were consistent with the findings of prior studies conducted by Harris and Harrington (2000), Parasuraman et al. (2005), Fuentes-Blasco et al. (2010), and Marimon et al. (2010). It should be emphasized that this study was conducted in the sports environment, which makes it novel.

Based on the findings, sports managers and sports marketers should do their best to deliver their websites and contents with the best quality to create customer loyalty and satisfaction. Although, we found "efficiency" as the most effective factor for e-loyalty and e-satisfaction, sports managers and sports marketers should put more weight on efficiency items that are relevant to sports websites. Increasing download speed, expanding websites' ease of use, and delivering classified and customized services are strongly recommended. A well-designed website results in better brand recognition (Liu et al., 2000). Zeithaml et al. (2002), Wolfinbarger and Gilly (2001), and Kim et al. (2006) suggested that information availability and content are also key aspects of online shopping.

Since electronic satisfaction has a mediating role between electronic service quality and electronic loyalty, sports managers and sports marketers need to incorporate proper strategies to satisfy sports fans with sports website features. Implementing website users' comments and recommendations for improving website quality, as well as inviting fans to participate in the process of designing and providing proper services, can be critical for creating satisfied and loyal sports fans.

The aim of clubs always is in creating fans who will be loyal to them. Thus, there must be respect for loyal fans, and consideration of the extent of their satisfaction toward club activities. The best advisers are fans, who are a no-cost way to improve business offerings. Fans are different, and their needs are different. Therefore, it is necessary to tailor each service to the moods of fans to achieve satisfaction.

The key is attraction and retention of customers, which requires improving their positive attitude about the supply of services. By improving the quality of services and customer satisfaction, they are more likely to use the services of a sports club and even suggest the club to others. To make loyal club fans, the club itself must prepare a comprehensive plan. The first step for sports clubs is to survey the audience and be aware of the level of their expectations for services. In the next step, the club should design functional and technical services that surpass customer expectations.

A better understanding of the dimensions of service quality by club managers will allow for improvement in the level of services provided to customers, along with an increase in the number of customers. In addition, the club will become more profitable. According to the quality of service, the satisfaction and loyalty of fans of sports clubs can play a role in the survival and profitability of clubs. Therefore, this research is important because it focuses on variables in all sports centers and compares metrics of service quality, satisfaction, and loyalty, which bring valuable results.

This study suggests that sports center managers consider all the variables of research and try to provide appropriate services and programs designed specifically for different age groups. Considering the reasonable price, sports centers should continuously evaluate customer satisfaction and loyalty and try to attract loyal customers with their business center.

Unfortunately, the study observed many managers who run centers without conducting any research about customers. They said that they know all the problems and needs of their customers, but they had no plans to solve those problems.

Unfortunately, due to the limited number of suitable recreation centers in Iran, the idea of providing better service than competitors has not been established and centers were providing any services attract a good number of customers.

The findings provide a large number of theoretical, managerial, and future research implications. However, interpretation of these implications should be with cautious due to some limitations. The current study has encountered certain limitations that make it difficult to apply the findings to other industries. Firstly, sports clubs, as well as their goods and services, are largely different from other industries. Secondly, compared to other industries, sports websites are mainly engaged in delivering intangible services, which makes them unique. The research population of the current study consisted of website users who subscribed to the website for the Persepolis football team, as one of the most popular teams in Iran; thus, according to structural, cultural, and personal differences, generalizing the findings to other teams could be difficult. The findings' validity is limited to a short period, which makes this field so uncertain. In case of data collection, online surveys are highly recommended. Using the online survey can cause some problems, such as taking a long time to collect data. Additionally, the results of this study are difficult to generalize because of the research context. Conduction of this study was in Iran, which is a developing country; therefore, this makes the generalization of the findings to developed countries more difficult. In addition, we received several incomplete questionnaires. We should take into account these limitations in the future.

REFERENCES

Akinci, S., Atilgan-Inan, E., & Aksoy, S. (2010). Re-assessment of E-S-Qual and E-RecS-Qual in a pure service setting. *Journal of Business Research*, *63*(1), 232–240. doi:10.1016/j.jbusres.2009.02.018

Al-Hawari, M., & Ward, T. (2006). The effect of automated service quality on Australian banks' financial performance and the mediating role of customer satisfaction. *Marketing Intelligence & Planning*, *24*(2), 127–147. doi:10.1108/02634500610653991

Allameh, S. M., Shekarchizadeh Esfahani, S., Khazaei Pool, J., & Hadinezhad, M. (2012). Studying Effective Factors on Accepting On-line Stock Transactions (Case Study: Investors of the Isfahan Stock Exchange). *American Journal of Scientific Research*, *77*(1), 54–66.

Anderson, R. E., & Srinivasan, S. S. (2003). E-satisfaction and e-loyalty: A contingent framework. *Psychology and Marketing*, *20*(2), 123–138. doi:10.1002/mar.10063

Audrain-Pontevia, A. F., N'Goala, G., & Poncin, I. (2013). A good deal online: The Impacts of acquisition and transaction value on E-satisfaction and E-loyalty. *Journal of Retailing and Consumer Services*, *20*(5), 445–452. doi:10.1016/j.jretconser.2013.04.002

Baida, Z., Gordijn, J., Akkermans, H., Saele, H., & Morch, A. Z. (2005). Finding e-service offerings by computer-supported customer need reasoning. *International Journal of E-Business Research*, *1*(3), 91–112. doi:10.4018/jebr.2005070105

Barrutia, J. M., & Gilsanz, A. (2013). Electronic Service Quality and Value: Do Consumer Knowledge-Related Resources Matter? *Journal of Service Research*, *16*(2), 231–246. doi:10.1177/1094670512468294

Bloemer, J., de Ruyter, K., & Wetzels, M. (1999). Linking perceived service quality and service loyalty: A multi-dimensional perspective. *European Journal of Marketing*, *33*(11/12), 1082–1107. doi:10.1108/03090569910292285

Boshoff, C. (2007). A psychometric assessment of E-S-QUAL: A scale to measure electronic service quality. *Journal of Electronic Commerce Research*, *8*(1), 101–114.

Butt, M. M., & Aftab, M. (2013). Incorporating attitude towards Halal banking in an integrated service quality, satisfaction, trust and loyalty model in online Islamic banking context. *International Journal of Bank Marketing*, *31*(1), 6–23. doi:10.1108/02652321311292029

Buttle, F., & Burton, J. (2002). Does service failure influence customer loyalty? *Journal of Consumer Behaviour*, *1*(3), 217–227. doi:10.1002/cb.67

Carlson, J., & O'Cass, A. (2010). Exploring the relationships between e-service quality, satisfaction, attitudes and behaviours in content-driven e-service web sites. *Journal of Services Marketing*, *24*(2), 112–127. doi:10.1108/08876041011031091

Chang, H., & Wang, H. (2011). The moderating effect of customer perceived value on online shopping behavior. *Online Information Review*, *35*(3), 333–359. doi:10.1108/14684521111151414

Cheng, T. C., Lai, L. C. F., & Yeung, A. C. (2008). The driving forces of customer loyalty: A study of internet service providers in Hong Kong. *International Journal of E-Business Research*, *4*(4), 26–42. doi:10.4018/jebr.2008100103

Craig-Lees, M. A., Harris, J., & Maulana, A. E. (2013). Websites and revisiting behaviour: An investigation of the relative role of predictors. *Marketing Intelligence & Planning*, *31*(3), 250–271. doi:10.1108/02634501311324609

Cristobal, E., Flavian, C., & Guinaliu, M. (2007). Perceived e-service quality (PeSQ): Measurement validation and effects on consumer satisfaction and website loyalty. *Managing Service Quality*, *17*(3), 317–340. doi:10.1108/09604520710744326

Esmaeili, M. (2014). Assessment of Users' Information Security Behavior in Smartphone Networks. *Assessment*, *6*, 5–2014.

Esmaeili, M., & Eydgahi, A. (2014, April 3-5). The Relationship of Active Learning Based Courses and Student Motivation for Pursuing STEM Classes. *Proceedings of the ASEE 2014 Zone1 Conference*, Bridgeport, CT, USA.

Eydgahi, A., & Esmaeili, M. (2014) Enhancing Engineering Education through Active Learning and Project Based Courses. *Proceedings of the 3rd conference on engineering education.*

Finn, A. (2011). Investigating the non-linear effects of e-service quality dimensions on customer satisfaction. *Journal of Retailing and Consumer Services*, *18*(1), 27–37. doi:10.1016/j.jretconser.2010.09.002

Fuentes-Blasco, M., Gil-Saura, I., Berenguer-Contrı´, G., & Moliner-Vela'zquez, B. (2010). Measuring the antecedents of e-loyalty and the effect of switching costs on website. *Service Industries Journal*, *30*(11), 1837–1852. doi:10.1080/02642060802626774

Gera, R. (2011). Modelling e-service quality and its consequences in India: An SEM approach. *Journal of Research in Interactive Marketing*, *5*(2/3), 203–225. doi:10.1108/17505931111187811

Giovanis, A. N., & Athanasopoulou, P. (2014). Gaining customer loyalty in the e-tailing marketplace: the role of e-service quality, e-satisfaction and e-trust. *International Journal of Technology Marketing 6, 9*(3), 288-304.

Ha, Y., & Im, H. (2012). Role of website design quality in satisfaction and word of mouth generation. *Journal of Service Management*, *23*(1), 79–96. doi:10.1108/09564231211208989

Harris, M., & Harrington, H. J. (2000). Service quality in the knowledge age – huge opportunities for the twenty first century. *Measuring Business Excellence*, *4*(4), 31–36. doi:10.1108/13683040010362562

Jih, W. J., Lee, S. F., & Tsai, Y. C. (2010). Effects of website Interactivity on e-loyalty: A social exchange perspective. [IJEBR]. *International Journal of E-Business Research*, *6*(4), 1–12. doi:10.4018/jebr.2010100101

Kim, J., Jin, B., & Swinney, J. (2009). The role of e-tail quality, e-satisfaction and e-trust in online loyalty development process. *Journal of Retailing and Consumer Services, 16*(4), 239–247. doi:10.1016/j.jretconser.2008.11.019

Kim, J., & Kim, C. (2010). E-service quality perceptions: a cross-cultural comparison of American and Korean consumers. *Journal of Research in Interactive Marketing*, 4(30), 257-275.

Kim, M., Kim, J. H., & Lennon, S. J. (2006). Online service attributes available on apparel retail websites: An E-S-QUAL approach. *Managing Service Quality, 16*(1), 51–77. doi:10.1108/09604520610639964

Kotler, P. (2003). *Marketing Management*. Englewood Cliffs, NJ: Prentice-Hall.

Ladhari, R. (2010). Developing e-service quality scales: A literature review. *Journal of Retailing and Consumer Services, 17*(6), 464–477. doi:10.1016/j.jretconser.2010.06.003

Lee, S., Jih, W. J., & Fang, S. R. (2006). Investigating the Impact of Customer Relationship Management Practices of E-Commerce on Online Customer's Web Site Satisfaction: A Model-Building Approach. *International Journal of E-Business Research, 2*(4), 61–77. doi:10.4018/jebr.2006100104

Lu, L. C., Chang, H. H., & Yu, S. T. (2013). Online shoppers' perceptions of e-retailers' ethics, cultural orientation, & loyalty: An exploratory study in Taiwan. *Internet Research, 23*(1), 47–68. doi:10.1108/10662241311295773

Marimon, F., Petnji Yaya, L. H., & Casadesus Fa, M. (2012). Impact of e-Quality and service recovery on loyalty: A study of e-banking in Spain. *Total Quality Management & Business Excellence, 23*(7-8), 769–787. doi:10.1080/14783363.2011.637795

Marimon, F., Vidgen, R., Barnes, S., & Cristobal, E. (2010). Purchasing behaviour in an online supermarket: The applicability of E-S-QUAL. *International Journal of Market Research, 52*(1), 111–129. doi:10.2501/S1470785310201089

Meng, J., & Mummalaneni, V. (2010). Measurement equivalency of web service quality instruments: A test on Chinese and African American consumers. *Journal of International Consumer Marketing, 22*(3), 259–269, 1528–7068. doi:10.1080/08961531003751165

Nam, J., Ekinci, Y., & Whyatt, G. (2011). Brand equity, brand loyalty and consumer satisfaction. *Annals of Tourism Research, 38*(3), 1009–1030. doi:10.1016/j.annals.2011.01.015

Oliver, R. L. (1999). Whence customer loyalty? *Journal of Marketing, 63*(4), 33–44. doi:10.2307/1252099

Parasuraman, A., Zeithaml, V. A., & Malhotra, A. (2005). E-S-QUAL: A multiple-item scale for assessing electronic service quality. *Journal of Service Research, 7*(3), 213–233. doi:10.1177/1094670504271156

Pearson, A., Tadisina, S., & Griffin, C. (2012). The role of e-service quality and information quality in creating perceived value: Antecedents to web site loyalty. *Information Systems Management, 29*(3), 201–215. doi:10.1080/10580530.2012.687311

Reichheld, F. F., & Schefter, P. (2000). E-loyalty: Your secret weapon on the web. *Harvard Business Review, 87*(4), 105–113.

Rezaei, H., Khazaei Pool, J., & Shabani, J. (2012). Investigating Intention to e-shopping Based on Expansion of Technology Acceptance Model. *New Marketing Research Journal*, *2*(1), 93–110.

Rezaei Dolatabadi, H., & Khazaei Pool, J. (2013). Analysis Electronic Service Quality through E-S-Qual Scale: The Case Study of Nowshahr Hotel, *Research Journal of Applied Sciences. Engineering and Technology*, *5*(7), 2321–2326.

Ribbink, D., van Riel, A. C. R., Liljander, V., & Streukens, S. (2004). Comfort your online customer: Quality, trust and loyalty on the internet. *Managing Service Quality*, *14*(6), 446–456. doi:10.1108/09604520410569784

Santos, J. (2003). E-service quality: A model of virtual service quality dimensions. *Managing Service Quality*, *13*(3), 233–246. doi:10.1108/09604520310476490

Shaemi, A., Khazaei Pool, J., Pormostafa, M., & Balouei, H. (2012). The classified Web Qual variable is based on Kano Model for the Evaluation of customer satisfaction of internet banking service quality. *New Marketing Research Journal*, *2*(2), 123–142.

Sheng, T., & Liu, C. (2010). An empirical study on the effect of e-service quality on online customer satisfaction and loyalty. *Nankai Business Review International*, *1*(3), 273–283. doi:10.1108/20408741011069205

Skogland, I., & Siguaw, J. (2004). Are your satisfied Customers loyal? *The Cornell Hotel and Restaurant Administration Quarterly*, *45*(3), 221–234. doi:10.1177/0010880404265231

Sousa, R. (2012). The moderating effect of channel use on the quality-loyalty relationship in multichannel e-services. *International Journal of Quality & Reliability Management*, *29*(9), 1019–1037. doi:10.1108/02656711211272935

Springer, M., Tyran, C., & Ross, S. (2013). Assessing the quality of a decision support e-service. *International Journal of E-Business Research*, *9*(2), 61–80. doi:10.4018/jebr.2013040105

Theodorakis, N. D., Alexandris, K., Tsigilis, N., & Karvounis, S. (2013). Predicting spectators' behavioural intentions in professional football: The role of satisfaction and service quality. *Sport Management Review*, *16*(1), 85–96. doi:10.1016/j.smr.2012.05.004

Vos, A., Marinagi, C., Trivellas, P., Eberhagen, N., Giannakopoulos, G., & Skourlas, C. (2014). Electronic service quality in online shopping and risk reduction strategies. *Journal of Systems and Information Technology*, *16*(3), 170–186. doi:10.1108/JSIT-01-2014-0008

Weathers, D., & Makienko, I. (2006). Assessing the Relationships between E-tail Success and Product and Website Factors. *Journal of interactivity marketing,* 20(2), 41-54.

Yang, Z., & Peterson, R. T. (2004). Customer perceived value, satisfaction, and loyalty: The role of switching costs. *Psychology and Marketing*, *21*(10), 799–822. doi:10.1002/mar.20030

This research was previously published in the International Journal of E-Business Research (IJEBR), 12(1); edited by Payam Hanafizadeh and Jeffrey Hsu, pages 43-57, copyright year 2016 by IGI Publishing (an imprint of IGI Global).

Chapter 25
The Rise of the Modern Sports Article:
Examining the Factors That Can Influence the Credibility of Online Sports News

Sean R. Sadri
Old Dominion University, USA

ABSTRACT

The evolution of online media has brought forth a new age of fandom online for sport enthusiasts with access to hundreds of new sports articles daily. This chapter touches on the perceived credibility of the modern sports article and provides evidence from scholarly studies, including the author's own sports credibility study. The study examines how article source, medium, fan identification, and user comment tone can all impact the credibility of a sports article. Study participants were randomly assigned to read a sports article in 1 of 12 stimuli groups. The article source was indicated to have appeared on a mainstream sports website, a sports blog, a social networking site, or a wire service as well as with positive comments, negative comments, or without comments. Analysis revealed that fan identification level was an important factor in credibility ratings as highly identified fans found the article to be significantly more credible than low identification fans as a whole. The study implications and factors influencing the credibility of an online sports article are explored.

INTRODUCTION

Few aspects of American life compare to an old-fashioned sports rivalry. Nearly every fan has a favorite team, and every team has a bitter rival. Coaches and players spend all season preparing for this rivalry game they desperately want to win. For the players, it's glory on the gridiron, the field, the rink, or the court, and a chance to establish themselves under the bright lights. For the fans, these games may mean even more. Crowds pack the parking lots hours before the game to tailgate with friends and support their team. Team logos are seen on clothing, windshields, and even license plates, and it clearly establishes

DOI: 10.4018/978-1-5225-5475-2.ch025

what side a fan is rooting for. Fans can easily spot their enemy. The attitude between opposing fans can get contentious, and this all happens before the game even starts. From the opening kickoff to the final whistle, the crowd is raucous and loud as fans from both teams realize what is at stake in a rivalry. When the game is over, the fans from the winning team go home ecstatic with a year of bragging rights. This may seem like insanity, but to a sports fan, this is completely ordinary.

Whether at a live game, in front of a television, or streaming from a cell phone, millions of fans around the world have felt the highs and lows of sport, which has turned sports media into a multi-billion dollar industry. American sports programming in 2014-15 generated $8.47 billion in sales for ABC, CBS, NBC and Fox, accounting for more than one-third (37%) of those companies' overall ad revenue for that period (Crupi, 2015). In 2014, Chevrolet, AT&T, Geico, Verizon, and Budweiser each invested over $250 million in advertising during live sporting events (Crupi, 2015). While digital video recorders (DVRs) have seemingly diminished the value of television ad marketing, sports continues to guarantee a reach of millions of live viewers for hundreds of games a year. Live sports media is also no longer relegated to just television screens. For the first time ever, the National Football League broadcast a regular-season game exclusively on the Internet: October 2015 marked the first time in which audiences around the country needed a computer or mobile device to watch an NFL game (Dougherty, 2015).

Sport has become a staple of American society as millions of fans are influenced by sport every day, and more individuals are becoming interested and active in sports (Wann, Melnick, Russell, & Pease, 2001). Sports and exercise have even come to carry cultural meanings that reflect the ideologies of our wider society and have been recognized as common elements of civic engagement (Beyer & Hannah, 2000). Robbins (2004) argued that in recreational sports (such as those with friends), all players are aware of the basic rules—and the repercussions of violating those rules—and take on roles as self-officiation. Players must create order "by creating a moral code of conduct or an ethos—the spirit of the game" (p. 315). An ethos, or spirit of a culture, is a meaningful system of morals, customs, norms, or practices of a group or society, which can often influence other norms or customs (Geertz, 1973; Robbins, 2004). The inherent competition that exists within sports has also been described by scholars as the ultimate struggle of good and evil, where "winning is a sign of goodness, rightness and divine approval" (Beyer & Hannah, 2000, p. 110).

The ethos of sport is not only manifested in the athletes themselves but also by their fans. Sport fandom is associated with an individual's affinity for specific sports teams. Many fans feel connected to a sports team in ways that go beyond the games themselves and carry over into a person's daily life. Some fans are so engulfed by their relationship to a team's successes and failures that it becomes a part of their social identity (Hu & Tang, 2010). Tajfel's (1981) social identity theory asserted that maintaining memberships in significant social networks would enhance a person's social identity, which in turn results in a more positive self-concept. These significant group memberships and relationships are used in social comparisons to develop and maintain one's self-esteem. The individuals within the group typically develop a system of social norms and values, which regulate their opinions and actions (Turner, 1982). In the sports realm, fan identity is the personal commitment or emotional involvement a person has with a sports organization (Milne & McDonald, 1999).

Fan identification has been shown to predict fan consumption behavior through sport media usage as highly identified fans are more likely to watch games through media or in person, pay more for tickets, and spend more on team merchandise (Laverie & Arnett, 2000). One study found that a person residing in the environment where the team is located, such as a fan of a college football team who lives on the university's campus, may gain enduring social connections (Wann, 2006). Sport fandom has become an important aspect of social relations, and social scientists are showing more interest in understanding fan involvement online (Wann, Friedman & McHale, 2003).

The shift to online-centric media can be felt throughout the journalism industry. The Pew Research Center found that cable news viewership has dropped 8% and newspaper circulation has dropped 3% from 2013 to 2014 (Mitchell, 2015). Newspaper advertising revenue has dropped 4% to $19.9 billion in that same timeframe, but digital ad revenue increased 18% to $50.7 billion. The modern media environment has also changed how individuals receive their news. In a survey of the current state of the news media, Pew Research Center found that half of Facebook users get their news from the social media website (Mitchell, 2014). The survey also suggested that the growth of social media and mobile phones offers media organizations the opportunity to reach more people than ever before.

The gains in online readership over the years may suggest high credibility for news and sports websites, but many of these websites lack proper factual verification, analysis of content, and editorial review (Chung, Kim, & Kim, 2010). The Information Age has diminished perceptions of media credibility in the eyes of citizens because people are generally skeptical of news from the three most popular channels: television, print, and online (Kiousis, 2001). Online credibility has been questioned since the early days of Internet news by some scholars (Newhagen & Levy, 1998), but the way individuals engage with media has changed drastically in the last twenty years.

BACKGROUND

Currently, there is no concrete consensus on the elements that build online credibility, so the present study outlined in this chapter aims to provide media theorists and media professionals a blueprint for what might work for audiences across media. Several facets of online journalism are addressed, including insights on the ever-growing realm of social media. The relevance of this study is amplified by the sheer lack of research on sports journalism and sports ethos. Oates and Pauly (2007) argued that the overall principles of online and traditional media credibility are applicable to sports. The authors argued that "sportswriting fundamentally resembles other forms of reporting and that journalism should not use sports as an ethical straw man against which to defend the virtue of its serious work" (Oates & Pauly, 2007, p. 332). However, the scope of this study is not limited to sports because all facets of news credibility can be dictated by some social identity, such as political partisanship. Ultimately, the present study is meant to bring insight and clarity to the evolving discourse on online credibility and digital ethos.

Digital Ethos and Credibility in the Modern Media Environment

Since the turn of the century, the Internet has been blamed by some scholars for the decline in media credibility (Johnson & Kaye, 2000). Because both traditional media and online media are being examined, it is useful to explore literature that compares the two. Kiousis (2001) examined the perceptions of news credibility for television, newspapers, and online, and found that news consumers are generally skeptical of news from all three channels. Newspapers were rated as having the highest credibility, followed by online news, and television news finished third. The author suggests that the dissemination of new technology often shifts opinions of older media. Essentially, access to the Internet may have increased the public trust of newspapers, while simultaneously reducing the trust in television (Kiousis, 2001). Modern news consumers are potentially experiencing a similar situation with cell phone technology and social media, where news is constantly being updated every minute, but there is so much information (much of it erroneous) that people are being disillusioned sifting through the facts and hearsay.

Recent technological advancements have made the job of the journalist easier, but have changed how people get their news and what they expect from it (Meyer, Marchionni & Thorson, 2010). In a study on online credibility, Meyer, Marchionni, and Thorson (2010) determined that an online author's perceived expertise is the strongest predictor of article and organization credibility. They argue that in the Digital Age, perceived expertise is predominantly determined by the level of shared meaning by the sender (journalist, blogger, Tweeter, etc.) and receiver (audience). Apostel and Folk (2005) examined how students evaluate the credibility of websites and online sources through digital ethos. The authors found that students will verify information on one website by trying to find that information on other websites. Students will also evaluate websites based on the design and their initial "feelings" of the site based on that design (characterized as technological ethos). Additionally, students experience citation ethos when other sources link *to* their chosen website. Essentially, credibility is bestowed by the link citations a website receives rather than the links it gives.

Digital ethos and a communal identity can also influence the ways in which news consumers perceive credibility. Gamie (2013) examined digital ethos construction and the sense of shared identity that was forged on the Facebook pages of two Egyptian groups during the 2011 Egyptian Revolution. The author found that anonymity played a profound role in digital discourses and created a sense of community by legitimizing calls for activism, reform, and revolutionary work. The author asserts that activist discourse can function more positively and safely in an anonymous environment as facelessness preserves digital ethos. However, when identities are exposed, individuals can become targets of regime operatives, thus making anonymity paramount.

Digital ethos has also been used to examine the credibility of Wikipedia and its dramatic influence on the Internet, popular culture, and the production and consumption of knowledge (McGrady, 2013). Wikipedia and other Wiki sites exhibit credibility through a community ethos that acknowledges the fallibility of its individual parts. The Wikipedia community has evolved over time, and rules within this community were created to standardize, organize, and mobilize masses to help eliminate the spread of erroneous information. The credibility of each page grows as more information becomes available and statements on pages can be validated with external links.

In the same way that Wikipedia has evolved with the Internet, online newspapers have become much more than simple web-based versions of a printed newspaper. They implement a bevy of additional content (such as videos, audio, and external hyperlinks) as well as provide users up-to-the-minute updates of the day's events. A survey on web 2.0 credibility (i.e., social networking, blogs, wikis, etc.) found that journalists in countries like Portugal consider these web 2.0 news sources to be unreliable (Serra & Canavilhas, 2013). However, a disconnect exists because the majority of journalists surveyed still use these sources to discover new stories and look for new stories. The authors assert that journalists rely on both the traditional means of assessing credibility (such as interviewing and reputation) and the newer means of credibility based on group assessments and collective intelligence.

The Internet has also given rise to the online-only news site, which can offer users a different perspective on national and global news. Chung, Kim, and Kim (2010) examined online newspaper credibility and divided online news into three distinct categories: mainstream, independent, and index. Their study determined that the mainstream type of online newspapers, such as *USAToday.com*, received the highest scores on most credibility items. However, the index type of news (or an online newsfeed providing news from various sources) was rated highest in creativeness, attractiveness, and having interesting items.

The authors argued that a website like *Google News* empowers users by offering them many choices of content. Online news consumers also have the freedom to subscribe to topics that interest them, such as sports news or entertainment news. The online-only independent news source had the lowest reported scores in expertise, attractiveness, and trustworthiness. Echoing these findings, Gunter (2006) determined that Internet users typically trust online news produced by established news providers more than news produced by independent online sources. The authors found that news credibility is mediated primarily by the reputation of the news supplier's brand and the relative partisanship or neutrality of news consumers on specific issues. This is analogous to sports fans who find articles disparaging of their favorite team and dismiss them for being biased, inaccurate, or untrue.

Fan Identification and the Perceived Credibility of Online Sports Articles

Social identity theory is inherently based in comparisons, so this theory can be applied to sports fans who often make comparisons between themselves and the outgroup (fans of rival teams). Wann, Dimmock, and Grove (2003) suggested that one "societal connection that may have important benefits for psychological health involves the strong ties fans often feel for their chosen sports team (i.e., those fans who are highly identified with their team)" (p. 289). Team identification has also been shown to facilitate a fan's well-being by increasing the likelihood of obtaining temporary and enduring social connections (Wann, 2006). Conversely, this beneficial relationship for fans is moderated by threats to a fan's social identity, such as a team's poor performance during the season.

The social connections established through sporting events and fan relationships are seemingly amplified through sports media. Wann and Branscombe (1992) found that the emotional responses to a sports article were different based on the level of identification with the sports team being covered. Highly identified fans experienced the most positive mood state when the article described a victory for the ingroup sports team, and whose author was an admitted loyal fan of that team. The most negative mood state was evoked when the team lost the competition and the article author was a disloyal fan of the participant's favorite team. The study also discovered that participants with low fan identification were not significantly influenced by the article author's group membership, the author's commitment to the team, or the game outcome.

Online readers have also been shown to seek out blogs that are tailored to their specific interests (Johnson & Kaye, 2004). Johnson and Kaye (2004) found that blog users judged blogs as highly credible and more credible than traditional media sources. Blog users in the study "rely on blogs because they provide more depth and more thoughtful analysis than is available in other media" (p. 633). Unbiased reporting is often considered a hallmark of traditional journalism, but the authors suggested that noticeable bias is seen as a virtue by blog users. For example, the majority of participants rated themselves as conservative, so they actively seek out conservative blogs that support their views and promote a community ethos. Sports fans will often seek out blogs that are dedicated to their favorite team but may not be objective and may refrain from being critical of that team.

For fans, the highs and lows experienced by wins and losses may even extend past the sports environment itself and validating their personal sports ethos. Van Leeuwen, Quick, and Daniel (2002) asserted that fans feel a sense of attachment to a university represented by the school's sports teams. The authors found that students at a university may feel closer to their university through sport than everyday college life, and social identity through college athletics goes well beyond on-field success. A similar study determined that college students list their parents, the talent of the players, geographical reasons (i.e., rooting for the home team), and the influence of one's friends and peers all ahead of team success as reasons they originally started following their favorite team (Wann, Tucker & Schrader, 1996). At certain universities, athletic programs also provide a sense of communal involvement within the institution, the local community, and, in some cases, an entire state (Melnick, 1993). Other scholars have found a positive relationship between identification for a university's men's basketball and football teams and a student's enjoyment and satisfaction with that university, the extent to which the university met expectations, as well as involvement and persistence at the university (Wann & Robinson, 2002).

In the field of sports broadcasting, Keene and Cummins (2009) examined the effects of a sports commentator's previous athletic experience on the perceived credibility of the broadcaster and viewer evaluations of game play. They found that athletic experience impacts perceptions of credibility, such that commentators without playing experience were viewed as least credible and participants rated their games as less enjoyable and exciting. Even a sportscaster's appearance has been shown to impact how audiences judge credibility. Scholars have found that physical attractiveness in a female sportscaster is positively correlated with competence, dynamism, expertness, and trustworthiness (Davis & Krawczyk, 2010).

The Impact of Anonymous User Comments on Credibility

The chapter author's present study also examines the impact of user comments on the perceived credibility of sports articles. The social identification/deindividuation (SIDE) model of computer-mediated communication effects is a useful tool for understanding the influence of visually anonymous peers (Reicher, Spears & Postmes, 1995). Based on previous research in this field (Lea, Spears, Watt & Rogers, 2000; Walther, DeAndrea, Kim & Anthony, 2010), this model asserts that an online reader's level of identification with online peer users can influence evaluations of credibility. Unlike Facebook wall posts from friends, the SIDE model puts primary emphasis on visual anonymity, which is essential for predicting and understanding online behavior (Lea et al., 2000). Applying the SIDE model to their study on YouTube comments, Walther et al. (2010) examined the influence of user comments on perceptions of YouTube anti-marijuana public service announcements (PSAs). The results showed that supportive or negative comments affected the study participant's evaluations of the PSAs, but did not affect a participant's attitude toward marijuana. However, the combination of user comments and the social identification of the participants to the users affected both PSA evaluations and attitudes towards marijuana positively or negatively, depending on the tone of those comments.

Scholars argue that an anonymous computer environment can give people the freedom to enact new identities and liberate themselves from the limitations brought on by reality, identity, expectations, and conventions (Turkle, 1996). Online identity is essentially a form of digital ethos in which individuals can recreate themselves into anything they imagine. Countering this argument, Postmes, Spears and Lea (1998) argued that even though a potential for identity replacement exists, people may not always want to free themselves from social constraints and look to the Internet to reinforce their real-world identities. The SIDE model suggests that an anonymous encounter in a group diverts attention from the individual level of interaction and focuses attention on the social level, which continually emphasizes social boundaries and the ingroup/outgroup dynamic (Postmes, Spears & Lea, 1998). This model is useful for examining the role of user comments in sports articles where the large majority of online users are completely anonymous. Thus, highly identified sports fans could be more likely to find an article as credible if the user comments are positive about their favorite team than if the comments are negative.

Additionally, participants with low fan identification often will not waver in their credibility assessments based on the user comments.

Ultimately, there are a multitude of factors that can affect the level of credibility attributed to online sports articles. The purpose of the study in this chapter is to examine the impact of the medium and the sports news source(s) on the credibility of sports articles for fans with both high and low identification. Looking specifically at differences in online media (sports website, social networking website, and sports blog) and comparing those with a more traditional form of media (wire service), this study tested the effects of sports fan identification on the perceived credibility of a sports article. Using social identity theory, fan identification, and the SIDE model as the primary theoretical frameworks, the study also analyzed how credibility assessments of a sports article are affected by positive and negative user comments. Building off of Chung, Kim, and Kim's (2010) study on online credibility, the present study examined the influence of the website itself on credibility by comparing a mainstream sports news source (ESPN.com), an independent sports news source (a sports blog), and an index sports news source (a Facebook note) in the experiment, and compared those to a traditional wire service (*Associated Press*).

STUDY DESIGN AND METHODOLOGY

The present study was an online experiment looking primarily at online news sources, so it was designed to reflect the natural setting of reading an online article and was administered online. A convenience sample of college students was used based on availability and accessibility to a sample population at a large public academic institution in the southeastern United States. Although a convenience sample is not ideal because the findings are less generalizable, the use of a convenience sample of college students has been utilized in previous scholarly studies involving sports fans. For example, Wann and Branscombe (1992) used college students in their study on fan emotional responses to the sports page, and Pham (1992) used a sample group of undergraduate students to study the effects of fan involvement and arousal on the recognition of sponsorship stimuli at a sporting event. In the present study, the participants were recruited from undergraduate mass communication classes, and extra credit was offered as an incentive for participation in the study. The present study had a total of 376 participants, all of whom were undergraduate students at the university. The mean age was 20.45 years old, and the majority of participants were female ($N = 255$) (Table 1).

Because the sample population had more female participants than male participants, a potential gender bias may have shifted the results. However, additional analysis was conducted after the data was collected, and the results showed that men and women had similar scores in nearly every scale used. Both genders had statistically similar scores on the fan identification scale ($F(1, 374) = 1.74, p = .190$), which was the basis for determining whether a participant was classified as a highly identified fan or low identification fan. Identification scores with the university ($F(1, 374) = 2.38, p = .124$) and with the anonymous users ($F(1, 250) = .82, p = .367$) were also close between the two genders. Additionally, males and females had similar evaluation ratings of the sports news sources ($F(1, 374) = 2.39, p = .123$), so the perceived gender bias did not have a profound impact on the study's results.

Additionally, threats to internal validity can impact the presumed causation between variables in an experiment (Shadish, Cook & Campbell, 2002), so a randomized-groups post-test only experimental design was used to counteract many internal validity threats. A pilot study was also run before conducting the experiment to fix any issues that could arise during the experiment. Appropriate adjustments were

Table 1. Profile of sample population

	Total (N = 376)	Percentage
Gender		
Male	121	32.2
Female	255	67.8
Age		
Average	20.45	
Standard Deviation	1.757	
Fan Identification Level		
Low Identification	174	46.3
High Identification	202	53.7

made to the study based on the outcome of the pilot study and recommendations of the participants. The present study was a 3 x 4 experimental design and participants were randomly assigned to one of twelve stimuli groups, each receiving the same sports article (Table 2). The article was taken from a previously published *Associated Press* article (Pells, 2012) about an NCAA Men's Basketball Tournament game involving the university being studied. The article recapped a basketball game in which the sample population's university had lost and was subsequently eliminated from the NCAA Tournament. Some minor changes to the article were made by the chapter author that did not affect the accuracy or factuality of the article itself.

During the experiment, one group of participants received the stimuli with a large ESPN.com banner at the top of the article, as well as the website's name beneath a fictional author's name. The bottom of the article had three positive user comments from users who support the university's men's basketball team, and the comments were aimed solely at the team, not at the article itself. The second group received the stimuli with a large banner for a popular sports blog that covers the university's athletic program at the top of the article, as well as the website's name beneath the fictional author's name. The bottom of the article also had three positive comments from supporters of the university's team. The third group received the stimuli as a Facebook note with the same fictional author and a large Facebook symbol at the top of the article. The note also had three positive comments at the end of the article. The large banners were all the same size and font and were designed to look nearly identical. The anonymous user comments were also identical for all three online sources.

The fourth, fifth, and sixth groups received the same initial stimuli with the same online sources as the previous three. However, these groups received a set of three negative user comments from users who

Table 2. 3 x 4 experimental design

ESPN.com Article	Sports Blog Article	Facebook Note	Wire Service Article
Positive User Comments (30*)	Positive User Comments (29)	Positive User Comments (33)	Positive User Comments (31)
Negative User Comments (32)	Negative User Comments (32)	Negative User Comments (32)	Negative User Comments (33)
No Comments (30)	No Comments (33)	No Comments (30)	No Comments (31)

*Note: Number denotes the number of participants that completed the study in each cell.

support a rival university's team at the bottom of the article. The user comments would be analogous to a Real Madrid fan posting disparaging comments on a soccer article about FC Barcelona immediately after Barcelona had been eliminated from the UEFA Champion's League tournament. The negative comments were targeted solely at the university's men's basketball team and were not disparaging of the article itself. The seventh, eighth, and ninth groups were control groups which received the article with one of the three online sources without any user comments. The comments and the fictional usernames used were all written by the chapter author, and the user comments were all reviewed in the pilot study and deemed as appropriate by the pilot study participants.

The final three groups received the stimuli as an article from a traditional wire service source, the *Associated Press*. The article had an *Associated Press* logo at the top of the article, as well as typed beneath the author's name. One group received only the article itself, while the two final groups received either positive or negative reader comments at the bottom of the page.

Because this experiment was focused on the potential impact of social identity, the manipulations of positive and negative user comment tone were measured by how positively or negatively participants identified with the anonymous users. The manipulations were analyzed after the experiment using an anonymous user comment scale, developed by Postmes, Spears, Sakhel, and de Groot (2001). Data analysis determined that the user comments with a positive tone ($M = 3.62$, $SD = 1.62$) garnered a higher identification score from participants than the user comments with a negative tone ($M = 2.19$, $SD = 1.35$). A univariate ANOVA was conducted, and it was determined that a significant difference existed between the two user comment tones ($F(1, 250) = 57.59$, $p < .001$), thereby validating the manipulations and suggesting that the user comments were appropriately constructed for this study.

The experiment began with a questionnaire that measured the participant's level of identification as a sports fan in general, as well as a fan of the university's men's basketball team. Total fan identification was measured by combining Shank and Beasley's (1998) refined sports involvement scale with Wann and Branscombe's (1993) team identification scale. The involvement scale asked participants to rate their personal feelings about sports using a 1 – 7 bipolar scale. Participants were asked to indicate if sports are: boring/exciting, uninteresting/interesting, valuable/worthless, unappealing/appealing, useful/useless, needed/not needed, irrelevant/relevant, and unimportant/important. For the present study, the scale was shown to be very reliable (Cronbach's $\alpha = .941$).

The team identification scale consisted of seven questions that addressed how participants feel about the university's men's basketball team (Wann & Branscombe, 1993). The questions asked participants to rate their feelings on a 1 – 8 bipolar scale and included questions regarding how important it is that the team wins, how strongly they see themselves as a fan, how strongly their friends see them as a fan, how closely they follow the team during the season, how important being a fan is to them, how much they dislike the university's biggest rivals, and how often they display the team's name or insignia at work or at home. The team identification scale was also shown to be very reliable for this study (Cronbach's $\alpha = .931$).

These two scales were combined for the purposes of this study to define participants categorized as highly identified fans or fans with low identification. The average score of the sports involvement scale and the team identification scale were summed, and a split of the summed means determined placement into a fan identification group for this study. A mean of the combined score was determined ($M = 9.98$, $SD = 2.93$), and participants with a total above or below that score were placed in the appropriate group. A one-way ANOVA showed that there was a significant difference in mean scores between the two fan identification groups ($F(1, 374) = 763.701$, $p < .001$). Nearly all the participants were at least minimally identified as sports fans, so identification level was defined as either high or low in this study. The initial questionnaire also concluded with a set of demographic questions about participant age, gender, and field of study.

After participants completed the initial questionnaire, they were randomly assigned a sports article in one of twelve groups listed earlier (Table 2). The online experiment was programmed to randomize each group and distribute the stimuli evenly. Before seeing the article, participants received a set of on-screen instructions asking them to read everything that appeared on the following screen and informing them that they will be asked to answer questions about what they have read. The article was the same for every participant, but it was indicated as to have originated from one of the four media organizations. Additionally, unless the participant was assigned to a control scenario, the participant also saw user comments (either positive or negative) at the bottom of the page.

After reading the article, the last aspect of the experiment was a final questionnaire, although certain aspects of the questionnaire varied based on the stimulus that the participant received. The first scale in the questionnaire measured a participant's attitude toward the website the article was said to originate from or the *Associated Press* (O'Cass & Carlson, 2010). Participants were asked to rate how they feel about ESPN.com, a popular sports blog covering the team, Facebook, or the *Associated Press* on a 1 – 7 Likert scale. They were given nine statements about their mood and level of excitement when using the media source, and they were asked to indicate their feelings from "strongly disagree" to "strongly agree." O'Cass and Carlson's (2010) scale was shown to be extremely reliable for the present study (Cronbach's $\alpha = .962$).

Participants were then asked to answer nine questions developed from a scale that measures the perceived credibility of the article (Bucy, 2003). The questions determined how the participants felt about the article itself and provided two contradictory items along a 7 – point bipolar scale. The scale included ratings of how fair, interesting, clear, enjoyable, accurate, believable, informative, and in-depth it was; it also measured nicely the article flowed. The credibility scale was also shown to be highly reliable for this experiment (Cronbach's $\alpha = .89$). For participants who received the stimuli with user comments, the next scale examined a participant's attitude toward the users who posted the anonymous comments (Walther et al., 2010). Participants were given five statements about their connection and identification with that group of people, and asked to rate their feelings on a 7-point bipolar scale ranging from "not at all" to "very much." The participants that were randomly selected for the control groups were not shown this set of statements. This group identity scale was also shown to be very reliable for the present study (Cronbach's $\alpha = .962$).

Because the entire sample population was made up of undergraduate students, the final scale of the experiment was designed to measure the participant's attitude toward the university and the university's relationship to that person's social identity (Mael & Tetrick, 1992). Participants were shown ten statements and asked to mark their opinions on a 7 – point Likert scale. The statements were made to judge how closely the participants identified as a member of the university's community and how emotionally connected they were to their school. Like the other scales used for this study, the university identification scale was shown to be very reliable (Cronbach's $\alpha = .896$). After answering all the questions in the final questionnaire, the participants were shown a post-experiment debrief explaining the purpose of the experiment and the experimental procedures. Finally, participants were thanked for their time and asked not to discuss the study with others while responses were still being collected.

SPORTS ARTICLE CREDIBILITY AND DIGITAL ETHOS: EXAMINING THE STUDY FINDINGS

Online journalism can be subject to the same credibility standards of traditional media, but the around-the-clock nature of the Internet has altered the media landscape and the way news is reported to consumers. News credibility has taken a hit with the public as new (and often unreliable) websites sprout up frequently (Gunter 2006). There is reason to believe this credibility phenomenon has impacted perceptions of media coverage outside of traditional news and translated to the sports world. Sports journalism, both online and offline, is built on the same principles as traditional journalism and can oftentimes be subject to the same ethical standards and guidelines (Oates & Pauly, 2007). Because a number of factors can impact one's perception of a sports article, different aspects of the sports article were examined under the scope of digital ethos to determine what factors make these stories credible.

Influence of Medium on Credibility

In previous studies (Bucy, 2003; Kiousis, 2001; Sundar & Nass, 2001), researchers found that article medium influenced participant evaluations of credibility, so the present study sought to determine how the medium may impact the credibility of a sports article. Looking specifically at the online medium and a wire service, there was no significant difference in credibility scores between the two media ($F(1, 374) = .091, p = .763$), as both were seen as slightly credible. This lack of significance contradicts earlier studies, such as Kiousis's (2001) study on medium credibility, where print was seen as significantly more credible than other types of news media, including online and television. The results of the present study may signify a distinction between sports and news coverage, and suggest that differences exist between the modern interests of sports and news media consumers.

Moreover, the credibility of the online medium for sports media consumers may now rival traditional media based on the dedication of established news organizations providing users with up-to-the-second sports news that is continually updated throughout the day. With cell phone and tablet apps that can stream sports content live, media consumers have become accustomed to online sports access literally at their fingertips. Traditional media, such as the *Associated Press*, may have maintained a level of public trust over the years with fact-checking procedures that may not exist for less-established websites, but there is an aspect of instant gratification and digital ethos that is severely lacking in traditional media. The speed with which the Internet can provide information would seemingly enhance its credibility among consumers, but this may have been offset by the amount of false information that can spread quickly online or game results that can easily be spoiled for fans through social media.

In 2012, NBC came under fire for broadcasting the major competitions of the 2012 London Olympics on tape delay (Levy, 2012). The absence of live coverage for many of the Olympics' major events caused a social media uproar and the trending Twitter hashtag, #NBCFail, from viewers who had the competition results ruined for them online (Levy, 2012). This social media outrage, as well as the same #NBCFail hashtag, continued during the 2014 Sochi Olympics in Russia. The network edited out parts of the opening ceremony, and, just as in London, major competitions were being broadcast on tape delay (Szklarski, 2014). Less than four days after the Olympic broadcasts had begun, #NBCFail was used more than 14,000 times on social media and a petition had been started to rescind the company's broadcast and distribution rights of the Olympics (Szklarski, 2014).

Although television was not tested as a medium in this study, this phenomenon illuminates the instant gratification and digital ethos that people desire from the online medium that is notably absent from all other media platforms. Traditional media is at an even larger disadvantage because media consumers now have the online platform to broadcast their joys or frustrations to followers, and the delay for sports articles and event results does not resonate with readers. Essentially, neither medium was seen as exceedingly credible, but the limitless nature of the Internet for streaming and reporting on sports stories as they occur is an issue for sports journalists and news organizations to consider when attempting to raise the credibility of their brand.

Influence of Article Source and Fan Identification on Credibility

The present study also sought to determine which online source would be regarded as the most credible: ESPN, a sports blog, or Facebook. Despite research to the contrary (Chung, Kim & Kim, 2010; Gunter, 2006), the credibility ratings of the three online sources were not significantly different ($F(2, 278) = 2.04$, $p = .131$), which reflects this study's earlier findings about medium credibility. The overall similarity in credibility scores among the three sources may have occurred because the study participants all received the same article, which was originally published by the *Associated Press*. Because the article covered a real-life sporting event that was factually accurate and may have still been in the participants' minds, it seems logical that participants would rate the article as moderately credible.

The article also covered a sporting event in which the sample population's identified team lost. In a previous fan identification study, Wann, Dolan, McGeorge, and Allison (1994) found that highly identified fans reported greater positive emotions after a win and greater negative emotions after a loss than fans with low identification. Highly identified fans have also been shown to enhance their well-being after a win—and protect it after a loss—by using biased descriptions about the game outcome (Wann, Morriss-Shirkey, Peters & Suggs, 2002). Although the fan identification scales appeared before the article in the present study, the outcome of the game may have impacted participant responses to credibility, and sports ethos may have played a factor. In a seemingly cathartic way, both fan identification groups may have been trying to placate the negative emotions of a team loss by rating the article as less credible than they would have rated a team win. Although fans grow accustomed to reading both positive and negative game outcomes during a season, this particular article recapped a loss in the final game of the season in which the university's team was eliminated from the NCAA tournament, so the effect on credibility ratings could have been more profound.

Wann and Branscobe (1992) determined that emotional responses to a sports article differed based on degree of identification with a sports team, so the present study sought to determine whether a relationship exists between credibility and fan identification. Interestingly, highly identified fans found the article to be significantly more credible as a whole than low identification fans ($F(1, 352) = 44.89$, $p < .001$) and also in eleven out of twelve stimuli groups (Table 3). The fans of a particular team found the article about that team significantly more credible, and this may be due to familiarity with the topic. Some scholars suggest that people are more inclined to judge an article as credible if they are familiar with the subject being covered (Henkel & Mattson, 2011). Topic familiarity may create an "illusion of truth" for statements when people lack cues regarding the reliability of a source. In the present study, highly identified fans are presumably much more familiar with the topic being reported and the sources providing the information, so it seems logical they would rate the article as more credible than low identification fans. Along with familiarity, highly identified fans have a stronger level of sports ethos and attachment

Table 3. Means of credibility scores for each stimuli group separated by identification level

Stimuli Group	N	Mean*	SD
Low Identification			
ESPN Positive	14	4.79	.88
ESPN Negative	11	4.85	1.09
ESPN Control	17	4.04	.86
Blog Positive	12	4.26	1.20
Blog Negative	15	4.01	.86
Blog Control	15	4.11	.86
Facebook Positive	12	4.00	.93
Facebook Negative	20	3.96	.79
Facebook Control	17	4.03	.85
AP Positive	13	4.63	.78
AP Negative	17	4.12	1.23
AP Control	11	4.26	.86
Low Identification Total	174	4.22	.95
High Identification			
ESPN Positive	16	5.26	.80
ESPN Negative	21	4.59	1.00
ESPN Control	13	4.94	.81
Blog Positive	17	5.12	1.09
Blog Negative	17	4.97	.94
Blog Control	18	5.04	.77
Facebook Positive	21	5.01	.91
Facebook Negative	12	4.86	.97
Facebook Control	13	4.70	1.39
AP Positive	18	4.96	1.09
AP Negative	16	4.92	.89
AP Control	20	4.70	.73
High Identification Total	202	4.92	.95

*Mean values can range from 1 to 7.

to the topic being discussed. Although the article was not targeted to an audience of either team's fan base, highly identified fans may have assumed that the article was tailored more toward their own fans, thus rating the article as more credible. Ultimately, the differing level of attachment to the team and the familiarity with the topic may have caused different levels of connection to the article, which resulted in a significant disparity in perceived credibility.

The significant differences in credibility scores may also be connected to the questions that were used to assess credibility. On Bucy's (2003) perceived credibility scale, for example, participants were asked questions regarding the flow and fairness of the article, but there were also asked to assess how enjoyable and interesting it was. A fan with low identification may rate the article as very fair and having a nice flow but may not find the article as enjoyable or interesting to read as a highly identified fan. Because all of these factors have been shown to impact credibility, all of them must be taken into account when researching it. Since highly identified fans already find the articles as moderately credible, sports news websites may try to adapt their stories to the needs of low identification fans in order to gain readership and appeal to a wider audience.

The stimuli groups that garnered the highest credibility scores from each identification group were also noteworthy. The stimuli group that was rated the highest by low identification fans was the ESPN.com group with negative user comments, and for highly identified fans, it was the ESPN.com group with positive user comments. Predictably, the stimuli group that would presumably score the highest from highly identified fans was rated highest by that group. The ESPN brand is established and carries weight in the sports community, and the comments may strike a chord with those participants in the study. Conversely, low identification fans preferred the ESPN article with negative user comments. Fans with low identification were either unaffected by the comments or a lack of connection to the team made the article seem more genuine with comments that do not reflect the common opinion of a fan of the university's basketball team. In a fan identity study, Wann et al. (2001) found that ingroup favoritism and outgroup bias are most likely when individuals are highly identified with their team and their identity has been threatened. In the present study, negative comments can be viewed as a threat to social identity and sports ethos for highly identified fans, which may have caused them to rate those articles harshly. These findings support the notion that high fan identification can significantly influence how readers perceive an article and view ingroup/outgroup members, and they also support the notion that low identification has a much milder effect.

Influence of User Comments on Credibility

User comments have become ubiquitous throughout online media and continue to evolve with technological advancements (Gsell, 2009). Although the impact of anonymous comments on credibility has not been thoroughly researched, the SIDE model suggests that anonymous online interactions can polarize a person's opinions either in favor or against an issue (Lee, 2007). In the present study, it was believed that the tone of the user comments may impact the credibility assessments of highly identified fans. However, there was no significant difference between the credibility scores based on the tone of the comments ($F(2, 299) = 1.61, p = .203$). Anonymous user comments have become a staple of online news and sports articles, and, perhaps, online news readers have become desensitized to user comments over time. The impact of the user comments could have been reduced because highly identified fans may have grown to block out both positive and negative user comments, especially if they do not post regularly in the comments section. The lack of influence on credibility may have also resulted from the intended message of the comments. Sports ethos could have played a factor because the anonymous user comments were directed at the participant's identified team, either lauding or disparaging the team and its season. The comments did not, however, praise or disparage the article itself, which may explain why the credibility ratings were not significantly different for the highly identified fans or the low identification fans ($F(2, 171) = 1.95, p = .145$).

The similarity in credibility scores for both identification groups based on the user comments gives credence to the assumption that people have come to ignore or block out comments in online articles. These findings contradict earlier research on the SIDE model (Walther et al., 2010) in which user comments were shown to influence evaluations of credibility. Walther et al. (2010) found that the perceived credibility of YouTube PSAs can be influenced by the tone of anonymous user comments discussing the serious issue of marijuana use. Controversial topics (e.g., terrorism) and polarizing political news (e.g., Donald Trump's presidential candidacy) may garner a more profound ethos response from readers who see comments that greatly support or oppose their viewpoints, but most sports articles rarely elicit this type of response. Discussing newspaper websites, Gsell (2009) argued that the initial creation of user comments was designed to be a natural complement to online articles with the open culture of the Internet, but that changed when user comments "attracted spam, profanity, harassment, and unpaid advertising onto the site, creating for staff the arduous daily duty of deleting off-color comments" (p. 16). The sheer amount of irrelevant, and often disrespectful, user comments that can be posted on a single article have changed the way online sports media consumers view these comments. Even if user comments have a small impact on news stories, the results of the present study suggest that user comments do not impact the credibility of online sports articles, especially as off-color and irrelevant comments become commonplace.

CONCLUSION

Using fan identification as the primary theoretical framework, this study examined the key factors that can impact the credibility of a sports article across media. Unlike previous findings on credibility (Kiousis, 2001; Sundar & Nass, 2001), medium had little impact on the perceived credibility of the sports article. The results suggest that credibility of all media has seemingly evened out since the turn of the century, where all platforms (print, radio, television, and online) have similar credibility perceptions from news consumers, but none are rated as overly credible. Online media has seemingly come the furthest to a point where people are comfortable using it, but still do not fully trust the information they are receiving.

While there was no significant difference in the perceived credibility of the online sources overall, there was a large disparity in the credibility scores between the two identification groups. Other studies have found similar reactions from highly identified fans regarding their favorite teams, although in different sports ethos areas (Fink et al., 2009, Wann & Branscombe, 1992; Wann & Robinson, 2002). Highly identified fans found the article to be significantly more credible than fans with low identification, which is beneficial for sports media organizations who are trying to maintain readers that already visit their website or read their newspaper. However, this large credibility gap can also become a burden for media organizations who are actively trying to attract new users and engage with their audience. The pressure is now on sports media professionals to deviate from the status quo and experiment with new tactics to draw in less identified fans, such as utilizing new article layouts or new storytelling techniques.

In today's media environment, sports journalists are facing new challenges as they work to appease fans who regularly have credibility concerns and unlimited access to coverage of their favorite teams from a multitude of competing sources. Sports fans, and news consumers in general, are looking for information that is both current and credible, and modern sports journalists must look for ways to break stories as they happen without sacrificing credibility. Ultimately, this study's findings suggest that medium, source, and user comments matter less to fans when making credibility assessments than the level of connection and identity they share with their favorite team. The onus, then, falls on sports journalists to create stories that exude creativity and manage to resonate with every fan, from the most causal to the most diehard. That may mean using data visualization to make statistics easier to follow, integrating social media in a more profound way that speaks directly to readers, or incorporating elements of text, audio, pictures, and video to fully encapsulate the whole story. Technological advancements have made the possibilities endless, and sports journalists need to embrace these possibilities in order to capitalize on technological ethos (Apostel & Folk, 2005) that helps to create content whose credibility connects with a wide readership. Not only will the fans benefit, but sports journalism as a whole will benefit as we enter a new digital age.

REFERENCES

Apostel, S., & Folk, M. (2005). First phase in-formation literacy on a fourth generation Web site: An argument for a new approach to Web site evaluation criteria. *Computers & Composition Online, Spring 2005*. Retrieved March 10, 2016 from http://www2.bgsu.edu/departments/english/cconline/apostelfolk/c_and_c_online_apostel_folk/

Beyer, J. M., & Hannah, D. R. (2000). The Cultural Significance of Athletics in U.S. Higher Education. *Journal of Sport Management*, *14*(2), 105.

Bucy, E. P. (2003). Media Credibility Reconsidered: Synergy Effects Between On-Air and Online News. *Journalism & Mass Communication Quarterly*, *80*(2), 247–264. doi:10.1177/107769900308000202

Chung, C. J., Kim, H., & Kim, J. H. (2010). An anatomy of the credibility of online newspapers. *Online Information Review*, *34*(5), 669–685. doi:10.1108/14684521011084564

Crupi, A. (2015, September 10). Sports Now Accounts for 37% of Broadcast TV Ad Spending: Big Four Nets $8.47 Billion in Ad Sales. *Advertising Age*. Retrieved November 2, 2015, from http://adage.com/article/media/sports-account-37-percent-all-tv-ad-dollars/300310/

Davis, D. C., & Krawczyk, J. (2010). Female Sportscaster Credibility: Has Appearance Taken Precedence? *Journal of Sports Media*, *5*(2), 1–34. doi:10.1353/jsm.2010.0004

Dougherty, P. (2015, October 22). Sports media: Bills-Jaguars telecast on Yahoo could be sign of the future. *TimesUnion.com*. Retrieved November 2, 2015, from http://www.timesunion.com/tuplus-sports/article/Bills-Jaguars-telecast-on-Yahoo-could-be-sign-of-6585347.php

Fink, J. S., Parker, H. M., Brett, M., & Higgins, J. (2009). Off-Field Behavior of Athletes and Team Identification: Using Social Identity Theory and Balance Theory to Explain Fan Reactions. *Journal Of Sport Management*, *23*(2), 142–155.

Gamie, S. (2013). The Cyber-Propelled Egyptian Revolution and the De/Construction of Ethos. In M. Folk & S. Apostel (Eds.), *Online Credibility and Digital Ethos: Evaluating Computer-Mediated Communication* (pp. 316–331). Hershey, PA: IGI Global. doi:10.4018/978-1-4666-2663-8.ch018

Geertz, C. (1973). *The interpretation of cultures: Selected essays*. New York: Basic.

Gsell, L. (2009). Comments Anonymous. *American Journalism Review*, *31*(1), 16–17.

Gunter, B. (2006). Who do online news consumers trust? *Library and Information Update*, *5*(9), 40–41.

Henkel, L. A., & Mattson, M. E. (2011). Reading is believing: The truth effect and source credibility. *Consciousness and Cognition*, *20*(4), 1705–1721. doi:10.1016/j.concog.2011.08.018 PMID:21978908

Hu, A. W., & Tang, L. (2010). Factors Motivating Sports Broadcast Viewership with Fan Identification as a Mediator. *Social Behavior & Personality: An International Journal*, *38*(5), 681–689. doi:10.2224/sbp.2010.38.5.681

Johnson, T. J., & Kaye, B. K. (2000). Using is Believing: The Influence of Reliance on the Credibility of Online Political Information Among Politically Interested Internet Users. *Journalism & Mass Communication Quarterly*, *77*(4), 865–879. doi:10.1177/107769900007700409

Johnson, T. J., & Kaye, B. K. (2004). Wag the Blog: How Reliance on Traditional Media and the Internet Influence Credibility Perceptions of Weblogs Among Blog Users. *Journalism & Mass Communication Quarterly*, *81*(3), 622–642. doi:10.1177/107769900408100310

Keene, J. R., & Cummins, R. G. (2009). Sports Commentators and Source Credibility: Do Those Who Can't Play. . . Commentate? *Journal of Sports Media*, *4*(2), 57–83. doi:10.1353/jsm.0.0042

Kiousis, S. (2001). Public trust or mistrust? Perceptions of media credibility in the information age. *Mass Communication & Society*, *4*(4), 381–403. doi:10.1207/S15327825MCS0404_4

Laverie, D. A., & Arnett, D. B. (2000). Factors affecting fan attendance: The influence of identity salience and satisfaction. *Journal of Leisure Behavior*, *32*(2), 225–246.

Lea, M., Spears, R., Watt, S. E., & Rogers, P. (2000). The InSIDE story: Social psychological processes affecting on-line groups. In T. Postmes, M. Lea, R. Spears, & S. Reicher (Eds.), *SIDE issues centre stage: Recent developments in studies of de-individuation in groups* (pp. 47–62). Amsterdam: KNAW.

Lee, E. J. (2007). Deindividuation effects on group polarization in computer-mediated communication: The role of group identification, public self-awareness, and perceived argument quality. *Journal of Communication*, *57*(2), 385–403. doi:10.1111/j.1460-2466.2007.00348.x

Levy, D. (2012, July 31). 2012 Olympics: NBC Finding New and Unique Ways to Fail American Viewers. *Bleacher Report*. Retrieved August 30, 2012, from http://bleacherreport.com/articles/1279506-2012-olympics-nbc-keeps-finding-new-and-unique-ways-to-fail-american-viewers

Mael, F., & Tetrick, L. (1992). Identifying Organizational Identification. *Educational and Psychological Measurement*, *52*(4), 813–824. doi:10.1177/0013164492052004002

McGrady, R. (2013). Ethos [edit]: Procedural Rhetoric and the Wikipedia Project. In M. Folk & S. Apostel (Eds.), Online Credibility and Digital Ethos: Evaluating Computer-Mediated Communication (pp. 114 -130). Hershey, PA: IGI Global.

Melnick, M. J. (1993). Searching for sociability in the stands: A theory of sports spectating. *Journal of Sport Management*, *7*, 44–60.

Meyer, H. K., Marchionni, D., & Thorson, E. (2010). The Journalist Behind the News: Credibility of Straight, Collaborative, Opinionated, and Blogged "News". *The American Behavioral Scientist, 54*(2), 100–119. doi:10.1177/0002764210376313

Milne, G. R., & McDonald, M. A. (1999). *Sport marketing: Managing the exchange process*. Sudbury, MA: Jones and Bartlett.

Mitchell, A. (2014, March 26). *State of the News Media 2014*. Pew Research Center. Retrieved November 15, 2015, from http://www.journalism.org/2014/03/26/state-of-the-news-media-2014-overview/

Mitchell, A. (2015, April 29). *State of the News Media 2015*. Pew Research Center. Retrieved November 16, 2015, from http://www.journalism.org/2015/04/29/state-of-the-news-media-2015/

Newhagen, J. E., & Levy, M. R. (1998). The future of journalism in a distributed communication architecture. In D. L. Borden & K. Harvey (Eds.), *The Electronic Grapevine: Rumor, Reputation, and Reporting in the New On-Line Environment* (pp. 9–21). Mahwah, NJ: Lawrence Erlbaum Associates.

O'Cass, A., & Carlson, J. (2010). Examining the effects of website-induced flow in professional sporting team websites. *Internet Research, 20*(2), 115–134. doi:10.1108/10662241011032209

Oates, T. P., & Pauly, J. (2007). Sports Journalism as Moral and Ethical Discourse. *Journal of Mass Media Ethics, 22*(4), 332–347. doi:10.1080/08900520701583628

Pells, E. (2012, March 25). Louisville in Final 4 with 72-68 Win over Florida. *The Associated Press*. Retrieved April 1, 2012, from http://www.lexisnexis.com

Pham, M. (1992). Effects of involvement, arousal and pleasure on recognition of sponsorship stimuli. *Advances in Consumer Research. Association for Consumer Research (U. S.), 19*(1), 85–93.

Postmes, T., Spears, R., & Lea, M. (1998). Breaching or building social boundaries: SIDE effects of computer-mediated communication. *Communication Research, 25*(6), 689–715. doi:10.1177/009365098025006006

Postmes, T., Spears, R., Sakhel, K., & de Groot, D. (2001). Social influence in computer-mediated communication: The effects of anonymity on group behavior. *Personality and Social Psychology Bulletin, 27*(10), 1243–1254. doi:10.1177/01461672012710001

Reicher, S. D., Spears, R., & Postmes, T. (1995). A social identity model of deindividuation phenomena. *European Review of Social Psychology, 6*(1), 161–198. doi:10.1080/14792779443000049

Robbins, B. (2004). "That's Cheap." The Rational Invocation of Norms, Practices, and an Ethos in Ultimate Frisbee. *Journal of Sport and Social Issues, 28*(3), 314–337. doi:10.1177/0193723504266992

Serra, P., & Canavilhas, J. (2013). The Credibility of Sources 2.0 in Journalism: Case Study in Portugal. In M. Folk & S. Apostel (Eds.), *Online Credibility and Digital Ethos: Evaluating Computer-Mediated Communication* (pp. 169–185). Hershey, PA: IGI Global. doi:10.4018/978-1-4666-2663-8.ch010

Shadish, W. R., Cook, T. D., & Campbell, D. T. (2002). *Experimental and quasi-experimental designs for generalized causal inference*. Boston: Houghton Mifflin.

Shank, M. D., & Beasley, F. M. (1998). Fan or fanatic: Refining a measure of sports involvement. *Journal of Sport Behavior, 21*(4), 435.

Sundar, S. S., & Nass, C. (2001). Conceptualizing sources in online news. *Journal of Communication*, *51*(1), 52–72. doi:10.1111/j.1460-2466.2001.tb02872.x

Szklarski, C. (2014, February 10). CBC Sochi 2014 Olympics Coverage Attracts Frustrated NBC Viewers. *Huffington Post*. Retrieved December 15, 2015, from http://www.huffingtonpost.ca/2014/02/10/cbc-sochi-2014-olympics_n_4763185.html

Tajfel, H. (1981). *Human groups and social categories*. Cambridge, UK: Cambridge University Press.

Turkle, S. (1996). Parallel lives: Working on identity in virtual space. In D. Grodin & T. R. Lindlof (Eds.), *Constructing the self in a mediated world* (pp. 156–175). Thousand Oaks, CA: Sage. doi:10.4135/9781483327488.n10

Turner, J. C. (1982). Towards a cognitive redefinition of the social group. In H. Tajfel (Ed.), *Social identity and intergroup relations*. Cambridge University Press.

Van Leeuwen, L., Quick, S., & Daniel, K. (2002). The sport spectator satisfaction model: A conceptual framework for understanding the satisfaction of spectators. *Sport Management Review*, *5*(2), 99–128. doi:10.1016/S1441-3523(02)70063-6

Walther, J. B., DeAndrea, D., Kim, J., & Anthony, J. C. (2010). The Influence of Online Comments on Perceptions of Antimarijuana Public Service Announcements on YouTube. *Human Communication Research*, *36*(4), 469–492. doi:10.1111/j.1468-2958.2010.01384.x

Wann, D. L. (2006). Understanding the Positive Social Psychological Benefits of Sport Team Identification: The Team Identification–Social Psychological Health Model. *Group Dynamics*, *10*(4), 272–296. doi:10.1037/1089-2699.10.4.272

Wann, D. L., & Branscombe, N. R. (1992). Emotional Responses to the Sports Page. *Journal of Sport and Social Issues*, *16*(1), 49–64. doi:10.1177/019372359201600104

Wann, D. L., & Branscombe, N. R. (1993). Sports Fans: Measuring Degree of Identification with Their Team. *International Journal of Sport Psychology*, *24*, 1–17.

Wann, D. L., Dimmock, J., & Grove, J. R. (2003). Generalizing the Team Identification–Psychological Health Model to a Different Sport and Culture: The Case of Australian Rules Football. *Group Dynamics*, *7*(4), 289–296. doi:10.1037/1089-2699.7.4.289

Wann, D. L., Dolan, T. J., McGeorge, K. K., & Allison, J. A. (1994). Relationships between spectator identification and spectators' perceptions of influence, spectators' emotions, and competition outcome. *Journal of Sport & Exercise Psychology*, *16*, 347–364.

Wann, D. L., Friedman, K., McHale, M., & Jaffe, A. (2003). The Norelco Sport Fanatics Survey: Examining Behaviors of Sport Fans. *Psychological Reports*, *92*(3), 930–936. doi:10.2466/pr0.2003.92.3.930 PMID:12841467

Wann, D. L., Melnick, M. J., Russell, G. W., & Pease, D. G. (2001). *Sport fans: The psychology and social impact of spectators*. New York: Routledge.

Wann, D. L., Morriss-Shirkey, P. A., Peters, E., & Suggs, W. L. (2002). Highly Identified Sport Fans and Their Conflict between Expression of Sport Knowledge and Biased Assessments of Team Performance. *International Sports Journal*, *6*(1), 153.

Wann, D. L., & Robinson, I. N. (2002). The Relationship Between Sport Team Identification and Integration into and Perceptions of a University. *International Sports Journal*, *6*(1), 36.

Wann, D. L., Tucker, K. B., & Schrader, M. P. (1996). An exploratory examination of the factors influencing the origination, continuation, and cessation of identification with sports teams. *Perceptual and Motor Skills*, *82*(3), 995–1101. doi:10.2466/pms.1996.82.3.995

KEY TERMS AND DEFINITIONS

Associated Press: An American nonprofit news organization founded in 1846 that provides news and information to other media organizations that subscribe to its service.

ESPN: A prominent American-based global sports broadcasting network operating on cable television, satellite television, and online.

Fan Identification: The level at which a sports fan identifies with a particular sport or team.

SIDE Model: The social identity model of deindividuation effects (SIDE) is a communication studies theory developed to describe the social effects of computer-mediated communication. The model suggests that anonymous interactions online can have a profound effect on group behavior.

Social Identity Theory: A social psychological theory asserting that a person's self-concept or identity is maintained through one's group memberships. These significant group memberships and relationships are used in social comparisons to develop and maintain one's self-esteem.

Sport Blog: A web journal that is frequently updated with entries appearing in reverse chronological order and focused specifically on a sport, sports team, or sports topic.

Sports Ethos: The "spirit of the game" for athletes, competitors, and sports fans.

User Comments: Comments posted by readers at the bottom of an online article.

This research was previously published in Establishing and Evaluating Digital Ethos and Online Credibility edited by Moe Folk and Shawn Apostel, pages 309-328, copyright year 2017 by Information Science Reference (an imprint of IGI Global).

Chapter 26
Between Sports Event and Media Event:
The Sochi 2014 Olympic Winter Games in Italian Newspapers

Marica Spalletta
Link Campus University, Italy

Lorenzo Ugolini
Sapienza University of Rome, Italy

ABSTRACT

Since its first edition (1896), modern Olympic Games have represented a far-reaching sport event, because they draw the attention of a wide audience and because their "festivity" breaks daily routines. According to Dayan and Katz (1992), Olympic Games are to be considered certainly as a sport event, but also as a media event. They also state that the affirmation of media events is strictly linked to their live broadcasting on TV. This chapter aims to understand if, referring to the Olympic Games, it is still possible to talk about "media events" in the shift between their representation in live broadcasting and their journalistic reports on printed news media. Through a qualitative media content analysis, the chapter examines the way in which two Italian significant newspapers (Corriere della Sera and La Gazzetta dello Sport) covered the Sochi 2014 Winter Olympic Games. The research shows that the analysis of Sochi 2014 as a media event cannot abstract from the current main features of sports journalism, that are hybridization, mediatization and popularization. Therefore, Sochi has represented a break of journalistic daily routine because of a journalistic coverage strongly hybridized but, on the other hand, it can't be fully considered as a "media event" because of the lack of mediatization and popularization.

DOI: 10.4018/978-1-5225-5475-2.ch026

INTRODUCTION AND CONTEXT[1]

Since its first edition in 1896, modern Olympic Games have represented a far-reaching sports event, the most awaited by athletes competing in nearly all the different disciplines (Toohey & Veal, 2007; Horne & Whannel, 2012): every athlete aims even only for taking part to the Olympics, because it constitutes the successful completion of his/her agonistic career; at the same time, when he/she wins an Olympic gold medal, immediately he/she becomes a Hall-of-Famer of his/her discipline (Miller, 2012).

However, as Toohey and Veal state (2007, pp. 6-7) "the Olympic Games are no longer – if they ever were – just a sporting event: they are a cultural, political and economic phenomenon. Particular interest see them as a media event, a tourism attraction, a marketing opportunity, a catalyst for urban development and renewal, a city image creator and booster, a vehicle for 'sport for all' campaigns, an inspiration for youth and a force for peace and international understanding".

Therefore, on one hand the Olympic Games are a very heterogeneous phenomenon, in which sports issues often blend with economic, social, cultural and political issues (Guttman, 2002; Toohey & Veal, 2007; Sugden & Tomlinson, 2012). For example, concerning the relationship between sport and politics, over the last century it has usually taken shape in three different ways: the Olympic Games have represented a *political topic* (i.e. the American boycott of Moscow 1980 and the following Soviet boycott of Los Angeles 1984) (Tomlinson & Young, 2006; Toohey & Veal, 2007), a *frame* in which political issues emerged (from Berlin 1936, that is the so-called "Hitler's Olympics", to the Munich 1972 massacre, not to say about the Square of the Three Cultures protest in coincidence with Mexico City 1968) (Hilton, 2006; Large, 2012; Witherspoon, 2013), finally a useful *tool* to promote the image of the host country (recently, Athens 2004 and Beijing 2008) (Panagiotopoulou, 2012).

On the other hand, the Olympic Games have to be considered as one of the main media events: as Toohey and Veal (2007, p. 1) state, "every four years, in recent decades, some 10,000 athletes from 200 countries, with a similar number of coaches and officials, as many as 15,000 accredited media representatives and hundreds of thousands of spectators have gathered for more two weeks to participate in, report on and watch a sporting event which is in turn viewed on television, listened to on radio, read about in the print media and followed by Internet by billions of people around the world". Therefore, according to Toohey and Veal all the media cover the Olympics, involving in the event a very heterogeneous audience, composed certainly by active participants and enthusiastic fans, but also by people generally not affected by sports, but interested in Olympics.

Over the last century, several authors have focused on the relationship between sport and media, highlighting the way in which the Olympic Games hybridity has affected and, at the same time, has been affected by the media and journalistic coverage (Spalletta & Ugolini, 2013). For example, McAloon (1984) states that Olympics are a hybrid meta-genre, composed of spectacle, festival, ritual and games, and this feature characterizes media reports about it. In the same way, according to Panagiotopoulou (2010, p. 233) "television has transformed the scope and the resources of [...] the Olympic Games", which "constitute one of the biggest mediated phenomena and a popular expression of our time". Considering the Olympic Games not merely as a sports event, but primarily as a media event is also one of the main topic explained by Dayan and Katz in their *Media Events* (1992). According to them, in fact, the Olympic Games constitute a media event because their "festivity" breaks the daily routines and, at the same time, because of their rituality and their capability to attract the wider media audiences in the history.

RESEARCH AIMS AND METHODOLOGY

Dayan and Katz (1992) state that the affirmation of media events is strictly linked to their live broadcasting on TV, and they focus their analysis on this topic. On the contrary, the aim of this paper is to understand what happens to media events like the Olympic Games in the shift between their representation in live broadcasting and their journalistic reports on print media, that is their news coverage on printed newspapers: is it still possible to talk about "media events" even if their narration is not in live broadcasting?

In order to answer this question, the paper focuses on the journalistic coverage of the XXII Olympic Winter Games, held in Sochi (Russia) from the 7th to the 23rd February 2014 (from now on: "Sochi 2014"). It presents the results of a qualitative media content analysis, studying the way in which two important Italian newspapers (the *Corriere della Sera* and *La Gazzetta dello Sport*) covered Sochi 2014. As far as methodology is concerned, we preferred a qualitative approach to the subject over a quantitative one (Altheide, 1987, 1995; Altheide & Schneider, 2013; Macnamara, 2005; Corbetta, 2003) because, rather than focusing on statistics and hard numbers, we are more interested in highlighting topics and trends shaping the way in which newspapers reported all the issues related to Sochi 2014. Even if we can't come to a general conclusion starting from a limited quantitative corpus, the qualitative approach allows us to answer three main questions, which emerge in the shift between Dayan and Katz's analysis about media events live broadcasting and the way in which media events take shape when we focus on their journalistic coverage in print media:

- Did the Sochi 2014 Olympic Winter Games represent a stop of daily routines?
- Did newspapers talk about it as contests, conquests and/or coronations?
- Did journalists cover this event with reverence and ceremony, suspending their normally critical stance?

The analysed corpus consists of 759 articles (200 from the *Corriere della Sera* and 559 from *La Gazzetta dello Sport*), published in both newspapers' printed editions from 1st January to 31st March 2014. We chose this time interval because it allows us to analyse the news coverage of the Olympic events, and also to understand what made the news about Sochi 2014 before and after the competitions. From this point of view, the articles published during the Olympic Games are 416 (98 from the *Corriere della Sera* and 318 from *La Gazzetta dello Sport*), while the ones published before and after the days of the competitions are 343 (102 from the *Corriere della Sera* and 241 from *La Gazzetta dello Sport*).

Referring to the analysed newspapers, we chose them for several reasons. First of all, the *Corriere della Sera* and *La Gazzetta dello Sport* are among the most historical and influential newspapers in Italy, and their circulation is similar and comparable (Agostini, 2012). Furthermore, the first one is considered the most important general interest daily Italian newspaper, as the second one is the most important Italian sports daily newspaper (Murialdi, 2006; Cucci & Germano, 2003). This choice allows us to analyse in depth the double nature of an event like the Olympic Games: its sports dimension (which is supposed to be prominent in a sports newspaper) and its non-sports one (which is supposed to be better analysed in a general interest newspaper) (Spalletta & Ugolini, 2013).

RESEARCH FINDINGS

Defining Media Events: Sochi 2014 as a Stop of Daily Routines

Dayan and Katz (1992, p. 5) affirm that media events "are *interruptions* of routine; they intervene in the normal flow of broadcasting and our lives", and specify that "regular broadcasting is suspended and preempted as we are guided by a series of special announcements and preludes that transform daily life into something special and, upon the conclusion of the event, are guided back again".

In order to analyse Sochi 2014 as a stop of daily routines, it is preliminarily necessary to understand what is supposed to be the "routine" that Sochi 2014 should have stopped. The central issue to be highlighted concerns how the concept of "regular broadcasting" can be interpreted when we move from TV to newspapers.

1. The first point to be underlined is the evolution of the news coverage of winter sports in the two analysed newspapers. In both cases, winter sports are included in the category of "other sports", which can be defined by its position in the newspaper (in *La Gazzetta dello Sport*) or in the sports pages (in the *Corriere della Sera*). Usually, the most covered and analysed sport is football, which occupies all the first pages (or the sports pages) of the newspapers. No other discipline can be compared to football from this point of view: only in some specific cases this "routine" can be broken, for example in *La Gazzetta dello Sport* during the most important cycling competitions (the *Tour de France* and the *Giro d'Italia*), or by some important Formula 1 or motorcycling races in the *Corriere della Sera*, but only if the football match day did not present a more important news – or was on Saturday (Spalletta & Ugolini, 2013).

Our research shows that the news coverage concerning winter sports changes during the Olympic Winter Games.

As we said in the introduction, *La Gazzetta dello Sport* is the most important Italian sports newspaper and it tends to cover all the disciplines, which are presented in a fixed order: first of all football (Serie A, Serie B, Lega Pro, foreign championships), then Formula 1/MotoGP, cycling and basketball, finally the other sports (including winter disciplines, and especially alpine skiing and figure skating). The Sochi 2014 Olympic Winter Games partially stop this layout: their coverage represents the front page's main topic only in the day after the opening ceremony and the Olympic competitions' report moves up the football's one in the day after the medals won by Armin Zöggeler and Christof Innerhofer. We have also to underline that, during the Olympic Games, *La Gazzetta dello Sport* covers several disciplines whose reports normally don't appear regularly (from cross country skiing to biathlon, from speed skating to short track, from hockey to snowboard); at the same time, these disciplines are quoted in the front page when there are great performances of Italian athletes.

In the *Corriere della Sera*, the reports of the winter sports competitions before the beginning of the Olympic Games are very few, quite short (Vanetti, 2014c) and mainly dedicated to alpine skiing: the only real exception is represented by the news coverage of one of the most popular Italian athletes, Carolina Kostner, and her participation to the European Figure Skating Championships in Budapest (Piccardi, 2014a). Moreover, in the sports pages the coverage of winter sports never comes before the one concerning football, nor "deserves" the front page of the newspaper. On the contrary, from 7th February on, winter sports disciplines are covered daily, with more and longer articles than before the beginning of the Olympic Games. Often situated before football news from Tuesday to Friday (but not during the weekend and on Monday, when football news have the upper hand back), these news concern the main athletes of all winter sports, especially the Italian ones who won a medal; in those cases, the news are frequently announced in the front page of the newspaper.

2. The second feature to analyse concerns the fact that, according to Dayan and Katz (1992, p. 7), "these events are pre-planned, announced and advertised in advance" and "there is an active period of looking forward, abetted by the promotional activity of the broadcasters". In our case, it is necessary to understand if the newspapers present a sort of "path" approaching the Olympic Games in the previous weeks.

In *La Gazzetta della Sport*, from the 1st of January to the 6th of February, all the articles focused on winter sports refer to Sochi, proving that the Olympic Games represent the 2014 main winter sport event. On one hand, the articles report the athletes' ambitions (Poli, 2014a) or their disappointments (Molinaro, 2014a), not to say about the Italian chances to win an Olympic medal (Arcobelli, 2014a). On the other hand, they focus on the issues related to the organization, highlighting delays (Merlo, 2014a), difficulties (Narducci, 2014a; Buongiovanni & Poli, 2014) and debates (Poli, 2014b; Piccioni & Galdi, 2014; Merlo, 2014b).

The *Corriere della Sera* offers a different approach: besides sport oriented articles, similar to the *La Gazzetta dello Sport* ones (Vanetti, 2014a, 2014b), the general interest newspaper offers several articles concerning sport policies in Italy, related to winter sports (Cotelli, 2014) and not only to them (Calcagno, 2014a).

However, according to us the most interesting point to underline is that – before the beginning of the Olympic Games – the two newspapers often focus on the non-sports issues related to Sochi 2014: politics (Buongiovanni, 2014b; Valentino, 2014a), economics (Poli, 2014c; Dragosei, 2014b), security/terrorism (Poli, 2014b; Anonymous, 2014a) and LGBT rights (Piccioni & Galdi, 2014; Dragosei, 2014a). In the *Corriere della Sera*, the articles focusing on these issues were written by non-sports journalists, and published in almost every case in non-sports pages (mainly in foreign affairs pages). In *La Gazzetta dello Sport*, the coverage of these issues increases but does not supersede the reporting about competitions.

Referring especially to the *Corriere della Sera*, two were the main controversies covered: the first one concerned the statements of the Italian International Olympic Committee member Mario Pescante, who claimed the inappropriateness of Barack Obama's choice to send in Sochi two homosexual sportswomen as American delegates (Calcagno, 2014b); the second one refers to the opportunity of the partecipation of Enrico Letta (who at the time was the Italian Prime Minister) at the Olympic Games opening ceremony (Valentino, 2014b): a polemic that pushed Letta himself to write an article (published in the front page) to explain his choice to attend the opening ceremony (Letta, 2014). Also *La Gazzetta dello Sport* covers these topics, but they don't represent the newspaper's "core business".

3. The third point to underline is related to the coming back to daily routines after the media event. According to us, the passage from broadcasting to newspaper from this point of view can be better understood referring to what Dayan and Katz (1992, p. 119) call "*rite de passage*": "a ritual of separation, of entry into a liminal period of trials and teachings, and of return to normal society, often in a new assumed role". In our research we focused on the news coverage of the Olympic

Games "principals" (using Dayan and Katz's words), that are the main athletes, after the end of competitions.

After the end of the Olympic Games, in *La Gazzetta dello Sport* winter sports' newsworthiness comes back to its daily routines and the coverage focuses especially on alpine skiing and figure skating. In this perspective, Sochi still remains a news value only in respect of the German athlete Maria Riesch and the Italian one Carolina Kostner: talking about their possible retirement, several articles underline that the Sochi 2014 Olympic Games could be the final act of their agonistic careers (Buongiovanni, 2014n; Molinaro, 2014c).

In the *Corriere della Sera*, the news coverage of winter sports and their champions is reduced to what it was before Sochi 2014 and progressively disappears, aided by the fact that the Olympic Games were one of the last competitions of the winter sports seasons. Yet again, Carolina Kostner represents an exception, with her participation to the World Figure Skating Championship held in Saitama at the end of March (Piccardi, 2014z). Only one article analyses the possible athletic future of Italian champions Zöggeler and Fontana (Piccardi, 2014v). It is interesting to underline that Sochi is mentioned very few times in relation to Olympic Games (or Paralympic Games, which were hold in Sochi just after the end of the Olympic Games), and quite often in relation with the news concerning Vladimir Putin and the critical diplomatic situation between Russia and Ukraine: Sochi was the planned location of a G8 summit in June 2014.

Scripting Media Events: Sochi 2014 as Contest, Conquest, and Coronation

Dayan and Katz (1992) separate media events into three categories: *conquests*, *coronations* and *contests*. Conquests are "one-time events": they "tend to break the rules" and strictly depend of the charisma of their protagonists. Coronations mark the rites of passage of the great, and they refer to all typologies of "parades" (therefore, not only to monarchic events). Finally, contests are the typical ceremonies of sports and politics, designed to identify the best contender or the best team; they are pure celebrations of achievement and the message they spread is that the winner won by playing by the rules.

According to Dayan and Katz, Olympic Games belong to the last category because of several reasons, most of which characterize the covering of Sochi 2014 Olympic Winter Games by the two analysed newspapers.

First of all, Dayan and Katz (1992, p. 33) argue that Olympic Games are "regularly recurrent", in the sense that they are "held once every four years at a given season". *La Gazzetta dello Sport* and the *Corriere della Sera* often underline this feature, highlighting that athletes consider Olympic Games as the most important moment of their career (Reichel, 2014; Vanetti, 2014n). No other victory, in fact, is comparable to an Olympic medal, as argued especially by those athletes forced to stay away from the competitions (Molinaro, 2014a; Anonymous, 2014b). The articles focused on this topic appear more frequently during the days before the competitions.

Secondly, Dayan and Katz (1992) state that Olympic Games are "rule-governed battles of champions" (p. 26) and they bid individuals and teams "to compete according to strict rules" (p. 33). Also this feature emerges in the journalistic coverage. *La Gazzetta dello Sport* often describes the rules of each competition, focusing especially on the new entries in the Olympic programme (and consequently unknown to the wider public) or the ones in which the most famous athletes are competing; this coverage ranges from slopestyle (Poli, 2014d) to figure skating (Buongiovanni, 2014c). Due to the different nature of the *Corriere della Sera*, this feature is less present, but still identifiable (Piccardi, 2014c).

According to the authors (1992, p. 35), another feature concerns the time orientation: contests are media events that take shape in the present and their journalistic coverage reflects this feature. The analysed articles prefer to focus on the agonistic race and on its protagonists, and they rarely refer to former champions in the straight reporting. On the contrary, news stories or feature articles talk about the Olympic history (Merlo, 2014d; Gregori, 2014; Vanetti, 2014g) or look to the future of the Olympic Games and their champions (Molinaro, 2014b; Piccardi, 2014l).

Finally, Dayan and Katz (1992, p. 31) argue that “what makes an event new, and electrifying, is the enhanced status of its personae”: therefore, the athletes’ personality and character make the shift between a sports event and a media event. This is probably one of the most important features that emerges in the journalistic coverage. Every agonistic race becomes newsworthy because of the athlete who is involved in it: *La Gazzetta dello Sport* and the *Corriere della Sera* talk about alpine skiing because of Tina Maze (Molinaro, 2014b; Vanetti, 2014h) and Christof Innerhofer (Poli, 2014e; Vanetti, 2014i); about figure skating because of Evgueny Plushenko (Buongiovanni, 2014d; Piccardi, 2014d) and Carolina Kostner (Buongiovanni, 2014m; Piccardi, 2014e); about luge because of Armin Zöggeler (Arcobelli, 2014e; Piccardi, 2014f); about short track speed skating because of Arianna Fontana (Buongiovanni, 2014f; Piccardi, 2014l). *La Gazzetta dello Sport* gives specific room also to cross country skiing because of Marit Bjørgen (Arcobelli, 2014c); about biathlon because of Ole Einar Bjørndalen (Arcobelli, 2014d). More clearly (and more “olympically”) the *Corriere della Sera* focuses on some athletes apart from their victories, reporting the participation of the famous violinist Vanessa Vanakorn Mae at the giant slalom for Thailand (Vanetti, 2014e), or the pleasant oddity represented by Jamaican bobsleigh team (Piccardi, 2014q). On the contrary, these topics are covered by *La Gazzetta dello Sport* only in the short news section.

In all that cases, the newsworthiness is certainly influenced by the news value of proximity (Hall *et al.*, 1978; Gans, 1979), but not totally dependent on it. On the *Corriere della Sera*, the news concerning Italian athletes are prominent, and the newsworthiness of other athletes depends on their capability to emerge, but rarely because of a great win (for example, the little or almost absent coverage concerning Marit Bjørgen, Ole Einar Bjørndalen and the Netherlands Skating team). Similarly, *La Gazzetta dello Sport* – which is inevitably more focused on sports – gives little coverage to the Kamil Stoch’s two gold medals in ski jumping; according to us, it happens because the Polish ski jumper appears to be lacking of charisma in terms of newsworthiness (even if he carried out great feats).

Therefore, according to Dayan and Katz Olympic Games normally appear as a contest. However, the authors (1992, p. 25) argue that “all media events [...], even those which strongly adhere to a given script, nevertheless contain echoes of their scripts which loom in the background or are given secondary status”. The shift between the different categories (contests, conquests and coronations) depends on the events’ protagonists: “almost all of these events – they write (1992, p. 12) – have heroic figures around whose initiatives the reintegration of society is proposed”, and each figure represents a different typology of “authorities” (Weber, 1946): *legal* (contest), *traditional* (coronation) and *charismatic* (conquest).

Our research confirms that the presence of heroic figures can transform a contest in a coronation or in a conquest; at the same time, it shows that the shift depends on the athlete’s character or on the dimension/importance of his/her victory (Merlo, 2014c). In fact, Olympic Games become a coronation when the coverage focused especially on Carolina Kostner, Christof Innerhofer or Arianna Fontana. In those cases, articles respectively celebrate the hopes and the victories of an unlucky champion (Buongiovanni, 2014m; Piccardi, 2014s), of a cheerful champion (Merlo, 2014f; Vanetti, 2014l) and of a champion who was a "child" at Torino 2006 and is a woman at Sochi 2014 (Buongiovanni, 2014i; Piccardi, 2014i, 2014t). On the contrary, Olympic victories represent conquests when the articles focus on Armin Zöggeler (Arcobelli, 2014e; Piccardi, 2014g), Ole Einar Bjørndalen (Arcobelli, 2014f) and Marit Bjørgen (Arcobelli, 2014h): their successes represent "giant leaps for mankind" after whose "life is not the same" (Dayan & Katz, 1992, p. 26).

The research also shows that there is one case in which the coverage embodies the three different typologies of sports/media events: when the newspapers focus on the Russian skater Evgueny Plushenko. Before the beginning of the Olympic Games, *La Gazzetta dello Sport* reports the dilemma about his participation in terms of contest (Buongiovanni, 2014a); Plushenko's victory in the team event is the celebration of a coronation (Buongiovanni, 2014d), while referring to the incoming men individual event he becomes a potential candidate for conquest (Buongiovanni, 2014g); after his retirement before the beginning of the individual event, the articles celebrate "the funeral of the king" (Buongiovanni, 2014h). In the *Corriere della Sera*, the coverage is similar: we find the contest (Piccardi, 2014b), the coronation (but only referring to the potential victory in the men individual event, the victory in the team event not being covered) (Piccardi, 2014d), then the funeral of the king (Piccardi, 2014m). The difference is that the *Corriere della Sera* gives more room, before (Piccardi, 2014b) and after (Piccardi, 2014o) the Olympic Games, to the controversies of Plushenko's participation to Sochi and its political interpretations: he was considered one of Vladimir Putin's favourites and, for this reason, preferred to other more competitive (but less charismatic) athletes.

This leads us to the last important aspect, which came to light from our research. The Dayan and Katz's idea of coronation emerges not only referring to the athletes, who should be the main protagonists of the Olympic Games, but also in respect of the Russian President Vladimir Putin. Especially in the days before and after the opening ceremony, both newspapers describe Sochi 2014 as "the Games of Vladimir Putin", underlining that he clearly aims to transform the Olympic Games in his personal international coronation (Arcobelli, 2014b; Buongiovanni, 2014b; Monti, 2014; Valentino, 2014a, 2014c). The Putin's coronation takes shape on 24th of February, when both newspapers write that Sochi 2014 represents a victory for Russia, but also for its President (Poli, 2014f; Valentino, 2014l).

Celebrating Media Events: The Journalistic Coverage Between Reverence and Critical Stance

Referring to the journalistic work related to media events, Dayan and Katz (1992, p. 7) state that "these broadcast events are presented with *reverence* and *ceremony*. The journalists who preside over them suspend their normally critical stance and treat their subject with respect, even awe". "One wonders whether the media events is not an expression of a neo romantic desire for heroic action by great men", the two authors affirm "in this sense, media events go beyond journalism in highlighting charisma and collective action, in defiance of established authority" (p. 21). In our case, we aim to understand if the journalists' attitude on newspapers corresponds, in whole or in part, to this "suspension" observed by Dayan and Katz.

The most interesting aspect emerging from our research concerns the different attitude of the journalists depending on the nature of the news. As we observed before, the news coverage offered by the two analysed newspapers gives room to sports news, but also to all the non-sports news related to Sochi 2014. In the first case, during the Olympic Winter Games the journalists describe with passion and emotional involvement the hopes (Piccardi, 2014r; Vanetti, 2014d; Narducci, 2014b), the victories (Vanetti,

2014f; Piccardi, 2014s; Narducci, 2014c) and the failures (Piccardi, 2014h; Vanetti, 2014m; Narducci, 2014d) of Italian athletes, and not only the Italian ones (Vanetti, 2014h; Valentino, 2014i; Poli, 2014a; Arcobelli, 2014c; Buongiovanni, 2014l).

The journalists' attitude changes when the topic of the news shifts from sports to the other issues we highlighted above, and the most significant differences between the two analysed newspapers emerge referring to this shift. In the *Corriere della Sera*, the analysis of Olympic Games from the point of view of the Italian sport policies is critical (Vanetti, 2014o; Piccardi, 2014p), but in particular the issues concerning politics (Valentino, 2014e; Venturini, 2014), economics (Piccardi, 2014n), security/terrorism (Valentino, 2014g) and LGBT rights (Valentino, 2014f) are analysed, though remaining in a sports context (also by non-sports journalists – in particular by Paolo Valentino, special envoy for foreign assignments – but almost always in the sports pages), with a more critical and analytical attitude, oriented to the symbolism of some competitions, in particular referring to LGBT rights (Valentino, 2014d).

We can place the two most meaningful examples at the beginning and at the end of the Olympic Games. The 8th of February, when the *Corriere della Sera* reports about the opening ceremony and the first day of competitions, the report is split in two parts: the first one, reporting all the political, economical and social issues, is situated at page 2 and 3 of the newspaper; the sports news, as usual, are situated at the end of the newspaper (at page 58 and 59). At the end of the Olympic Games, taking stock of the event, the sports journalists focus on the good results of Sochi 2014, from both sports and non-sports points of view (Piccardi, 2014u; Valentino, 2014l), while in the other parts of the newspaper the attention moved to the critical diplomatic situation between Russia and Ukraine, with its repercussions on the Olympic Games (Valentino, 2014h) and the general political consequences (Caretto, 2014).

Referring to *La Gazzetta dello Sport*, the journalists' critical stance takes shape certainly in respect of the non-sports news: topics like LGBT rights and security are always analysed focusing on their effects on the political balances and especially referring to the relationship between United States and Russia (Merlo, 2014e; Piccioni & Galdi, 2014; Monti, 2014). The same attitude emerges also when the articles focus on the issues of doping (Narducci, 2014e).

However, a different attitude emerges also depending on the journalists that are involved. In fact, sports reporters, as Andrea Buongiovanni, Marisa Poli, Stefano Arcobelli and Pierangelo Molinaro, tend to cover sports news with reverence and ceremony, focusing on the agonistic issues and their protagonists. On the contrary, sports columnists as Gianni Merlo or Fausto Narducci (not to say the editor Andrea Monti) tend to analyse with critical stance the non-sports news. The only two cases in which the first attitude blends clearly with the second one concern the Ukraine success in biathlon team event – which is celebrated and analysed because it sounds as a "feat for peace" (Arcobelli, 2014g) – and the gold medal won by the Netherlands skater Ireen Wüst – which embodies the spirit of the Olympic Games also because of her homosexuality (Buongiovanni, 2014e). In the first case, journalists highlight the political meaning of a sports performance, while in the second case they underline the sports meaning of a performance which could be celebrated because of its strong political meaning.

Discussion

The qualitative analysis we carried out allows us to answer the three main questions we introduced in the second paragraph, highlighting some significant topics and trends in respect of the way in which Sochi 2014 constituted a media event in the printed news media.

1. *Did the Sochi 2014 Olympic Winter Games represent a stop of daily routines?*

In the "Defining media events" paragraph, we observed that the Sochi 2014 Olympic Winter Games represented a stop of daily routines during the Olympic events: in fact, the two analysed newspapers covered several disciplines normally not reported. However, these reports didn't break the coverage routines, in the sense that the news about Olympic Games rarely come before the reports about football (on both newspapers) or the ones related to other journalistic genres (on the *Corriere della Sera*). According to us, it happens because the newsworthiness of Sochi 2014 doesn't satisfy the news value of leaderization, which is sports journalism's typical feature (Mazzoleni, 2012; Allan, 2005). Today, in fact, sports journalism tends to detach the figures of charismatic athletes from the context of what they do, creating a narrative and a hype around the athlete as an individual and new scenarios in which he/she competes with his/her opponents, with his/her own ability to deliver, with the history of the sport he/she practices, and above all with other leaders such as him/herself (Spalletta & Ugolini, 2013). In this perspective, media events' newsworthiness is strictly related to athletes' great performances and it is enhanced when there is an Italian athlete. Referring to Sochi 2014, the lack of a "charismatic leader" in the Italian team (as Alberto Tomba at Calgary 1998 or Manuela Di Centa at Lillehammer 1994) and the failure to win a gold medal don't allow the event's "holiday experience" to take completely shape. On the contrary if a charismatic athlete as Christof Innerhofer had won the gold medal in men downhill (that is the most important event in a very popular sport as alpine skiing), this achievement would probably have been covered in the newspapers' first pages.

2. *Did newspapers talk about it as contests, conquests and/or coronations?*

In the "Scripting media events" paragraph, we underline that both the analysed newspapers script Sochi 2014 as contests, conquests or coronations; we also notice that the shift from the first category to the other ones is strictly related to the heroic figures around whom media events and journalistic tales take shape. Our research shows that both the analysed newspapers tended to focus on the Sochi 2014's "personae", like the athletes (both Italian and non-Italian ones), or like the Russian President Vladimir Putin, who is one of the main protagonists of the XXII Olympic Winter Games. According to us, it happens certainly because celebrating "personae" depends on a sports journalism's typical feature, which consists in *personalization* (Mazzoleni, 2012): today in fact, sports journalists tend to shift the focus of their reporting from sports as a collective phenomenon (even in individual sports) to its most famous and representative protagonists. As a result, what makes the news is not alpine skiing, luge or figure skating anymore, but the most important and well-known athletes, as Christof Innerhofer, Armin Zöggeler or Carolina Kostner (Spalletta & Ugolini, 2013). Athletes like Armin Zöggeler, Christof Innerhofer, Carolina Kostner, Arianna Fontana, Marit Bjørgen, Ole Einar Bjørndalen or Evgueny Plushenko allow journalists to personalize their reports.

3. *Did journalists cover this event with reverence and ceremony, suspending their normally critical stance?*

In the "Celebrating media events" paragraph, we note that journalists report Sochi 2014 with reverence and ceremony, that is one of the main features of media events but also a traditional feature of sports journalism. Since its beginnings, in fact, sports journalism has highlighted the epic nature of a game, and has built triumphal or tragic narratives about athletes drawing from their past history (Boyle, 2006; Rowe, 2004). However, we also underline that this attitude emerges only when the reports focus on sports news. On the contrary, when journalists have to cover no-sports news involved in the Sochi 2014 Olympic Winter Games, they get back their critical stance, and their tales don't represent ceremonies but analysis. According to us, it happens because sports journalism's newsworthiness is deeply changed, and today sports journalism covers on one hand what happens *before*, *during* and *after* sports performances (Spalletta & Ugolini, 2013; Sorrentino & Bianda, 2013), on the other hand a variety of topics related to the sport it focuses on, whether they are economic, political, scientific, medical, or concerning the personal life of athletes. Academic literature (Andrews, 2013; Boyle, 2006; Rowe, 2004; Sorrentino & Bianda, 2013) defines these phenomena as "hybridization". Referring to these topics, journalists have to get back their objectivity.

CONCLUSION

In the paper's introduction, we underlined that Dayan and Katz (1992, p. 14) consider the Olympic Games as a typical example of media events because they are ceremonies: "A ceremony interrupts the flow of daily life (syntactics); it deals reverently with sacred matters (semantics); and it involves the response (pragmatics) of a committed audience". They also state (pp. 4-7) that media events constitute a new television genre, which is pre-planned, organized outside the media and, above all, live broadcasted. Finally, in respect of journalistic coverage, according to Dayan and Katz (p. 7) media events are presented with reverence and ceremony, and the journalists suspend their normally critical stance.

Break of daily routines, live broadcasting and reverential journalistic attitude create a media event out of a political debate (Kennedy *vs* Nixon), a state funeral (Sadat, Gandhi, Kennedy, etc.), particularly meaningful official journeys (from Sadat in Jerusalem to John Paul II in Poland), sports events like Olympic Games (p. 4).

Finally, according to Dayan and Katz (pp. 25-27) media events can be split in three categories: contests, conquests and coronations. As political events, also the sports ones (Olympic Games or Football World Cup) usually belong to the first category. However, because the boundaries between contests, conquests and coronations are not so defined, sports events can become conquests or coronations.

The theoretical frame proposed by Dayan and Katz represents the starting point of our research, which focuses on a specific edition of Winter Olympic Games (Sochi 2014) and on a specific typology of journalistic coverage (the printed newspapers). These choices don't allow us to draw a general conclusion; nonetheless, we are able to highlight meaningful trends in respect of our research question: *Referring to Sochi 2014, can we talk about "media events" in the shift from their live broadcasting to their journalistic coverage in printed newspapers?*

Starting from these premises, we can try to answer our research question starting from its first topic: applying Dayan and Katz' categories, have Sochi 2014 represented a media event on the analysed newspapers? Our research suggests us to answer "probably not", because it didn't respect totally the parameters quoted before.

First of all, Sochi 2014 has represented a break of both newspapers' daily routines only in respect of few, specific cases: the opening ceremony and the related involvement of international authorities, Vladimir Putin's endorsement to Russian Olympic Games and how Sochi 2014 has been affected by the Russian President's political strategies, finally some Olympic medals won by Italian athletes (like the luger Armin Zöggeler and the alpine skier Christof Innerhofer); in this way, Sochi 2014 has certainly modified but not revolutionized the newspapers' traditional newsworthiness.

Second, journalists have covered Sochi 2014 with reverence and ceremony only when their reports strictly focused on competitions; on the contrary, when they have to cover non-sports news (political, economic, social, cultural or human interest) they have maintained their critical stance. We have to underline that this difference is very significant, because today the idea of "sports news" consists also of non-sports issues related to sport.

Finally, referring to the three categories of media events proposed by Dayan and Katz (contests, conquests, coronations), Sochi 2014 has certainly belonged to the first one in respect of sports issues covered by the analysed newspapers, while it can be considered a conquest or a coronation in respect of the other quoted issues.

Therefore, at first blush Sochi 2014 doesn't appear to be adequately relevant to the Dayan and Katz's definition of "media event". However, our research shows that, over the Olympic Games, the journalistic coverage of winter sports has been wider and deeper than in the other days: the winter sports newsworthiness peaks during the Olympics. This forces us to re-think our answer, wondering why Sochi 2014 has represented a break of journalistic daily routine.

In order to answer this question, we need to focus on our textual corpus, and our answer couldn't work referring to other typologies of media coverage of Sochi 2014. Furthermore, a preliminary consideration about the idea of "television live broadcasting" would be necessary, especially in respect of its meaning in a media scenario currently composed by several typologies of live broadcasting (from web streaming to live tweeting, not to say about the new-born Periscope). However, this isn't the aim of our research.

On the contrary, focusing on our textual corpus the research shows that Sochi 2014 has represented a break of journalistic daily routines because it has respected the first of the three features of today sports journalism: hybridization, mediatization and popularization (Spalletta & Ugolini, 2013).

Referring to the first one, our research clearly shows that in the coverage of Sochi 2014 sports issues blend with political, economic and social ones, especially when the journalistic tale focuses on the Russian President Vladimir Putin and his policies, the international relationship between Russia and other countries (for example, in respect of the participation of Italian Prime Minister Enrico Letta in the opening ceremony), finally the Ukraine crisis which began during the competition. In this way, winter sports' newsworthiness grows in respect of the traditional reasons why they were reported, and these disciplines reach an unusual journalistic coverage (for example: the front page of the *Corriere della Sera*).

Therefore, referring to hybridization Sochi 2014 has represented a break of daily routines, because of a journalistic coverage strongly hybridized. On the contrary, it can't be considered as a "media event" because of the lack of mediatization and popularization.

Concerning mediatization (and especially its quoted systemic effects), our research shows that the journalistic coverage of Sochi 2014 has been certainly spectacularized (because a contest is a "drama" by its nature), in most cases personalized (winter sports tend to be identified with their most representative athletes), but barely leaderized.

This lack of leaderization affects negatively the journalistic coverage of Sochi: there has not been a strong leader (like Alberto Tomba or Manuela Di Centa, referring to past Olympic editions) in important disciplines (from this point of view, an athlete like Arianna Fontana, which would play a leading role, competes in a sport less newsworthy than alpine skiing or cross-country), while potentially strong leaders (as Carolina Kostner or Ole Einar Bjørndalen, Marit Bjørgen and Evgueny Plushenko) are not so considered by journalists because of their past Olympic failures or because they are not Italian athletes (and for the analysed newspapers, proximity is one of the main news values).

Referring to popularization, it takes shape when sports journalism reports on competitions as well as on popular aspects, like athletes' personal lives, relationships, and all the topics related to the news value of human interest (Street, 1997; Van Zoonen, 2005; Mazzoleni & Sfardini, 2009). According to us, Sochi 2014 newsworthiness is affected by a lack of popularization, which is certainly due to the quoted lack of leaderization, but also to an additional and meaningful development of leaderized and popularized sports journalism: *celebritization*, that is the athletes' talent to act – and to be covered – as celebrities (Wheeler, 2013; Spalletta & Ugolini, 2014). Our research shows that – without this talent, which belongs to the athlete more than to his journalistic tale – the shift from break of journalistic daily routines to media event appears to be difficult, not to say impossible.

REFERENCES

Agostini, A. (2012). *Giornalismi*. Bologna: il Mulino.

Allan, S. (Ed.). (2005). *Journalism: Critical Issues*. Maidenhead, UK: Open University Press.

Altheide, D. L. (1987). Ethnographic Content Analysis. *Qualitative Sociology*, *10*(1), 65–77. doi:10.1007/BF00988269

Altheide, D. L. (1995). *Qualitative Media Analysis*. London: Sage.

Altheide, D. L., & Schneider, C. J. (2013). *Qualitative Media Analysis*. Newbury Park, CA: Sage.

Andrews, P. (2013). *Sports Journalism. A Practical Introduction*. London: Sage.

Anonymous. (2014a, January 23). Email di minacce agli atleti italiani. «Non è credibile». *Corriere della Sera*, p. 10.

Anonymous. (2014b, January 28). Sci: oggi slalom, Reichelt ko. *Corriere della Sera*.

Arcobelli, S. (2014a, January 7). Italia, le ambizioni vanno veloci. *La Gazzetta dello Sport*, p. 30.

Arcobelli, S. (2014b, February 5). Felini, film e polemiche. Il primo giorno di Putin. *La Gazzetta dello Sport*, p. 25.

Arcobelli, S. (2014c, February 9). Bjoergen senza tempo. Il fondo elegge la sua regina. *La Gazzetta dello Sport*, p. 26.

Arcobelli, S. (2014d, February 9). Infinito Bjoerndalen. Mister Biathlon è nella leggenda. *La Gazzetta dello Sport*, p. 26.

Arcobelli, S. (2014e, February 10). Il mito Zoeggeler. Sei Olimpiadi, sei medaglie. Da vent'anni a 140 km all'ora. *La Gazzetta dello Sport*, p. 6.

Arcobelli, S. (2014f, February 20). Leggenda Bjoerndalen, nessuno come lui: ciao Daehlie. *La Gazzetta dello Sport*, p. 24.

Arcobelli, S. (2014g, February 22). La festa e il dolore. Ucraina, un'impresa per la pace. *La Gazzetta dello Sport*, p. 33.

Arcobelli, S. (2014h, February 23). La regina delle nevi. Sesto oro: nessuna come la Bjoergen. *La Gazzetta dello Sport*, p. 30.

Boyle, R. (2006). *Sports Journalism: Context and Issues*. London: Sage.

Buongiovanni, A. (2014a, January 19). Fernandez ancora d'oro. Russia, caos per Plushenko. *La Gazzetta dello Sport*.

Buongiovanni, A. (2014b, January 31). Miracolo Russia. «Vietato sbagliare. Sono i Giochi di Putin». *La Gazzetta dello Sport*, p. 29.

Buongiovanni, A. (2014c, February 5). Cinquanta: «La gara a squadre vi conquisterà». *La Gazzetta dello Sport*, p. 24.

Buongiovanni, A. (2014d, February 10). Plushenko è lo zar dei Giochi russi. E Putin applaude, *La Gazzetta dello Sport*, p. 13.

Buongiovanni, A. (2014e, February 10). Wust, il trionfo non guarda alle discriminazioni. *La Gazzetta dello Sport*, p. 13.

Buongiovanni, A. (2014f, February 11). Una Fontana insaziabile. «Inseguo quattro finali». *La Gazzetta dello Sport*, p. 28.

Buongiovanni, A. (2014g, February 13). Volosozhar-Trankov che show. L'oro della programmazione. *La Gazzetta dello Sport*, p. 29.

Buongiovanni, A. (2014h, February 14). Le tribune in silenzio. Plushenko si ritira. Il triste finale dello zar di Russia. *La Gazzetta dello Sport*, p. 28.

Buongiovanni, A. (2014i, February 19). Bimba a Torino 2006, nella storia a Sochi. *La Gazzetta dello Sport*, p. 29.

Buongiovanni, A. (2014l, February 20). La Russia è gelata. Belli senz'anima. I fenomeni sono fuori ai quarti. *La Gazzetta dello Sport*, p. 28.

Buongiovanni, A. (2014m, February 21). Kostner, inno alla vita. Entra nella storia con un bronzo capolavoro. *La Gazzetta dello Sport*, p. 22.

Buongiovanni, A. (2014n, March 26). L'ultima Kostner?. *La Gazzetta dello Sport*, p. 31.

Buongiovanni, A. & Poli, M. (2014, February 4). Sicurezza olimpica. Impianti perfetti e paesi inventati. I Giochi artificiali. *La Gazzetta dello Sport*, p. 26.

Calcagno, D. (2014a, January 15). «Italiani troppo tifosi e poco sportivi. Per risalire investiremo sulla scuola». *Corriere della Sera*, p. 43.

Calcagno, D. (2014b, January 16). Pescante all'attacco di Obama: «Manda gay ai Giochi di Sochi». *Corriere della Sera*, p. 43.

Caretto, E. (2014, February 23). «Vladimir non starà a guardare. Attenti alle mosse a sorpresa». *Corriere della Sera*, p. 5.

Corbetta, P. (2003). Metodologie e tecniche della ricerca sociale. Vol. 1. Bologna: il Mulino.

Cotelli, M. (2014, January 27). Strategia sbagliata dei dirigenti. Ma a pagare saranno gli atleti. *Corriere della Sera*, p. 41.

Cucci, I., & Germano, I. S. (2003). *Tribuna stampa. Storia critica del giornalismo sportivo da Pindaro a Internet*. Roma: Il Minotuaro.

Dayan, D., & Katz, E. (1992). *Media events. The Live Broadcasting of History*. Cambridge, MA: Harvard University Press.

Dragosei, F. (2014a, January 20). Quando Putin fa l'amico dei gay. *Corriere della Sera*, p. 12.

Dragosei, F. (2014b, January 26). Piste, treni, maxi investimenti. Come oligarchi e amici di Putin hanno messo le mani sui Giochi. *Corriere della Sera*, p. 13.

Gans, H. (1979). *Deciding What's News. A Study of CBS Evening News, NBC Nightly News, «Newsweek» and «Time»*. New York: Pantheon Books.

Gregori, C. (2014, February 12). Boicottaggi, duelli, Belov e il Miracolo. Quei giganti che si sfidano da sempre. *La Gazzetta dello Sport*, pp. 20-21.

Guttman, A. (2002). *The Olympics. A History of the Modern Games*. Chicago: University of Illinois Press.

Hall, S., Critcher, C., Jefferson, T., Clarke, J., & Roberts, B. (1978). *Policing the Crisis. Mugging, the State, and Law and Order*. London: MacMillan. doi:10.1007/978-1-349-15881-2

Hilton, C. (2006). *Hitler's Olympics. The 1936 Berlin Olympic Games*. Stroud: Sutton Pub. Ltd.

Horne, J., & Whannel, G. (2012). *Understanding the Olympics*. New York: Routledge.

Large, D. C. (2012). *Munich 1972. Tragedy, Terror and Triumph*. Lanham: Rowman & Littlefield.

Letta, E. (2014, February 7). «Perché ho deciso di essere a Sochi con i nostri atleti». *Corriere della Sera*, pp. 1.11.

Macnamara, J. (2005). Media Content Analysis: Its Uses, Benefits and Best Practice Methodology. *Asia Pacific Public Relations Journal*, *6*(1), 1–34.

Mazzoleni, G. (2012). *La comunicazione politica*. Bologna: il Mulino.

Mazzoleni, G. & Sfardini, A. (2009). *Politica pop. Da "Porta a Porta" a "L'isola dei famosi"*. Bologna: il Mulino.

McAloon, J. (Ed.). (1984). *Rite, Drama, Festival, Ritual: Rehearsals Toward a Theory of Cultural Performance*. Philadelphia: ISHI.

Merlo, G. (2014a, February 1). Lavori in corso. E le camere non ci sono. *La Gazzetta dello Sport*, p. 32.

Merlo, G. (2014b, February 4). Bach: «Putin ci ha dato garanzie su diritti di lavoratori e omosessuali». *La Gazzetta dello Sport*, p. 27.

Merlo, G. (2014c, February 9). Cannibali diversi con il dna dell'oro. *La Gazzetta dello Sport*, p. 27.

Merlo, G. (2014d, February 10). Se Plank nel '76 avesse avuto gli sci nuovi.... *La Gazzetta dello Sport*, p. 11.

Merlo, G. (2014e, February 13). La guerra dei Roses e quei gesti di fair play. *La Gazzetta dello Sport*, p. 28.

Merlo, G. (2014f, February 15). Innerhofer: simpaticamente narciso, intellettuale e giocatore in borsa. *La Gazzetta dello Sport*, p. 19.

Miller, D. (2012). *The Official History of the Olympic Games and the IOC*. Edinburgh, UK: Mainstream Publishing Company.

Molinaro, P. (2014a, January 8). La Vonn rinuncia all'Olimpiade. «Sono a pezzi». *La Gazzetta dello Sport*.

Molinaro, P. (2014b, February 14). Premio alla carriera. L'oro della Maze: «E non è finita». *La Gazzetta dello Sport*, p. 29.

Molinaro, P. (2014c, March 21). Riesch smette. «È meglio ora, sono al vertice». *La Gazzetta dello Sport*, p. 29.

Monti, A. (2014, February 8). I Giochi di Putin, l'Olimpiade di tutti. *La Gazzetta dello Sport*, pp. 1.23.

Murialdi, P. (2006). *Storia del giornalismo italiano*. Bologna: il Mulino.

Narducci, F. (2014a, January 19). Punteggi in diretta per combattere combine e favori. *La Gazzetta dello Sport*.

Narducci, F. (2014b, February 6). L'Italia vuole ribaltare i pronostici. Si riparte dalla grinta di Londra. *La Gazzetta dello Sport*, p. 19.

Narducci, F. (2014c, February 10). Giornata storica. E non è finita. *La Gazzetta dello Sport*, pp. 2-3.

Narducci, F. (2014d, February 13). Sochi e i quarti posti azzurri. Medaglie di legno, anzi di neve.... *La Gazzetta dello Sport*, p. 19.

Narducci, F. (2014e, February 22). L'Italia olimpica macchiata dal doping. Brutte figure da Schwazer a Frullani. *La Gazzetta dello Sport*, p. 23.

Panagiotopoulou, R. (2010). Sports Events: the Olympics in Greece. In N. Couldry, A. Hepp & F. Krotz (Eds.). (pp. 233-249). Media Events in a Global Age. New York: Routledge.

Panagiotopoulou, R. (2012). Nation Branding and the Olympic Games: New Media Images for Greece and China. *The International Journal of the History of Sport*, *29*(16), 2337–2348. doi:10.1080/09523367.2012.744527

Piccardi, G. (2014a, January 18). Un bronzo di mestiere e d'orgoglio. Carolina lascia il trono d'Europa. *Corriere della Sera*, p. 51.

Piccardi, G. (2014b, January 19). Plushenko scatena la Russia connection. *Corriere della Sera*, p. 32.

Piccardi, G. (2014c, February 3). Italia, beata gioventù senza paura. La medaglia è un atto di fede. *Corriere della Sera*, p. 38.

Piccardi, G. (2014d, February 6). I Giochi dello Zar. *Corriere della Sera*, p. 40.

Piccardi, G. (2014e, February 8). Il sogno di Carolina: una gara perfetta per fare pace con l'Olimpiade. *Corriere della Sera*, p. 59.

Piccardi, G. (2014f, February 9). Pronte le frecce tricolori: per Zoeggeler e uomini jet gran voglia di medaglia. *Corriere della Sera*, p. 38.

Piccardi, G. (2014g, February 10). Il collezionista. *Corriere della Sera*, p. 33.

Piccardi, G. (2014h, February 12). In fondo cadono tutti. *Corriere della Sera*, pp. 42-43.

Piccardi, G. (2014i, February 13). Arianna prepara uno sprint da podio. *Corriere della Sera*, p. 51.

Piccardi, G. (2014l, February 14). Caduta nell'argento. *Corriere della Sera*, p. 64.

Piccardi, G. (2014m, February 14). Ultimo tango al veleno per Plushenko: è l'addio. *Corriere della Sera*, p. 64.

Piccardi, G. (2014n, February 15). Campione chi? Gli illustri sconosciuti che preoccupano le grandi aziende. *Corriere della Sera*, pp. 66-67.

Piccardi, G. (2014o, February 15). Plushenko, caso politico, in un pattinaggio che non è per «vecchi». *Corriere della Sera*, p. 67.

Piccardi, G. (2014p, February 17). Come siamo caduti in fondo. *Corriere della Sera*, p. 38.

Piccardi, G. (2014q, February 17). Giamaica, la felicità di arrivare ultimi. *Corriere della Sera*, p. 38.

Piccardi, G. (2014r, February 18). La grande bellezza. I giorni della Kostner: «Una sfida con me stessa. In pista cerco la felicità». *Corriere della Sera*, pp. 50-51.

Piccardi, G. (2014s, February 21). Bronzo magico. *Corriere della Sera*, p. 62.

Piccardi, G. (2014t, February 22). Le signore dei Giochi. *Corriere della Sera*, p. 64.

Piccardi, G. (2014u, February 24). Tanto tuonò che non successe nulla. Che belli i Giochi meno freddi della storia. *Corriere della Sera*, p. 48.

Piccardi, G. (2014v, March 19). Malagò fa festa alle medaglie (e agli otto legni). *Corriere della Sera*, p. 43.

Piccardi, G. (2014z, March 28). L'Ave Maria strega Saitama. Kostner seconda dopo il corto: «Più nervosa che a Sochi». *Corriere della Sera*, p. 59.

Piccioni, V. & Galdi, M. (2014, February 3). Letta va a Sochi fra le proteste. «Fai come Obama». *La Gazzetta dello Sport*, p. 37.

Poli, M. (2014a, January 3). Mikaela Shiffrin: «Giovane, ambiziosa e felice: la mia vita è una sfida sugli sci». *La Gazzetta dello Sport*.

Poli, M. (2014b, January 8). Sochi blindata, sono Giochi di guerra. *La Gazzetta dello Sport*.

Poli, M. (2014c, January 29). Russia, i Paperoni dello sport. Più di 51 miliardi per i Giochi. *La Gazzetta dello Sport*, p. 32.

Poli, M. (2014d, February 9). Slopestyle da applausi. Kotsenburg trova l'oro con il salto mai tentato. *La Gazzetta dello Sport,* p. 27.

Poli, M. (2014e, February 15). Torna il Serial Winner. La forza del campione: il meglio quando conta. *La Gazzetta dello Sport*, p. 27.

Poli, M. (2014f, February 24). Impianti e spettacolo. Lo zar è stato di parola. *La Gazzetta dello Sport*, p. 33.

Reichel, C. (2014, January 24): Parla Morgenstern: «Sochi, sarò pronto. Ho visto la caduta. Cancellerò la paura». *La Gazzetta dello Sport*, p. 27.

Rowe, D. (2004). *Sport, Culture and the Media*. Maidenhead, UK: Open University Press.

Sorrentino, C., & Bianda, E. (2013). *Studiare giornalismo. Ambiti, logiche, attori*. Roma: Carocci.

Spalletta, M. & Ugolini, L. (2013). *SportNews. Modi e mode del giornalismo sportive italiano*. Roma-Napoli: UCSI-UniSOB.

Spalletta, M., & Ugolini, L. (2014). Hybridity in Italian sports journalism: From sportswomen to celebrities. In *Proceedings of Hybridity and the News. Hybrid Forms of Journalism in the 21st Century conference*. Retrieved from http://www.vub.ac.be/sites/vub/files/nieuws/users/jellmast/Hybridity%20and%20the%20News%20Electronic%20Proceedings2.pdf

Street, J. (1997). Remote control? Politics, technology and "electronic democracy". *European Journal of Communication*, *1*(1), 27–42. doi:10.1177/0267323197012001003

Sudgen, J., & Tomlinson, A. (Eds.). (2012). *Watching the Olympics. Politics, Power and Representation*. New York: Routledge.

Tomlinson, A., & Young, C. (2006). *National Identity and Global Sports Events. Culture, Politics and Spectacle in the Olympics and the Football World Cup*. Albany, NY: State University of New York Press.

Toohey, K., & Veal, A. J. (2007). *The Olympic Games. A Social Science Perspective*. Wallingford: CABI. doi:10.1079/9781845933463.0000

Valentino, P. (2014a, February 3). Giochi grandiosi, il messaggio che Putin manda al mondo. *Corriere della Sera*, p. 39.

Valentino, P. (2014b, February 4). Letta a Sochi mandi un segnale chiaro e forte. *Corriere della Sera*, p. 13.

Valentino, P. (2014c, February 7). Si aprono i Giochi di Putin. Dall'Onu dure critiche alle discriminazioni sui gay. *Corriere della Sera*, pp. 10-11.

Valentino, P. (2014d, February 14). Miracolo a Sochi: Putin abbraccia la Wüst, lesbica d'oro. *Corriere della Sera*, p. 65.

Valentino, P. (2014e, February 15). Russia-Usa, la perenne rivincita. E Putin sfoggia la spilla americana. *Corriere della Sera*, p. 67.

Valentino, P. (2014f, February 17). Sochi, Luxuria arrestata e liberata. Aveva la bandiera «Gay è ok». *Corriere della Sera*, p. 39.

Valentino, P. (2014g, February 19). Pussy Riot, fermo e rilascio: «La polizia è stata violenta». *Corriere della Sera*, p. 59.

Valentino, P. (2014h, February 21). Disertare Sochi? La tregua di Bubka (ma il disagio degli atleti resta). *Corriere della Sera*, p. 5.

Valentino, P. (2014i, February 22). Obama perde la scommessa. Il Canada batte gli Usa e va a giocarsi l'oro dell'hockey. *Corriere della Sera*, pp. 64-65.

Valentino, P. (2014l, February 24). I Giochi sono fatti, adesso è tempo di sfide. *Corriere della Sera*, p. 41.

Van Zoonen, L. (2005). *Entertaining the Citizen. When Politics and Popular Culture Converge*. Lanham, MD: Rowman & Littlefield.

Vanetti, F. (2014a, January 8). Giochi già finiti per la Vonn. «Non posso, devo farmi operare». *Corriere della Sera*, p. 43.

Vanetti, F. (2014b, January 18). Visintin: «Gioco a rollerball sulla tavola». *Corriere della Sera*, p. 51.

Vanetti, F. (2014c, January 24). I velocisti azzurri all'esame di Kitzbuehel. *Corriere della Sera*, p. 51.

Vanetti, F. (2014d, February 8). Gli uomini-jet azzurri alla discesa della verità. *Corriere della Sera*, p. 58.

Vanetti, F. (2014e, February 9). Vanessa in musica da Mozart al gigante: «Lo sci è come il violino, ci vuole ritmo». *Corriere della Sera*, p. 39.

Vanetti, F. (2014f, February 10). Christof d'argento. *Corriere della Sera*, pp. 32-33.

Vanetti, F. (2014g, February 12). La missione della Russia. Cancellare la beffa Usa. *Corriere della Sera*, p. 43.

Vanetti, F. (2014h, February 14). Tina, discese ardite e risalite: «Ho imparato dalle sconfitte». *Corriere della Sera*, p. 65.

Vanetti, F. (2014i, February 15). Il replicante. Dopo l'argento, Innerhofer è di bronzo: «Ma come ho fatto?». *Corriere della Sera*, pp. 66-67.

Vanetti, F. (2014l, February 16). Innerhofer chiude in superG inseguendo un tris storico. *Corriere della Sera*, p. 33.

Vanetti, F. (2014m, February 17). Innerhofer, niente tris: «Ma fatemi un sorriso». *Corriere della Sera*, p. 39.

Vanetti, F. (2014n, February 21). Razzoli, una medaglia per cancellare quattro anni da buttare. *Corriere della Sera*, p. 63.

Vanetti, F. (2014o, February 24). Soddisfatti, non contenti. *Corriere della Sera*, pp. 48-49.

Venturini, F. (2014, February 8). La roulette di Putin. *Corriere della Sera*, p. 1.

Weber, M. (1946). *From Max Weber: essays in sociology*. New York: Oxford University Press.

Wheeler, M. (2013). *Celebrity Politics*. Cambridge, MA: Polity Press.

Witherspoon, K. B. (2013). *Before the Eyes of the World: Mexico and the 1968 Olympic Games*. Chicago: Northern Illinois University Press.

ENDNOTE

[1] This essay is the joint work of both authors. However, the paragraphs entitled "Introduction and context", "Research aims and methodology", "Scripting media events" and 'Conclusion" are to be attributed to Marica Spalletta; the paragraphs entitled "Defining media events", "Celebrating media events" and "Discussion" are to be attributed to Lorenzo Ugolini.

This research was previously published in Global Perspectives on Media Events in Contemporary Society edited by Andrew Fox, pages 173-193, copyright year 2016 by Information Science Reference (an imprint of IGI Global).

Chapter 27
Bollywood Sporting Spectacles:
Indian Premier League Cricket as a Bollywoodized Media Event

Sony Jalarajan Raj
MacEwan University, Canada

Rohini Sreekumar
Amity University, India

ABSTRACT

Indian Premier League (IPL) has evolved as a popular event for the large entertainment savvy middle class as well as sports enthusiasts who equally enjoy the new live spectacle on television. Most of the franchised team is owned by Bollywood stars or at least branded or heralded by film star. This made cricket match an extremely glamorized event with all the mix of a Bollywood film. This revolutionized the entertainment culture of public where they are now witnessing the merging of the most popular entertainment outlet – film and sports. The chapter argues that the concept of IPL as a media event is identified by the public as a glorified Bollywood film where it set an ideology that every second should be enjoyed with a similar enthusiasm of a masala Bollywood film. This chapter situates IPL with the larger framework provided by Dayan and Katz (1992) in defining a media event.

INTRODUCTION

India, aiming to become one of the super powers of the world (Follath, 2012), has only a faded image in the sports arena. Despite the population of one billion and a growing economy, India's poor performances in world sports have been a major discussion during any prestigious sports events like Olympics or Asian Games (Shetty, 2014; Lal, 2008). However, all these disregards has been positively contemplated to the popularity of cricket, a game of spirit and entertainment that the Indians vie and die for. Even when India's failure in the global athletic events has always been highlighted, India is known for the craziest audience for cricket. Cricket is enthusiastically appreciated by the Indian population irrespective of age gender or religious differences. Brought by the British colonists in India, cricket remains as an incom-

DOI: 10.4018/978-1-5225-5475-2.ch027

parable trade mark left by the colonial rule. This gradually evolved into a mania in India, where the dream of an average kid is to become a cricketer. Lezard (2003), while reviewing the book A Corner of a Foreign Field: The Indian History of a British commented that cricket would be the major factor that undermined the caste system in India. Apart from cricket, an equally popular entertainment medium in India is Bollywood, which is now a global entity. Bollywood has been always receptive to changing social and political scenarios in their thematic adaptations (Dudrah, 2006). In Bollywood, though sports films seized the interest among the filmmakers only recently, it is rapidly becoming the favourite genre as they try to plot the films over popular games and sports in India. By the beginning of 1980s onwards, Bollywood films began to give prior consideration to sport movies, which gradually evolved into a particular genre in Bollywood. It has already become a globalized cultural industry and a cinema of attractions packaged with romance, melodrama, action, costumes, songs and dance extravaganzas. While establishing a devoted fan base around the world, Bollywood entered into a lucrative area of cross-media entertainment by stepping into the world of sports entertainment. Bollywood stretches its long business tentacles with the Indian version of twenty20 cricket, popularly known as Indian Premier League (IPL), the money making machine which is now as competitive and profitable as English Premier League Football. Nevertheless, IPL is now one of the much celebrated events in the global sporting world where the celebrity film stars and business tycoons sponsor and organize the team. This nexus of Bollywood stars with the global business leaders and international cricketers fetched an easy revenue of 200 billion dollars in the beginning year. As IPL reached the sixth season of its triumphs and tribulations, it has become a prototype of a new age business entity which has been adopted in different parts of the world. This chapter identifies IPL as a 'media event' and, equates and evaluates the ways in which this qualifies as a media event by juxtaposing it with the the major aspects provided by Dayan and Katz (1992).

CONTEXT AND THEORETICAL FRAMEWORK

Bollywood actors' entry into the cricket field made the sport the most glamorous event in Indian entertainment scenario. In the present era, people are searching for countless ways to get entertained. Entertainment is the core of most of the popular television programs. Previously, the presence of any celebrity in the pavilion excited both the live audience and the television audience equally. On the contrary, now cricket turned out to be star-studded event bedecked with cheer-girls that made the televised world to compete for the telecast rights. This revolutionized the entertainment culture of public by merging two of the most popular entertainment media– film and sports. This not only merged two big industries, but brought together their audiences to the same platform. Now audience witness their favourite stars like Shah Rukh Khan, Preety Zinta and Shilpa Shetty cheering for his/her team, and the celebrity or star image that the players are getting due their presence and involvement in styling the players according to their image. Here the game of cricket is getting the image of a 2-3 hour Bollywood film of anticipation, sentiments, joy, sorrow, and where, the dance and song sequence is replaced by the cheer girls, live-drum beats and theme songs, and the highly emotional reaction by the stars on the pavilion provides the best scene of the day (as Shahrukh's quarrel with the security staff of a stadium in Mumbai after the victory of his team Kolkota Knight Riders that banned him from entering the stadium for five years).

While much have been written on these two popular entertainment media, a nexus between them either as a film genre or as a entrepreneurship have been scarcely taken into consideration in the academic parlance. The proposed chapter situates IPL within the original description of media event provided by Dayan and Katz (1992) where they posited that these "events electrify a large audience...cause audience to celebrate the event by gathering before the television sets in groups" (p.9). Furthermore, they argue that these events integrate societies in a collective heartbeat. On a simple terms, Dayan and Katz identified three main aspects that distinguish any live broadcasts from media events - it has to be an interruption to the routine television broadcasting, has to be ceremonious and it should excite a large and collective audience. Though this aspects that make a broadcast a media event has been widely criticised and questioned with the increasing number of live television channels that sensitise and glamorize every petty incidents, this chapter proposes that Dayan and Katz original description could still be found relevant in understanding any a broadcast as a media event. In this chapter we argue that the festivity is achieved through the presence of a glamorous industry like Bollywood in the sports that gave the whole game structure an entirely new face and reception aesthetics. Moreover it not only provides a cinematic touch to the game, but captures a large, but divided audience based on specific region/territory each of which is headed by a celebrity mainly Bollywood film stars, leading to the celebration and reconciliation among the States.

Starting with a general introduction on Bollywood and its global entertainment and cultural prospect, the chapter moves on to the definition of entertainment in this ICT era, and the transformation of the most popular sport, cricket into a new format of 20 overs reducing its timespan. This is followed by the Indian adaptation of T20 and the arrival of betting of players and a new revenue model and media entertainment culture.

METHODOLOGY

The chapter is purely a qualitative study considering mainly newspaper reports to elucidate the relation between Bollywood and Cricket, and the factors that make this sports event a glamorous media ritual.

Commercialized Cricket: IPL and Bollywood

As previously discussed, though in global games India could not make a mark, she has already conquered the world with its 'soft power' (Tharoor, 2012; as quoted in "Shashi Tharoor: Soft Power"). The recent franchised cricket tournament is yet another kind of a cultural conquest. Indian Premier League (IPL), which Forbes Magazine labelled as the 'World's hottest Sports League', is the brain child of the Board of Control for Cricket in India (BCCI), who modelled this upon other professional sports confederacies like English Premier League and Major League Baseball. The first season of IPL commenced on April 2008. BCCI's brain child IPL is an attempt to track the 99 million television audience in India. Targeted towards the billionaires, corporate celebrities and film stars, IPL is aimed at tracking previously unseen revenue assimilation. As Sinha (2011) opined, branding of IPL was achieved through segmentation, according to which the teams are segmented so that it will appeal to local as well as global audience and which could add glamour as well be able to pump huge revenue into the game.

It is cricket's version of tabloid journalism. It is much more now about glamour and entertainment than about what happens between the players," said Rajdeep Sardesai, the son of a professional Indian cricketer and editor in chief of CNN-IBN, a news channel. (Sengupta, 2008)

Let's take a glance at the popular English Premier league which could be considered as the inspirational model for Indian Premier League. Barclays Premier League is said to be the most watched premier leagues in the world marking its television turn over alone to be £1.2 billion. While the teams of Premier League are 20 football clubs from various parts of Europe, IPL is a consortium of 8 teams under the banner of the most prominent personalities/celebrities from different states of India rather than any cricket clubs. This include Bollywood stars' owned teams like Shahrukh Khan/ Juhi Chawla leading West Bengal (*Kolkata Knight Riders*), Shilpa Shetty for Rajasthan (*Rajastan Royals*) and Priti Zinta for Punjab (*Kings XI Punjab*), and Corporates' owned teams like *Mumbai Indians* (owned by Mukhesh Ambani), *Sunrisers Hyderabad* owned by Sun Group (a media conglomerate), *Chennai Super Kings* by India Cements, Delhi Daredevils by GMR Group and Royal Challengers Bangalore owned by UB group. Premier League football games are for hard core football fans who sometimes follow their favourite team in different stadium around the world. The 90 minutes match is played with all eyes on the players, with no distractions of celebrity. Here players are the heroes and there chants/terrace chats form the extravaganza of the match. The suspense is created in these matches with the hooligan activities which is a direct reflection of the response of the highly devoted sports followers (Ingle, 2013).

One of the main reasons for a global popularity of IPL was the presence of celebrities like film stars and corporate icons as the franchisors of the teams. The subject gets such a prominence as it is a nexus between two global entertainment outlets, sports and Bollywood. There is a huge marketing strategy behind formulating IPL, brand elements and marketing elements. Major share of its marketing and branding activities are conducted through television, thereby creating a mediated fandom and sports consumption. The global broadcasting rights for IPL was procured by partnership between Sony Entertainment Television Network and World Sport Group (Based in Singapore) for US 1.026 billion, who in turn resold the rights to other foreign broadcasters for their local telecasting in respective countries (Sinha, 2011). Since mostly depending on the broadcasting rights, Bollywood celebrities find this an added advantage to further their screen presence across the world. For them, it is dual victory as while propagating the team through television, they are also targeting their film audience. 64% of the total amount earned through television right return to the hands of franchisers. The central argument thus is how the presence of film fraternities in the sports tournament and in its ownership gave a significant boost to the marketing of the sports in a global arena. For the audience who have seen their stars as sportsman only in the big screen, this was a chance to experience their real-life dedication to sports. The main star presence in the games is none other than the King of Bollywood, Shah Rukh Khan, the owner of the team/franchise, 'Kolkata Knight Riders'. Other prominent film stars are Prita Zinta, owner of the team Kings XI Punjab, Shilpa Shetty, owner of Rajasthan Royals, along with the presence of an array for ambassadors like Katrina Kaif and Deepika Padukone from respective states to encourage the players and the team.

In the contemporary world, where sports events are increasingly going global, one of the effective ways to brand it would be through celebrities who has already gained name in the global cultural scenario. In many ways, IPL is an adaptation of English Premier League, where by the teams are regionalized and franchised on a profit mission apart from sports enthusiasm. As Rowe and Gilmour (2009) opined on the hybridized global/local culture of sports consumption in Asian countries,

These shifts are manifested in the growing popularity of sports entertainment cultures that reflect the rise of emergent media and leisure economies, combining global aspirational cosmopolitanism with an assertion of local cultural identities and histories.

Hence propagating IPL could not be more effective than giving it into the hands of film personalities (few at least) who can lift the image of the league to a global sports entertainment scenario. The major success of the show hence lies in the way it has met with audience need for entrainment and their expectations from a film- glamour, heroes, villains, sentiments, emotions, conflicts, and victory.

As when the consumption and conception of sports become culturally adapted and identified, for India, Bollywood being the major commodity showing India in a global map, there is no other better strategy that could connect the game with the glamorous film industry, but to associate it with Bollywood. Such a nexus is a double edged coin, where by on one side the profit generation is an advantage for both the parties, on the other side, it provides an opportunity to brand himself/herself or their films. Moreover, the new culturally adapted sports event is also a novel way to address the limitations of both the medium; traditional cricket lacked a glamour, and Bollywood, though has filmed cricket, lacked a direct showcase of their sports spirit. Here the pivotal game of cricket has been diluted to only part of a giant extravaganza, where laser shows, cheer leaders, responsive film stars in the pavilion has captured most of the space.

Bollywood in the Pitch: When Glamour Meets Sports

Rather than looking at the revenue generated, this article looks at the way this IPL was projected as a visual extravagance, there by reformatting the stage, scenario and the reception of cricket as a media event. This remains as a perfect example of how the traditional definition of cricket or a Premier League has been redefined by the modern celebrity society.

Bollywood is the most popular entertainment industry in India (Rajadhyaksha, 2003) and it is based on this factor that IPL became a celebrated media event. While getting into the game in itself, the event is organized in such a manner that every second of the game hold complete glamorous extravagance as it is also telecasted live through television around the globe apart from the live audience in the stadium. Here the attempt is to showcase cricket as a glamorous Bollywood event. Every match is a 3 hour show packed with the filmic elements of anticipation, sentiments, joy, sorrow, and where, the dance and song sequence is replaced by the cheer girls, live-drum beats and theme songs. More than the players, it is the stars in the pavilion towards whom the camera focuses most of the time to capture the highly emotional reaction by them, making it sometimes the best scene of the day. In fact IPL could be considered as a televised sports spectacle as a Bollywood masala film.

Bollywood is globally popular for its song and dance sequences. IPL, the televised spectacle was not devoid of this. One of the main elements that has been criticized as well as encouraged during the game was the presence of cheer girls, a group of seductively dressed girls who cheered, swayed and applaud on the ground. 'Dancing beauties' as they are often referred to could be compared to the recent trend of 'item dancers' in Bollywood films, where by a sexy dancer number often by some popular actress in Bollywood (who just have a cameo appearance through this song) is included in the film, which has no relation to the plot, but just to market the film and the songs. As with the item girls and item numbers in the film, cheerleaders also met with many criticisms. Moreover, most of these cheer girl groups are taken from Europe, Australia and US. This also is a globalizing trend of Bollywood, where by films increasingly cast foreign characters, both as a significant element of its storyline, and also to support the dance and song sequences. The role of these cheer girls are questioned from politicians to religious leaders. Bharatiya Janata Party, President (Maharashtra) commented that while the dance bars are banned in Maharashtra, why these cheer girls are not bought under the same legislature being similar or sometimes worse than bar girls (Raghunath, 2008). However being a Bollywood star-studded event, the role of cheerleaders is easily understood as a point to maximize the glamour. Even before the commencement of the season, news about its music performances used to take the sports and entertainment section of all media. There was a huge publicity in 2011 for IPL's fourth season that Shahrukh khan is planning to share screen with Pop singer Shakira for his teams' theme music. However, though the news have been never confirmed nor did the song ever happened, audience was patiently following up with the star activities in the IPL in a similar way as they do prior to the release of his film. Again in 2013, Shahrukh Khan was dragged into the news when Jennifer Lopez turned down the offer put forward by his team Kolkata Knight Riders to perform in inaugural ceremony of the sixth season of IPL.

When coming to the music, IPL team Themes songs have been much discussed and debated in the media and particularly on YouTube. Shilpa's Rajastan Royals chose Sunidhi Chauhan whereas Kings XI Punjab owned by Priti Zinta made the Punjabi pop singer Daler Mehandi, brand ambassador to give a musical touch to their team.

Shah Rukh Khan and his team Kolkata Knight Riders would be the best case study of analysis in this glamorised sports event. SRK's team is considered commercially the most successful because it has a high number of sponsors. SRK's star power acts as a money puller for the team. Being unbeatable in the film industry and a global icon, Shah Rukh himself is the brand ambassador of his team, and is one of the highest revenue making team in the event. An year before the commencement of the first season of IPL, Shah Rukh captured the box office with an unique character as a Hockey coach in the film, Chak de India (2007). This in fact gave a boost to the star value of the actor when he took the leadership of a cricket team. Much of the drama in the IPL seasons are provided by him through his emotional response in pavilion. To give a glamorous touch to his team, the jersey for his players were designed by the renowned Bollywood fashion designer, Manish Malhotra ("Kolkata Knight", 2008) and under the directorship of the prominent choreographer and director Farah Khan, a music video album was made with an African background ("No new", 2010).

In the seasons starting from 2008 to 2012, Bollywood directors deferred the release of the films during the initial season of the IPL earing that the films get unnoticed because of the gaining popularity of the cricket extravaganza (Das, 2012). Sinha (2012) commented that during the first three seasons of IPL, multiplexes remained almost unutilized, with some of them showing IPL promos, rather than film. However, by 2012, as the popularity of IPL began to wane, Bollywood filmmakers made the IPL vent itself as a stage for promoting the films and actors. According to Rowe (2004) the positive image of a global sports event is exploited for promoting films among the sports fans, so that more audience will be attracted both to the sports ground as well to the film theatres. Recent trend of film team owners to encourage the promotional activities is also a similar stunt to track the audience, as the TRP ratings of IPL is gradually waning as the years pass ("IPL's television rating", 2013). As such film personalities increasingly began to use the event as a platform to promote the films and other causes, as the IPL itself is a complete package of visual treat. The latest in the list is Shah Rukh's film *Chennai Express* (2013), whose promo is released in the final match of IPL Season 6. Moreover, social causes also find this platform more helpful. As such Farhan Akhtar promoted his MARD (Men against Rape and Discrimination) campaign, raising voice against gender inequality and atrocities against women. The match chosen for the promotion is also notable; biggest matches between Shah Rukh Khan's team Kolkatta Knight Riders and Priety Zinta's Kings 11 Punjab with a whole pavilion wearing black big moustache.

As Bollywood also is known for its highly emotional and sensational melodrama and conflict, the game is also not devoid of conflicts and media bash. Two of the cheer girls from Kings XI Punjab was asked to leave the stadium at Mohali by the team's event management company Wizcraft International Entertainment pointing on their dark skin (Banerjee, 2008). This shook the society with global media bashing against the racist approach of the company. The King of the show, Shah Rukh left no chances to make this event no less than a Bollywood films with his highly poignant response to issues. IN the first season of IPL, Shahrukh made a huge cry when ICC anti-corruption Unit prohibited him from entering the dressing room and the dugout area ("SRK say he", 2008). Expressing disappointment and frustration the actor announced that he will boycott the matches. To add with it, in 2012, for misbehaving and man-handling the security personals, he was banned for five years from entering the MCA (Mumbai Cricket Association) premises including Wankhede Stadium ("Shah Rukh Khan banned", 2012). Though the response came after the victory of his team in the match, for the public, this anti-climax was no less than watching a thriller. Filmic moments were incessant in the IPL seasons that filled the air space of both new and entertainment media. During the IPL season 5 in 2012, five players were suspended from BCCI for spot-fixing which was actually caught in a sting operation by a private news channel (Ramanujam, 2012).

These factors provide the game of cricket the frontage of a three hour colourful extravaganza as similar to a film. Becoming a model for all other regional films, Bollywood sets the status of an 'all-India cinema' (Mishra, 2002), creating a shared experience and transforming them to an abstract national subject. This also helps in surpassing language, class and cultural differences, by catering to varied sections of society, from "illiterates" to "sophisticated urbanites" (Ibid., p. 4). The presence of such an industry's association and influence with cricket (a popular sport in India) not only provides the game with a glamorous facade, but unites a large and collective audience in the way way as it does with its films. According to a survey done by Business Standard in 2014, IPL has the highest reach in India when compared to other sports event (As quoted in "IPL is the largest reached", 2015). In 2015, IPL saw an increase in viewership of 41% (IPL T20 Official website, 2015). According to Tam Media Research, 2015, 36% of IPL viewers are women for which Santosh Desai, a social commentator, responds that the credit for this goes to the programming and packaging (Raghavendra & Sharma, 2015). This percentage of women viewership is significant because Indian female viewers have been always criticized for their craze for soap operas which captures the prime time space in television owing to its popularity (Raj & Kumar, 2010). In this way IPL was able to draw a large collective audience, thus satisfying the three main factors posited by Elihu and Katz - ceremonious event drawing a large collective audience with an interruption to routine telecast.

Evaluating IPL under the tagline of a Media event provides many more justifications. TV Channel 'Colors' owned by Viacom and Network 18 unleashed four shows taking into its ambit the audience of Bollywood and cricket. IPL Rockstar, a music talent reality show is one among the ambitious project in which the Bollywood team owners like Shahrukh, Shilpa Shetty and Preity Zinta taking turns to be in the judgment seat making the experience of the cricket even to more heights. While the IPL Award Night was organized to honour the performers on field IPL Khatron Ke Khiladi, reality show like Fear Factor was organized whereby cricketers perform stunts. The list has been filled by a series of Fashion shows and music events organized by different franchises of IPL (Chandran, 2010). Rajesh, the chief executive of Colors commented,

Cricket is a national passion. Bollywood is a religion. If you can bring both of them together, it can't get any bigger than that... (Leahy, 2010)

Meanwhile, Star Plus has conducted the Bollywood award night CINTAA award in conjunction with the third season of IPL. As television channel vie to attach shows to the popularity of IPL and Bollywood, this in-turn has helped the films fraternities to use these platform to market their films.

It could be said that the democratisation of cricket happened with IPL as family audience began to frequent stadium. This is in stiff response to the positives of IPL like less duration, presence of their favourite celebrities, music, dance and drama within an affordable ticket price to enter the stadium (Bastian, 2012). To make the show enjoyable for the non-English speaking group, Sony Six commenced the Hindi commentary for the matched telecasting in their channel. This has also reflected in the television viewership of IPL which rose to a record of 140 million in its sixth season (Srivastava, 2013).

The trend of using sports celebrities for product endorsement has been looked at as a marketing tactics to increase the emotional tie between consumer and the celebrity (Stone, Joseph, Jones, 2003). Particularly in India, high performing sports personalities are the highest endorsers. For instance, Forbes Magazine ranked Mahendra Singh Dhoni, the Indian cricket team captain the 31st in the list of richest sportsperson far ahead of Wayne Rooney and Usain Bolt. Out of his income, 90 percent came from his endorsements that make him one of the wealthiest sportsperson in the world. It's quite amusing to note that half of the products that he endorse have no particular relation to his personae; the products include Mysore Sandal soap, Dabur Honey and Videocon. As Carlson and Donavan (2008) opined, the fan's identification with the celebrity has a positive impact on the marketing of that product due to the emotional attachment called para-social relationship. In this particular case, the product or event is marketed by film stars where by the para-social relationship has doubled with the presence of Bollywood stars who has also made use of the fandom of sports stars to increase the brand of their franchise. However, even though cricket became a household name in India with IPL, these games are known for its celebrity/film star presence rather than the glory of the game in the same way a film is popular for its star presence.

CONCLUSION

The latest result of a global mediated cultural extravaganza is the Bollywoodized cricket tournament named Indian Premier League. As Rowe and Gilmour (2009) quoted, the tagline of contemporary global sports is 'a mediated live cultural form'. While being constituted by a culture, in the present world, the consumption of that event remains global, though being local. IPL is a perfect example of how the overpowering entrainment world has captured the scope of sports in furthering their business interest and vice versa. Cricket and Bollywood being the two pop culture of India, the coming together of these two huge revenue-makers rewrite the entertainment aesthetics.

As contrary to the belief that the IPL can negatively affect the Bollywood film release, it has proved that cricket and Bollywood can go hand in hand when it reached its sixth season. Films have proved that if the story is good the success is certain. Though IPL brought forward the commercialisation of cricket previously unseen in India or elsewhere, this also have democratised the sports with the participation of all sectors of society. However the spirit of the game have far been removed from the stadium due to its capsule effect and the distractions in the stadium like star presence. One of the constructive service that these franchises could do to the society is to dedicate a part of their profit for entertaining cricket clubs in their respective states that could encourage young cricketers to come forward. Each franchisers should make sure that their teams have a few new faces from these clubs. This will make the league in all ways democratic.

For cricket as well as the Bollywood industry, it is a win-win situation, as both flourish on the reputation of either. The nexus proved well as it tracked a combination of audience, both local and global, consisting of both the sports as well as the film fans. The important element, the game itself, has been pushed aside by the presence of star entrepreneurs and film stars. Bollywood entrepreneurs left no chance to make the event an extravagance where the sports stadium could be transformed to a film location, not devoid of any elements that make a cinematic ambience. The chapter also shows that amidst the soaring amount of live news channels and live broadcastings, the separation of these events from the definition given by Dayan and Katz (1992) still be found significant.

Though the article gave prior concern to the bollywoodizing trend of IPL, it also shed light on the non-western flow of culture. Though adapted from the western concept of premier leagues, IPL has interpreted it such a way that it gave a locally-rooted cultural touch, branding it as an entertainment extravaganza with global players, thus making it a global sport event. Such a contextualized sports event is important as it characterised by the non-western world, thus realigning the power structure of the world.

REFERENCES

Baker, A. (2003). *Contesting Identities: Sports in American Film*. Urbana, IL: University of Illinois Press.

Banerje, P. (2008, May 20). 'Colour of skin' comes into play 'Dark' girls told to leave. *The Telegraph*. Retrieved from http://www.telegraphindia.com/1080520/jsp/frontpage/story_9295090.jsp

Bastian, N. (2012). Fun for the whole family. *ESPN Cricinfo*. Retrieved from http://www.espncricinfo.com/magazine/content/story/566303.html

Bergan, R. (1982). *Sports in the movies*. London: Proteus.

Carlson, B. D., & Donavan, D. T. (2008). Concerning the effect of athlete endorsements on brand and team-related intentions. *Sport Marketing Quarterly*, *17*, 154–162.

Chandran, A. (2010). Colors charges premium on IPL shows to recover costs. *Live Mint*. Retrieved from http://www.livemint.com/Companies/a0toFOYhX0DII2tIQbn5pK/Colors-charges-premium-on-IPL-shows-to-recover-costs.html

Das, S. (2012, June 7). How Bollywood braved the IPL storm. *Indiantelevision.com*. Retrieved from http://www.indiantelevision.com/aac/y2k12/aac699.php

Dudrah, R. (2006). *Bollywood; Sociology goes to the movies*. New Delhi: Sage Publication India Pvt Ltd.

Follath, E. (September 09, 2012). India at Crossroads on Path to Superpower Status. *ABC News*. Retrieved from http://abcnews.go.com/International/india-crossroads-path-superpower-status/story?id=17173228

Fowler, A. (1989). Genre. In E. Barnouw (Ed.), *International Encyclopedia of Communications* (Vol. 2, pp. 215–217). New York: Oxford UniversityPress.

Gupta, A. (2004). The globalization of cricket: The rise of the non-West. *The International Journal of the History of Sport*, *21*(2), 257–276. doi:10.1080/0952336041000168l975

Ingle, S. (2013). Football hooliganism, once the English disease, is more like a cold sore now. *The Guardian*. Retrieved from http://www.theguardian.com/football/blog/2013/nov/03/english-football-hooliganism

IPL is the largest reached sports event. (2015). *Indiatelevision.com*. Retrieved from http://www.indiantelevision.com/specials/event-coverage/ficci-frames/ipl-is-the-largest-reached-sports-event-in-2014-ficci-kpmg-report-150330

IPL's television ratings slightly down from 2012. (2013, April13). *ESPN cricinfo*. Retrieved fromhttp://www.espncricinfo.com/indian-premier-league-2013/content/story/629700.html

Is cricket killing other sports in India. (2011). *Sportstar*. Retrieved from http://www.sportstaronnet.com/tss2724/stories/20040612009908200.htm

Joshi, S. (2012). BCCI not a 'charitable organisation'. *The Hindu*. Retrieved form http://www.thehindu.com/sport/cricket/article2910033.ece

Katz, E., & Liebes, T. (2007). "No More Peace!": How disaster, terror and war have upstaged media events. *International Journal of Communication*, *1*(2), 157–166.

Kolkata Knightriders launched amidst gloom. (2008, March 11). *Hindustan Times*. Retrieved from http://www.hindustantimes.com/Cricket/CricketNews/Kolkata-Knightriders-launched-amidst-gloom/Article1-281360.aspx

Kress, G. (1988). *Communication and Culture: An Introduction*. Kensington, NSW: New South Wales University Press.

Kumar, S. (2011). An India beyond cricket. *The Diplomat*. Retrieved from http://thediplomat.com/indian-decade/2011/04/10/an-india-beyond-cricket/

Lal, N. (August 08, 2008). India's failure of Olympic proportions. *Asia Times*. Retrieved from http://www.atimes.com/atimes/South_Asia/JH08Df03.html

Leahy, J. (2010). Viacom and News Corp targeting India. *Financial Times*. Retrieved from http://www.ft.com/intl/cms/s/0/7cf107fa-248a-11df-8be0-00144feab49a.html#axzz2rIYjTyMO

Lezard, N. (2003). How cricket conquered India. *The Guardian*. Retrieved from http://www.theguardian.com/books/2003/may/03/featuresreviews.guardianreview5

Majumdar, B. (2001). Politics of Leisure in Colonial India: 'Lagaan': Invocation of a Lost History? *Economic and Political Weekly*, *36*(35), 3399–3404.

Mishra, V. (2002). *Bollywood Cinema: Temples of Desire*. New York: Routledge.

O'Brien, T. (1990). The Screen of America: Movies and Values from Rocky to Rain Man. Academic Press.

PEPSI IPL 2015 opens with a 41% increase. (2015). *IPL T20 Official Website*. Retrieved from http://www.iplt20.com/news/2015/announcements/6068/pepsi-ipl-2015-opens-with-a-41-increase-in-tv-viewership

Raghavendra, N., & Sharma, R. T. (May 21, 2015). Competitive Premier League drawing more women into audience. *The Economic Times*. Retrieved from http://articles.economictimes.indiatimes.com/2015-05-21/news/62459722_1_mumbai-indians-ipl-royal-challengers-bangalore

Raghunath, P. (2008, April 25). Cheerleaders pose a 'moral dilemma'. *Gulf News*. Retrieved from http://gulfnews.com/news/world/india/cheerleaders-pose-a-moral-dilemma-1.99456

Raj, S. J., & Sreekumar, R. (2010). Reaching The Middle Class? Commoditized Soap Opera in The Indian Media Paradigm. *Mass Communicator*, *4*(3), 15–25.

Rajadhyaksha, A. (2003). The 'Bollywoodization' of the Indian cinema: Cultural nationalism in a global arena. *Inter-Asia Cultural Studies*, *4*(1), 26–39. doi:10.1080/1464937032000060195

Ramanujam, S. (2012, May 16). Has cricket become just a money making venture? *The Times of India*. Retrieved from http://www.kathoram.com/malayalam/south-north-indian-kerala-traditional-non-vegetarian-recipe-pachakam-adukkala/taste-time/29592-taste-time-.html

Rowe, D. (1998). If you film it, will they come? Sports on Film. *Journal of Sport and Social Issues*, *22*(4), 350–359. doi:10.1177/019372398022004002

Rowe, D. (Ed.). (2004). *Critical readings: Sports, culture and the media*. Maidenhead, UK: Open University Press.

Rowe, D., & Gilmour, C. (2009). Global sport: Where Wembley Way meets Bollywood Boulevard. *Continuum (Perth)*, *23*(2), 171–182. doi:10.1080/10304310802710512

Sarris. (1980). Why sports movies don't work. *Film Comment, 16*(6), 49-53.

Sengupta, S. (2008, May 7). Bright Lights and Big Money in India's New Cricket League. *The New York Times*. Retrieved from www.nytimes.com/2008/05/07/sports/othersports/07cricket.html?pagewanted=all&_r=0 1/

Shah Rukh Khan banned from Wankhede stadium for 5 years. (2012, May 23). *The Indian Express*. Retrieved from http://www.indianexpress.com/news/shah-rukh-khan-banned-from-wankhede-stadium-for-5-years/950969/

Shetty, A. (2014). *Why does a country as big and able as India fail to produce top class athletes?* Retrieved from http://www.cricketzone.in/Thread-Why-does-a-country-as-big-and-able-as-India-fail-to-produce-top-class-athletes

Sinah. (2011). The Creation of a successful brand. In *Cases in Management*. New Delhi: PHI Learning Private Limited.

Singh, P. (2013). Indian Premier League blues no more for Bollywood? *The Hindustan Times*. Retrieved from http://www.hindustantimes.com/entertainment/bollywood/indian-premier-league-blues-no-more-for-bollywood/article1-1037080.aspx

Sinha. (2012, April 2). IPL clash gets bigger as Bollywood enters the picture. *The Times of India*. Retrieved from http://articles.timesofindia.indiatimes.com/2012-04-02/india/31275098_1_ipl-games-small-budget-films-film-industry

Srivastava, P. (2013). IPL 6 mania reaches new high, first 16 games record a staggering 140 million viewership. *India Today*. Retrieved from http://indiatoday.intoday.in/story/first-16-games-of-ipl-6-record-staggering-140-million-viewership/1/267963.html

SRK says he will boycott remaining matches of IPL. (2008, May 23). *IBN Live*. Retrieved from http://ibnlive.in.com/news/srk-says-he-will-boycott-remaining-matches-of-ipl/65781-5.html

Stone, G., Joseph, M., & Jones, M. (2003). An exploratory study on the use of sports celebrities in advertising: A content analysis. *Sport Marketing Quarterly*, *12*, 94–102.

Upala, K. B. R. (2010, February 24). No new videos for IPL teams. *Mid-Day*. Retrieved from http://entertainment.oneindia.in/bollywood/features/2010/no-ipl-videos-240210.html

Why does India perform so poorly at the Olympics? (2012). *Euro News*. Retrieved from http://www.euronews.com/2012/07/19/why-does-india-perform-so-poorly-at-the-olympics/

World Cup final had highest rating: TAM. (2011, April 7). *The Economic Times*. Retrieved from http://articles.economictimes.indiatimes.com/2011-04-07/news/29392442_1_peak-rating-highest-rating-star-cricket

This research was previously published in Global Perspectives on Media Events in Contemporary Society edited by Andrew Fox, pages 211-223, copyright year 2016 by Information Science Reference (an imprint of IGI Global).

Chapter 28
Sport Omnibus Events as Media Shows

Diana-Luiza Dumitriu
National University of Political Studies and Public Administration, Romania

ABSTRACT

Inside the wider commodification process that the social field of sport has been subject to, sport events are not only about the competition itself, but they have become a global multilayered show. The 'symbiotic relationship' (Valgeirsson & Snyder, 1986, p. 131) between sport and media made them one of the most successful entertaining products as they provide an intense spectatorship experience. The main aim of this chapter is to focus on the media-sport nexus in order to understand the impact that this hybridization process between the two social fields had on sport events? How media reflect and redefine sport competitions as media events? What are the main aspects that make sport events so competitive on the wider entertaining (media) market? Despite the undisputable transformative effects brought by sport competitions entering the media logic, I will argue that there is also a reverse effect that major sport events exert upon the media field, focusing mainly on their interruptive quality (Dayan & Kats, 1992) in terms of media and social agenda. In discussing these aspects I will narrow down the analysis on the major sport competitions, as they are the most complex media-sport constructs. The 'fun factor' (Kellner, 2003, p. 3) and the emotional flow of the competition reach their most spectacular form through what I call omnibus events. By omnibus events I refer to major competitions on the sport global map that are defined as impressive shows, involving world wide audiences, significant number of sport acts and actors and high commercial value (i.e. The Olympic Games, The World Cup). More important, their vortextual nature (Whannel, 2002) makes them referential for the public agenda, drawing everyone's attention and building alternative ways to connect large number of people to them. The chapter will approach these sport omnibus events as media shows by analyzing their multilayered structure: the dramaturgical dimension of sport acts and its corollary management of impression, the ritual dimension of sport ceremonial practices, the axiological dimension of sport events as social values' system, the commercial dimension of sport events as products on the entertaining and celebrity market, the aesthetic dimension of sport

DOI: 10.4018/978-1-5225-5475-2.ch028

acts as expressive media constructs and their emotional dimension in terms of spectatorship experience. On this last dimension there are two main aspects that I will focus on, one regarding the live-remote experience and the other one directed towards the multiplication process of sport competition related events (from special TV shows, social media events, to thematic parties or marketing events). Media's centrality inside the social field of sport came with a consistent spectacularization effect, contributing to sport competition becoming resourceful media shows in terms of public impact and commercial value, a process that this chapter manages to lay emphasis on by addressing the multilayered nature of such events.

INTRODUCTION

The quid pro quo relationship between sport and media, which has been mainly built on commercial grounds, led to an entire reconfiguration of the sport acts and the spectatorship experiences. When most of our sport experiences are, in fact, mediated ones, media's centrality inside the social field of sport has become somehow truistic. It is more and more difficult to think about sport outside the media logic, as media not only conquered the world of sport, but they have also profoundly transformed it (Whannel, 1992).This symbolic colonization of the sport imagery by the media came with a consistent spectacularization effect, contributing to sport events becoming resourceful media shows in terms of public impact and commercial value. Inside the wider commodification process that sport has been subject to, sport events are no longer only about the competition itself, but more and more about the global-scale show that they end up providing.

The main aim of this chapter is to discuss the impact that the sport media events have in terms of multilayered entertainment constructs. From the overcrowded pool of sport events which managed to rise to the media event status? What are the premises that facilitate the conversion of sport events into such impressive media events? What are the main aspects that make sport media events so competitive on the wider entertaining market?

Despite the compelling structural force exerted by the media (Bourdieu, 1996, p.64) over sport competitions as transcultural phenomena (Hepp & Couldry, 2010), I will argue that some of them are more than ritual media events (Couldry, 2003; Hepp, 2004) or 'high holydays of mass communication' (Dayan & Kats, 1992, p.1). When crowned with the media events' halo, they go way beyond the interruptive festive viewing (Dayan & Kats, 1992), becoming subject to an impressive multiplication process. Therefore, the sport media event is rather a conventional formula for what I call the sport omnibus events, because, de facto, when addressing such global scale phenomena, we are actually speaking about a consistent cluster or mosaic of micro-events.

In order to understand why and how sport events can push the media events framework even further in terms of engagement, transformative and vortextual nature (Whannel, 2002), I will focus on the three constitutive dimensions of such events: the dramaturgical richness embedded in sport performances, the commercial spiral that they manage to fuel and their impressive emotional capital. For this reason I would argue that sport media events are a multilayered construct that should be placed at the junction between the sport, the media and the marketing ethos, acting as a powerful social, cultural and economic palimpsest. The dynamics of such events is, thus, strongly connected to the increasing role of popular culture within today's society (Grindstaff, 2008; McGuigan, 2010) and the successful evolution of the sport industry within the global market economy.

THE RISE OF THE SPORT OMNIBUS EVENTS ON THE GLOBALIZED PUBLIC AGENDA

From local to global sport events, from well-known sport disciplines to new ones, the sport-events' calendar has become very crowded. While, Roy Panagiotopoulou (2010) says that we are facing an "eventization" of the field of sport, I would rather argue that sport per se is structurally an event-based social phenomenon. However, in order to enter on the globalized public agenda, sport events have to meet some generic criteria such as wide audiences, high quality of the performance, high symbolic capital for both the sport actors and the publics, strategic value for sport geopolitics and high marketing potential. Therefore, aiming to win a place under the spotlight, sport events end up competing with each other 'for the conquest of public attention, as all aspire to the privilege of being on all media at one' (Dayan, 2010) and being under the commercial radar.

While entering the wider commodification process that sport has been subject to, sport events themselves have become a resourceful commodity, enriching the media-sport offer on the entertainment market. This symbolic hegemony of the market logic has generated a strong transformative pressure upon the design and the dynamics of the sport events, making them a more and more sophisticated product. However, the sine qua non condition in increasing their market value is that they need to be 'mediazable', providing an attractive media product for the audience. This is how competition and entertainment have become the two sides of the same coin when sport events are at stake, converting the sport mega-events into impressive transcultural phenomena (Hepp & Couldry, 2010).

Sharing the commercial grounds of this media-sport hybridization process, some sport events managed to conquer the global scene. Nevertheless, in a world where almost every social field was affected by the symbolic imperialism of entertainment, when it comes to sport, entertainment as well as competition reach their most spectacular form through what can be called: omnibus events. By *omnibus events* I refer to both the quantitative dimension of their world wide audience, time frame, significant number of participants and impressive financial investments, as well as to the qualitative dimension regarding the spectacular show they are providing and the rich social imagery built around them. When it comes to sport events, The Olympic Games, The World Cup, The FIFA Champions League, The Super Bowl, The Grand Slam Tournaments like Wimbledon or Roland Garros are such examples of omnibus events. They are as famous as any individual sport superstar. Therefore, working as a distinct type of commodity on the celebrity market, they end up generating a whole event-related social imagery and corollary market, acting as a hybrid sport-entertainment product.

The reason why I choose to call them omnibus events and not just megaevents (Roche, 2000; Whannel, 2002) is that the latter term is rather focused on the quantitative dimension of the event in terms of participants and audiences. The omnibus event, however, is a better suited concept to express the multilayered structure of such events, the heterogeneity of both the actors and the actions involved in or related to the sport event. The Latin term "omnibus", which means "for all", including, or dealing with numerous items at once, can thus refer not only to the wide-addressability of these events, but also to their manifold structural mosaic of actors and performances. This integrative and versatile nature of the concept makes it fitted in describing the complexity of such events in terms of sport and cultural signification, soft power (Nye, 2004), entertainment or marketing value.

The global and globalizing nature of such events, as well as their 'vortextual' character (Whannel, 2002), that is the rapid diffusion of all elements connected to these events towards a large and heterogeneous public, are strongly related to their reconfiguration as media events. In other words, what Whannel calls vortextual effect is, de facto, a phenomenon of contamination and convergence in terms of media agenda, described by a consistent and quick-acting coverage and corollary public debates articulated around the events. Nevertheless, within the infinite variety of sport events, only the omnibus ones meet the media events' criteria, hanging a halo over the television set and transforming the viewing experience (Dayan & Kats, 1992, p.1). Why and how do these omnibus sport events become such exciting media events? What favored this successful reconfiguration of sport omnibus events into media events?

First of all I would argue that sport omnibus events involve all three forms of contest, conquest and coronation that Dayan and Kats (1992) refer to when speaking about media events. Competition or contest is the constitutive component of any sport event, while conquest can be related to the symbolic sport geopolitics and war-frame logic. As for the coronation component, it is probably the most intense ritual manifestation within sport omnibus events, activating strong identity and identification mechanisms that link sport actors to their supporters and that provide sport acts with such significant symbolic capital. Who hasn't been moved to tears when the national anthem was played or his favorite athlete kissed the field after a winning performance? All these components converge in creating the proper stage for heroes and stars, for exemplary actions and emerging legends, confirming media-events genre as an 'expression of a neo-romantic desire for heroic action by great men' (Dayan & Kats, 1992, p.21). Moreover, in a celebrity-saturated world, where everyone seems to be involved in either producing or consuming celebrities, I want to lay stress on the commercial value of this desire for heroism, as it is now translated in terms of celebrity-driven consumption behavior. And what better celebrity stage than media sport events?

From media coverage to marketing instrumentalization, the sport omnibus events enter the storytelling reframing process, mixing the tension and the spectacularity of the performance with the inspirational rhetoric of sport acts. The contest-conquest-coronation triad embedded in sport omnibus events becomes a solid pole of public interest as 'one serves to <qualify> the hero (our contest), a second shows the hero reaching beyond human limits (conquest) and the third sets the stage for recognition and <glorification> of the hero (coronation)' (Dayan & Kats, 1992, p.29). People all over the world remember not only the legendary sport figures or the new born stars, but rather a more contextualized event-related frame of glorification, putting sport omnibus events themselves on the celebrity map. It is Nadia's 1976 Montreal Olympic Games first 10 in gymnastics history, Isner and Mahut 2010 Wimbledon Grand Slam 11 hours and 5 minutes marathon match, the 1999 UEFA Champions League Final when Manchester United won by scoring two last-minute goals against Bayern Munich (min. 90+1 and 90+3) or Brazil 2014 FIFA World Cup when Germany trounce Brazil in the semifinals with 7-1. Thus, the walk of fame is not only about teams and athletes, goals or records, but also about the sport omnibus events that hosted their performances.

Back to the grand-scale dimension of sport omnibus events, they reach impressive audiences through media broadcasting, capitalizing on 'the unique potential of the electronic media to command attention universally and simultaneously in order to tell a primordial story about current affairs'(Dayan & Kats, 1992, p.1). In terms of accessibility and popularity, everybody all over the world knows about them, speaks about them and, sooner or later, comes across the show-ball effect produced by them. Whether you like it or not, you find yourself more or less related to these events, the news or the products created by or around them. From live broadcasting, to pre or post competition news, from limited editions of soft-drinks, to T-shirts and travel packs, sport omnibus events, as any media event in this global age, end up reaching 'a wide and diverse multiplicity of audiences and participants' (Hepp & Couldry, 2010).

The vortextual effect (Whannel, 2002) of these media events explains their transformative power (Dayan & Kats, 1992). All the public fussiness created around sport omnibus events, which are very popular and enjoy a high public exposure, reflects their social impact in terms of symbolic and commercial power, as well as in terms of event-viewers and consumers of event-related products. These aspects 'carry semantic meaning: they speak of the greatness of the event and they have a pragmatic aspect as well' (Dayan & Kats, 1992, p.10), since sport omnibus events are both spectacular cultural and commercial global phenomena. Nevertheless, each media sport event acts as a product that needs not only to impress, but most of all to sell. Therefore, going beyond the cultural frame, sport omnibus events 'have been transformed into the focal point of intense commercial activity, in which the commodified spectacle generates huge cash flows' (Whannel, 2009, p.215). This is why they should be understood within the macro-context of the market economy and, moreover, within the wider capitalist framework of a global entertaining market they are part of.

The final aspect that I will refer to in explaining why sport *omnibus* events fall under the heading of media events, before focusing on their constitutive dimensions, is related to their time-frame. Besides the fact that they are 'preplanned, announced and advertised in advance'(Dayan & Kats, 1992, p.7), like any other media event, there is a consistent cyclicity of the sport omnibus events' calendar. While competing for audiences, media coverage and marketing budgets, there is a quite rigid calendar that these events have to keep to. This contributes to increasing the predictability in terms of their schedule, enhancing the ritual dimension of such events and, in marketing terms, maintaining the canibalization between them (as commodities) at low levels. The chance to have The Super Bowl, The FIFA Champions League Final, The Olympic Games and the US Open Grand Slam Tournament all at the same time is only a hypothetic script, with minimum to zero odds of happening, as nobody would benefit from such a situation, whether they are athletes, fans, media or sponsors.

So, beyond the actual competition for the broadcasting rights of sport omnibus events and their contribution in converting them into impressive media events, media also had to cope with their interruptive function. Sport omnibus events interfere with our daily routine, especially in terms of media consumption and entertainment choices. Therefore, they bring significant changes in the normal scheduling of television stations, not only through the actual media coverage of the live-broadcasting of the event, but also through the news, the TV-shows and the ad-hoc debates related to them. Moreover, there is a clear prime-time synchronicity effect, both the media and the sport actors acting towards scheduling a sport omnibus event inside the prime-time period in order to maximize its attraction power. In commercial terms, timing is as important as the product itself and sport events make no exception to this rule, as prime time means larger audiences and, hence, profitability for both the media and the sport actors. The event-centric or temporary monopoly exerted by such media events on the public agenda also explains the closure effect (Bourdieu, 1996) within the media field, that is the high convergence in terms of top-list subjects that dominate the media channels.

But what makes sport omnibus push attractiveness to addictiveness, spectacularity to commercial magnetism? Which are the defining aspects that explain their competitiveness on the entertainment market and on the global public agenda? Far from providing an exhaustive explanatory frame of sport omnibus events, I would focus on what I consider to be the constitutive dimensions of these sport media events and discuss the multiplication process that they are subject to.

THE CONSTITUTIVE DIMENSIONS OF THE SPORT MEDIA EVENTS

Sport omnibus events as complex media events are a multilayered entertainment construct, providing one of the most spectacular global-scale forms of emotional engagement. However, I would argue that, despite the macro-contextual factors that have favoured their emergence, there are three constitutive dimensions that led to such impressive rise of the sport media events on the public agenda: the dramaturgical component embedded in the performances' hosted by such events, their commercial value and the emotional capital on which they have managed to build their strong attraction chains. While addressing these defining aspects of the sport media events, I will lay stress on the overall impact that they have in terms of spectatorship experience and engagement. This, in turn, will help in understanding the addictive consumption that they are object to and the halo effect of such 'high holydays of mass communication'(Dayan & Kats, 1992, p.1). Moreover, they will converge in bringing to the fore the global multiplicative lattice generated by the sport media events.

The *Dramaturgical* Dimension of the Sport Media Events

The 'show' metaphor has been constitutive for the sport ethos, providing a resourceful input for what has been converted into one of the most spectacular forms of media shows. Every sport event involves a dialogic form of social performance that brings together competitive means and entertaining ends, as sport acts are designed to be put on stage in front and, moreover, for the audiences. The performers – audience dyad, which defines these 'platform performances' (Goffman, [1982]/1983, p.7), is, in fact, the sine qua non condition of any sport (media) show, as 'both sets of roles are normative, organically linked, and necessary to the performance' (Cheska, 1979, p.54).

From local to global mega-events, the dynamics of sport performances lays under this meta-metaphor of show, engaging a consistent dramaturgical repertoire of social representations and practices. Hence, due to the recreational dimension and the public nature of the sport acts, the dramaturgical analogy comes as natural in relating to the sport performances. From spatiality, which is inherent to sport (Kennedy & Hills, 2009, p.152), to role-playing, cultural and expressive value, the sport events go beyond the competitive frame, engaging both performers, mediators and spectators (live or remote) in building up impressive shows where 'meaning is a constitutive production in and through group performance' (Rawls, 1987, p.141).

I would argue that, in a context where sport, along with drama and war, have become the dominant metaphors of our time (Manning, 1996, p.261), sport omnibus events have won the foreground because they are actually mobilizing all three dominant metaphors at once. The dramaturgical dimension of sport acts is actually the one that pushed forward their successful reconfiguration as media shows. To some extent it was all about taking the genuine sport show to another level. But, what makes sport events so attractive for the audience and so resourceful for media constructs in terms of dramaturgical potential? Which are the main dramaturgical coordinates embedded in sport performances?

A first aspect that makes a sport event such a great media show is related to the spatiality of the performances and the corollary mapping of the boundaries of perception. Using Goffman's model of performances' regions ([1959]/2003), which is tributary to the theatre metaphor, the sport events provide us with an interesting (social) negotiation of their boundaries. The actual sport performance on the front stage (the game, the race, the confrontation etc.) is, for sure, the most spectacular and engaging part of the sport event, but, the backstage, the zone of transition, or the residual region have become more and more intriguing for the audiences.

Media whetted audiences' appetite for the show behind and beyond the public stage, leading to a constant redefinition of the performances' regions and, moreover, to a hybridization process between them. Thus, by bringing backstage aspects or aspects related to the residual region under the spotlight, media manipulate the boundaries of perception and create that triggering exposure effect. This, in turn, was used for amplifying the sensationalism and spectacularity of the sport media shows. Under the pressure of word's hypervisibility and transparency (Baudrillard, [1987]/1997), sport media shows are no longer only about the actual competition moment, but rather about an entire set of acts connected to this foreground play. From preparing for the competition, to the post-competition reactions, media reconfigured the sport event into a composite stage or what can be called a show in multiple acts, within which the sport actors find it hard to set a clear difference between self as performer and self as performed, experiencing high face threatening situations (Goffman, 1967, 1971). Thus, the feeling of complicity in feeding the audiences' curiosity and providing them with access to things that were not meant for the public eye, works as a bait that media use to win the public interest for both the sport event per se, but also for satellite news related to it. Moreover, it is a resourceful field of pseudo-events, which are 'made for and by media' (Sartori, [1998]/2005, p.65), attesting to the multiplication mechanism that sport omnibus events are subject to.

Another aspect that media brought out in terms of spatiality, when converting sport omnibus events into media shows, is related to the spectatorship experiences, which 'became defined by patterns of deterritorialized consumption that altered the polarity of longstanding [...] place/identity relations' (Ruddock, Hutchins & Rowe, 2010, p.328). Globalization and the fast technological evolution provided the media with the tools to redefine the spectator's role and experience, moving the focus from bringing fans to the sport events to bringing the sport events to fans throughout these media shows.

Now, when we speak about sport audiences as defining component of the sport media shows, we are not talking only about the actual public from the stadium or sport halls, but rather about the infinite remote audiences that are sharing this experience all around the world. Physical distance is no longer a constraint in enjoying sport events. Moreover, the rise of sport mediated live experiences is considered, to some extent, better than the genuine ones. Through panoramic views, multiple angles perspective, replays, close-ups, real time statistics and background information, this hyperreality of sport events as media shows made the 'televisual experience of live sport, for many, superior to the experience obtained by viewing in person' (Whannel, 2009, p.205).

Embracing the opportunities provided by media, spectators are not space-dependent anymore, becoming part of a global sport media show which is first of all defined by the emotional and not by the physical distance towards the event. Media managed to turn 'this enormous mass of people from various countries, of various convictions, different nationalities and cultures into one world stadium' (Milshteyn & Molchanov, 1976, p.71), intensifying the spectacularity and the grandeur of sport events as high holydays of mass communication (Dayan & Kats, 1992). Moreover, media (especially new media), provided us with new ways of spectatorship engagement, redefining the role of the audiences within the wider sport event and responding to the imperative of giving them a more active role in building up these impressive media shows.

This reconfiguration of the sport omnibus events and corollary spectatorship experiences provided by media confirm their media events status, as they imply the transplantation of reality on air/ TV/ online and the relocation of the public space into the domestic zone (Dayan & Kats, 1992). Therefore, we are living a time when the experience of the sport media events is not defined by a set of constrains, but rather by a wide spectrum of possibilities in terms of audiences' participation and engagement. It is all about a multiplication of the sport performances' arenas, a multiplication of the viewing contexts, as well as a multiplication of the media shows formats that are reconfiguring the sport omnibus event.

As any dramaturgical construct, sport events are defined by an interesting mixture of scripts and improvisations, by well-defined and emerging roles and plots. However, beyond their competitive and entertaining dimensions, 'actions that occur within the magic circle of sporting events are full of symbolic meaning' (Cheska, 1979, p.64). I would go even further by saying that they are subject to a wide spectrum of symbolic meanings, as these meanings are socially and contextually build. Around these globally staged social dramas (Turner, 1974, 1975), both the conflictive as well as the ritual dimensions of sport performances contribute to the symbolic opulence of the sport media events, favoring the event-related multiplication process on a semantic level.

The sport events work as routinized social situations during which the sport actors are oriented towards fulfilling the social expectations attached to their roles and reaffirming social values. They are also great social ceremonies, 'serving as an arena for the creation of symbolic leaders and the display of heroic action'(Birell, 1981, p.356).This ritual dimension of the sport media shows provides a great expressive richness in terms of both sport actors' and spectatorship experiences, involving 'dramatization and theatrealization of social and institutional relations, acting, first of all, as a vast spectacle that society provides itself and about itself'(Lardellier, 2003, p.171). Nevertheless, what makes sport omnibus events such attractive media shows is their capacity to redefine this ritual heritage within a global marketing logic, converting them into an eclectic cultural and entertainment construct. And what can be more engaging and newsworthy than a media event that capitalizes on the spectacularity and the symbolism of the sport acts that are performed on the global scene?

The *Emotional* Dimension of the Sport Media Events

Probably the aspect that best defines the media sport events is that, beyond the actual competing performance on the field and on the screen, they are 'primarily about shared experiences' (Hilvoorde, Elling & Stokvis, 2010). The spectacularity of these events, as well as the symbolic capital that they build on, are grounded on a strong emotional component embedded in both the sport actors' and the audiences' experiences. This emotional power exerted by such grand scale social dramas (Craig & Beedie, 2008; Turner, 1974, 1975) makes sport events a resourceful entertainment input and favors the rise of what can be called an affective snowball effect. From athletes and organizers, to journalists, marketers, politicians and world-wide audiences, everyone is emotionally engaged in experiencing sport omnibus events. Moreover, the media sport events are not only about individual, but mostly about collective emotions, about sharing, contextualizing and responding to emotional stimuli.

The prominence of the emotional dimension in building up the media sport events is strongly related to the fact that media themselves encourage the public's identification with the sport actors. Sport events are redefined in terms of intense emotional experiences such as pride, shame, joy, disappointment, euphoria or anger. In this context, sport actors' performances during sport omnibus events speaks about ourselves and takes our engagement to these events even further. 'Questions of identity and identification are of critical importance' (Dunning, 1999, p.3) for sport events and, therefore, the duality of sport competitions as both 'unifying and divisive' (Eitzen, 1999) gave rise to strong emotional reactions from both the sport actors' and audiences' part.

What makes sport omnibus events so attractive to the public is this affective richness, as 'our relationship to sport is one of those remarkably naturalized social phenomena that seemingly seep into our pores of sensibility' (Wenner, 2010, p.1571). While converting sport omnibus events into media ones, the informative dimension becomes less and less important in favor of the persuasive and expressive components of the sport event as media construct. The audience is invited to take part in these exciting events, to live and share the tension of the competition, as well as to empathize with the sport actors during their performances.

Thus, the media sport events act as an intense 'emotional symbiosis' (Ponomariev, 1980, p.77) and favor what can be called the *'affective public'* (Beciu, 2009, p.57) that is drawn by this emotional experience promise. Along with the 'fun factor' (Kellner, 2003, p.3) embedded in every sport performance, the 'exhilarating festive feeling' (Ponomariev, 1980, p.76) brought out by the sport omnibus events made them 'always to be understood in terms of the changing cultural patterns of affect control, the control of the emotions and associated behaviors' (Tomlinson, Markovits & Young, 2003, p.1464). Moreover, I would argue that the shared experiences are not about uniformity within our event-related experiences, but rather about a shared intensity and synchronicity in our emotional engagement. Sport omnibus events are, hence, not about a certain emotion; they are about a wide spectrum of emotions.

The new media managed to provide a public expression for these engagement behaviors, making the global emotional synchronization even more explicit. The 35.6 millions of tweets for the Brazil versus Germany match during the FIFA World Cup 2014 (according to statista.com portal) do not speak only about the spectacularity of the performance or its strategic value for the teams, but rather about people's emotional reaction to it. Likes and tweets, shares and followers reflect an emotional reaction to a media sport event that audiences recognize as both 'an invitation -even a command- to stop their daily routine and join in a holiday experience (Dayan & Kats, 1992:1), as well as an invitation to show their engagement and take a public position to the sport act.

The spectacularization and dramatization that the 'neo-television' (Casetti & Odin, 1990) adds to a sport event are meant not only to rise the newsworthy of the event, but rather to magnify the emotional engagement of its audiences. It is all part of the wider 'seduction imagery', which aims to captivate the public (Soulage, 1998, p.134) and to convert sport omnibus events into spectacular media shows by enhancing both their expressive and impressive power. On these grounds, the sport media events serve a transformative function (Dayan & Kats, 1992) and give rise to their festive vortextual effect (Whannel, 2002).

Whether we speak about the Olympic Games, World Championships, Grand Slam Tournaments, FIFA Champion League or Super Bowl, people remember and relate to them primary in terms of their emotional experiences. Their success as dramaturgical or commercial construct depends on the emotional trigger they manage to activate in terms of spectatorship experience. Good sport media events provide a spectacular show and a high engagement level from the audience part; great sport media shows provide unforgettable feelings, which have a significant multiplication power.

The *Commercial* Dimension of the Sport Media Events

Sport media events are not only about the 'festive viewing of television' (Dayan & Kats, 1992, p.1) or the thrilling emotional experiences shared by the worldwide audiences, but also about a commercial El Dorado. Beyond this 'symbiotic relationship' (Valgeirsson & Snyder, 1986, p.131) between sport and media lays a shared commercial aim that allowed for the honeymoon to begin for 'the ménage á trois among owners, broadcasters and advertisers' (Lever & Wheeler, 1993, p.130). The audience-dependency of sport events has considerably been intensified when media gained their centrality within the sport field, and throughout this constant pressure of the rating targets, the market logic ended up dominating sport as field of cultural production (Bourdieu, 1996, p.29).

Compared to media, sport omnibus events are facing a double standard in terms of audiences' targets: the ad-hoc audience from the arena (the ticket audience) and the distant audience of the media sport event (the remote/distant audience).The aim is to enlarge both of these categories, as each of them has its role in the overall sport show and profitability of the event. Audiences have become the ultimate indicator of a sport event success and a tool for legitimizing the mega-show status as both cultural and commercial phenomenon. However, audiences are not an aim per se, but rather play an instrumental role in terms of their commercial value and money flows that they give rise to. The evolution of the revenue generated on the global sports market from 2006 to 2014 went from 107,5 to 146,5 billion U.S. dollars (according to statista.com portal), making the battle for audiences a strategic one. The multiplication of possible audiences brought along a multiplication of the possible marketing opportunities linked to a sport event. And what can better attract wide audiences and foster their consumer appetite for sport-related products and services than a great sport media show?

Media provide audiences not only with access to worldwide sport omnibus events, but also to sport-related brands and markets, while, at the same time providing marketers with access to global arenas of customers. In this marketing logic that sport events have entered, audiences are first of all addressed in terms of potential versus real consumer pool. Therefore, all the 'interconnections between sport, the media and advertising have helped to create the impression that the pivotal social and personal experience of the modern age is to be a consumer' (Craig & Beedie, 2008, p.130), even when sport events are at stake.

Sport media events have been converted into a huge collage of competition, advertising and entertainment elements. From the actual confrontation on the field, goals and time-records, to event-related adds or entire marketing campaigns, spectacular opening and closing ceremonies, dedicated TV shows and special social media pages, banners and billboards that wrap up the field, cloth collections, special travel packages or Smartphone applications, sport media events have become a huge marketing playground or, to keep to the sport imagery, a race track for marketing concepts and products. With a global reach of 3.6 billion people in 220 countries and territories around the world for the London 2012 Olympic Games (according to the International Olympic Committee's Marketing Report on London 2012 Olympic Games), an average audience of 111.5 million viewers for the 2014 Super Bowl XLVIII (according to Nielsen monitoring) and an estimated 3.2 billion people for the Brazil 2014 World Cup, these sport omnibus events are continuously redefining the parameters of spectacular media shows. There is no wonder that, during such media events, marketers themselves are prone to brake records or at least to achieve great results.

Facts like the tops of the most viewed FIFA 2014 World Cup ads on YouTube show that global brands like Activia (*La la la* - 133.9 million views), Nike (*Winner Stays* - 79.7 million views & *The Last Game* - 48.4 million views), Samsung (The Training -54.3 million views) or Adidas (*The Dream: all in or nothing* - 35.2 views & House Mach - 16.2 million views) manage to reach over millions of views in a couple of weeks (according to statista.com portal). These marketing figures come to confirm the that the sport media events are without any doubt thrilling events that reach the largest audiences in the history of the world and are able to create their own constituencies (Dayan & Kats, 1992, pp. 13-15).

Sport omnibus events work as both commodities and commercial bait for selling other products and services. People watch, but, moreover, come to the sport events not just for the game, the race or the fight, but for the overall show that they want to be part of and to enjoy before, during and after the competitive act itself. Similar to the pop scene, which, in many cases can be integral part of the sport show (see the top artists that are performing at the sport omnibus events opening and closing ceremonies), the sport scene is one of the 'creators of contemporary myths' (Tolleneer, 1986, p. 234). It brings together the tension and the heroism of the battles on the field with the glow and the entertainment of celebrity storytelling (Andrews, & Jackson, 2001; Ogden, & Rosen, 2010; Rojek, 2012; Smart, 2005). Alternative marketing strategies and ad-hoc activities are build around such resourceful media events, capitalizing on both the quantitative dimension of the sport audiences, as well as on the qualitative dimension of their emotional engagement.

To some extent, it can be said that the sport media events emerge from treasuring up the celebrity of sport superstars, based on a mechanic cumulative principle: the more celebrities taking part in the event, the more popular the event. People all around the world are interested in seeing the sport celebrities in action and every event that manages to gather them under the same roof holds true for becoming a great (media) show. Such media events host exciting clash of the sport titans and, therefore, embrace their celebrity status by proximity. But, are there sport events popular because of the sport celebrities they bring together or are the sport actors famous because they take part in such sport media events? I would rather argue that the fame transitivity goes both ways and, moreover, that there is a contamination fame effect between the sport superstars and sport media events.

Here comes the reverse drift of what I have called the contamination fame effect. Sport media events can work as symbolic godfathers for new born sport stars. Their brand value, which reaches impressive figures (464 million U.S. dollars for the Super Bowl, 348 million U.S. dollars for the Summer Olympic Games, 160 million U.S. dollars for the for the FIFA World Cup, according to statista.com portal), makes them a celebrity loading dock. Just like sport actors or clubs, sport events themselves have gained their place on the celebrity market, becoming a sport brand in their own right. They are no longer just the host for sport celebrities, but act as a global celebrity spot drawing everyone's attention. Winning an Olympic medal, breaking a world record, scoring in the World Cup Final or getting yourself notices due to your performance during the Super Bowl can work as a celebrity baptism for the sport actors.

This contamination fame effect is not only about a reciprocal celebrity transfer between sport actors and sport media events, but rather about a spiral mechanism of fame in which both of them are involved in a continuous process of gaining, maintaining and increasing their celebrity 'stocks'. Moreover, I would argue that, understanding the marketing logic they have to cope with for remaining competitive on the celebrity market, they are strategically involved in this complicity of fame transfer, consolidating their win-win relation and conquering new media coverage and marketing fruitful lands. By doing this, they actually generate a multiplication process of the marketing opportunities, consolidating sport actors' top position among brand ambassadors, as well as the prominence of the sport events related contexts in the marketing arena.

CONCLUSION: FROM THE MEDIA SPORT EVENT TO THE MEDIA SPORT EVENT MOSAIC

Whether we speak about the multiple sport performances hosted by a sport omnibus event, the parallel worldwide tribunes, the rich spectrum of emotional experiences of all the people linked to these events or the commercial actions revolving around them, the sport media events are far from a monolithic construct.

Their episodic nature, hosting both simultaneous and sequential acts, is the mere element that triggers the multiplication helix. Many actors, many performances, many scenes and stages, many supporters and much more remote viewers engaging in providing and consuming these transcultural masterpieces. This scattering model of sport media events is, in fact, the defining aspect that makes them so addictive in terms of entertaining products.

The overwhelming feeling that comes along with such grand scale shows is based on this impressive mosaic construct. Under the umbrella of a sport omnibus event like the Olympic Games you can probably find the most complex, yet harmonic diversity tribute: from age, gender, skin color, nationality, rituals and values, to consumers' preferences and behaviors. Sport media events are not only staging the 'ultimate meritocracy' (Bell, 2009, p.54), but also a spectacular form of the modern Babylonian concept. Nevertheless, multiplication reflects only the quantitative dimension of the vortextual effect of sport media events. Along with it, what makes sport omnibus events so engaging is the contextualization process. National media redefine sport omnibus events and build distinct frames around them. Brands and marketers can provide us with alternative scenarios and customer experiences with sport events' related products. We ourselves can create multiple reconfigurations of the same sport media event, contributing to this reconfiguration black box.

The emotional richness attached to the sport events lays in their symbolic polysemy: everyone can provide its own interpretation and live a distinct experience of the same event. While the media events are all defined by their premediated / preplanned character, what the sport media events add to this is the infinite number of satellite actions related to them. From macro to micro-scale events, engaging global communities or just our small group of friends, we are witnessing marketing campaigns, online activities, street events, parties and reunions that are all somehow connected to the same sport omnibus event.

In this context, the rise of the social media provided us with even more effective tools of accelerating the multiplication mechanism, enriching both the spectatorship as well as the customer contexts of engagement that defines the sport participatory consumption (Rowe, 2011). In line with Puijk's idea that the media events, like the Olympic Games, should rather be analysed as a layered series of events of varying strength and meaning (Puijk, 2000), I argue that the sport media events are a mosaic construct of sport, media, commercial, cultural and socio-politic clusters of events. Starting with the sport performances from the field, which constitute the hard-core nucleus of these events, the sport media events are defined by an impressive multiplication power, giving rise to a cascade circuit of satellite events on both macro and micro-scale, offline and online contexts.

Nevertheless, what makes the sport omnibus events distinguish themselves from other media events and maintain their competitiveness on the entertainment market is the symbolic capital of these grand scale war-shows (Dumitriu, 2012) that triggers such intense emotional experiences and engagement. The spectacularity of the sport performances, the outstanding number of actors they are involving and the emotional capital they manage to activate work like a multi-stage amplifier for other event-related manifestations. The event nucleus that we can identify in the sport host-arena and within the strict competitive time-frame becomes object to an impressive media and marketing blossom, giving rise to concurrent satellite events challenging the ones on the sport field.

A sport omnibus event is thus not a static, but rather a dynamic cluster of events, which converge in building up these multilayered sport media show constructs. It means much more than the sum of all these mosaic elements, going way beyond a mechanic cumulative principle, because the mere act of linking them under the same thematic-frame contributes to the multiplication and the emotional intensification processes. There is no wonder that, when the global tendency is to move towards event-driven economies (Nauright, 2004), sport media events are leading the way, providing reference marks, while breaking spectaculariy, audiences and marketing records.

ACKNOWLEDGMENT

This chapter was possible with the financial support of the Sectoral Operational Programme for Human Resources Development 2007-2013, co-financed by the European Social Fund, under the project number POSDRU/159/1.5/S/134650 with the title "Doctoral and Postdoctoral Fellowships for young researchers in the fields of Political, Administrative and Communication Sciences and Sociology".

REFERENCES

Andrews, D. L., & Jackson, S. J. (Eds.). (2001). *Sport Stars: The Cultural Politics of Sporting Celebrity*. New York: Routledge. doi:10.4324/9780203463543

Baudrillard, J. (1997). The other one through himself (Romanian version: Celălalt prin sine însuşi, translated by Ciprian Mihaili). Cluj Napoca: Casa Cărţii de Ştiinţă.

Beciu, C. (2009). Comunicare şi discurs mediatic. O lectură sociologică (Communication and media discourse. A sociological lecture). Bucharest: Comunicare.ro.

Bell, B. (2009). *Sport Studies*. Exeter: Learning Matters.

Birrell, S. (1981). Sport as Ritual: Interpretations from Durkheim to Goffman. *Social Forces*, *60*(2), 354–376. doi:10.1093/sf/60.2.354

Bourdieu, P. (1996). *On television (Romanian version: Despre televiziune. Dominatia jurnalismului, translated by Bogdan Ghiu)*. Bucharest: Meridiane.

Casetti, F., & Odin, R. (1990). De la Paleo à la Neo-Télévision: Approche Semio-Pragmatique. *Communications*, *51*(1), 9–26. doi:10.3406/comm.1990.1767

Cheska, A. T. (1979). Sports Spectacular: A Ritual Model of Power. *International Review for the Sociology of Sport*, *14*(2), 51–72. doi:10.1177/101269027901400204

Couldry, N. (2003). *Media Rituals: A Critical Approach*. London: Routledge.

Craig, P., & Beedie, P. (Eds.). (2008). *Sport Sociology.* Parkstone: Learning Matters.

Dayan, D. (2010). Beyond media events: disenchantment, derailment, disruption. In Media Events in a Global Age (pp. 23-31). London: Routledge.

Dayan, D., & Katz, E. (1992). *Media Events. The Live Broadcasting of History.* Cambridge, MA: Harvard University Press.

Dumitriu, D. L. (2012). Media Framing of Sports Competitions. Going Beyond the War and the Show Frames of Sports Events. *Romanian Journal of Communication and Public Relations*, *14*(4), 47–64.

Dunning, E. (1999). *Sport Matters: sociological studies of sport, violence and civilization.* London: Routledge.

Eitzen, D. S. (1999). *Fair and Foul. Beyond the Myths and Paradoxes of Sport.* Lanham, MD: Rowman & Littlefield.

Goffman, E. (1967). *Interaction ritual: Essays on face to face behavior.* Garden City, NY: Anchor Books.

Goffman, E. (1971). *Relations in public.* New York: Harper & Row.

Goffman, E. (1982). (1983). The Interaction Order: American Sociological Association, 1982 Presidential Address. *American Sociological Review*, *48*(1), 1–17. doi:10.2307/2095141

Goffman, E. (2003). The Presentation of Self in Everyday Life (Romanian edition: Viaţa cotidiană ca spectacol, translated by Simona Dragan & Laura Albulescu). Bucharest: Comunicare.ro.

Grindstaff, L. (2008). Culture and Popular Culture: A Case for Sociology. *The Annals of the American Academy of Political and Social Science*, *619*(1), 206–222. doi:10.1177/0002716208318520

Hepp, A. (2004). Radio and Popular Culture in Germany. Radio Culture between Comedy and Eventization. In A. Crisell (Ed.), *More Than a Music Box. Radio in a MultiMedia World* (pp. 189–212). New York: Berghan Press.

Hepp, A., & Couldry, N. (2010). Introduction: Media events in globalized media cultures. In Media Events in a Global Age. London: Routledge.

International Olympic Committee Marketing Report London 2012. (n.d.). Retrieved July 24, 2014 fromhttp://www.olympic.org/Documents/IOC_Marketing/London_2012/LR_IOC_MarketingReport_medium_res1.pdf

Kellner, D. (2003). *Media Spectacle.* London: Routledge. doi:10.4324/9780203166383

Kennedy, E., & Hills, L. (2009). *Sport, Media and Society.* Oxford, UK: Berg.

Lardellier, P. (2003). *The theory of ritual relations. Antropology and communication (Romanian version: Teoria legăturilor ritualice. Antropologie şi comunicare, translated by Valentina Pricopie).* Bucharest: Tritonic.

Lever, J., & Wheeler, S. (1993). Mass Media and the Experience of Sport. *Communication Research, 20*(1), 125–143. doi:10.1177/009365093020001006

Manning, K. (1996). Dramaturgy, Politics And The Axial Media Event. *The Sociological Quarterly, 37*(2), 261–278. doi:10.1111/j.1533-8525.1996.tb01749.x

McGuigan, J. (2010). *Cultural Analysis*. London: Sage Publications.

Milshteyn, O. A., & Molchanov, S. V. (1976). The Shaping of Public Opinion Regarding Sport by the Mass Media as a Factor Promoting International Understanding. *International Review for the Sociology of Sport, 11*(3), 71–84. doi:10.1177/101269027601100305

Nauright, J. (2004). Global games: Culture, political economy and sport in the globalised world of the 21st century. *Third World Quarterly, 25*(7), 1325–1336. doi:10.1080/014365904200281302

Nielsen Monitoring Report. (n.d.). *Super Bowl XLVIII Draws 111.5 Million Viewers, 25.3 Million Tweets.* Retrieved July 24, 2014 from http://www.nielsen.com/us/en/insights/news/2014/super-bowl-xlviii-draws-111-5-million-viewers-25-3-million-tweets.html

Nye, J. S. (2004). *Soft power: the means to success in world politics*. New York: Public Affairs.

Ogden, D. C., & Rosen, J. N. (2010). *Fame To Infamy: Race, Sport, and the Fall from Grace*. Mississippi: University Press of Mississippi. doi:10.14325/mississippi/9781604737516.001.0001

Panagiotopoulou, R. (2010). Sports events: The Olympics in Greece. In Media Events in a Global Age. London: Routledge.

Ponomariev, N. I. (1980). Sport as a Show. *International Review for the Sociology of Sport, 15*(3-4), 73–79. doi:10.1177/101269028001500306

Puijk, R. (2000). A global media event? Coverage of the 1994 Lillehammer Olympic Games. *International Review for the Sociology of Sport, 35*(3), 309–330. doi:10.1177/101269000035003005

Rawls, A. W. (1987). The Interaction Order Sui Generis: Goffman's Contribution to Social Theory. *Sociological Theory, 5*(2), 136–149. doi:10.2307/201935

Rein, I., Kotler, P., & Stoller, M. (1997). *High visibility: The making and marketing of professionals into celebrities*. Chicago: NTC Books.

Roche, M. (2000). *Mega-events and Modernity: Olympics and Expos in the Growth of Global Culture*. London: Routledge.

Rojek, C. (2012). *Fame attack: The inflation of celebrity and its consequences*. London: Bloomsbury.

Rowe, D. (2011). *Global media sport: Flows, forms and futures*. New York: Bloomsbury Academic.

Ruddock, A., Hutchins, B., & Rowe, D. (2010). Contradictions in media sport culture: The reinscription of football supporter traditions through online media. *European Journal of Cultural Studies*, *13*(3), 323–339. doi:10.1177/1367549410363200

Sartori, G. (1998). Homo videns. The hebetation through television and the post-thinking (Romanian version: Home videns. Imbecilizarea prin televiziune şi post-gândirea, translated by Mihai Elin), Bucharest. *Humanitas*.

Smart, B. (2005). *The Sport Star: Modern Sport and the Cultural Economy of Sporting Celebrity*. London: Sage.

Soulages, J. C. (1998). *Les mises en scène visuelles de l'information. Étude comparée France, Espagne, États-Uni*. Paris: INA/De Boeck Université.

Statista Portal. (n.d.). *Most-tweeted football matches during the FIFA World Cup 2014, ranked by number of tweets (in millions)*. Retrieved August 5, 2014 from http://www.statista.com/statistics/308185/most-tweets-matches-world-cup/

Statista.com Portal. (n.d.a). *Global sports market - total revenue from 2006 to 2015 (in billion U.S. dollars)*. Retrieved July 27, 2014 from http://www.statista.com/statistics/194122/sporting-event-gate-revenue-worldwide-by-region-since-2004/

Statista.com Portal. (n.d.b). *Most viewed FIFA World Cup ads on YouTube as of June 19, 2014 (in millions)*. Retrieved July 25, 2014 from http://www.statista.com/statistics/306751/most-viewed-fifa-world-cup-ads-youtube/

Statista.com Portal. (n.d.c). *Most valuable sports events brands worldwide in 2014 (in million U.S. dollars)*. Retrieved July 25, 2014 from http://www.statista.com/statistics/253353/brand-value-of-sport-events-worldwide/

Tolleneer, J. (1986). The Sports Scene and the Pop Scene: A Comparative Structural-Functional Analysis. *International Review for the Sociology of Sport*, *21*(2-3), 229–238. doi:10.1177/101269028602100211

Tomlinson, A., Markovits, A. S., & Young, C. (2003). Introduction: Mapping Sports Space. *The American Behavioral Scientist*, *46*(11), 1463–1475. doi:10.1177/0002764203046011001

Turner, V. (1975). Symbolic Studies. *Annual Review of Anthropology*, *4*(1), 145–161. doi:10.1146/annurev.an.04.100175.001045

Turner, V. W. (1974). *Dramas, Fields, and Metaphors: Symbolic Action in Human Society*. New York: Cornell University Press.

Valgeirsson, G., & Snyder, E. E. (1986). A Cross-Cultural Comparison of Newspaper Sports Sections. *International Review for the Sociology of Sport*, *21*(2-3), 131–139. doi:10.1177/101269028602100205 van Hilvoorde, I., Elling, A., & Stokvis, R. (2010). How to influence national pride? The Olympic medal index as a unifying narrative. *International Review for the Sociology of Sport*, *45*(1), 87–102. doi:10.1177/1012690209356989

Wenner, L. A. (2010). Sport, Communication, and the Culture of Consumption: On Language and Identity. *The American Behavioral Scientist*, *53*(2), 1571–1573. doi:10.1177/0002764210368085

Whannel, G. (1992). *Fields in Vision - Television sport and cultural transformation*. London: Routledge.

Whannel, G. (2002). *Media sport stars, masculinities and moralities*. London: Routledge.

Whannel, G. (2009). Television and the Transformation of Sport. *The Annals of the American Academy of Political and Social Science*, *625*(1), 205–218. doi:10.1177/0002716209339144

This research was previously published in Global Perspectives on Media Events in Contemporary Society edited by Andrew Fox, pages 194-210, copyright year 2016 by Information Science Reference (an imprint of IGI Global).

Index

P

R

S

T

U

V

W

www.ingramcontent.com/pod-product-compliance
Lightning Source LLC
LaVergne TN
LVHW080620300926
849162LV00005B/1213